INTRODUCTION TO ECONOMICS

MARC LIEBERMAN

NEW YORK UNIVERSITY

ROBERT E. HALL

STANFORD UNIVERSITY

South-Western College Publishing
Thomson Learning™

Australia • Canada • Denmark • Japan • Mexico • New Zealand • Philippines
Puerto Rico • Singapore • South Africa • Spain • United Kingdom • United States

Introduction to Economics, by Marc Lieberman and Robert Hall
Acquisitions Editor: Keri L. Witman
Developmental Editor: Dennis Hanseman
Marketing Manager: Lisa L. Lysne
Sr. Production Editor: Sharon L. Smith
Manufacturing Coordinator: Charlene Taylor
Internal Design: Joe Devine
Cover Designer and Illustrator: Joe Devine
Photo Researcher: Cary Benbow
Production House: Pre-Prsess Company, Inc.
Printer: World Color—Taunton, MA

Printed in the United States of America
5 6 02

For more information, contact South-Western College Publishing, 5191 Natorp Boulevard,

Mason, Ohio, 45040 or find us on the Internet at http://www.swcollege.com

For permission to use material from this text or product, contact us by
• **telephone: 1-800-730-2214**
• **fax: 1-800-730-2215**
• **web: http://www.thomsonrights.com**

Library of Congress Cataloging-in-Publication Data

Lieberman, Marc
  Introduction to Economics / Marc Lieberman, Robert E. Hall.
    p.   cm.
  Includes bibliographical references and index.
  ISBN 0-324-00879-1
  1. Economics.   I. Hall, Robert E.   II. Title.
HB171.5.L7135 1999
  330—dc21   99-30970

This book is printed on acid-free paper.

PREFACE

To the Instructor

This book provides an introduction to economic *principles*—and how those principles are applied in the real world. It's based on our well-received one-year principles book (*Economics: Principles and Applications,* by Robert Hall and Marc Lieberman, 1st edition, 1998), but redesigned and substantially rewritten for a *one-semester course* in economic principles that combines both micro- and macroeconomics.

Our philosophy is to treat fewer topics, and to treat them fully. We have tried to stick to a simple rule: If a topic can't be covered in a fully satisfying way, don't introduce it at all. The result is a book that provides a comprehensive introduction to economic principles and applications, yet one that can be read and absorbed in one semester.

The overall approach of *Introduction to Economics* can be summed up as follows:

- **We stress the basic principles of economics.** Economic theory makes repeated use of some fundamental ideas that appear again and again in many contexts. To truly understand what economics is all about, students need to learn what these central ideas are, and they need to see them in action in different contexts. We've identified and stressed eight *basic principles of economics* in this text. These are:

  - Maximization Subject to Constraints
  - Opportunity Cost
  - Specialization and Exchange
  - Markets and Equilibrium
  - Policy Tradeoffs
  - Marginal Decision Making
  - Short-Run versus Long-Run Outcomes
  - The Importance of Real Values

 A full statement of each principle appears in Chapter 1 (pp. 13–14), and that full statement appears again later when each principle is used for the first time. Thereafter, whenever the principle is used, it is identified with a key symbol shown in the margin.

- **We avoid nonessential material.** When we believed a topic was not essential to a basic understanding of economics, we left it out. We have also avoided interviews, news clippings, and boxed inserts with only remote connections to the core material. The features your students *will* find in our book are there to help them understand basic economic theory itself, or to help them explore sources of information on their own, using the Internet.

- **We explain difficult concepts patiently.** Because we have avoided the encyclopedic approach, we can explain the topics we *do* cover thoroughly and patiently. We try to lead students, step-by-step, through each aspect of the theory, through each graph, and through each numerical example. Moreover, in the process of developing this book, we asked other experienced teachers to tell us which aspects of economic theory are hardest for their students to learn, and we've paid special attention to the trouble spots.

- **We use concrete examples.** Students learn best when they see how economics can explain the world around them. Whenever possible, we develop the theory using real-world examples. When we employ hypothetical examples, because they illustrate the theory more cleanly, we try to make them realistic. In addition, each chapter ends with a thorough, extended application of the material.

SPECIAL PEDAGOGICAL FEATURES. We've chosen features that reinforce the basic theory, rather than distract from it. Here is a list of the most important ones, and how we believe they help students focus on essentials.

- *Using the Theory* sections, which present extended applications, appear near the end of each chapter. While there are plenty of real-world examples in the body of each chapter, helping to illustrate each step along the way, we also felt it important to have one extended application that unifies the material in the chapter. In the "Using the Theory" sections, students see how the tools they've learned can explain something about the world—something that would be difficult to explain without those tools.

- *Dangerous Curves* explanations are designed to eliminate confusion that sometimes arises as students read the text—the kinds of mistakes we see year after year in their exams.
- *Internet references* point students to resources that contain up-to-the-minute information. We prefer Internet references, rather than the traditional approach of including news stories in the text, for two reasons. First, we want to minimize distractions; and second, what is current news at the time of writing may be stale by the time the book is read.

WHAT'S DIFFERENT IN CONTENT, AND WHY. In addition to the special features just described, you will find some important differences in topical approach and arrangement. These, too, are designed to make the theory stand out more cleanly, and to make learning easier. These are not pedagogical experiments, nor are they innovation for the sake of innovation. The pedagogical differences you will find in this text are the product of years of classroom experience.

A few of the differences may require minor adjustments in class lectures, and these are listed below. But we would be remiss if we merely listed them without also pointing out why we believe they are improvements. Please indulge us a bit as you read through this list.

Innovations in Microeconomics

- **Scarcity, Choice, and Economic Systems** (Chapter 2): This early chapter, while covering standard material like opportunity cost, also introduces some central concepts much earlier than other texts. Most importantly, the chapter introduces the concept of *comparative advantage,* and the basic principle of *specialization and exchange.* We have placed them near the front of our book because we believe they provide important building blocks for much that comes later. For example, economies of scale (Chapter 5) can result from comparative advantage and specialization *within* the firm. International trade (Chapter 18) can be seen as a special application of these principles, extending them to trade between nations.
- **The Theory of the Firm** (Chapter 6): Many texts introduce the theory of the firm within the model of perfect competition. We believe this is an unfortunate choice because it forces students to master the

logic of profit maximization and the details of a rather special kind of market at the same time. Students quite naturally think of firms as facing downward-sloping demand curves—not horizontal ones. We've found that they have an easier time learning the theory of the firm in a more familiar context.

Further, by treating the theory of the firm in a separate chapter—before perfect competition—we can group together those concepts that apply in *all* market structures (the shapes of marginal cost and average cost curves, the marginal cost and marginal revenue rule, the shut-down rule, etc.), and distinguish them from concepts that are unique to perfect competition (the horizontal demand curve facing the firm, marginal revenue equals price, etc.)

- **Monopoly, Monopolistic Competition, and Oligopoly** (Chapter 8): Two features of our treatment are worth noting here. First, we emphasize price discrimination, a key feature of imperfect competition. We find that students are very interested in this topic. Second, we have omitted older theories of oligopoly that raised more questions than they answered, such as the kinked demand curve model. Our treatment of oligopoly is strictly game-theoretic, but we've taken great care to keep it simple and clear.
- **Description vs. Assessment** (Chapters 7, 8, and 10): In treating each of the four basic product market structures (perfect competition, monopoly, monopolistic competition, and oligopoly), most texts switch back and forth between the *description* of different markets and the *assessment* of market outcomes. In our view, this has several drawbacks. First, students often confuse the two. Second, it can make learning about market structure overwhelming. It is hard enough for first-time economics students to understand what happens in each type of market, let alone learn what is good and bad about each one at the same time. Finally, by mixing description and assessment, the all-important concept of economic efficiency is lost in the shuffle; it is diffused throughout the book, rather than treated comprehensively as a unified topic.

Our book collects the material on economic efficiency into a single chapter. This has several advantages. First, it permits you to focus on *description* and *prediction* when teaching about the four market structures—a full plate, in our experience. Second, having a chapter devoted to efficiency and market failure allows a more comprehensive treatment of the topic than we've seen elsewhere. Finally, our approach—in which students learn about efficiency *after* they have mastered the four market structures—allows them to study efficiency with the perspective needed to really understand it.

Innovations in Macroeconomics

- **Long-Run Macroeconomics** (Chapter 14): This text presents long-run growth before short-run fluctuations. But unlike many other texts, which treat growth in an entirely descriptive way, our treatment is analytical. We use a very simple supply and demand framework to explain the causes—and costs—of economic growth in both rich and poor countries.

  We believe it is better to treat the long run before the short run, for two reasons. First, the long-run model makes full use of the tools of supply and demand, and thus provides for an easier transition from microeconomics to macroeconomics. Second, we believe that economic fluctuations and their transitory nature are best understood by viewing them as deviations from a long-run trend. This, of course, requires a prior treatment of how that long-run trend is determined.

- **Aggregate Demand and Aggregate Supply** (Chapter 17): One of our pet peeves about other introductory texts is the too-early introduction of aggregate demand and aggregate supply curves, *before* teaching where these curves come from. Students then confuse the *AD* and *AS* curves with their microeconomic counterparts, requiring corrective action later. In this text, the *AD* and *AS* curves do not appear until Chapter 17, where they are fully explained. Our treatment of aggregate supply is based on a very simple mark-up model that our students have found very accessible.

BUILDING A SYLLABUS. We have arranged the contents of each chapter, and the table of contents as a whole, according to the order of presentation that we recommend. But we've also built in some flexibility. For example, Chapter 4 develops consumer theory with both marginal utility and (in an appendix) indifference curves, allowing you to present either method in class. If you wish to highlight international trade, you could assign Chapter 18 immediately after Chapter 3.

Finally, we have included only those chapters that we thought were both essential and teachable in a one-semester course. But nothing in Chapter 9 (Labor Markets and Wages) or Chapter 10 (Economic Efficiency and the Role of Government) is required to understand the other

chapters in the book. And the treatment of macroeconomics could, in a pinch, end with Chapter 16, leaving out Chapter 17 (Aggregate Supply and Demand). Finally, an instructor could drop Chapter 18 (International Trade and Comparative Advantage), since comparative advantage as a general concept is fully treated earlier, in Chapter 2.

TEACHING AIDS FOR THE INSTRUCTOR

- The Instructor's Manual contains chapter summaries, lecture ideas, teaching tips and activities, ideas for interactive teaching, and solutions to end-of-chapter problems and exercises.
- The Test Bank contains thousands of multiple-choice questions. It is available in both printed and electronic forms.
- Full-color transparencies are available for most of the key graphs and illustrations in the text.
- Our Web site gives students access to a variety of perspectives on economic issues of the day. It contains a series of accessible position papers that explain competing viewpoints on key policy issues. The site also contains news updates linked to the text, teaching and learning resources, and a variety of other interesting features. (http://hall-lieb.swcollege.com)
- Tutorial software allows students to create, modify, and use key graphs.
- A CNN video provides a variety of short video clips on various aspects of economics.
- Many of the text's figures and tables are available as Microsoft PowerPoint files.

A REQUEST. Although we've worked hard on this book, we know we'll be able to improve it further in future editions. For that, our fellow users are indispensable. We invite your comments and suggestions wholeheartedly. We especially welcome your suggestions for additional "Dangerous Curves" and "Using the Theory" sections. You may send your comments to either of us care of South-Western College Publishing.

Marc Lieberman
Robert Hall

ACKNOWLEDGMENTS

This book is a case study of the principle of specialization and exchange. So many people contributed their valuable skills and expertise, especially the staff of South-Western College Publishing. As with our previous text, our largest debt of gratitude is owed to our development editor, Dennis Hanseman. Not only does he hold a Ph.D. in economics, but he also possesses a rare ability to take the viewpoint of someone new to the field. His knack for spotting potential areas of confusion, his stubborn insistence on absolute clarity at every turn, and his innumerable contributions in planning and executing the project were immensely valuable. Jack Calhoun, now team director at South-Western, originally signed us as authors, so it is fair to say that this book would not exist without him. He was a relentless advocate for South-Western as a superior publishing company (a description that turned out to be entirely accurate), and a great problem solver once the project was under way. Keri Witman, the acquisitions editor for this project, worked hard to make it a reality, and showed tremendous patience and creativity in breaking through the inevitable logjams that arise when not every contingency can be anticipated in a contract. Lisa Lysne—with a combination of exceptional talent and long hours—did a superior job of marketing and advertising this book and coming up with creative ways to explain what it was all about. Joe Devine created the design features for the text, and accomplished a near impossible task: designing a cover that both authors like a lot.

In addition to those at South-Western, we would like to thank the staff of Pre-Press Company, who turned our manuscript into a beautiful book. Bruce Watson and Jennifer Stephan contributed many of the end-of-chapter questions. Geoffrey Jehle, of Vassar College, and Heinz Kohler, of Amherst College, also made important contributions. Chaitan Narsule deserves special thanks for reading every page of the manuscript, and showing remarkable skill and taste in suggesting changes.

Finally we would like to thank the instructors who provided numerous suggestions that we found most helpful in developing this book. While we had no intention of writing a book that would be "all things to all people," and could not incorporate every suggestion, these individuals helped us make the book "more things for more people."

Ali Akarca
University of Illinois, Chicago

James Burnell
College of Wooster

Barbara Craig
Oberlin College

Arthur Gibb
U.S. Naval Academy

Geoffrey Jehle
Vassar College

David Jaeger
Hunter College

Roger Little
U.S. Naval Academy

Paul Munyon
Grinnell College

Greg Pizzigno
St. John's University

Laura Randall
Hunter College

Mark Walbert
Illinois State University

Robert Whaples
Wake Forest University

James Whitney
Occidental College

Michael Zweig
SUNY/Stony Brook

Personal Note from Marc Lieberman. I want to especially thank four people for helping me with this project in ways that are impossible to measure. Geoffrey Jehle, Professor of Economics at Vassar College, provided excellent advice on writing, organizing, and thinking about the material. Lori Strasberg provided emotional support, and made sure that I had fun when work was done for the day. And my parents, Harold and Charlene Lieberman, were both patient and supportive when their son—once again—had to postpone a family visit to make a deadline.

Personal Note from Bob Hall. Charlotte Pace, who keeps my office humming at Stanford, contributed in many ways, especially raising the art of copy checking and proofreading to new levels of excellence. My son Chris served as college culture consultant for the book. My wife, Susan Woodward—a financial economist—helped in so many ways, and happily tolerated the domestic dislocations that inevitably accompany a project like this one. She read and commented on many of the chapters and drafted material in her areas of interest. And she made Marc very happy by cooking dinner for him.

TO THE STUDENT

You may have already noticed that this note is substantially shorter than our note to instructors. And for good reason. The entire book has been written with you in mind. Here, we just want to give you some advice on using some special features of this book, and suggest some helpful supplements.

- **Getting started:** The first chapter tells you what economics is, and gives some tips on how to study it.
- **The Basic Principles:** As you will see, much of economic theory boils down to a small number of fundamental ideas, which appear again and again in many contexts. In this book, we've identified eight of them, and we call them the *basic principles of economics*. The entire list is presented in Chapter 1, and each principle is discussed, in more detail, in a later chapter when it is first used. Throughout the

book, each time the principle appears again, it is identified with a key symbol, as shown at left. When you see one of these keys, it's a signal to stop and think about how the principle is being used.

- **Dangerous Curves:** Professors *do* talk about other things besides the mistakes their students make on exams. But when the subject comes up, it is surprising that our experiences are so similar. Year after year, no matter how hard we try, the same confusions pop up. We've tried to identify the most common ones in our "Dangerous Curves" feature, which you will find throughout the text. You may want to skip them as you read through the chapter the first time, and concentrate on them later—especially before exam time.

- **Using the Theory:** Each chapter ends with an application that demonstrates how the tools you've learned can help you understand something new about the world, something that would be hard to understand *without* those tools.

- The Lieberman/Hall **Web site** contains a variety of helpful features that will enrich your study of economics. Check it out on a regular basis at http://hall-lieb.swcollege.com.

- **Mathematical Appendix:** For the most part, the only math you need to understand this book is what you learned in high school—and only a small part of that. The required math, as well as the basics of graphs, are reviewed in the mathematical appendix at the end of the book. If you are very rusty, you might want to read the appendix in its entirety, early on. Otherwise, just know that it's there, and refer to it when you need it.

LEARNING AIDS. The following items are also available to help you learn economics:

- **The Study Guide:** Learning is different from memorizing. This textbook has been written to help you understand each concept. Nevertheless, to really master the material, there is nothing like repeated problem solving. Much as practicing helps a pianist, the Study Guide written to accompany this book will help you strengthen your knowledge of economics. (ISBN: 0-324-00880-5)

- **ECONOMICS ALIVE!** is a pair of exciting CD-ROMs that contain animated lessons, economic tool-building exercises, and simulations that will help you learn economics interactively. (For microeconomics, ISBN: 0-538-84650-X. For macroeconomics, ISBN: 0-538- 85471-5.)

These learning aids can be ordered through your campus bookstore.

We are honored to help your instructor welcome you to the field of economics. We hope you find the experience of reading this book a fulfilling one—as fulfilling as the experience we had writing it.

Marc Lieberman
Robert Hall

ABOUT THE AUTHORS

MARC LIEBERMAN

is Clinical Associate Professor of Economics at New York University. He received his Ph.D. from Princeton University, and has presented his extremely popular Principles of Economics course at New York University, Harvard, Vassar, the University of California/Santa Cruz, and the University of Hawaii. Lieberman is co-editor and contributor to *The Road to Capitalism: Economic Transformation in Eastern Europe and the Former Soviet Union.* In addition, he has consulted with the Bank of America and the Educational Testing Service. In his spare time, he is a professional screenwriter. He cowrote the script for *Love Kills,* a thriller that aired on the USA Cable Network, and he currently teaches screenwriting at Gotham Writer's Workshop in New York City.

ROBERT E. HALL

is a prominent applied economist. He is the Robert and Carole McNeil Professor of Economics at Stanford University and Senior Fellow at Stanford's Hoover Institution, where he conducts research on inflation, unemployment, taxation, monetary policy, and the economics of high technology. He received his Ph.D. from MIT and has taught there as well as at the University of California, Berkeley. Hall is director of the research program on Economic Fluctuations of the National Bureau of Economic Research, and chairman of the Bureau's Committee on Business Cycle Dating, which maintains the semiofficial chronology of the U.S. business cycle. He has published numerous books and articles in scholarly journals, and is the co-author of the popular intermediate text *Macroeconomics: Theory, Performance, and Policy.* Hall has advised the Treasury Department and the Federal Reserve Board on national economic policy, and has testified on numerous occasions before congressional committees.

BRIEF CONTENTS

CONTENTS

PART 2

MICROECONOMIC DECISION MAKERS

PART 3

MARKETS, PRICES, AND RESOURCE ALLOCATION

PART 4

MACROECONOMICS: BASIC CONCEPTS

PART 5

THE BEHAVIOR OF THE MACROECONOMY

PART 6

INTERNATIONAL TRADE

PHOTO CREDITS

CHAPTER

1

WHAT IS ECONOMICS?

Economics. The word conjures up all sorts of images: monolithic corporate headquarters, highly paid executives in business suits, complicated graphs and charts, manic stock traders on Wall Street, an economic summit meeting in a European capital, a somber television news anchor announcing good or bad news about the economy. . . . You probably hear about economics several times each day. But what *is* economics? How does it fit into human knowledge? How does the world benefit from it?

First, economics is a *social science*. It studies those aspects of human behavior relating to working, producing goods, distributing them, and consuming them.

Second, economics has practical value to people, businesses, and government. An economist designed the system used by the Public Broadcasting System to decide what TV shows to produce. Economists have developed theories that have reduced risk in financial markets, enabled more people to obtain insurance against fire and theft, and helped to protect consumers against defective products. And economic principles have influenced decisions about taxes, Social Security, unemployment insurance, business regulations, international trade, and many other government programs and policies that affect our lives in important ways.

Many people have only vague ideas about the field of economics . . . and sometimes incorrect ideas. If you have never studied economics before, you may have some misconceptions about what it is all about. Let's dispel some of these misconceptions right now.

MYTHS ABOUT ECONOMICS

"ECONOMICS IS THE SAME AS *BUSINESS*." The confusion between business and economics is easy to understand, because economics has much to say about business. Indeed, a mastery of economic principles will help anyone planning to start a business or to work for an established firm. But since economics is a social science, its goal is to understand how business activities fit into the broader picture of our society. The field of business, by contrast, takes an exclusively how-to approach.

"ECONOMICS IS ABOUT MAKING MONEY IN STOCKS, BONDS, AND REAL ESTATE." A knowledge of economics will certainly help you understand what goes on in financial markets, and it is indispensable for anyone hoping to become a savvy investor. There is even a branch of economics—called *finance*—that focuses on markets such as those for stocks and bonds. But economics is not about the ins and outs of trading things for profit. Indeed, economics teaches us that it is very difficult to beat the market on a continuing basis and that most of those who claim they can do so are deluding themselves and their clients.

"SINCE THE ECONOMY ITSELF IS SO COMPLEX, ONLY SPECIALISTS WITH YEARS OF TRAINING CAN HOPE TO UNDERSTAND IT." Our global, national, and even local economies *are* very complex. But this does not mean that studying economic principles needs to be complex. In this text, you will see that some simple ideas can give you surprisingly powerful insights into the economy. Indeed, the art of economics—and the main activity of those who practice it—is to extract simple, understandable truths from an increasingly complex world.

"ECONOMICS IS BORING." Economics deals with questions like these:

- Why, in recessions, are millions of Americans who want to work unable to find jobs?
- Why might a government purposely create an economic downturn, throwing millions of people out of work?
- Is it true that going to war is good for the economy?
- What does it mean for a country's currency—or its entire economy—to "collapse," as happened to Thailand, Indonesia, and several other Asian countries in 1997?
- Where will the jobs be when you graduate from college, and which professions will pay the highest salaries?
- Why do highly trained physicians earn $200,000 per year, while actors like Jim Carrey and Demi Moore earn more than fifty times that amount to star in movies?
- Why does the cost of many services, such as long-distance telephone calls, continue to fall, while the cost of others—for example, college education—keeps rising relentlessly?

If you find these questions uninteresting, then you may as well close this book now. Economics will, indeed, bore you. But if you are like most people—curious, but often confused by what goes on in the world—you will find economics to be interesting and perhaps even fascinating.

ECONOMICS, SCARCITY, AND CHOICE

As a *social science*, economics seeks to explain something about *society*. In this sense, it has much in common with psychology, sociology, and political science. But economics differs from these other social sciences, both in terms of *what* economists study and *how* they study it. Economists ask fundamentally different questions, and they answer them using tools that other social scientists find rather exotic.

A useful definition of economics, which stresses the difference between economics and other social sciences, is the following:

> *Economics is the study of <u>choice</u> <u>under</u> <u>conditions</u> of <u>scarcity</u>.*

ECONOMICS The study of choice under conditions of scarcity.

This definition may appear strange to you. Where are the familiar words we ordinarily associate with economics, words such as "money," "stocks and bonds," "prices," and "budgets"? As you will soon see, economics deals with all of these things and more. It even reaches beyond what we ordinarily think of as the economy. Let's take a closer look at the concept of scarcity, and how it helps define the field of economics.

SCARCITY AND THE INDIVIDUAL

Think for a moment about your own life—the activities of your day, the possessions you enjoy, the surroundings in which you live. Is there anything you don't have right now that you would *like* to have? Anything that you have, but that you would like *more* of? If your answer is "no," then congratulations—either you are well advanced on the path of Zen self-denial, or else you are a close relative of Bill Gates. The rest of us, however, would benefit from an increase in our material standard of living. This simple truth is at the very core of economics. It can be restated this way: We all face the problem of **scarcity.**

SCARCITY A situation in which the amount of something available is insufficient to satisfy the desire for it.

At first glance, it seems that you suffer from an infinite variety of scarcities. There are so many things you might like to have right now—a larger room or apartment, a new car, more clothes . . . the list is endless. But a little reflection suggests that your limited ability to satisfy these desires is based on two basic limitations: scarce *time* and scarce *spending power*.

> *As individuals, we face a scarcity of time and spending power. Given more of either, we could each have more of the goods and services that we desire.*

The scarcity of spending power is no doubt familiar to you. We've all wished for higher incomes, or greater wealth, so that we could more easily afford to buy the things we want. But the scarcity of time is equally important. So many of the activities we enjoy—seeing a movie, taking a vacation, making a phone call—require time as well as money. Just as we have limited spending power, we also have a limited number of hours in each day to satisfy our desires.

Because of the scarcities of time and spending power, each of us is forced to make choices. We must allocate our scarce *time* to different activities: work, play, education, sleep, shopping, and more. We must allocate our scarce *spending power* among different goods and services: housing, food, furniture, travel, and many others. And each time we choose to buy something or do something, we are also choosing *not* to buy or do something else.

Economists study the choices we make as individuals and how those choices shape our economy. For example, the goods that each of us decides to buy ultimately determine which goods business firms will produce. This, in turn, explains which firms and industries will hire new workers and which will lay them off.

Economists also study the more subtle and indirect effects of individual choice on our society. Will most Americans continue to live in houses, or—like Europeans—will most of us end up in apartments? Will we have an educated and well-informed citizenry? Will museums and libraries be forced to close down? Will traffic congestion in our cities continue to worsen, or is there relief in sight? These questions hinge, in large part, on the separate decisions of millions of people. To answer them requires an understanding of how people make choices under conditions of scarcity.

SCARCITY AND SOCIETY

Now let's think about scarcity from *society's* point of view. What are the goals of our society? We want a high standard of living for our citizens, clean air, safe streets, good schools, and more. What is holding us back from accomplishing all of these goals in a way that would satisfy everyone? You probably already know the answer: scarcity.

In society's case, the problem is a scarcity of **resources**—the things we use to make goods and services that help us achieve our goals. Economists classify resources into three categories:

1. **Labor** is the time human beings spend producing goods and services.
2. **Capital** consists of the long-lasting tools that people use to produce goods and services along with their labor. This includes *physical capital* such as buildings, machinery, and equipment, as well as **human capital**—the *skills and training of the labor force.*
3. **Land** is the physical space on which production takes place, and also the natural resources found under it or on it, such as oil, iron, coal, and lumber.

> *As a society, we face a scarcity of resources—labor, capital, and land.*

Anything produced in the economy comes, ultimately, from some combination of these resources. Think about the last lecture you attended at your college. You were consuming a service—a college lecture. What went into producing that service? Your instructor was supplying labor. Many types of capital were used as well. The physical capital included desks, chairs, a blackboard or transparency projector, and the classroom building itself. It also included the computer your instructor may have used to write out his or her lecture notes. In addition, there was human capital—your instructor's specialized knowledge and lecturing skills. Finally, there was land—the property on which your classroom building sits.

Besides the three resources, other things were used to produce your college lecture. Chalk, for example, is a tool used by your instructor, so you might think it should be considered capital, but it is not. Why not? Because it is not *long lasting.* Typically, economists consider a tool to be capital only if it lasts for a few years or longer. Chalk tends to be used up as the lecture is produced, so it is considered a *raw material* rather than capital.

But a little reflection should convince you that a piece of chalk is itself produced from some combination of the three resources (labor, capital, and land). In fact, all of the raw materials needed to produce the lecture—the energy used to heat or cool your building, the computer paper used for your instructor's lecture notes, and more—come, ultimately, from society's three resources. And the scarcity of resources, in turn, causes the scarcity of all goods and services produced from them.

Goods and services are not important to us just as individuals; we also use them to accomplish our social goals. Safe streets, for example, are an important social goal. To achieve this goal, we must have police protection, and this requires resources—police vehicles, police stations, courthouses, and more. To produce these things, we use the labor of autoworkers, bricklayers, and electricians; natural re-

RESOURCES The land, labor, and capital that are used to produce goods and services.

LABOR The time human beings spend producing goods and services.

CAPITAL Long-lasting tools used in producing goods and services.

HUMAN CAPITAL The skills and training of the labor force.

LAND The physical space on which production occurs, and the natural resources that come with it.

sources such as sand, iron, and copper; and machinery like cement mixers, cranes, and electric drills. These very same resources, however, could instead be used to produce *other* desirable things, such as new homes, hospitals, automobile factories, or schools. As a result, every society must have some method of *allocating* its scarce resources—choosing which of our many competing desires will be fulfilled and which will not be.

Many of the big questions of our time center on the different ways in which resources can be allocated. The cataclysmic changes taking place in Eastern Europe and the former Soviet Union arose from a very simple fact: The method these countries used to allocate resources was not working. The never-ending debates between Democrats and Republicans in the United States, and similar debates throughout the world's democracies, reflect subtle but important differences of opinion about how to allocate resources. Often, these are disputes about whether the private sector can handle the allocation of resources on its own or whether the government should be involved.

SCARCITY AND ECONOMICS

The scarcity of resources—and the choices it forces us to make—is the source of all of the problems you will study in economics. Households have limited incomes for satisfying their desires, so they must choose carefully how they allocate their spending among different goods and services. Business firms try to make profit, but they must pay for their inputs, so they must carefully choose *what* to produce, *how much* to produce, and *how* to produce it. Local, state, and federal governments must work with limited budgets, so they must carefully choose which goals to pursue. Economists study these decisions made by households, firms, and governments to explain how our economic system operates, to forecast the future of our economy, and to suggest ways to make that future even better.

THE WORLD OF ECONOMICS

The field of economics is surprisingly broad. It extends from the mundane—why does a pound of steak cost more than a pound of chicken?—to the personal and profound—how do couples decide how many children to have? With a field this broad, it is useful to have some way of classifying the different types of problems economists study and the different methods they use to analyze them.

MICROECONOMICS AND MACROECONOMICS

The field of economics is divided into two major parts: microeconomics and macroeconomics. **Microeconomics** comes from the Greek word *micros*, meaning "small." It takes a close-up view of the economy, as if looking through a microscope. Microeconomics is concerned with the behavior of *individual actors* on the economic scene—households, business firms, and governments. It looks at the choices made by these actors and how they interact with each other in *specific markets*. What will happen to the cost of movie tickets over the next five years? How many jobs will open up in the fast-food industry? How would the Japanese electronics industry be affected by a U.S. tax on imports? These are all microeconomic questions, because they analyze individual *parts* of the economy, rather than the whole.

Macroeconomics—from the Greek word *macros*, meaning "large"—takes an *overall view* of the economy. Macroeconomics is not concerned about individual

Resources for Economists on the Internet
Vast index of Web sites with economic information and data on the web.
http://www.rfe.org

MICROECONOMICS The study of the behavior of individual households, firms, and governments, the choices they make, and their interaction in specific markets.

MACROECONOMICS The study of the economy as a whole.

firms, individual households, or even individual industries; rather, it concentrates on what is happening in the economy as a whole. Instead of focusing on the production of carrots or computers, macroeconomics lumps all goods and services together and looks at the economy's *total output*. Instead of focusing on employment in the fast food industry or the manufacturing sector, it considers *total employment* in the economy. Instead of asking why credit card loans carry higher interest rates than home mortgage loans, it asks what makes interest rates *in general* rise or fall. In all of these cases, macroeconomics focuses on the big picture and ignores the fine details.

POSITIVE AND NORMATIVE ECONOMICS

POSITIVE ECONOMICS The study of what *is,* of how the economy works.

NORMATIVE ECONOMICS The study of what *should be;* it is used to make value judgments, identify problems, and prescribe solutions.

The micro versus macro distinction is based on the level of detail we want to consider. Another useful distinction has to do with the *purpose* in analyzing a problem. **Positive economics** deals with what *is*—with *how* the economy works, plain and simple. If we lower income tax rates in the United States next year, will the federal-budget surplus decrease? If so, by how much? And what effect will this have on total employment? These are all positive economic questions. We may disagree about the answers, but we can all agree that there *are* correct answers to these questions—if only we can discover them.

Normative economics concerns itself with what *should be*. It is used to make judgments about the economy, identify problems, and prescribe solutions. While positive economics is concerned with just the facts, normative economics requires us to make value judgments. When an economist advises that we cut government spending—an action that will benefit some citizens and harm others—the economist is engaging in normative analysis.

Positive and normative economics are intimately related in practice. For one thing, we cannot properly argue about what we should or should not do unless we know certain facts about the world. Every normative analysis is therefore based on an underlying positive analysis. But while a positive analysis can, at least in principle, be conducted without value judgments, a normative analysis is always based, at least in part, on the values of the person conducting it.

WHY ECONOMISTS DISAGREE. The distinction between positive and normative economics can help us understand why economists so often disagree. Suppose you are watching a television interview in which two economists are asked whether the United States should eliminate all government-imposed barriers to trading with the rest of the world. The first economist says, "Yes, absolutely," while the other says, "No, definitely not." Why the sharp disagreement?

The difference of opinion may be *positive* in nature: The two economists may have sharply divergent views about what would actually happen if trade barriers were eliminated. Differences like this sometimes arise because our knowledge of the economy is imperfect.

More likely, however, the disagreement will be *normative*. Economists, like everyone else, have different values. In this case, both economists might agree that opening up international trade would benefit *most* Americans, but harm *some* of them. Yet they may still disagree about the wisdom of this policy move because they have different values. The first economist might put more emphasis on benefits to the overall economy, while the second might put more emphasis on preventing harm to a particular group. Here, the two economists have come to the same *positive conclusion*, but their *different values* lead them to different *normative conclusions*.

Unless these two economists are given ample time to express the basis for their opinions—which rarely happens in news articles and happens even more rarely on television—the public will hear only the disagreement. People may then conclude that economists cannot agree about how the economy works, when the *real* disagreement is over which goals are more important for our society.

One of the most important things you will learn in introductory economics is the distinction between normative and positive disagreements. You will see that there is much more agreement on positive economic issues than on normative ones. Economists know more about how the economy works than the never-ending arguments over policy would suggest.

WHY STUDY ECONOMICS?

Students take economics courses for all kinds of reasons.

TO UNDERSTAND THE WORLD BETTER

Much of what happens in the world can be better understood by applying the tools of economics. The list ranges from the global and cataclysmic—wars, famines, epidemics, and depressions—to the local and personal—the worsening traffic conditions in your city, the raise you did or didn't get last month, or the long line of people waiting to buy tickets for a popular concert. Economics has the power to help us understand these phenomena because they result, in large part, from the choices we make under conditions of scarcity.

Economics has its limitations, of course. But it is hard to find any aspect of life about which economics does not have *something* important to say. Economics cannot explain why so many Americans like to watch television, but it *can* explain how networks and cable stations decide which programs to offer. Economics cannot protect you from a robbery, but it *can* explain why some people choose to become thieves and why no society has chosen to eradicate crime completely. Economics will not help you solve the problems of your love life, resolve unconscious conflicts from your childhood, or help you overcome a fear of flying, but it *can* explain how many skilled therapists, ministers, and counselors there will be to help us solve these problems.

TO GAIN SELF-CONFIDENCE

Understanding basic economic principles will expand your grasp of world events and increase your confidence as you face the future. You need no longer feel that mysterious, inexplicable forces are shaping your life, buffeting you like the bumpers in a pinball machine, determining whether or not you'll be able to find a job, what your salary will be, whether you'll be able to afford a home, and in what kind of neighborhood. After learning economics, you may be surprised to find that you no longer toss out the business page of your local newspaper because it appears to be written in a foreign language. You may no longer flip to another channel the instant the TV news announcer says, "And now for news about the economy. . . ." You may find yourself listening to economic reports with a critical ear, catching mistakes in logic, misleading statements, or out-and-out lies. When you master economics, you gain a sense of mastery over the world, and thus over your own life as well.

TO ACHIEVE SOCIAL CHANGE

If you are interested in making the world a better place, economics is indispensable. There is no shortage of serious social problems worthy of our attention—

unemployment, hunger, poverty, disease, child abuse, drug addiction, violent crime—and economic factors play a key role in all of them. Economics can help us understand the origins of these problems, explain why previous efforts to solve them have failed, and enable us to design new, more effective solutions.

TO HELP PREPARE FOR OTHER CAREERS

Economics has long been the most popular college major for individuals intending to work in business. But in the last two decades it has also become popular among those planning careers in politics, international relations, law, medicine, engineering, psychology, and more. This is for good reason: Practitioners in each of these fields often find themselves confronting economic issues. For example, lawyers increasingly face judicial rulings based on the principles of economic efficiency. Doctors need to understand the consequences of proposed changes in national health-care policy. Industrial psychologists need to understand the economic implications of any workplace changes they advocate.

TO BECOME AN ECONOMIST

Only a tiny minority of this book's readers will decide to become economists themselves. This is welcome news to the authors, and after you have studied labor markets in Chapter 9, you will understand why. But if you do decide to pursue a career as an economist—obtaining a master's degree or even a Ph.D.—you will find many possibilities for employment. Of 16,780 members of the American Economic Association who responded to a recent survey,[1] 65 percent were teachers at colleges or universities. The rest were engaged in a variety of activities in both the private sector (21 percent) and government (14 percent). Economists are hired by banks to assess the risk of investing abroad; by manufacturing companies, to help them determine new methods of producing, marketing, and pricing their products; by government agencies, to help design policies to fight crime, disease, poverty, and pollution; by international organizations, to help create aid programs for less developed countries; by the media, to help the public interpret global, national, and local events; and even by nonprofit organizations, to provide advice on controlling costs and raising funds more effectively.

THE METHOD OF ECONOMICS

One of the first things you will notice as you begin to study economics is the heavy reliance on *models*. Indeed, the discipline goes beyond any other social science in its insistence that every theory be represented by an explicit, carefully constructed model.

MODEL An abstract representation of reality.

> A *model* is an abstract representation of reality.

Children play with model trains, model planes, and model people—dolls. Architects build cardboard models of buildings before construction begins. These are physical models: three-dimensional replicas that you can pick up and hold. Economic models, on the other hand, are built not with cardboard, plastic, or metal, but with words, diagrams, and mathematical statements.

---

1. *American Economic Review*, December 1993, p. 635.

THE ART OF BUILDING ECONOMIC MODELS

Look back at the definition of the word "model." The two key words are *abstract* and *representation*. A model is not supposed to be exactly like reality. Rather, it *represents* the real world by *abstracting*, or taking from it, that which will help us understand it. There is much in the real world that a model must leave out.

When you build a model, how can you know which details to include and which to leave aside? There is no simple answer to this question. The right amount of detail depends on your purpose in building the model in the first place. There is, however, one guiding principle:

> *A model should be as simple as possible to accomplish its purpose.*

This means that a model should contain all *necessary* details—but no *unnecessary* ones.

To help make this more concrete, think about a map. A map is a model—it represents the earth's three-dimensional surface by collapsing it into two dimensions; it leaves out many details of the real world, such as trees and houses and potholes; and it is much smaller than the area it represents. When you buy a map, how much detail are you looking for?

Let's say you are in San Francisco, and your purpose—the reason you need a map—is to find the best way to drive from Fisherman's Wharf to the downtown civic center. In this case, you would want a very detailed city map, with every street, park, and plaza in San Francisco clearly illustrated and labeled. A highway map—which ignores these details—wouldn't do at all.

But now suppose your purpose is different: to select the best driving route from San Francisco to Cincinnati. Now, you want a highway map. A map showing every street between San Francisco and Cincinnati would have *too much* detail. All of that extraneous information would only obscure what you really need to see.

Although economic models are more abstract than road maps, the same principle applies in building them: The level of detail that would be just right for one purpose will usually be too much or too little for another. When you feel yourself objecting to a model in this text because something has been left out, keep in mind the purpose for which the model is built. In introductory economics, the purpose is entirely educational. The models are designed to help you understand some simple, but powerful, principles about how the economy operates. Keeping the models simple makes it easier to see the basic principles at work and remember them later.

Of course, economic models have other purposes besides education. They can help businesses make decisions about pricing and production, help households decide how and where to invest their savings, and help governments and international agencies formulate policies. Models built for these purposes will be much more detailed than the ones in this text, and you will learn about them if you take more advanced courses in economics. But even complex models are built around a very simple framework, the same framework you will be learning here.

ASSUMPTIONS AND CONCLUSIONS

Every economic model begins with *assumptions* about the way decision makers in the economy behave. There are two types of assumptions in a model: simplifying assumptions and critical assumptions.

A **simplifying assumption** is just what it sounds like—a way of making a model simpler, without affecting any of its important conclusions. The purpose of a simplifying assumption is to rid a model of extraneous detail, so its essential features

SIMPLIFYING ASSUMPTION Any assumption that makes a model simpler without affecting any of its important conclusions.

can stand out more clearly. A road map, for example, makes the simplifying assumption, "There are no trees," because trees on a map would only get in the way. Similarly, in an economic model, we might assume that there are only two goods that households can choose from or that there are only two nations in the world. We make such assumptions *not* because they are true, but because they make a model easier to follow and do not change any of the important insights we can get from it.

A **critical assumption,** by contrast, is an assumption that affects the conclusions of a model in important ways. When you use a road map, you make the critical assumption, "All of these roads are open." If that assumption is wrong, your conclusion—the best route to take—might be wrong as well.

In an economic model, there are always one or more critical assumptions. You don't have to look very hard to find them, because economists like to make these assumptions explicit, right from the outset. For example, when we study the behavior of business firms, our model will assume that firms try to earn the highest possible profit for their owners. By stating this conclusion up front, we see immediately where the model's conclusions spring from.

CRITICAL ASSUMPTION Any assumption that affects the conclusions of a model in an important way.

TWO FUNDAMENTAL ASSUMPTIONS

The economy is complex. In the twenty seconds or so that it takes you to read this sentence, America's 250 million people will produce about $5 million worth of goods and services, the U.S. government will collect about $1 million in taxes and spend about the same, and U.S. firms will buy about $600,000 worth of goods and services from foreign firms in more than a hundred different countries.

Economists make sense of all this activity—and more—in two steps. First, the decision makers in the economy are divided into three broad groups: households, business firms, and government agencies. In *micro*economic models, the focus is on the behavior of *individual* households, firms, and government agencies and how they interact with each other. In *macro*economic models, we group these decision makers together into sectors—the household sector, the business sector, the government sector, and the foreign sector—and study how each sector interacts with the others.

The next step in understanding the economy is to make two critical assumptions about decision makers. These two assumptions are so universal in economic models that we may fairly consider them part of the foundation of economic thought.

FIRST FUNDAMENTAL ASSUMPTION. The first assumption has to do with *what* it is that individual decision makers are trying to accomplish. It can be stated as follows:

> *Every economic decision maker tries to make the best out of any situation.*

Typically, making the best out of a situation means *maximizing some quantity.* Business firms, for example, are usually assumed to maximize profit. Households maximize utility—their well-being or satisfaction. In some cases, however, we might want to recognize that firms or households are actually groups of individuals with different agendas. While a firm's owners might want the firm to maximize profits, the managers might want to consider their own power, prestige, and job security. These goals may conflict, and the behavior of the firm will depend on how the conflict is resolved.

While economists often have spirited disagreements about *what* is being maximized, there is virtually unanimous agreement that any economic model should begin with the assumption that *someone* is maximizing *something.* Even the behavior of groups—like the decision makers in a firm or officials of the federal government—is assumed to arise from the behavior of different maximizing individuals, each pursuing his or her own agenda.

The first fundamental assumption seems to imply that we are all engaged in a relentless, conscious pursuit of narrow goals—an implication contradicted by much of human behavior. As you read this paragraph, are you consciously trying to maximize your own well-being? Perhaps. You may be fully aware that reading this will improve your grade in economics; that, in turn, will help you achieve other important goals. But most likely, you aren't thinking about any of this. In truth, we only rarely make decisions with conscious, hard calculations. Why, then, do economists assume that people make decisions consciously, when, in reality, they often don't?

This is an important question. Economists answer it this way: The ultimate purpose of building an economic model is to *understand and predict behavior*—the behavior of households, firms, government, and the overall economy. As long as people behave *as if* they are maximizing something, then we can build a good model by *assuming that they are.* Whether they *actually, consciously* maximize anything is an interesting philosophical question, but the answer doesn't affect the usefulness of the model. Thus, the belief behind the first fundamental assumption is that people, for the most part, behave *as if* they are maximizing something.

One last thought about the assumption that people maximize something: It does not imply that people are selfish or that economists think they are. On the contrary, economists are very interested in cases where people take the interests of others into account. For example, much economic life takes place in the family, where people care a great deal about each other. Our first fundamental assumption would then be applied to the family as a whole. That is, we would assume that the entire family, rather than any one individual within it, is trying to make the best out of any situation.

Economics also recognizes that people often care about their friends, their neighbors, and the broader society in which they live. Useful economic models have been built to explore charitable giving by individuals and corporations, volunteer activity, and ethical behavior such as honesty, fairness, and respect for fellow citizens.

SECOND FUNDAMENTAL ASSUMPTION. A second critical assumption underlying all economic models is a simple fact of life:

> *Every economic decision maker faces constraints.*

Society's overall scarcity of resources constrains each of us individually in much the same way as the overall scarcity of space in a crowded elevator limits each rider's freedom of movement. Because of the scarcity of resources, households are constrained by limited incomes, business firms are constrained by requirements that they pay for all of the inputs they use, and government agencies are constrained by limited budgets.

Together, the two fundamental assumptions help define the approach economists take in answering questions about the world. To explain why there is poverty, illiteracy, and crime, to explain the rise and fall of industries and the patterns of trade among nations, or to explain why some government policies succeed while others fail, economists always begin with the same three questions:

1. Who are the individual decision makers?
2. What are they maximizing?
3. What constraints do they face?

This approach is used so heavily by economists that it is one of the *basic principles of economics* you will learn in this book.

A FEW WORDS ON MACROECONOMICS

In *micro*economics, it is easy to see the two fundamental assumptions at work, since the decision makers, what they maximize, and their constraints are spelled out right from the beginning. In *macro*economics, however, we focus not on *individual* households, firms or government agencies, but on household, business, or government *sectors*. As a result, the individual decision makers are somewhat hidden in the background. Still, every macroeconomic model is based on the actions of individual decision makers, who are each assumed to be maximizing something subject to constraints. And in recent decades, macroeconomists have striven to clarify the role of the two fundamental assumptions in their models, to build the "microfoundations" of macroeconomics.

"HOW MUCH MATH DO I NEED?"

Economists often express their ideas using mathematical concepts and a special vocabulary. Why? Because these tools enable economists to express themselves more precisely than with ordinary language. For example, someone who has never studied economics might say, "When used textbooks are easy to buy, students won't buy new textbooks." A student of economics would say, "When the price of used textbooks falls, the demand curve for new textbooks shifts leftward."

Does the second statement sound strange to you? It should. First, it uses a special term—a *demand curve*—that you haven't yet learned. Second, it uses a mathematical concept—a *shifting curve*—with which you might not be familiar. But while the first statement might mean a number of different things, the second statement—as you will see in Chapter 3—can mean only *one* thing. By being precise, we can steer clear of unnecessary confusion. If you are worried about the special vocabulary of economics, you can relax. All of the new terms will be defined and carefully explained as you encounter them.

But what about the math? Here, too, you can relax. While professional economists often use sophisticated mathematics to solve problems, only a little math is needed to understand basic economic *principles*. And virtually all of this math comes from high-school algebra and geometry.

Still, you may have forgotten some of your high-school math. If so, a little brushing up might be in order. This is why we have included a *Mathematical Appendix* at the end of the book. It covers some of the most basic concepts—such as the equation for a straight line, the concept of a slope, and the calculation of percentage changes—as well as a few special tools that you may not have encountered before. You may want to glance at this appendix now, just so you'll know what's there. Then, from time to time, you'll be reminded about it when you're most likely to need it.

THE BASIC PRINCIPLES OF ECONOMICS

As you learn economics, you will encounter a variety of different theories, ideas, and techniques, each suited to analyzing a particular problem. But a few of these ideas are so central that they are used again and again in a variety of different contexts. And these ideas are not only useful in their own right; they also form the foundation on which the rest of economic theory is built. In this book, we call these ideas *basic principles of economics:*

*The **basic principles of economics** are ideas that are used again and again to analyze economic problems. They form the foundation upon which economic theory is built.*

In this sense, the body of economic theory is like an upside-down pyramid, with a few basic principles at the narrow bottom and the many ideas that spring from them forming the wider top.

In this book, you will learn eight basic principles of economics. A "key" symbol will appear each time one of them is introduced for the first time. Then, each time the principle is *used* in the text—to analyze a problem or to help form a more specific theory—you'll be alerted with the same key symbol, in the margin.

For example, earlier in this chapter, you learned about the two *fundamental assumptions* that economists use when analyzing almost any problem. Together, these two assumptions form the first of the basic principles you will learn about. Let's now introduce this principle formally:

> ⚷ *Basic Principle #1: Maximization Subject to Constraints*
> *The economic approach to understanding a problem is to identify the decision makers, and then determine what they are maximizing and the constraints that they face.*

As you will see, the principle of *maximization subject to constraints* will be used again and again in this book.

What about the rest of the basic principles? Following is the complete list, along with the pages on which you will find important conclusions derived from each principle. (The bolded page number indicates the first time the principle is introduced.) You are welcome to read the list now, but don't expect to understand it . . . yet. By the time you've finished reading this book, however, you will understand what these principles mean, how they are used, and why they are so basic to economics.

The Eight Basic Principles of Economics

- **Basic Principle #1—Maximization Subject to Constraints:** *The economic approach to understanding a problem is to identify the decision makers, and then determine what they are maximizing and the constraints that they face.*

- **Basic Principle #2—Opportunity Cost:** *All economic decisions made by individuals or society are costly. The correct way to measure the cost of a choice is its opportunity cost—that which is given up to make the choice.*

- **Basic Principle #3—Specialization and Exchange:** *Specialization and exchange enable us to enjoy greater production and higher living standards than would otherwise be possible. As a result, all economies exhibit high degrees of specialization and exchange.*

- **Basic Principle #4—Markets and Equilibrium:** *To understand how the economy behaves, economists organize the world into separate markets and then examine the equilibrium in each of those markets.*

- **Basic Principle #5—Policy Tradeoffs:** *Government policy is constrained by the reactions of private decision makers. As a result, policy makers face tradeoffs: Making progress toward one goal often requires some sacrifice of another goal.*

- **Basic Principle #6—Marginal Decision Making:** *To understand and predict the behavior of individual decision makers, we focus on the incremental or marginal effects of their actions.*

BASIC PRINCIPLES OF ECONOMICS A small set of basic ideas that are used repeatedly in analyzing economic problems. They form the foundation of economic theory.

- **Basic Principle #7—Short-Run versus Long-Run Outcomes:** *Markets behave differently in the short run than in the long run. In solving a problem, we must always know which of these time horizons we are analyzing.*

- **Basic Principle #8—The Importance of Real Values:** *Since our economic well-being depends, in part, on the goods and services we can buy, it is important to translate from nominal values—which are measured in current dollars—to real values—which are measured in purchasing power.*

You may want to flip back to this list from time to time, especially when you see the "key" symbol in the margin and need to refresh your memory about the principle that it refers to.

HOW TO STUDY ECONOMICS

As you read this book or listen to your instructor, you may find yourself nodding along and thinking that everything makes perfect sense. Economics may even seem easy. Indeed, it *is* rather easy to follow economics, since it's based so heavily on simple logic. But *following* and *learning* are two different things. You will eventually discover—preferably *before* your first exam—that economics must be studied actively, not passively.

If you are reading these words lying back on a comfortable couch, a phone in one hand and a remote control in the other, you are, sorry to say, going about it in the wrong way. Active studying means reading with a pencil in hand and a blank sheet of paper in front of you. It means closing the book periodically and *reproducing* what you have learned. It means listing the steps in each logical argument, retracing the cause-and-effect links in each model, and drawing the graphs that represent the model. It means *thinking* about the basic principles of economics and how they relate to what you are learning. It is hard work, but the pay-off is a good understanding of economics and a better understanding of your own life and the world around you.

⌐ S U M M A R Y ¬

Economics is the study of choice under conditions of scarcity. As individuals, and as a society, we have unlimited desires for goods and services. Unfortunately, the *resources*—land, labor, and capital—needed to produce those goods and services are scarce. Therefore, we must choose which desires to satisfy and how to satisfy them. Economics provides the tools that explain those choices.

The field of economics is divided into two major areas. *Microeconomics* studies the behavior of individual households, firms, and governments as they interact in specific markets. *Macroeconomics,* by contrast, concerns itself with the behavior of the entire economy. It considers variables such as total output, total employment, and the overall price level.

Economics makes heavy use of *models*—abstract representations of reality. These models are words, diagrams, and mathematical statements that help us understand how the economy operates. All models are simplifications, but a good model will have just enough detail for the purpose at hand.

Almost all economic models are based on two fundamental assumptions. The first is that every decision maker tries to make the best out of any situation; the second is that every decision maker faces constraints. In every problem that economists analyze, the starting point is determining (1) Who are the decision makers, (2) what are they maximizing, and (3) what constraints do they face?

K E Y   T E R M S

economics	capital	macroeconomics	simplifying assumption
scarcity	human capital	positive economics	critical assumption
resources	land	normative economics	basic principles of economics
labor	microeconomics	model	

R E V I E W   Q U E S T I O N S

1. Discuss how scarcity arises for households, businesses, and governments. Which of the two fundamental assumptions of economics embodies the phenomenon of scarcity?

2. Explain whether the following would be classified as microeconomics or macroeconomics.
   a. Research into why the economy has prospered in the 1990s
   b. A theory of how consumers decide what to buy
   c. An analysis of Microsoft's share of the computer software market
   d. Research on why interest rates were unusually high in the late 1970s and early 1980s

3. Discuss whether the following statements are examples of positive economics or normative economics, or whether they contain elements of both:
   a. An increase in the federal government's budget deficit causes interest rates to rise.
   b. The goal of any country's economic policy should be to increase the welfare of its poorest, most vulnerable, citizens.
   c. Excess regulation of small business is stifling the economy. Small business has been responsible for most of the growth in employment over the last 10 years, but regulations are putting a severe damper on the ability of small businesses to survive and prosper.
   d. The 1980s were a disastrous decade for the U.S. economy. Income inequality increased to its highest level since before World War II.

4. What determines the level of detail that an economist builds into a model?

5. How would an economist respond to the following criticism?
   "The problem with economics is that so much of it is unrealistic. Take, for example, the idea that consumers try to maximize their utility, or well-being. When I go into a store to buy something, I don't stand in the aisles with my calculator trying to compute exactly which purchase will make me the happiest."

P R O B L E M S   A N D   E X E R C I S E S

1. Come up with a list of critical assumptions that could lie behind each of the following statements. Discuss whether each assumption would be classified as normative or positive.
   a. The United States is a democratic society.
   b. European movies are better than American movies.
   c. The bigger the city, the higher the quality of the newspaper.

2. It's a good idea to practice finding economic information on the Web. To get started, visit Resources for Economists on the Internet at http://www.rfe.org. On the introductory page, you will see the words "Table of Contents" highlighted. Click there and browse the categories. Then go to the category "Newspapers and other News Media" and browse some of the on-line sources of economic news. Bookmark one or two and plan to check back regularly for economic news of the day.

CHAPTER 2

SCARCITY, CHOICE, AND ECONOMIC SYSTEMS

What does it cost you to go to the movies? If you answered seven or eight dollars, because that is the price of a movie ticket, then you are leaving a lot out. Most of us are used to thinking of "cost" as the money we must pay for something. A Big Mac costs $2.50, a new Toyota Corolla costs $15,000, and so on. Certainly, the money we pay for a good or service is a *part* of its cost. But economics takes a broader view of costs, recognizing monetary as well as nonmonetary components.

THE CONCEPT OF OPPORTUNITY COST

The total cost of any choice we make—buying a car, producing a computer, or even reading a book—is everything we must *give up* when we take that action. This cost is called the *opportunity cost* of the action, because we give up the opportunity to have other things that we value.

> *The **opportunity cost** of any choice is what we give up when we make that choice.*

Opportunity cost is the most accurate and complete concept of cost—the one we should use when making decisions.

OPPORTUNITY COST FOR INDIVIDUALS

Virtually every action we take as individuals uses up scarce money or scarce time or both. Hence, every action we choose requires us to sacrifice other enjoyable goods and activities for which we could have used our money and time. For exam-

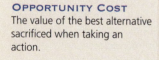

OPPORTUNITY COST
The value of the best alternative sacrificed when taking an action.

16

ple, it took a substantial amount of the authors' time to write this textbook. Suppose that the time devoted to writing the book could instead have been used by one of the authors to either (1) go to law school, (2) write a novel, or (3) start a profitable business.

Do all of these alternatives together make up the opportunity cost of writing this book? Not really. Choosing not to write the book would have released some time, but not enough time to pursue all of these activities. To measure opportunity cost, we should look only at the alternatives that *would* have been chosen—the *next best* alternatives that must be given up. Suppose that, for one of the authors, the next best alternative was to start a profitable business. Then the opportunity cost of co-authoring this book was the value of the forgone opportunity to start the business. Since the other, less valuable alternatives would not have been chosen anyway, they are not part of the cost of writing the book.

To explore this notion of opportunity cost further, let's go back to an earlier question: What does it cost to see a movie? That depends on who is seeing the movie. Suppose some friends ask Jessica, a college student, to go with them to a movie located ten minutes from campus. To see the movie, Jessica will use up scarce *funds* to buy the movie ticket and scarce *time* traveling to and from the movie and sitting through it. Suppose the *money* she uses for the movie ticket would otherwise have been spent on a long-distance phone call to a friend in Italy—her next best use of the money—and the *time* would otherwise have been devoted to studying for her economics exam—her next best use of time. For Jessica, then, the opportunity cost of the movie consists of two things given up: (1) a phone call to her friend *and* (2) a higher score on her economics exam. Seeing the movie will require Jessica to sacrifice *both* of these valuable alternatives, since the movie will cost Jessica both money and time.

Now consider Samantha, a highly paid consultant who lives in New York City, a few miles from the movie theater, and who has a backlog of projects to work on. As in Jessica's case, seeing the movie will use scarce funds and scarce time. But for Samantha, both costs will be greater. First, the direct money costs: There is not only the price of the movie ticket, but also the round-trip cab fare, which could bring the direct money cost to $20. However, this is only a small part of Samantha's opportunity cost. Let's suppose that the time it takes Samantha to find out when and where the movie is playing, hail a cab, travel to the movie theater, wait in line, sit through the previews, and travel back home is three hours—not unrealistic for seeing a movie in Manhattan. Samantha's next best alternative for using her time would be to work on her consulting projects, for which she would earn $150 per hour. In this case, we can measure the entire opportunity cost of the movie in monetary terms: first, the direct money costs of the movie and cab fare ($20), and second, the *forgone income* associated with seeing the movie ($150 × 3 hours = $450), for a total of $470!

At such a high price, you might wonder why Samantha would ever decide to see a movie. Indeed, the same reasoning applies to almost everything Samantha does besides work: It is very expensive for Samantha to talk to a friend on the phone, eat dinner, or even sleep. Each of these activities requires her to sacrifice the direct money costs plus another $150 per hour of forgone income. Would Samantha ever choose to pursue any of these activities? The answer for Samantha is the same as for Jessica or anyone else: yes—*if* the activity is more highly valued than what is given up. It is not hard to imagine that, after putting in a long day at work, leisure activities would be very important to Samantha—worth the money cost *and* the forgone income required to enjoy them.

With an understanding of the concept of opportunity cost and how it can differ among individuals, you can understand some behavior that might otherwise appear strange. For example, why do high-income people rarely shop at discount stores like Kmart, and instead shop at full-service stores where the same items sell for much higher prices? It's not that high-income people *like* to pay more for their purchases. But discount stores are generally understaffed and crowded with customers, so shopping there takes more time. While discount stores have lower *money* cost, they impose a higher *time* cost. For high-income people, these stores are actually more costly than stores with higher price tags.

We can also understand why the most highly paid consultants, entrepreneurs, attorneys, and surgeons often lead such frenetic lives, doing several things at once and packing every spare minute with tasks. Since these people can earn several hundred dollars for an hour of work, every activity they undertake carries a correspondingly high opportunity cost. Brushing one's teeth can cost $10, and driving to work can cost hundreds! By combining activities—making phone calls while driving to work, thinking about and planning the day while in the shower, or reading the morning paper in the elevator—the opportunity cost of these routine activities can be reduced.

OPPORTUNITY COST AND SOCIETY

From an individual's point of view, it is useful to think of opportunity cost as arising from the *scarcity* of *time or money*. But when we switch our perspective to society as a whole, opportunity cost arises from a different source: the *scarcity of society's resources*. Since human wants are unlimited, while society's resources are finite, no society can produce enough of everything to satisfy everyone's desires simultaneously. Therefore,

> *All production carries an opportunity cost: To produce more of one thing, society must shift resources away from producing something else.*

Consider a goal on which we can all agree: better health for our citizens. What would be needed to achieve this goal? Perhaps more medical checkups for more people and greater access to top-flight medicine when necessary. These, in turn, would require more and better trained doctors, more hospital buildings and laboratories, and more high-tech medical equipment such as CAT scanners and surgical lasers. In order for us to produce these goods and services, we would have to pull resources—land, labor, and capital—out of producing other goods and services that we also enjoy. The opportunity cost of improved health care, then, consists of these other goods and services we would have to do without.

PRINCIPLE OF OPPORTU-NITY COST All economic decisions made by individuals or society are costly. The correct way to measure the cost of a choice is its opportunity cost—that which is given up to make the choice.

THE PRINCIPLE OF OPPORTUNITY COST

Opportunity cost is one of the most important ideas you will encounter in economics. The concept sheds light on virtually every problem that economists study, whether it be explaining the behavior of consumers or business firms or understanding important social problems like poverty or racial discrimination. In all of these cases, economists apply the **principle of opportunity cost.**

> *Basic Principle #2: Opportunity Cost*
> *All economic decisions made by individuals or society are costly. The correct way to measure the cost of a choice is its opportunity cost—that which is given up to make the choice.*

PRODUCTION POSSIBILITIES FRONTIERS

Let's build a simple model to help us see how the principle of opportunity cost can be applied to society's choices. We'll start with a *simplifying assumption*—that the production of all goods and services in a society has been predetermined, except for those in *two* categories: health care and movies. In this way, we narrow down society's choices: There can be more health care, but only at the cost of fewer movies. Alternatively, more movies can be produced, but only at the cost of less health care. This may seem like a strange juxtaposition: How can we pit health care—which requires inputs such as doctors, laboratories, and medical equipment—against movies—which require inputs such as actors, writers, film, studios, and theaters? The answer is that all of these inputs are ultimately made from the same general categories of resources: land, labor, and capital. To have more health care, we must pull these resources out of other production—in our example, out of movie production.

To be even more specific, let's measure health care by the *number of lives saved* and movies by the *number of high-budget feature films produced*. Then, with all other production held constant, society would face a clear tradeoff: saving more lives would require a shift of resources from movies to health care, so there would be fewer films produced each year.

Figure 1 illustrates this tradeoff for society in graphical form. The curve in the figure is society's **production possibilities frontier (PPF)**, *giving the different combinations of goods that can be produced with the resources and technology currently available.* The number of lives saved through medical intervention is measured along the vertical axis, and the number of feature films produced appears along the horizontal axis. The PPF tells us the *maximum quantity* of movies that can be produced for each quantity of lives saved, or the maximum number of lives saved for each different quantity of films. Positions beyond the frontier are unattainable with

PRODUCTION POSSIBILITIES FRONTIER (PPF) A curve showing all combinations of two goods that can be produced with the resources and technology currently available.

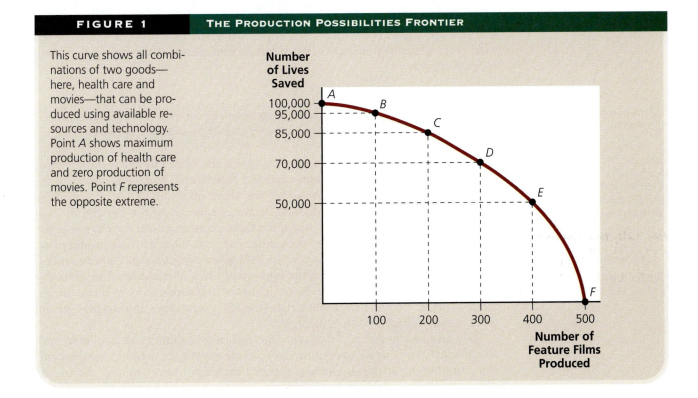

| FIGURE 1 | THE PRODUCTION POSSIBILITIES FRONTIER |

This curve shows all combinations of two goods—here, health care and movies—that can be produced using available resources and technology. Point *A* shows maximum production of health care and zero production of movies. Point *F* represents the opposite extreme.

the technology and resources at the economy's disposal. Society's choices are limited to points *on* or *inside* the PPF.

Point *A* represents one choice this society could make: to devote all the resources for the two goods—health care and movies—to health care alone. In this case, there would be zero movies, but 100,000 lives would be saved each year with the health-care system. Point *F* represents the opposite extreme: All resources available for the two goods would go into film production and none into health care. There would be 500 major movies produced each year, but society would have to forgo every opportunity to save lives.

If points *A* and *F* seem absurd to you, remember that they represent two *possible* choices for this society, but choices it would be unlikely to make. People want entertainment as well as physical health, so a realistic choice would include a *mix* of health care and movies.

Suppose this society desires such a mix, but the economy, for some reason, is currently operating at the undesirable point *A*—maximal health care, zero films. Then some resources must be shifted from health care to films. A move from point *A* to point *B* would result in 100 movies each year, but, as a consequence, there would be a cutback on health care and 5,000 fewer lives would be saved. The opportunity cost of 100 additional films, then, would be 5,000 human lives.

INCREASING OPPORTUNITY COST. The move from point *A* to point *B* in Figure 1 got us 100 more movies, but cost us 5,000 in lives saved. From point *B*, let us once again imagine shifting enough resources out of health care to produce an additional 100 movies. Notice that, this time, there is an even *greater* cost: 10,000 fewer lives saved. The opportunity cost of movies has risen. You can see that as we continue to increase movie production by increments of 100—moving from point *C* to point *D* to point *E*—the opportunity cost of movies keeps right on rising, until the last 100 films cost an additional 50,000 lives.

The behavior of opportunity cost described here—that the more films we produce, the greater the opportunity cost of producing still more of them—applies to a wide range of choices facing society. It can be generalized as the *law of increasing opportunity cost.*

🔑 **OPPORTUNITY COST**

LAW OF INCREASING OPPORTUNITY COST The more of something that is produced, the greater is the opportunity cost of producing one more unit.

Due to the law of diminishing returns

> *According to the **law of increasing opportunity cost,** the more of something we produce, the greater is the opportunity cost of producing still more.*

The law of increasing opportunity cost causes the PPF to have a *concave* shape, becoming steeper as we move rightward and downward. To understand why, remember—from high-school math—that the slope of a line or curve is just the change along the vertical axis divided by the change along the horizontal axis. Along the PPF, as we move rightward, the slope corresponds to the change in the number of lives saved divided by the change in the number of films produced or, equivalently, the change in the number of lives saved *per additional film produced.* The absolute value of this slope is the opportunity cost of one more film. Since the opportunity cost increases as we move rightward and produce more films, the absolute value of the PPF's slope must rise—the PPF gets steeper and steeper—giving us the concave shape we see in the figure.

You may be wondering if the law of increasing opportunity cost applies in both directions. That is, as we save more lives, do we experience a rise in the opportunity cost of saving a life? A glance at Figure 2 should convince you that the answer

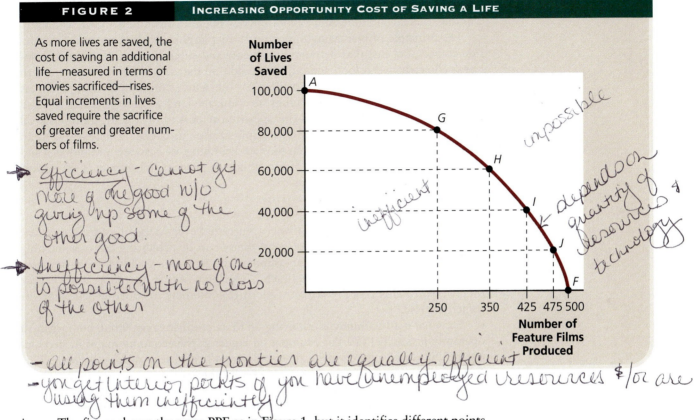

FIGURE 2 — INCREASING OPPORTUNITY COST OF SAVING A LIFE

As more lives are saved, the cost of saving an additional life—measured in terms of movies sacrificed—rises. Equal increments in lives saved require the sacrifice of greater and greater numbers of films.

[Handwritten margin notes:]

Efficiency - Cannot get more of one good w/o giving up some of the other good.

Inefficiency - more of one is possible with no loss of the other

impossible

inefficient

K dependent on quantity of resources & technology

- all points on the frontier are equally efficient
- you get interior points if you have unemployed resources &/or are using them inefficiently

---

is yes. The figure shows the same PPF as in Figure 1, but it identifies different points along the frontier. Notice that equal increments in lives saved require the sacrifice of greater and greater numbers of films.

Why should there be a law of increasing opportunity cost? Why must it be that the more of something we produce, the greater the opportunity cost of producing still more?

There is a very good reason. Most resources, by their very nature, are better suited to some purposes than to others. At point *F,* where only films are produced, movie production is using many resources that are poorly suited to this purpose and that would be much better suited for work in health care. For example, at point *F,* potentially brilliant surgeons are employed as film directors, actors, camera operators, and so on; hospitals are used as film studios; and laser equipment originally designed for eye surgery might instead be used to provide special effects.

As we move leftward along the PPF, shifting resources out of movies and into health care, we would first shift those resources *best suited to health care*—for example, a surgeon who could save many lives in the emergency ward, but is not doing too well as a film editor. For example, moving from *F* to *J* in Figure 2, we shift resources that were not really contributing all that much to film production, but will contribute quite a bit to health care. This is why, at first, the PPF is very steep: We get a *large* increase in lives saved for only a *small* decrease in the number of films made. As we continue moving leftward, however, we are forced to shift into health care resources that are better and better suited to making films. As a result, the PPF becomes flatter. Finally, we arrive at point *A,* where all resources, no matter how well suited for moviemaking, are working in the health-care industry. Film studios would be used as hospital wards and spotlights used to illuminate operating rooms.

Harrison Ford might be your ophthalmologist, Arnold Schwarzenegger might be working a suicide hot line, and Sandra Bullock might be operating a CAT scanner.

The principle of increasing opportunity cost applies to all of society's production choices, not just that between health care and entertainment. If we look at society's choice between food and oil, we would find that some land is better suited to growing food and some land to drilling for oil. As we continue to shift resources out of food production and into oil production, the land we are shifting is less and less suited to producing oil, and the opportunity cost of producing additional oil will therefore increase. The same principle applies in choosing between civilian goods and military goods, between food and clothing, or between automobiles and public transportation: The more of something we produce, the greater is the opportunity cost of producing still more.

THE SEARCH FOR A FREE LUNCH

At the beginning of this chapter, it was argued that every decision to produce *more* of something requires us to pay an opportunity cost by producing less of something else. Economist Milton Friedman summarized this idea in his famous remark: "There is no such thing as a free lunch." The logic of this statement is seen every time we *move along* a PPF: We must sacrifice something in order to have more of something else.

But what if an economy is not living up to its productive potential, but is instead operating *inside* its PPF? For example, in Figure 2, the economy might be producing 250 films and enough medical care to save 40,000 lives—a point *inside* its PPF. (Identify this point in Figure 2.) Shouldn't it be able to produce more of both goods by simply moving *to* its PPF, with no opportunity cost whatsoever? Here it looks as if Milton Friedman was wrong—there *can be* such a thing as a free lunch! But why would an economy ever be operating inside its PPF? There are two possibilities.

TECHNICAL INEFFICIENCY. One case where economies operate inside their PPFs arises when resources are being wasted.

For example, suppose a plywood manufacturer can figure out a way to produce the same amount of output using less lumber *and no more of any other input.* Any manager who did not take advantage of an opportunity like this would be wasting lumber, a valuable resource. Eliminating this waste would make the manufacturer better off—since production could increase without any increase in costs—and make society better off—since there could be more plywood without having to sacrifice anything. When all waste of this sort has been eliminated, production is **technically efficient**—the maximum possible output is being produced from a given collection of inputs.

TECHNICAL EFFICIENCY
A situation in which the maximum possible output is being produced from a given collection of inputs.

Technical *in*efficiency is illustrated in Figure 3, where the PPF is drawn for the choice between plywood and paper, two goods that use lumber and labor as key inputs. Once again, we assume that production of all other goods remains constant, and focus only on the choice between two goods: plywood and paper. Point *A* on the PPF shows us that, given plywood production of 400 units, the maximum production of paper would be 600 units. However, with technical inefficiency, the economy might be at a point like *B*—inside the PPF. In that case, the economy is not producing the maximum possible output from the resources—for example, lumber—at its disposal. Eliminating the technical inefficiency would allow us to move from point *B* inside the PPF to a point *on* the PPF. We could move from point *B* to point *C* and produce more plywood; from *B* to *A*, producing more paper; or from *B* to *E,* producing more of *both* goods. In any of these cases, we can have more of

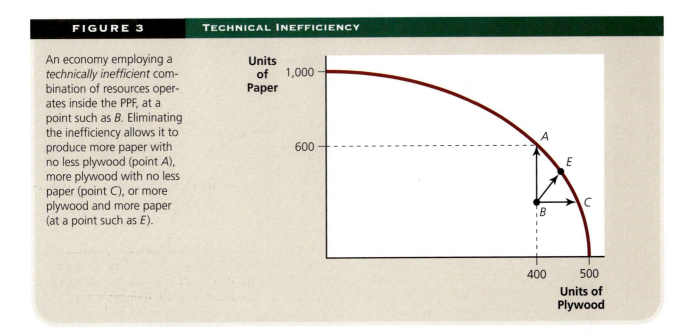

| FIGURE 3 | TECHNICAL INEFFICIENCY |

An economy employing a *technically inefficient* combination of resources operates inside the PPF, at a point such as *B*. Eliminating the inefficiency allows it to produce more paper with no less plywood (point *A*), more plywood with no less paper (point *C*), or more plywood and more paper (at a point such as *E*).

one thing without having to produce less of anything else, and so we can avoid paying any opportunity cost for the additional production.

Before you get the idea that finding free lunches like this is an easy task, be forewarned that cases of technical inefficiency are rare. When you study microeconomics, you will see that owners and managers of firms have powerful incentives to eliminate most instances of technical inefficiency.

RECESSIONS. Another situation where an economy operates inside its PPF is a *recession*—a slowdown in overall economic activity. During recessions, many resources are idle. There is widespread unemployment—people want to work, but are unable to find jobs. Factories shut down, so we are not using all of our available capital or land, either. An end to the recession would move the economy from a point *inside* its PPF to a point *on* its PPF—using idle resources to produce more goods and services without sacrificing anything.

This simple observation can help us understand, in part, why the United States and the Soviet Union had such different economic experiences during World War II. In the United States, the average standard of living improved considerably as we entered the war; in the Soviet Union, it deteriorated severely. Why?

Figure 4 helps to solve this puzzle. Here, the PPFs illustrate the choice between military goods and civilian goods. When the United States entered the war in 1940, it was still suffering from the Great Depression—the most serious and long-lasting economic downturn in modern history, which began in 1929 and hit most of the developed world. For reasons you will learn when you study macroeconomics, joining the allied war effort ended the depression in the United States and moved our economy from a point like *A*, inside the PPF, to a point like *B*, *on* the frontier. Military production increased, but so did the production of civilian goods. Although there were shortages of some consumer goods, the overall result was a rise in the material well-being of the average U.S. citizen.

In the Soviet Union, things were very different. In the 1930s, the Soviet economy—which was internationally isolated—was able to escape entirely the effects of

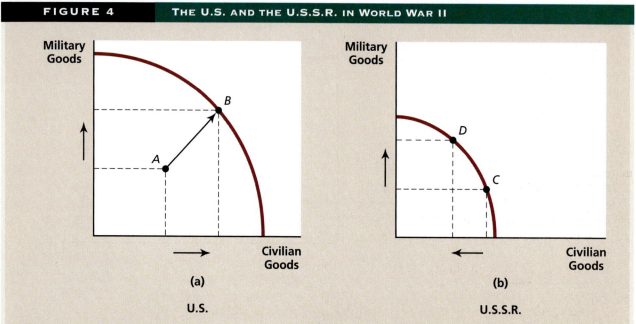

FIGURE 4   **THE U.S. AND THE U.S.S.R. IN WORLD WAR II**

At the onset of World War II, the U.S. economy was experiencing unemployment, at point *A* in panel (a). War production eliminated the unemployment, and the economy moved *onto* its PPF at point *B,* with more military goods *and* more civilian goods. The Soviet Union, by contrast, began the war with no unemployed resources. It could increase military production only by moving *along* its PPF and sacrificing civilian goods, from point *C* to point *D.*

the depression that plagued the rest of the world. Thus, before the war, it was already operating on or near its PPF, at a point like C. Entering the war—which meant an increase in military production—required a movement *along* its PPF, to a point like *D.* For the Soviet Union, the drop in civilian production—and the resulting drop in living standards—was the opportunity cost that had to be paid in order to fight the war.[1]

An economic downturn—such as the Great Depression of the 1930s—does seem to offer a clear-cut free lunch, but even here, appearances can be deceiving. When you study macroeconomics, you will see that a variety of government policies might help to end recessions. But these policies come with their own costs. Of course, we may feel that it is worth paying these costs to end a recession, but that is a different matter. Once again, we see that a truly free lunch is not so easy to find.

ECONOMIC SYSTEMS

As you read these words—perhaps sitting at home or in the library—you are experiencing a very private moment. It is just you and this book; the rest of the world might as well not exist. Or so it seems. . . .

---

1.   Another explanation for the different experiences of the United States and Soviet Union can also be illustrated with PPFs. Since the war was not fought on our turf, we had no significant destruction of physical capital within the 48 states. But large parts of the Soviet Union were decimated. Similarly, while the human loss for the United States was significant, the Soviet loss was even worse—about 20 times greater. In the Soviet Union, the huge decreases in labor and capital shifted the PPF significantly *inward*—with fewer resources, there could be less production of civilian goods for a given amount of military goods. This was another reason for the decline in Soviet living standards.

Actually, even in this supposedly private moment, you are connected to the rest of the world in ways you may not have thought about. In order for you to be reading this book, we, the authors, had to write it. Someone (his name is Dennis Hanseman) had to edit it, to help make sure that all necessary material was covered and explained as clearly as possible. Someone else had to prepare the graphics. Others had to run the printing presses and the binding machines, and still others had to pack the book, ship it, unpack it, put it on a store shelf, and then sell it to you. And there is more: People had to manufacture paper and ink, the boxes used for shipping, the computers used to keep track of inventory, and so on. It is no exaggeration to say that thousands of people were involved in putting this book in your hands.

And there is still more. The chair or couch upon which you are sitting, the light shining on the page, the heat or the air conditioning in the room, the clothes you are wearing—these are all things that you are using right now, things produced by *somebody else*. At this very moment, then, you are economically linked to others in many different ways.

Take a walk in your town or city, and you will see even more evidence of our economic interdependence: People are collecting garbage, helping schoolchildren cross the street, transporting furniture across town, constructing buildings, repairing roads, painting houses. Everyone is producing goods and services for *other people*.

Why is it that so much of what we consume is produced by somebody else? Why are we all so heavily dependent on each other for our material well-being? Why doesn't each of us—like Robinson Crusoe on his island—produce our own food, clothing, housing, and anything else we desire? And how did it come about that *you*—who did not produce any of these things yourself—are able to consume them?

These are all questions about our *economic system*—the way our economy is organized. Ordinarily, we take our economic system for granted, like the water that runs out of our tap. But now it's time to take a closer look at the plumbing: to learn how our economy serves so many millions of people, enabling them to survive and prosper.

SPECIALIZATION AND EXCHANGE

If we were forced to, most of us could become economically self-sufficient. We could stake out a plot of land, grow our own food, make our own clothing, and build our own homes. But no society is characterized by such extreme self-sufficiency. On the contrary, every economic system over the past 10,000 years has been characterized by two features: (1) **specialization**, in which each of us concentrates on a limited number of productive activities; and (2) **exchange**, in which most of what we desire is obtained by trading with others, rather than producing for ourselves. These two features are at the heart of a basic principle of economics:

> ⚷ *Basic Principle #3: Specialization and Exchange*
> *Specialization and exchange enable us to enjoy greater production, and higher living standards, than would otherwise be possible. As a result, all economies exhibit high degrees of specialization and exchange.*

There are three reasons that specialization and exchange enable us to enjoy greater production. The first has to do with human capabilities: Each of us can learn only so much in a lifetime. By limiting ourselves to a narrow set of tasks—fixing plumbing, managing workers, writing music, or designing computer software— we are each able to hone our skills and become experts at one or two things, instead

SPECIALIZATION A method of production in which each person concentrates on a limited number of activities.

EXCHANGE The act of trading with others to obtain what we desire.

of remaining amateurs at a lot of things. It is easy to see that an economy of experts will produce more than an economy of amateurs.

A second gain from specialization results from the time needed to switch from one activity to another. When people specialize, and spend more time doing one task, there is less unproductive "downtime" from switching activities.

Before considering the third gain from specialization, it is important to note that these first two gains—acquiring expertise and minimizing downtime—would occur even if all workers were identical. To see why, let's consider an extreme example. Suppose that three identical triplets—Sherrie, Gerri, and Kerry—decide to open up their own photocopy shop. They quickly discover that there are three primary tasks to be accomplished each day: making photocopies, dealing with customers, and servicing the machines.

Suppose first that the triplets decide *not* to specialize. Each time a customer walks in, *one* of the triplets will take the order, walk to the photocopy machine, make the copies, walk back to the counter, collect the money, make the change, and give a receipt. In addition, each time a machine runs out of paper or ink, the triplet who is using the machine must remedy the problem. You can see that there will be a great deal of time spent going back and forth between the counter, the copy machines, and the supply room. Moreover, none of the triplets will become an expert at servicing the machines, dealing with customers, or making photocopies. As a result of the downtime between tasks, and the lack of expertise, the triplets will not be able to make the maximum possible number of copies or handle the maximum possible number of customers each day.

Now, let's rearrange production to take advantage of specialization. We'll put Sherrie at the counter, Gerri at the photocopy machine, and Kerry at work keeping the machines in working order. Suddenly, all of that time spent going back and forth is now devoted to more productive tasks. Moreover, Sherrie becomes an expert at working the cash register, since she does this all day long. Gerri becomes an expert at making copies, figuring out the quickest ways to select the proper settings, position originals, and turn pages. And Kerry learns how to quickly diagnose and even anticipate problems with the machines. Each task is now performed by an expert. You can see that specialization increases the number of copies and customers that the triplets can handle each day, even though there is no difference in their basic abilities or talents.

Adam Smith first explained these gains from specialization in his book, *An Inquiry into the Nature and Causes of the Wealth of Nations,* published in 1776. Smith explained how specialization within a pin factory dramatically increased the number of pins that could be produced there. In order to make a pin, he wrote,

> *One man draws out the wire, another straightens it, a third cuts it, a fourth points it, a fifth grinds it at the top for receiving the head; to make the head requires three distinct operations; to put it on is a [separate] business, to whiten the pins is another; it is even a trade by itself to put them into the paper; and the important business of making a pin is, in this manner, divided into about eighteen distinct operations, which, in some manufactories, are all performed by distinct hands.*

Smith went on to observe that 10 men, each working separately, might make 200 pins in a day, but through specialization, they were able to make 48,000! What is true for a pin factory or a photocopy shop can be generalized to the entire economy: Even when workers are identically suited to various tasks, total production will increase when workers specialize.

Of course in the real world, workers are *not* identically suited to different kinds of work. Nor are all plots of land, all natural resources, or all types of capital equip-

TABLE 1	TIME REQUIREMENTS FOR BERRIES AND FISH	
	1 Quart of Berries	**1 Fish**
Maryanne	1 hour	1 hour
Gilligan	1½ hours	3 hours

ment identically suited for different tasks. This observation brings us to the *third* source of gains from specialization.

FURTHER GAINS FROM SPECIALIZATION: COMPARATIVE ADVANTAGE.

Imagine a shipwreck in which there are only two survivors—let's call them Maryanne and Gilligan—who wash up on opposite shores of a deserted island. Initially they are unaware of each other, so each is forced to become completely self-sufficient. Each has 12 hours of daylight to perform two tasks necessary for survival: catching fish and picking berries.

On one side of the island, Maryanne finds that it takes her one hour to pick one quart of berries or to catch one fish, as shown in Table 1. She decides to devote five hours to berry picking and seven hours to fishing, and her total production—five quarts of berries and seven fish—is entered in the first row of Table 2.

On the other side of the island, Gilligan—who is less adept at both tasks—requires an hour and a half to pick a quart of berries and three hours to catch one fish, as listed in Table 1. Gilligan decides to spend three hours picking berries—yielding two quarts—and nine hours fishing—catching three fish, as listed in the second row of Table 2. The last row of Table 2 shows total production on the island, obtained simply by adding up the berries and fish produced by these two stranded castaways.

One day, Maryanne and Gilligan discover each other. After rejoicing at the prospect of human companionship, they decide to develop a system of production that will work to their mutual benefit. Let's rule out any gains from specialization that might arise from minimizing downtime or from becoming an expert, as occurred in the photocopy shop example. Will it still pay for these two to specialize? The answer is yes, as you will see after a small detour.

Absolute Advantage: A Detour. When Gilligan and Maryanne sit down to figure out who should do what, they might fall victim to a common mistake: basing their decision on *absolute advantage*. An individual has an **absolute advantage** in the production of some good when he or she can produce it using *fewer resources* than another individual can. On the island, the only resource being used is labor time, so the reasoning might go as follows: Maryanne can pick one quart of berries more quickly than Gilligan (see Table 1), so she has an *absolute advantage* in berry picking. It seems logical, then, that Maryanne should be the one to pick the berries.

> **ABSOLUTE ADVANTAGE**
> The ability to produce a good or service using fewer resources than other producers use.

TABLE 2	PRODUCTION UNDER SELF-SUFFICIENCY	
	Quarts of Berries	**Number of Fish**
Maryanne	5	7
Gilligan	2	3
Total Island	7	10

But wait! Maryanne can also catch fish more quickly than Gilligan (see Table 1), so she has an absolute advantage in fishing as well. If absolute advantage is the criterion for assigning work, then Maryanne should do both tasks. This, however, would leave Gilligan doing nothing, which is certainly *not* in the pair's best interests. What can we conclude from this example? That absolute advantage is an unreliable guide for allocating tasks to different workers.

Comparative Advantage. The correct principle to guide the division of labor on the island is comparative advantage:

OPPORTUNITY COST

> A person has a **comparative advantage** in producing some good if he or she can produce it with a smaller opportunity cost than some other person can.

COMPARATIVE ADVANTAGE The ability to produce a good or service at a lower opportunity cost than other producers.

Notice the important difference between absolute advantage and comparative advantage: You have an *absolute advantage* in producing a good if you can produce it with *fewer resources* than someone else can. But you have a *comparative advantage* if you can produce it with a *smaller opportunity cost*. As you'll see, these are not necessarily the same thing.

Let's determine who has a comparative advantage in fishing. For Maryanne, catching one fish takes an hour, time which could instead be used to pick one quart of berries. Thus, for her, the opportunity cost of one fish is one quart of berries. For Gilligan, however, catching one fish takes three hours, time which he could instead use to pick two quarts of berries. The opportunity cost of one fish for Gilligan, then, is two quarts of berries. Comparing the two numbers, we see that Maryanne can catch fish with a lower opportunity cost in berries, so she has a *comparative advantage* in catching fish.

Now let's turn to berry picking. In the time it takes Maryanne to pick one quart of berries (one hour), she could alternatively catch one fish. Thus, for Maryanne, the opportunity cost of one quart of berries is one fish. For Gilligan, however, an extra quart of berries takes an hour and a half, while catching a fish takes three hours. Thus, for Gilligan, the opportunity cost of one quart of berries is just *half* a fish. Hence, it is Gilligan, and not Maryanne, who has the lower opportunity cost for a quart of berries. Therefore, Gilligan—who has an *absolute* advantage in nothing—has a *comparative* advantage in berry picking.

Now let's see what happens if the two decide to specialize according to their respective comparative advantage. Maryanne would devote her twelve hours to fishing, catching twelve fish each day. Gilligan would pick berries all day, getting eight quarts. (Remember: each quart requires an hour and a half of Gilligan's time.) These results are summarized in Table 3. Comparing them with Table 2, you can see that when each of the two specializes according to his or her comparative advantage, total production on the island is greater. The two can produce one more quart of berries, and two more fish each day.

TABLE 3	**PRODUCTION WITH SPECIALIZATION**	
	Quarts of Berries	**Number of Fish**
Maryanne	0	12
Gilligan	8	0
Total Island	8	12

What is true for our shipwrecked island dwellers is also true for the entire economy:

> *Total production of every good or service will be greatest when individuals specialize according to their comparative advantage. This is another factor behind the basic principle of specialization and exchange.*

SPECIALIZATION AND EXCHANGE

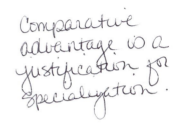

Comparative advantage is a justification for specialization.

Notice that comparative advantage identifies a gain from specialization that is conceptually distinct from the gains discussed earlier. In this example, we have not assumed that either Maryanne or Gilligan becomes better at either task due to specialization, nor have we assumed any time saving from not having to switch between tasks. The gains discussed here—from comparative advantage—come about for an entirely different reason: because each individual is relatively better suited to some tasks than others. More specifically, some people can produce some goods with a lower opportunity cost than other people can. When everyone is producing according to comparative advantage, we ensure that the opportunity cost of everyone's production is as low as possible. In this way, society can produce more of everything with the same resources, as the principle of specialization and exchange tells us.

Now let's turn from our fictional island to the real world. Do we observe that production is, in fact, consistent with the principle of comparative advantage? Indeed, we do. A journalist may be able to paint her house more quickly than a housepainter, giving her an *absolute* advantage in painting her home. Will she paint her own home? Except in unusual circumstances, no. The journalist no doubt has a *comparative* advantage in writing news articles. Indeed, most journalists—like most college professors, attorneys, architects, and other professionals—hire housepainters, leaving themselves more time to practice the professions in which they enjoy a comparative advantage.

Even comic-book superheroes seem to behave consistently with comparative advantage. Superman could no doubt cook a meal, fix a car, chop wood, and do virtually *anything* faster than anyone else on the earth. Superman, we could say, had an absolute advantage in everything, but a clear comparative advantage in catching criminals and saving the known universe from destruction, which is exactly what he spent his time doing.

SPECIALIZATION IN PERSPECTIVE. The gains from specialization, whether they arise from developing expertise, from minimizing downtime, or from pursuing comparative advantage, can explain many features of our economy. For example, college students need to select a major and then, upon graduating, to decide on a career. Those who follow this path are rewarded with higher incomes than those who dally. This is an encouragement to specialize. Society is better off if you specialize, since you will help the economy produce more, and society rewards you for this contribution with a higher income.

Another phenomenon: Most of us end up working for business firms that employ dozens, or even hundreds or thousands, of other employees. Why do these business firms exist? Why isn't each of us a self-employed expert, exchanging our production with other self-employed experts? Part of the answer is that organizing production into business firms pushes the gains from specialization still further. Within a firm, some people can specialize in working with their hands, others in managing people, others in marketing, and still others in keeping the books. Each firm is a kind of minisociety within which specialization occurs. The result is greater production and a higher standard of living than we would achieve if we were all self-employed.

Specialization has enabled societies everywhere to achieve standards of living unimaginable to our ancestors. But it can have a downside as well, if it goes too far. In the old film *Modern Times,* Charlie Chaplin plays a poor soul standing at an assembly line, attaching part number 27 to part number 28 thousands of times a day. In the real world, specialization is rarely this extreme. Still, it has caused some jobs to be repetitive and boring. In some plants, workers are deliberately moved from one specialty to another to relieve boredom.

Nor is maximizing our material standard of living our only goal. In some instances, we might be better off *increasing* the variety of tasks we do each day, even if this meant some sacrifice in production and income. For example, in many societies, one sex specializes in work outside the home and the other specializes in running the home and taking care of the children. Might families be better off if children had more access to *both* parents, even if this meant a somewhat lower family income? This is an important question. While specialization gives us material gains, there may be *opportunity costs* to be paid in the loss of other things we care about. The right amount of specialization can be found only by balancing the gains against these costs.

RESOURCE ALLOCATION

It was only 10,000 years ago—a mere blink of an eye in human history—that the Neolithic revolution began, and human society switched from hunting and gathering to farming and simple manufacturing. At the same time, human wants grew beyond mere food and shelter to the infinite variety of things that can be *made*. Ever since, all societies have been confronted with three important questions:

1. *Which* goods and services should be produced with society's resources?
2. *How* should they be produced?
3. *Who* should get them?

RESOURCE ALLOCATION
A method of determining which goods and services will be produced, how they will be produced, and who will get them.

Together, these three questions constitute the problem of **resource allocation**. The way a society chooses to answer these questions—i.e., the method it chooses to allocate its resources—will in part determine the character of its economic system.

Let's first consider the *which* question. Should we produce more health care or more movies, more goods for consumers or more capital goods for businesses? Where on the production possibilities frontier should the economy operate? As you will see, there are different methods societies can use to answer these questions.

The *how* question is more complicated. Most goods and services can be produced in a variety of different ways, each method using more of some resources and less of others. For example, there are many ways to dig a ditch. We could use *no capital at all* and have hundreds of workers digging with their bare hands. We could use *a small amount of capital* by giving each worker a shovel and thereby use less labor, since each worker would now be more productive. Or we could use *even more capital*—a power trencher—and dig the ditch with just one or two workers. In every economic system, there must always be some mechanism that determines how goods and services will be produced from the infinite variety of ways available.

Finally, the *who* question. Here is where economics interacts most strongly with politics. There are so many ways to divide ourselves into groups: men and women, rich and poor, workers and owners, families and single people, young and old . . .

the list is endless. How should the output of our economy be distributed among these different groups and among individuals within each group?

Determining *who* gets the output is always the most controversial aspect of resource allocation. Over the last half-century, our society has become more sensitized to the way goods and services are distributed, and we increasingly ask whether that distribution is fair. We have observed that men get a disproportionately larger share of output than women do, whites get more than African-Americans and Hispanics, and middle-aged workers get more than the very old and the very young. We have also focused on the distribution of particular goods and services. Should scarce donor organs be rationed to those who have been waiting the longest, so that everyone has the same chance of survival? Or should they be sold to the highest bidder, so that those willing and able to pay the most will get them? Should productions of Shakespeare's plays be subsidized by the government to permit more people—especially more poor people—to see them? Or should the people who enjoy these plays pay the full cost of their production?

THE THREE METHODS OF RESOURCE ALLOCATION. Throughout history, there have been three primary mechanisms for allocating resources. In a **traditional economy,** *resources* are allocated according to the long-lived practices of the past. Tradition was the dominant method of resource allocation for most of human history and remains strong in many tribal societies and small villages in parts of Africa, South America, Asia, and the Pacific. Typically, traditional methods of production are handed down by the village elders, and traditional principles of fairness govern the distribution of output.

Traditional village economies tend to be stable and predictable, but they have one serious drawback: They don't grow. With everyone locked into the traditional patterns of production, there is little room for innovation and technological change. Traditional economies are therefore likely to be stagnant economies.

In a **command economy,** resources are allocated by explicit instructions from some higher authority. *Which* goods and services should we produce? The ones we're *ordered* to produce. *How* should we produce them? The way we're *told* to produce them. *Who* will get the goods and services? Whomever the authority *tells* us should get them.

In a command economy, a government body *plans* how resources will be allocated. That is why command economies are also called centrally planned economies. But command economies are disappearing fast. Until a few years ago, examples would have included the former Soviet Union, Poland, Rumania, Bulgaria, Albania, and many others. Beginning in the late 1980s, all of these nations have abandoned central planning. The only examples left are Cuba, China, and North Korea, and even these economies—though still dominated by central planning—are moving away from it.

The third method of allocating resources—and the one with which you are no doubt most familiar—is the market, a system in which resources are allocated as a result of individual decision making. In a **market economy,** neither long-held traditions nor commands from above guide our economic behavior. Instead, we are largely free to make choices ourselves. *Which* goods and services are produced? Whichever ones producers *choose* to produce. How are they produced? However producers *choose* to produce them. *Who* gets these goods and services? Anyone who *chooses* to buy them.

There are, of course, limitations on freedom of choice in a market economy. Some restrictions are imposed by government to ensure an orderly, just, and productive society. We cannot kill, steal, or break contracts—even if that is our desire—

TRADITIONAL ECONOMY An economy in which resources are allocated according to long-lived practices from the past.

COMMAND ECONOMY An economy in which resources are allocated according to explicit instructions from a central authority.

MARKET ECONOMY An economy in which resources are allocated through individual decision making.

without suffering serious consequences, and we must pay taxes to fund government services. But the most important limitations we face in a market economy—as in any type of economy—are from the overall scarcity of resources.

This last point is crucial: Even in a market system, individuals are not simply free to do what they want—they are constrained by the resources they control. And in this respect, we do not all start in the same place in the economic race. Some of us—like the Rockefellers and the Kennedys—have inherited great wealth; some—Bill Gates, the novelist Joyce Carol Oates, and the model Claudia Schiffer—have inherited great intelligence, talent, or beauty; and some, such as the children of successful professionals, are born into a world of helpful personal contacts. Others, unfortunately, will inherit none of these advantages. In a market system, those who control more resources will have more choices available to them than those who control fewer resources. Still, in spite of the limitations imposed by government and the constraints imposed by the resources at our disposal, the market relies heavily on individual choice to allocate resources.

But wait . . . If each person acts according to his or her own desires, with no guidance from command or tradition, won't chaos ensue? How, in such a free-for-all, are resources actually *allocated*?

The answer is contained in a single word: *prices*.

PRICE The amount of money that must be paid to a seller to obtain a good or service.

THE IMPORTANCE OF PRICES. A **price** is how much money a buyer must pay to a seller for a good or service. Price is not the same as *cost*. In economics, as you've learned, cost means *opportunity cost*—*everything* that is sacrificed to buy the good. While the price of a good is a *part* of its opportunity cost—since the money spent on the good could have been used to buy something else—it is not always the entire cost. For example, the price does not include the value of the *time* sacrificed to buy something. Buying a new jacket will require you to spend time traveling to and from the store, trying on different styles and sizes, and waiting in line at the cash register. In some cases—like Samantha's decision to go to a movie—the value of the time sacrificed is so great that the cost is much greater than the price.

Still, in most cases, the price of a good is a significant part of its opportunity cost. For large purchases, such as a home or automobile, the price will be the *most* important part of opportunity cost. And this is why prices are so important to the overall working of the economy: They confront individual decision makers with the costs of their choices. Consider the example of buying a new car, where the price makes up most of the cost. The price, together with your limited income, makes it easy to see that buying a new car will require you to buy less of other things. In this way, the opportunity cost to *society* of making another car is converted to an opportunity cost *for you*. If you value a new car more highly than the other things you must sacrifice for it, you will buy it. If not, you won't buy it.

Why is it so important that people face the opportunity costs of their actions? The following thought experiment can answer this question. Imagine that the government passed a new law: When anyone buys a new car, the government will reimburse that person for it immediately. The consequences would be easy to predict. First, on the day the law was passed, everyone would rush out to buy new cars. Why not, if cars are free? The entire stock of existing automobiles would be gone within days—maybe even hours. Many people who didn't value cars much at all, and who hardly ever used them, would find themselves owning several—one for each day of the week, or to match the different colors in their wardrobe. Others, who weren't able to act in time—including some who desperately needed a new car for their work or to run their households—would be unable to find one at all.

Over time, automobile companies would step up their production to meet the surge in demand for cars, and then we would face another problem: the government's yearly "automobile budget," which would be hundreds of billions of dollars. Ultimately, we would all bear the cost of the increased car production, since the government would have to raise taxes. But we would pay as taxpayers, not as car owners. And our hefty tax bill would be supporting some rather frivolous uses for cars. Chances are, we would all be worse off because of this new policy. By eliminating a price for automobiles, and severing the connection between the opportunity cost of producing a car and the individual's decision to get one, we would have created quite a mess for ourselves.

> *When resources are allocated by the market, and people must* pay *for their purchases, they are forced to consider the opportunity cost to society of their individual actions.*

MAXIMIZATION
SUBJECT TO
CONSTRAINTS

OPPORTUNITY
COST

UNDERSTANDING THE MARKET. The market is simultaneously the most simple and the most complex of the systems for allocating resources. From the point of view of individuals, the market is simple, in that there are no traditions or commands to be memorized and obeyed. Instead, each of us responds to the prices we face as we *wish* to, unconcerned about the overall process of resource allocation.

But from the economist's point of view, the market is quite complex. Resources are allocated indirectly, as a *by-product* of individual decision making, rather than through easily identified traditions or commands. As a result, it often takes some skillful economic detective work to determine just how individuals are behaving and how resources are being allocated as a consequence. To reinforce your understanding of economics, it helps to do some of this detective work yourself, sorting out the mysteries of resource allocation from the behavior that you observe in the real world. This book will provide plenty of examples, but you can find many more on your own.

RESOURCE ALLOCATION IN THE UNITED STATES. The United States has always been considered one of the strongest examples of a market economy. Each day, millions of distinct products are traded in markets. Our grocery stores are always stocked with broccoli and tomato soup, the drugstore always has Kleenex and aspirin—all due to the choices of individual producers and consumers. The goods that are traded, the way they are traded, and the price at which they are traded are determined by the traders themselves. No direction from above is needed to keep markets working.

But even in the United States, there are numerous cases of resource allocation *outside* the market. For example, families are important institutions in the United States, and many economic decisions are made within them. Families tend to operate like traditional villages, not like market economies—few families charge prices for the goods and services provided inside the home.

One can find examples of command in our economy as well. Various levels of government collect, in total, about a third of our incomes as taxes. We are *told* how much tax we must pay, and there are serious penalties for noncompliance, including imprisonment. This affects the distribution of output in important ways, since we can freely make purchases only with the income we have left after we pay taxes. Government also produces certain services—such as mail delivery and law enforcement. In these cases, decisions about *which* specific goods to produce and *how* to produce them are made by government agencies and passed down the chain of government command to those actually providing the services.

The Brookings Institution
Public policy "think tank" located in Washington D.C. Visit Brookings for a selection of recent Op-Ed pieces written by scholars at the Institution.
http://www.brook.edu/es/oped/default.htm

There are also other ways, aside from strict commands, that the government limits our market freedoms. Regulations designed to protect the environment, maintain safe workplaces, and ensure the safety of our food supply are just a few examples of government-imposed constraints on our individual choice.

What are we to make, then, of resource allocation in the United States? There are cases where markets are constrained, but these are the exception rather than the rule. For each example we can find where resources are allocated by tradition or command, or where government restrictions seriously limit some market freedom, we can find hundreds of examples where individuals make choices according to their own desires. The things we buy, the jobs at which we work, the homes in which we live—in almost all cases, these come to us as a result of market choices. The market, though not pure, is certainly the dominant method of resource allocation in the United States.

RESOURCE OWNERSHIP

So far, we've been concerned with how resources are allocated. Another important feature of an economic system is *how resources are owned*. The owner of a resource—a parcel of land, a factory, or one's own labor time—determines how it can be used and receives income when others use it.

Under *communal* ownership, resources are owned by everyone—or by no one, depending on your point of view. They are simply there for the taking, with no person or organization imposing any restrictions on their use or charging any fees. It is hard to find economies with significant communal ownership of resources. Karl Marx believed that, in time, all economies would evolve toward communal ownership, and he names this predicted system **communism,** although none of the economies that invoked Marx's principles ever achieved this goal. This is not surprising: Communal ownership on a broad scale can work only when individuals have no conflicts over how resources are used. In other words, a prerequisite for the arrival of communism is the *end of scarcity*—an unlikely prospect in the foreseeable future.

COMMUNISM A type of economy in which most resources are owned in common.

Nevertheless, there are examples of communal ownership on a smaller scale. Traditional villages maintain communal ownership of land and sometimes cattle. In some of the cooperative farms in Israel—called *kibbutzim*—land and capital are owned by everyone, and there may be a single television set, a single kitchen, or a single dining room—all communally owned. Conflicts may result when individuals differ over how these resources should be used, but these conflicts are resolved by consensus, rather than by decree or by charging fees for their use. Consensus works in this case because the communal ownership applies only *within* the kibbutz, so only small numbers of people are involved.

In many countries, including the United States, families operate on the principle of communal ownership. The house, furniture, television set, telephone, and food in the refrigerator are treated as if owned jointly. We can also find examples of communal property in the broader economy. Who "owns" our sidewalks, streets, and public beaches? Really, no one. And in practice, all citizens are free to use them as much and as often as they would like.

SOCIALISM A type of economy in which most resources are owned by the state.

Under **socialism,** the *state* owns all or most of the resources. The prime example is the former Soviet Union, where the state owned all of the land and capital equipment in the country. In many ways, it also owned the labor of individual households, since it was virtually the only employer in the nation and unemployment was considered a crime.

Examples of state ownership of resources abound in nonsocialist economies as well. In the United States, national parks, state highway systems, military bases, public colleges and universities, and government buildings are all state-owned resources. Over a third of the land in the country is owned by the federal government. The military, even under our current volunteer system, is an example in which the state owns the labor of soldiers—albeit for a limited period of time.

When most resources are owned *privately*—as in the United States—we have **capitalism.** Take the book you are reading right now. If you turn to the title page, you will see the imprint of South-Western College Publishing Company. This is a *private company,* owned by another company—International Thomson Publishing—which, in turn, is owned by *private individuals.* These individuals, in the end, own the facilities of South-Western: the buildings, the land under them, the office furniture and computer equipment, and even the reputation of the company. When these facilities are used to produce and sell a book, the private owners receive the income, mostly in the form of company profits. Similarly, the employees of South-Western are private individuals. They are *selling* a resource they own—their labor time—to South-Western, and receive income—wages and salaries—in return.

The United States is one of the most capitalistic countries in the world. But even the United States is not purely capitalist. Many resources, as we've seen, are owned by the state, and some are owned communally. In addition, the government often restricts how resources can be used, through environmental regulations, zoning laws, and licensing requirements. Moreover, the government—through various taxes—takes from us some of the income we earn by supplying resources. Still, it is fair to say that the dominant mode of resource ownership in the United States is *private* ownership. Resource owners keep most of the income from supplying their resources, and have broad freedom in deciding how their resources can be used.

CAPITALISM A type of economy in which most resources are owned privately.

TYPES OF ECONOMIC SYSTEMS

We've used the phrase *economic system* a few times already in this book. But now it's time for a formal definition.

> An **economic system** *is composed of two features: a mechanism for allocating resources and a mode of resource ownership.*

ECONOMIC SYSTEM A system of resource allocation and resource ownership.

Let's ignore the rare economies in which communal ownership or allocation by tradition are dominant. Then we are left with four basic types of economic systems, indicated by the four quadrants in Figure 5. In the upper left quadrant, we have *market capitalism* (often called the **market system**), in which resources are allocated primarily by the market and owned primarily by private individuals. Today, most of the economies of the world are market capitalist systems, including all of the countries of North America and Western Europe, and most of those in Asia, Latin America, and Africa.

In the lower right quadrant is *centrally planned socialism,* under which resources are mostly allocated by command and owned mostly by the state. This was the system in the former Soviet Union and the nations of Eastern Europe until the late 1980s. But in less than a decade, these countries' economies have gone through cataclysmic change, moving from the lower right quadrant of the diagram to the upper left. That is, these nations have simultaneously changed both their systems of resource allocation and their systems of resource ownership.

MARKET SYSTEM An economic system involving resource allocation by the market and private resource ownership.

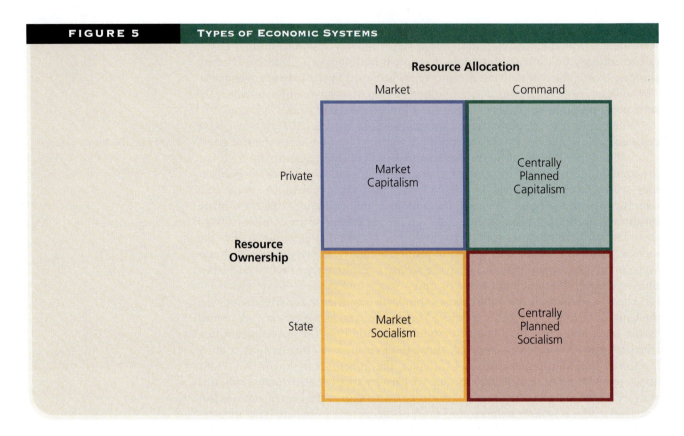

FIGURE 5 — **TYPES OF ECONOMIC SYSTEMS**

Although market capitalism and centrally planned socialism have been the two paramount economic systems in modern history, there have been others. The upper right quadrant represents a system of *centrally planned capitalism,* in which resources are owned by private individuals, yet allocated by command. Countries such as Sweden and Japan—where the government is more heavily involved in allocating resources than in the United States—flirt with this type of system. Nations at war—like the United States during World War II—also move in this direction, as governments find it necessary to direct resources by command in order to ensure sufficient military production.

Finally, in the lower left quadrant is *market socialism,* in which resources are owned by the state, yet allocated by the market mechanism. The possibility of market socialism has fascinated many social scientists, who believed it promised the best of both worlds: the freedom and efficiency of the market mechanism and the fairness and equity of socialism. There are, however, serious problems—many would say, unresolvable contradictions—in trying to mix the two. The chief examples of market socialism in modern history were short-lived experiments—in Hungary and Yugoslavia in the 1950s and 1960s—in which the results were mixed at best.

ECONOMIC SYSTEMS AND THIS BOOK. In this book, you will learn how market capitalist economies operate. This means that the other three types of economic systems in Figure 5 will be consciously ignored. Ten years ago, these statements would have been accompanied by an apology that would have gone something like this: "True, much of the world is characterized by alternative economic systems, but there is only so much time in one course . . ." In the past decade, however, the world has changed dramatically: About 400 million people have come under the sway of the market as their nations have abandoned centrally planned socialism; another billion or so may soon be added as China changes course. The study of modern economies is now, truly, the study of market capitalism. No more apologies are needed.

OPPORTUNITY COST AND THE INTERNET

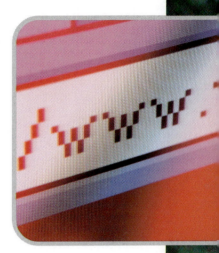

The Internet raises interesting and challenging questions about resource ownership and resource allocation. More than 40 million people around the world used the Internet by the end of 1996, and the number has been doubling every year. Huge quantities of resources have been diverted from producing other goods and services to make the Internet available to more people for more hours. Among these resources are labor (to install the lines, maintain the servers, and provide technical assistance to users) and capital (modems, computers, and fiber-optic cable). Use of the Net often strains the capacity of service providers and the capacity of the system as a whole. Each time usage increases, society must either divert resources to increasing capacity or allow worsened congestion on the Net. So far, society has chosen to increase capacity: The Internet infrastructure has been growing at near incredible speed, and, for the most part, serious congestion has been avoided.

Who pays for the Internet? In the United States, the payment comes from a variety of sources. Taxpayers bore part of the burden of creating the Internet, because the government provided millions of dollars in subsidies to help establish the network initially. Organizations that provide Internet service to their members also pay part of the cost. Large universities, for example, often pay yearly fees of $100,000 or more to maintain their connection. Commercial Internet service providers—such as America Online, AT&T, and Sprint—must also pay these access fees. And all service providers—colleges and universities as well as commercial providers—must pay for their own equipment and user support.

But what is *your* cost when you use the Internet to send an e-mail to a friend or to search for information on the World Wide Web? If you use your college's computer system, you almost certainly face a price (a direct money cost) of zero. Your college pays the yearly fee, and you can stay on-line as long as you want, without paying a penny. Thus, the only opportunity cost *you* face is the value of your time spent on-line. If there is nothing pressing, rewarding, or particularly fun for you to do some afternoon, the value of your time will be relatively low. As a result, you might stay on line for an hour or more while composing an e-mail, downloading a two-hundred-megabyte file of uncertain value, or watching an Internet video.

These sorts of choices—by you and millions of other college students—affect the allocation of resources in our society: More resources are diverted toward the Internet and away from other uses. And ultimately, you and others will pay the cost. For example, your college may have to pay higher Internet fees, and they will be passed on to you in the form of higher tuition payments. But, unless your college changes its policy on Internet use, you will probably *not* be charged a fee each time you use the Internet. That is, the direct price will probably remain zero.

Is this bad for society? It may very well be. As you learned in this chapter, when individuals do not face the opportunity cost of their choices, their choices are likely to make *everyone* worse off. (Think of the example of the free automobiles.) And in 1996, something happened that showed clearly what can happen when people overuse the Internet because they face no direct money price.

First, some background. Until 1996, it was only at colleges, universities, or government organizations that Net users paid no direct price. Those who subscribed to commercial services paid a fixed monthly fee, with an additional charge for each hour of use over some preset number. For these commercial users, there *was* a price for spending another hour on the Net.

But in 1996, all that changed. In February of that year, AT&T, in order to attract customers to its new Internet service, offered a special deal: a flat rate of $19.95 per month for *unlimited* time on line. Other commercial providers quickly matched the flat-rate policy. While users were still paying a price to *subscribe* to the commercial service, the price for *additional hours* on-line was suddenly eliminated. Usage shot up and the Internet became clogged: At peak times, users around the country faced slower response times and annoying delays in hooking up.

Then, on December 1, the situation worsened dramatically: America Online—the largest commercial provider, with more than seven million customers—finally joined the rest of the industry and offered its own $19.95 monthly flat rate. This vastly increased the number of users who faced no price for additional hours. The effect was almost immediate. Within days, America Online found that its users were hooking up 30 percent more frequently and staying on-line 20 percent longer. Over the next two weeks, the company found itself in a vicious circle. Due to congestion, many of its customers faced hours of delays while trying to hook up. As a result, they were reluctant to let go once they connected. Since the only price they paid was a few cents per minute in local phone bills, customers would leave their computers hooked up while they went to lunch, walked the dog, or even went to sleep for the night. This, of course, made it more difficult for others to hook up, which made them hang on even longer when they were finally connected, and so on. When America Online responded by automatically disconnecting its users after a few minutes of inactivity, some users responded by downloading special programs to simulate active use and maintain their connections. One reporter described the situation this way: "It's as if a diner at a fixed-price buffet had someone hang on to his seat after lunch, so he could still have a place for dinner."[2]

What does all this have to do with resource allocation? First, it tells us that the policy of not charging for additional time on the Internet—whether through commercial providers or universities—can cause resources to be *overallocated* toward the Internet: When people use the Net in ways that have low value, we must sacrifice other valuable goods and services in order to increase the Net's capacity. Second, it tells us that resources may be allocated *among* Net users in a rather haphazard way. Instead of allocating time on-line to those who value it most and are willing to pay the most for it, time is allocated to those lucky enough to hook up at a particular moment, regardless of the value they place on the service. If some users remain logged on while walking their dog, others can't hook up at all. These include surgeons waiting to receive crucial information about a pending operation, businesses trying to close important deals with their clients, and government officials tracking everything from data on the economy to the military activities of hostile countries.

The recent experience with the Internet reinforces two important ideas discussed in this chapter: the principle of opportunity cost and the crucial role of prices in allocating resources. It is largely through *prices* that our society's opportunity cost becomes *our own* opportunity cost. When a price is reduced to zero—like the price of

---

2   Peter H. Lewis, "An 'All You Can Eat' Price Is Clogging Internet Access," *New York Times,* December 17, 1996, p. A1.

additional hours on the Net—much of our individual opportunity cost disappears, so we do not properly incorporate the costs to our society into our own decision making. The result is an allocation of resources that we are not very happy about.

As the Internet becomes a more central part of our lives, it is likely that more of the resource allocation tools of the market economy will be used to solve congestion problems. Instead of flat monthly fees, service providers will charge for time, just as long-distance phone companies charge by the minute for phone calls. Then the personal cost of using the Internet will better reflect the opportunity cost to society.

S U M M A R Y

One of the most fundamental concepts in economics is *opportunity cost*. The opportunity cost of any choice is what we give up when we make that choice. At the individual level, opportunity cost arises from the scarcity of time or money; for society as a whole, it arises from the scarcity of resources—land, labor, and capital. To produce and enjoy more of one thing, we must shift resources away from producing something else. The *principle of opportunity cost* tells us that the correct measure of cost is not just the money price we pay, but the opportunity cost—what we give up when we make a choice. The *law of increasing opportunity cost* tells us that the more of something we produce, the greater the opportunity cost of producing still more.

In a world of scarce resources, each society must determine its economic system—its way of organizing economic activity. All *economic systems* feature *specialization*—where each person and firm concentrates on a limited number of productive activities—and *exchange*—through which we obtain most of what we desire by trading with others. Specialization and exchange enable us to enjoy higher living standards than would be possible under self-sufficiency.

Every economic system determines how resources are owned and how they are allocated. In a market system, resources are owned primarily by private individuals and allocated primarily through markets. Prices play an important role in markets. Prices signal the relative scarcity of goods and resources to individual decision makers, and force them to take account of society's opportunity cost when they make choices.

K E Y   T E R M S

opportunity cost
principle of opportunity cost
production possibilities frontier (PPF)
law of increasing opportunity cost

technical efficiency
specialization
exchange
absolute advantage
comparative advantage
resource allocation

traditional economy
command economy
market economy
price
communism
socialism

capitalism
economic system
market system

R E V I E W   Q U E S T I O N S

1. How might the concept of opportunity cost be used to explain the fact that people often stop at convenience stores to buy items that are available at lower prices in large grocery stores?

2. "Warren Buffett is one of the world's wealthiest men, worth billions of dollars. For someone in his income bracket, the principle of opportunity cost simply doesn't apply." True or false? Explain.

3. What are some reasons why a country might be operating inside its PPF?

4. Why is a PPF concave, i.e., bowed out from the origin?

5. What are three distinct reasons why specialization leads to a higher standard of living?

6. List the three questions any resource allocation mechanism must answer. Briefly describe the three primary methods of resource allocation that have evolved to answer these questions.

7. What is the chief allocative mechanism in a market economy? How does it help to determine answers to the three questions mentioned in question 6?

8. Why can't the United States economy be described as a *pure market system?*

9. True or false?: "Resource allocation and resource ownership are essentially the same thing. Once you know who owns the resources in an economy, you also know by what mechanism those resources will be allocated." Explain your answer.

P R O B L E M S   A N D   E X E R C I S E S

1. You are considering what to do with an upcoming weekend. Here are your options, from least to most preferred: (1) Study for upcoming midterms; (2) fly to Colorado for a quick ski trip; (3) go into seclusion in your dorm room and try to improve your score on the computer game "Doom." What is the opportunity cost of a decision to play the computer game all weekend?

2. You and a friend have decided to work jointly on a course project. Frankly, your friend is a less than ideal partner. His skills as a researcher are such that he can review and outline only two articles a day. Moreover, his hunt-and-peck style limits him to only 10 pages of typing a day. On the other hand, in a day you can produce six outlines or type 20 pages.
    a. Who has an absolute advantage in outlining, you or your friend? . . . in typing?
    b. Who has a comparative advantage in outlining? . . . in typing?
    c. According to the principle of comparative advantage, who should specialize in which task?

3. Suppose that one day, Gilligan eats a magical island plant that turns him into an expert at everything. In particular, it now takes him just half an hour to pick a quart of berries, and 15 minutes to catch a fish.

    a. Redo Table 2, showing production for Gilligan, Maryanne, and the island under self-sufficiency.
    b. Who has a comparative advantage in picking berries? In fishing? When the castaways discover each other, which of the two should specialize in which task?
    c. Redo Table 3, showing production for Gilligan, Maryanne, and the entire island under specialization. Can *both* castaways benefit from Gilligan's new abilities? How?

4. Among other things, the World Bank collects data on a variety of economic and social indicators for many developing countries. Visit their site at http://www.worldbank.org/html/extdr/regions.htm. Choose three countries and read the "Country Brief" for each. What mechanisms of resource allocation and ownership are used in these countries? Where do you see these countries fitting into the scheme in Figure 5? How might each country's location in that figure affect its economic development?

C H A L L E N G E   Q U E S T I O N S

1. Graph the PPF for an economy that faces constant, rather than increasing, opportunity costs in the production of two goods.

2. How would you show economic growth, i.e., an increase in the overall productive capacity of an economy, in terms of one or more PPF curves?

3. Consider an economy devastated by war. What would happen to its PPF for the production of any two goods?

CHAPTER

3

SUPPLY AND DEMAND

Father Guido Sarducci, a character on *Saturday Night Live,* once observed that a few years after we graduate from college, we remember only about five minutes' worth of material. Then why not have a Five Minute University, Sarducci asked, where you'd learn only this five minutes' worth of knowledge and dispense with the rest? The economics course would require just ten seconds, during which all students would learn to recite three words: "supply and demand."

Of course, there is much more to economics than these three words. What is interesting about Sarducci's observation, however, is that so many people do regard the phrase "supply and demand" as synonymous with economics. And surprisingly few people actually understand what the phrase means. In a debate about health care, poverty, or the high price of housing, you might hear someone say, "Well, it's just a matter of supply and demand," as a way of dismissing the issue entirely. Others use the phrase with an exaggerated reverence, as if supply and demand were an inviolable physical law, like gravity, about which nothing can be done. So what does this oft-repeated phrase really mean?

Supply and demand is just an economic model—nothing more and nothing less. It's designed to explain *how prices are determined in a market system.* Why has this model taken on such an exalted role in the field of economics? Because prices, themselves, play such an exalted role in the economy, guiding the actions of individual buyers and sellers and determining how our resources are allocated. In a market system, once the price of a good has been determined, only those willing to pay that price will get the good. Thus, prices determine which households will get which goods and services and which firms will get which resources. If you want to know why the laptop computer industry is expanding while the daily newspaper industry is shrinking, or why homelessness is a more pervasive problem in the United States than hunger, you need to understand how prices are determined.

Thus, supply and demand, by explaining how prices are determined, helps us understand the workings of particular industries, and also the operation of the economy as a whole.

In this chapter, you will learn how the model of supply and demand works and how to use it. You will also learn about the strengths and limitations of the model. It will take more time than Guido Sarducci's ten-second economics course, but in the end you will know much more than just three little words.

MARKETS

Listen to an economist for any length of time, and sooner or later you'll hear the word "market." In ordinary language, a market is an actual location where buying and selling take place, such as a supermarket, an outdoor market, or a flea market. In economics, a market is something different. It is defined not by its location, but by its participants:

> A *market* is a group of buyers and sellers with the potential to trade.

MARKET A group of buyers and sellers with the potential to trade.

Economists think of the economy as a collection of individual markets. In each market, the set of buyers and sellers will be different, depending on what is being traded. There is a market for oranges, another for automobiles, another for real estate, and still others for corporate stocks, French francs, and anything else that is bought and sold.

THE SIZE OF THE MARKET

In some cases, the buyers and sellers in a market—those who have the potential to trade with each other—will be residents of the same town. In other cases, they will be spread around the country or even the world. The market for haircuts is a local market, since most of us will not travel long distances for a haircut and few barbers or hairdressers will travel long distances to see customers at rates we would pay. The market for oil, however, is a global market, since oil is relatively cheap to transport and buyers and sellers anywhere in the world can easily communicate and trade with each other.

Often, we have some latitude in defining the geographic breadth of a market, and the choice will depend on our purpose. To explain how and why real estate prices differ from one place to another, we would define our markets locally. There would be one market for real estate in Poughkeepsie, another in Kalamazoo, and so on. But if the purpose is to explain the overall rise in real estate prices in the United States over the last 20 years, it is better to define the market more broadly, lumping all buyers and sellers in the country into a single, national market.

COMPETITION IN MARKETS

In some markets, either the buying or the selling side is dominated by a few large players. Did you eat cereal for breakfast this morning? Then chances are your cereal came from one of four large *sellers*—Kelloggs, Post, General Mills, or Quaker—since, together, they sell about 90 percent of all breakfast cereal in the United States. Similarly, the market for windshield wiper motors is dominated by a few large *buyers*—the carmakers.

When there are relatively few buyers or sellers in a market, each one will have some influence on the price of the product. Kelloggs knows that it can charge a higher price for its cereal if it is willing to sell fewer boxes, or that it can lower the price and attract additional customers. Similarly, General Motors knows that it can influence the price it pays for wiper motors by negotiating with its suppliers or changing the quantity it buys.

> *When a buyer or seller has some ability to influence the price of a product, we say that the market is **imperfectly competitive**.*

The markets for automobiles, computer software, hospital care, and magazines are all imperfectly competitive.

In other markets, by contrast, there are so many buyers and sellers that each is just a tiny part of the whole. Wheat, for example, is grown on thousands of U.S. farms and purchased by thousands of millers. It is easily transported, so any farmer can sell to any miller in the country. If a single farm doubles or triples its production of wheat, or a single flour mill dramatically increases its purchases of wheat, nothing will happen to the market price for wheat. In this market, the individual buyer and seller are just too small to have any impact. Therefore, each one treats the price of wheat as something predetermined, outside of his control.

> *In a **perfectly competitive market** (or just **competitive market**), there are so many buyers and sellers that each is too small to affect the price. Each buyer and seller treats the market price as a given.*

What has this got to do with supply and demand? Earlier, you learned that supply and demand is useful for understanding how prices are determined in a *market system*. Now, we will narrow down the meaning of supply and demand even more:

> *Supply and demand explains how prices are determined in competitive markets.*

To restrict the application of supply and demand to *competitive* markets might make you think that the model isn't very useful. After all, very few markets strictly satisfy the requirement of perfect competition; most markets are—at least to some degree—imperfectly competitive. So can we use our model of supply and demand in the real world?

Very much so. Even when competition is somewhat imperfect, so that buyers and sellers have *some* influence on price, supply and demand often provides a good approximation to what is going on. This is why it has proven to be the most versatile and widely used model in the economist's tool kit. Neither personal computers nor orange juice are traded in perfectly competitive markets. But ask an economist to tell you why computer prices have come down over the last 15 years or why the price of orange juice rises after a freeze in Florida, and she will invariably reach for supply and demand to find the answer.

Supply and demand are like two blades of a scissors: The demand blade tells us how much of something people want to buy, and the supply blade tells us how much sellers want to sell. To analyze a market, we need both blades—and they must both be sharp. In this and the next section, we will be sharpening those blades, learning separately about supply and demand. Then, when we have a thorough understanding of each one, we'll put them together—and put them to use. Let's start with demand.

IMPERFECTLY COMPETITIVE MARKET A market in which a single buyer or seller has the power to influence the price of the product.

PERFECTLY COMPETITIVE MARKET A market in which no buyer or seller has the power to influence the price.

add:
# of firms affects supply curve

DEMAND

Listen to the way people talk about their desires. "I *want* a car," or "I *must* join a gym this year," or "I *need* to go to California this summer." From these simple declarations, we might conclude that the "demand" for a good or service is an absolute, not subject to change. But we would be mistaken. Suppose that buying a car was so expensive that you wouldn't have enough money left over for food. Might you decide it's best *not* to buy a car? Or suppose that joining a gym cost so much that you'd have to sacrifice going out on weekends all year. Would you figure out some other way to get exercise?

Economics deals with *choices* rather than needs or wants. In deciding on our purchases, we make the best choices we can, given the constraints we face. The concept of *choice* is the key to understanding the *quantity demanded* in a market:

> **QUANTITY DEMANDED** The total amount of a good that all buyers in a market would choose to purchase at a given price.

*The **quantity demanded** of any good is the total amount that buyers in a market would choose to purchase at a given price.*

Notice that quantity demanded tells us about *buyers' choices*—not about what will actually happen in a market. We don't worry—yet—about how much buyers will *actually* be able to buy in the market. That will be sorted out later, when we put demand and supply together.

There are a few other things to keep in mind about quantity demanded. First, it can refer either to an individual buyer—"the quantity of running shoes demanded by Leticia"—or to *all* buyers in a market—"the quantity of running shoes demanded in the United States." The interpretation depends on the problem we are analyzing. In this chapter, we focus on quantity demanded in an entire market.

Second, the definition of quantity demanded refers to *buyers*. Who are they? In general, buyers of goods can be households, other business firms, or government agencies. For example, business firms and government agencies buy computers, aircraft, and automobiles. But in markets for consumer goods and services—hamburgers, rental apartments, dry-cleaning services, bus rides, and so on—the buyers are *households*. This chapter deals primarily—but not exclusively—with consumer markets, in which households are the buyers.

Finally, notice that the quantity of a good demanded depends on the price of the good. Of course, price is not the only influence on buyers' choices, and we will discuss some of the others a little later. But the definition of quantity demanded stresses price for a good reason: because the supply and demand model is designed to explain how prices are determined in markets. It seems natural, then, to begin our exploration of demand with the influence of prices.

THE LAW OF DEMAND

How does a change in price affect quantity demanded? You probably know the answer to this already: When something is more expensive, people buy less of it. This common observation applies to walnuts, air travel, magazines, education, and virtually everything else that people buy. For all of these goods and services, price and quantity are negatively related—that is, when price rises, quantity demanded falls; when price falls, quantity demanded rises. This negative relationship is observed so regularly in markets that economists call it the *law of demand*:

> **LAW OF DEMAND** As the price of a good increases, the quantity demanded decreases.

*The **law of demand** states that when the price of a good rises, and everything else remains the same, the quantity of the good demanded will fall.*

Read that definition again, and notice the very important words, "everything else remains the same." The law of demand tells us what would happen *if* all of the other influences on buyers' choices remained unchanged, and only one influence—the price of the good—changed.

This is an example of a common practice in economics. In the real world, many variables change simultaneously. But to understand the economy, we must understand the effect of each variable *separately.* Imagine that you were trying to discover which headache remedy works best for you. You wouldn't gain much information if you took an Advil, a Tylenol, and a Bayer aspirin all at the same time. Instead, you should take just *one* of these pills the next time you get a headache and observe its effects. To understand the economy, we go through the same process—conducting mental experiments in which only one thing changes at a time. The law of demand tells us what happens when we change *just* the price of the good and assume that all other influences on buyers' choices remain constant.

THE DEMAND SCHEDULE AND THE DEMAND CURVE

To make our discussion more concrete, let's look at a specific market: the market for maple syrup in Wichita. Table 1 shows a hypothetical **demand schedule** for maple syrup in this market. This is *a list of different quantities demanded at different prices, with all other variables held constant.* For example, the demand schedule tells us that when the price of maple syrup is $2.00 per bottle, the quantity demanded will be 6,000 bottles per month. Notice that the demand schedule obeys the law of demand: As the price of maple syrup increases, the quantity demanded falls.

Now look at Figure 1. It shows a diagram that will appear again and again in our study of economics. In the figure, each price-and-quantity combination in Table 1 is represented by a point. For example, point *A* represents the price $4.00 and quantity 4,000, while point *B* represents the pair $2.00 and 6,000. When we connect all of these points with a line, we obtain the famous *demand curve,* labeled with a *D* in the figure.

> The **demand curve** shows the relationship between the price of a good and the quantity demanded, holding constant all other variables that affect demand. Each point on the curve shows the quantity that buyers would choose to buy at a specific price.

The demand curve in Figure 1—like virtually all demand curves we might observe—follows the law of demand: A rise in the price of the good causes a decrease in the quantity demanded. Graphically, this means that *the demand curve slopes downward.*

> The law of demand tells us that demand curves slope downward.

DEMAND SCHEDULE A list showing the quantities of a good that consumers would choose to purchase at different prices, with all other variables held constant.

DEMAND CURVE The graphical depiction of a demand schedule; a curve showing the quantity of a good or service demanded at various prices, with all other variables held constant.

demand can be aggregated, demand supply cannot

TABLE 1	DEMAND SCHEDULE FOR MAPLE SYRUP IN WICHITA	
	Price (per bottle)	**Quantity Demanded (bottles per month)**
	$1.00	7,500
	$2.00	6,000
	$3.00	5,000
	$4.00	4,000
	$5.00	3,500

higher price = less demand

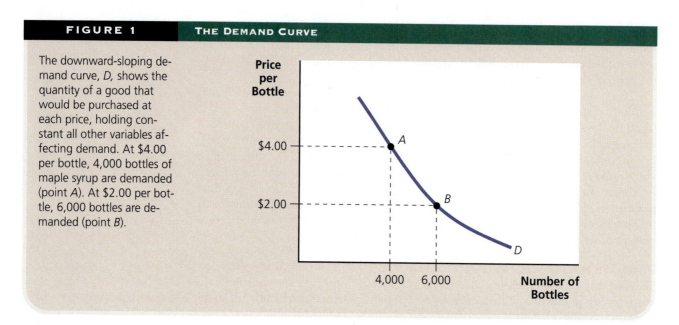

FIGURE 1   THE DEMAND CURVE

The downward-sloping demand curve, *D,* shows the quantity of a good that would be purchased at each price, holding constant all other variables affecting demand. At $4.00 per bottle, 4,000 bottles of maple syrup are demanded (point *A*). At $2.00 per bottle, 6,000 bottles are demanded (point *B*).

CHANGES IN QUANTITY DEMANDED

As you will see in this chapter, markets are affected by a variety of different events: changes in households' incomes, changes in the prices of other goods, changes in technology, and so on. These events can affect the demand for a good in different ways. Some events will cause us to *move along* the demand curve for a good. Other events will cause the entire demand curve to *shift.* It is crucial to distinguish between these two very different effects on demand, and economists have adopted a language-convention that helps us keep track of the distinction.

Let's go back to Figure 1. There, you can see that if the price of maple syrup rises from $2.00 to $4.00 per bottle, the number of bottles demanded falls from 6,000 to 4,000. This is a movement *along* the demand curve, from point *B* to point *A,* and we call it a *decrease in quantity demanded.* More generally,

> *A change in a good's price causes us to* move along *the demand curve. We call this a **change in quantity demanded.***

CHANGE IN QUANTITY DEMANDED A movement along a demand curve in response to a change in price.

A rise in price causes a leftward movement along the demand curve—a *decrease in quantity demanded.* A fall in price causes a rightward movement along the demand curve—an *increase in quantity demanded.*

CHANGES IN DEMAND

Whenever we draw a demand curve, we are always assuming something about the other variables that affect buyers' choices. For example, the demand curve in Figure 1 might tell us the quantity demanded at each price, *assuming* that average household income in Wichita is $40,000. In the real world, of course, average household income in a market might change. What happens then? Then buyers would choose to buy *more or less* of the good at any given price.

To see this more clearly, let's take a specific example. Suppose that the average household income in Wichita rose from $40,000 to $45,000. Then we would expect households to buy more maple syrup at any given price. This is illustrated in Table 2. For example, at the original income level, households would choose to buy

TABLE 2	INCREASE IN DEMAND FOR MAPLE SYRUP IN WICHITA		
	Price (per bottle)	Original Quantity Demanded (bottles per month)	New Quantity Demanded after Increase in Income (bottles per month)
	$1.00	7,500	9,500
	$2.00	6,000	8,000
	$3.00	5,000	7,000
	$4.00	4,000	6,000
	$5.00	3,500	5,500

6,000 bottles of maple syrup at a price of $2.00. But after income rises, they would choose to buy 8,000 bottles at that same price. The same holds for any other price for maple syrup: after income rises, households will choose to buy more than before. In other words, *the entire relationship between price and quantity demanded has changed.*

Figure 2 plots the new demand curve from the quantities in the third column of Table 2. The new demand curve lies to the *right* of the old curve. For example, at a price of $2.00, the old demand curve told us that the quantity demanded was 6,000 bottles (point *B*). But after the increase in income, buyers would want to buy 8,000 bottles at that price (point *C*). Notice that the rise in household income has *shifted the demand curve to the right.* We call this an *increase in demand*, because the word "demand" means the entire relationship between price and quantity demanded. More generally,

A change in any determinant of demand—except for the good's price—causes the demand curve to shift. We call this a change in demand.

When buyers choose to purchase more at any price, the demand curve shifts rightward—an *increase in demand*. When buyers choose to purchase less at any price, the demand curve shifts leftward—a *decrease in demand*.

Now let's look at the different variables that can cause demand to change and shift the demand curve.

INCOME AND WEALTH. We've already discussed how a change in income can affect the demand for a good, but now let's be more precise. Your **income** is what you earn over a period of time—say, $3,000 per month or $36,000 per year. Your **wealth**—if you are fortunate enough to have some—is the total value of everything you own—cash, bank accounts, stocks, bonds, real estate, valuable artwork, or any other valuable property—minus everything you owe—home mortgage, credit card debt, auto loan, student loans, and so on.

CHANGE IN DEMAND A shift of a demand curve in response to a change in some variable other than price.

INCOME The amount that a person or firm earns over a particular period.

WEALTH The total value of everything a person or firm owns at a point in time, minus the total value of everything owed.

Language is important when speaking about demand. If you say, "People demand more maple syrup," you might mean that we are moving along the demand curve, like the move from point *A* to point *B* in Figure 1. Or you might mean that the entire demand curve has shifted, like the shift from D_1 to D_2 in Figure 2.

To avoid confusion (and mistakes on exams!), always use the special language that distinguishes between these two cases. When we *move along* the demand curve, we call it a *change in quantity demanded*. A change in quantity demanded is always caused by a change in the good's price. But when the entire demand curve shifts, we call it a *change in demand*. A change in demand is always caused by a change in something *other* than the good's price.

DANGEROUS CURVES

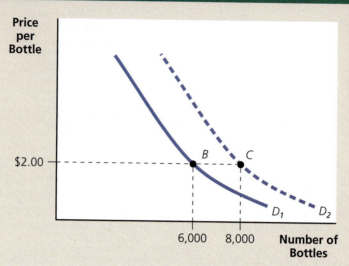

FIGURE 2   **A SHIFT IN THE DEMAND CURVE**

A change in any influence on demand besides the price of the good causes the entire demand curve to shift. An increase in income, for example, causes the demand for maple syrup, a normal good, to shift from D_1 to D_2. At each price, more bottles are demanded after the shift.

NORMAL GOOD A good that people demand more of as their income rises.

Increases in income and increases in wealth have similar effects on demand. A rise in income or wealth will *increase* demand for most goods. We call these **normal goods.** Housing, airline travel, and health club memberships are all examples of normal goods.

> The demand for most goods (normal goods) is positively related to income or wealth. A rise in either income or wealth will increase demand for these goods, and shift the demand curve to the right.

INFERIOR GOOD A good that people demand less of as their income rises.

But for some goods, a rise in income or wealth could *decrease* demand. Such goods are called **inferior goods,** and there are many examples. Ground chuck is a cheap source of protein, but not most people's idea of a fine dining experience. Higher income or wealth would enable consumers of ground chuck to buy steaks, decreasing their demand for ground chuck. For similar reasons, Greyhound bus tickets, low-rent housing units, and single-ply paper towels are probably inferior goods. For all of these goods, an increase in consumers' income or wealth would decrease demand, shifting the demand curve to the left.

DANGEROUS CURVES

It's easy to confuse *income* with *wealth*. Although both are measured in dollars and either can be used to buy goods and services, they are not the same thing. Income is measured *over a period of time*. (You earn $10.00 *per hour* or $400 *per week*.) Wealth, by contrast, is measured *at a moment in time*. (On January 1, 1999, you had $5,436 in wealth.)

To see the difference between income and wealth, it helps to realize that a household can have a high value for one and very little of the other. For example, some highly paid professionals spend all of their income every year. Their incomes are high, but they have very little wealth.

On the other hand, when the French accountant Paul Gaugin moved to a South Seas island in 1891 to become a painter, he sold everything he owned and paid back all of his debts. The assets he had left over were his wealth, which was very high. But his income during the next several years was virtually zero.

PRICES OF RELATED GOODS. A substitute is a good that can be used in place of another good and that fulfills more or less the same purpose. For example, many people use maple syrup to sweeten their pancakes, but they could use a number of other things instead: bananas, sugar, fruit, or jam. Each of these can be considered a substitute for maple syrup.

When the price of a substitute rises, people will choose to buy more of the good itself. For example, when the price of jam rises, some jam users will switch to maple syrup.

> *When the price of a substitute rises, the demand for a good will increase, shifting the demand curve to the right.*

Of course, if the price of a substitute falls, we have the opposite result: Demand for the original good decreases, shifting its demand curve to the left.

There are many examples in which a change in a substitute's price affects demand. A rise in the price of postage stamps would increase the demand for electronic mail. A drop in the rental price of videos would decrease the demand for movies at theaters. In each of these cases, we assume that the price of the substitute is the only price that is changing.

A **complement** is the opposite of a substitute: It is some thing used together with the good we are interested in. Pancake mix is a complement to maple syrup, since these two goods are used frequently in combination. If the price of pancake mix rises, the cost of eating a pancake breakfast rises too. In response, some consumers will switch to other breakfasts—bacon and eggs, for example—that don't include maple syrup. The demand for maple syrup will then decrease. In general,

> *a rise in the price of a complement decreases the demand for a good, shifting the demand curve to the left.*

This is why we expect a higher price for automobiles to decrease the demand for gasoline and a lower price for movie-tickets to increase the demand for movie-theater popcorn.

POPULATION. Over time, as the population increases in an area, the number of buyers will ordinarily increase as well. This is why an increase in population generally causes an increase in demand for a good. The growth of the U.S. population over the last 50 years has been an important reason (but not the only reason) for rightward shifts in the demand curves for food, rental apartments, telephones, and many other goods and services.

EXPECTATIONS. Expectations of future events can affect demand. For example, if buyers anticipate a rise in the price of maple syrup, they may choose to purchase more *now*, to stock up before the price hike. The demand curve would shift to the right. If people expect the price of a good to drop, they may postpone buying, hoping to take advantage of the lower price later. This would shift the demand curve leftward. Expectations are particularly important in markets for financial assets such as stocks and bonds and in the market for real estate. For example, you would be more likely to buy a new home at any current price if you thought the price would rise over the next few years, rather than fall or remain the same.

SUBSTITUTE A good that can be used in place of some other good and that fulfills more or less the same purpose.

COMPLEMENT A good that is used together with some other good.

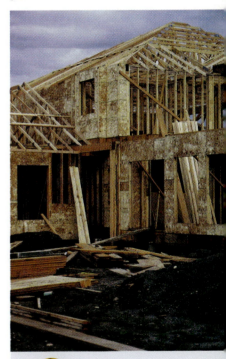

U.S. Department of Commerce
Federal agency collecting economic, social and demographic data on the U.S. economy. Two rich data sources within the Commerce Department are the Bureau of the Census and the Bureau of Economic Analysis.
Commerce: http://www.doc.gov/
B.E.A.: http://www.bea.doc.gov/
Census: http://www.census.gov/

DANGEROUS CURVES

A troubling thought may have occurred to you. In the list of variables that shift the demand curve in Table 3, shouldn't we include the amount supplied by sellers? Or, to put the question another way, doesn't demand depend on supply?

The answer is no. The demand curve tells us how much buyers *would choose* to buy at alternative prices. It provides answers to a series of hypothetical questions: "How much maple syrup *would* consumers choose to buy if the price were $3.00 per bottle? . . . if the price were $3.50 per bottle . . . ," and so on. Sellers' decisions have no effect on the demand curve, since they do not affect the answers to these hypothetical questions.

"But wait," you object. "Surely, if sellers decide to sell more, people will buy more." True, but *not* because of a shift in the demand curve. As you'll see a bit later, if sellers want to sell more, consumers will indeed buy more—but only because the *price* of the good will decrease. This is represented by a movement *along* the demand curve, not a shift of the curve itself.

TASTES. Suppose we know the number of buyers in Wichita, their expectations about the future price of maple syrup, the prices of all related goods, and the average levels of income and wealth in Wichita. Do we have all the information we need to draw the demand curve for maple syrup in Wichita? Not really. Because we do not yet know how consumers in Wichita *feel* about maple syrup. How many of them eat breakfast? Of these, how many make pancakes or waffles? How often? How many of them *like* maple syrup, and how much? And what about all of the other goods and services competing for Wichita consumers' dollars: How do buyers feel about *them*?

The questions could go on and on, identifying various characteristics about buyers that influence their attitudes toward maple syrup. The approach of economics is to lump all of these characteristics of buyers together and call them, simply, *tastes*. Economists do not try to explain where these tastes come from or what makes them change—that is left to other social scientists. Instead, economists concern themselves with the consequences of a change in tastes, whatever the reason for its occurrence.

When tastes change *toward* a good (people favor it more), demand increases and the demand curve shifts to the right. When tastes change *away* from a good, demand decreases and the demand curve shifts to the left. In general, tastes tend to be rather stable, so economists most often look elsewhere when trying to explain a change in demand. But there are cases where changes in tastes are important. For example, intense antismoking advertising and laws restricting smoking have changed tastes away from cigarettes over the past three decades. This has decreased the demand for cigarettes, shifting the demand curve to the left.

Table 3 summarizes the important variables that change demand and shift the demand curve.

TABLE 3	**CAUSES OF A CHANGE IN DEMAND**
Demand decreases, and the demand curve shifts leftward, when:	**Demand increases, and the demand curve shifts rightward, when:**
income ↓ (normal good)	income ↑ (normal good)
wealth ↓ (normal good)	wealth ↑ (normal good)
price of substitute ↓	price of substitute ↑
price of complement ↑	price of complement ↓
expected future price ↓	expected future price ↑
tastes change away from the good	tastes change toward the good

SUPPLY

Now we switch our focus from the buying side to the selling side of the market. When we introduced demand, we discussed a common error: the tendency to regard our desire for something as a fixed amount, instead of viewing it as a variable that can change. We often make a similar mistake with supply. We might hear someone say, "There is only so much oil we can drill from the ground," or "There is no place left to build new office space in Manhattan." And yet, our known oil reserves have increased dramatically over the last quarter century, as oil companies have found it worth their while to look harder for oil. Similarly, the amount of office space in Manhattan continues to grow, as 12-story buildings are knocked down and replaced with 50-story ones. Supply, like demand, can *change*. And the amount of a good supplied in a market will depend on the *choices* made by those who produce it.

> The **quantity supplied** of any good is the total amount that sellers in a market would choose to produce and sell at a given price.

QUANTITY SUPPLIED The total amount of a good or service that all producers in a market would choose to produce and sell at a given price.

Notice that quantity supplied—like quantity demanded—tells us about sellers' *choices*. The amount that will *actually* be sold will be discussed later, when we put demand and supply together.

There are some other things to keep in mind when thinking about quantity supplied. First, it can refer to an individual seller, like your local Kinko's copy shop, or to the combined choices of *all* sellers in a market—all photocopy shops in your area. In this chapter, we'll focus on quantity supplied to an entire market.

Second, the definition of quantity supplied refers to *sellers* in general. Typically, the sellers are business firms that produce goods and services, as in the markets for coffee, haircuts, new cars, and airline travel. In these markets, each business firm will choose to produce and sell the quantity of output that gives it the highest possible profit. But in some markets, households are the sellers. For example, households sell their labor time to the business firms that employ them in the labor market. Households are also often sellers in markets for real estate, stocks and bonds, and used cars. This chapter, however, deals primarily with markets in which the sellers are business firms.

Finally, the quantity of a good supplied depends on the *price* of the good. There are other influences on sellers' choices besides the price of the good they are selling—and we'll discuss these other influences soon. But since the prices of goods play such an important role in resource allocation, they are a natural starting point for our analysis of quantity supplied.

THE LAW OF SUPPLY

How does a change in price affect quantity supplied? When a seller can get a higher price for a good, producing and selling it becomes more profitable. Producers will devote more resources toward its production and increase the quantity they would like to sell. For example, a rise in the price of vases will encourage ceramics manufacturers to shift resources out of the production of other things (coffee mugs, dishes, and so on) and toward the production of vases.

In general, price and quantity supplied are *positively related:* When the price of a good rises, the quantity supplied will rise as well. This relationship between price and quantity supplied is called the *law of supply,* the counterpart to the law of demand we discussed earlier.

LAW OF SUPPLY As the price of a good increases, the quantity supplied increases.

> The **law of supply** states that when the price of a good rises, and everything else remains the same, the quantity of the good supplied will rise.

Once again, notice the very important words, "everything else remains the same." Although many other variables influence the quantity of a good supplied, the law of supply tells us what would happen if all of them remained unchanged as the price of the good changed.

THE SUPPLY SCHEDULE AND THE SUPPLY CURVE

Let's continue with our example of the market for maple syrup in Wichita. Who are the suppliers in this market? Since maple syrup is easy to transport, any producer on the continent can sell in Wichita. In practice, these producers are located mostly in the forests of Vermont, in upstate New York, and in Canada. The quantity supplied is the amount of maple syrup all of these producers together would offer for sale in Wichita at each price for maple syrup.

SUPPLY SCHEDULE A list showing the quantities of a good or service that firms would choose to produce and sell at different prices, with all other variables held constant.

Table 4 shows the **supply schedule** for maple syrup in Wichita—a *list of different quantities supplied at different prices, with all other variables held constant.* As you can see, the supply schedule obeys the law of supply: As the price of maple syrup rises, the quantity supplied rises along with it.

Now look at Figure 3, which shows a very important curve—the counterpart to the demand curve we drew earlier. In the figure, each point represents a price-quantity pair taken from Table 4. For example, point *F* in the figure corresponds to a price of $2.00 per bottle and a quantity of 4,000 bottles per month, while point *G* represents the price-quantity pair $4.00 and 6,000 bottles. Connecting all of these points with a solid line gives us the *supply curve* for maple syrup, labeled with an *S* in the figure.

SUPPLY CURVE A graphical depiction of a supply schedule; a curve showing the quantity of a good or service supplied at various prices, with all other variables held constant.

> The **supply curve** shows the relationship between the price of a good and the quantity supplied, holding constant the values of all other variables that affect supply. Each point on the curve shows the quantity that sellers would choose to sell at a specific price.

Notice that the supply curve in Figure 3—like all supply curves for goods and services—is *upward sloping*. This is the graphical representation of the law of supply: An increase in price causes an increase in quantity supplied.

> The law of supply tells us that supply curves slope upward.

TABLE 4	SUPPLY SCHEDULE FOR MAPLE SYRUP IN WICHITA	
	Price (per bottle)	**Quantity Supplied (bottles per month)**
	$1.00	2,500
	$2.00	4,000
	$3.00	5,000
	$4.00	6,000
	$5.00	6,500

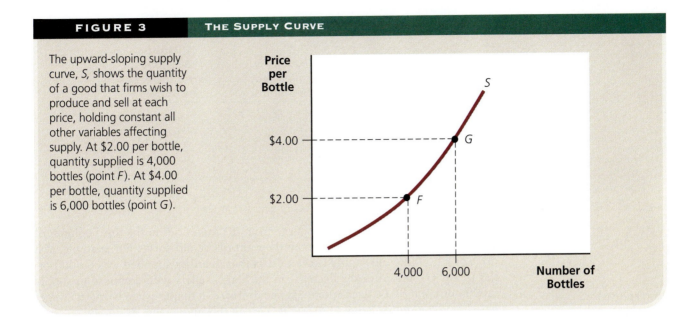

FIGURE 3   **THE SUPPLY CURVE**

The upward-sloping supply curve, *S,* shows the quantity of a good that firms wish to produce and sell at each price, holding constant all other variables affecting supply. At $2.00 per bottle, quantity supplied is 4,000 bottles (point *F*). At $4.00 per bottle, quantity supplied is 6,000 bottles (point *G*).

CHANGES IN QUANTITY SUPPLIED

Sellers' choices about how much to sell are affected by many different variables. One of these variables—the price of the good—causes sellers to *move along* a given supply curve. The other variables cause the entire supply curve to *shift*. To avoid confusion, economists use the same language convention for supply that we discussed earlier for demand. Look once again at Figure 3. Notice that when the price of maple syrup rises from $2.00 to $4.00, the number of bottles supplied rises from 4,000 to 6,000. This is a movement *along* the supply curve, from point *F* to point *G*, and we call it an *increase in quantity supplied*. More generally,

> *A change in a good's price causes us to move* along *the supply curve. We call this a **change in quantity supplied.***

A rise in price causes a rightward movement along the supply curve—an *increase in quantity supplied.* A fall in price causes a leftward movement along the supply curve—a *decrease in quantity supplied.*

CHANGES IN SUPPLY

Both the supply schedule in Table 4 and the supply curve in Figure 3 hold constant all other variables that might affect supply. For example, let's suppose that the supply curve in Figure 3 tells us the quantity supplied at each price *if maple syrup workers are paid $10 per hour.* But what would happen if these workers' wages fell to $7 per hour? Then, at any given price for maple syrup, firms would find it more profitable to produce and sell maple syrup, and they would no doubt choose to sell more. This is illustrated in Table 5. For example, at the original wage of $10, maple syrup producers would choose to sell 6,000 bottles when the price is $4.00. But if they could pay the lower wage of $7, they would choose to sell 8,000 bottles at that same price. The same holds for any other price for maple syrup: after the wage falls, sellers would choose to sell more than before. In other words, *the entire relationship between price and quantity supplied has changed.*

CHANGE IN QUANTITY SUPPLIED A movement along a supply curve in response to a change in price.

TABLE 5	INCREASE IN SUPPLY OF MAPLE SYRUP IN WICHITA		
	Price (per bottle)	**Quantity Supplied (bottles per month)**	**Quantity Supplied after Increase in Supply**
	$1.00	2,500	4,500
	$2.00	4,000	6,000
	$3.00	5,000	7,000
	$4.00	6,000	8,000
	$5.00	6,500	8,500

Figure 4 plots the new supply curve from the quantities in the third column of Table 5. The new supply curve lies to the right of the old curve. For example, at a price of $4.00, the old supply curve told us that quantity supplied was 6,000 bottles (point G). But after the decrease in the wage, sellers would choose to supply 8,000 bottles at $4.00 each (point J). The decrease in maple-syrup workers' wages has *shifted the supply curve to the right.* We call this an *increase in supply.*

CHANGE IN SUPPLY A shift of a supply curve in response to some variable other than price.

*A change in any influence on supply—except for the good's price—causes the supply curve to shift. We call this a **change in supply.***

When sellers choose to sell more at any price, the supply curve shifts rightward—an *increase in supply.* When sellers choose to sell less at any price, the supply curve shifts leftward—a *decrease in supply.*

Table 5 illustrates how an increase in supply affects the supply schedule: The quantity supplied at each price increases. Figure 4 shows the old and new supply curves after an increase in supply. Notice that the new supply curve lies to the right of the old curve. For example, at a price of $4.00, the quantity supplied is 6,000 bottles on the old curve (point G) and 8,000 bottles on the new curve

FIGURE 4	A SHIFT IN THE SUPPLY CURVE

A change in any nonprice determinant of supply causes the entire supply curve to shift. A decrease in labor costs, for example, causes the supply of maple syrup to shift from S_1 to S_2. At each price, more bottles are supplied after the shift.

(point *J*). Changes in supply are represented by a *shift* in the supply curve. When supply increases, the supply curve shifts to the right; when supply decreases, the supply curve shifts to the left.

Now let's take a look at the different variables that can cause a change in supply and shift the supply curve.

To avoid confusion, always apply the same language convention for supply that we discussed earlier for demand. When we *move along* the supply curve, we call it a *change in quantity supplied*. A change in quantity supplied is always caused by a change in the good's price. When the entire supply curve shifts, we call it a *change in supply*. A change in supply is caused by a change in something *other* than the good's price.

DANGEROUS CURVES

PRICES OF INPUTS. Producers of maple syrup use a variety of inputs: land, maple trees, water, labor, glass bottles, bottling machinery, transportation, and more. A higher price for any of these means a higher cost of producing and selling maple syrup, making it less profitable. As a result, we would expect producers to shift some resources out of maple syrup production, causing a decrease in supply.

In general,

> *a rise in the price of an input causes a decrease in supply, shifting the supply curve to the left. A fall in the price of an input causes an increase in supply, shifting the supply curve to the right.*

Figure 4 illustrates what happens when the wage rate paid to maple syrup workers (an input for maple syrup producers) falls: the supply of maple syrup increases and the supply curve shifts to the right. The same holds in any market. For example, we would expect a rise in the price of rubber to decrease the supply of tires and a decline in the price of paper to increase the supply of paperback books.

PRICES OF ALTERNATE GOODS. Firms can often choose among a variety of goods and services to produce and sell, all of which use roughly the same inputs. A maple syrup producer could cut down its maple trees and supply lumber instead. Or it could dry its maple syrup and produce maple *sugar*. These other goods that firms *could* produce are called **alternate goods.**

> *A rise in the price of an alternate good will decrease the supply of a good, shifting the supply curve leftward.*

ALTERNATE GOODS Other goods that a firm could produce using some of the same types of inputs as the good in question.

If the price of maple *sugar* rises, it will become more profitable, so producers will devote more of their output to maple sugar, *decreasing* the supply of maple syrup. Using similar logic, a higher price for oats decreases the supply of wheat, and a lower price for hardcover books should increase the supply of paperbacks.

TECHNOLOGY. Suppose there is a technological advance in producing maple syrup, say, a new, more efficient tap or a new bottling method. If this reduces the cost of producing maple syrup, producers will want to make and sell more of it at any price. In general, cost-saving technological advances will increase the supply of a good, shifting the supply curve to the right. Over the past two decades, cost-saving technological changes have dramatically increased supply in the markets for telephone calls, computers, cable television service, fax machines, photocopies, and more.

TABLE 6	CAUSES OF A CHANGE IN SUPPLY	
	Supply decreases, and the supply curve shifts leftward, when:	**Supply increases, and the supply curve shifts rightward, when:**
	price of an input ↑	price of an input ↓
	price of an alternate good ↑	price of an alternate good ↓
	productive capacity in the industry ↓	productive capacity in the industry ↑
	expectations of future price ↑	expectation of future price ↓
		there is a cost-saving technological advance

DANGEROUS CURVES

The list of variables that shift the supply curve in Table 6 does not include the amount that buyers want to buy. Is this a mistake? Doesn't demand affect supply?

The answer is no. The supply curve tells us how much sellers *would choose* to sell at alternative prices. It provides answers to a series of hypothetical questions, such as "How much maple syrup would firms choose to sell if the price were $4.00 per bottle? . . . if the price were $3.50 per bottle . . . ," and so on. Buyers' decisions don't affect the answers to these questions, so they cannot shift the supply curve.

But if people want to buy more, won't sellers want to sell more? Yes, but not because of any shift in the supply curve. As you'll see a bit later, an increase in demand will result in an increase in quantity supplied, but only by increasing the price of the good. This is represented by a movement *along* the supply curve, not a shift in the curve itself.

PRODUCTIVE CAPACITY. An increase in the number of firms in an industry or an increase in the size of each firm will increase supply, shifting the supply curve rightward. If half of the maple trees in Vermont perished, the total productive capacity of maple syrup suppliers would shrink, decreasing the supply of maple syrup. If more firms moved into the market and started their own maple syrup farms, supply would increase. Over the past several years, many new firms have begun producing laptop computers, leading to an increase in productive capacity and an increase in supply in this market.

EXPECTATIONS OF FUTURE PRICES. Imagine that you are the president of Sticky's Maple Syrup, Inc., and your research staff has just determined that the price of maple syrup will soon rise dramatically. What would you do? You should *postpone* producing—or at least selling—your output until later, when the price will be higher and profits will be greater. Applying this logic more generally,

> *A rise in the* expected *price of a good will decrease the supply, shifting the supply curve leftward.*

Using similar logic, a belief that the price of commercial lots in Trenton is about to fall will increase the supply of such lots—more of them will be offered for sale at any given price.

Table 6 summarizes the different variables that change the supply of a good and shift the supply curve.

PUTTING SUPPLY AND DEMAND TOGETHER

What happens when buyers and sellers, each having the desire and the ability to trade, come together in a market? The two sides of the market have different agendas: Buyers would like to pay the lowest possible price, while sellers would like to charge the highest possible price. Is there chaos when they meet, with buyers and sellers endlessly chasing after each other or endlessly bargaining for advantage, so that trade never takes place? A casual look at the real world suggests not. In most markets, most of the time, there is order and stability in the encounters between buyers and sellers. In most cases, prices do not fluctuate wildly from moment to moment but seem to hover around a stable value. This stability may be short lived—lasting only a day, an hour, or even a minute in some markets—but still, for this short time, the market seems to be at rest. Whenever we study a market, therefore, we look for this state of rest—a price and quantity at which the market will settle, at least for a while.

Economists use the word *equilibrium* when referring to a state of rest. More formally,

> *an **equilibrium** is a situation that, once achieved, will not change unless something we have been holding constant changes.*

EQUILIBRIUM A state of rest; a situation that, once achieved, will not change unless some external factor, previously held constant, changes.

What will be the price of maple syrup in Wichita? And how much will people actually buy each month? We can rephrase these questions as follows: What is the equilibrium price of maple syrup in Wichita, and what is the equilibrium quantity of maple syrup exchanged? These are precisely the questions that the supply-and-demand model is designed to answer.

Look at Figure 5, which combines the supply and demand curves for maple syrup in Wichita. We'll use the figure to find the equilibrium in this market, through the process of elimination. Let's first ask what would happen if the price of maple syrup in Wichita were $1.00 per bottle. At this price, we see that buyers would choose to buy 7,500 bottles each week, while sellers would offer to sell only 2,500 per week. We say that there is an **excess demand** of 5,000 bottles. What will happen? Buyers will compete with each other to get more maple syrup than is available, offering to pay a higher price rather than do without. The price will then rise. You can see that $1.00 per bottle is *not* the equilibrium price since—if the price *were* $1.00— it would automatically tend to rise. $1.00 is *not* a point of rest in this market.

EXCESS DEMAND At a given price, the excess of quantity demanded over quantity supplied.

shortage

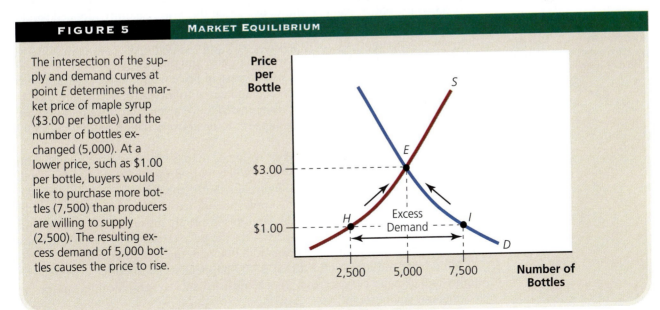

| FIGURE 5 | MARKET EQUILIBRIUM |

The intersection of the supply and demand curves at point *E* determines the market price of maple syrup ($3.00 per bottle) and the number of bottles exchanged (5,000). At a lower price, such as $1.00 per bottle, buyers would like to purchase more bottles (7,500) than producers are willing to supply (2,500). The resulting excess demand of 5,000 bottles causes the price to rise.

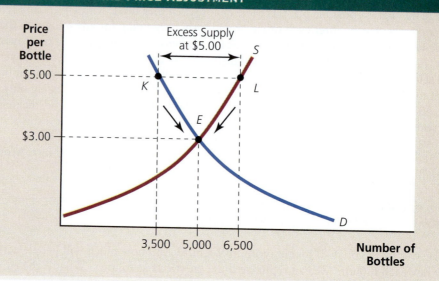

FIGURE 6   ° **EXCESS SUPPLY AND PRICE ADJUSTMENT**

At any price above $3.00 per bottle, the market for maple syrup will be out of equilibrium. The excess supply of 3,000 bottles at a price of $5.00 causes the market price to fall. As the price falls, quantity supplied decreases and quantity demanded increases. At point E, the market is back in equilibrium.

EXCESS SUPPLY At a given price, the excess of quantity supplied over quantity demanded.

Before we consider other possible prices, let's look more closely at the changes we would see in this market as the price rose. First, there would be a decrease in quantity demanded—movement along the demand curve leftward from point *I*. At the same time, we would see an increase in quantity supplied—a movement along the supply curve rightward from point *H*. As these movements continued, the excess demand for maple syrup would shrink and, finally—at a price of $3.00—disappear entirely. At this price, there would be no reason for any further price change, since quantity supplied and quantity demanded both would equal 5,000 bottles per month. There would be no disappointed buyers to offer higher prices. In sum, if the price happens to be below $3.00, it will rise to $3.00 and then stay put.

Now let's see what would happen if, for some reason, the price of maple syrup were $5.00 per bottle. Figure 6 shows us that, at this price, quantity supplied would be 6,500 bottles per month, while quantity demanded would be only 3,500 bottles—an **excess supply** of 3,000 bottles. Sellers would compete with each other to sell more maple syrup than buyers wanted to buy, and the price would fall, so $5.00 cannot be the equilibrium price. The decrease in price would move us along both the supply curve (leftward) and the demand curve (rightward), decreasing the excess supply of maple syrup until it disappeared, once again, at a price of $3.00 per bottle. Our conclusion: If the price happens to be above $3.00, it will fall to $3.00 and then stop changing.

You can see that any price higher or lower than $3.00 is *not* the equilibrium price. If the price is higher than $3.00, it will tend to drop, and if it is lower, it will tend to rise. You can also see—in Figure 6—that if the price were exactly $3.00, there would be neither an excess supply nor an excess demand. Sellers would choose to sell 5,000 bottles per week, and this is exactly the quantity buyers would choose to buy. There would be no reason for the price to change. Thus, $3.00 must be our sought-after equilibrium price and 5,000 our equilibrium quantity.

No doubt, you have noticed that $3.00 happens to be the price at which the supply and demand curves cross. This leads us to an easy, graphical technique for locating our equilibrium:

> To find the equilibrium price and quantity in a competitive market, draw the supply and demand curves. The equilibrium is the point where the two curves intersect.

The intersection of the supply and demand curves helps us to understand the concept of equilibrium even more clearly. At the intersection, the market is operating on both the demand and the supply curves. When the price is $3.00, buyers and sellers can *actually* buy and sell the quantities they *would choose* to buy and sell at $3.00. There are no dissatisfied buyers unable to find the goods they want to purchase, nor are there unhappy sellers unable to find buyers for the products they have brought to the market. This is why $3.00 is the equilibrium price. In this state of rest, there is a balance between the quantity supplied and the quantity demanded.

But that point of rest will not necessarily be a lasting one. Remember that in order to draw the supply and demand curves in the first place, we had to assume particular values for all the other variables—besides price—that affect demand and supply. If any one of these variables changes, then either the supply curve or the demand curve shifts, and our equilibrium will change as well. Economists are very interested in how and why the equilibrium changes in a market, so this is what we'll explore next.

WHAT HAPPENS WHEN THINGS CHANGE?

Point E in Figure 7 shows our initial equilibrium—a price of $3.00 and quantity of 5,000 bottles—in the market for maple syrup in Wichita. But now suppose that average household income in Wichita increases. We have already seen that the demand curve will shift rightward from D_1 to D_2. At the original price of $3.00 per bottle, there will be an excess demand of 2,000 bottles, forcing the price up. The rise in price will move us along the supply curve, from point E to point E'. Using our terminology, we would say that *an increase in demand* causes an increase in price, which, in turn, causes *an increase in quantity supplied*.

FIGURE 7	A SHIFT IN DEMAND AND A NEW EQUILIBRIUM

An increase in household incomes increases demand from D_1 to D_2. At the old price of $3.00 per bottle, there is now an excess demand. As a result, price rises until excess demand is eliminated at point E'. In the new equilibrium, quantity demanded again equals quantity supplied. The price is higher and more bottles are produced and sold.

FIGURE 8	A SHIFT IN SUPPLY AND A NEW EQUILIBRIUM

A decrease in wages causes supply to increase from S_1 to S_2. At the old equilibrium price of $3.00, there is now an excess supply. As a result, the price falls until excess supply is eliminated at point E'. In the new equilibrium, quantity demanded again equals quantity supplied. The price is lower, and more bottles are produced and sold.

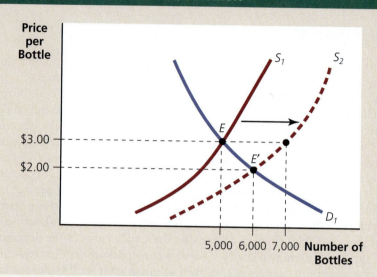

The end result is an increase in the equilibrium price—from $3.00 to $4.00—and a rise in the equilibrium quantity—from 5,000 to 6,000 bottles. In general,

Any change that shifts the demand curve rightward will increase both the equilibrium price and the equilibrium quantity.

Similarly,

Any change that shifts the demand curve leftward will cause the equilibrium price and quantity to decrease.

Figure 8 illustrates another type of change. Here, the wages of workers in the maple syrup industry have decreased, so the supply curve shifts rightward, from S_1 to S_2. Now, we have an excess supply of 2,000 bottles at the original price of $3.00, so the price will decline. The fall in price moves us rightward along the demand curve, from point E to point E'. Here, an *increase in supply* causes the price to fall, which causes an *increase in quantity demanded*. Our new equilibrium occurs along S_2, at a lower price—$2.00—and a higher quantity—6,000 bottles. To generalize,

Any change that shifts the supply curve rightward will decrease the equilibrium price and increase the equilibrium quantity.

Similarly, any change in the opposite direction will shift the supply curve to the left and give us the opposite results:

Any change that shifts the supply curve leftward will cause the equilibrium price to rise and the equilibrium quantity to fall.

So far, we've considered the consequences of a change in a single variable only. But what happens to the market equilibrium when two or more variables are al-

FIGURE 9   **A Simultaneous Shift of Supply and Demand**

A decrease in the price of pancake mix causes demand to increase to D_2, while a rise in the price of maple *sugar* causes supply to decrease to S_2. Both price and quantity adjust until a new equilibrium is attained at point E' with a higher price and a higher quantity.

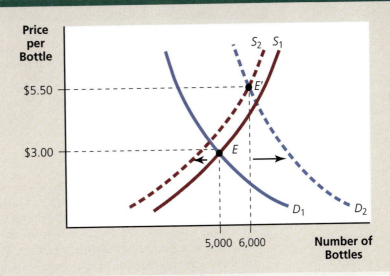

lowed to change simultaneously? Figure 9 illustrates how we would analyze a situation like this. Here, we assume that there is a decrease in the price of pancake mix, a complement to maple syrup, and, simultaneously, a rise in the price of maple *sugar,* an alternate good. The drop in the price of the complementary good shifts the demand curve for maple syrup rightward, from D_1 to D_2, while the rise in the price of the alternate good shifts the supply curve leftward, from S_1 to S_2. The impact on the equilibrium *price* is unambiguous: It must increase, since each of these shifts pushes the equilibrium price higher. The effect on the equilibrium *quantity,* however, is ambiguous: It could go either way, depending on which of the shifts—supply or demand—is greater. The figure illustrates the case where equilibrium quantity increases, because the rightward shift in demand—making quantity increase—is greater than the leftward shift in supply—making quantity decrease. You may want to prove to yourself that we could just as easily have illustrated a *decrease* in equilibrium quantity, simply by making the supply shift a bit larger or the demand shift a bit smaller.

Figure 9 illustrates only one of the possible combinations of shifts in supply and demand. But there are others. Table 7 summarizes what we know will happen to the equilibrium price (P) and quantity (Q) and what remains uncertain, in each case. For example, to find what happens when demand increases and supply decreases, look at the bottom, leftmost cell: The equilibrium price rises, while the equilibrium quantity might rise, fall, or remain the same.

Remember the advice in Chapter 1—to study economics actively, rather than passively. This would be a good time to put down the book, pick up a pencil and paper, and see whether you can work with supply and demand curves, rather than just follow along as you read. Try to draw diagrams that illustrate each of the possibilities in Table 7.

It's tempting to say that the demand or supply curves shift "up" or "down" rather than "rightward" or "leftward." But it's best to avoid this temptation. To see why, look at the supply shift in Figure 9. Supply *decreases,* yet the supply curve shifts *upward.* Since we measure quantity on the horizontal axis, always describe shifts as "rightward" or "leftward."

DANGEROUS CURVES

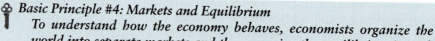

TABLE 7	EFFECT OF SUPPLY AND DEMAND SHIFTS ON EQUILIBRIUM PRICE (*P*) AND QUANTITY (*Q*)		
	Increase in Demand (rightward shift)	No Change in Demand	Decrease in Demand (leftward shift)
Increase in Supply (rightward shift)	P? Q↑	P↓ Q↑	P↓ Q?
No Change in Supply	P↑ Q↑	No change in P or Q	P↓ Q↓
Decrease in Supply (leftward shift)	P↑ Q?	P↑ Q↓	P? Q↓

THE PRINCIPLE OF MARKETS AND EQUILIBRIUM

In this chapter, you've seen an example of how economists approach a problem. We began by asking how the prices of the things we buy are actually determined. To answer that question, we abstracted from the complex, real-world economy and viewed it as a number of distinct *markets*. We then chose to analyze one of those markets—the market for maple syrup—by looking for its *equilibrium* price and quantity. The supply-and-demand model is just one example of a more general approach: to identify a market and examine its equilibrium.

> 🔑 *Basic Principle #4: Markets and Equilibrium*
> *To understand how the economy behaves, economists organize the world into separate markets and then examine the equilibrium in each of those markets.*

You have already seen one of the payoffs to this approach: It can explain how the price in a market is determined and what causes that price to change. But the approach takes us even further. It helps us predict important changes in the economy and prepare for them. And it helps us design government policies to accomplish our social goals and avoid policies that are likely to backfire. In the next section, we apply the principle of *markets and equilibrium* to some cases where government intervention is unlikely to accomplish our goals and may even cause unintended harm. In later chapters, you will see some examples of effective government policies that can help market economies work even better.

GOVERNMENT INTERVENTION IN MARKETS

In our discussion so far, we've seen how competitive markets—through the mechanism of supply and demand—will settle at an equilibrium price and quantity. But society, or some groups within society, may be unhappy with this equilibrium. Most often, there is dissatisfaction with the equilibrium price: Apartment dwellers often complain that their rents are too high, while dairy farmers complain that the price of milk is too low.

Responding to this dissatisfaction, governments will sometimes intervene to prevent the market from attaining its equilibrium. Although these interventions often enjoy strong political support, they may have perverse effects. Economic analysis usually recommends alternative ways to accomplish the same goals at lower cost.

PRICE CEILINGS

Look at Figure 10, which shows the market for maple syrup in Wichita, with an equilibrium price of $3.00 per bottle. Suppose a government agency, in order to help maple syrup buyers, imposes a **price ceiling** in this market—a regulation preventing the price from rising above the ceiling.

PRICE CEILING A government-imposed price that may not legally be exceeded.

More specifically, suppose the ceiling is $2.00 per bottle, and it is strictly enforced. Then producers will no longer be able to charge $3.00 for maple syrup, but will have to content themselves getting $2.00 instead. In Figure 10, we will move down along the supply curve, from point *E* to point *R*, decreasing quantity supplied from 5,000 bottles to 4,000. At the same time, the fall in price will move us along the demand curve, from point *E* to point *V*, increasing quantity demanded from 5,000 to 6,000. These changes in quantities supplied and demanded together create an excess demand for maple syrup of 6,000 – 4,000 = 2,000 bottles each month. Ordinarily, the excess demand would force the price back up to $3.00. But now the price ceiling prevents this from occurring. What will happen?

There is a practical observation about markets that helps us arrive at an answer:

> *When quantity supplied and quantity demanded differ, the* ***short side of the market****—whichever of the two quantities is less—will prevail.*

SHORT SIDE OF THE MARKET At a given price, the smaller of quantity demanded and quantity supplied.

This simple rule follows from the voluntary nature of exchange in a market system: No one can be forced to buy or sell more than they want to. With an excess demand, sellers are the short side of the market. Since we cannot force them to sell any more than they want to—4,000 units—buyers will not be able to purchase all they want.

But this is not the end of the story. Because of the excess demand, all 4,000 bottles produced each month will quickly disappear from store shelves, and many buyers will be disappointed. The next time people hear that maple syrup has become available, everyone will try to get there first, and we can expect long lines at stores. In addition, people may have to go from store to store, searching for scarce maple syrup. When we include the opportunity cost of the time spent waiting in line or

FIGURE 10 PRICE CEILINGS AND BLACK MARKETS

A government-imposed price ceiling of $2.00 per bottle reduces the legal quantity sold to 4,000 bottles, leaving an excess demand of 2,000 bottles. A black market may arise in which scalpers purchase the available 4,000 bottles and sell them (illegally) at the highest price consumers are willing to pay for that quantity—$4.00 per bottle, determined at point *T* on the demand curve.

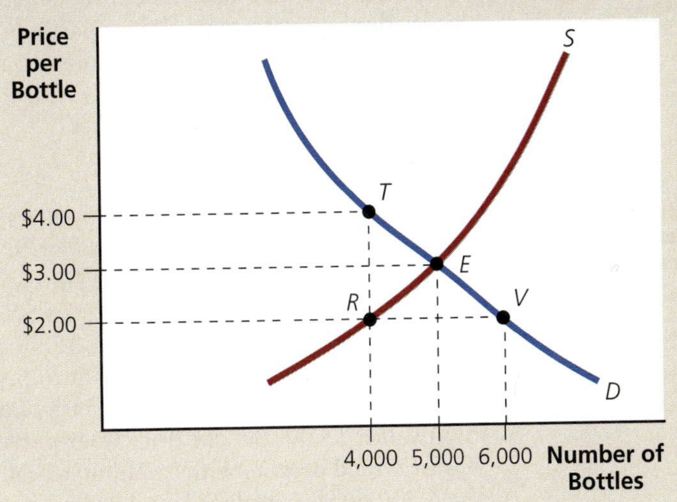

shopping around, the ultimate effect of the price ceiling may be a *higher* cost of maple syrup for many consumers.

OPPORTUNITY COST

> *A price ceiling creates a shortage and increases the time and trouble required to buy the good. While the price decreases, the* opportunity cost *may rise.*

And there is still more. Suppose the price ceiling cannot be perfectly enforced. With so many unsatisfied potential buyers—many of whom would pay more than $2.00 per bottle if they could only find a willing seller—suppliers will be tempted to violate the price ceiling. And even if suppliers abide by the law, other individuals can try to buy maple syrup at $2.00 per bottle and sell it for a higher price. The result: a **black market,** where goods are sold illegally at prices higher than the legal ceiling.

BLACK MARKET An illegal market in which goods are sold at prices above the legal ceiling.

Ironically, the black-market price will typically exceed the original, freely determined equilibrium price—$3.00 per bottle in our example. To see why, look at Figure 10 again. With a price ceiling of $2.00, sellers supply 4,000 bottles per month. Suppose all of this is bought by middlemen—maple syrup scalpers, if you will—who then sell it at the highest price they can get. What price can they charge? We can use the demand curve to find out. At $4.00 per bottle (point T), the scalpers would just be able to sell all 4,000 bottles. They have no reason, therefore, to charge any less than this.

The unintended consequences of price ceilings—long lines, black markets, and, sometimes, higher prices—explain why they are generally a poor way to bring down prices. Experience with price ceilings has generally confirmed this judgment, so in practice they are rare. There are two exceptions, however.

First, governments impose a price ceiling of *zero* on certain trades that society finds unacceptable to treat as market transactions at all. For example, organs for transplant operations—such as hearts and livers—can be donated, but not sold. The result is shortages, although so far, there is no organized black market in donor organs.

RENT CONTROLS A government-imposed maximum on rents that may be charged for apartments or homes.

The other exception is **rent controls**—city ordinances that specify a maximum monthly rent on many apartments and homes. If you live in a city with rent control, you will be familiar with its consequences. In any case, you may want to reread this section with the market for apartments in mind. How are shortages and long lines manifested? Do rent controls always decrease the cost of apartments to renters? (Think: opportunity cost.) And who are the middlemen—the "apartment scalpers"—who profit in this market?

PRICE FLOORS

PRICE FLOOR A government-imposed minimum price below which a good or service may not be sold.

Sometimes, governments try to help sellers of a good by establishing a **price floor**—a minimum amount below which the price is not permitted to fall.

For example, suppose that the Maple Syrup Producers Association convinces the government to set a price floor of $5.00 per bottle. To see the effects on the market, look back at Figure 6. At $5.00 per bottle, producers would like to sell 6,500 bottles, while consumers want to purchase only 3,500. The excess supply of 6,500 − 3,500 = 3,000 would ordinarily push the market price down to its equilibrium value, $3.00. But the price floor prevents this. Our short-side rule tells us that buyers would determine the amount actually traded. They would purchase 3,500 of the 6,500 bottles produced, and producers would be unable to sell the remainder.

What would happen then? Producers would have an incentive to violate the price floor by selling some of their maple syrup for less than $5.00. A black market would develop for cheap maple syrup. As you can see, price floors can be just as hard to enforce as price ceilings.

But there is a foolproof strategy the government could use to prevent a black market from developing. It's a strategy that governments around the world typically use when they establish price floors. In our example, the government would establish a special agency—let's call it the Maple Syrup Board—that promises to buy maple syrup from any seller at $5.00 per bottle. With this policy, no supplier would ever sell at any price below $5.00, since it could always sell to the government instead. With the price effectively stuck at $5.00, private buyers will buy 3,500 bottles per month—point K on the demand curve in Figure 6. But since quantity supplied is 6,500, the government will find itself buying 6,500 − 3,500 = 3,000 bottles each month. In other words, the government maintains the price floor by buying up the entire excess supply. This prevents the excess supply from doing what it would ordinarily do: drive the price down to its equilibrium value.

And this is not the end of the story. Maintaining a price floor, as described here, would cause the government to endlessly accumulate growing stocks of food. To deal with this, governments will often try to limit supply. Our Maple Syrup Board might gain the power to limit the number of trees each producer could tap. In this way, price floors often get the government deeply involved in production decisions, rather than leaving them to the market.

Governments in many countries have a long history of using price floors in agricultural markets to prop up the incomes of farmers. In the United States, price floors for milk, cheese, eggs, and a variety of fruits and vegetables have been established. This policy has many critics—including most economists. They argue that the government spends too much money buying surplus agricultural products, and that the resulting higher prices distort the public's buying and eating habits—often to their nutritional detriment. Moreover, many of the farmers who benefit from price floors are wealthy individuals or large, powerful corporations, which do not need the assistance.

THE BASIC PRINCIPLE OF POLICY TRADEOFFS

In our discussion of government intervention in markets, you may have noticed something interesting: A policy designed to help us achieve one goal causes us to compromise on some other goal. For example, if one of our goals is to maintain high incomes for farmers, we can achieve it by establishing a price floor on farm goods. But we *also* want low tax rates on households and businesses, and the price floor may interfere with this. How? As we've seen, as a result of the price floor, individual farmers will want to sell more farm goods, and individual consumers will want to buy fewer of them. When these reactions from buyers and sellers are taken into account, we discover that there will be a surplus of farm goods on the market that the government will have to deal with. Whether the government decides to establish a costly program to limit production, or to buy the surpluses itself, it will need more tax dollars, and may have to raise tax rates.

This is just one example of a more general principle. In fact, as you will see throughout this text, there are virtually always tradeoffs involved in government policy making. For this reason, we consider government policy tradeoffs to be one of the basic principles of economics.

> **Basic Principle #5: Policy Tradeoffs**
> *Government policy is constrained by the reactions of private decision makers. As a result, policy makers face tradeoffs: making progress toward one goal often requires some sacrifice of another goal.*

Economics is famous for making the public aware of policy tradeoffs. Whenever we think we've found an easy solution to one of society's vexing problems, economic analysis makes us aware of some other social goal that must be sacrificed if we pursue that solution. Although this knowledge is sometimes unpleasant, it can help us formulate wiser policies and—at a minimum—prevent even more unpleasant surprises.

SUPPLY AND DEMAND AND NORMATIVE ECONOMICS

Supply and demand offers us important lessons about the economy. The lessons are both positive—telling us *what* will happen when there is a change in a market—and normative—suggesting what sorts of policies we *should or should not* pursue.

Most economists believe that the mechanism of supply and demand is an effective way to allocate resources. "Let the market determine prices," they say, "and let each of us respond to those prices as we wish." When someone proposes to interfere with this mechanism, economists listen—but skeptically. The burden of proof, they believe, should lie with those who favor intervention. Why do economists feel this way?

Answering this question requires a more thorough understanding of the economy than we can provide after just three chapters of this book. Be assured, though, that when you finish your introductory study of economics, you will know why economists treat supply and demand with such respect.

ANTICIPATING A PRICE CHANGE

In the late 1980s, many East Coast colleges purchased expensive equipment that would enable them to switch rapidly from oil to natural gas as a source of heat. The idea was to protect the colleges from a sudden rise in oil prices, like the one they had suffered earlier, in the 1970s.

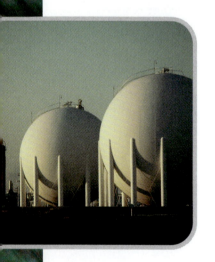

In the fall of 1990, when Iraq invaded Kuwait, the colleges finally got a chance to put their new equipment to use. Oil prices skyrocketed, and the colleges switched from burning oil to burning natural gas. But college administrators, expecting big savings on their energy bills, were in for a shock: They did not save much at all. When they received the bills from their local utilities, they found that the price of natural gas—like the price of oil—had risen sharply. Many of these administrators were angry at the utility companies and accused them of price gouging. Iraq's invasion of Kuwait, they reasoned, had not affected natural gas supplies at all, so there was no reason for the price of natural gas to rise.

Were the college administrators right? Was this just an example of price gouging by the utility companies, taking advantage of an international crisis to increase their profits? A simple supply-and-demand analysis will give us the answer. More specifically, it will enable us to answer two questions: (1) Why did Iraq's invasion of Kuwait cause the price of oil to rise; and (2) Why did the price of natural gas rise as well?

Figure 11 shows supply and demand curves in the world market for oil. Before the invasion, the market was in equilibrium at E, with price P_1 and total output Q_1. Iraq's invasion and continued occupation of Kuwait—one of the largest oil producers in the world—led to a worldwide embargo of oil from Iraq and Kuwait. As far as the oil market was concerned, it was as if these nations' oil fields no longer existed—a significant decrease in the oil industry's productive capacity. If you look back at Table 6, you will see that a change in productive capacity is one of the causes of a shift in the supply curve. In this example, in which productive capacity

FIGURE 11 — THE MARKET FOR OIL

Before the Iraqi invasion of Kuwait, the oil market was in equilibrium at point E. The invasion and the resulting embargo on Iraqi oil decreased supply to S_2. Price increased to P_2 and the quantity exchanged fell to Q_2.

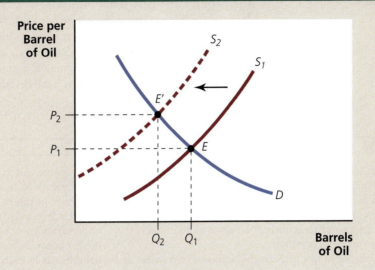

decreased, the supply curve for oil shifted to the left. The new equilibrium at E' occurred at a lower quantity and a higher price. This change in the oil market was well understood by most people—including the college administrators—and no one was surprised when oil prices rose.

But what has all this got to do with natural gas prices? Everything, as the next part of our analysis will show. Oil is a *substitute* for natural gas. A rise in the price of a substitute, we know, will increase the demand for a good. (Look back at Table 3 if you need a reminder.) In this case, the increase in the price of oil (depicted in Figure 11) caused the demand curve *for natural gas*—depicted in Figure 12—to shift rightward. The price of natural gas rose, from P_3 to P_4.

FIGURE 12 — THE MARKET FOR NATURAL GAS

Oil is a substitute for natural gas. A rise in the price of oil increases the demand for natural gas. Here, demand increased from D_1 to D_2 and price rose from P_3 to P_4.

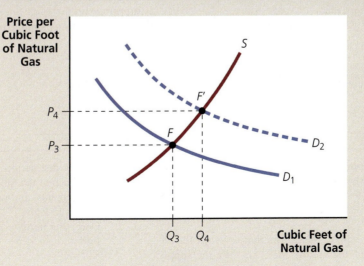

The administrators were right that the invasion of Kuwait did not affect the supply of natural gas. What they missed, however, was the invasion's effect on the *demand* for natural gas. With a fuller understanding of supply and demand, they could have predicted—*before* investing in their expensive switching equipment—that any rise in oil prices would cause a rise in natural gas prices. Armed with this knowledge, they would have anticipated a much smaller saving in energy costs from switching to natural gas and might have decided that there were better uses for their scarce funds.

S U M M A R Y

In a market economy, prices are determined through the interaction of buyers and sellers in *markets*. *Perfectly competitive* markets have many buyers and sellers, and none of them individually can affect the market price. If at least one buyer or seller has the power to influence the price of a product, the market is *imperfectly competitive*.

The model of *supply and demand* explains how prices are determined in perfectly competitive markets. The *quantity demanded* of any good is the total amount buyers would choose to purchase at a given price. The *law of demand* states that quantity demanded is negatively related to price; it tells us that the demand curve slopes downward. The demand curve is drawn for given levels of income, wealth, tastes, and prices of substitute and complementary goods. If any of those factors changes, the demand curve will shift.

The *quantity supplied* of a good is the total amount sellers would choose to produce and sell at a given price. According to the *law of supply*, the supply curves slope upward. The supply curve will shift if there is a change in the price of an input, the price of an alternate good, productive capacity, or expectations of future prices.

The *principle of markets and equilibrium* tells us that to understand how the economy operates, we should think of the economy as a system of markets, and then examine the equilibrium in each of those markets. Equilibrium price and quantity in a market are found where the supply and demand curves intersect. If either of the curves shifts, price and quantity will change as the market moves to a new equilibrium.

Governments often intervene in markets, to change the equilibrium price. *Price ceilings* are imposed in an attempt to hold a price below its equilibrium value. *Price floors* are an attempt to keep the price above the equilibrium value. Economists tend to be skeptical about price ceilings and price floors, since they are often ineffective and have unintended consequences that undermine the government's goals.

K E Y   T E R M S

market	change in demand	law of supply	excess supply
imperfectly competitive market	income	supply schedule	price ceiling
perfectly competitive market	wealth	supply curve	short side of the market
quantity demanded	normal good	change in quantity supplied	black market
law of demand	inferior good	change in supply	rent controls
demand schedule	substitute	alternate goods	price floor
demand curve	complement	equilibrium	
change in quantity demanded	quantity supplied	excess demand	

R E V I E W   Q U E S T I O N S

1. How does economists' use of the word "market" differ from its use in everyday speech?

2. List and briefly explain the factors that can shift the demand curve, and the factors that can shift the supply curve.

3. Discuss the distinction between substitutes and complements. Which of the following pairs are substitutes, which are complements, and which are neither?
   a. Coke and Pepsi
   b. Computer hardware and computer software
   c. Beef and chicken
   d. Salt and sugar
   e. Ice cream and frozen yogurt

4. Rank each of the following markets according to how close it comes to perfect competition:
   a. Wheat
   b. Personal computer hardware
   c. Gold
   d. Airline tickets from New York to Kalamazoo, Michigan

5. Are the following goods more likely to be normal or inferior?
   a. Lexus automobiles
   b. Second-hand clothes
   c. Imported beer
   d. Baby-sitting services
   e. Recapped tires
   f. Futons
   g. Home haircutting tools
   h. Restaurant meals

6. What does the term "equilibrium" mean in economics?

7. Explain why the price in a free market cannot stay above or below equilibrium for long, unless there is outside interference.

8. What does it mean to say that the "short side of the market prevails"?

9. State whether each of the following will cause a change in demand or a change in supply, and in which direction:
   a. Input prices increase.
   b. Income in an area declines.
   c. The price of an alternate good increases.
   d. Tastes shift away from a good.

PROBLEMS AND EXERCISES

1. Throughout the 1970s and 1980s, red meat fell out of favor with many consumers. On a supply-and-demand diagram, illustrate the effect of such a change on equilibrium price and quantity in the market for beef.

2. Discuss, and illustrate with a graph, how each of the following events will affect the market for coffee:
   a. A blight on coffee plants kills off much of the Brazilian crop.
   b. The price of tea declines sharply.
   c. Coffee workers organize themselves into a union and gain higher wages.
   d. Coffee is shown to cause cancer in laboratory rats.
   e. Coffee prices are expected to rise rapidly in the near future. *The only ∆ that affects both S & D*

3. The following table gives hypothetical data for the quantity of gasoline demanded and supplied in Los Angeles per month.

Price per Gallon	Qty. Demanded (millions of gals.)	Qty. Supplied (millions of gals.)
$1.20	170	80
$1.30	156	105
$1.40	140	140
$1.50	123	175
$1.60	100	210
$1.70	95	238

   a. Graph the demand and supply curves.
   b. Find the equilibrium price and quantity.
   c. Illustrate on your graph how a rise in the price of automobiles would affect the gasoline market.
   d. The California state government, alarmed by recent increases in gas prices, imposes a price ceiling of $1.20 per gallon. How will this affect the market? Specifically, calculate the resulting shortage or surplus.

4. How will each of the following affect the market for blue jeans in the United States? Illustrate each answer with a supply-and-demand diagram.
   a. The price of denim cloth increases.
   b. An influx of immigrants arrives in the United States. (Explicitly state any assumptions you are making.)
   c. A recession causes household incomes to decrease.

5. Indicate which curve shifted which way to account for each of the following?
   a. The price of furniture rises as the quantity bought and sold falls.
   b. Apartment vacancy rates increase while average monthly rent on apartments declines.
   c. The price of personal computers continues to decline as sales skyrocket.

6. The market for rice has the following supply-and-demand schedule:

P (per ton)	Q_D (in tons)	Q_S (in tons)
10	100	0
20	80	30
30	60	40
40	50	50
50	40	60

To support rice producers, the government imposes a price floor of $30 per ton. What quantity will be traded in this market? Why?

7. The Economic Research Service of the U.S. Department of Agriculture regularly forecasts demand and supply of agricultural products worldwide. Information on specific crops is available through "Briefing Rooms" listed at http://www.econ.ag.gov/briefing/.
   a. Go to "Data" in the "Corn Briefing Room" at http://www.econ.ag.gov/briefing/corn/ for the latest information on corn prices. (If you can't read PDF files on your browser, get the free plug-in at http://www.adobe.com/prodindex/acrobat/readstep.html.)
   b. Did the average price of corn rise or fall between the last two months reported? Name two factors affecting the demand for corn that could have caused this change in price. Name two factors affecting the supply of corn that could have led to the same impact on price.

   (The questions in part c are based on material contained in the Appendix to Chapter 3.)
   c. Suppose the demand curve for corn has remained unchanged in recent months. If the demand for corn is *inelastic,* with price elasticity of demand equal to $E_D = 0.75$, will the change in price you noted in (b) cause total expenditure of corn buyers to increase, decrease, or remain unchanged? What percentage change in total expenditure on corn do you predict?

CHALLENGE QUESTIONS

1. Let demand be given by the equation $Q_D = 500 - 50P$ and supply by the equation $Q_S = 50 + 25P$. What will be the equilibrium price and quantity?

2. A Wall Street analyst observes the following equilibrium price-quantity combinations in the market for soft drinks over a 4-year period:

Year	P	Q
1	10	20
2	15	30
3	20	40
4	25	50

She concludes that the market defies the law of demand. Is she correct? Why or why not?

3. Assume the labor market for aircraft workers is in equilibrium. However, defense cutbacks result in decreased demand for airplanes and hence for aircraft workers. Will the result inevitably be unemployment in the aircraft industry? Why or why not? (Hint: In a labor market, how would you label the vertical and horizontal axes? That is, what is being supplied and demanded, and what is its price?)

4. Consider the following labor market scenario. You observe an influx of new workers into a region, the unemployment rate rises, but there is no decline in the wage. What is the most likely explanation for this situation?

5. As discussed in this and the preceding chapter, prices act as an allocative mechanism, determining how available supply is distributed among all who want a particular good. In the case of a price ceiling, this price mechanism is frustrated. Consider the market for rental housing. If a price ceiling is set below the market price:
   a. Will there be a shortage or a surplus of rental housing?
   b. Since price can no longer allocate housing, what other mechanisms might emerge? What factors might determine who gets a rent-controlled apartment and who does not? (You might find it helpful to read an article about rent control in cities such as Berkeley, California, or New York.)

APPENDIX: ELASTICITY OF DEMAND

The law of demand tells us that when price increases, quantity demanded will fall, and when price decreases, quantity demanded will rise. But it doesn't tell us *how much* quantity demanded will change. For some goods, quantity demanded is sensitive to price changes, while for other goods, there is almost no sensitivity at all. If we want be more specific about what happens when a price changes, we need a way to measure the sensitivity of quantity demanded to a change in price. Economists have developed just such a measure, called the *price elasticity of demand.*

The price elasticity of demand (E_D) *(or just* elasticity of demand, *for short) is the absolute value of the percentage change in quantity demanded divided by the percentage change in price:*

$$E_D = \left| \frac{\% \Delta Q^D}{\% \Delta P} \right|.$$

To understand how the elasticity of demand measures price sensitivity, think about what happens when the price of a good rises by, say, 2 percent. The denominator of our measure will be 2. We know the numerator will be *negative,* because a rise in the price of the good will cause quantity demanded to fall. However, since we take the absolute value of the final fraction, we can ignore the negative sign. Thus, the numerator will tell us the percentage by which quantity demanded falls when the price rises by 2 percent.

Now, the more sensitive quantity demanded is to this 2 percent price change, the greater the fall in quantity demanded, the greater the numerator will be, and the greater E_D will be. Thus, *the more sensitive quantity demanded is to price, the greater will be the price elasticity of demand.* For example, if a 2 percent rise in the price of newspapers causes a 3 percent drop in the quantity of newspapers demanded, then $E_D = | \% \Delta Q^D / \% \Delta P | = 3\%/2\% = 1.5$. We would say, "The price elasticity of demand for newspapers is 1.5." If that same 2 percent rise in price instead causes a 6 percent drop in the quantity demanded, then $E_D = | \% \Delta Q^D / \% \Delta P | = 6\%/2\% = 3.0$. In the second case, quantity demanded is more sensitive to price, and our measure of elasticity is larger: 3.0 rather than 1.5.

The elasticity of demand for a good has a straightforward interpretation: It tells us the percentage change in quantity demanded *per 1 percent increase* in price. An elasticity of 3.0, for example, tells us that when price rises by 1 percent, quantity demanded falls by 3.0 percent. When price rises by 2 percent, quantity demanded falls by 6.0 percent, and so on.

Finally, keep in mind that a demand elasticity number tells us the response of quantity demanded to a price change *when all other influences on demand remain unchanged.* We are interested in the pure effect of a price change on quantity demanded, uncluttered by changes in other prices, income, tastes, or other variables. Elasticity tells us the change in quantity we *would* observe if just the price of the good changed, and nothing else did. In other words,

A price elasticity of demand tells us the quantity response to a price change as we move along a demand curve, from one point to another.

CALCULATING PRICE ELASTICITY OF DEMAND

Suppose that you actually know the demand curve for a product; that is, you know what quantity consumers in a market would like to buy at each possible price. You would still have one more task in order to calculate a demand elasticity: measuring the *percentage change* in both quantity demanded and price.

PERCENTAGE CHANGES FOR ELASTICITIES. A percentage change is *usually* defined as the change in a variable divided by its starting or base value. (See the mathematical appendix on percentage changes.) But this method of calculating percentage changes can create a problem when determining elasticities. For example, look at Table A1, which shows the quantity of peanuts demanded at two different prices. (For now, ignore the columns referring to macadamia nuts.) Let's first calculate the percentage change in the price of peanuts when the price rises from $1.50 per pound to $2.50 per pound—a change of $1. Since the starting value is $1.50, the percentage change in price would be $1/$1.50 = 0.66, or 66 percent. But what if—instead of increasing from $1.50 to $2.50—the price had *decreased* from $2.50 to $1.50? In this case, our starting price would be $2.50, and our percentage change in price would now become –$1/$2.50 = –0.40, or –40 percent. This example shows us that, if we calculate percentage changes in the standard way, the number we get will depend on whether the price is rising or falling along any interval. That is, a price change from $1.50 to $2.50 is a percentage rise of 66 percent, while a price change from $2.50 to $1.50 is a percentage fall of 40 percent. The same is true for changes in quantity demanded: The percentage change in quantity demanded—calculated in the standard way—would depend on the *direction* of the change.

But that won't do for calculating an elasticity. Why? Elasticity of demand measures price sensitivity over an *interval* along the demand curve. We want this measure to be the same regardless of which end of the interval we start at. To ensure this, we adopt a special convention for measuring percentage changes for elasticities: *The base value used to calculate a percentage change in a variable is always midway between the initial value and the new value.* Thus, if the price rises from $1.50 to $2.50 or falls from $2.50 to $1.50, we use as our base price the value midway between these two prices, found by calculating their simple average: ($1.50 + $2.50)/2 = $2.00. This way, we are using the same base value, regardless of the direction of the price change. And our percentage change in price will be the same (except for sign) whether price rises from $1.50 to $2.50, or falls from $2.50 to $1.50.

More generally, when price changes from any value P_0 to any other value P_1, we define the percentage change in price as

$$\%\Delta P = \frac{(P_1 - P_0)}{(P_1 + P_0)/2}.$$

The term in the numerator is the change in price; the term in the denominator is the base price—the midpoint between the two prices. If you plug the preceding numbers into this formula, you'll see that when price rises from $1.50 to $2.50, the percentage rise in price is $1.00/$2.00 = 0.50; when price falls from $2.50 to $1.50, the percentage fall is $1.00/$2.00 = 0.50.

The percentage change in quantity demanded is calculated in a similar way. When quantity demanded changes from Q_0 to Q_1, the percentage change is calculated as

$$\%Q^D = \frac{(Q_1 - Q_0)}{(Q_1 + Q_2)/2}.$$

Once again, we are using the number midway between the initial and the new quantity demanded as our base quantity.

TABLE A1	DEMAND SCHEDULES FOR PEANUTS AND MACADAMIA NUTS			
	Peanuts		**Macadamia Nuts**	
	Price (per pound)	**Quantity (pounds per year)**	**Price (per pound)**	**Quantity (pounds per year)**
	$1.50	500,000	$8.00	15,000
	$2.50	490,000	$9.00	5,000

USING THE FORMULA. Now let's calculate the elasticity of demand for both peanuts and macadamia nuts, using the hypothetical data in Table A1. For peanuts, when price rises from $1.50 to $2.50, quantity demanded falls from 500,000 to 490,000, so we have

$$\%\Delta Q^D = \frac{(Q_1 - Q_0)}{[(Q_1 + Q_0)/2]}$$

$$= \frac{(490,000 - 500,000)}{495,000}$$

$$= -0.02, \text{ or } -2.0 \text{ percent}$$

$$\%\Delta P = \frac{(P_1 - P_0)}{[(P_1 + P_0)/2]}$$

$$= \frac{(\$2.50 - \$1.50)}{\$2.00}$$

$$= -0.50, \text{ or } 50.0 \text{ percent}$$

$$E_D = \left| \frac{-2.0 \text{ percent}}{50.0 \text{ percent}} \right| = 0.04.$$

We find that the quantity of peanuts demanded falls by 0.04 percent for each 1 percent increase in price. Not much price sensitivity at all here.

For macadamia nuts, the same price change of $1.00—but from $8.00 to $9.00 in this case—causes quantity demanded to fall from 15,000 to 5,000, so we have:

$$\%\Delta Q^D = \frac{(Q_1 - Q_0)}{[(Q_1 + Q_0)/2]}$$

$$= \frac{(5,000 - 15,000)}{10,000}$$

$$= -1.0, \text{ or } -100 \text{ percent}$$

$$\%\Delta P = \frac{(P_1 - P_0)}{[(P_1 + P_0)/2]}$$

$$= \frac{(\$9.00 - \$8.00)}{\$8.50}$$

$$= 0.118, \text{ or } 11.8 \text{ percent}$$

$$E_D = \left| \frac{-100 \text{ percent}}{11.8 \text{ percent}} \right| = 8.5$$

Here, each 1 percent increase in price causes quantity demanded to drop by about 8.5 percent. Macadamia nuts, unlike peanuts, exhibit a great deal of price sensitivity.

CATEGORIZING GOODS BY ELASTICITY

When the numerical value of the price elasticity of demand is *between 0 and 1.0*, we say that demand is *inelastic*. When demand for a good is inelastic, the elasticity will be smaller than unity, i.e.,

$$\left| \frac{\%\Delta Q^D}{\%\Delta P} \right| < 1$$

Or, rearranging, we obtain

$$\left| \%\Delta Q^D \right| < \left| \%\Delta P \right|$$

In words, inelastic demand means that the percentage change in quantity demanded will be *smaller* than the percentage change in price. For example, if price rises by 4 percent, quantity demanded will fall, but by *less* than 4 percent. When demand is inelastic, quantity demanded is *not* very sensitive to price.

An extreme case of inelastic demand occurs when a change in price causes absolutely no change in quantity demanded at all. In this case, since $\%\Delta Q^D = 0$, the elasticity will equal zero. We call this special case *perfectly inelastic* demand. Panel (a) of Figure A1 shows what the demand curve for a good would look like if demand were perfectly inelastic at every price. The demand curve is vertical: No matter what the price, quantity demanded is the same.

Although perfectly inelastic demand is interesting from a theoretical point of view, it is difficult to find examples of goods with zero elasticity of demand in the real world. With zero demand elasticity, the good would have to be one that consumers want only in a fixed quantity. One example might be insulin—the drug needed by

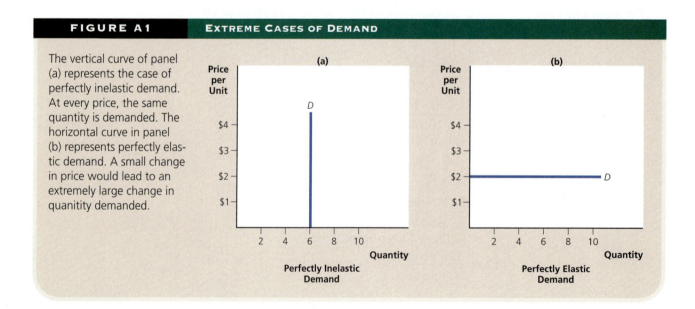

FIGURE A1	**EXTREME CASES OF DEMAND**

The vertical curve of panel (a) represents the case of perfectly inelastic demand. At every price, the same quantity is demanded. The horizontal curve in panel (b) represents perfectly elastic demand. A small change in price would lead to an extremely large change in quanitity demanded.

diabetics to control their blood sugar. Insulin has no use other than in the management of diabetes. For diabetics, quantity requirements for insulin are quite rigid, and there are no substitutes for its use. A drop in price will not encourage diabetics to use more, nor will a modest rise in price cause diabetics to economize on its use.

When $E_D > 1.0$, we say that demand is *elastic*. In this case, the elasticity will be greater than unity:

$$\left| \frac{\%\Delta Q^D}{\%\Delta P} \right| > 1$$

Or, rearranging, we get

$$\left| \%\Delta Q^D \right| > \left| \%\Delta P \right|$$

When demand is elastic, the percentage change in quantity demanded is *larger* than the percentage change in price. For instance, if price rises by 4 percent, quantity demanded will fall by *more* than 4 percent. Elastic demand means that quantity demanded is *sensitive* to price.

An extreme case of price sensitivity occurs when demand is *perfectly* or *infinitely elastic*. Even the tiniest change in price causes a huge change in quantity demanded, so huge that, for all intents and purposes, we can call the response infinite. When demand is perfectly elastic, then no matter how much people are buying, the demand curve will be a horizontal line—as shown in panel (b) of Figure A1. The demand for a single brand of salt may fall into this category. If the price of Brand X salt rose a little, while other brands next to it on the supermarket shelf continued to cost the same, virtually everyone would switch to the other brands, causing the quantity of Brand X salt demanded to plummet.

Finally, when elasticity of demand is exactly equal to 1, we have *unitary elasticity*. In this case, we would have $\left| \%\Delta Q^D \right| = \left| \%\Delta P \right|$, and demand for the good is exactly at the boundary between elastic and inelastic. Many consumer products seem to have price elasticities near 1.0. In addition, a price elasticity of 1.0 is important as a benchmark case, as you will see in the next section.

ELASTICITY AND TOTAL EXPENDITURE

When the price of a good increases, the law of demand tells us that people will demand less of it. But this does not necessarily mean that they will *spend* less on it. After the price rises, fewer units will be purchased, but each unit will cost more. It turns out that whether total spending on a good rises or falls depends on the price elasticity of demand for the good.

To see this more formally, note that the total expenditure (*TE*) on a good is defined as

$$TE = P \times Q$$

where P is the price per unit and Q is the quantity purchased. We can use a rule about percentage changes, explained in the Mathematical Appendix: *When two numbers are both changing, the percentage change in their product is the sum of their individual percentage changes.* Applying this to total expenditure, we can write

$$\%\Delta TE = \%\Delta P + \%\Delta Q$$

TABLE A2	EFFECTS OF PRICE CHANGES ON EXPENDITURE		
Where demand is:		**A price increase will:**	**A price decrease will:**
inelastic	$(\%\Delta Q^D < \%\Delta P)$	increase expenditure	decrease expenditure
unitary elastic	$(\%\Delta Q^D = \%\Delta P)$	cause no change in expenditure	cause no change in expenditure
elastic	$(\%\Delta Q^D > \%\Delta P)$	decrease expenditure	increase expenditure

Now let's assume that P rises by, say, 10 percent. What will happen to total expenditure? If demand is *unitary elastic,* then Q will fall by 10 percent, so we will have

$$\%\Delta TE = 10 \text{ percent} + (-10 \text{ percent}) = 0$$

The percentage change in total expenditure is zero, meaning that total expenditure does not change at all! If demand is *inelastic,* a 10 percent rise in price will cause quantity demanded to fall by *less* than 10 percent, so we have

$$\%\Delta TE = 10 \text{ percent} + (\text{something less negative than} -10 \text{ percent}) > 0$$

The percentage change in total expenditure is greater than zero, so total expenditure rises. Finally, if demand is *elastic,* so that Q falls by more than 10 percent, TE will fall:

$$\%\Delta TE = 10 \text{ percent} + (\text{something more negative than} -10 \text{ percent}) < 0$$

Of course, the results we just obtained for a price increase of 10 percent would hold for any price increase. Our conclusions about elasticity and total expenditure are presented in Table A2. They can be summarized as follows:

> *Where demand is price inelastic, total expenditure moves in the same direction as price. Where demand is elastic, total spending moves in the opposite direction to price. Finally, where demand is unitary elastic, total expenditure remains the same as price changes.*

Let's check the statements in Table A2, using our hypothetical data for peanuts and macadamia nuts. Repeating the information from our earlier example, and adding a column for total expenditure, we have:

Macadamia Nuts

Price per pound (P)	Quantity Demanded (pounds per year) (Q)	Total Yearly Expenditure (P × Q)
$8.00	15,000	$120,000
$9.00	5,000	$ 45,000

Peanuts

Price per pound (P)	Quantity Demanded (pounds per year) (Q)	Total Yearly Expenditure (P × Q)
$1.50	500,000	$ 750,000
$2.50	490,000	$1,225,000

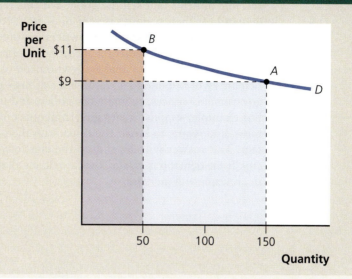

FIGURE A2   **ELASTICITY AND TOTAL EXPENDITURE**

Any point along a demand curve defines a rectangle whose area indicates total expenditure on the good at that point. At point *A*, where price is $9 per unit and 150 units are demanded, expenditure is $1,350. At point *B*, expenditure is $550. Moving from *A* to *B*, expenditure decreases, so demand must be elastic over that range.

Notice what happens to total expenditure in each case. Demand for macadamia nuts, you recall, was price elastic ($E_D = 8.5$) when price rose from $8 to $9. According to the rules in Table A2, we would expect a price rise to reduce total expenditure, and that is exactly what happens: The $1.00 rise in price causes total expenditure to decrease from $120,000 to $45,000. Peanuts, on the other hand, were price inelastic ($E_D = 0.04$) when price rose from $1.50 to $2.50, and our rules tell us that a rise in price should increase total expenditure. Indeed, the $1.00 price hike causes total expenditure on peanuts to rise from $750,000 to $1,225,000.

There is an easy way to see how a change in price changes the total expenditure of buyers, using a graph of the demand curve. At point *A* in Figure A2, price is $9 per unit and quantity demanded is 150 units. Total revenue is price × quantity = $9 × 150 = $1,350. But this is exactly equal to the *area* of the blue shaded rectangle, which has a width of 150 and a height of $9. Thus, the area of this rectangle shows total expenditure on the good when price is $9. More generally,

> *At any point on a demand curve, buyers' total expenditure is the area of a rectangle with width equal to quantity demanded and height equal to price.*

Now suppose that price rises from $9 to $11, so we move along the demand curve to point *B*, where quantity demanded drops to 50 units. Here, total expenditure is $11 × 50 = $550, given by the area of the red rectangle, with width equal to 50 and height equal to $11. You can see that the area of the wider, blue rectangle is greater than the area of the narrower, red rectangle. This tells us that total expenditure is greater at a price of $9 than it is at $11. In other words, the rise in price from $9 to $11 causes total expenditure to decrease.

As you've learned, a price increase causes total expenditure on a good to decrease only when demand for the good is *elastic*. So our diagram tells us that, for the good depicted in the figure, demand is elastic for a price change from $9 to $11 or from $11 to $9.

Knowing the price elasticity of demand for a good and understanding the link between elasticity and total expenditure is helpful in many different contexts. For example, the total amount that consumers spend on a good is also the *total sales revenue* of firms that sell the good. For this reason, knowing the price elasticity of demand for their product is very important to firms. Producers of goods and services—doctors, bakers, theater owners, manufacturers, and others—use price elasticity of demand to predict the impact of a price change on their total sales revenue. And government policy makers—who need to anticipate how private market participants will respond to government actions—use demand elasticities to price many government services, to make tax policy, and to design programs to help the needy. For example, suppose a city government is considering an increase in mass transit fares, and wants to know the impact on the total revenue of the mass transit system. The answer will depend on the elasticity of demand for mass transit in that city. If the demand is *elastic,* the fare hike will *decrease* revenue; if demand is *inelastic,* revenue will *increase.*

CHAPTER

4

CONSUMER CHOICE

You are constantly making economic decisions. Some of them are rather trivial: Should you buy those delicious-looking vine-ripened tomatoes or the cheaper variety? Should you meet your friend for dinner at that fancy Italian restaurant or at Burger King? Should you buy a cup of coffee at Starbucks or make it more cheaply at home?

Other economic decisions can have a profound impact on the way you live. Should you buy a car because it is more convenient or rely on your bicycle or public transportation because it is cheaper? Should you live with roommates to pay lower rent or live on your own and pay more? Should you go to work after college or invest in an expensive professional degree so that you can get a higher paying job in the future?

The economic nature of all these decisions is rather obvious, since they all involve *spending*. In other cases, the economic nature of your decisions may be less obvious. Did you get up early today in order to do things you needed to do, or did you sleep in? Which leisure activities—movies, concerts, sports, hobbies—do you engage in, and how often do you decline an opportunity to have fun for lack of time? At this very moment, what have you decided *not* to do in order to make time to read this chapter? All of these are economic choices, too, because they require you to allocate your scarce *time* among different alternatives.

How can we hope to analyze economic decisions when they all seem so different from each other? Our starting point is basic principle #1, maximization subject to constraints, which you first encountered in Chapter 1.

> *The economic approach to understanding a problem is to identify the decision makers and then determine what they are maximizing and the constraints that they face.*

MAXIMIZATION SUBJECT TO CONSTRAINTS

When we apply this principle to individual decision making, we immediately face two questions: What are individuals trying to maximize? And what are their constraints?

In economics, we assume that most people try to maximize their overall level of *satisfaction*. This may mean just momentary pleasure, but it can also mean self-improvement, a secure future, the right balance between work and play, or anything else that people value. As we attempt to satisfy these desires, we come up against constraints: too little income or wealth to buy everything we might enjoy and too little time to enjoy it all.

In this chapter, you will learn the economic model of individual choice. In most of the chapter, we will focus on choices about *spending:* how people decide what to buy. This is why the theory of individual decision making is often called "consumer theory." Later, in the "Using the Theory" section, we'll see how the theory can be broadened to include decisions about allocating scarce *time* among different activities.

THE BUDGET CONSTRAINT

The principle of *maximization subject to constraints* calls for us to look for the constraints decision makers face as they try to pursue their objectives. For *consumers*, the constraints arise from two simple facts of economic life: (1) Consumers have to pay prices for the goods and services they buy, and (2) they have limited funds to spend. These two facts are summarized by the consumer's *budget constraint:*

> *A consumer's **budget constraint** identifies which combinations of goods and services the consumer can afford with a limited budget, at given prices.*

BUDGET CONSTRAINT The different combinations of goods a consumer can afford with a limited budget, at given prices.

Consider Max, a devoted fan of both movies and concerts, who has a total budget of $150 to spend on both each month. For each movie, Max must pay a direct money cost of $10 (the ticket price plus the cost of transportation), and for each concert, a direct money cost of $30. If Max were to spend all of his $150 budget on concerts at $30 each, he could see at most five each month. If he were to spend it all on movies at $10 each, he could see 15 of them.

But Max could also choose to spend part of his budget on concerts and part on movies. In this case, for each number of concerts, there is some *maximum* number of movies that he could see. For example, if he goes to 1 concert per month, it will cost him $30 of his $150 budget, leaving $120 available for movies. Thus, if Max were to choose 1 concert, the maximum number of films he could choose would be 12.

Figure 1 lists, for each number of concerts, the maximum number of movies that Max could see. Each combination of goods in the table is affordable for Max, since each will cost him exactly $150. Combination *A*, at one extreme, represents 0 concerts and 15 movies. Combination *F*, the other extreme, represents 5 concerts and no movies. In each of the combinations between *A* and *F*, Max attends both concerts and movies.

The graph in Figure 1 plots the number of movies along the vertical axis and the number of concerts along the horizontal. Each of the points *A* through *F* corresponds to one of the combinations in the table. If we connect all of these points with a straight line, we have a graphical representation of Max's budget constraint, which we call Max's **budget line.**

BUDGET LINE The graphical representation of a budget constraint.

Reality

Note that any point below or to the left of the budget line is affordable. For example, 2 concerts and 6 movies—indicated by point *G*—would cost only

FIGURE 1   THE BUDGET CONSTRAINT

The budget line shows all combinations of concerts and movies Max could obtain by spending $150 each month. At point *A*, he could attend 15 movies, but no concerts. At *F*, he could attend 5 concerts, but no movies. At points *B–E*, he attends both movies *and* concerts. The slope of the line ($-P_{concert}/P_{movie} = -3$) shows that the opportunity cost of another concert is 3 movies.

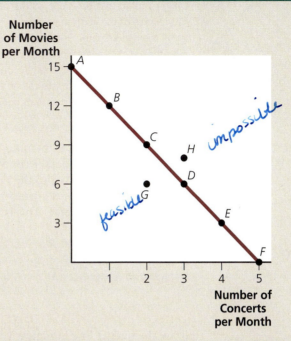

Max's Consumption Possibilities with Income of $150

	Concerts at $30 each:		Movies at $10 each:	
	Quantity	Total Expenditure on Concerts	Quantity	Total Expenditure on Movies
A	0	$ 0	15	$150
B	1	$ 30	12	$120
C	2	$ 60	9	$ 90
D	3	$ 90	6	$ 60
E	4	$120	3	$ 30
F	5	$150	0	$ 0

$60 + $60 = $120. Max could certainly afford this combination. On the other hand, he *cannot* afford any combination above or to the right of this line. Point *H*, representing 3 concerts and 8 movies, would cost $90 + $80 = $170, which is beyond Max's budget. The budget line therefore serves as a border between those combinations that are affordable and those that are not.

Let's look at Max's budget line more closely. The *vertical intercept* is 15, the number of movies Max could see if he attended 0 concerts. Starting at the vertical intercept (point *A*), notice that each time Max increases 1 unit along the horizontal axis (attends 1 more concert), he must decrease 3 units along the vertical (see 3 fewer movies). Thus, the slope of the budget line is equal to –3. The slope tells us Max's *opportunity cost* of 1 more concert. That is, the opportunity cost of 1 more concert is 3 movies forgone.

There is an important relationship between the *prices* of two goods and the opportunity cost of having more of one or the other. The prices Max faces tell us how many dollars he must give up to get another unit of each good. If, however, we

DANGEROUS CURVES

It's tempting to think that the slope of the budget line should be $-P_y/P_x$, where the price of the vertical-axis good, P_y, is in the numerator, rather than in the denominator. But this is wrong. The budget line's slope is the change in *quantity* along the vertical axis divided by the change in *quantity* along the horizontal. As our example shows, when the slope is expressed in terms of *prices* rather than quantities, the formula is $-P_x/P_y$, with the price of the *horizontal*-axis good in the numerator.

RELATIVE PRICE The price of one good relative to the price of another.

🔑 **OPPORTUNITY COST**

divide one money price by another money price, we get what is called a **relative price**—the price of one good *relative* to the other. Since $P_{concert} = \$30$ and $P_{movie} = \$10$, the *relative price of a concert* is the ratio $P_{concert}/P_{movie} = \$30/\$10 = 3$. Notice that "3" is the opportunity cost of another concert in terms of movies, and—except for the absence of a minus sign—it is also the slope of the budget line. That is, *the relative price of a concert, the opportunity cost of another concert, and the slope of the budget line* have the same absolute value. This is one example of a general relationship:

> *The slope of the budget line indicates the trade-off between one good and another. If P_y is the price of the good on the vertical axis and P_x is the price of the good on the horizontal axis, then the slope of the budget line is $-P_x/P_y$.*

CHANGES IN THE BUDGET LINE

To draw the budget line in Figure 1, we have assumed given prices for movies and concerts and a given income that Max can spend on them. These "givens"—the prices of the goods and the consumer's income—are always *held constant* as we move along a budget line; if any one of them changes, the budget line will change as well. Let's see how.

CHANGES IN INCOME. If Max's available income increases from $150 to $300 per month, then he can afford to see more movies, more concerts, or more of both, as shown by the change in his budget line in Figure 2(a). If Max were to devote *all* of his income to movies, he could now see 30 of them each month, instead of the 15 he was able to see before. Devoting his entire income to concerts would enable him to attend 10, rather than 5. Moreover, for any number of concerts, he will be able to see more movies than before. For example, before, when his budget was only $150, choosing 2 concerts would allow Max to see only 9 movies. Now, with a budget of $300, he can have 2 concerts and *24* movies.

Notice that the old and new budget lines in Figure 2(a) are parallel—they have the same slope of –3. This is because we changed Max's income but *not* prices. Since $P_{concert}/P_{movie}$ has not changed, the trade-off between movies and concerts remains the same. Thus,

> *An increase in income will shift the budget line upward (and rightward). A decrease in income will shift the budget line downward (and leftward). These shifts are parallel—changes in income do not affect the budget line's slope.*

CHANGES IN PRICE. Now let's go back to Max's original budget of $150 and explore what happens to the budget line when a price changes. Suppose the price of a movie falls from $10 to $5. The graph in Figure 2(b) shows Max's old and new budget lines. When the price of a movie falls, the budget line rotates outward—the vertical intercept moves higher. The reasoning is this: When movies cost

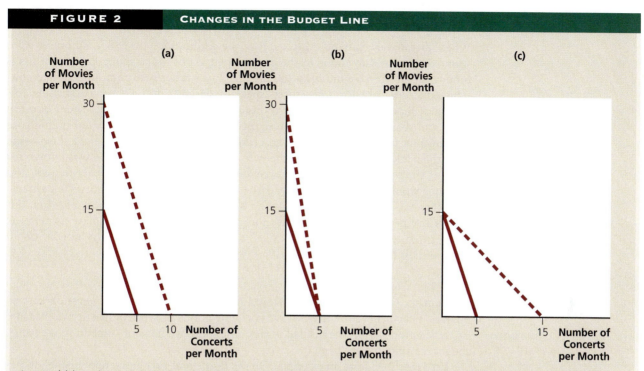

FIGURE 2   CHANGES IN THE BUDGET LINE

In panel (a), an increase in income leads to a rightward, parallel shift of the budget line. In panel (b), a decrease in the price of a movie causes the budget line to rotate upward; the horizontal intercept is unaffected. In panel (c), a decrease in the price of a concert leads to a rightward rotation of the budget line.

$10, Max could spend his entire $150 on them and see 15; now that they cost $5, he can see a maximum of 30. The horizontal intercept—representing how many concerts Max could see with his entire income—doesn't change at all, since there has been no change in the price of concerts. Notice that the new budget line is also *steeper* than the original one, with slope equal to $-P_{concert}/P_{movie} = -\$30/\$5 = -6$. Now, with movies costing $5, the trade-off between movies and concerts is 6 to 1, instead of 3 to 1.

Panel (c) of Figure 2 illustrates another price change—this time, a fall in the price of *concerts* from $30 to $10. Once again, the budget line rotates, but this time, it is the horizontal (concerts) intercept that changes and the vertical (movies) intercept that remains fixed.

We could draw similar diagrams illustrating a *rise* in the price of movies or concerts, but you should try to do this on your own. In each case, one of the budget line's intercepts will change, as well as its slope:

> *When the price of a good changes, the budget line rotates: Both its slope and one of its intercepts will change.*

The budget constraint, as illustrated by the budget line, is one side of the story of consumer choice. It indicates the trade-off consumers *are able* to make between one good and another. But just as important is the trade-off that consumers *want* to make between one good and another, and this depends on consumers' *preferences*, the subject of the next section.

CONSUMER PREFERENCES

When dictator Ferdinand Marcos fled the Philippines in 1985, Filipinos were stunned by what they found in the private quarters of Malacañang Palace, the long-time home of Marcos and his wife, Imelda. Just off her bedroom, Imelda had constructed a series of enormous closets specially designed to hold her astonishing collection of shoes. Among her many thousands of pairs could be found shoes of every color and shape imaginable—from dainty slippers the faintest blush of orchid rose to four-inch spiked heels in blazing crimson. Obviously, Imelda liked shoes—she liked them a lot. What's more, as the wife of a longtime dictator who was known for treating the national treasury as his own, Imelda had only to snap her fingers, and someone would deliver whatever pair she fancied, in whatever quantity she desired.

Why, you might ask, would anyone want so many shoes? A good question, but here is another one: If Imelda liked shoes so much, and if she could have as many as she wanted, why did she have "only" a few thousand pairs? Why not 20 or 30 thousand? Why not more?

EARLY INSIGHTS

Economists a hundred years ago would have found the preceding question easy to answer. They believed that when we consume goods or services, we derive pleasure or satisfaction—what they called **utility.** The more we have of something we value, the more utility we get from it.

UTILITY Pleasure or satisfaction obtained from consuming goods and services.

Let's take Imelda as an example. On the horizontal axis in the upper panel of Figure 3, we'll measure the number of pairs of shoes she owns. On the vertical axis, we'll measure the utility Imelda derives from having them. If Imelda values shoes, her utility will increase as she acquires more of them, as it does in the figure. There we see that when she has 1,000 pairs, Imelda enjoys total utility of 30 "utils," but when she has 2,000 pairs, her total utility grows to 50 utils, and so on. Throughout the figure, the total utility Imelda derives from consuming shoes keeps rising as she owns more and more pairs.

But notice something interesting—and important: Although Imelda's utility increases every time she acquires more shoes, the *additional* utility she derives from each *successive* 1,000 pairs gets smaller and smaller as she gets more pairs. We call the *change in utility derived from consuming an additional unit* of a good the *marginal utility* of that additional unit of consumption:

MARGINAL UTILITY The change in total utility an individual obtains from consuming an additional unit of a good or service.

> **Marginal utility** is the change in utility an individual enjoys from consuming an additional unit of a good.

In our example, a "unit" of shoes is 1,000 pairs, so Imelda's marginal utility is her change in total utility from consuming an additional 1,000 pairs of shoes. What we've observed about Imelda's utility can be restated this way: As she gets more and more shoes, her *marginal utility* from shoes declines. In the nineteenth and early twentieth centuries, economists thought this pattern was typical of virtually *all* consumers consuming virtually any good or service, and they gave it a name: the **law of diminishing marginal utility.** The great economist Alfred Marshall (1842–1924) put it this way:

LAW OF DIMINISHING MARGINAL UTILITY As consumption of a good or service increases, marginal utility decreases.

> The marginal utility of a thing to anyone diminishes with every increase in the amount of it he already has.[1]

---

1. *Principles of Economics,* vol. 3, (Macmillan & Co., 1930), ch. 3 appendix, notes 1 and 2.

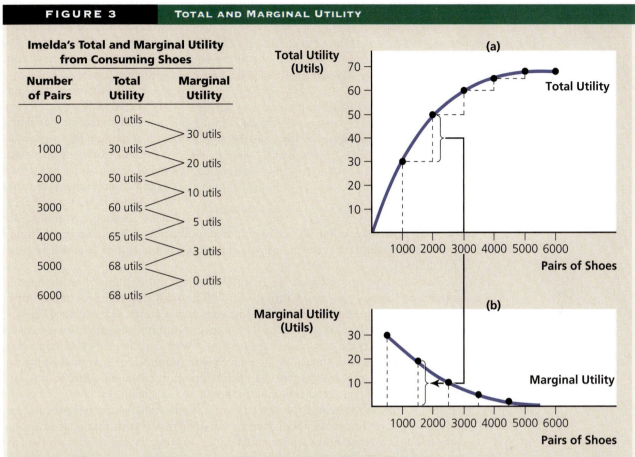

FIGURE 3	TOTAL AND MARGINAL UTILITY

Imelda's Total and Marginal Utility from Consuming Shoes

Number of Pairs	Total Utility	Marginal Utility
0	0 utils	
		30 utils
1000	30 utils	
		20 utils
2000	50 utils	
		10 utils
3000	60 utils	
		5 utils
4000	65 utils	
		3 utils
5000	68 utils	
		0 utils
6000	68 utils	

Panel (a) shows the total utility to Imelda Marcos from her shoe collection. As the collection increases, so does her total utility. Panel (b) shows the corresponding marginal utility. *MU* falls as the collection grows, indicating that each additional thousand pairs provide less *additional* utility than the previous thousand did.

According to the law of diminishing marginal utility, when you consume your first unit of some good, like a pair of shoes, you derive some amount of utility. When you get your second pair, you enjoy greater satisfaction than when you only had one pair, but the *extra* satisfaction you derive from the second pair is likely to be smaller than the satisfaction you derived from the first. Adding the third pair of shoes to your collection will no doubt increase your utility further, but again the *marginal utility* you derive from that third pair is likely to be less than the marginal utility you derived from the second. Figure 3 will again help us see what's going on. On the right is a table summarizing the information in the total utility graph. The first two columns show, respectively, the quantity of shoes Imelda consumes and the total utility she receives from consuming that many shoes. The third column is new. It shows the marginal utility she receives from each successive 1,000 pairs she consumes. As you can see glancing down the third column, Imelda's total utility keeps increasing (marginal utility is always positive) until she consumes 5,000 pairs, but the rate at which total utility increases gets smaller and smaller (her marginal utility diminishes) as her consumption increases.

The marginal utility numbers from the table are plotted in the lower left panel of the figure. Because marginal utility is the increment in utility caused by a *change*

DANGEROUS CURVES

The word "marginal" is one you will encounter again and again in your study of economics. Literally, a margin is an "edge," or something *beyond*. In economics, marginal means "additional" or "incremental" and is used to describe what happens when a decision maker considers a small *change* from his current situation.

It is easy to confuse a *total* measure of something with its associated *marginal* measure, because they are both measured in the same units. But they are not the same thing. The marginal always tells us the *change in the total* caused by *one more* of something. For example, both total utility and marginal utility are measured in utils. But marginal utility tells us the *change* in *total utility* when a consumer gets one more unit of a good.

in consumption from one level to another, we plot each marginal utility entry *between* the old and new consumption levels.

Notice the close relationship between the graph of total utility in the top panel and the corresponding graph of marginal utility in the lower panel. Look closely at the two graphs, and you will see that for every 1,000-unit increment in Imelda's shoes, her marginal utility is equal to the *change* in her total utility. The downward-sloping curve in the lower panel gives us a vivid illustration of the law of diminishing marginal utility.

One last thing about Figure 3: Because marginal utility diminishes for Imelda, by the time she has consumed a total of 5,000 pairs of shoes, the marginal utility she derives from an additional 1,000 pairs has fallen all the way to zero. That is, she is fully *satiated* and gets no extra satisfaction or utility from additional pairs of shoes. This gives us the answer to the question, "Why does Imelda's collection contain *only* 5,000 pairs of shoes?" It is because, with diminishing marginal utility, by the time she consumes 5,000 pairs, additional pairs provide no additional utility whatsoever. There is no reason to add further to her collection.

Today, economists believe that we can understand consumer preferences and analyze consumer choices without assuming that there are such things as utility or marginal utility. Nonetheless, the insights of the early approach, along with the language of utility and marginal utility analysis, are still very much alive and widely used. In the sections that follow, we'll continue to use these concepts to analyze consumer preferences. Then, in the appendix to this chapter, you'll learn an alternative theory of consumer choice that does not rely on the concept of utility at all.

RATIONALITY

In order to predict *how* people make choices, we need to believe that they *can* make choices. In economics, we assume that any decision maker is able to look at two alternatives and *compare* them. That is, you can state either that you prefer one to the other or that you are entirely indifferent between the two—you value them equally. In addition, it is assumed that these comparisons a consumer makes are *logically consistent,* or *transitive*. If, for example, you prefer a sports car to a jeep, and a jeep to a motorcycle, then we assume that you will also prefer a sports car to a motorcycle. When a consumer can make comparisons, and when all her comparisons are logically consistent in this manner, we say that she has **rational preferences**.

RATIONAL PREFERENCES
Preferences that satisfy two conditions: (1) Any two alternatives can be compared and either one is preferred, or the two are valued equally; and (2) the comparisons are logically consistent.

Notice that rationality is a matter of how you make your choices, and *not what choices you make*. You can be rational and like apples better than oranges, or oranges better than apples. You can even be rational if you like anchovies or brussels sprouts! What matters is that you make choices consistently, and most of us usually do. Imagine for a moment what it might be like if you didn't. How would you figure out what to order in a restaurant if you prefer the chef's salad to the Reuben sandwich and the Reuben to the hamburger, but prefer the hamburger to the chef's salad! Clearly, choosing consistently is an important part of just being able to choose.

TASTES

While economists assume that consumers are rational, they are reluctant to be too specific when it comes to describing a person's tastes. The reason is obvious: People are different. They like different things. American teens delight in having a Coke with dinner, while the very idea makes a French person shudder. What would satisfy a Buddhist monk would hardly satisfy the typical American. And even among "typical Americans," there is little consensus about tastes. Some read Jane Austen, while others pick John Grisham. Some like to spend their vacations traveling to distant lands, whereas others would prefer to stay home and sleep in every day. And while some Americans would define happiness as a nice house in a safe, peaceful suburb, others prefer the excitement, variety, and social diversity found in big cities. In the face of such wide differences in consumer tastes, economists look for common denominators—things that seem to be true for a wide variety of people.

One of those things is this: We generally feel that *more is better*. Specifically, if we get more of some good or service, and nothing else is taken away from us, we will generally feel better off. Since marginal utility measures the change in utility from getting one more unit of a good, we can also state the "more is better" assumption this way: *Marginal utility is positive.*

This condition seems to be satisfied for the vast majority of goods we all consume. Of course, there are exceptions. If you hate eggplant, then the more of it you have, the worse off you are. In this case, the marginal utility of eggplant would be negative, violating the assumption. Similarly, a dieter who says, "Don't bring any ice cream into the house—I don't want to be tempted," also violates the assumption. The model of consumer choice in this chapter is designed for preferences that satisfy the "more is better" condition, and it would have to be modified to take account of exceptions like these.

In addition to presuming that "more is better," we'll make one other assumption about peoples' tastes: that the more of a good someone consumes, the less *additional* satisfaction that person will get from consuming still more of it. Here, we are assuming that *marginal utility diminishes as more of a good is consumed*. This is what we assumed for Imelda and her shoes, and it seems plausible that it would hold for most things that we value. Once again, there may be exceptions. If a fan takes special pride in owning every CD ever recorded by Garth Brooks, then each time she acquires another one, she comes closer to her goal, and her marginal utility might *rise* with each additional CD acquired. But—as with "more is better"—these exceptions would be rare.

CONSUMER DECISION MAKING

So far in this chapter, you've learned quite a bit about the consumer's budget constraint. But our characterization of consumer preferences has been rather minimal. We have made only three assumptions: that consumers are rational, that the marginal utility of a good is positive, and that marginal utility declines as more of the good is consumed. With so little to go on, what can we hope to say about the *choices* a consumer will actually make? Surprisingly, we can say quite a bit. Our first conclusion about consumer choice is very basic:

the consumer will always choose a point on the budget line, rather than a point below it.

U.S. Consumer Gateway
A "one-stop" link to federal information useful to consumers. *ScamAlert!* offers current information on deceptive practices in the marketplace. *In the Spotlight* has useful information on consumer-awareness campaigns.
http://www.consumer.gov/

MAXIMIZATION SUBJECT TO CONSTRAINTS

FIGURE 4   CONSUMER DECISION MAKING

The budget line shows the maximum number of movies Max could attend for each number of concerts he attends. He would never choose an interior point like *G* because there are affordable points—on the line—that make him better off. Max will choose a point *on* the budget line. More specifically, he will choose the point at which the marginal utility per dollar spent on movies and concerts are equal. From the table below, this occurs at point *D*.

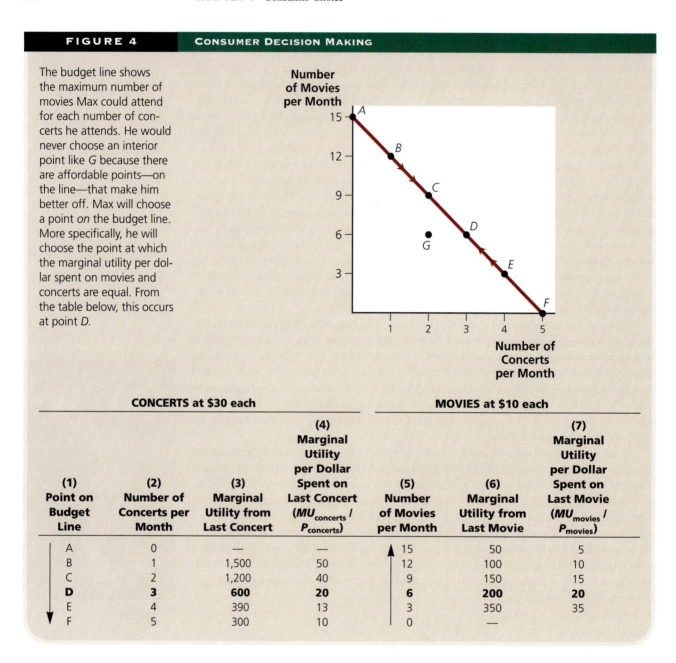

	CONCERTS at $30 each			MOVIES at $10 each		
(1) Point on Budget Line	**(2)** Number of Concerts per Month	**(3)** Marginal Utility from Last Concert	**(4)** Marginal Utility per Dollar Spent on Last Concert ($MU_{concerts}$ / $P_{concerts}$)	**(5)** Number of Movies per Month	**(6)** Marginal Utility from Last Movie	**(7)** Marginal Utility per Dollar Spent on Last Movie (MU_{movies} / P_{movies})
A	0	—	—	15	50	5
B	1	1,500	50	12	100	10
C	2	1,200	40	9	150	15
D	**3**	**600**	**20**	**6**	**200**	**20**
E	4	390	13	3	350	35
F	5	300	10	0	—	

To see why this is so, look at Figure 4. There you'll see Max's budget line, reproduced from Figure 1, where the price of concerts is $30, the price of movies is $10, and his monthly budget is $150. Max would never choose point *G,* representing 2 concerts and 6 movies, since there are affordable points—on the budget line—that we know make him better off. For example, point *C* has the same number of concerts (2), but more movies (9). "More is better" tells us that Max will prefer *C* to *G,* so we know *G* won't be chosen. For the same reason, Max must prefer point *D,* with 3 concerts and 6 movies, to point *G.* Indeed, if we look at any point below the budget line, we can always find at least one point *on* the budget line that is preferred, as long as more is better.

Knowing what Max will not do—knowing he *will not* choose a point inside his budget line—is helpful. It tells us that we can narrow our search for the point he *will* choose to just the ones along the budget line *AF.* But how can Max find the one point along the budget line that gives him a higher utility than all the others?

To answer this question, we'll introduce one of the basic principles of economics: *marginal decision making:*

> ⚷ *Basic Principle #6: Marginal Decision Making*
> *To understand and predict the behavior of individual decision makers, we focus on the incremental or marginal effects of their actions.*

Marginal decision making can be compared to the children's game in which one child is blindfolded and must find a hidden object. As she changes position, the others tell her only "warmer" or "colder" to indicate whether she is moving closer or farther away from the object. Eventually she will find it—without anyone ever telling her where the object is hidden. In consumer theory, we can think of "maximum utility" as the hidden object the consumer is looking for, and we imagine her deciding whether some change in her collection of goods makes her better or worse off—"warmer" or "colder." If she continually makes changes that make her better off, until no such changes are left, then she will discover the combination that makes her as well off as possible.

Marginal decision making is a central concept in economics in general and consumer theory in particular. Before we put it to use, however, a small warning: Taken literally, consumer theory will seem hopelessly unrealistic. "Surely," you may think, "people don't actually *use* concepts like budget lines or marginal utility when they make decisions." And you would be absolutely correct. After all, you've been making economic decisions all your life without even knowing about these concepts.

But keep in mind that consumer theory, like many theories in economics, is an "as-if" theory. Economists do not claim that the model of consumer choice describes the psychological mechanics consumers actually use when they make decisions. Rather, they claim that consumers generally choose their goods and services *as if* they follow the model. This is why our highly structured way of looking at decision making—while not a realistic description of *how* people make choices—has proven so useful in explaining the nature of those choices.

With this perspective in mind, let's apply marginal decision making to Max and his choice between movies and concerts. To do this, we need hypothetical information about Max's preferences, which is provided in the table below Max's budget constraint, in Figure 4.

Each row of the table corresponds to a different point on Max's budget line. For example, the row labeled *"C"* corresponds to point *C* on the budget line. The second entry in each row tells us the number of concerts that Max attends each month, and the third entry tells us the marginal utility he gets from consuming *the last* concert. For example, at point *C*, Max attends two concerts, and the second one gives him an additional 1,200 utils beyond the first. Notice that as we move *down* along the budget line, from point *A* to *B* to *C* and so on, the number of concerts increases, and the marginal utility numbers in the table get smaller, consistent with the law of diminishing marginal utility.

The fourth entry in each row shows something new: the *marginal utility per dollar* spent on concerts, obtained by dividing the marginal utility of the last concert by the price of a concert ($MU_{concerts}/P_{concerts}$). This tells us the gain in utility Max gets for each dollar he spends on the last concert. For example, at point *C*, Max gains

1,200 utils from his second concert during the month, so his marginal utility per dollar spent on that concert is 1,200 utils / \$30 = 40 utils per dollar. Marginal utility per dollar, like marginal utility itself, declines as more concerts are consumed.

The last three entries in each row give us similar information for movies: the number of movies attended, the marginal utility derived from the last movie, and the marginal utility per dollar spent on the last movie (MU_{movies}/P_{movies}). As we travel *up* this column, Max attends more movies, and both marginal utility and marginal utility per dollar decline—once again, consistent with the law of diminishing marginal utility.

To understand how Max can find the best point on his budget line—the one that gives him the highest utility—suppose that he is initially at point *B*: 1 concert and 12 movies. Is he maximizing his utility? Let's see. Comparing the fourth and seventh entries in row *B* of the table, we see that Max's marginal utility per dollar spent on concerts is 50 utils, while his marginal utility per dollar spent on movies is only 10 utils. Since he is gaining more additional utility from each dollar spent on concerts than from each dollar spent on movies, he should shift some of his dollars from movies to concerts. That is, he should travel farther down his budget line.

Now suppose that, after shifting his spending from movies to concerts, Max arrives at point *C* on his budget line. What should he do then? At point *C*, Max's *MU* per dollar spent on concerts is 40 utils, while his *MU* per dollar spent on movies is 15 utils. Once again, he would gain utility by shifting from movies to concerts, traveling down his budget line once again.

Now suppose that Max arrives at point *D*. At this point, the *MU* per dollar spent on both movies and concerts is the same: 20 utils. There is no further gain from shifting spending from movies to concerts. At point *D*, Max has exploited all opportunities to make himself better off by moving down the budget line. He has maximized his utility.

But wait . . . what if Max had started at a point on his budget line *below* point *D*, with too many movies and too few concerts? Would he still end up at the same place? Yes, he would. Suppose Max finds himself at point *E*, with 4 concerts and 3 movies. Here, marginal utilities per dollar are 13 utils for concerts and 35 utils for movies. Now, Max could make himself better off by shifting spending away from concerts and toward movies. He will travel *up* the budget line, once again arriving at point *D*, where no further move will improve his well-being.

As you can see, whether Max begins at a point on his budget line above point *D* or below it, marginal decision making will always bring him back to point *D*. What is so special about point *D*? It is the only point on the budget line where *marginal utility per dollar* is the same for both goods. When this condition holds, there is nothing to gain by shifting spending in either direction.

What is true for Max and his choice between movies and concerts is true for *any* consumer and *any* two goods. We can generalize our result this way: For any two goods *x* and *y*, with prices P_x and P_y, whenever $MU_x/P_x > MU_y/P_y$, a consumer is made better off shifting spending away from *y* and toward *x*. When $MU_y/P_y > MU_x/P_x$, a consumer is made better off by shifting spending away from *x* and toward *y*. This leads us to an important conclusion:

MAXIMIZATION SUBJECT TO CONSTRAINTS

MARGINAL DECISION MAKING

> *A utility-maximizing consumer will choose the point on the budget line where marginal utility per dollar is the same for both goods ($MU_x/P_x = MU_y/P_y$). At that point, there is no further gain from reallocating expenditures in either direction.*

We can generalize even further. Suppose there are more than two goods an individual can buy. For example, we could imagine that Max wants to divide his entertainment budget among movies, concerts, plays, football games, and what have you. Or we can think of a consumer who must allocate her entire income among thousands of different goods and services each month: different types of food, clothing, entertainment, transportation, and so on. Does our description of the optimal choice for the consumer still hold? Indeed, it does. No matter how many goods there are to choose from, when the consumer is doing as well as possible, it must be true that $MU_x/P_x = MU_y/P_y$ for any pair of goods x and y. For if this condition is *not* satisfied, the consumer will be better off consuming more of one and less of the other good in the pair.[2]

In finding the utility-maximizing combination of goods for a consumer, why do we use marginal utility *per dollar* instead of just marginal utility? Shouldn't the consumer always shift spending wherever *marginal utility* is greater? The answer is no. The following thought experiment will help you see why. Imagine that you like to ski and you like going out for dinner. Further, given your current combination of skiing and dining out, your marginal utility for one more skiing trip is 2,000 utils, and your marginal utility for an additional dinner is 1,000 utils. Should you shift your spending from dining out to skiing? It might seem so, since skiing has the higher marginal utility.

But what if skiing costs $200 per trip, while a dinner out costs only $20? Then, while it's true that another skiing trip will give you twice as much utility as another dinner out, it's also true that *skiing costs ten times as much*. You would have to sacrifice *10* restaurant meals for 1 skiing trip, and that would make you *worse* off. Instead, you should shift your spending in the other direction: from skiing to dining out. Money spent on additional skiing trips will give you 1,000 utils/$200 = 5 utils per dollar, while money spent on additional dinners will give you 1,000 utils/$20 = 50 utils per dollar. Dining out clearly gives you "more bang for the buck" than skiing. The lesson of this example is: When trying to find the utility-maximizing combination of goods, compare marginal utilities *per dollar*, not marginal utilities alone.

DANGEROUS CURVES

WHAT HAPPENS WHEN THINGS CHANGE?

If every one of our decisions had to be made only once, life would be much easier. But that's not how life is. Just when you think you've figured out what to do, things change. In a market economy, as you've learned, prices can change for any number of reasons. (See Chapter 3.) Consumers' incomes can change as well. They may lose a job or find a new one; they may get a raise or a cut in pay. Changes in our incomes or the prices we face cause us to rethink our spending decisions: What maximized utility before the change is unlikely to maximize it afterward. The result is a change in our behavior.

CHANGES IN INCOME

Figure 5 illustrates how an increase in income might affect Max's choice between movies and concerts. As before, we assume that movies cost $10 each, that concerts cost $30 each, and that these prices will remain constant. Initially, Max has $150 in income to spend on the two goods, so his budget line is the solid line from point A to point F. As we've already seen, under these conditions, Max would choose point D (3 concerts and 6 movies) to maximize utility.

---

2. There is one exception to this statement: Sometimes the optimal choice is to buy *none* of some good. For example, if $MU_y/P_y > MU_x/P_x$ no matter how small a quantity of good x a person consumes, it will always pay to reduce consumption of good x further, until its quantity is zero. Economists call this a "corner solution," because—when there are only two goods being considered—the individual will locate at one of the endpoints of the budget line, in a corner of the diagram.

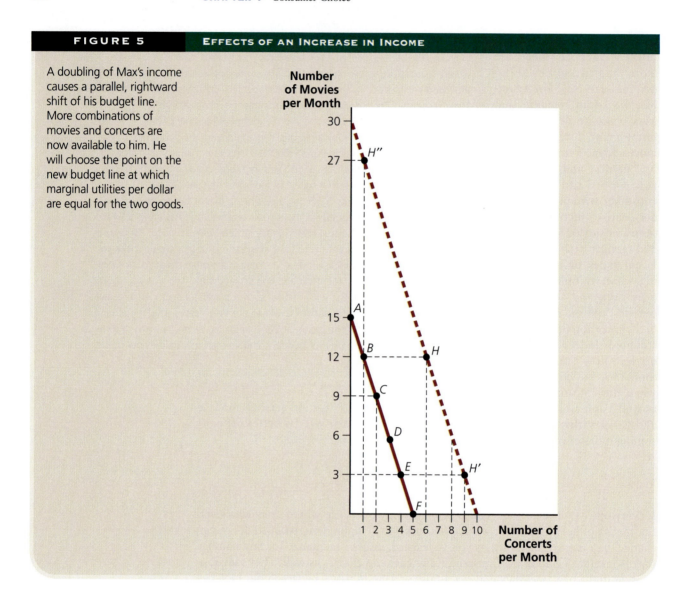

FIGURE 5   **EFFECTS OF AN INCREASE IN INCOME**

A doubling of Max's income causes a parallel, rightward shift of his budget line. More combinations of movies and concerts are now available to him. He will choose the point on the new budget line at which marginal utilities per dollar are equal for the two goods.

Number of Movies per Month

Number of Concerts per Month

If Max's income increases to $300, his budget line will shift upward and outward in the figure. How will he respond? As always, he will search along his budget line until he finds the point where the marginal utility per dollar spent on both goods is the same. Without more information—such as that provided in the table in Figure 4—we can't be certain which point will satisfy this condition. But we can discuss some of the possibilities.

Figure 5 illustrates three alternative possibilities. If Max's best combination ends up being point *H*, he would attend 12 movies and 6 concerts. If we compare his initial choice (point *D*) with this new choice (point *H*), we see that the rise in income has caused him to consume more of *both* goods. As you learned in Chapter 3, when an increase in income causes a consumer to buy *more* of something, we call that thing a *normal good*. If, for Max, point *H* happens to be where the marginal utilities per dollar for the two goods are equal, then, for him, both movies and concerts are normal goods.

Alternatively, Max's marginal utilities per dollar might be equal at a point like H', with 9 concerts and 3 movies. In this case, the increase in income would cause Max's consumption of concerts to increase (from 3 to 9), but his consumption of movies to *fall* (from 6 to 3). Movies would be an *inferior good* for Max—one for which demand decreases when income increases—while concerts would be a *normal* good.

It's tempting to think that *inferior* goods are of lower quality than *normal* goods. But economists don't define normal or inferior based on the intrinsic properties of a good, but rather by the choices people make when their incomes increase. For example, Max may think that both movies and concerts are high-quality goods. When his income is low, he may see movies on most weekends because, being cheaper, they enable him to have some entertainment every weekend. But when his income increases, he can afford to switch from movies to concerts on some of his weekends. If Max makes this choice—and attends fewer movies—then his *behavior* tells us that movies are inferior for him. If instead he chose to see more movies and fewer concerts when his income increased, then concerts would be the inferior good.

DANGEROUS CURVES

Finally, let's consider another possible outcome for Max: point H''. At this point, he attends more movies and fewer concerts compared to point D. If point H'' is where Max's marginal utilities per dollar are equal after the increase in income, then *concerts* would be the inferior good, while movies would be normal.

CHANGES IN PRICE

In Chapter 3, you were introduced to the *law of demand,* which holds that a rise in the price of a good reduces the quantity demanded, and a fall in price increases quantity demanded. In this section, we use the tools of consumer theory to analyze what is *behind* the law of demand, to see *why* consumers behave as they do when a price changes. In the process, you will learn why exceptions to the law of demand are so rare.

Let's explore what happens to Max when the price of a concert decreases from $30 to $10 while his income remains at $150 and the price of a movie remains $10. The drop in the price of concerts will rotate Max's budget line rightward, pivoting around its vertical intercept, as illustrated in the upper panel of Figure 6. What will Max do after his budget line rotates in this way? Again, he will select the combination of movies and concerts on his budget line that makes him as well off as possible. This will be the combination at which the marginal utility per dollar spent on both goods is the same. In the figure, we assume that this occurs at point J on the new budget line, where Max consumes 4 concerts and 11 movies.

If the price of concerts drops once again, to $5, the budget line rotates rightward again. In the figure, Max will now choose point K, attending 6 concerts and 12 movies.

THE INDIVIDUAL'S DEMAND CURVE. You've just seen that each time the price of concerts changes, so does the quantity of concerts Max will want to see. The lower panel of Figure 6 highlights this relationship by plotting the quantity of concerts demanded on the horizontal axis and the price of concerts on the vertical axis. For example, in both the upper and lower panels, point D tells us that when the price of concerts is $30, Max will see 3 of them. When we connect points like D, J, and K in the lower panel, we get Max's **individual demand curve,** which shows *the quantity of a good demanded by an individual at each different price.* Notice that Max's demand curve for concerts slopes downward—a fall in the price of concerts increases the quantity demanded—showing that Max's responses to price changes obey the law of demand.

INDIVIDUAL DEMAND CURVE A curve showing the quantity of a good or service demanded by a particular individual at each different price.

FIGURE 6   **DERIVING THE DEMAND CURVE**

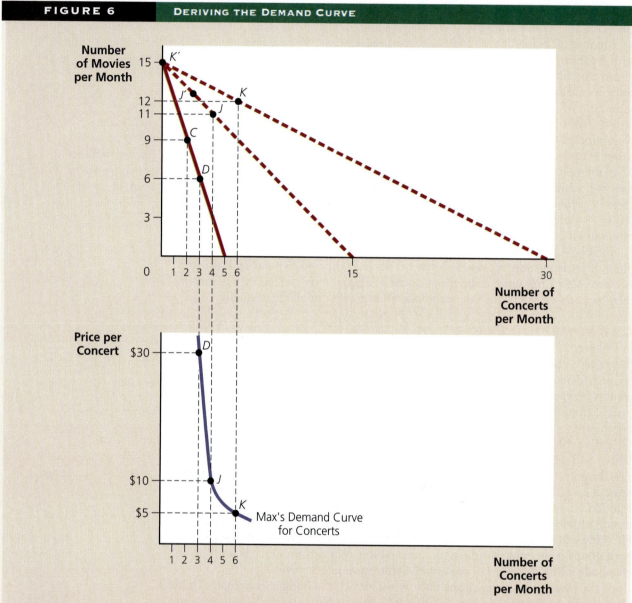

In the upper panel, a decrease in the price of concerts causes Max's budget lines to rotate outward. At $30 per concert, he maximizes utility at point *D* in both panels and attends 3 concerts. If the price falls to $10 per concert, he increases his consumption to 4 concerts per month, at point *J*. At a price of $5 each, he attends 6 concerts, shown at point *K*. Max's demand curve (lower panel) is obtained by connecting points such as *D, J,* and *K*.

But if Max's preferences had been different, could his response to a price change have violated the law of demand? In particular, could he have chosen points such as *J'* and *K'* instead of *J* and *K* in the upper panel of Figure 6? If he did, a fall in the price of concerts would have led him to want *fewer* of them, and his demand curve (which you are invited to draw for yourself) would have sloped *up-ward*. Is that possible?

The answer is yes . . . and no. Yes, it is theoretically possible; but no, it does not seem to happen in practice. To understand why, we must look deeper into the effects of a price change on quantity demanded. In doing so, we'll gain more insight into the process of consumer decision making.

THE SUBSTITUTION EFFECT. When a good's price changes, we can identify two separate effects on quantity demanded. As you will see, these two effects sometimes work together and sometimes work in opposite directions.

Suppose the price of a good falls. Then it becomes less expensive *relative to* other goods whose prices have not fallen. Some of these other goods are *substitutes* for the now cheaper good—they are different goods, but they are used to satisfy the same general desire. (For example, Coke and Pepsi are very close substitutes for each other, since they both satisfy the same desire for a carbonated cola drink with a little caffeine.) When one of the ways of satisfying a desire becomes relatively cheaper, consumers will purchase more of it, and purchase less of the substitute good.

In Max's case, concerts and movies, while different, both satisfy the desire to be entertained. When the price of a concert falls, so does its relative price (relative to movies). Max can now get more entertainment from his budget by substituting concerts for movies, so he will demand more concerts.

This impact of a price decrease is called a **substitution effect**—the consumer substitutes *toward* the good whose price has decreased and away from other goods whose prices have remained unchanged.

> *The* substitution effect *of a price change arises from a change in the relative price of a good, and it always moves quantity demanded in the* opposite direction *to the price change. When price decreases, the substitution effect works to increase quantity demanded; when price increases, the substitution effect works to decrease quantity demanded.*

The substitution effect is a powerful force in the marketplace. For example, while the price of personal computers has fallen in recent years, the prices of typewriters and other writing tools have remained more or less the same. This fall in the relative price of computers has caused consumers to substitute toward them and away from typewriters, which, in turn, has caused several typewriter manufacturers to leave the market. Similarly, over the past 20 years, the price of Broadway plays has increased much more rapidly than the price of movies. As a result, the *relative price* of plays has increased, and consumers have *substituted* movies for plays, a major cause of financial distress on Broadway.

The substitution effect is also important from a theoretical perspective: It is the main factor responsible for the law of demand. Indeed, if the substitution effect were the *only* effect of a price change, the law of demand would be more than a law; it would be a logical necessity. But as we are about to see, a price change has another effect as well.

THE INCOME EFFECT. In Figure 6, when the price of concerts decreases from $30 to $10, Max's budget line rotates rightward. Max now has a wider range of

---

SUBSTITUTION EFFECT
As the price of a good decreases, the consumer substitutes that good in place of other goods whose prices have not changed.

driven by diminishing marginal utility

options than before: He can consume more concerts, more movies, or *more of both*. The price decline of *one* good has increased Max's total purchasing power over *both* goods.

A price cut gives the consumer a gift, which is rather like an increase in *income*. Indeed, in a sense, it *is* an increase in *available* income: Point *D* (3 concerts and 6 movies) originally cost Max $150, but after the decrease in the price of concerts, the same combination would cost him just (6 × $10) + (3 × $10) = $90, leaving him with $60 in *available income* to spend on more movies or concerts or both. This leads to the second effect of a change in price:

INCOME EFFECT As the price of a good decreases, the consumer's purchasing power increases, causing a change in quantity demanded for the good.

> The **income effect** of a price change is the impact on quantity demanded that arises from a change in purchasing power over both goods. A drop in price increases purchasing power, while a rise in price decreases purchasing power.

How will a change in purchasing power influence the quantity of a good demanded? That depends. Recall that an increase in income will increase the demand for normal goods and decrease the demand for inferior goods. The same is true for the *income effect* of a price cut: It can work to either *increase* or *decrease* the quantity of a good demanded, depending on whether the good is normal or inferior. For example, if concerts are a normal good for Max, then the income effect of a price cut will lead him to consume more of them; if concerts are inferior, the income effect will lead him to consume fewer.

COMBINING SUBSTITUTION AND INCOME EFFECTS. Now let's look again at the impact of a price change, considering the substitution and income effects together. A change in the price of a good changes both the relative price of the good (the substitution effect) and the overall purchasing power of the consumer (the income effect). The ultimate impact of the price change on quantity demanded will depend on *both* of these effects. In most cases, these two effects work together to push quantity demanded in the same direction, but they can occasionally oppose each other. To help clarify this, we'll consider the total impact of a price change on different types of goods.

Normal Goods. Normal goods are the easiest category to consider. When the price of a normal good falls, the substitution effect *increases* quantity demanded. The price drop will also increase the consumer's purchasing power, and—for a normal good—*increase* quantity demanded even further. The opposite occurs when price increases: The substitution effect decreases quantity demanded, and the decline in purchasing power further decreases it. Figure 7 summarizes how the substitution and income effects combine to make the price and quantity of a normal good move in opposite directions:

> For normal goods, the substitution and income effects work together, causing quantity demanded to move in the opposite direction of the price. Normal goods, therefore, must always obey the law of demand.

Inferior Goods. Now let's see how a price change affects the demand for *inferior* goods. As an example, consider the cassette tape. Many people own stereo equipment that can play both cassettes and compact discs. For some of these people, cassettes will be an inferior good: A rise in income would decrease demand for them,

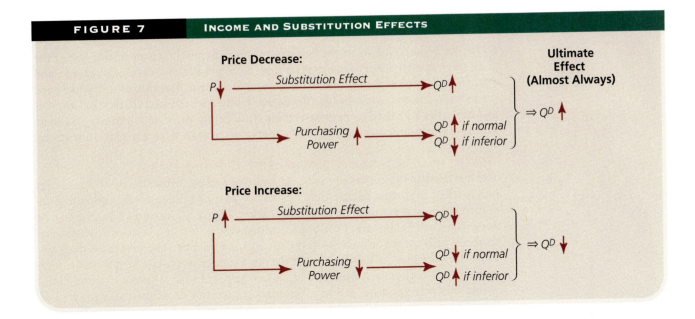

FIGURE 7   INCOME AND SUBSTITUTION EFFECTS

since it would make compact discs—a preferable alternative—more affordable. If the price of cassettes falls, the substitution effect would work, as always, to *increase* quantity demanded. The price cut will also, as always, increase the consumer's purchasing power. But if cassette tapes are inferior, the rise in purchasing power will *decrease* quantity demanded. Thus, we have two opposing effects: the substitution effect, increasing quantity demanded, and the income effect, decreasing quantity demanded. In theory, either of these effects could dominate the other, so the quantity demanded could move in either direction. In practice, however, the substitution effect almost always dominates for inferior goods.

Why does the substitution effect almost always dominate? Because we consume such a wide variety of goods and services that a price cut in any one of them changes our purchasing power by only a small amount. For example, suppose you have an income of $20,000 per year, and you spend $500 per year on cassette tapes. If the price of cassettes falls by, say, 20 percent, this would save you $100—like a gift of $100 in income. But $100 is only ½ percent of your income. Thus, a 20 percent fall in the price of cassette tapes would cause only a ½ percent rise in your purchasing power. Even if cassette tapes are, for you, an inferior good, we would expect only a tiny decrease in your quantity demanded when your purchasing power changes by such a small amount. Thus, the income effect should be very small. On the other hand, the *substitution* effect should be rather large: With cassette tapes now 20 percent cheaper, you will likely substitute away from other purchases (such as compact discs) and buy many more tapes.

For inferior goods, the substitution and income effects of a price change work against each other. The substitution effect moves quantity demanded in the opposite direction of the price, while the income effect moves it in the same direction as the price. But since the substitution effect virtually always dominates, consumption of inferior goods—like normal goods—will virtually always obey the law of demand.

CONSUMERS IN MARKETS

So far, we've looked only at the behavior of an individual consumer. But one of the goals of consumer theory is to explain how large *groups* of individuals react to and are affected by changes in their economic environment. For this purpose, we need the *market demand curve*. In Chapter 3, you learned what a market demand curve is and how it can be used to help determine equilibrium price and quantity in a market. In this section, we revisit the market demand curve to learn where it comes from.

FROM INDIVIDUAL TO MARKET DEMAND

The market demand curve tells us the quantity of a good demanded by all consumers in a market, so it makes sense that we can derive it by adding up the individual demand curves of every consumer in that market. Figure 8 illustrates how this can be done in a small local market for bottled water, where, for simplicity, we assume that there are only three consumers—Jerry, George, and Elaine. The first three diagrams show the individual demand curves. If the market price were, say, $2 per bottle, Jerry would buy 4 bottles each week (point *c*), George would buy 6 (point *c'*), and Elaine would buy zero (point *c''*). Thus, the market quantity demanded at a price of $2 would be 4 + 6 + 0 = 10, which is point *C* on the market demand curve. To obtain the entire market demand curve, we repeat this procedure at each different price, adding up the quantities demanded by each individual to obtain the total quantity demanded in the market. (Verify on your own that points *A, B, D,* and *E* have been obtained in the same way.) In effect, we obtain the market demand curve by summing horizontally across each of the individual demand curves:

> *The market demand curve is found by horizontally summing the individual demand curves of every consumer in the market.*

Notice that as long as each individual's demand curve is downward sloping (and this will virtually always be the case), then the market demand curve will also be downward sloping. More directly, if a rise in price makes each consumer buy fewer units, then it will reduce the quantity bought by *all* consumers as well. Indeed, the market demand curve can still obey the law of demand even when *some* individuals violate it. Thus, although we are already quite confident about the law of demand at the individual level, we can be even more confident at the market level. This is why we always draw market demand curves with a downward slope.

CHALLENGES TO CONSUMER THEORY

In some circumstances, our model of consumer choice will not work well, at least not without some modification. One problem is *uncertainty*. In our model, the consumer knows with certainty the outcome of any choice—so many movies and concerts—and knows with certainty how much income is available for spending. But in many real-world situations, you make your choice and you take your chances. When you buy a car, it might be a lemon; when you pay for some types of surgery, there is a substantial risk that it will be unsuccessful; and when you buy a house, you cannot be sure of its condition or how much you will like the neighborhood. Income, too, is often uncertain. Employees risk being laid off, and even self-employed lawyers, doctors, and small-business owners cannot be sure of their in-

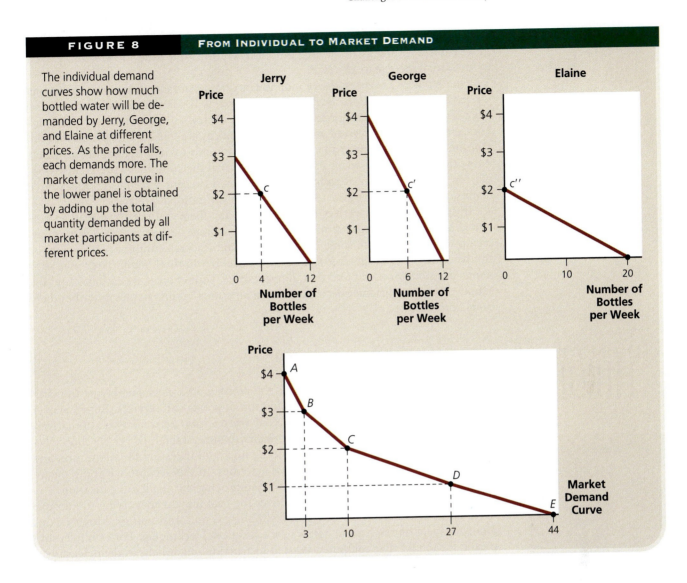

FIGURE 8   FROM INDIVIDUAL TO MARKET DEMAND

The individual demand curves show how much bottled water will be demanded by Jerry, George, and Elaine at different prices. As the price falls, each demands more. The market demand curve in the lower panel is obtained by adding up the total quantity demanded by all market participants at different prices.

comes. When uncertainty is an important aspect of consumer choice, economists use other, more complex models. But even these models are based heavily on the one you have learned in this chapter.

Another problem is *imperfect information.* In our model, consumers are assumed to know exactly what goods they are buying and the prices at which they can buy them. But in the real world, we must sometimes spend time and money to get this information. Prices can be different in different stores and even on different days, depending on whether there is a sale, so we might have to make phone calls or shop around. To be sure of the quality of our purchases, we may have to subscribe to *Consumer Reports* magazine or spend time inspecting goods or getting advice from others. Over the past few decades, economists have been intensely interested in imperfect information and its consequences for decision-making behavior.

A third problem is that people can spend more than their incomes in any given year by borrowing funds or spending out of savings; or they may spend less than their incomes, because they choose to save or pay back debts. Economic models have been built to deal with all of these complications. In these models, consumers make choices for this year and for future years at the same time and are constrained by their total income in *all* years.

Finally, there are cases where individuals do not, in fact, choose rationally—as we have defined the term. For example, people will sometimes *judge quality by price*. Diamonds, designer dresses, men's suits, doctor's services, and even automobiles are sometimes perceived as better if their prices are higher. This means that the consumer cannot compare any two bundles of goods by themselves; he must first know their prices. And when prices change, so will the consumer's preferences—violating our description of rational preferences. In recent years, economists have teamed up with psychologists to study violations of rational preferences.

In sum, there are a variety of cases where the theory of the consumer, as presented in this chapter, would not work well. Economists have developed more complex models to deal with some of these cases, and research continues on the others. But we should not exaggerate their importance. If you think about your own economic decisions, you will find that, in most cases, your choices *are* rational, and the simple theory of consumer decision making presented in this chapter describes them quite accurately.

IMPROVING EDUCATION[3]

So far in this chapter, we've considered the problem of a consumer trying to maximize utility by selecting the best combination of goods and services. But consumer theory can be extended to consider almost *any* decision between two alternatives. Economists use the model of consumer theory to understand how people choose between work and leisure, between spending now and investing for the future, and even between honest work and criminal activities. In this section, we apply the insights of consumer theory to another issue: improving the quality of education.

Billions of dollars have been spent over the past few decades trying to improve the quality of education in our schools, colleges, and universities. Much of this money is spent on research to assess new educational techniques. For example, suppose it is thought that computer-assisted instruction might help students learn better or more quickly. A typical research project to test this hypothesis would be a *controlled experiment* in which one group of students would be taught with the computer-assisted instruction and the other group would be taught without it. Then students in both groups would be tested. If the first group scores significantly higher, computer-assisted instruction will be deemed successful; if not, it will be deemed unsuccessful. To the disappointment of education researchers, most promising new techniques are found to be unsuccessful: Students seem to score about the same, no matter which techniques are tried.

Economists find these studies highly suspect, since the experimenters treat students as passive responders to stimuli. Presented with a stimulus (the new technique), students are assumed to give a simple response (scoring higher on the exam). Where in this model, economists ask, are students treated as *decision makers* like the rest of us? In particular, where is the recognition that students must make *choices* about allocating their scarce time?

---

3.   This section is based on ideas originally published in Richard B. McKenzie and Gordon Tullock, *New World of Economics,* 3d ed. (Burr Ridge, Ill.: Irwin, 1981).

FIGURE 9	TIME ALLOCATION

Panel (a) shows combinations of French and economics test scores that can be obtained for a given amount of study time. The slope of –2 indicates that each additional point in French requires a sacrifice of two points in economics. The student chooses point C. Panel (b) shows that computer-assisted French instruction causes the budget line to rotate outward; French points are now less expensive. The student might move to point D, attaining a higher French score. Or she might choose F, using all of the time freed up in French to study economics. Or she might choose an intermediate point such as E.

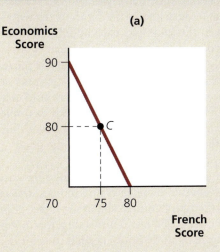

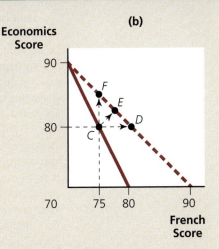

Let's apply our model of consumer choice to a student's time allocation problem. To keep things simple, we'll assume a bleak world in which there are only two activities: studying economics and studying French. Instead of costing money, each of these activities costs *time*, and there is only so much time available. And instead of buying quantities of two goods, students "buy" points on their exams with hours of studying.

Panel (a) of Figure 9 shows how we can represent the time allocation problem graphically. The economics test score is measured on the vertical axis and the French score on the horizontal axis. The straight line in the figure is the student's budget line, showing the tradeoff between economics and French scores. Our student can achieve any combination of scores on this budget line with her scarce time.

A few things are worth noting about the budget line in the figure. First, the more study time you devote to a subject, the better you will do on the test. But that means *less* study time for the other subject and a lower test score there. Thus, the opportunity cost of scoring better in French is scoring lower in economics, and vice versa. This is why the budget line has a negative slope: The higher the score in French, the lower will be the score in economics. As our student moves downward along the budget line, she is shifting hours away from studying economics and toward studying French.

Second, notice that the vertical and horizontal axes both start at "70," rather than "0." This is to keep our example from becoming too depressing. If our student devotes *all* her study time to economics and none to French, she would score 90 in economics, but still be able to score 70 (rather than 0) in French, just by attending class and paying attention. If she devotes all her time to French, she would score 80 in French and 70 in economics. (Warning: Do not try to use this example to convince your economics instructor you deserve at least a 70 on your next exam.)

Finally, the budget line in the figure is drawn as a straight line with a slope of −2. Therefore, in this example, each additional point in French requires our student to sacrifice two points in economics, regardless of where she is on her budget line. This assumption just helps make the analysis more concrete; none of our conclusions would be different if we assumed a different slope for the budget line, or even a curved budget line, where the tradeoff would change as we moved along it. But let's take a moment to understand what our example implies.

As you've learned, the slope of any budget line is $-P_x/P_y$, where x is the good measured on the horizontal axis and y is the good measured on the vertical axis. In our example, $-P_x/P_y$ translates into $-P_{French\ point}/P_{econ\ point}$. But what is the "price" of a test point in French or economics? Unlike the case of Max, who had to allocate his scarce *funds* between concerts and movies, our student must allocate her scarce *time* between the two "goods" she desires: test points in French and test points in economics. The *price* of a test point is therefore not a money price, but rather a *time price*: the number of study hours needed to achieve an additional point. For example, if it takes an additional two hours of studying to achieve another point in French, then the price per point in French is two hours. In our example, we assume that the price remains constant no matter how many hours are spent studying a subject. That is, it takes an additional two hours of study time to increase the French score from 70 to 71, from 71 to 72, and so on. Moreover, in the figure, we assume that the price per point in economics is one-half the price per point in French. The slope of the budget line is therefore $-P_{French\ point}/P_{econ\ point} = -2$.

Now let's turn our attention to student decision making. Our student derives utility from both her economics score and her French score—the greater either score, the greater is her utility. But among all those combinations of scores on her budget line, which will give her the highest total utility? We can answer this question using the same technique we used for Max and his decision between concerts and movies, but with one important difference: Instead of looking for the combination of two goods such that marginal utilities *per dollar* are equal, we look for the combination of test points in the two subjects such that marginal utilities *per hour* are equal. After all, it is hours that must be spent on additional test points, not dollars. In general:

> *In allocating time between two activities that provide utility, an individual will select the combination of activities such that the marginal utility per hour of one activity is equal to the marginal utility per hour of the other activity.*

MAXIMIZATION SUBJECT TO CONSTRAINTS

MARGINAL DECISION MAKING

Suppose this condition is satisfied for our student at point C, where she scores 80 in economics and 75 in French. This is where the marginal utility per hour in French is equal to the marginal utility per hour in economics.

Now, let's introduce a new computer-assisted technique in the French class, one that is, in fact, remarkably effective: It enables students to learn more French with the same study time or to study less and learn the same amount. This is a *decrease* in the price of French points—it now takes fewer hours to earn a point in French—so the budget line will rotate outward, as shown in panel (b) of Figure 9. On the new budget line, if our student devotes all of her time to French, she can score higher than before—90 instead of 80—so the horizontal intercept moves rightward. But since nothing has changed in her economics course, the vertical intercept remains unaffected. Notice, too, that the budget line's slope has changed, to –1; now, the opportunity cost of an additional point in French is one point in economics, rather than two.

After the new technique is introduced in the French course, our *decision-making* student will locate at a point on her new budget line the point where marginal utilities per hour are equal in the two courses. Where that point is, of course, will depend on her preferences, and panel (b) illustrates some alternative possibilities. At point *D,* her performance in French would improve, but her economics performance would remain the same. This seems to be the kind of result education researchers have in mind when they design their experiments: If a successful technique is introduced in the French course, we should be able to measure the impact with a French test.

Point *F* illustrates a different choice: *Only* the economics performance improves, while the French score remains unchanged. Here, even though the technique in French is successful (it does, indeed, shift the budget line), none of its success shows up in higher French scores.

But wait: How can a new technique in the French course improve performance in economics, but not at all in French? The answer is found by breaking down the impact of the new technique into our familiar income and substitution effects. You can see that the new technique lowers the time cost of getting additional points in French. The substitution effect (French points are relatively cheaper) will tend to improve her score in French as she substitutes her time away from studying economics and toward studying French. But there is also an *"income"* effect: The "purchasing power" of her time has increased, since now she could use her fixed allotment of study time to "buy" higher scores in *both* courses. If performance in French is a "normal good," this increase in "purchasing power" will work to increase her French score; but if it is an "inferior good," it could work to *decrease* her French score. Point *F* could come about because French performance is *such* an inferior good, that the negative income effect exactly cancels out the positive substitution effect. In this case, the education researchers will incorrectly judge the new technique a complete failure—it does not affect French scores at all.

Could this actually happen? Perhaps. It is easy to imagine a student deciding that 75 in French is good enough and using any time savings from better French instruction to improve her performance in some other course. More commonly, we expect a student to choose a point such as *E,* somewhere between points *D* and *F,* with performance improving in *both* courses. But even in this case, the higher French score measures just a *part* of the impact of the technique; the remaining effect is seen in a higher economics score.

This leads us to a general conclusion: When we recognize that students make *choices,* we expect only some of the impact of a better technique to show up in the course in which it is used. In the real world, college students typically take several courses at once and have other competing interests for their time as well (cultural events, parties, movies, telephone calls, exercising, and so on). Any time saved due to better teaching in a single course might well be "spent" on *all* of these alternatives, with only a little devoted to performing better in that single course. Thus, we cannot fully measure the impact of a new technique by looking at the score in one course alone. This suggests why educational research is conducted as it is: A more accurate assessment would require a thorough accounting for all of a student's time, which would be both expensive and difficult to achieve. Nevertheless, we remain justified in treating this research with some skepticism.

S U M M A R Y

Consumers face two simple facts of life: They have to pay for the goods and services they buy, and they have limited incomes to spend. These facts are summarized in the consumer's *budget constraint.* Given their preferences, consumers decide which goods to consume by choosing the combination along their budget constraint that yields the greatest *utility,* or satisfaction.

According to the *law of diminishing marginal utility,* the marginal, or additional, utility derived from a good declines as more of it is consumed. A utility-maximizing consumer will choose the combination of goods along his or her budget constraint at which the marginal utility per dollar spent is the same for all goods. This is an example of the *principle of marginal decision making.*

An increase in income shifts the budget constraint outward. The consumer responds by choosing more of all normal goods and less of inferior goods. A change in the price of a good causes the budget constraint to rotate. The consumer responds by purchasing more of a good whose price has fallen and less of a good whose price has risen. By tracing out a consumer's reaction to a series of prices, we can generate a downward-sloping *demand curve* for a good. The downward slope reflects the interaction of the *substitution effect* and the *income effect.* For a normal good, both effects contribute to the downward slope of the demand curve. For an inferior good, we can have confidence that the substitution effect dominates the income effect, so—once again—the demand curve will slope downward.

K E Y   T E R M S

budget constraint
budget line
relative price
utility

marginal utility
law of diminishing marginal utility
rational preferences
individual demand curve

substitution effect
income effect

R E V I E W   Q U E S T I O N S

1. What variables are held constant along a budget line?

2. What kinds of changes will shift or rotate the budget line?

3. Explain the relationship between a total quantity and a marginal quantity.

4. State and explain the law of diminishing marginal utility. Can you think of a good or service you consume that is not subject to this law? Could marginal utility be negative? Give an example.

5. Economists usually assume that consumer preferences are logically consistent. What does that mean? What are some other assumptions economists make about preferences?

6. Discuss the following statement: "Economists' assumption of consumer rationality is too strong. For example, anyone who smokes cigarettes is clearly being irrational."

7. What condition will be satisfied when a consumer has chosen the combination of goods that maximizes utility subject to a budget constraint?

8. What are income and substitution effects? How are they related to the law of demand?

9. "The demand curve for an inferior good is upward sloping." True or false? Explain.

10. How is a market demand curve derived?

P R O B L E M S   A N D   E X E R C I S E S

1. Parvez, a pharmacology student, has allocated $120 per month to spend on paperback novels and used CDs. Novels cost $8 each; CDs cost $6 each. Draw his budget line. What would happen to that budget line if the price of a CD increased to $10?

2. Parvez, our consumer from the previous question, is spending $120 monthly on paperback novels and used CDs. For novels, *MU/P* = 5; for CDs, *MU/P* = 4. Is he maximizing his utility? If not, should he consume (1) more novels and fewer CDs or (2) more CDs and fewer novels?

3. Anita consumes both pizza and Pepsi. The following tables show the amount of utility she obtains from different amounts of these two goods:

Pizza		Pepsi	
Quantity	**Utility**	**Quantity**	**Utility**
4 slices	115	5 cans	63
5 slices	135	6 cans	75
6 slices	154	7 cans	86
7 slices	171	8 cans	96

Suppose Pepsi costs $0.50 per can, pizza costs $1 per slice, and Anita has $9 to spend on food and drink. What combination of pizza and Pepsi will maximize her utility?

4. Oprah is trying to decide how to allocate a fifteen-minute segment between two guests on an upcoming show. Pauly Shore's antics start to wear thin fast; her marginal utility from his appearance is given by $MU = 500 - 20T$, where T is the number of minutes Pauly is on. (So, the first minute Pauly is on gives Oprah 480 utils; the second minute, 460; and so on.) Tony Randall, however, is always a solid guest. Oprah can count on him for a constant 200 utils every minute he is in front of the camera. Pauly demands $200 per minute for his appearance; Tony is happy with $100 a minute. To maximize her utility, how much time should Oprah give each guest?

5. Three people have the following individual demand schedules for Count Chocula cereal showing how many boxes each would purchase monthly at different prices:

Price	Person 1	Person 2	Person 3
$5.00	0	1	2
$4.50	0	2	3
$4.00	0	3	4
$3.50	1	3	5

a. What is the market demand schedule for this cereal? (Assume that these three people are the only buyers.) Draw the market demand curve.

b. Why might the three people have different demand schedules?

6. What would happen to the market demand curve for polyester suits—an inferior good—if consumers' incomes rose?

7. Larsen E. Pulp, head of Pulp Fiction Publishing Co., just got some bad news: the price of paper, the company's most important input, has increased.

a. On a supply/demand diagram, show what will happen to the price of Pulp's output (novels).

b. Explain the resulting substitution and income effects for a typical Pulp customer. For each effect, will the customer's quantity demanded increase or decrease? Be sure to state any assumptions you are making.

8. The Bureau of Labor Statistics (BLS), a division of the U.S. Department of Labor, regularly tracks consumer income and spending in its *Consumer Expenditure Survey*. To see a summary of the survey, go to http://stats.bls.gov/news.release/cesan.toc.htm and click on the link to Consumer Expenditures in the most recent year available. Read the brief report and study the data in the table.

a. Did the income of the average consumer rise or fall between the two most recent years reported?

b. What are the eight major categories into which consumer expenditures are divided in the table?

c. Which category of expenditure increased the most between the two most recent years reported? If all prices had remained unchanged over that year, how would you explain that change in expenditure? Considered as a group, are the goods in that category normal goods or inferior goods for the average consumer?

d. Did expenditure decrease in any category between the two most recent years reported? If so, are goods in that category normal or inferior goods for the average consumer?

CHALLENGE QUESTIONS

1. The Smiths are a low-income family, with $10,000 available annually to spend on food and shelter. Food costs $2 per unit, and shelter costs $1 per square foot per year. The Smiths are currently dividing the $10,000 equally between food and shelter.

a. Draw their budget constraint on a diagram with food on the vertical axis and shelter on the horizontal axis. Label their current consumption choice. How much do they spend on food? On shelter?

b. Suppose the price of shelter rises to $2 per square foot. Draw the new budget line. Can the Smiths continue to consume the same amounts of food and shelter as previously?

c. In response to the increased price of shelter, the government makes available a special income supplement. The Smiths receive a cash grant of $5,000 that must be spent on food and shelter. Draw their new budget line and compare it to the line you derived in part (a). *Could* the Smiths consume the same combination of food and shelter as in part (a).

d. With the cash grant and with shelter priced at $2 per square foot, *will* the family consume the same combination as in (a)? Why, or why not?

APPENDIX: CONSUMER THEORY WITH INDIFFERENCE CURVES

One of the drawbacks in the theory of consumer choice presented in the body of this chapter—based on marginal utility—is that you could never "see" any of the important information about the consumer's preferences. But there is another way to characterize preferences that is much more visual: using *indifference curves*. This appendix assumes that you have read the section on the budget constraint in the chapter. However, it does not assume any familiarity with marginal utility theory.

Consider Kate, whose sister is spending her junior year abroad in Moscow. Kate likes to talk to her sister on the phone, but, like every consumer, she faces a limited budget. To make our example more realistic, we'll recognize that Kate buys a number of different goods—not just two—and that her budget constraint requires that all of her purchases together must fall within her budget. How can we use a two-dimensional diagram to indicate purchases of more than two goods? By using an economist's trick: On one axis, we measure long-distance phone calls, and on the other we measure units of "all other goods" together. In Figure A1, the horizontal axis measures the minutes of phone time each week, and the vertical axis measures units of *all other goods combined.* Point *G,* for example, represents a combination where Kate speaks to her sister for 10 minutes each week and buys 50 units of all other goods.

What will we assume about Kate's preferences? We discussed two of our assumptions in the body of the chapter: that her choices are logically consistent (rational) and that more is better for every good. Now we introduce one more feature that seems common among people's tastes: With many types of goods and services, people tend to show at least some preference for variety over extremes in what they consume, other things being equal. To be more precise, suppose you were indifferent between having 10 new release videos and having 10 hit CDs. That is, you will find either of these two collections of goods equally satisfying. According to the preference for diversity in consumption, if offered a basket containing, instead, 5 of the videos along with 5 of the new CDs, you would prefer that alternative with variety to either of the two extreme options that concentrate your consumption on just one good. Of course, there are exceptions to this rule, too: Someone who collects both stamps and coins might prefer a complete collection of either one to a half-complete collection of each. Such instances seem special and rare, however, so economists generally assume at least some preference for diversity in a person's consumption.

Now let's begin characterizing Kate's preferences by picking a point at random, such as point *G* in the figure. Next, we ask Kate to tell us how much we can reduce her consumption of all other goods if we give her one more minute of conversation with her sister, so that she will be no better and no worse off after the change. Suppose she tells us, "I'd trade 20 units of all other goods for one more minute of conversation with my sister and feel no better and no worse off for the change." Then Kate must be indifferent between point *G* on the one hand and point *H* on the other, since point *H* gives her one more minute of phone time and 20 units less of all other goods than point *G.*

Next, we ask Kate to imagine herself at point *H,* and we ask her the same question. If she answers, "I'd trade off 15 units of other goods for another minute of conversation," then she must be indifferent between point *H* and point *J,* since *J* gives her one more minute of phone time and 15 units less in other goods than point

| **FIGURE A1** | **AN INDIFFERENCE CURVE** |

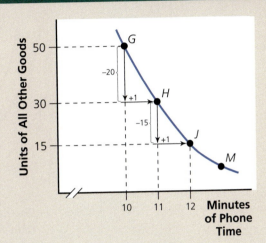

This curve shows all combinations of phone time and other goods that make Kate equally happy. At point G, when Kate is spending little time on the phone, the curve is relatively steep. She is willing to trade a lot of "all other goods" for one more minute of phone time. At M, the curve is flatter, indicating that she is willing to trade fewer "other goods" for an additional minute of phone time.

H. Now we know that Kate is indifferent between point *J* and point *H* and between point *H* and point *G*. So long as she is rational, she must be entirely indifferent among all three points—*G*, *H*, and *J*. (Remember, rational choice requires consistent choice.) By continuing in this way, we can trace out a set of points that—as far as Kate is concerned—are equally satisfying and so give her the same total utility from her consumption. When we connect these points with a line, we obtain one of Kate's indifference curves.

> An **indifference curve** represents all combinations of two categories of goods that make the consumer equally well off.

Notice two things about the indifference curve in Figure A1. First, it slopes downward. Second, it bows away from the origin, becoming flatter as we move southeasterly along it. Each of these results from the assumptions we've made about preferences. The indifference curve slopes down because every time we give Kate one more minute of phone time, we make her better off (more is better). In order to find another point on her original indifference curve, we must make her worse off by the same amount, *taking away* spending on other goods. Thus, each time we move rightward along an indifference curve, we must also move downward.

The slope of the indifference curve—the change along the vertical axis divided by the change along the horizontal axis as we move along it—tells us the rate at which Kate could trade all other goods for phone calls and still remain indifferent. But what about the *curvature* of her indifference curve? Why has it been drawn negatively sloped *and* bowed away from the origin? Interestingly, this kind of shape must result whenever preferences satisfy the "principle of diversity." At points such as *G*, high on her indifference curve, Kate consumes a lot of "all other goods" and relatively few phone calls compared to points lower down, such as *M*. When Kate has a preference for variety in her consumption, she will be quite willing to trade off a lot of her other goods for one more minute of phone calls, and this is reflected by the relatively steep slope of the indifference curve at *G*. Similarly, when Kate is spending a lot of time on the phone and consumes relatively little other goods, as is the case at point *M*, she will

FIGURE A2   AN INDIFFERENCE MAP

These three indifference curves are part of Kate's indifference map. She prefers higher curves to lower ones.

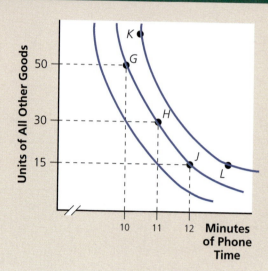

There are two common mistakes students make when drawing indifference curves. One is to allow the ends of the curve to "curl up," like the curve through point *B* in the following figure, so that the curve slopes upward at the ends. This violates our assumption of "more is better." To see why, notice that point *A* has more of both goods than point *B*, so as long as "more is better," *A* must be preferred to *B*. But then *A* and *B* are not indifferent, so they cannot lie on the same indifference curve. For the same reason, points *M* and *N* cannot lie on the same indifference curve. Remember that indifference curves cannot slope upward.

DANGEROUS CURVES

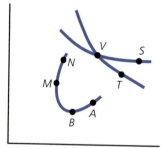

The second mistake is to allow two indifference curves to cross. For example, consider the two indifference curves passing through point *V*. *V* and *T* are on the same indifference curve, so the consumer must be indifferent between them; but *V* and *S* are also on the same indifference curve, so the consumer is indifferent between them, too. Since rationality requires the consumer's preferences to be consistent, the consumer must then also be indifferent between *T* and *S*, but this is impossible, because *S* has more of both goods than *T*, a violation of "more is better." Remember that indifference curves cannot cross.

be very reluctant to trade off any more of her now relatively scarce other goods for more time on the phone. This is reflected in the relatively flat slope of the indifference curve at *M*. Thus, we can expect that whenever preferences show some taste for variety in consumption, an indifference curve will become flatter as we move along it downward and rightward.

THE INDIFFERENCE MAP

To trace out the indifference curve in Figure A1, we began at a specific point—point *G*. In Figure A2 we've reproduced the indifference curve through *G*, *H*, and *J*. But now consider the new point *K*, which involves more phone time and more of other goods than point *G*. We know that point *K* is preferred to point *G* ("more is better"), so it is not on the indifference curve that goes through *G*. However, we can use the same procedure we used earlier to find a *new* indifference curve, connecting all points indifferent to point *K*. Indeed, we can repeat this procedure for any initial starting point we might choose, tracing out dozens, hundreds, or even thousands of Kate's indifference curves—as many as we'd like.

The result would be an *indifference map*—a set of indifference curves that describe Kate's preferences, like the three curves in Figure A2. Although we cannot say how much satisfaction Kate experiences on any particular indifference curve, we do know that she would always prefer any point on a higher indifference curve to any point on a lower one. For example, consider the points *G* and *L*. *L* involves more phone time, but less of other goods than *G*. How can we know if Kate prefers *L* to *G*, or *G* to *L*? Kate's indifference map tells us that she *must* prefer *L* to *G*. Why? We know that she prefers *K* to *G*, since *K* has more of both phone time and other goods. We also know that Kate is indifferent between *L* and *K*, since they are on the same indifference curve. Since she is indifferent between *L* and *K*, but prefers *K* to *G*, then she must also prefer *L* to *G*.

The same technique could be used to show that

> *any point on a higher indifference curve is preferred to any point on a lower one.*

Thus, Kate's indifference map tells us how she ranks all alternatives imaginable. This is why we say that an indifference map gives us a complete characterization of someone's preferences: It allows us to look at any two points and—just by seeing which indifference curves they are on—immediately know which, if either, is preferred.

THE MARGINAL RATE OF SUBSTITUTION

The slope of the indifference curve along any one of its segments tells us the rate at which a consumer can trade off one good for another and still remain indifferent. The *absolute value* of this slope is called the *marginal rate of substitution,* or *MRS*. The *MRS* plays an important role in the indifference curve approach, so let's define it. When the quantity of good *y* is measured on the vertical axis and the quantity of good *x* is measured on the horizontal axis,

> *the marginal rate of substitution of good* y *for good* x *($MRS_{y,x}$) along any segment of an indifference curve is (the absolute value of) the indifference curve's slope along that segment. The MRS tells us the decrease in the quantity of good* y *needed to accompany a one-unit increase in good* x, *in order to keep the consumer indifferent to the change.*

Although the *MRS* has a technical definition, its meaning is quite simple. Look back at Figure A1. If Kate were currently consuming at point *G*, she could tell us the following: "If you gave me one more minute on the phone with my sister (good *x*), and took away 20 units of all other goods (good *y*), then I'd be just as well off as I am now." Then Kate would be telling us that her *MRS* is 20. As you can see in the figure, this is also equal to the absolute value of the indifference curve's slope along the segment *GH*. (The decrease along the vertical axis is 20, and the increase along the horizontal axis is 1, so the absolute value of the slope is 20/1 = 20.)

CONSUMER DECISION MAKING

Now we can combine everything you've learned about budget lines in the chapter, and what you've learned about indifference maps and the marginal rate of substitution in this appendix, to determine the combination of goods Kate should choose. Figure A3

FIGURE A3 · **CONSUMER DECISION MAKING**

Kate's most preferred combination of phone calls and "all other goods" is at point *E*. It is a point on the highest indifference curve attainable, given her budget and the prices of the two goods. At a point like *R*, her *MRS* exceeds the slope of her budget line, so she would be better off increasing her phone time and moving to a higher indifference curve. At *S*, her *MRS* is less than the slope of the line, so she would be better off cutting back on phone time.

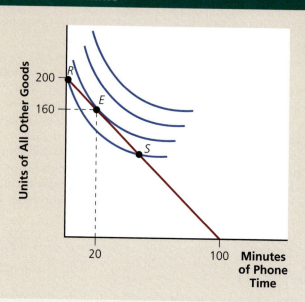

adds Kate's budget line to her indifference map. In drawing the budget line, we suppose that she has a weekly budget of $200 to spend on phone calls and all other goods, and that long-distance phone rates are $2 per minute during the time that Kate likes to call her sister. We also assume that the price of a unit of all other goods is $1.

If Kate devotes all of her income to phone calls and none to other goods, she could have 100 minutes of phone time per month. This is the horizontal intercept of her budget line in the figure. On the other hand, she could choose 0 phone time and 200 units of all other goods—the vertical intercept. Since the price of a minute of phone time (good x) is $2, and the price of a unit of all other goods (good y) is $1, the slope of Kate's budget line is $-P_x/P_y = -\$2/\$1 = -2$. Each additional minute of phone time requires Kate to give up $2 in other goods.

Kate's optimal combination of phone calls and other goods will satisfy two criteria: (1) It will be a point on her budget line, and (2) it will lie on the highest indifference curve possible. Kate can find this point by traveling down her budget line, passing through a variety of indifference curves. At first, each indifference curve is higher than the one before, until she reaches the highest curve possible. This occurs at point *E*, where she buys 160 units of other goods and 20 minutes of long-distance calls per week. Any further moves down the budget line will put her on lower indifference curves, so these moves would make her worse off. Point *E* is her optimal choice, then.

Notice two things about point *E*. First, it occurs where the indifference curve and the budget line touch but don't cross. As you can see in the diagram, when an indifference curve actually crosses the budget line, we can always find some other point on the budget line that lies on a higher indifference curve.

Second, at point *E*, the slope of the indifference curve is the same as the slope of the budget line. Does this make sense? It should, when you think about it this way: The slope of the indifference curve is minus the marginal rate of substitution between two goods. The *MRS* tells us the rate at which the consumer could trade one good for the other and remain indifferent. The slope of the budget line, by contrast, tells us the rate at which the consumer *is actually able* to trade one good for the other. If there is any difference between the rate at which a consumer could trade one good for the other with indifference and the rate at which she is *able* to trade, she can always make herself better off by moving to another point on the budget line. For example, suppose Kate were at point *R*, where her indifference curve is steeper (slope = −10) than her budget line (slope = −2). Since her *MRS* at point *R* is 10, she could give up 10 units of other goods for 1 more minute of phone time and remain indifferent. But Kate's budget line tells us that she *is able* to trade just 2 units of other goods for another minute of phone time. If trading away 10 units of other goods for another minute would leave her indifferent, but she *actually* has to give up only 2 units, then she must be better off by making the trade. We conclude that *when Kate's indifference curve is steeper than her budget line, she should spend more on phone calls and less on other goods.*

Using similar reasoning, convince yourself that Kate should make the opposite move—spending less on phone calls and more on other goods—if her indifference curve is flatter than her budget line, as it is at point *S*. Only when the indifference curve and the budget line have the same slope—when they touch but do not cross—is Kate as well off as possible. More generally,

> *the optimal combination of goods for a consumer is that combination on the budget line at which the indifference curve has the same slope as the budget line.*

MAXIMIZATION SUBJECT TO CONSTRAINTS

MARGINAL DECISION MAKING

Now remember that (the absolute value of) the slope of an indifference curve at any point is equal to the marginal rate of substitution between the two goods ($MRS_{y,x}$), while (the absolute value of) the slope of the budget line is equal to P_x/P_y. Using these two facts, our conclusion about the consumer's optimal choice can be expressed this way:

> *The optimal combination of two goods* x *and* y *is that combination on the budget line for which* $MRS_{y,x} = P_x/P_y$.

If this condition is not met, there will be a difference between the rate at which a consumer could trade good *y* for good *x* and remain indifferent, and the rate at which she *could actually* make the trade. This will always give the consumer an opportunity to make herself better off.[4]

INDIFFERENCE CURVES AND THE INDIVIDUAL DEMAND CURVE

We can also use indifference curves to derive Kate's demand curve for long-distance phone calls. In panel (a) of Figure A4, we show what happens when long-distance rates fall from $2.00 per minute to $1.00 per minute. First, the horizontal intercept

---

4.   The body of this chapter covers the marginal utility approach to consumer theory. You might be wondering whether the indifference curve approach leads to a different consumer choice. The answer is no: Both approaches lead to the same optimal combination of goods. Here is the proof:

First, note that $MRS_{y,x} = MU_x/MU_y$ for any change along an indifference curve. Why? The $MRS_{y,x}$ tells us the decrease in good *y* per unit change in good *x* that keeps the consumer indifferent. When good *y* decreases, utility falls by $MU_y \times \Delta_y$ (the change in utility per unit change in *y*, times the change in *y*). When *x* increases, utility increases by $MU_x \times \Delta x$. Now remember that, as we move along an indifference curve, total utility must remain unchanged to keep the consumer indifferent. Thus, as we move along an indifference curve, it must be that $MU_y \times \Delta y = MU_x \times \Delta x$, or $\Delta y/\Delta x = MU_x/MU_y$. The left-hand side is the change in *y* per unit change in *x* that keeps the consumer indifferent, or $MRS_{y,x}$, so we have $MRS_{y,x} = MU_x/MU_y$.

Now, in the marginal utility approach, the consumer chooses a combination of goods such that $MU_x/P_x = MU_y/P_y$, or, rearranging, $MU_x/MU_y = P_x/P_y$. In the indifference curve approach, the consumer chooses the combination such that $MRS_{y,x} = P_x/P_y$. Since $MU_x/MU_x = MRS_{y,x}$, using the marginal utility approach or the *MRS* approach will give us the same optimal combination of goods.

FIGURE A4   DERIVING THE DEMAND CURVE

At $2 per minute of phone time, Kate chooses point *E* in panel (a) and spends 20 minutes on the phone. If the price falls to $1 per minute, her budget line rotates outward; she moves to point *F,* consuming 30 minutes of phone time. The demand curve in panel (b) is obtained by connecting price-quantity combinations like *E* and *F.*

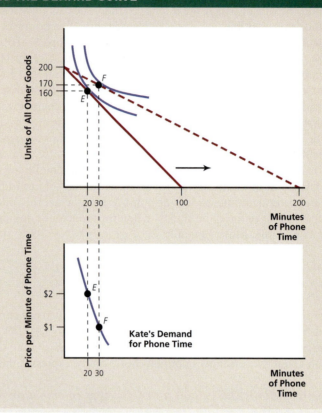

of Kate's budget line will move rightward, from 100 minutes to 200 minutes. Second, Kate will travel down her new budget line until she reaches point *F,* which places her on the highest indifference curve possible. At this point, she spends $170 on other goods and speaks to her sister for 30 minutes each week. Panel (b) shows Kate's demand curve for long-distance phone time, based on the information in panel (a). At $2.00 per minute, she buys 20 minutes of phone time, and at $1 per minute, she buys 30 minutes. Notice that Kate's demand curve for long-distance phone calls satisfies the law of demand: A drop in long-distance rates increases the quantity of phone time demanded.

CHAPTER
5

PRODUCTION AND COST

In the early 1990s, the Russian Federation began a remarkable transformation from centrally planned socialism to market capitalism. One of the crucial steps was to *privatize* most of Russia's production facilities—to transfer ownership of factories and stores from the government to private citizens. But Russian officials were worried: Wouldn't wealthy Americans, Japanese, Germans, French, and British swarm into the country and buy up most of Russia's manufacturing plants?

To the surprise of many Russian officials, the feared "foreign invasion" never occurred. Although foreigners sniffed around a bit, and a few took the plunge, most investors stayed away. One important reason was their strong belief that Russian manufacturing firms would be unable to compete with Western firms after Russia opened its borders to international trade. There was something peculiar about Russian firms. After you have read this chapter, you'll understand just what that peculiarity was.

In this chapter, we begin our study of the business firms that produce and sell goods and services. The first section addresses some very general, but important, questions. What are business firms? What advantages do business firms enjoy over other ways of organizing production? Why do so many of us work as employees of firms? Then, in the remainder of the chapter, we turn our attention to the nature of production and cost. You will see that there are many different ways of measuring costs, each telling us something different about the firm.

THE NATURE OF THE FIRM

> A **business firm** is an organization, owned and operated by private individuals, that specializes in production.

Your first image when you hear the word "production," may be a busy, noisy factory where goods are assembled, piece by piece, and then carted off to a warehouse for eventual sale to the public. Large manufacturers may come to mind—General Motors, Boeing, or even Ben and Jerry's. All of these companies produce things, but the word "production," encompasses more than just manufacturing.

> Production is the process of combining inputs to make outputs.

Some outputs are, indeed, physical *goods*, like automobiles, aircraft, or ice cream. But outputs can also be *services*. Indeed, many of America's largest corporations produce services. Think of Citicorp (banking services), American Airlines (transportation services), Bell Atlantic (telecommunications services), and Wal-Mart (retailing services).

Figure 1 illustrates the relationships between the firm and those with whom it must deal. Notice that we have put the firm's management in the center of the diagram. It is the managers who must decide what the firm will do, both day to day and over a longer time horizon. When we refer to the firm as a *decision maker*, we mean the manager or managers who actually make the decisions.

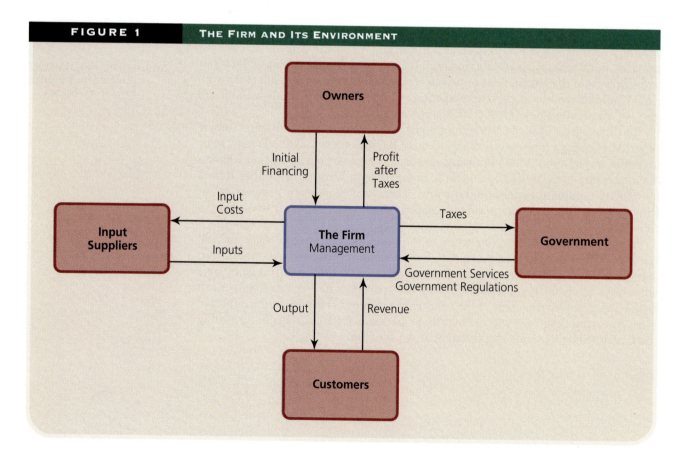

FIGURE 1   **THE FIRM AND ITS ENVIRONMENT**

As you can see in the figure, the firm must deal with a variety of individuals and organizations. It sells its output to *customers*—which can be households, government agencies, or other firms—and receives *revenue* in return. For example, Ford Motor Company sells its automobiles to households, to other firms (such as rental car companies), and to government agencies (such as local police departments). Ford earns revenue from all of these customers.

Where does the revenue go? Much of it pays for the inputs the firm uses. Ford must pay for labor, machinery, steel, rubber, electricity, factory buildings, and the land underneath them, and much, much more. The total of all of these payments makes up the firm's *costs* of production. When costs are deducted from revenue, what remains is the firm's **profit:**

PROFIT Total revenue minus total cost.

$$\text{Profit} = \text{Revenue} - \text{Costs}$$

Figure 1 shows that some of this profit goes to the government as taxes, and the remainder—profit after taxes—accrues to the owners of the firm.

TYPES OF BUSINESS FIRMS

There are about 20 million business firms in the United States, and each of them falls into one of three legal categories, based on the rules and conditions of ownership. In a **sole proprietorship,** a single individual starts the firm, owns it, and is entitled to all of the profit after taxes. In Figure 2, you can see that most business firms are sole proprietorships. This is not surprising since they are the easiest form of business to start: In many cases, the owner just begins doing business. For tax purposes, the firm's profit is simply treated as part of the owner's personal income and is subject to the personal income tax.

SOLE PROPRIETORSHIP A firm owned by a single individual.

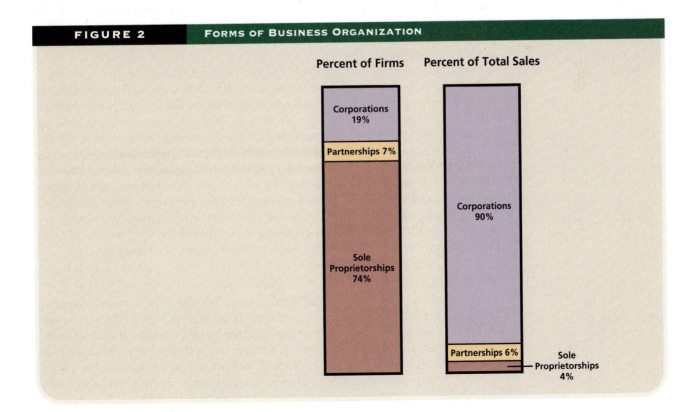

FIGURE 2 **FORMS OF BUSINESS ORGANIZATION**

Percent of Firms   Percent of Total Sales

Corporations 19%
Partnerships 7%
Sole Proprietorships 74%

Corporations 90%
Partnerships 6%
Sole Proprietorships 4%

PARTNERSHIP A firm owned and usually operated by several individuals who share in the profits and bear personal responsibility for any losses.

In a **partnership,** responsibilities are shared among several co-owners. One clear advantage of a partnership is that each owner can take time off, leaving the others in charge. In addition, partners can often share many inputs—such as secretaries, advertising, and reception areas—reducing the costs for each partner. Of course, the profits must be shared with the co-owners as well. Partnerships are common among professionals, such as doctors, lawyers, and architects.

Although sole proprietorships and partnerships are easy to create, they share two problems that ultimately make many owners decide against them. The first is *unlimited liability:* In either of these types of businesses, each owner is held personally responsible for the obligations of the firm. If the business runs up debts and closes down, or is successfully sued for a large sum of money, the owners will usually have to honor these obligations out of their own pockets.

The second problem is the difficulty of raising money to expand the business. In a sole proprietorship or partnership, owners must think very carefully before bringing in new partners—especially strangers—because each partner bears full responsibility for the poor judgment of any one of them. Thus, when owners need additional funds, they must usually use their own money or borrow from a bank. In either case, the current owners bear all the risk if the business fails.

CORPORATION A firm owned by those who buy shares of stock and whose liability is limited to the amount of their investment in the firm.

These drawbacks lead many business firms to choose the third type of organization: a **corporation.** In this type of firm, ownership is divided among those who buy shares of *stock.* Each share of stock entitles its owner to a vote for the board of directors, which in turn hires the corporation's managers. And each share of stock entitles its owner to a share of the corporation's profit—some of which is paid out each quarter as *dividends.* The corporate form of organization makes it easier to raise additional funds: The corporation simply sells additional shares of stock, thereby bringing in new owners. People are less hesitant to become co-owners of a corporation because of its other chief advantage: *limited liability.* The owners (stockholders) of a corporation can lose only what they have paid for the stock they own; they will never have to reach into their own pockets to honor the firm's obligations.

Why, then, doesn't every firm choose the corporate form? Because a corporation, in addition to its many advantages, must also bear some additional costs. To set up a corporation, government documents must be filed, and lawyers and accountants are usually hired to help with the job. And once you incorporate, you are subject to a variety of laws and regulations that apply only to corporations. Finally, owners of corporations suffer *double taxation.* First, the corporation pays taxes on its total profit. Then, households must pay income taxes on the portion of profit they receive as dividends. Each dollar of profits is thus taxed twice: once as corporate profits and again as household income. Still, for the largest firms, the advantages of incorporating outweigh the disadvantages. Although only a minority—about 20 percent—of businesses choose to be corporations, they tend to be large firms, producing about 90 percent of our national output (see Figure 2).

WHY EMPLOYEES?

Most firms have *employees*—people who work for the firm, receive a wage or salary, but are not themselves owners. Indeed, most of us will spend the greater part of our lives working as employees of firms owned by other people. We are so accustomed to this arrangement that we rarely think about it. But life didn't have to be this way. There is no law to prevent each of us from operating our own one-person firms as independent contractors. Indeed, there would be many advantages to this sort of arrangement: We could each determine our own hours, we could set our own work rules, and no one could fire us, no matter what we did. So why don't more of us do it?

To understand why so many people work as employees, consider the alternative: each of us working as independent contractors. In such an economy, we would each specialize in a craft or profession and trade with each other, but *work* only for ourselves. If you wanted to buy a couch, you would go to an independent couch maker. The couch maker, in turn, would buy her saw from an independent saw maker, her lumber from a lumber cutter, and so on, throughout the economy. We would each operate on our own. And we would each concentrate on an activity in which we had a comparative advantage, learn to do it well, and buy the materials we needed from other individuals. Such an arrangement would offer us many benefits. But we would not be enjoying the highest standard of living possible.

To see why, let's conduct the following thought experiment. Suppose that, in this economy of independent contractors, someone got a brilliant idea: to set up a new organization, a *firm with employees,* to produce couches. In this firm, hundreds or even thousands of employees would promise to show up for work every day in exchange for an agreed-upon wage or salary. Would this kind of production have major advantages over production by independent contractors? Absolutely.

GAINS FROM SPECIALIZATION. One advantage of production by firms with employees is the possibility of further gains from specialization. When many people work within a single organization, assembly-line methods, in which each worker specializes in *one aspect* of production, become feasible. Whereas the independent contractor must design the couch, make the couch, deal with customers, and advertise her services, at the couch factory each of these tasks would be performed by different individuals who would work full-time at their activity. This increases the gains from specialization.

LOWER TRANSACTION COSTS. Another advantage for a firm with employees is lower **transaction costs**—a term economists use for the hassles of doing business. It takes time to find reliable suppliers of cloth, wood, and tools, and time to negotiate deals with each of them. In a world of independent contractors, where business relationships would be more temporary and flexible, each of us would spend a great deal of time searching for high-quality, reliable suppliers and negotiating contracts with them. As a result, transaction costs would be high.

In a firm with employees, however, many supplies and services can be produced *inside* the organization, by *employees*. The firm's owners negotiate just *one* contract with each person—an employment contract—specifying the responsibilities and obligations of both sides. As long as employee turnover isn't too great, the firm can enjoy significant savings on transaction costs.

REDUCED RISK. Finally, the large firm with employees offers opportunities for everyone involved to reduce *risk*. When workers join firms and agree to work for a stable wage or salary, they receive a kind of insurance that protects them against fluctuations in their incomes. The protection is not complete—there is always the possibility of being laid off when times are bad—but it is understood by both firms and workers that those who remain on the job will continue to receive their regular

TRANSACTION COSTS The time costs and other costs required to carry out market exchanges.

wage or salary, regardless of business conditions. Many people—preferring not to gamble with the source of their livelihood—place a high value on this feature of employment contracts, a feature not available to the independent contractor.

But how can firms provide this kind of protection to employees? Doesn't offering stable wages, even when business is bad, increase the variability of the firm's profits? Won't this increase the risk faced by the firm's owners?

DIVERSIFICATION The process of reducing risk by spreading sources of income among different alternatives.

Perhaps. But large firms create opportunities for owners to reduce their risk, too, through **diversification**. To *diversify* is to spread the source of your income among several different alternatives, as suggested by the saying, "Don't put all your eggs in one basket." With large firms, two kinds of diversification are possible. First, the firm itself can produce several different product lines, so that if one is selling poorly, another may be selling well. This is diversification *within the firm.*

Second, owners need not limit themselves to ownership of just one firm; instead, they can spread their investment, buying shares in a *portfolio* of firms. The portfolio can be carefully chosen so that when some firms are doing poorly, others are likely to be doing well. This is diversification *among firms,* and it allows the income of each owner to be more stable than the profits at any one firm.

You can see that a large firm with employees offers several advantages over independent contractors. These advantages help it attract customers, workers, and potential owners. Here's why:

- The greater gains from specialization and the savings on transaction costs allow the firm with employees to produce a given amount of output using fewer resources than would a collection of independent contractors.
- Since the firm can produce its output using fewer resources, it can charge lower prices—attracting *customers* away from independent contractors.
- Since the firm saves on resources, it can afford to pay a higher wage rate to its workers than they could earn as independent contractors. The firm can also provide its workers with valuable insurance against income fluctuations. These advantages induce many independent contractors to become *employees*.
- Opportunities for diversification within and among firms help reduce the risk to potential *owners,* enticing them to organize firms.

Since modern firms with employees have such an edge in winning customers, attracting workers, and enticing potential owners, it is not surprising that they produce so much of our output.

THE LIMITS TO THE FIRM

From all of this, you might be tempted to conclude that bigger is always better—that the larger the firm, the greater will be the cost savings. But if that were true, there would be just one enormous firm in the economy, and we'd all be working for it! In fact, there are limits to the gains from specialization, the savings on transaction costs, and opportunities for diversification. Bigger is not *always* better.

Why? Because as firms expand in size, they begin to encounter difficulties. For one thing, larger firms have more layers of management than small firms. Major corporations like IBM, General Motors, and Bell Atlantic each have several hundred high-level managers, and thousands more at lower levels. In a firm with so many managers, communication and decision making become more complex and time consuming. Indeed, for much of the 1980s, IBM was criticized by its stockholders for failing to keep up with rapid changes in the market for small computers. According to its critics, IBM had grown so large that decision making had become sluggish.

Large firms also have difficulty *monitoring* their workers, to prevent shirking or sloppy work. These problems increase costs at the firm, counteracting the cost advantages of bigness described earlier. Eventually, as a firm continues to grow, a point is reached at which the advantages of further growth are outweighed by the disadvantages. This explains why firms do not grow indefinitely larger.

In some types of production, the disadvantages of bigness set in right away, and independent contractors will have the advantage. Plumbing, shoe repair, gardening, and psychotherapy are almost always provided by independent contractors rather than large firms. These are jobs where it is best to have a single professional or craftsperson perform a *variety* of tasks; further specialization *within* the craft would create losses rather than gains. (Imagine the disadvantages of a plumbing firm in which each worker specializes: One finds your problem, another removes your old pipes, another locates a replacement pipe, another writes the bill, and so on.)

National Bureau of Economic Research
As the leading nonprofit economic research organization in the United States, the NBER sponsors research on all aspects of the economy. Ongoing research programs include the NBER/Sloan Productivity Project aimed at understanding how technology affects production.
http://www.nber.org/

THINKING ABOUT PRODUCTION

When you think of production, it is quite natural to think of *outputs*—the things firms make—and *inputs*—the things firms use to make outputs. Inputs include resources (labor, capital, and land), as well as raw materials and other goods and services provided by other firms. For example, to produce this book, South-Western College Publishing Company used a variety of inputs: *labor* (including that provided by the authors, editors, artists, printers, and company managers); *human capital* (the knowledge and skills possessed by each of the preceding laborers); *physical capital* (including computers, delivery trucks, and a company headquarters building in Cincinnati); and *land* (under the headquarters). The company also used many inputs that were produced by *other firms,* including raw materials such as paper and ink, as well as the services of trucking companies, telephone companies, and Internet access providers.

The way in which these inputs may be combined to produce output is the firm's **technology.** We leave it to engineers and scientists to spell out a firm's technology and to discover ways to improve it. Economists consider technology as a given, a *constraint* on the firm's production. This constraint is spelled out by the firm's *production function*:

> *For each different combination of inputs, the **production function** tells us the maximum quantity of output a firm can produce over some period of time.*

The idea behind a production function is illustrated in Figure 3. Quantities of each input are plugged into the box representing the production function, and the maximum quantity of goods or services produced pops out. The production function itself—the box—is a mathematical function relating inputs and outputs.

When a firm uses many different inputs, production functions can be quite complicated. For example, the production function for a shoe manufacturer would tell us how many shoes can be produced with each different combination of leather, rubber, cloth, workers, factory floor space, leather-cutters, awls, and so on.

TECHNOLOGY A method by which inputs are combined to produce a good or service.

PRODUCTION FUNCTION A function that indicates the maximum amount of output a firm can produce over some period of time from each combination of inputs.

FIGURE 3	THE FIRM'S PRODUCTION FUNCTION

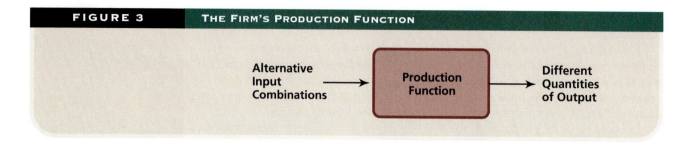

In this chapter, to keep things simple, we'll spell out the production function for a mythical firm that uses only two inputs: capital and labor. Our firm is Spotless Car Wash, whose output is a service: the number of cars washed. The firm's capital is the number of automated car-washing lines, and its labor is the number of full-time workers who drive the cars onto the line, drive them out, towel them down at the end, and deal with customers.[1]

THE SHORT RUN AND THE LONG RUN

When a firm alters its level of production, its input requirements will change. Some inputs, such as labor, can be adjusted relatively quickly. Other inputs—for example, capital equipment—may be more difficult to change. Why? Leases or rental agreements may commit the firm to keep paying for equipment over some period of time, whether the equipment is used or not. Or there may be practical difficulties in adjusting capital, like a long lead time needed to acquire new equipment or sell off existing equipment. These considerations make it useful to categorize firms' decisions into one of two sorts: *long-run decisions* and *short-run decisions*. The **long run** is a time horizon long enough for a firm to vary *all* of its inputs.

LONG RUN A time horizon long enough for a firm to vary all of its inputs.

The long run will be different for different firms. For a surgeon who would need several months to obtain a new surgical laser, to find a buyer for the one he has, or to find a larger or a smaller office, the long run is several months or more. At Spotless Car Wash, it might take a year to acquire and install additional automated lines, or to sell the ones it already has. For Spotless, then, the long run would be any period longer than a year.

When a firm makes long-run decisions, it makes choices about *all* of its inputs. But firms must also make decisions over shorter time horizons, during which some of its inputs *cannot* be adjusted.

SHORT RUN A time horizon during which at least one of the firm's inputs cannot be varied.

*The **short run** is a time horizon during which at least one of the firm's inputs cannot be varied.*

For Spotless Car Wash, the short run would be any period *less* than a year, the period during which it is stuck with a certain number of automated lines.

You can think of the short run and long run as two different lenses a firm's manager must look through in making her decisions. When she is using the short-run lens, at least one of her inputs appears to be fixed; but when she looks through the long-run lens, all of her inputs are variable. To guide the firm over the next several years, she will use the long-run lens; to determine what the firm should do next week, the short-run lens.

---

1.   Of course, a car wash would use other inputs besides just capital and labor: water, washrags, soap, electricity, and so on. But the costs of these inputs would be minor when compared to the costs of labor and capital. To keep our example simple, we will ignore these other inputs entirely.

PRODUCTION IN THE SHORT RUN

In this section, we'll be describing important features of production in the short run. Remember that in the short run, at least one of the firm's inputs cannot be varied. As a result, the firm will have two types of inputs:

> *Fixed inputs are those whose quantity remains constant, regardless of how much output is produced. Variable inputs are those whose quantity changes as the level of output changes.*

FIXED INPUT An input whose quantity remains constant, regardless of how much output is produced.

VARIABLE INPUT An input whose usage changes as the level of output changes.

When firms make short-run decisions, there is nothing they can do about their fixed inputs: They are stuck with whatever quantity they have. They can, however, make choices about their variable inputs. Indeed, we see examples of such short-run decisions all the time. Chrysler Corporation might decide *this month* to cut output by 5 percent and lay off thousands of workers, even though it cannot change its factory buildings or capital equipment for another year or more. For Chrysler, labor is variable, while its factory and equipment are fixed. Levi Strauss might decide to increase production of blue jeans over the next quarter by obtaining additional workers, cotton cloth, and sewing machines, yet continue to make do with the same factory. Here, workers, cloth, and sewing machines are all variable, while only the factory building is fixed.

Spotless Car Wash uses only two inputs to produce its output—labor and capital. Its only variable input is labor, and its only fixed input is capital. The three columns in Table 1 describe Spotless's production function in the short run. Column 1 shows the quantity of the fixed input, capital (K); column 2 the quantity of the variable input, labor (L). Note that in the short run, Spotless is stuck with one unit of capital—one automated line—but can take on as many or as few workers as it wishes.

Column 3 shows the *total product* of the firm (Q).

> *Total product is the maximum quantity of output that can be produced from a given combination of inputs.*

TOTAL PRODUCT The maximum quantity of output that can be produced from a given combination of inputs.

For example, the table shows us that with one automated line but no labor, total product is zero. With one line and six workers, output is 185 car washes per day.

Figure 4 shows Spotless's *total product curve*. The horizontal axis represents the number of workers, while the vertical axis measures units of output. (The amount of capital—which is held fixed at one automated line—is not shown on the graph.) Notice that each time the firm hires another worker, output increases, so the total product curve slopes upward. The vertical arrows in the figure show precisely *how*

TABLE 1	SHORT-RUN PRODUCTION AT SPOTLESS CAR WASH	
Quantity of Capital	**Quantity of Labor**	**Total Product**
1	0	0
1	1	30
1	2	90
1	3	130
1	4	155
1	5	172
1	6	185

(handwritten annotations between Total Product values: 30, 40, 40, 25, 17, 13)

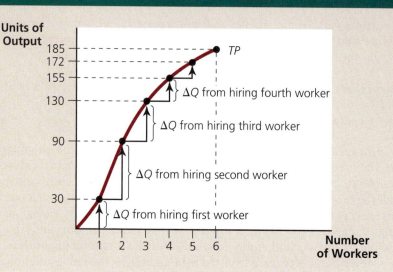

FIGURE 4   **TOTAL AND MARGINAL PRODUCT**

The total product (*TP*) curve shows the total amount of output that can be produced using various numbers of workers. The marginal product of labor (*MPL*) curve is the change in total product when another worker is hired. The *MPL* for each change in employment is indicated by the length of the vertical arrows.

Units of Output

- 185
- 172
- 155
- 130
- 90
- 30

TP

ΔQ from hiring fourth worker

ΔQ from hiring third worker

ΔQ from hiring second worker

ΔQ from hiring first worker

1 2 3 4 5 6   **Number of Workers**

much output increases with each one-unit rise in employment. We call this rise in output the *marginal product of labor.*

MARGINAL PRODUCT OF LABOR (MPL) The additional output produced when one more worker is hired.

> *The **marginal product of labor** (MPL) is the additional output produced when one more worker is hired. Mathematically, the marginal product of labor is the change in total product (ΔQ) divided by the change in the number of workers hired (ΔL): MPL = $\Delta Q/\Delta L$.*

For example, when employment rises from 2 to 3 workers, total product rises from 90 to 130, so the marginal product of labor for *that* change in employment is 130 − 90 = 40 units of output.

MARGINAL RETURNS TO LABOR

Look at the vertical arrows in Figure 4, which measure the marginal product of labor, and you may notice something interesting. As more and more workers are hired, the MPL first increases (the vertical arrows get longer), and then decreases (the arrows get smaller). This pattern is believed to be typical at many types of firms, so it's worth exploring.

INCREASING RETURNS TO LABOR. When the marginal product of labor increases with a rise in employment, we say there are **increasing marginal returns to labor.** Each time a worker is hired, total output rises by more than it did when the previous worker was hired. Why does this happen? One reason is that additional workers may allow production to become more specialized. Another reason is that at very low levels of employment, there may not be enough workers to properly operate the available capital. In either case, the additional worker not only produces some additional output as an individual, but also makes all other workers more productive.

At Spotless Car Wash, increasing returns to labor are observed up to the hiring of the second worker. Why? While one worker could operate the car wash alone, he or she would have to do everything: drive the cars on and off the line, towel them down,

INCREASING MARGINAL RETURNS TO LABOR The marginal product of labor increases as more labor is hired.

and deal with customers. Much of this worker's time would be spent switching from one task to another. The result, as we see in Table 1, is that one worker can wash only 30 cars each day. Add a second worker, though, and now specialization is possible. One worker can collect money and drive the cars onto the line, and the other can drive them off and towel them down. Thus, with two workers, output rises all the way to 90 car washes per day; the second worker adds more to production (60 car washes) than the first (30 car washes), by making *both* workers more productive.

DIMINISHING RETURNS TO LABOR. When the marginal product of labor is decreasing, we say there are **diminishing marginal returns to labor:** Output rises when another worker is added, but the rise is smaller and smaller with each successive worker. Why does this happen? For one thing, as we keep adding workers, additional gains from specialization will be harder and harder to come by. Moreover, each worker will have less and less of the fixed inputs with which to work.

This last point is worth stressing. It applies not just to labor, but to any variable input. In all kinds of production, if we keep increasing the quantity of any one input, while holding the others fixed, diminishing marginal returns will eventually set in. If a farmer keeps adding additional pounds of fertilizer to a fixed amount of land, the yield may continually increase, but eventually the *amount* of the increase—the marginal product of fertilizer—will begin to come down. If a small bakery continues to acquire additional ovens without hiring any workers or enlarging its floor space, eventually the additional output of bread—the marginal product of ovens—will decline. This tendency is so pervasive and widespread that it has the force of a law, and economists have given that law a name:

> The **law of diminishing (marginal) returns** states that as we continue to add more of any one input (holding the other inputs constant), its marginal product will eventually decline.

The law of diminishing returns is a physical law, not an economic one. It is based on the nature of production—on the physical relationship between inputs and outputs with a given technology.

At Spotless, the law of diminishing returns sets in after two workers have been hired. Beyond this point, the firm is crowding more and more workers into a car wash with just one automated line. Output continues to increase—since there is usually *something* an additional worker can do to move the cars through the line more quickly—but the increase is less dramatic each time.

This section has been concerned with *production*—the *physical* relationship between inputs and outputs. But a more critical concern for a firm is: What will it *cost* to produce any level of output? Cost is measured in dollars and cents, not the physical units of inputs or outputs. But as you are about to see, what you've learned about production will help you understand the behavior of costs.

DIMINISHING MARGINAL RETURNS TO LABOR The marginal product of labor decreases as more labor is hired.

LAW OF DIMINISHING MARGINAL RETURNS As more and more of any input is added to a fixed amount of other inputs, its marginal product will eventually decline.

THINKING ABOUT COSTS

Talk to people who own or manage businesses, and it won't be long before the word "cost" comes up. People in business worry about measuring costs, controlling costs, and—most of all—reducing costs. This is not surprising: Owners want their firms to earn the highest possible profit, and costs must be subtracted from a firm's revenue to determine its profit. We will postpone a thorough discussion of profit until the next chapter. Here, we focus on just the costs of production: how economists think about costs, how costs are measured, and how they change as the firm adjusts its level of output.

Let's begin by revisiting a familiar notion. In Chapter 2 you learned that economists always think of cost as *opportunity cost*—what we must give up in order to do something. This concept applies to the firm as well:

OPPORTUNITY COST

> *A firm's total cost of production is the opportunity cost of the owners—everything they must give up in order to produce output.*

This notion—that the cost of production is its opportunity cost—is at the core of economists' thinking about costs. It can help us understand a common mistake people make when thinking about the costs of a decision.

THE IRRELEVANCE OF SUNK COSTS

Suppose you bought a used car for $5,000 last year. During the year, you've paid $3,000 for various repairs, and now the car is acting up again. A trustworthy mechanic tells you that the car needs a major overhaul, which will cost you $7,000. On the other hand, he knows someone selling the same model of car—with no defects—for $6,000. What should you do?

Some people faced with this decision might be tempted to repair the car they own. They might reason that a $7,000 repair job is worth it to prevent the loss of a car that has already cost them $8,000. ($5,000 to purchase it plus $3,000 in repairs). But this would be faulty reasoning. The $8,000 already paid is an example of a *sunk cost*:

OPPORTUNITY COST

SUNK COST A cost that was incurred in the past and does not change in response to a present decision.

> *A **sunk cost** is a cost that was paid in the past and will not change regardless of your present decision. Sunk costs should be ignored when making current decisions.*

Why ignore sunk costs? Because they are not part of the *opportunity cost* of the action you are considering. Opportunity cost, remember, is what you must give up when you choose some action. But sunk costs have *already* been given up, so they are not part of the cost of making your choice. In the case of your car, the $8,000 you have paid is gone, whether you buy another car or have yours repaired. The only costs that are relevant are those that *depend* on your decision and will change with it. Since you would have to pay $7,000 to repair your car, but only $6,000 to buy an equivalent one, you are better off giving up on your car and buying the replacement.

In many personal decisions, sunk costs are lurking in the background, tempting the decision maker to miscalculate and make a poor choice. For example, if you have completed two years of medical school and then discover you'd rather be a lawyer than a doctor, you might be tempted to stay in medical school because you have already spent so much money and time on it. But those costs you have already paid are sunk, and irrelevant to your decision. The only costs that matter now are those that will *change* with your decision: the costs of your *remaining* years of medical school on the one hand, or completing three years of law school on the other.

Sunk costs should be ignored in business decisions as well. For example, South-Western Publishing Company has paid a number of costs to put this book in your hands. One of these costs was management's salaries. Suppose South-Western sells out the entire first printing and is considering whether to print another 20,000 copies. Should it consider the costs of management salaries? Absolutely not. These salaries are sunk costs and have no relevance to the decision. The only costs that matter are those that will *change* if the second printing is ordered: the costs of printing, binding, and shipping the books. Business firms, like other decision makers, should ignore sunk costs when making choices. Only costs that are *not* sunk should enter the decision-making process.

EXPLICIT VERSUS IMPLICIT COSTS

The concept of opportunity cost also helps us classify costs into two types. Table 2 lists several different costs an owner might have to bear. On the left-hand side are the firm's **explicit costs**—instances where the firm actually pays out money for its inputs. These payments include *wages* and *salaries* for its workers, *rent* for its use of buildings and property, *interest* on any loans that were taken out to buy equipment, and payments for raw materials. Payments such as these are clearly part of an owner's opportunity cost, since the owners could have used the funds paid out to buy other valuable things.

> **EXPLICIT COSTS** Money actually paid out for the use of inputs.

But money payments are not the only costs to the firm. On the right-hand side of the table are some other possible costs an owner might bear. These we call **implicit costs** because, although they are indeed costs to the firm, *no money actually changes hands*. Let's consider them one at a time.

Suppose you own a restaurant, and you also happen to own the building and the land underneath. You don't have to pay any rent, so under "rent paid out," your explicit cost would be zero. Does this mean that the building and the land are free? To an accountant—who focuses on actual money payments—the answer is yes. But to an economist—who thinks of opportunity cost—the answer is *absolutely not*. By choosing to use your land and building for your restaurant, you are sacrificing the opportunity to rent them to someone else. This *forgone rent* is an implicit cost, and it is as much a cost of production as the rent you would pay if someone else owned the building. In both cases, something is given up to produce your output.

> **IMPLICIT COSTS** The cost of inputs for which there is no direct money payment.

Now suppose that instead of borrowing the money to start up your restaurant— to buy ovens, dishes, tables, chairs, and an initial inventory of food—you used your own money. You therefore have no debts and no interest to pay on them, so your interest on loans is zero. But there is still a cost to be considered: You *could* have put your money in a bank account, lent it to someone else, or invested it elsewhere. In any of these cases, you would have earned *investment income* on your money.

TABLE 2	A FIRM'S COSTS
Explicit Costs	**Implicit Costs**
Rent paid out	Opportunity cost of:
Interest on loans	Owner's land (rent forgone)
Managers' salaries	Owner's money (investment income forgone)
Hourly workers' wages	Owner's time (labor income forgone)
Cost of raw materials	

Economists measure the opportunity cost of funds you invest in a business as the income you *could* have earned on these funds by investing them elsewhere. This *forgone investment income* is an implicit cost of doing business.

Finally, suppose you decide to manage your restaurant yourself. Have you escaped the costs of hiring a manager? Not really, because you are still paying an opportunity cost: You could have done something else with your time. We measure the value of your time as the income you *could* have earned by devoting your labor to your next-best income-earning activity. This *forgone labor income*—the wage or salary you could be earning elsewhere—is an implicit cost of your business.

COSTS IN THE SHORT RUN

Remember that, in the short run, one or more of the firm's inputs are fixed. No matter how much output is produced, the quantity of these fixed inputs remains the same. Other inputs, by contrast, can be varied as output changes. Because the firm has these two different types of inputs in the short run, it will also face two different types of costs.

FIXED COSTS Costs of fixed inputs.

The costs of a firm's fixed inputs are called, not surprisingly, **fixed costs.** Like the fixed inputs themselves, fixed costs remain the same no matter what the level of output. In most businesses, we can treat rent, and interest—whether explicit or implicit—as fixed costs, since producing more or less output in the short run will not cause any of these costs to change. Managers typically refer to these costs as their *overhead costs* or, simply, overhead.

VARIABLE COSTS Costs of variable inputs.

The costs of obtaining the firm's variable inputs are its **variable costs.** These costs, like the usage of variable inputs themselves, will rise as output increases. In most businesses, we treat the wages of hourly employees and the costs of raw materials as variable costs, since quantities of both labor and raw materials can usually be adjusted rather rapidly.

MEASURING SHORT-RUN COSTS

In Table 3, we return to our mythical firm—Spotless Car Wash—and ask: What happens to *costs* as output changes in the short run? The first three columns of the table give the relationship between inputs and outputs—the production function—just as in Table 1, which was discussed earlier. But there is one slight difference: In Table 3, we've reversed the order of the columns, putting total output first. We are changing our perspective slightly: Now we want to observe how a change in the quantity of *output* causes the firm's *inputs*—and therefore its *costs*—to change.

In addition to Spotless's production function, we need to know one more thing before we can analyze its costs: what it must *pay* for its inputs. In Table 3, the price of labor is set at $60 per worker per day, and the price of each automated car-washing line at $75 per day.

How do Spotless's short-run costs change as its output changes? Get ready, because there are a surprising number of different ways to answer that question, as illustrated in the remaining columns of Table 3.

TOTAL FIXED COST (TFC) The cost of all inputs that are fixed in the short run.

TOTAL COSTS. Columns 4, 5, and 6 in the table show three different types of total costs. In column 4, we have Spotless's **total fixed cost (TFC)**—the cost of all inputs that are fixed in the short run. Like the quantity of fixed inputs themselves, fixed costs remain the same no matter what the level of output. For Spotless Car Wash, the daily cost of renting or owning one automated line is $75, so total fixed cost is $75. Running down the column, you can see that this cost—because it is fixed—remains the same no matter how many cars are washed each day.

Column 5 shows **total variable cost** (TVC)—the cost of all variable inputs. For Spotless, labor is the only variable input. As output increases, more labor will be needed, so TVC will rise. For example, to wash 90 cars each day requires 2 workers, and each worker must be paid $60 per day, so TVC will be $2 \times \$60 = \$120$. But to wash 130 cars requires 3 workers, so TVC will rise to $3 \times \$60 = \$180$.

Finally, column 6 shows **total cost** (TC)—the sum of all fixed and variable costs:

$$TC = TFC + TVC.$$

For example, at 90 units of output, $TFC = \$75$ and $TVC = \$120$, so $TC = \$75 + \$120 = \$195$. Because total variable cost rises with output, total cost rises as well.

Now look at Figure 5, where we've graphed all three total-cost curves for Spotless Car Wash. Both the TC and TVC curves slope upward—since these costs increase with output. Notice that there are *two* ways in which TFC is represented in the graph. One is the TFC curve, which is a horizontal line, since TFC has the same value at any level of output. The other is the *vertical distance* between the rising TVC and TC curves, since TFC is always the *difference* between TVC and TC. In the graph, this vertical distance must remain the same, at $75, no matter what the level of output.

AVERAGE COST. While total costs are important, sometimes it is more useful to track a firm's costs *per unit* of output, which we call its *average cost*. There are three different types of average cost, each obtained from one of the total cost concepts just discussed.

The firm's **average fixed cost** (AFC) is its total fixed cost divided by the quantity of output:

$$AFC = TFC/Q$$

TOTAL VARIABLE COST (TVC) The cost of all variable inputs used in producing a particular level of output.

TOTAL COST (TC) The costs of all inputs—fixed and variable.

AVERAGE FIXED COST (AFC) Total fixed cost divided by the quantity of output produced.

understand this table

$(4)+(5)$ $\frac{\Delta(6)}{\Delta(1)}$ $(4)/(1)$ $(5)/(1)$ $(6)/(1)$

TABLE 3			SHORT-RUN COSTS FOR SPOTLESS CAR WASH						
(1) Output (per day)	(2) Capital	(3) Labor	(4) TFC	(5) TVC	(6) TC	(7) MC	(8) AFC	(9) AVC	(10) ATC
0	1	0	$75	$0	$75	-	-	-	-
						$2.00			
30	1	1	$75	$60	$135		$2.50	$2.00	$4.50
						$1.00			
90	1	2	$75	$120	$195		$0.83	$1.33	$2.17
						$1.50			
130	1	3	$75	$180	$255		$0.58	$1.38	$1.96
						$2.40			
155	1	4	$75	$240	$315		$0.48	$1.55	$2.03
						$3.53			
172	1	5	$75	$300	$375		$0.44	$1.74	$2.18
						$4.62			
185	1	6	$75	$360	$435		$0.41	$1.95	$2.35

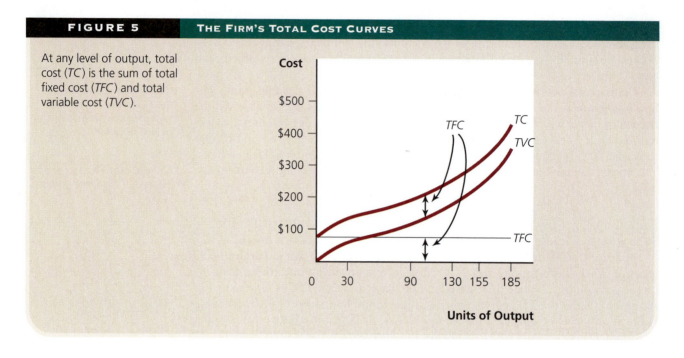

FIGURE 5   **THE FIRM'S TOTAL COST CURVES**

At any level of output, total cost (*TC*) is the sum of total fixed cost (*TFC*) and total variable cost (*TVC*).

No matter what kind of production or what kind of firm, *AFC* will always fall as output rises. Why? Because *TFC* remains constant, so a rise in *Q must* cause the ratio *TFC/Q* to fall. Business managers often refer to this decline in *AFC* as "spreading their overhead" over more output. For example, a restaurant has overhead costs for its buildings, furniture, and cooking equipment. The more meals it serves, the lower will be its overhead cost per meal. Does *AFC* fall with output at Spotless Car Wash? Look at Table 3. When output is 30 units, *AFC* is $75/30 = $2.50. But at 90 units of output, *AFC* drops to $75/90 = $0.83. And *AFC* keeps declining as we continue down the column. The more output produced, the lower is the fixed cost per unit of output.

AVERAGE VARIABLE COST (AVC) Total variable cost divided by the quantity of output produced.

Average variable cost (*AVC*)—in column 9 of the table—is the cost of the variable inputs per unit of output:

$$AVC = TVC/Q$$

For example, at 30 units of output, *TVC* = $60, so *AVC* = *TVC/Q* = $60/30 = $2.00.

What happens to *AVC* as output rises? Based on mathematics alone, we can't be sure. On the one hand, a rise in *Q* raises the denominator of the fraction *TVC/Q*. On the other hand, *TVC* increases, so the numerator rises as well. Thus, it's possible for *AVC* to either rise or fall, depending on whether *TVC* or *Q* rises by a greater percentage. But if you run your finger down the *AVC* column in the table, you'll see a pattern: The *AVC* numbers first decrease and then increase. Economists believe that this pattern of decreasing and then increasing average variable cost is typical at many firms. When plotted in Figure 6, this pattern causes the *AVC* curve to have a *U*-shape. We'll discuss the reason for this characteristic *U*-shape later.

AVERAGE TOTAL COST (ATC) Total cost divided by the quantity of output produced.

Average total cost (*ATC*)—shown in column 10—is the total cost per unit of output:

$$ATC = TC/Q$$

FIGURE 6   AVERAGE AND MARGINAL COSTS

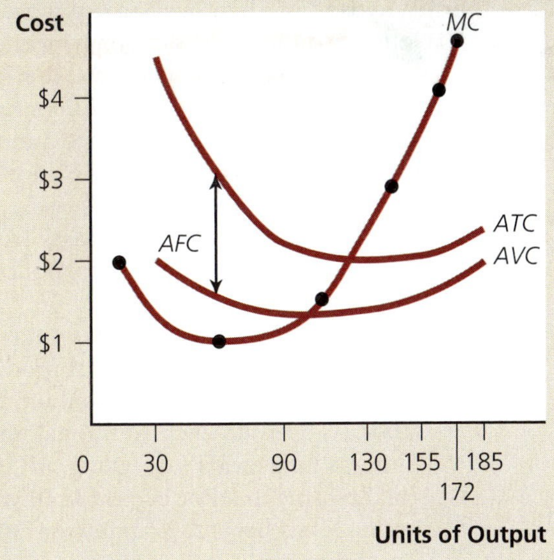

Average variable cost (AVC) and average total cost (ATC) are U-shaped, first decreasing and then increasing. Average fixed cost (AFC)—the vertical distance between ATC and AVC—gets smaller as output increases.

The marginal cost (MC) curve is also U-shaped, reflecting first increasing and then diminishing marginal returns to labor. MC passes through the minimum points of both the AVC and ATC curves.

understand this graph of ufo on 127.

For example, at 90 units of output, TC = $195, so ATC = TC/Q = $195/90 = $2.17. As output rises, ATC, like AVC, can either rise or fall, since both the numerator and denominator of the fraction TC/Q rises. But we usually expect ATC, like AVC, to first decrease and then increase, so the ATC curve will also be U-shaped. However—as you can see in Figure 6—it is not identical to the AVC curve. At each level of output, the difference between the two curves is average *fixed* cost (AFC).

Since AFC declines as output increases, the ATC curve and the AVC curve must get closer and closer together as we move rightward.

MARGINAL COST. The total and average costs we've considered so far tell us about the firm's cost at a particular *level* of output. For many purposes, however, we are more interested in how cost *changes* when output *changes*. This information is provided by another cost concept:

Marginal cost (MC) is the increase in total cost from producing one more unit of output. Mathematically, MC is calculated by dividing the change in total cost (ΔTC) by the change in output (ΔQ):

MARGINAL COST (MC) The increase in total cost from producing one more unit of output.

$$MC = \Delta TC / \Delta Q$$

For Spotless Car Wash, marginal cost is entered in column 7 of Table 3 and graphed in Figure 6. Since marginal cost tells us what happens to total cost *when output changes*, the entries in the table are placed *between* one output level and another. For example, when output rises from 90 to 130, total cost rises from $195 to $255. For this change in output, we have ΔTC = $255 – $195 = $60, while ΔQ = 40, so MC = $60/40 = $1.50. This entry is listed *between* the output levels 90 and 130 in the table and plotted *between* them in Figure 6.

EXPLAINING THE SHAPE OF THE MARGINAL COST CURVE

As you can see in Table 3 (and also in Figure 6), *MC* first declines and then rises. Why is this? Here, we can use what we learned earlier about marginal returns to labor. At low levels of employment and output, there are increasing marginal returns to labor: $MPL = \Delta Q/\Delta L$ is rising. Its reciprocal, $\Delta L/\Delta Q$, must therefore be *falling*. This tells us that *additional units of output can be produced with less and less additional labor*. But since additional labor is the firm's only cost of increasing production, the cost of an additional unit of output (*MC*) must be falling as well. Thus, as long as *MPL* is rising, *MC* must be falling. For Spotless, since *MPL* rises when employment increases from 1 to 2 workers, *MC* must fall as the firm's output rises from 35 units (produced by 1 worker) to 90 units (produced by 2 workers).

At higher levels of output, we have the opposite situation: Diminishing marginal returns set in, and the marginal product of labor ($\Delta Q/\Delta L$) falls. Therefore, its reciprocal ($\Delta L/\Delta Q$) rises: Additional units of output require more and more additional labor. As a result, each additional unit of output costs more and more to produce. Thus, as long as *MPL* is falling, *MC* must be rising. For Spotless, diminishing marginal returns to labor occur for all workers beyond the second, so *MC* rises for all output levels beyond 90 units (the amount produced by 2 workers).

To sum up:

> When MPL *rises*, MC *falls; when* MPL *falls,* MC *rises. Since* MPL *ordinarily rises and then falls,* MC *will ordinarily fall and then rise. This is why the* MC *curve is* U-*shaped.*

THE RELATIONSHIP BETWEEN AVERAGE AND MARGINAL COSTS

Although marginal cost and average cost are not the same, there is an important relationship between them. Look again at Figure 6, and notice that all three curves—*MC*, *AVC* and *ATC*—first fall and then rise, but not all at the same time. The MC curve bottoms out before either the AVC or ATC curve. Further, the *MC* curve intersects each of the average curves *at its lowest point*. These graphical features of Figure 6 are no accident; indeed, they follow from the laws of mathematics. To understand this, let's consider a related example with which you are probably more familiar.

AN EXAMPLE: AVERAGE AND MARGINAL TEST SCORES. Suppose you take five tests in your economics course during the term, with the results listed in Table 4. To your immense pleasure, you score 100 on your first test. Your total score—the total number of points you have received thus far during the term—is 100. Your marginal score—the *change* in your total caused by the most recent test—will also be 100, since your total rose from 0 to 100. Your average score so far is 100 as well.

Now suppose that, for the second test, you forget to study actively. Instead, you just read the text while simultaneously watching music videos and eavesdropping on your roommate's phone conversations. As a result, you get a 50. Your marginal score—the rise in the total—is 50. Since this score is lower than your previous average of 100, the second test will pull your average down. Indeed, whenever you score lower than your previous average, you will always decrease the average. In the table, we see that your average after the second test falls to 75.

TABLE 4	AVERAGE AND MARGINAL TEST SCORES			
Number of Tests Taken	**Total Score**	**Marginal Score**	**Average Score**	
0	0		-	
		100		
1	100		100	
		50		
2	150		75	
		60		
3	210		70	
		70		
4	280		70	
		80		
5	360		72	

Now you start to worry, so you turn off the TV while studying, and your performance improves a bit: you get a 60. Does the improvement in your score—from 50 to 60—increase your *average* score? Absolutely not. Your average will decrease once again, because your *marginal* score of 60 is still lower than your previous average of 75. As we know, when you score lower than your average, you pull the average down—even if you're improving. In the table, we see that your average now falls to 70.

For your fourth exam, you study a bit harder and score a 70. This time, since your score is precisely *equal* to your previous average, the average remains unchanged at 70.

Finally, on your fifth and last test, your score improves once again, this time to 80. This time, you've scored *higher* than your previous average, pulling your average up from 70 to 72.

This example may be easy to understand, because you are used to figuring out your average score in a course as you take additional exams. But the relationship between marginal and average spelled out here is universal—it is the same for grade point averages, batting averages . . . and costs.

AVERAGE AND MARGINAL COST. Now let's apply our previous discussion to a firm's cost curves. Whenever marginal cost is below average cost, we know that the cost of producing *one more* unit of output is *less* than the average cost of all units produced so far. Therefore, producing one more unit will bring the average down. That is, when marginal cost is below average cost, average cost will come down. This applies to both average *variable* cost and average *total* cost.

For example, when Spotless is producing 30 units of output, its *ATC* is $4.50 and its *AVC* is $2.00. But if it increases from 30 to 90 units of output, the marginal cost of these *additional* units is just $1.00. Since *MC* is less than both *ATC* and *AVC* for this change, it pulls both averages down. Graphically, when the *MC* curve lies below one of the average curves (*ATC* or *AVC*), the average curve will slope downward.

Now consider a change in output from 90 units to 130 units. Marginal cost for this change is $1.50. But the *AVC* at 90 units is $1.33. Since *MC* is greater than *AVC*, this change in output will pull *AVC* up. Accordingly, the *AVC* curve begins to slope upward. However, *ATC* at 90 units is $2.17. Since *MC* is still *less* than *ATC*, the *ATC* curve will continue to slope downward.

Finally, consider the change from 130 to 155 units. For this change in output, *MC* is $2.40, which is greater than the previous value of both *AVC* ($1.38) and *ATC* ($1.96). If the firm makes this move, both *AVC* and *ATC* will rise.

Now, let's put together what we know about marginal cost, and what we know about the relationship between marginal and average cost. Remember that marginal cost drops rapidly when the firm begins increasing output from low levels of production, due to increasing marginal returns to labor. Thus, *MC* will initially drop *below* *AVC* and *ATC*, pulling these averages down. But if the firm keeps increasing its output, diminishing returns to labor will set in. *MC* will keep on rising, until it *exceeds* *AVC* and *ATC*. Once this happens, further increases in output will *raise* both *AVC* and *ATC*.

When we state this argument in terms of the curves graphed in Figure 6, we can finally understand why the *AVC* and *ATC* curves are *U*-shaped.

> *At low levels of output, the* MC *curve lies below the* AVC *and* ATC *curves, so these curves will slope downward. At higher levels of output, the* MC *curve will rise above the* AVC *and* ATC *curves, so these curves will slope upward. Thus, as output increases, the average curves will first slope downward and then slope upward. That is, they will have a U-shape.*

There is one more important observation to make before we leave the short run. We've just seen that whenever the *MC* curve lies *below* the *ATC* curve, the *ATC* curve is falling. But when the *MC* curve crosses the *ATC* curve and rises *above* it, the *ATC* curve will be rising. As a result, the *MC* curve must intersect the *ATC* curve at its *minimum* point, as it does in Figure 6. And the same is true of the *AVC* curve.

> *The* MC *curve will intersect the minimum points of the* AVC *and* ATC *curves.*

TIME TO TAKE A BREAK. By now, your mind may be swimming with concepts and terms: total, average, and marginal cost curves; fixed and variable costs; explicit and implicit costs. . . . We are covering a lot of ground here and still have a bit more to cover: production and cost in the *long run*.

As difficult as it may seem to keep these concepts straight, they will become increasingly easy to handle as you use them in the chapters to come. But it's best not to overload your brain with too much new material at one time. So if this is your first trip through this chapter, now is a good time for a break. Then, when you're fresh, come back and review the material you've read so far. When the terms and concepts start to feel familiar, you are ready to move on to the long run.

PRODUCTION AND COST IN THE LONG RUN

Most of the business firms you have contact with—such as your supermarket, the stores where you buy new clothes, and your telephone company—plan to be around for quite some time. They have a long-term planning horizon, as well as a short-term one. But so far, we've considered the behavior of costs only in the short run.

In the long run, costs behave differently because the firm can adjust *all* of its inputs in any way it wants:

> *In the long run, there are no fixed inputs or fixed costs; all inputs and all costs are variable. The firm must decide what* combination *of inputs to use in producing any level of output.*

How will the firm choose? Its goal is to earn the highest possible profit, and to do this, it must follow the *least-cost rule:*

> *To produce any given level of output, the firm will choose the input mix with the lowest cost.*

Let's apply the least-cost rule to Spotless Car Wash. Suppose we want to know the cost of washing 185 cars per day. In the short run, of course, Spotless does not have to worry about how it would produce this level of output: It is stuck with one automated line, and the only way to wash 185 cars is to hire 6 workers (see Table 3). Total cost in the short run will be $6 \times \$60 + \$75 = \$435$.

In the long-run, however, Spotless can vary the number of automated lines as well as the number of workers. Its *long-run* production function will tell us all the different combinations of *both* inputs that can be used to produce any output level. Suppose four different input combinations can be used to wash 185 cars per day. These are listed in Table 5. Combination *A* uses the least capital and the most labor—no automated lines at all and 9 workers washing the cars by hand. Combination *D* uses the most capital and the least labor—3 automated lines with only 3 units of labor. Since each automated line costs $75 per day and each worker costs $60 per day, it is easy to calculate the cost of each production method. Spotless will choose the one with the lowest cost—combination *C*, with 2 automated lines and 4 workers, for a total cost of $390 per day.

Retracing our steps, we have found that if Spotless wants to wash 185 cars per day, it will examine the different methods of doing so and select the one with the least cost. Once it has determined the cheapest production method, the other, more expensive methods can be ignored.

Table 6 shows the results of going through this procedure for several different levels of output. The second column, **long-run total cost (LRTC)**, tells us the cost of producing each quantity of output *when the least-cost input mix is chosen.* For each output level, different production methods are examined, the cheapest one is chosen, and the others are ignored. Notice that the *LRTC* of 0 units of output is $0. This will always be true for any firm. In the long run, all inputs can be adjusted as the firm wishes, and the cheapest way to produce 0 output is to use *no* inputs at all.

LONG-RUN TOTAL COST (LRTC) The cost of producing each quantity of output when the least-cost input mix is chosen in the long run.

TABLE 5	FOUR WAYS TO WASH 185 CARS PER DAY		
Quantity of Method	**Quantity of Capital**	**Labor**	**Cost**
A	0	$9	$540
B	1	$6	$435
C	2	$4	$390
D	3	$3	$405

TABLE 6	LONG-RUN COSTS FOR SPOTLESS CAR WASH	
Output	LRTC	LRATC
0	$0	-
30	$100	$3.33
90	$195	$2.17
130	$255	$1.96
155	$315	$2.03
172	$360	$2.09
185	$390	$2.11
200	$450	$2.25
250	$650	$2.60
300	$1,200	$4.00

DANGEROUS CURVES

When you read the *least-cost rule* of production, you might begin to think that the firm's goal is to have the *least possible cost.* But this is not true. To convince yourself, just realize that the least possible cost would be zero, and in the long run this could be achieved by not using any inputs and producing nothing!

The least-cost rule says that any *given* level of output should be produced at the lowest possible cost. The firm's goal is to maximize *profit,* and the least-cost rule helps it do that. For example, if the firm is considering producing 10 units of output, and there are two ways to produce that number of units—one costing $6,000 and the other costing $5,000—the firm should always choose the latter, because it is cheaper. If it chose the former, and it ended up producing 10 units of output, it would not be earning the highest possible profit. But notice that $5,000 is not the "lowest possible cost" for the firm; it is the lowest possible cost *for producing 10 units.*

LONG-RUN AVERAGE TOTAL COST (LRATC) The cost per unit of output in the long run, when all inputs are variable.

(For comparison, what is the *short*-run total cost of producing 0 units? Why can it never be $0?)

The third column in Table 6 gives the **long-run average total cost (LRATC)**, the cost per unit of output in the long run:

$$LRATC = LRTC/Q.$$

Long-run average total cost is similar to average total cost defined earlier: Both are obtained by dividing total cost by the level of output. There is one important difference, however: In calculating *LRATC*, we use long-run total cost (*LRTC*) in the numerator; to calculate *ATC*, we use short-run total cost (*TC*). Thus, *LRATC* tells us the cost per unit when the firm can vary all of its inputs and always chooses the cheapest input mix possible. *ATC*, however, tells us the cost per unit when the firm is stuck with some collection of fixed inputs.

THE RELATIONSHIP BETWEEN LONG-RUN AND SHORT-RUN COSTS

If you compare Table 6 (long run) with Table 3 (short run), you will see something important: for some output levels, *LRTC* is smaller than *TC*. For example, Spotless can wash 185 cars for an *LRTC* of $390. But earlier, we saw that in the short run, the *TC* of washing these same 185 cars was $435. To understand the reason for this difference, look back at Table 5, which lists the four different ways of washing 185 cars per day. In the short run, the firm is stuck with just one automated line, so its only option is method *B*. In the long run, however, the firm can change *all* of its inputs, so it can choose any of the five methods of production, including method *C*, which is the cheapest. In many cases, the freedom to choose among different production methods enables the firm to select a cheaper input mix in the long run than it can in the short run. Thus, in the long run, the firm may be able to save money.

But not always. At some output levels, the freedom to adjust all inputs doesn't save the firm a dime. To wash 130 cars, for example, the long-run cost—the cost when using the cheapest input mix—is the same as the short-run total cost ($LRTC = TC = \$255$). For this output level, it must be that the *short-run* input mix is also the least-cost input mix. Thus, if Spotless wants to wash 130 cars per day, it would choose in the long run the same production method it is already using in the short run. At this output level, the firm could not save money by adjusting its capital in the long run. (There are other output levels listed in the tables for which $LRTC = TC$. Can you find them?)

What we have found for Spotless Car Wash is true for all firms:

> *Long-run total cost can be less than or equal to, but never greater than, short-run total cost (LRTC ≤ TC).*

We can also state this relationship in terms of *average costs*. That is, we can divide both sides of the inequality by Q, and obtain $LRTC/Q \leq TC/Q$. Using our definitions, this translates to $LRATC \leq ATC$. Long-run average cost can be less than or equal to, but never greater than short-run average total cost ($LRATC \leq ATC$).

AVERAGE COST AND PLANT SIZE. Often, economists refer to the collection of fixed inputs at the firm's disposal as its **plant**. For example, the plant of a computer manufacturer such as Compaq would consist of its factory building and the assembly lines inside it. The plant of the Hertz car-rental company would include all of its automobiles and rental offices. For Spotless Car Wash, we've assumed that the plant is simply the company's capital equipment—the automated lines for washing cars. If Spotless were to add to its capital, then each time it acquired another automated line, it would have a different—and larger—plant. Viewed in this way, we can distinguish between the long run and the short run as follows: in *the long run, the firm can change the size of its plant; in the short run, it is stuck with its current plant.*

Now think about the *ATC* curve, which tells us the firm's average total cost in the short run. This curve is always drawn for a specific plant. That is, the *ATC* curve tells us how average costs behave in the short run, *when the firm uses a plant of a given size*. If the firm had a different size plant, it would be moving along a different *ATC* curve. In fact, there is a different *ATC* curve for each different plant the firm could have. In the long run, then, the firm can choose on which *ATC* curve it wants to operate. And, as we know, it will always choose that *ATC* curve—among all of the *ATC* curves available—that gives it the lowest possible average total cost. This insight tells us how we can graph the firm's *LRATC* curve.

GRAPHING THE LRATC CURVE. Look at Figure 7, which shows several different *ATC* curves for Spotless Car Wash. There is a lot going on in this figure, so let's take it one step at a time. First, find the curve labeled ATC_1. This is our familiar *ATC* curve—the same one shown in Figure 6—which we used to find Spotless's average total cost in the short run, when it was stuck with one automated line. The other *ATC* curves refer to *different* plants that Spotless *might* have had instead. For example, the curve labeled ATC_0 shows how average total cost would behave if Spotless had a plant with 0 automated lines; ATC_2 shows average total cost with 2 automated lines, and so on. Since, in the long run, the firm can choose what size plant to operate, it can also choose on which of these *ATC* curves it wants to operate. And, as we know, in the long run it will always choose the plant with the lowest possible average total cost.

PLANT The collection of fixed inputs at a firm's disposal.

| FIGURE 7 | LONG-RUN AVERAGE TOTAL COST |

Average-total cost curves ATC_0, ATC_1, ATC_2, and ATC_3 show average costs when the firm has 0, 1, 2, and 3 production lines, respectively. The *LRATC* curve combines portions of all the firm's *ATC* curves. The firm will choose the lowest cost *ATC* curve for each level of output.

Envelope of short-run average cost curves

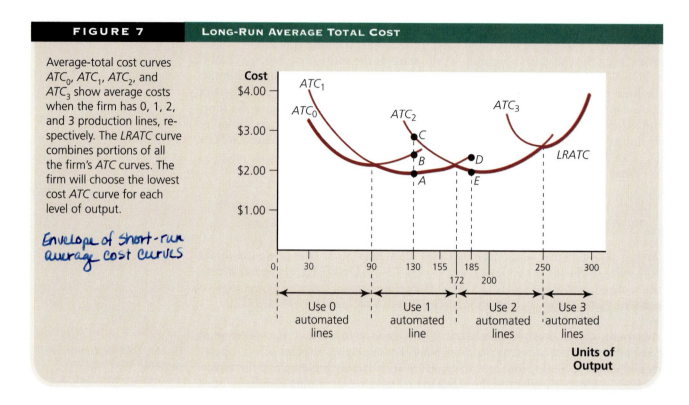

Let's take a specific example. Suppose that Spotless decides it wants to wash 130 cars per day. In the long run, what size plant should it choose? Scanning the different *ATC* curves in Figure 7, we see that the lowest possible per-unit cost—$1.96 per car—is at point *A* along ATC_1. The best plant, therefore, will have just one automated line. For this output level, Spotless would never choose a plant with 0 lines, since it would then have to operate on ATC_0 at point *B*. Since point *B* is higher than point *A*, we know that point *B* represents a larger per-unit cost. Nor would the firm choose a plant with 2 lines—operating on ATC_2 at point *C*—for this would mean a still larger per-unit cost. Of all the possibilities, only point *A* along ATC_1 enables Spotless to achieve the lowest per-unit cost for washing 130 cars. Thus, to produce 130 units of output in the long run, Spotless would choose to operate at point *A* on ATC_1. Thus, point *A* is the *LRATC* of 130 units.

Now suppose instead that Spotless wanted to produce 185 units of output in the long run. A plant with 1 automated line is no longer the best choice. Instead, the firm would choose a plant with 2 automated lines. How do we know? For an output of 185, the firm could choose point *D* on ATC_1, or point *E* on ATC_2. Since point *E* is lower, it is the better choice. At this point, average total cost would be $2.00, so this would be the *LRATC* of 185 units.

Continuing in this way, we could find the *LRATC* for every output level Spotless might produce. To produce any given level of output, the firm will always operate on the *lowest ATC* curve available. As output increases, it will move along an *ATC* curve until another, lower *ATC* curve becomes available—one with lower costs. At that point, the firm will increase its plant size, so it can move to the lower *ATC* curve. For example, as Spotless increases its output level from 90 to 172 units of output, it will continue to use a plant with 1 automated line, and move along ATC_1. But if it wants to produce more than 172 units in the long run, it will increase its plant to 2 automated lines, and begin moving along ATC_2.

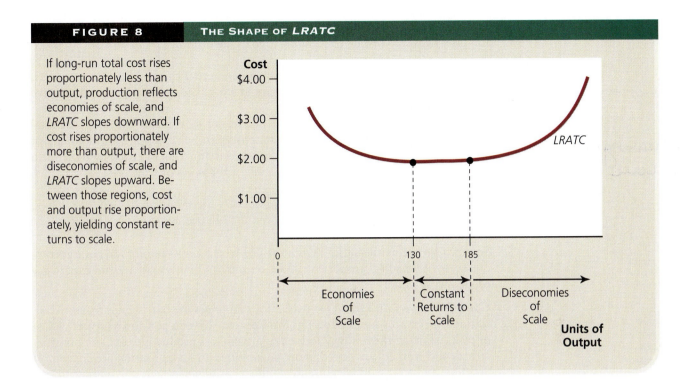

FIGURE 8 — **THE SHAPE OF *LRATC***

If long-run total cost rises proportionately less than output, production reflects economies of scale, and *LRATC* slopes downward. If cost rises proportionately more than output, there are diseconomies of scale, and *LRATC* slopes upward. Between those regions, cost and output rise proportionately, yielding constant returns to scale.

Thus, we can trace out Spotless's *LRATC* curve by combining just the lowest portions of all the *ATC* curves from which the firm can choose. In the figure, this is the thick, scalloped-shaped curve. A firm's *LRATC* curve combines portions of each *ATC* curve available to the firm in the long run. For each output level, the firm will always choose to operate on the *ATC* curve with the lowest possible cost.

Figure 7 also gives us a clear view of the different options facing the firm in the short run and the long run. Once Spotless builds a plant with 1 automated line, its options in the short run are limited—it can only move along ATC_1. If it wants to increase its output from 130 to 185 units, it must move from point *A* to point *D*. But in the long run, it can move along its *LRATC* curve—from point *A* to point *E*—by changing the size of its plant.

More generally,

> *In the short run, a firm can only move along its current* ATC *curve. In the long run, however, it can move from one* ATC *curve to another, by varying the size of its plant. As it does so, it will also be moving along its* LRATC *curve.*

EXPLAINING THE SHAPE OF THE *LRATC* CURVE

In Figure 7, the *LRATC* curve has a scalloped look, because the firm can only choose among four different plants. But many firms—especially large ones—can choose among hundreds or even thousands of different plant sizes. Each plant would be represented by a different *ATC* curve, so there would be hundreds of *ATC* curves crowded into the figure. As a result, the scallops would disappear, and the *LRATC* curve would appear as a smooth curve, like the dashed line in Figure 7.

In Figure 8, which reproduces this smoothed-out *LRATC* curve, you can see that the curve is U-shaped—much like the *AVC* and *ATC* curves you learned about earlier. That is, as output increases, long-run average costs first decline, then remain constant, and finally rise. Although there is no law or rule of logic that requires an

LRATC curve to have all three of these phases, in many industries this seems to be the case. Let's see why, by considering each of the three phases in turn.

ECONOMIES OF SCALE. When an increase in output causes *LRATC* to decrease, we say that the firm is enjoying **economies of scale:** The more output produced, the lower is cost per unit.

On a purely mathematical level, economies of scale mean that long-run total cost is rising by a smaller proportion than output. For example, if a doubling of output (*Q*) can be accomplished with less than a doubling of costs, then the ratio *LRTC/Q* = *LRATC* will decline, and. . .voilà! Economies of scale.

> *When long-run total cost rises proportionately less than output, production is characterized by economies of scale, and the* LRATC *curve slopes downward.*

So much for the mathematics. But in the real world, *why* should total costs ever increase by a smaller proportion than output? Why should a firm experience economies of scale?

Gains from Specialization. One reason for economies of scale is gains from specialization. At very low levels of output, workers may have to perform a greater variety of tasks, slowing them down and making them less productive. But as output increases and workers are added, more possibilities for specialization are created. At Spotless, an increase in output and employment might permit one worker to specialize in taking cash from customers, a second to drive the cars onto the line, a third to towel them down, a fourth to work on advertising, and so on. Since each worker is more productive, output will increase by a greater proportion than costs.

The greatest opportunities for increased specialization occur when a firm is producing at a relatively low level of output, with a relatively small plant and small workforce. Thus, economies of scale are more likely to occur at lower levels of output.

More Efficient Use of Lumpy Inputs. Another explanation for economies of scale involves the "lumpy" nature of many types of plant and equipment. By this, we mean that some types of inputs cannot be increased in tiny increments, but rather must be increased in large jumps.

A doctor, for example, needs the use of an x-ray machine in order to serve her patients. Unless she can share with other doctors (which may not be possible), she must buy one or more *whole* machines—she cannot buy a half or a fifth of an x-ray machine. Suppose a single machine can service up to 500 patients per month and costs $2,000 per month (in interest payments or forgone investment income). Then the more patients the doctor sees (up to 500), the lower will be the cost of the machine per patient. For example, if she sees 100 patients each month, the cost per patient will be $2,000/100 = $20; if she sees 500 patients, the cost per patient drops to $2,000/500 = $4. If much of the doctor's plant and equipment are lumpy in this way, her *LRATC* curve might continue to decline over some range of output.

We see this phenomenon in many types of businesses: Plant and equipment must be purchased in large lumps, and a low cost per unit is achieved only at high levels of output. If you decide to start a pizza-delivery business on campus, you will have to purchase or rent at least one pizza oven. If you can make 200 pizzas per day with a single oven, then your fixed (oven) costs will be the same whether you bake 1, 10, 50, 100, or 200 pizzas.

Other inputs besides equipment can also be lumpy in this way. Restaurants must pay a yearly license fee and are not permitted to buy part of a license if their output is small. An answering service must have a receptionist on duty at all times, even if only a few calls come in each day. A theater must have at least one ticket seller and one projectionist, regardless of how many people come to see the show. In all of these cases, an increase in output allows the firm to spread the cost of lumpy inputs over greater amounts of output, lowering cost *per unit of output*.

Making more efficient use of lumpy inputs will have more impact on *LRATC* at low levels of output, when these inputs make up a greater proportion of the firm's total costs. At higher levels of output, the impact is smaller. For example, suppose a restaurant must pay a yearly license fee of $1,000. If output doubles from 1,000 to 2,000 meals per year, license costs per meal served will fall from $1.00 to $0.50. But if output doubles from 10,000 to 20,000 meals, license costs per meal drop from $0.10 to $0.05—a hardly noticeable difference. Thus, spreading lumpy inputs across more output—like the gains from specialization—is more likely to create economies of scale at relatively low levels of output. This is another reason why the typical *LRATC* curve—as illustrated in Figure 8—will slope downward at relatively low levels of output.

A look at Table 6 tells us that there are, indeed, economies of scale for Spotless at low levels of output. While it costs $100 to wash 30 cars, it costs only $195 to wash 90 cars. Output triples, but costs increase by only $95/$100, or 95 percent, so *LRATC* falls. Spotless is clearly enjoying economies of scale. Indeed, Figure 8 shows that it will experience economies of scale for all output levels up to 130 units.

DISECONOMIES OF SCALE. As output continues to increase, most firms will reach a point where bigness begins to cause problems. This is true even in the long run, when the firm is free to increase its plant size as well as its workforce. For example, a large firm may require more layers of management, so communication and decision making become more time consuming and costly. It may also be more difficult to screen out misfits among new hires and to monitor those already working at the firm, so there is an increase in mistakes, shirking of responsibilities, and even theft from the firm. All of these problems contribute to rises in *LRTC* as output increases therefore work in the opposite direction to the forces helping to create economies of scale. Eventually, these problems may become so serious that a doubling of output will cause *more* than a doubling of total cost. When this happens, *LRATC* will rise. More generally,

> When long-run total cost rises more than in proportion to output, there are **diseconomies of scale**, and the LRATC curve slopes upward.

While economies of scale are more likely at low levels of output, *di*seconomies of scale are more likely at higher output levels. In Figure 8, you can see that Spotless experiences noticeable diseconomies of scale when it is washing more than 185 cars per day.

CONSTANT RETURNS TO SCALE. In Figure 8, you can see that for output levels between 130 and 185, the smoothed out *LRATC* curve is roughly flat. Over this range of output, *LRATC* remains approximately constant as output increases. Here, output and *LRTC* rise by roughly the same proportion:

> When both output and long-run total cost rise by the same proportion, production is characterized by **constant returns to scale**, and the LRATC curve is flat.

Why would a firm experience constant returns to scale? We have seen that as output increases, the impact of specialization and more efficient use of lumpy inputs

DISECONOMIES OF SCALE
Long-run average total cost increases as output increases.

CONSTANT RETURNS TO SCALE Long-run average total cost is unchanged as output increases.

will diminish, while the problems of bigness become more serious. At some level of production, these forces may just cancel out, so that an increase in output does not change *LRATC* at all. The firm will then have constant returns to scale until the problems of bigness begin to dominate. Constant returns to scale are most likely to occur at some *intermediate* range of output.

In sum, when we look at the behavior of *LRATC*, we often expect a pattern like the following: economies of scale (decreasing *LRATC*) at low levels of output, constant returns to scale (constant *LRATC*) at some intermediate level of output, and diseconomies of scale (increasing *LRATC*) at high levels of output. This is why *LRATC* curves—like the one drawn in Figure 8—are typically *U*-shaped.

Of course, even *U*-shaped *LRATC* curves will have different appearances at different firms. Indeed, *LRATC* curves need not be *U*-shaped at all. In later chapters, you will see that the shape of an *LRATC* curve has much to tell us about the economy: about the size of firms, the nature of competition among them, and the problems faced by government regulators. But you have already learned enough about production and costs to understand an important and ongoing problem in another country—one caused, at least in part, by a failure to understand the logic of cost curves.

USING THE THEORY

COST CURVES AND ECONOMIC REFORM IN RUSSIA

At the beginning of this chapter, it was suggested that Russian manufacturing firms may be different from their counterparts in other countries. Now we can discuss one of the important differences: Russian firms seem to require more inputs—labor, capital, energy, and raw materials—than, say, American firms producing similar product. There are many reasons for this: an antiquated capital stock, poor infrastructure (e.g., roads and telecommunications), and the absence of management skills suited to the privately owned firm. But the problem has been exacerbated by a simple misunderstanding of production and cost made by generations of Soviet leaders.

First, a fact: The Soviet economy relied heavily on *monopolies*—single enterprises that were the sole producers of a good for the entire country. As late as 1991, Soviet government economists reported that out of 7,664 major product lines, 5,884 were manufactured by a single producer![2] Most of these enterprises remain intact today, and as a result, they operate on a much larger scale than their Western counterparts.

Why so many monopolies? There were essentially two reasons. First, in a command economy, it was easier for the state to monitor and control fewer large enterprises than a greater number of small ones. Second, there was an ideological bias toward bigness: Soviet leaders from Vladimir Lenin to Leonid Brezhnev viewed the capitalist practice of having many firms, each producing the same item, as unnecessarily wasteful and duplicative. Why, they asked, should several firms make different brands of toothpaste that are more or less the same when a single manufacturer can produce toothpaste? Why have several competing automobile companies, each with its own separate design divisions, management teams, and distribution network, when a single enterprise would need only *one* design division, *one* management team, and *one* distribution network? Soviet leaders believed that avoiding wasteful duplication would enable their industries to operate more efficiently than those in the capitalist world would, using fewer inputs for any level of output. In effect, they believed that their enterprises could continue to enjoy economies of scale until each one was producing for the entire Soviet market. This view of costs

2.   Marshall Goldman, *What Went Wrong with Perestroika* (New York: W.W. Norton, 1992), p. 154.

FIGURE 9 — THE SOVIET VIEW OF PRODUCTION

Planners in the former Soviet Union imagined—incorrectly—that their enterprises could enjoy economies of scale until each was producing for the entire market.

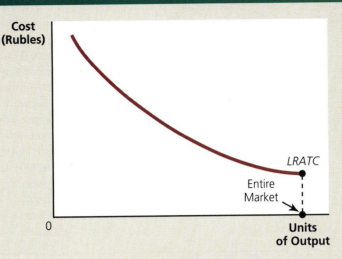

FIGURE 10 — SOVIET PRODUCTION

Newly privatized Russian firms have been operating in the region of diseconomies of scale—at levels like Q_2. If they reduce output in the short run to Q_3, they will find average costs rising along *ATC*.

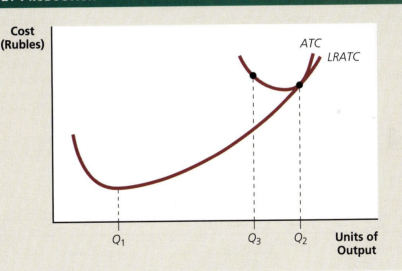

is illustrated in Figure 9, where the *LRATC* curve slopes downward over the entire range of output.[3] Had the Soviet leadership been right—had Figure 9 been an accurate portrayal of a typical firm's *LRATC* curve—then having monopoly enterprises producing for the entire market might have made sense.

But they were not right: With the transformation to a market economy, it has become apparent that production in Russia—as elsewhere—is mostly characterized by *U*-shaped *LRATC* curves, like the one in Figure 10. For years, the huge Russian enterprises have been operating in the region of *dis*economies of scale, at output levels like Q_2. As a result, their per-unit costs have been pushed higher than necessary.

---

3. In later chapters, you will see that there are, indeed, firms whose *LRATC* curves slope everywhere downward. But these firms are the exception, not the rule.

If production had been organized differently—with several firms, each producing a smaller quantity of output, like Q_1—costs per unit could have been lower.

Today, the newly privatized Russian firms are in a serious jam, both in the short run and in the long run. In the short run, when plant size is fixed, any reduction in output would move the firm along its *ATC* curve, not its *LRATC* curve. Thus, reducing output—say, to Q_3—might *raise* per-unit costs rather than lower them.

But even over a longer time horizon, these firms will not find it easy to change their scale of operations and move along their *LRATC* curves. Unlike many large Western firms—which have grown large by taking over smaller firms or building multiple plants in different parts of the country—many huge Russian firms were *built* as single-plant enterprises. The factory, the equipment, the technology—all were designed for a single plant, so it is not so easy to reduce plant size by spinning off a part of the operation. In many cases, the entire facility will have to be redesigned from the ground up in order for the firm to move down its *LRATC* curve and lower its costs per unit. For these Russian firms, the long run will be very long indeed.

S U M M A R Y

Business firms combine inputs to produce outputs. While some production takes place in the household, production through business firms with employees allows gains from specialization (each worker may specialize in one aspect of production), lower transaction costs, and reduced risk for employees.

A firm's *production function* describes the maximum output it can produce using different quantities of inputs. In the *short run*, at least one of the firm's inputs is fixed. In the *long run*, all inputs can be varied.

A firm's *cost of production* is the opportunity cost of its owners—everything they must give up in order to produce output. In the short run, some costs are *fixed* and independent of the level of production. Other costs—*variable costs*—change as production increases. *Marginal cost* is the change in total cost from producing one more unit of output. The *mar-*

ginal cost curve has a *U* shape, reflecting the underlying marginal product of labor. A variety of average cost curves can be defined. *The average variable cost curve* and the *average total cost curve* are each U-shaped, reflecting the relationship between average and marginal cost.

In the long run, all costs are variable. The profit-maximizing firm's *long-run total cost curve* indicates the cost of producing each quantity of output with the least-cost input mix. The related *long-run average total cost (LRATC) curve* is formed by combining portions of different *ATC* curves—each portion representing a different plant size. The shape of the *LRATC* reflects the nature of returns to scale. It slopes downward when there are economies of scale, slopes upward when there are diseconomies of scale, and is flat when there are constant returns to scale.

K E Y   T E R M S

business firm	fixed input	sunk costs	marginal cost (MC)
profit	variable input	explicit costs	long-run total cost (LRTC)
sole proprietorship	total product	implicit costs	long-run average total cost
partnership	marginal product of labor	fixed costs	(LRATC)
corporation	(MPL)	variable costs	plant
transaction costs	increasing marginal returns	total fixed cost (TFC)	economies of scale
diversification	to labor	total variable cost (TVC)	diseconomies of scale
technology	diminishing marginal returns	total cost (TC)	constant returns to scale
production function	to labor	average fixed cost (AFC)	
long run	law of diminishing marginal	average variable cost (AVC)	
short run	returns	average total cost (ATC)	

R E V I E W   Q U E S T I O N S

1. What are the three types of business firm? Discuss the pros and cons of each type.

2. Why is most production activity carried out by firms, rather than by independent contractors?

3. A home builder incurs the following costs. Which are examples of transaction costs? Why?
   a. Cost of lumber
   b. Lawyer's fees for handling the legal work connected with the purchase of land
   c. Interest expense on a loan to buy new equipment
   d. Opportunity cost of time spent gathering bids from subcontractors

4. During the 1980s, there was a series of mergers between firms. Often, these brought together firms that made totally different products. Explain one possible motive for these combinations.

5. Given the advantages of larger firm size, why don't we expect companies to grow larger without limit?

6. Discuss the distinction between the short run and the long run as those terms relate to production.

7. Which of the following inputs would likely be classified as fixed and which as variable over a time horizon of one month? Why?
   a. Ovens to the Nabisco bakery
   b. Wood to the La-Z-Boy Chair Co.
   c. Oranges to Minute Maid Juice Co.
   d. Labor to a McDonald's hamburger franchise
   e. Cars to the Hertz Car-Rental Company.

8. Explain the difference between the total output of a firm and the marginal product of labor (*MPL*) at that firm. How are they related?

9. Classify the following as fixed or variable costs for a time horizon of 6 months. Justify your categorization.
   a. GM's outlay for steel
   b. Pillsbury's spending on flour
   c. *Tenured* professors' salaries at Ohio State
   d. The cost of newsprint for the *New York Times*

10. At home on Vulcan one summer, Mr. Spock spent all his time working on an invention to give McCoy a severe shock whenever he said, "Damn it, Jim, I'm a doctor." Alas, the invention didn't work. Spock consoled himself with the idea that, since he had used Starfleet's equipment and lab, at least his failed attempt hadn't cost him anything. Is his thinking "logical"? Explain.

11. Can long-run total cost (*LRTC*) ever be greater than short-run total cost (*TC*)? Why or why not?

12. Explain the "*U*" shape of a typical long-run average cost curve. Specifically, why is the curve downward sloping at lower levels of output and upward sloping at higher levels?

13. Explain the dilemma faced by many Russian enterprises today.

PROBLEMS AND EXERCISES

1. The following table shows total output (in tax returns completed per day) of the accounting firm of Hoodwink and Finagle:

Number of Accountants	Number of Returns per Day
0	0
1	5
2	12
3	17
4	20
5	22

   Assuming the quantity of capital (computers, adding machines, desks, etc.) remains constant at all output levels:
   a. Calculate the marginal product of each accountant.
   b. Over what range of employment do you see increasing returns to labor? Diminishing returns?
   c. Explain why *MPL* might behave this way in the context of an accounting firm.

2. The following table gives the short-run and long-run total cost for various levels of output of Consolidated National Acme, Inc.:

Q	TC₁	TC₂
0	0	350
1	300	400
2	400	435
3	465	465
4	495	505
5	560	560
6	600	635
7	700	735

   a. Which column, *TC₁* or *TC₂*, gives long-run total cost, and which gives short-run total cost? How do you know?
   b. For each level of output, find short-run *TFC*, *TVC*, *AFC*, *AVC*, and *MC*.
   c. At what output level would the firm's short-run and long-run input mixes be the same?
   d. When producing two units, Consolidated's managers decide to double production to four units. So they simply double all of their inputs in the long run. Comment on their managerial skill.
   e. Over what range of output do you see economies of scale? Diseconomies of scale? Constant returns to scale?

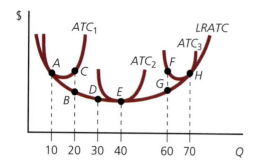

3. Ludmilla's House of Schnitzel is currently producing 10 schnitzels a day at point *A* on the preceding diagram. Ludmilla's business partner, Hans (an impatient sort), orders her to double production immediately.

   a. What point will likely illustrate Ludmilla's cost situation for the near future? Why?

   b. If Ludmilla wants to keep producing 20 schnitzels, at what point does she want to be eventually? How can she get there?

   c. Eventually, Ludmilla and company do very well, expanding until they find themselves making 70 schnitzels a day. But after a few years Ludmilla discovers that profit was greater when she produced 20 schnitzels per day. She wants to scale back production to 20 schnitzels per day—laying off workers, selling off equipment, renting less space, and producing fewer schnitzels. Hans wants to reduce output by just

   cutting back on flour and milk and laying off workers. Who's right? Discuss the situation with reference to the relevant points on the diagram.

   d. Does the figure tell us what output Ludmilla should aim for? Why or why not?

4. In a recent year, a long, hard winter gave rise to stronger-than-normal demand for heating oil. The following summer was characterized by strong demand for gasoline by vacationers. Show what these two events might have done to the short-run *MC*, *AFC*, *AVC*, and *ATC* curves of Continental Airlines.

5. Ever think about starting your own business when you finish school? One thing to consider carefully is the opportunity cost of your own time, and that will depend on what you *could have* earned, had you taken your next best employment opportunity instead. For current information on earnings by occupation in your state, consult the *Occupational Employment Statistics* on the Bureau of Labor Statistics Web site at http://stats.bls.gov/oes/state/oessrch2.htm.

   Think about the job you would most likely have if you worked for somebody else. Now go to the BLS Web site and find out the opportunity cost of working for yourself, instead.

CHALLENGE QUESTIONS

1. Draw the long-run total cost and long-run average cost curves for a firm that experiences:

   a. Constant returns to scale over all output levels

   b. Diseconomies of scale over low levels of output, constant returns to scale over intermediate levels of output, and economies of scale over high output levels. Does this pattern of costs make sense? Why or why not?

2. The following curve shows the *marginal product* of labor for a firm at different levels of output.

   a. Show what the corresponding total product curve would look like (in a diagram like Figure 4).

   b. Do the total and marginal product curves for this firm ever exhibit diminishing marginal returns to labor? Increasing marginal returns to labor?

CHAPTER 6

HOW FIRMS MAKE DECISIONS: PROFIT MAXIMIZATION

In early 1996, the managers of Nintendo America, Inc., knew that they had a winner on their hands: the Nintendo 64 video-game player. With this new product, players would be able to jump, fly, and even swim through a variety of three-dimensional fantasy worlds, with images more spectacular and action much faster than in any competing product.

Then came the hard questions. Where should the new product be produced: Japan, the United States, or perhaps Hong Kong? How should the company raise the funds to pay the costs of production? When should it bring the product to market? How much should it spend on advertising and in which types of media? And finally, what price should the company charge, and how many units should it plan to produce?

These last decisions—how much to produce and what price to charge—are the focus of this chapter. In the end, Nintendo planned to produce 500,000 units, and decided to charge $199. But why didn't it charge a lower price that would allow it to sell more output? Or a higher price that would give it more profit on each unit sold?

Although this chapter concentrates on firms' decisions about price and output level, the tools you will learn apply to many other firms' decisions. How much should MasterCard spend on advertising? How late should Starbucks keep its coffee shops open? How many copies should *Newsweek* give away free to potential subscribers? Should movie theaters offer Wednesday afternoon showings that only a few people attend? This chapter will help you understand how firms answer these sorts of questions.

THE GOAL OF PROFIT MAXIMIZATION

To analyze decision making at the firm, let's go back to one of the basic principles, first introduced in Chapter 1: *maximization subject to constraints*. What is the firm trying to maximize?

Economists have given this question a lot of thought. Some firms—especially large ones—are complex institutions where many different groups of people work together. A firm's owners will usually want the firm to earn as much profit as possible. But the workers and managers who actually run the firm may have other agendas. They may try to divert the firm away from profit maximization in order to benefit themselves. For now, let's assume that workers and managers are faithful servants of the firm's owners. That is:

MAXIMIZATION SUBJECT TO CONSTRAINTS

> *We will view the firm as a single economic decision maker whose goal is to maximize its owners' profit.*

Why do we make this assumption? Because it has proven so useful in understanding how firms behave. Toward the end of the chapter, we'll come back to the important topic of different groups within the firm and the potential conflicts among them.

UNDERSTANDING PROFIT

Profit is defined as the firm's *sales revenue* minus its *costs of production*. There is widespread agreement over how to measure the firm's revenue, the flow of money into the firm. But there are two different conceptions of the firm's costs, and each of them leads to a different definition of profit.

TWO DEFINITIONS OF PROFIT

One conception of costs is that used by accountants. With a few exceptions, accountants consider only *explicit* costs, where money is actually paid out.[1] If we deduct only the costs recognized by accountants, we get one definition of profit:

ACCOUNTING PROFIT Total revenue minus accounting costs.

$$\text{Accounting profit} = \text{Total revenue} - \text{Accounting costs}$$

But economics, as you have learned, has a much broader view of cost—*opportunity cost*. For the firm's owners, opportunity cost is the total value of *everything* sacrificed to produce output. This includes not only the explicit costs recognized by accountants—such as wages and salaries and outlays on raw materials—but also *implicit costs,* when something is given up but no money changes hands. For example, if an owner contributes his own time or her own money to the firm, there will be forgone wages or forgone investment income—both implicit costs for the firm.

This broader conception of costs leads to a second definition of profit:

ECONOMIC PROFIT Total revenue minus all costs of production, explicit and implicit.

$$\text{Economic profit} = \text{Total revenue} - All \text{ costs of production}$$
$$= \text{Total revenue} - (\text{Explicit costs} + \text{Implicit costs})$$

---

1.   One exception is *depreciation,* a charge for the gradual wearing out of the firm's plant and equipment. Accountants include this as a cost even though no money is actually paid out.

The difference between economic profit and accounting profit is an important one; when they are confused, some serious (and costly) mistakes can result. An example might help make the difference clear.

Suppose you own a firm that produces T-shirts, and you want to calculate your profit over the year. Your bookkeeper provides you with the following information:

Total Revenue from Selling T-shirts	**$300,000**
Cost of raw materials	$80,000
Wages and salaries	$150,000
Electricity and phone	$20,000
Advertising cost	$40,000
Total Explicit Cost	**$290,000**
Accounting Profit	**$10,000**

From the look of things, your firm is earning a profit, so you might feel pretty good. Indeed, if you look only at *money* coming in and *money* going out, you have indeed earned a profit—$10,000 for the year . . . in *accounting* profit.

But suppose that in order to start your business you invested $100,000 of your own money—money that could have been earning $6,000 in interest if you'd put it in the bank instead. Also, you are using two extra rooms in your own house as a factory—rooms that could have been rented out for $4,000 per year. Finally, you are managing the business full-time, without receiving a separate salary, and you could instead be working at a job earning $40,000 per year. All of these costs—the interest, rent, and salary you *could* have earned—are implicit costs that have not been taken into account by your bookkeeper. They are part of the opportunity cost of your firm, because they are sacrifices you made to operate your business.

Now let's look at this business from the economist's perspective and calculate your *economic* profit.

Total Revenue from Selling T-shirts	**$300,000**
Cost of raw materials	$80,000
Wages and salaries	$150,000
Electricity and phone	$20,000
Advertising cost	$45,000
Total Explicit Costs	**$290,000**
Investment income forgone	$6,000
Rent forgone	$4,000
Salary forgone	$40,000
Total Implicit Costs	**$50,000**
Total Costs	**$340,000**
Economic Profit	**–$40,000**

From an economic point of view, your business is not profitable at all, but is actually losing $40,000 per year! But wait: How can we say that your firm is suffering a loss when it takes in more money than it pays out? Because, as we've seen, your *opportunity cost*—the value of what you are giving up to produce your output—includes more than just money costs. When *all* costs are considered—implicit as well as explicit—your total revenue is not sufficient to cover what you have sacrificed to run your business. You would do better by shifting your time, your money, and your spare room to some alternative use.

Which of the two definitions of profit is the correct one? Either one of them, depending on the reason for measuring it. For tax purposes, the government is interested in profits as measured by accountants. The government cares only about the money you've earned, not what you *could* have earned had you done something else with your money or your time.

However, for our purposes—understanding the behavior of firms—economic profit is clearly better. Should your T-shirt factory stay in business? Should it expand or contract in the long run? Will other firms be attracted to the T-shirt industry? It is economic profit that will help us answer these questions, because it is economic profit that you and other owners care about.

**OPPORTUNITY
COST**

> *The proper measure of profit for understanding and predicting the behavior of firms is* economic *profit. Unlike accounting profit, economic profit recognizes* all *the opportunity costs of production—both explicit costs and implicit costs.*

Let's apply these ideas to Microsoft Corporation. In the year ending in June 1998, Microsoft had an accounting profit of $4.5 billion. But this was not its economic profit. Microsoft's owners—its shareholders—had invested $16.3 billion in the company—money that could have earned interest in a bank or some other financial investment. The forgone investment earnings must be included as part of the opportunity cost paid by Microsoft's owners. Let's suppose that they could have earned 5 percent by putting their money into some other investment. Then, the forgone investment income was $16.3 billion × 0.05 = $0.8 billion (after rounding). If the forgone investment income were the only implicit cost for Microsoft, we can deduct it from the accounting profit of $4.5 billion to obtain an *economic* profit of $4.5 billion − $0.8 billion = $3.7 billion.[2]

WHY ARE THERE PROFITS?

When you look at the income received by households in the economy, you see a variety of payments. Those who provide firms with land receive *rent*—the payment for land. Those who provide labor receive a wage or salary. And those who lend firms money so they can purchase capital equipment receive interest. The firm's profit goes to its owners. But what do the owners of the firm provide that earns them this payment?

Economists view profit as a payment for two contributions that are just as necessary for production as are land, labor, or machinery. These two contributions are *risk* and *innovation*.

Consider a restaurant that happens to be earning profit for its owner. The land, labor, and capital the restaurant uses to produce its meals did not simply come together magically. Someone—the owner—had to be willing to take the initiative to set up the business, and this individual assumed the risk that the business might fail and the initial investment might be lost. Because the consequences of loss are so

---

2. *Source:* Morningstar Principia Pro database, 11/30/98. Some of Microsoft's owners are also workers or managers in the firm. We do not count their sacrifice of time as part of the owners' implicit cost, because these owners receive a separate salary to compensate for their time.

severe, the reward for success must be large in order to induce an entrepreneur to establish a business.

On a larger scale, Ted Turner risked hundreds of millions of dollars in the late 1970s when he created Cable News Network (CNN). Now that CNN has turned out to be so successful, it is easy to forget how risky the venture was at the outset. At the time, many respected financial analysts forecast that the project would fail and Turner would be driven into bankruptcy.

Profits are also a reward for *innovation*. Ted Turner was the first to create a 24-hour global news network, just as Steven Jobs and Steven Wozniak—when they formed the Apple Computer Company in the 1970s—were the first to produce a usable personal computer for the mass market. These are obvious innovations.

But innovations can also be more subtle, and they are more common than you might think. When you pass by a successful laundromat, you may not give it a second thought. But someone, at some time, had to be the first one to realize, "I bet a laundromat in this neighborhood would do well"—an innovation. There can also be innovations in the production process, such as that improvement in mass production that made the disposable contact lens possible.

In almost any business, if you look closely you will find that some sort of innovation was needed to get things started. Innovation, like taking on the risk of losing substantial wealth, makes an essential contribution to production. Profit is, in part, a reward to those who innovate.

THE FIRM'S CONSTRAINTS

If the firm were free to set its revenue and costs at will, it would always set its revenue infinitely high, set its costs equal to zero, and earn infinite profit for its owners. This would make the owners very happy. Unfortunately for owners, though, the firm is not free to do this; it faces *constraints* on both its revenue and its costs. In Chapter 5, you saw that once the firm chooses its output level, it has also determined its cost of production—a constraint. In this section, you will see that the choice of output level also determines the firm's revenue.

THE DEMAND CURVE FACING THE FIRM

Our starting point in understanding the firm's revenue constraint is to study a familiar concept: the demand curve. A demand curve always tells us the quantity of a good buyers wish to buy at different prices. But which buyers? And from which collection of firms are they buying? Depending on how we answer these questions, we might be talking about any of several different types of demand curves.

Market demand curves—like the ones we studied in Chapter 3—tell us the quantity demanded by all consumers from all firms in a market. The *individual demand curve* we studied in Chapter 4 told us the quantity of a good demanded by one consumer only. In this chapter, we look at yet another kind of demand curve:

> The **demand curve facing a firm** tells us, for different prices, the quantity of output that customers will choose to purchase from that firm.

DEMAND CURVE FACING A FIRM A curve that indicates, for different prices, the quantity of output that customers will purchase from a particular firm.

Notice that this new demand curve—the demand curve facing the firm—refers to only *one* firm and to *all buyers* who are potential customers of that firm.

FIGURE 1 — THE DEMAND CURVE FACING THE FIRM

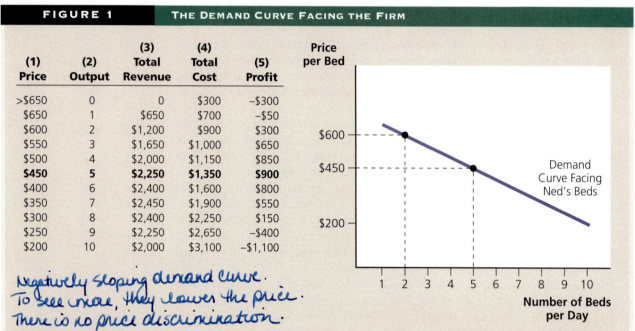

(1) Price	(2) Output	(3) Total Revenue	(4) Total Cost	(5) Profit
>$650	0	0	$300	–$300
$650	1	$650	$700	–$50
$600	2	$1,200	$900	$300
$550	3	$1,650	$1,000	$650
$500	4	$2,000	$1,150	$850
$450	**5**	**$2,250**	**$1,350**	**$900**
$400	6	$2,400	$1,600	$800
$350	7	$2,450	$1,900	$550
$300	8	$2,400	$2,250	$150
$250	9	$2,250	$2,650	–$400
$200	10	$2,000	$3,100	–$1,100

Negatively sloping demand curve. To see more, they lower the price. There is no price discrimination.

The table presents information about Ned's Beds. Data from the first two columns are plotted in the figure to show the demand curve facing the firm. At any point along that demand curve, the product of price and quantity equals total revenue, which is given in the third column of the table.

Let's consider the demand curve faced by Ned, the owner and manager of Ned's Beds—a manufacturer of bed frames. Figure 1 lists the different prices that Ned could charge for each bed frame and the number of them (per day) he can sell at each price. The figure also shows a graph of the demand curve facing Ned's firm. At each price (on the vertical axis), it shows us the quantity of output the firm can sell (on the horizontal axis). Notice that, like the other types of demand curves we have studied, the demand curve facing the firm slopes downward. In order to sell more bed frames, Ned must lower his price.[3]

The definition of the demand curve facing the firm suggests that by selecting a price, the firm determines how much output it will sell. But it is often useful to flip the demand relationship around: By selecting an output level, the firm determines the price it can charge. This leads to an alternative definition:

> *The demand curve facing the firm shows us the maximum price the firm can charge to sell any given amount of output.*

Looking at Figure 1 from this perspective, we see that the horizontal axis shows alternative levels of output and the vertical axis shows the price Ned should charge if he wishes to sell each quantity of output.

These two different ways of defining the firm's demand curve show us that it is, indeed, a constraint for the firm. The firm can freely determine *either* its price *or* its

---

3.   The downward-sloping demand curve tells us that Ned's Beds sells its output in an *imperfectly competitive market*—a market where the firm can *set* its price. Most firms operate in this type of market. If a manager thinks, "I'd like to sell more output, but then I'd have to lower my price, so let's see if it's worth it," we know he operates in an imperfectly competitive market. In a *perfectly competitive market,* by contrast, the firm would have to accept the market price as given—a case we'll take up in the next chapter.

level of output. But once it makes the choice, the other variable is automatically given by the firm's demand curve. Thus, the firm has only *one* choice to make. Selecting a particular price implies a level of output, and selecting an output level implies a particular price. And we could choose to focus on either one of these variables, with the other implied. Economists typically focus on the choice of output level, with the price implied. We will follow that convention in this textbook.

TOTAL REVENUE

There is another way of viewing the constraint imposed on the firm by the demand curve it faces. Each time it chooses a level of output, it also determines its **total revenue**—the total inflow of receipts from selling output. Why? Because once we know the level of output, we also know the price the firm can charge. Total revenue—which is the number of units of output times the price per unit—follows automatically.

> **TOTAL REVENUE** The total inflow of receipts from selling a given amount of output.

The third column in Figure 1 lists the total revenue of Ned's Beds. Each entry is calculated by multiplying the quantity of output (column 2) by the price per unit (column 1). For example, if Ned's firm produces 2 bed frames per day, he can charge $600 for each of them, so total revenue will be $2 \times \$600 = \$1,200$. If Ned increases output to 3 units, he must lower the price to $550, earning a total revenue of $3 \times \$550 = \$1,650$. Because the firm's demand curve slopes downward, Ned must lower his price each time his output increases, or else he will not be able to sell all he produces. With more units of output, but each one selling at a lower price, total revenue could rise or fall. Scanning the total revenue column, we see that for this firm, total revenue first rises and then begins to fall. This will be discussed in greater detail later on.

TOTAL COST

Just as the firm faces constraints on its revenue, it also faces constraints imposed by its costs. That is, once the firm decides how much to produce, it must pay for the necessary inputs. The fourth column of Figure 1 lists Ned's total cost—the lowest possible cost of producing each quantity of output. More output always means greater costs, so the numbers in this column are always increasing. For example, at an output of 0, total cost is $300. This tells us we are looking at costs in the short run, over which some of the firm's costs are *fixed*. (What would be the cost of producing 0 units if this were the long run?) If output increases from 0 to 1 bed frame, total cost rises from $300 to $700. This increase in total costs—$400—is caused by an increase in *variable* costs, such as labor and raw materials.

We can sum up our discussion of the firm's constraints as follows:

> *The firm faces constraints that limit its choices of revenue and costs. For each level of output the firm might choose, its demand curve determines the price it can charge and the total revenue it will receive, and its production technology determines the total cost it must bear.*

MAXIMIZATION SUBJECT TO CONSTRAINTS

THE PROFIT-MAXIMIZING OUTPUT LEVEL

In this section, we ask a very simple question: How does a firm find the level of output that will earn it the greatest possible profit? We'll look at this question from several angles, each one giving us further insight into the behavior of the firm.

THE TOTAL REVENUE AND TOTAL COST APPROACH

At any given output level, we know how much revenue the firm will earn, and we know its cost of production. We can then easily calculate profit, which is just the difference between total revenue *(TR)* and total cost *(TC).*

MAXIMIZATION SUBJECT TO CONSTRAINTS

> *In the total revenue and total cost approach, the firm calculates profit = TR – TC at each output level and selects the output level where profit is greatest.*

LOSS A negative profit—when total cost exceeds total revenue.

Let's see how this works for Ned's Beds. Column 5 of Figure 1 lists total profit at each output level. If the firm were to produce no bed frames at all, total revenue *(TR)* would be 0, while total cost *(TC)* would be $300. Total profit would be *TR – TC* = 0 – $300 = –$300. We would say that the firm earns a profit of negative $300 or a **loss** of $300 per day. Producing one bed frame would raise total revenue to $650 and total cost to $700, for a loss of $50. Not until the firm produces 2 bed frames does total revenue rise above total cost and the firm begin to make a profit. At 2 bed frames per day, *TR* is $1,200 and *TC* is $900, so the firm earns a profit of $300. Remember that as long as we have been careful to include *all* costs in *TC*—implicit as well as explicit—the profits and losses we are calculating are *economic* profits and losses.

In the total revenue and total cost approach, finding the profit-maximizing output level is straightforward: We just scan the numbers in the profit column until we find the largest value—$900—and the output level at which it is achieved—5 units per day. We conclude that the profit-maximizing output for Ned's Beds is 5 units per day.

THE MARGINAL REVENUE AND MARGINAL COST APPROACH

There is another way to find the profit-maximizing level of output. This approach, which uses *marginal* concepts, gives us some powerful insights into the firm's decision-making process. Recall that *marginal* cost is the *change* in total cost from producing one more unit of output. Now, let's consider a similar concept for revenue.

 MARGINAL REVENUE (MR) The change in total revenue from producing one more unit of output.

> *Marginal revenue (MR) is the change in total revenue from producing one more unit of output. Mathematically, MR is calculated by dividing the change in total revenue (ΔTR) by the change in output (ΔQ): MR = ΔTR/ΔQ.*

Table 1 reproduces the *TR* and *TC* columns from Figure 1, but adds columns for marginal revenue and marginal cost. (In the table, output is always changing by one unit, so we can use ΔTR alone as our measure of marginal revenue.) For example, when output changes from 2 to 3 units, total revenue rises from $1,200 to $1,650. For this output change, *MR* = $450. As usual, marginals are placed *between* different output levels because they tell us what happens as output *changes* from one level to another.

There are two important things to notice about marginal revenue. First, when *MR* is *positive*, an increase in output causes total revenue to *rise*. In the table, *MR* is posi-

DANGEROUS CURVES

You may be tempted to forget about profit, and think that the firm should produce where its total revenue is maximized. As you can see in the third column in Figure 1, total revenue is greatest when the firm produces 7 units per day, but at this output level, profit is not as high as it could be. The firm does better by producing only 5 units. True, revenue is lower at 5 units, but so are costs. It is the difference between revenue and cost that matters, not revenue alone.

TABLE 1	MORE DATA FOR NED'S BEDS					
Output	Total Revenue	Marginal Revenue	Total Cost	Marginal Cost	Profit
0	0		$300		−$300
		$650		$400	
1	$650		$700		−$50
		$550		$200	
2	$1,200		$900		$300
		$450		$100	
3	$1,650		$1,000		$650
		$350		$150	
4	$2,000		$1,150		$850
		$250		$200	
5	**$2,250**		**$1,350**		**$900**
		$150		$250	
6	$2,400		$1,600		$800
		$50		$300	
7	$2,450		$1,900		$550
		−$50		$350	
8	$2,400		$2,250		$150
		−$150		$400	
9	$2,250		$2,650		−$400
		−$250		$450	
10	$2,000		$3,100		−$1,100

(handwritten note in margin: No different prices per unit)

tive for all increases in output from 0 to 7 units. When *MR* is *negative,* an increase in output causes total revenue to *fall,* as occurs for all increases beyond 7 units.

The second thing to notice about *MR* is a bit more complicated: Each time output increases, *MR* is *smaller* than the price the firm charges at the new output level. For example, when output increases from 2 to 3 units, the firm's total revenue rises by $450—even though it sells the third unit for a price of $550. This may seem strange to you. After all, if the firm increases output from 2 to 3 units, and it gets $550 for the third unit of output, why doesn't its total revenue rise by $550?

The answer is found in the firm's downward-sloping demand curve, which tells us that to sell more output, the firm must cut its price. When output increases from 2 to 3 units, the firm must lower its price from $600 to $550. Moreover, the new price of $550 will apply to *all three* units the firm sells.[4] This means it *gains* some revenue—$550—by selling that third unit. But it also *loses* some revenue—$100— by having to lower the price by $50 on each of the two units of output it could have otherwise sold at $600. Marginal revenue will always equal the *difference* between this gain and loss in revenue—in this case, $550 − $100 = $450.

> *When a firm faces a downward-sloping demand curve, each increase in output causes a revenue gain—from selling additional output at the new price—and a revenue loss—from having to lower the price on all previous units of output. Marginal revenue is therefore less than the price of the last unit of output.*

---

4. Some firms can charge two or more different prices for the same product. We'll explore some examples in Chapter 9.

USING *MR* AND *MC* TO MAXIMIZE PROFITS. Now we'll see how marginal revenue, together with marginal cost, can be used to find the profit-maximizing output level. The logic behind the *MC* and *MR* approach is this:

> *An increase in output will always raise profit as long as marginal revenue is greater than marginal cost (MR > MC).*

Notice the word *always*. Let's see why this rather sweeping statement must be true. Table 1 tells us that when output rises from 2 to 3 units, *MR* is $450 while *MC* is $100. This change in output causes both total revenue and total cost to rise, but it causes revenue to rise by *more* than cost ($450 > $100). As a result, profit must increase. Indeed, looking at the profit column, we see that increasing output from 2 to 3 units *does* cause profit to increase, from $300 to $650.[5] The converse of this statement is also true:

> *An increase in output will always lower profit whenever marginal revenue is less than marginal cost (MR < MC).*

For example, when output rises from 5 to 6 units, *MR* is $150 while *MC* is $250. For this change in output, both total revenue and total cost rise, but cost rises *more*, so profit must go down. In the table, you can see that this change in output does indeed cause profit to decline, from $900 to $800.

These insights about *MR* and *MC* lead us to the following simple guideline the firm should use to find its profit-maximizing level of output:

> *The firm should increase output whenever* MR > MC, *and lower output when* MR < MC.

Let's apply this rule to Ned's Beds. In Table 1 we see that when moving from 0 to 1 unit of output, *MR* is $650 while *MC* is only $400. Since *MR* is larger than *MC*, making this move will increase profit. Thus, if the firm is producing 0 beds, it should always increase to 1 bed. Should it stop there? Let's see. If it moves from 1 to 2 beds, *MR* is $550 while *MC* is only $200. Once again, *MR* > *MC*, so the firm should increase to 2 beds. You can verify from the table that if the firm finds itself producing 0, 1, 2, 3, or 4 beds, *MR* > *MC* for an increase of 1 unit, so it will always make greater profit by increasing production.

Until, that is, output reaches 5 beds. At this point, the picture changes: From 5 to 6 beds, *MR* is $150 while *MC* is $250. For this move, *MR* < *MC*, so profits would decrease. Thus, if the firm is producing 5 beds, it should *not* increase to 6. The same is true at every other output level beyond 5 units: The firm should *not* raise its output, since *MR* < *MC* for each increase. We conclude that Ned maximizes his profit by producing 5 beds per day—the same answer we got using the *TR* and *TC* approach earlier.[6]

Invest Smart

Think you're good at spotting profitable companies? Test your skills on the free stock market simulation game provided by ThinkQuest.

http://library.advanced.org/10326/index.html

MARGINAL DECISION MAKING

---

5. You may have noticed that the rise in profit of ($350) is equal to the difference between *MR* and *MC* in this example. This is no accident. *MR* tells us the *rise* in revenue; *MC* tells us the *rise* in cost. The difference between them will always be the *rise* in profit.

6. It sometimes happens that *MR* is precisely equal to *MC* for some change in output, although this does not occur in Table 1. In this case, increasing output would cause *both cost and revenue* to rise by equal amounts, so there would be *no* change in profit. The firm should not care whether it makes this change in output or not.

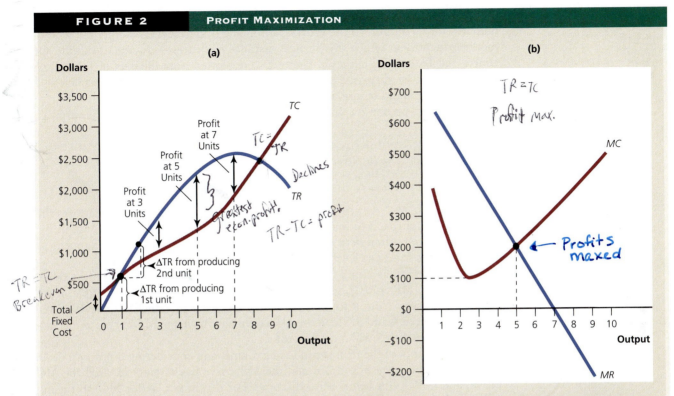

FIGURE 2   PROFIT MAXIMIZATION

Panel (a) shows the firm's total revenue (*TR*) and total cost (*TC*) curves. Profit is the vertical distance between the two curves at any level of output. Profit is maximized when that vertical distance is greatest—at 5 units of output. Panel (b) shows the firm's marginal revenue (*MR*) and marginal cost (*MC*) curves. (As long as *MR* lies above the horizontal axis, the *TR* curve slopes upward.) Profit is maximized at the level of output closest to where the two curves cross—at 5 units of output.

PROFIT MAXIMIZATION USING GRAPHS

Both approaches to maximizing profits (using totals or using marginals) can be seen even more clearly when we use graphs. In Figure 2(a) and (b), the data from Table 1 have been plotted—the *TC* and *TR* curves in the left panel, and the *MC* and *MR* curves in the right one.

Note the important relationship between the *MR* and *TR* curves. ==MR tells us the *change* in total revenue as output increases.== Thus, as long as the *MR* curve lies above the horizontal axis (*MR* > 0), *TR* must be increasing, and the *TR* curve must slope upward. In the figure, *MR* > 0 and the *TR* curve slopes upward from 0 to 7 units. When the *MR* curve dips below the horizontal axis (*MR* < 0), *TR* is decreasing, so the *TR* curve begins to slope downward. In the figure, this occurs beyond 7 units of output. ==As output increases in Figure 2, *MR* is first positive and then turns negative, so the *TR* curve will first *rise* and then *fall*.==

THE *TR* AND *TC* APPROACH USING GRAPHS. Now let's see how we can use the *TC* and *TR* curves to guide the firm to its profit-maximizing output level. We know that the firm earns a profit at any output level where *TR* > *TC*—where the *TR* curve lies *above* the *TC* curve. In Figure 2(a), you can see that all output levels between 2 and 8 units are profitable for the firm. The *amount* of profit is simply the *vertical distance* between the *TR* and *TC* curves, whenever the *TR* curve lies above

the *TC* curve. Since the firm cannot sell part of a bed frame, it must choose whole numbers for its output, so the profit-maximizing output level is simply the whole-number quantity at which this vertical distance is greatest—5 units of output. Of course, the *TR* and *TC* curves in Figure 2 were plotted from the data in Table 1, so we should not be surprised to find the same profit-maximizing output level—5 units—that we found before when using the table.

We can sum up our graphical rule for using the *TR* and *TC* curves this way:

> *To maximize profit, the firm should produce the quantity of output where the vertical distance between the* TR *and* TC *curves is greatest, and the* TR *curve lies above the* TC *curve.*

THE *MR* AND *MC* APPROACH USING GRAPHS. Figure 2 also illustrates the *MR* and *MC* approach to maximizing profits. As usual, the marginal data in the lower panel are plotted *between* output levels, since they tell us what happens as output changes from one level to another.

In the diagram, as long as output is less than 5 units, the *MR* curve lies above the *MC* curve (*MR* > *MC*), so the firm should produce more. For example, if we consider the move from 4 to 5 units, we compare the *MR* and *MC* curves at the midpoint between 4 and 5. Here, the *MR* curve lies above the *MC* curve, so increasing output from 4 to 5 will increase profit.

But now suppose the firm is producing 5 units and considering a move to 6. At the midpoint between 5 and 6 units, the *MR* curve has already crossed the *MC* curve, and now it lies *below* the *MC* curve. For this move, *MR* < *MC*, so raising output would *decrease* the firm's profit. The same is true for every increase in output beyond 5 units: The *MR* curve always lies below the *MC* curve, so the firm will decrease its profits by increasing output. Once again, we find that the profit-maximizing output level for the firm is 5 units.

Notice that the profit-maximizing output level—5 units—is the level closest to where the *MC* and *MR* curves cross. This is no accident. For each change in output that *increases* profit, the *MR* curve will lie above the *MC* curve. The first time that an output change *decreases* profit, the *MR* curve will cross the *MC* curve and dip below it. Thus, the *MC* and *MR* curves will always cross closest to the profit-maximizing output level.

With this graphical insight, we can summarize the *MC* and *MR* approach this way:

> *To maximize profit, the firm should produce the level of output closest to the point where* MC = MR, *that is, the level of output at which the* MC *and* MR *curves intersect.*

This rule is very useful, since it allows us to look at a diagram of *MC* and *MR* curves and *immediately* identify the profit-maximizing output level. In this text, you will often see this rule. When you read, "The profit-maximizing output level is where *MC* equals *MR*," translate to, "The profit-maximizing output level is closest to the point where the *MC* curve crosses the *MR* curve."

AN IMPORTANT PROVISO. There is one important exception to this rule. Sometimes the *MC* and *MR* curves cross at two different points. In this case, the profit-maximizing output level is the one at which the *MC* curve crosses the *MR* curve *from below*.

FIGURE 3   **TWO POINTS OF INTERSECTION**

Sometimes the *MR* and *MC* curves intersect twice. The profit-maximizing level of output is always found where *MC* crosses *MR* from below.

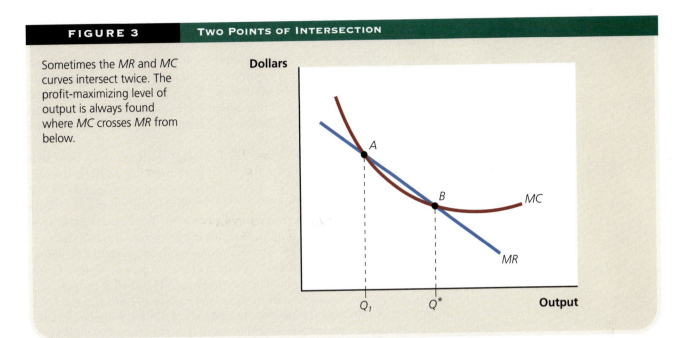

Figure 3 shows why. At point *A*, the *MC* curve crosses the *MR* curve from *above*; our rule tells us that the output level at this point—Q_1—is *not* profit-maximizing. Why not? Because at output levels lower than Q_1, *MC* > *MR*, so profit *falls* as we increase output toward Q_1. Also, profit *rises* as we increase output *beyond* Q_1, since *MR* > *MC* for these moves. Since it never pays to increase *to* Q_1, and profit rises when increasing *from* Q_1, we know that Q_1 cannot possibly maximize the firm's profit.

But now look at point *B*, where the *MC* curve crosses the *MR* curve from below. You can see that when we are at an output level lower than *Q**, it always pays to increase *to Q**, since *MR* > *MC* for these moves. You can also see that, once we have arrived at *Q**, further increases will reduce profit, since *MC* > *MR*. *Q** is thus the profit-maximizing output level for this firm—the output level at which the *MC* curve crosses the *MR* curve *from below*.

WHAT ABOUT AVERAGE COSTS?

You may have noticed that this chapter has discussed *most* of the cost concepts introduced in Chapter 5. But it has not yet referred to *average* cost. There is a good reason for this. We have been concerned about how much the firm should produce if it wishes to earn the greatest possible level of profit. To achieve this goal, the firm should produce more output whenever doing this *increases* profit, and it needs to know only *marginal* cost and *marginal* revenue for this purpose. The different types of average cost (*ATC*, *AVC*, and *AFC*) are simply irrelevant. Indeed, a common error—

A common error is to think the firm should produce the level of output at which the difference between *MR* and *MC* is as large as possible, like 2 or 3 units of output in Figure 2. Let's see why this is wrong. If the firm produces 2 or 3 units, it would leave many profitable increases in output unexploited—increases where *MR* > *MC*. As long as *MR* is even a tiny bit larger than *MC*, it pays to increase output, since doing so will add more to revenue than to cost. The firm should be satisfied only when the difference between *MR* and *MC* is as *small* as possible—not as large as possible.

DANGEROUS CURVES

sometimes made even by business managers—is to use average cost in place of marginal cost in making decisions.

For example, suppose a yacht maker wants to know how much his total cost will rise in the short run if he produces another unit of output. It is tempting—*but wrong*—for the yacht maker to reason this way: "My cost per unit (*ATC*) is currently $50,000 per yacht. Therefore, if I increase production by 1 unit, my total cost will rise by $50,000; if I increase production by 2 units, my total cost will rise by $100,000; and so on."

There are two problems with this approach. First, *ATC* includes many costs that are *fixed* in the short run—including the cost of all fixed inputs, such as the factory and equipment and the design staff. These costs will *not* increase when additional yachts are produced, and they are therefore irrelevant to the firm's decision making in the short run. Second, *ATC changes* as output increases. The cost per yacht may rise above $50,000 or fall below $50,000, depending on whether the *ATC* curve is upward or downward sloping at the current production level. Note that the first problem—fixed costs—could be solved by using *AVC* instead of *ATC*; the second problem—changes in average cost—remains even when *AVC* is used.

The correct approach, as we've seen in this chapter, is to use the *marginal cost* of a yacht and to consider increases in output one unit at a time. Alternatively, the firm can cut to the chase and produce where its *MC* curve crosses its *MR* curve from below. Average cost doesn't help at all; it only confuses the issue.

Does this mean that all of your efforts to master *ATC* and *AVC*—their definitions, their relationship to each other, and their relationship to *MC*—were a waste of time? Far from it. As you'll see, average cost will prove *very* useful in the chapters to come. But average cost should *not* be used in place of marginal cost as a basis for decisions.

MARGINAL DECISION MAKING: A BROADER VIEW

The *MC* and *MR* approach for finding the profit-maximizing output level is actually a very specific application of a more general principle:

> The **marginal approach to profit** states that a firm should take any action that adds *more* to its revenue than to its cost.

MARGINAL DECISION MAKING

MARGINAL APPROACH TO PROFIT A firm maximizes its profit by taking any action that adds more to its revenue than to its cost.

In this chapter, the action we've been considering is to increase output by 1 unit, and we've learned that the firm should take this action whenever *MR* > *MC*. Since *MR* is how much this action *adds to revenue* and *MC* is how much it *adds to cost*, you can see that all along we have, indeed, been using a particular application of the more general marginal approach to profit. But this principle can be applied to any other decision facing the firm.

How can we be so bold as to say *any* decision facing the firm? Any action we can imagine that increases the firm's revenue more than its costs will, *by definition*, increase its profits. Suppose that having the president of the company sing the "Star Spangled Banner," each morning while standing on his head would add more to revenue than to cost. Then—to earn maximum profit—the firm should have the president do just that. But we needn't dwell on absurd actions, since there are plenty of realistic ones to illustrate this principle.

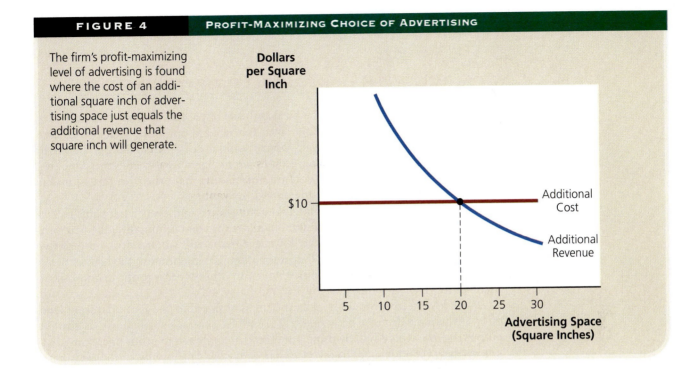

FIGURE 4   **PROFIT-MAXIMIZING CHOICE OF ADVERTISING**

The firm's profit-maximizing level of advertising is found where the cost of an additional square inch of advertising space just equals the additional revenue that square inch will generate.

Consider the manager of a movie theater who must decide what size advertisement to take out in the local paper. Suppose each square inch of advertising space costs $10. Figure 4 shows the theater's additional cost curve for advertising, which will be a horizontal line at $10—each time the advertisement increases by 1 square inch, total cost *rises* by $10.[7] Suppose also that the larger the ad, the greater the revenue from selling tickets, but that the additional revenue declines as the ad grows larger and larger in square-inch increments. In this case, the marginal revenue curve for advertising is downward sloping, like the one drawn in the figure. The marginal profit principle tells us that the firm should keep increasing the size of the ad as long as the additional revenue from doing so is greater than the additional cost of doing so. Notice that we are assuming that the added viewers attracted by additional ads don't increase the theater's cost. As you can see in the diagram, the firm should select the ad size where the two curves cross, or 20 square inches. Any ad larger or smaller than this would cause the theater to earn a smaller profit.

The marginal approach to profit explains much of a firm's behavior that we see in the real world. It tells us that a profit-maximizing firm will take any action that adds more to its revenue than it adds to its costs, whether that action is lobbying the government for special treatment, extending the hours that a store is open, recalling a defective product, or giving free samples of merchandise. (You may want to think about how firms would decide on each of these actions using the marginal

---

7.   Don't be confused by this horizontal line. The "additional-cost" curves we've considered so far have all been *MC* curves. These were *U*-shaped because they tracked the additional cost of producing more *output* when returns to labor were first increasing, and then diminishing. In this example, we are looking at the additional cost *not* of producing more output, but of buying more *advertising space*. Since ad space costs a constant $10 per square inch, the additional cost of 1 more square inch will be constant at $10 as well.

approach to profits.) Two more examples of this technique are discussed in greater detail in the "Using the Theory" section at the end of this chapter.

DEALING WITH LOSSES: THE SHUTDOWN RULE

So far, we have dealt only with the pleasant case of profitable firms and how they select their profit-maximizing output level. But what about a firm that cannot earn a positive profit at *any* output level? What should it do? At first glance, you might think that such a firm should always shut down its operation, even in the short run. After all, why keep producing if you are not making any profit? In fact, it makes sense for some unprofitable firms to continue operating.

Consider a firm with the *TC* and *TR* curves shown in the left-hand panel of Figure 5 (ignore the *TVC* curve for now). No matter at what output level the firm produces, the *TC* curve lies above the *TR* curve, so it will suffer a loss—a negative profit. For this firm, the goal is still profit maximization. But now, the highest profit will be the one with the *least negative value*. In other words, profit maximization becomes *loss minimization*.

If the firm keeps producing, then the smallest possible loss is at an output level of *Q**, where the distance between the *TC* and *TR* curves is smallest. *Q** is also the output level we would find by using our marginal approach to profit (increasing output whenever it adds more to revenue than to costs). This is why, in the right-hand panel of Figure 5, the *MC* and *MR* curves must intersect at (or very close to) *Q**.

The question is: should this firm produce at *Q**, and suffer a loss? The answer is yes, *if* the firm would lose even *more* if it stopped producing and shut down its operation. Remember that, in the short run, a firm must continue to pay its total fixed cost (*TFC*) no matter what level of output it produces—even if it produces nothing at all. If the firm shuts down, it will therefore have a loss equal to its *TFC*, since it

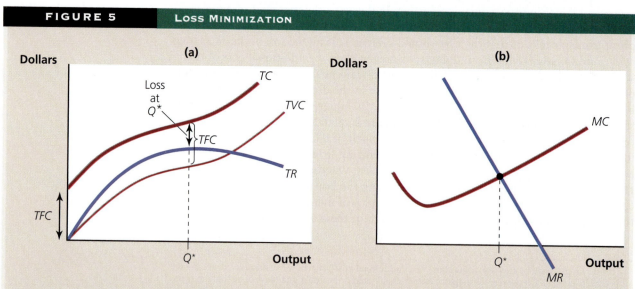

FIGURE 5	**LOSS MINIMIZATION**

The firm shown here cannot earn a positive profit at *any* level of output. If it produces anything, it will minimize its loss by producing where the vertical distance between *TR* and *TC* is smallest. Because *TR* exceeds *TVC* at *Q**, the firm will produce there in the short run.

will not earn any revenue. But if, by producing some output, the firm can cut its loss to something *less* than *TFC*, then it should stay open and keep producing.

To understand the shut-down decision more clearly, let's think about the firm's total variable costs. Business managers often call *TVC* the firm's *operating cost*, since the firm only pays these variable costs when it continues to operate. If a firm, by staying open, can earn more than enough revenue to cover its operating costs, then it is making an *operating profit* (*TR* > *TVC*). It should not shut down, because its operating profit can be used to help pay its fixed costs. But if the firm cannot even cover its operating cost when it stays open—that is, if it would suffer an *operating loss* (*TR* < *TVC*)—it should definitely shut down. Continuing to operate only adds to the firm's loss, increasing the total loss beyond fixed costs.

This suggests the following guideline—called the **shutdown rule**—for a loss-making firm:

> Let *Q** be the output level at which MR = MC. Then, in the short run:
>   If *TR* > *TVC* at *Q**, *the firm should keep producing.*
>   If *TR* < *TVC* at *Q**, *the firm should shut down.*
>   If *TR* = *TVC* at *Q**, *the firm should be indifferent between shutting down and producing.*

Look back at Figure 5. At *Q**, the firm is making an operating profit, since its *TR* curve is above its *TVC* curve. This firm, as we've seen, should continue to operate.

Figure 6 is drawn for a different firm, one with the same *TC* and *TVC* curves as the firm in Figure 5, but with a lower *TR* curve. This firm cannot earn an operating profit, since its *TR* curve lies below its *TVC* curve everywhere—even at *Q**. This firm should shut down.

The shutdown rule is a powerful predictor of firms' decisions to stay open or cease production in the short run. It tells us, for example, why some seasonal businesses—such as ice-cream shops in summer resort areas—shut down in the winter when *TR* drops so low that it becomes smaller than *TVC*. And it tells us why producers of steel, automobiles, agricultural goods, and television sets will often keep producing output for some time even when they are losing money.

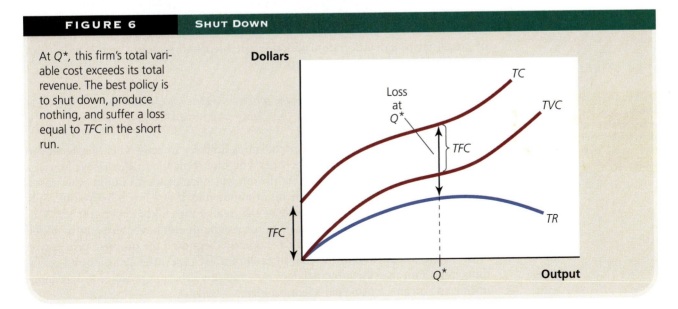

| FIGURE 6 | SHUT DOWN |

At *Q**, this firm's total variable cost exceeds its total revenue. The best policy is to shut down, produce nothing, and suffer a loss equal to *TFC* in the short run.

Keep in mind that the shutdown rule applies only in the short run, a time horizon too short for the firm to escape its commitments to pay for fixed inputs such as plant and equipment. In the long run, as you know, there *are* no fixed costs, since all inputs can be varied. Therefore, a firm facing a long run loss has another option, one not available in the short run. It can sell its plant and equipment and *exit* the industry for good, reducing its total cost, as well as its loss, to zero.

> *A firm should exit the industry when it has any size loss in the long run.*

We will look more closely at the exit decision and other long-run considerations in the next chapter.

THE GOAL OF THE FIRM REVISITED

So far in this chapter, we've assumed that a firm will make decisions that maximize its profit. That is, we've assumed that the firm is operated on behalf of its owners, who receive its profits. But in large firms, the owners hire managers to run the firm, and the managers, in turn, hire workers. Can we be sure that the workers and managers will maximize profit, as the owners want? Or can workers and managers pursue their *own* goals that reduce the firm's profit?

THE PRINCIPAL-AGENT PROBLEM

The relationships among workers, managers, and owners within the firm are examples of what economists call *principal-agent relationships*.

> *A **principal** is a person or group who hires someone to do a job. An **agent** is the person hired to do that job.*

SPECIALIZATION AND EXCHANGE

PRINCIPAL A person or group that hires someone to do a job.

AGENT A person hired to do a job.

Principal-agent relationships can be seen everywhere in the economy. Your economics professor, for example, is an *agent* of the university and its trustees, who are the principals. If someone cleans your house or apartment, that person is your agent, and you are the principal. Principal-agent relationships are a natural consequence of specialization. If each of us specializes in one type of good or service, we will always find ourselves producing for others. Thus, principal-agent relationships, by enabling specialization in production, enable us all to enjoy high standards of living. But they are often problematic.

> *The **principal-agent problem** arises when an agent has (1) interests that conflict with the principal's, and (2) the ability to pursue those interests.*

PRINCIPAL-AGENT PROBLEM The situation that arises when an agent has interests that conflict with the principal's, and has the ability to pursue those interests.

In practice, the principal-agent problem is unlikely to arise when the agent can be closely monitored. For example, when you hire someone to clean your house, a quick inspection will tell you whether the job was done properly. But in other cases, this kind of monitoring may be difficult or impossible. If you hire a baby-sitter, only the baby-sitter knows for sure how he or she treated the child in your absence. Similarly, most people who take their cars in for repairs do not have the expertise to tell whether the mechanic (their agent) has honestly diagnosed the problem or has even done all the work listed in the bill. In each of these cases, the agent knows something important that the principal does not, and this situation prevents proper monitoring and creates a principal-agent problem.

THE PRINCIPAL-AGENT PROBLEM AT THE FIRM

In business firms, there are two important principal-agent relationships—one between owners and managers and another between managers and workers. Each of these relationships can be plagued by conflicting goals. Managers are certainly interested in keeping their jobs and being promoted, giving them strong incentive to please owners by striving for high profits. But managers may also be interested in *other* things that can inflate the firm's costs and reduce its profits. These include high salaries, long vacations, the prestige of managing a great number of employees, or company perks such as first-class air travel, large offices with nice views, and extravagant expense accounts. Managers may also use company property such as telephones, photocopiers, and computers for personal use.

What about workers? They are interested in keeping their jobs and being promoted and thus have some incentive to please their managers. But they, too, may have other goals that conflict with profit maximization—for example, not working too hard, taking long lunch breaks, and (like managers) using company property for personal use.

We can see that agents at the firm have interests that conflict with those of their principals. That is one of the requirements for a principal-agent problem. But is the second requirement satisfied? Do the agents have the *ability* to pursue their interests?

Indeed they do. Owners can, to some extent, monitor the actions of managers by reading quarterly reports of the firm's profits. But owners can never know as much as managers about conditions and events at the firm, and so they cannot always tell whether management's decisions have led to the *highest profit possible.* Similarly, managers can observe how much output workers are producing, but because they cannot be everywhere at once, they cannot know whether workers are performing *as well as they could be.*

The principal-agent problem is likely to be more serious in large firms than in smaller ones. If you own a small ice-cream shop and hire a helper to scoop ice cream while you deal with customers, you will know how hard your employee is working and the length of his breaks, and you will have a good chance of catching him if he begins stealing ice cream to bring home to his friends. But a large firm like Ben and Jerry's, with hundreds of managers and thousands of workers, has a serious problem on its hands. The stockholders cannot be sure that management expense accounts are being used solely for company purposes or that each promotion or pay hike is justified. And if management wants to expand the firm—say, by starting a new product line—are they doing it with higher profits in mind, or merely to increase opportunities for promotion within the firm? Similarly, managers have a hard time preventing hourly workers from slacking off when they aren't being watched or ensuring that each worker punches in his or her own time card.

Economists have thought a lot about the principal-agent problem. Using models that view the firm as a collection of different groups—workers, managers, and owners—economics is discovering new ways in which the principal-agent problem affects the behavior of business firms, as well as nonprofit organizations like hospitals and universities and government agencies like police departments and the military. These models help us understand why firms can and do deviate from profit-maximizing behavior and how different types of supervision and pay arrangements can help solve the principal-agent problem in different types of organizations.

THE ASSUMPTION OF PROFIT MAXIMIZATION

From the preceding discussion, it might seem that the profit-maximizing assumption underlying most of this chapter is somewhat naive. After all, because of the principal-agent problem, the firm may *not always* maximize profits, even though that is what the owners want. Why, then, did we base our theory of firm behavior on such a simple assumption? Why not go back and view the firm in light of the principal-agent problem?

For one very good reason: The assumption of profit maximization, while not completely accurate, is reasonably accurate in most cases. While profit maximization is not the *only* goal of decision makers at the firm, it seems to be the driving force behind most management decisions. Remember that an economic model *abstracts* from reality. To stay simple and comprehensible, it leaves out many real-world details and includes only what is relevant for the purpose at hand. If the purpose is to explain *conflict within the firm,* or *deviations from profit-maximizing behavior,* the principal-agent problem would be a central element of the model. But when the purpose is to explain how firms decide what price to charge and how much to produce, how much to spend on advertising, or whether to shut down or continue operating in the short run, the assumption of profit maximization has proven to be sufficient. It explains what firms actually do with reasonable—and often remarkable—accuracy.

Even in larger firms, profit maximization seems to be the most important force driving firms' decisions. How can this be, when principal-agent problems can be so serious in large firms? In part, because the market provides some *solutions* to the principal-agent problem of large firms. Although far from perfect, they prevent firms from straying *too* far from the profit-maximizing course.

For example, when a firm's managers significantly inflate costs and reduce profit, the company's stock will become less attractive to potential buyers and its price will fall. Management will then face one of two consequences: (1) a **stockholder revolt**, in which owners, seeing that their firm is less profitable than others in the industry, replace the management team with another that promises to do better; or (2) a **hostile takeover**, in which outsiders buy up a majority of the firm's shares at low prices, often with the goal of sacking the current managers and replacing them with better ones. (The term "hostile" is from the viewpoint of the current managers.) In large corporations, poor management decisions can reduce profits by millions or even billions of dollars. Since there is so much at stake, stockholder revolts and hostile takeovers are not at all uncommon.

A recent example of a stockholder revolt occurred at Kmart Corporation. When profits declined in late 1994 and early 1995, stockholders blamed the management. The stockholders pointed to the much higher profits at competing discount retailers, such as Wal-Mart, which were operating under the same business conditions. In March 1995, Kmart's board of directors, elected by its shareholders, fired the company's president and four out of five vice-presidents and replaced them with another team believed to be better able to maximize the firm's profit.

A hostile takeover is more complicated than a stockholder revolt, because the current managers, who are the likely losers in a hostile takeover, can attempt a variety of measures to foil it. A recent example—and one that illustrates some of the vocabulary you will see in the business pages of your local newspaper—is the case of John Labatt Ltd., the Canadian beer maker. When Labatt's profits dwindled in late 1994 and the price of its stock dropped to 19 Canadian dollars per share, the financial press blamed poor management decisions. Sensing the firm was ripe for a hostile takeover, Labatt's managers tried to forestall it with a variety of actions designed to make the firm less attractive to outsiders, such as selling off valuable assets or taking on especially risky new projects. But at the com-

STOCKHOLDER REVOLT When owners, dissatisfied with the profits they are earning, replace the firm's management team.

HOSTILE TAKEOVER When outsiders buy up a firm's shares with the goal of replacing the management team and increasing profits.

pany's annual shareholder meeting, the shareholders voted to reject these moves. They *wanted* a takeover so they could sell their shares at a price reflecting the firm's *potential* profit under new management. Sure enough, the hostile takeover attempt came in early 1995 when an outsider—Onex Corporation—offered to buy all Labatt shares for 24 Canadian dollars each. Labatt's management responded by trying to arrange a **friendly takeover** by another firm deemed less likely to fire them. The **white knight** that came to their rescue was Interbrew SA, a Belgian beer maker. Interbrew was eager to expand into Canada to fulfill its own strategic plan, and it made an even more generous offer to Labatt's shareholders—28.5 Canadian dollars per share. In June 1995, Labatt's board of directors, representing the shareholders, happily agreed to the acquisition, and Labatt's management survived—temporarily. But unless they are able to better serve their masters—now the shareholders of Interbrew—their jobs will be threatened once again.

The threat of being fired is a powerful incentive for managers to worry about profits, but many firms use positive incentives as well. End-of-year *bonuses*—payments in addition to regular wages or salary—are often tied to total profit at the firm. In many cases, these bonuses are a substantial portion of a manager's total compensation. **Stock options**—which give managers the right to buy shares of the company's stock at a prespecified price—are another positive incentive. If the managers perform well, the market value of the firm's stock will rise. The managers can then *exercise* their stock options—purchasing the stock at the prespecified low price—and, if they choose, they can immediately sell the stock at the higher, market price and pocket the difference.

Incentives like bonuses and stock options on the one hand and threats of stockholder revolt or hostile takeover on the other are usually enough to keep management's eye on company profits. When this carrot-and-stick approach doesn't work, then *actual* revolts or takeovers—and the dumping or disciplining of management—ensure that poor managers do not survive for long. At any given time, therefore, we can expect *most* managers to try to maximize profits *most* of the time.

Similar mechanisms help ensure that hourly workers contribute to maximum profit at the firm. There are, indeed, plenty of opportunities to shirk or otherwise frustrate management's goals, but these can be pursued *only up to a point,* or the worker can expect to be fired. Television's Homer Simpson has on numerous occasions spilled coffee into the control panel of the nuclear reactor he operates, stolen expensive equipment for home use, and taken snoozes while the reactor goes into meltdown. Nobody in the real world would survive in a job with his record.

For all of the reasons just discussed, assuming that firms maximize profit for their owners is not too far off the mark. The principal-agent problem does exist, and it helps us understand many aspects of firm behavior, such as conflicts that arise within the firm, the structure of pay, and the methods used to supervise workers and managers. However, if our goal is to achieve a reasonably accurate prediction of firm decisions, profit maximization works pretty well.

Ask a physicist to predict when a bowling ball dropped from the top of the Empire State building will hit the ground, and she will assume it is falling in a perfect vacuum. Ask an economist to predict how much output a firm will produce and what price it will charge, and he will assume the firm's only goal is to maximize profit. In both cases the assumptions lead to very accurate—if not perfectly accurate—predictions.

FRIENDLY TAKEOVER When a firm's management arranges a takeover by another firm deemed unlikely to fire them.

WHITE KNIGHT A firm that undertakes a friendly takeover.

STOCK OPTIONS Rights to purchase shares of stock at a prespecified price.

GETTING IT WRONG AND GETTING IT RIGHT

Today, almost all managers have a good grasp of the concepts you've learned in this chapter, largely because microeconomics has become an important part of every business school curriculum. But if we go back a few decades—to when fewer managers had business degrees—we can find two examples of how management's failure to understand the basic theory of the firm led to serious errors. In one case, ignorance of the theory caused a large corporation to go bankrupt; in the other, a large corporation was able to outperform its competitors because *they* remained ignorant of the theory.

GETTING IT WRONG: THE FAILURE OF FRANKLIN NATIONAL BANK

In the mid-1970s, Franklin National Bank—one of the largest banks in the United States—went bankrupt. The bank's management had made several errors, but we will focus on the most serious one.

First, a little background. A bank is very much like any other business firm: It produces output (in this case a service, making loans) using a variety of inputs (land, labor, capital, and raw materials). The price of the bank's output is the interest rate it charges to borrowers. For example, with a 5 percent interest rate, the price of each dollar in loans is 5 cents per year.

Unfortunately for banks, they must also *pay* for the money they lend out. The largest source of funds is customer deposits, for which the bank must pay interest. If a bank wants to lend out more than its customers have deposited, it can obtain funds from a second source, the *federal funds market,* where banks lend money to one another. To borrow money in this market, the bank will usually have to pay a higher interest rate than it pays on customer deposits.

In mid-1974, John Sadlik, Franklin's chief financial officer, asked his staff to compute the average cost to the bank of a dollar in loanable funds. At the time, Franklin's funds came from three sources, each with its own associated interest cost:

Source	Interest Cost
Checking Accounts	2.25 percent
Savings Accounts	4 percent
Borrowed Funds	9–11 percent

What do these numbers tell us? First, each dollar deposited in a Franklin *checking account* cost the bank 2.25 cents per year,[8] while each dollar in a *savings account* cost Franklin 4 cents. Also, Franklin—like other banks at the time—had to pay between 9 and 11 cents on each dollar borrowed in the federal funds market. When Franklin's accountants were asked to figure out the average cost of a dollar in loans, they divided the total cost of funds by the number of dollars lent out. The number they came up with was 7 cents.

This average cost of 7 cents per dollar is an interesting number, but, as we know, it should have *no relevance to a profit-maximizing firm's decisions.* And this is where Franklin went wrong. At the time, all banks—including Franklin—were charging interest rates of 9 to 9.5 percent to their best customers. But Sadlik decided

---

8.   This cost was not actually a direct interest payment to depositors, since in the 1970s banks generally did not pay interest on checking accounts. But banks *did* provide free services, such as check clearing, monthly statements, free coffee, and even gifts (e.g., toasters) to their checking account depositors, and the cost of these freebies was computed to be 2.25 cents per dollar of deposits.

that since money was costing an *average* of 7 cents per dollar, the bank could make a tidy profit by lending money at 8 percent—earning 8 cents per dollar. Accordingly, he ordered his loan officers to approve any loan that could be made to a reputable borrower at 8 percent interest. Needless to say, with other banks continuing to charge 9 percent or more, Franklin National Bank became a very popular place from which to borrow money.

But where did Franklin get the additional funds it was lending out? That was a problem for the managers in *another* department at Franklin, who were responsible for *obtaining* funds. It was not easy to attract additional checking and savings account deposits, since, in the 1970s, the interest rate that banks could pay was regulated by the government. That left only one alternative: the federal funds market. And this is exactly where Franklin went to obtain the funds pouring out of its lending department. Of course, these funds were borrowed not at 7 percent, the average cost of funds, but at 9 to 11 percent, the cost of borrowing in the federal funds market.

To understand Franklin's error, let's look again at the average cost figure it was using. This figure included an irrelevant cost, the cost of funds obtained from customer deposits. This cost was irrelevant to the bank's lending decisions, since *additional* loans would not come from these deposits, but rather from the more expensive federal funds market. Further, this average figure was doomed to rise as Franklin expanded its loans. How do we know this? The *marginal* cost of an additional dollar of loans—9 to 11 cents per dollar—was greater than the *average* cost—7 cents. As you know, whenever the marginal is greater than the average, it pulls the average up. Thus, Franklin was basing its decisions on an average cost figure that not only included irrelevant sunk costs but was bound to increase as its lending expanded.

More directly, we can see Franklin's error through the lens of the marginal approach. The *marginal revenue* of each additional dollar lent out at 8 percent was 8 cents, while the *marginal cost* of each additional dollar—since it came from the federal funds market—was 9 to 11 cents. *MC* was greater than *MR,* so Franklin was actually losing money each time its loan officers approved another loan! Not surprisingly, these loans—which never should have been made—caused Franklin's profits to *decrease,* and within a year the bank had lost hundreds of millions of dollars. This, together with other management errors, caused the bank to fail.[9]

GETTING IT RIGHT: THE SUCCESS OF CONTINENTAL AIRLINES

In 1962, Continental Airlines was doing something with its jets that seemed like a horrible mistake. All other airlines at the time were following a simple rule: They would only offer a flight if, on average, 65 percent of the seats could be filled with paying passengers, since only then could the flight break even. Continental, however, was flying jets filled to just 50 percent of capacity and was actually expanding flights on many routes. When word of Continental's policy leaked out, its stockholders were angry, and managers at competing airlines smiled knowingly, waiting for Continental to fail. Yet Continental's profits—already higher than the industry average—continued to grow. What was going on?

There *was,* indeed, a serious mistake being made—but by the *other* airlines, not Continental. This mistake should by now be familiar to you: using average cost instead of marginal cost to make decisions. The "65 percent of capacity" rule used throughout the industry was derived more or less as follows: The total cost of the

---

9.   For more information on the failure of Franklin National Bank, see Sanford Rose, "What Really Went Wrong at Franklin National," *Fortune,* October 1974, pp. 118–226.

airline for the year (*TC*) was divided by the number of flights during the year (*Q*) to obtain the average cost of a flight (*TC/Q* = *ATC*). For the typical flight, this came to about $4,000. Since a jet had to be 65 percent full in order to earn ticket sales of $4,000, the industry regarded any flight that repeatedly took off with less than 65 percent as a money loser and canceled it.

As usual, there are two problems with using *ATC* in this way. First, an airline's average cost per flight includes many costs that are fixed and are therefore irrelevant to the decision to add or subtract a flight. These include the cost of running the reservations system, paying interest on the firm's debt, and fixed fees for landing rights at airports—none of which would change if the firm added or subtracted a flight. Also, average cost ordinarily changes as output changes, so it is wrong to assume it is constant in decisions about changing output.

Continental's management, led by its vice-president of operations, had decided to try the marginal approach to profits. Whenever a new flight was being considered, every department within the company was asked to determine the *additional* cost they would have to bear. Of course, the only additional costs were for additional *variable* inputs, such as additional flight attendants, ground crew personnel, in-flight meals, and jet fuel. These additional costs came to only about $2,000 per flight. Thus, the *marginal* cost of an additional flight—$2,000—was significantly less than the marginal revenue of a flight filled to 65 percent of capacity—$4,000. The marginal approach to profits tells us that when *MR* > *MC*, output should be increased, which is just what Continental was doing. Indeed, Continental correctly drew the conclusion that the marginal revenue of a flight filled at even 50 percent of capacity—$3,000—was *still* greater than its marginal cost, and so offering the flight would increase profit. This is why Continental was expanding routes even when it could fill only 50 percent of its seats.

In the early 1960s, Continental was able to outperform its competitors by using a secret—the marginal approach to profits. Today, of course, the secret is out, and all airlines use the marginal approach when deciding which flights to offer.[10]

---

10. For more information about Continental's strategy, see "Airline Takes the Marginal Bone," *Business Week*, April 20, 1963, pp. 111–114.

S U M M A R Y

In economics, we view the firm as a single economic decision maker with the goal of maximizing the owners' profit. Profit is total revenue minus *all* costs of production—explicit and implicit. In their pursuit of maximum profit, firms face two constraints. One is embodied in the demand curve the firm faces; it indicates the maximum price the firm can charge to sell any amount of output. This constraint determines the firm's revenue at each level of production. The other constraint is imposed by costs: More output always means greater costs. In choosing the profit-maximizing output, the firm must consider both revenues and costs.

One approach to choosing the optimal level of output is to measure profit as the difference between total revenue and total cost at each level of output, and then select the output level at which profit is greatest. An alternate approach uses *marginal revenue (MR)*—the change in total revenue from producing one more unit of output—and *marginal cost (MC)*—the change in total cost from producing one more unit. The firm should increase output whenever *MR* > *MC*, and lower output when *MR* < *MC*. The profit-maximizing output level is the one closest to the point where *MR* = *MC*. If profit is negative, but total revenue exceeds total variable cost, the firm should continue producing in the short run. Otherwise, it should shut down and suffer a loss equal to its fixed cost.

All of this assumes that the firm will be run with the owners' best interest in mind. However, a principal-agent problem may exist in which workers or managers pursue their own interest to the detriment of the owners' interests. Still, firms' owners have come up with a variety of incentives to keep managers' and workers' eyes on profits. The assumption of profit maximization, while not completely accurate, is accurate enough to be useful.

KEY TERMS

accounting profit
economic profit
demand curve facing a firm
total revenue

loss
marginal revenue (*MR*)
marginal approach to profit
shut-down rule

principal
agent
principal-agent problem
stockholder revolt

hostile takeover
friendly takeover
white knight
stock options

REVIEW QUESTIONS

1. What is the difference between accounting profit and economic profit?

2. Profit can be viewed as payment for what two intangible aspects of the production process?

3. What are the three kinds of demand curve we have studied so far in this book? What does each tell us?

4. What are the constraints on the firm's ability to earn profit? How does each constraint arise? How does the firm select the level of output where profit is greatest in:

a. The total revenue and total cost approach?
b. The marginal revenue and marginal cost approach? How is each approach illustrated graphically?

5. What are the two conditions necessary for the principal-agent problem to arise?

6. Discuss the following statement: "The assumption that a firm's only goal is profit maximization is completely unrealistic. Different groups within a company typically pursue their own agendas, which frequently have nothing to do with profit."

PROBLEMS AND EXERCISES

1. You have a part-time work-study job at the library that pays $10 per hour 3 hours per day on Saturdays and Sundays. Some friends want you to join them on a weekend ski trip leaving Friday night and returning Monday morning. They estimate your share of the gas, motel, lift tickets, and other expenses to be around $30. What is your total cost (considering both explicit and implicit costs) for the trip?

2. Until recently, you worked for a software development firm at a yearly salary of $35,000. After a couple of years, you decide to open your own business. Planning to be the next Bill Gates, you quit your job, cash in a $10,000 savings account (which pays 5 percent interest), and use the money to buy the latest computer hardware to use in your business. You also convert a basement apartment in your house, which you have been renting for $250 a month, into a work space for your new software firm.

   You lease some office equipment for $3,600 a year and hire two part-time programmers, whose combined salary is $25,000 a year. You also figure it costs around $50 a month to provide heat and light for your new office.

   a. What are the total annual explicit costs of your new business?
   b. What are the total annual implicit costs?
   c. At the end of your first year, your accountant cheerily informs you that your total sales for the year amounted to $55,000. She congratulates you on a profitable year. Are her congratulations warranted? Why or why not?

3. The following data are price/quantity/cost combinations for Titan Industry's mainframe computer division:

Quantity	Price per Unit	Total Cost of Production
0	above $225,000	$200,000
1	$225,000	$250,000
2	$175,000	$275,000
3	$150,000	$325,000
4	$125,000	$400,000
5	$90,000	$500,000

a. What is the marginal revenue if output rises from 2 to 3 units? (Hint: Calculate total revenue at each output level first.) What is the marginal cost if output rises from 4 to 5 units?
b. What quantity should Titan produce to maximize total revenue? Total profit?
c. What is Titan's fixed cost? How do Titan's marginal costs behave as output increases? Provide a plausible explanation as to why a computer manufacturer's marginal costs might behave in this way.

4. Discuss how serious you think the principal-agent problem would be in each of the following situations:
a. You leave your computer at a shop for repair.
b. You and a friend buy and run a business together.
c. A couple hires you to house-sit while they're in Europe for 2 months.
d. An employee owns shares in the company for which he works. His supervisor is out sick for a week.

5. Each entry in this table shows marginal revenue and marginal cost when a firm increases output to the given quantity:

Quantity	MR	MC
10	30	40
11	29	35
12	27	30
13	25	25
14	23	20
15	21	15
16	19	19
17	17	23

What is the profit-maximizing level of output?

6. The following tables give the cost/price situation for two firms. In the short run, how much should each produce?

Firm A

Quantity	Price	Total Cost
0	above $125	$250
1	$125	$400
2	$100	$500
3	$ 75	$550
4	$ 50	$600
5	$ 25	$700

Firm B

Quantity	Price	Total Cost
0	above $500	$500
1	$500	$700
2	$400	$900
3	$300	$1,100
4	$200	$1,300
5	$100	$1,500

7. The U. S. Securities and Exchange Commission (http://www.sec.gov/) enforces trading and reporting laws to help maintain orderly financial markets and the free flow of accurate financial information. Much of the information that the SEC collects is made public through its EDGAR database. One source of information on EDGAR is Form 10-K, an annual report on business and financial activities every publicly traded firm must file.
   a. Visit EDGAR at http://www.sec.gov/edgarhp.htm. Click on "Search the EDGAR Database," then on "Quick Forms Lookup." Select Form 10-K, and enter the company name "Gateway 2000." Search the entire database and locate Gateway's most recent 10-K filing. Use your browser to search the page for the table titled "Consolidated Financial Data." Look through those tables and find "Net income" and "Stockholders' equity" for the most recent year. Note that "net income" is Gateway's accounting profit (or loss) for the year, and "stockholders' equity" is the amount invested in the firm by Gateway's owners.
   b. How much total *accounting* profit (or loss) did Gateway's owners realize last year?
   c. If Gateway's owners could have earned 5 percent last year by investing their money elsewhere, how much *economic* profit (or loss) did they realize last year?

CHALLENGE QUESTIONS

1. A firm's *marginal profit* can be defined as the change in its profit when output increases by one unit.
   a. Compute the marginal profit for each change in Ned's Beds' output in Table 1.
   b. State a complete rule for finding the profit-maximizing output level in terms of marginal profit.

2. Howell Industries specializes in precision plastics. Their latest invention promises to revolutionize the electronics industry, and they have already made and sold 75 of the miracle devices. They have estimated average costs as given in the following table:

Unit	AC
74	$10,000
75	$12,000
76	$14,000

Backus Electronics has just offered Howell $150,000 if they will produce the 76th unit. Should Howell accept the offer and manufacture the additional device?

CHAPTER 7

PERFECT COMPETITION

No one knows exactly how many different types of goods and services are offered for sale in the United States, but the number must be somewhere in the tens of millions. Each of these goods is traded in a market, where buyers and sellers come together, and these markets have several things in common. Sellers want to sell at the *highest* possible price, buyers seek the *lowest* possible price, and all trade is *voluntary*. But here, the similarity ends.

When we observe buyers and sellers in action, we see that different goods and services are traded in vastly different ways. Consider advertising. Every day, we are inundated with sales pitches on television, radio, and newspapers for a long list of products: toothpaste, perfume, automobiles, computers, cat food, automobile tune-ups, banking services, and more. But have you ever seen a farmer on television trying to convince you to buy *his* wheat, rather than the wheat of other farmers? Do shareholders of major corporations like General Motors sell their stock by advertising in the newspaper? Why, in a world where virtually everything seems to be advertised, do we not see ads for wheat, corn, crude oil, gold, copper, shares of stock, or foreign currency?

Or consider profits. Anyone starting a business hopes to make as much profit as possible. Yet some companies—Microsoft, Quaker Oats, and Pepsico, for example—earn sizable profit for their owners year after year, while at other companies, such as Trans World Airlines and most small businesses, economic profit is generally low.

We could say, "That's just how the cookie crumbles," and attribute all of these observations to pure randomness. But economics is all about explaining such things—finding patterns amidst the chaos of everyday economic life. When economists turn their attention to differences in trading, such as these, they think immediately about *market structure*:

MARKET STRUCTURE The characteristics of a market that influence how trading takes place.

> By **market structure,** *we mean all the characteristics of a market that influence the behavior of buyers and sellers when they come together to trade.*

To determine the structure of any particular market, we begin by asking three simple questions:

1. *How many* buyers and sellers are there in the market?
2. Are the sellers offering a *standardized product,* more or less indistinguishable from that offered by other sellers, or are there significant differences between the products of different firms?
3. Are there any *barriers to entry or exit,* or can outsiders easily enter and leave this market?

The answers to these questions help us to classify a market into one of four basic types: *perfect competition, monopoly, monopolistic competition,* or *oligopoly.* In this and the next chapter, you will learn about the four different market structures. Our focus will be on *understanding* how a firm will behave in each type of market and how it will be affected by its trading environment. Later on (in Chapter 10), we will concern ourselves with *assessment*—the advantages and disadvantages of different market structures from society's point of view.

WHAT IS PERFECT COMPETITION?

When you hear the word "competition," you may think of an intense, personal rivalry, like that between two fighters competing in a ring or two students competing for the best test score in a small class. But there are other, less personal forms of competition. If you took the SAT exam to get into college, you were competing with thousands of other test takers in rooms just like yours, all across the country. But the competition was *impersonal:* You were trying to do the best that you could do, trying to outperform others in general, but not competing with any one individual in the room. In economics, the term "competition" is used in the latter sense. It describes a situation of diffuse, impersonal competition in a highly populated environment. The market structure you will learn about in this chapter—perfect competition—is an example of this notion.

THE THREE REQUIREMENTS OF PERFECT COMPETITION

PERFECT COMPETITION A market structure in which there are many buyers and sellers, the product is standardized, and sellers can easily enter or exit the market.

> *Perfect competition* is a market structure with three important characteristics:
>
> 1. *There are large numbers of buyers and sellers, and each buys or sells only a tiny fraction of the total quantity in the market.*
> 2. *Sellers offer a standardized product.*
> 3. *Sellers can easily enter into or exit from the market.*

These three conditions probably raise more questions than they answer, so let's see what each one really means.

A VERY LARGE NUMBER OF BUYERS AND SELLERS. In perfect competition, there must be many buyers and sellers. How many? It would be nice if we could specify a number, like 32,456, for this requirement. Unfortunately, we cannot, since what constitutes a large number of buyers and sellers can be different under different conditions. What is important is this:

In a perfectly competitive market, the number of buyers and sellers is so large that no individual decision maker can significantly affect the price of the product by changing the quantity it buys or sells.

Think of the market for wheat. On the selling side, there are thousands of individual wheat farmers in the United States, each producing only a small fraction of the total market quantity. If any one farm were to double, triple, or even quadruple its production, the impact on total market quantity and market price would be negligible. The same is true on the buying side: There are so many small buyers that no one of them can affect the market price by increasing or decreasing its quantity demanded.

Most agricultural markets conform to the large-number–small-participant requirement, as do markets for precious metals such as gold and silver and markets for the stocks and bonds of large corporations. For example, more than 6 million shares of General Motors stock are bought and sold *every day,* at a price (as this is written) of about $50 per share. A decision by a very large stockholder to sell, say, $1 million dollars worth of this stock—20,000 shares—would cause only a barely noticeable change in quantity supplied on any given day.

But now think about the market for notebook computers. Here, four large producers—Toshiba, Compaq, IBM, and Apple—account for 75 percent of total sales in the United States. If any one of these producers decided to change its output by even 10 percent, the impact on total quantity supplied—and market price—would be *very* noticeable. The market for notebook computers thus fails the large-number–small-participant requirement, so it is not an example of perfect competition.

A STANDARDIZED PRODUCT OFFERED BY SELLERS. In a perfectly competitive market, buyers do not perceive significant differences between the products of one seller and another. For example, buyers of wheat will ordinarily have no preference for one farmer's wheat over another's, so wheat would surely pass the standardized product test. The same is true of many other agricultural products, such as corn syrup and soybeans. It is also true of commodities like crude oil or pork bellies, precious metals like gold or silver, and financial instruments such as the stocks and bonds of a particular firm. (One share of AT&T stock is indistinguishable from another.)

When buyers *do* notice significant differences in the outputs of different sellers, the market is not perfectly competitive. For example, most consumers perceive differences among the various brands of coffee on the supermarket shelf and may have strong preferences for one particular brand. Coffee, therefore, fails the standardized product test of perfect competition. Other goods and services that would fail this test include personal computers, automobiles, houses, colleges, and medical care.

EASY ENTRY INTO AND EXIT FROM THE MARKET. Entry into a market is rarely free—a new seller must always incur *some* costs to set up shop, begin production, and establish contacts with customers. But a perfectly competitive market has no *significant* barriers to discourage new entrants: Any firm wishing to enter can do business on the same terms as firms that are already there. For example, anyone with the right background in farming can begin planting and growing wheat by paying the same costs as veteran wheat farmers. The same is true of anyone wishing to sell leather wallets, to open up a dry-cleaning shop, or to set up a new restaurant. Each of these examples would pass the free-entry test of perfect competition.

In many markets, however, there are significant barriers to entry. These are often imposed by government. Sometimes, the government imposes *absolute* restrictions on the number of market participants allowed. For example, the number of taxicabs licensed to operate in New York City is fixed, determined by the city government. From the 1930s until 1996, this number was set at 11,787. In mid-1996, the city finally issued 133 additional licenses, bringing the total to 11,920. Unless the city issues more licenses in the future, true entry into this market will be impossible—the licenses may change hands, but the total number of legally operated taxis cannot increase. Another example of government barriers to entry are *zoning laws*. These place strict limits on how many businesses such as movie theaters, supermarkets, or hotels can operate in a local area.

Barriers to entry can also arise without any government action, simply because existing sellers have an important advantage new entrants cannot duplicate. The brand loyalty enjoyed by existing producers of breakfast cereals, instant coffee, and soft drinks would require a new entrant to wrest customers away from existing firms—a very costly undertaking. Or significant economies of scale may give existing firms a cost advantage over new entrants. We will discuss these and other barriers to entry in more detail in later chapters.

In addition to easy entry, perfect competition requires easy *exit*: A firm suffering a long-run loss must be able to sell off its plant and equipment and leave the industry for good, without obstacles. Some markets satisfy this requirement, and some do not. Plant-closing laws or union agreements can require lengthy advance notice and high severance pay when workers are laid off. Or capital equipment may be so highly specialized—like an assembly line designed to produce just one type of automobile—that it cannot be sold off if the firm decides to exit the market. These and other barriers to exit do not conform to the assumptions of perfect competition.

IS PERFECT COMPETITION REALISTIC?

The three assumptions a market must satisfy to be perfectly competitive (or just "competitive" for short) are rather restrictive. Do any markets satisfy all these requirements? How broadly can we apply the model of perfect competition when we think about the real world?

First, remember that perfect competition is a *model*—an abstract representation of reality. No model can capture *all* of the details of a real-world market, nor should it. Still, in some cases, the model fits remarkably well. We have seen that the market for wheat, for example, passes all three tests for a competitive market: many buyers and sellers, standardized output, and easy entry and exit. Indeed, many other agricultural markets satisfy the strict requirements of perfect competition quite closely, as do many financial markets (stocks, bonds, commodities, foreign currency) and some markets for consumer goods and services (notebook paper, staples, fresh-cut flowers).

But in the vast majority of markets, one or more of the assumptions of perfect competition will, in a strict sense, be violated. This might suggest that the model can be applied only in a few limited cases. Yet when economists look at real-world markets, they use perfect competition more often than any other market structure. Why is this?

First, with perfect competition, we can use simple techniques to make some strong predictions about a market's response to changes in technology, consumer tastes, and government policies. While other types of market structure models also yield valuable predictions, they are often more cumbersome and the predictions less definitive. Second, economists believe that many markets—while not strictly perfectly competitive—come *reasonably* close. The more closely a real-world market fits the model, the more accurate our predictions will be when we use it.

We can even—with some caution—use the model to analyze markets that violate all three assumptions. Take the worldwide market for color televisions. There are about a dozen major sellers in this market. Each of them knows that its output decisions will have *some* effect on the market price, but no one of them can have a *major impact* on price. Consumers do recognize the difference between one brand and another, but their preferences are not very strong, and most recognize that quality has become so standardized that different brands are actually close substitutes for one another. And there are indeed barriers to entry—existing firms have supply and distribution networks that would be difficult for new entrants to replicate—but these barriers are not *so* great that they would keep out new entrants in the face of high potential profit. Thus, although the market for televisions does not strictly satisfy any of the requirements of perfect competition, it is not *too* far off on any one of them. The model will not perform as accurately for televisions as it does for wheat, but depending on how much accuracy we need, it may do just fine.

In sum, perfect competition can approximate conditions and yield accurate-enough predictions in a wide variety of markets. This is why you will often find economists using the model to analyze the markets for crude oil, consumer electronic goods, fast-food meals, medical care, and higher education, even though in each of these cases one or more of the requirements may not be strictly satisfied.

THE PERFECTLY COMPETITIVE FIRM

When we stand at a distance and look at conditions in a competitive market, we get one view of what is occurring; when we stand close and look at the individual competitive *firm*, we get an entirely different picture. But these two pictures are very closely related. After all, a market is a collection of individual decision makers, much as a human body is a collection of individual cells. In a perfectly competitive market, the individual cells of firms and consumers and the overall body of the market affect each other through a variety of feedback mechanisms. This is why, in learning about the competitive firm, we must also discuss the competitive market in which it operates.

Figure 1(a) applies the tools you have already learned—supply and demand—to the competitive market for gold. The market demand curve slopes downward: As price rises, buyers will want to purchase less. The supply curve slopes upward: As price rises, the total quantity supplied by firms in the market will rise. The intersection of the supply and demand curves determines the equilibrium price of gold, which, in the figure, is $400 per ounce. This is all familiar territory. But now let's

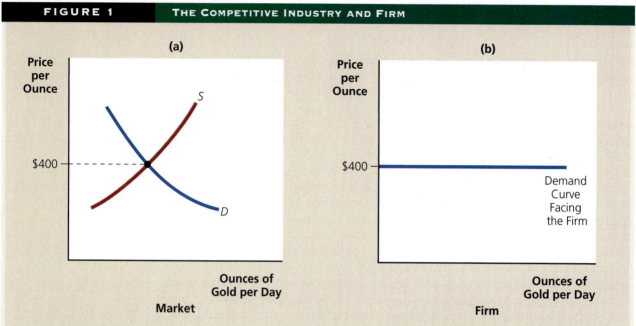

FIGURE 1   **THE COMPETITIVE INDUSTRY AND FIRM**

(a)

(b)

In panel (a) the market supply and demand curves intersect to determine a market price of $400 per ounce. The typical firm in panel (b) can sell all it wants at that price. The demand curve facing the competitive firm is a horizontal line at the market price.

switch lenses and see how an individual gold-mining company views the market for its *own* output.

THE DEMAND CURVE FACING A COMPETITIVE FIRM

Figure 1(b) shows the demand curve facing Small-Time Gold Mines, a small mining company. The curve is horizontal—infinitely price elastic—telling us that no matter how much gold Small-Time produces, it will always sell it at the same price—$400 per troy ounce.[1] Why should this be?

First, in perfect competition, output is standardized—buyers do not distinguish the gold of one mine from that of another. If Small-Time were to charge a price even a tiny bit higher than other producers, it would lose all of its customers—they would simply buy from Small-Time's competitors, whose prices would be lower. The horizontal demand curve captures this effect. It tells us that if Small-Time raises its price above $400, it will not just sell *less* output; it will sell *no* output.

Second, Small-Time is only a tiny producer, relative to the entire gold market. No matter how much it decides to produce, it cannot make a noticeable difference in market quantity supplied and so cannot affect the market price. Once again, the horizontal demand curve describes this effect perfectly: The firm can increase its production without having to lower its price.

---

1.   Gold is sold by the troy ounce, which is about 10 percent heavier than a regular ounce.

All of this means that Small-Time has no control over the price of its output—it simply accepts the market price as a given:

*In perfect competition, the firm is a **price taker**—it treats the price of its output as given.*

The horizontal demand curve facing the firm and the resulting price-taking behavior of firms are hallmarks of perfect competition. If a manager thinks, "If we produce more output, we will have to lower our price," then the firm faces a *downward-sloping* demand curve and is not a competitive firm. The manager of a competitive firm will always think, "We can sell all the output we want at the going price, so how much should we produce?"

COST AND REVENUE DATA FOR A COMPETITIVE FIRM

Now let's get more specific about our firm. Table 1 shows cost and revenue data for Small-Time Gold.

In the first two columns are different quantities of gold that Small-Time could produce each day and the maximum price that it could charge. Because Small-Time is a competitive firm—a price taker—the price remains constant at $400 per ounce, no matter how much gold it produces.

Run your finger down the total revenue and marginal revenue columns. Since price is always $400, each time the firm produces another ounce of gold, total

TABLE 1	COST AND REVENUE DATA FOR SMALL-TIME GOLD					
Output (troy ounces of gold per day)	Price (per troy ounce)	Total Revenue	Marginal Revenue	Total Cost	Marginal Cost	Profit
0	$400	$0		$550		−$550
			$400		$450	
1	$400	$400		$1,000		−$600
			$400		$200	
2	$400	$800		$1,200		−$400
			$400		$50	
3	$400	$1,200		$1,250		−$50
			$400		$100	
4	$400	$1,600		$1,350		$250
			$400		$150	
5	$400	$2,000		$1,500		$500
			$400		$250	
6	$400	$2,400		$1,750		$650
			$400		$350	
7	$400	$2,800		$2,100		$700
			$400		$450	
8	$400	$3,200		$2,550		$650
			$400		$550	
9	$400	$3,600		$3,100		$500
			$400		$650	
10	$400	$4,000		$3,750		$250

FIGURE 2	PROFIT MAXIMIZATION IN PERFECT COMPETITION

Panel (a) shows a competitive firm's total revenue (TR) and total cost (TC) curves. TR is a straight line with slope equal to the market price. Profit is maximized at 7 ounces per day, where the vertical distance between TR and TC is greatest. Panel (b) shows that profit is maximized where marginal cost (MC) intersects the horizontal demand (d) and marginal revenue (MR) curve.

revenue rises by $400. This is why marginal revenue—the additional revenue from selling one more ounce of gold—remains constant at $400.

Figure 2 plots Small-Time's total revenue and marginal revenue. Notice that the total revenue (TR) curve, in the upper panel, is a *straight line* that slopes upward—each time output increases by one unit, TR rises by the same $400. That is, the slope of the TR curve is equal to the price of output.

The marginal revenue (MR) curve is a *horizontal* line at the market price. In fact, the MR curve is the same horizontal line as the demand curve:

> *For a competitive firm, marginal revenue at each quantity is the same as the market price. For this reason, the marginal revenue curve and the demand curve facing the firm are the same—a horizontal line at the market price.*

In the lower panel of the figure, we have labeled the horizontal line "$d = MR$," since this line is both the firm's demand curve (d) *and* its marginal revenue curve (MR).[2]

The next two columns of Table 1 show total cost and marginal cost for Small-Time Gold Mines. There is nothing special about cost data for a competitive firm. In the figure, you can see that marginal cost (MC)—as usual—first falls and then rises. Total cost, therefore, rises first at a decreasing rate and then at an increasing rate. (You may want to look at Chapter 6 to review why this cost behavior is so common.)

FINDING THE PROFIT-MAXIMIZING OUTPUT LEVEL

A competitive firm—like any other firm—wants to earn the highest possible profit, and to do so, it should use the principles you learned in Chapter 6. Although the diagrams look a bit different for competitive firms, the ideas behind them are the same. We can use either Table 1 or Figure 2 to find the profit-maximizing output level. And we can use the techniques you have already learned: the total-revenue and total-cost approach, or the marginal-revenue and marginal-cost approach.

THE TOTAL-REVENUE AND TOTAL-COST APPROACH. In the *TR* and *TC* approach, profit at each output level—entered in the last column of Table 1—is equal to *TR* − *TC*. Scan the profit entries until you find the highest value—$700 per day. The output level at which the firm earns this profit—7 ounces per day—is the profit-maximizing output level. Alternatively, use the graph in the upper panel of Figure 2. Profit is the distance between the *TR* and *TC* curves, and this distance is greatest when the firm is producing 7 units of output, verifying what we found in the table.

THE MARGINAL-REVENUE AND MARGINAL-COST APPROACH. In the *MR* and *MC* approach, the firm should continue to increase output as long as marginal revenue is greater than marginal cost. You can verify, using the table, that if the firm is initially producing 1, 2, 3, 4, 5, or 6 units, *MR* > *MC*, so producing more will raise profit. Once the firm is producing 7 units, however, *MR* < *MC*, so further increases in output will reduce profit. Alternatively, using the graph, we look for the output level at which *MR* = *MC*. As the graph shows, there are two output levels at which the *MR* and *MC* curves intersect. However, we can rule out the first crossing point because there, the *MC* curve crosses the *MR* curve from above. Remember that the profit-maximizing output is found where the *MC* curve crosses the *MR* curve *from below*. Once again, this occurs at 7 units of output.

You can see that finding the profit-maximizing output level for a competitive firm requires no new concepts or techniques; you have already learned everything you need to know in Chapter 6. In fact, the only difference is one of appearance. Ned's Beds—our firm in Chapter 6—did *not* operate under perfect competition. As a result, both its demand curve and its marginal revenue curve sloped *downward*.

---

2.   In this and later chapters, lowercase letters refer to the individual firm and uppercase letters to the entire market. For example, the demand curve facing the firm is labeled "*d*," while the market demand curve is labeled "*D.*"

Small-Time, however, operates under perfect competition, so its demand and *MR* curves are the same horizontal line.

MEASURING TOTAL PROFIT

You have already seen one way to measure a firm's total profit on a graph: the vertical distance between the *TR* and *TC* curves. In this section, you will learn another graphical way to measure profit.

To do this, we start with the firm's *profit per unit*, which is the revenue it gets on each unit minus the cost per unit. Revenue per unit is just the price (*P*) of the firm's output, and cost per unit is our familiar *ATC*, so we can write:

$$\text{profit per unit} = P - ATC$$

In Figure 3(a), Small-Time's *ATC* curve has been plotted from the data in Table 1. When the firm is producing at the profit-maximizing output level, 7 units, its *ATC* is $300. Since the price of output is $400, profit *per unit* = *P* − *ATC* = $400 − $300 = $100. This is just the vertical distance between the firm's demand curve and its *ATC* curve at the profit-maximizing output level.

Once we know Small-Time's profit per unit, it is easy to calculate its *total* profit: Just multiply profit per unit by the number of units sold. Small-Time Gold is earning $100 profit on each ounce of gold, and it sells 7 ounces in all, so total profit is $100 × 7 = $700.

Now look at the blue shaded rectangle in Figure 3(a). The height of this rectangle is profit per unit, and the width is the number of units produced. The *area* of the rectangle—height × width—equals Small-Time's profit:

> *A firm earns a profit whenever* P > ATC. *Its total profit at the best output level equals the area of a rectangle with height equal to the distance between* P *and* ATC *and width equal to the level of output.*

In the figure, Small-Time is fortunate: At a price of $400, there are several output levels at which it can earn a profit. Its problem is to select the one that makes its profit as great as possible. We should all have such problems.

But what if the price had been lower than $400—so low, in fact, that Small-Time could not make a profit at *any* output level? Then the best it can do is to choose the smallest possible loss. Just as we did in the case of profit, we can measure the firm's total loss using the *ATC* curve.

Panel (b) of Figure 3 reproduces Small-Time's *ATC* and *MC* curves from panel (a). This time, however, we have assumed a lower price for gold—$200—so the firm's *d* = *MR* curve is the horizontal line at $200. Since this line lies everywhere below the *ATC* curve, profit per unit (*P* − *ATC*) is always negative: Small-Time cannot make a positive profit at *any* output level.

With a price of $200, the *MC* curve crosses the *MR* curve from below at 5 units of output. Thus, unless Small-Time decides to shut down (we'll discuss shutting

DANGEROUS CURVES

In Figure 3, we are using the *ATC* curve to help us *measure* profit and loss. Do not make the mistake of using *ATC* in place of *MC* to *find* the profit-maximizing output level. In particular, it is tempting—but *wrong*—to think that the firm should produce where profit *per unit* (*P* − *ATC*) is greatest. The firm's goal is to maximize *total* profit, not profit per unit. Using Table 1 or Figure 3, you can verify that while Small-Time's profit *per unit* is greatest at 6 units of output, its *total* profit is greatest at 7 units.

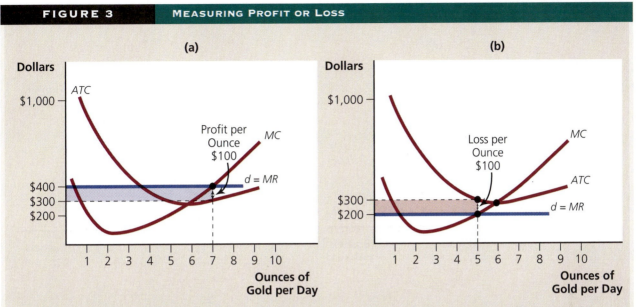

FIGURE 3 — **MEASURING PROFIT OR LOSS**

The competitive firm in panel (a) produces where marginal cost equals marginal revenue, or 7 units of output per day. Profit per unit at that output level is equal to revenue per unit ($400) minus cost per unit ($300), or $100 per unit. Total profit (indicated by the blue-shaded rectangle) is equal to profit per unit times the number of units sold, $100 × 7 = $700. In panel (b), the firm faces a lower market price of $200 per ounce. The best it can do is to produce 5 ounces per day and suffer a loss shown by the red area. It loses $100 per ounce on each of those 5 ounces produced, so the total loss is $500—the area of the red-shaded rectangle.

down later), it should produce 5 units. At that level of output, *ATC* is $300, and profit per unit is $P - ATC = \$200 - \$300 = -\$100$, a *loss* of $100 per unit. The total loss is loss per unit times the number of units produced, or $-\$100 \times 5 = -\$500$. This is equal to the area of the red shaded rectangle in Figure 3(b), with height equal to $100 and width equal to 5 units:

> *A firm suffers a loss whenever* P < ATC *at the best level of output. Its total loss equals the area of a rectangle with height equal to the distance between* P *and* ATC *and width equal to the level of output.*

THE FIRM'S SHORT-RUN SUPPLY CURVE

A competitive firm is a price taker: It takes the market price as given and then decides how much output it will produce at that price. If the market price changes for any reason, the price taken as given will change as well. The firm will then have to find a new profit-maximizing output level. Let's see how the firm's choice of output changes as the market price rises or falls.

Figure 4(a) shows *ATC, AVC,* and *MC* curves for a competitive producer of soybeans. The figure also shows 5 hypothetical demand curves the firm might face, each corresponding to a different market price for soybeans. If the market price were $7 per bushel, the firm would face demand curve d_1, and its profit-maximizing output level—where $MC = MR$—would be 7,000 bushels per year. If the price dropped to $5 per bushel, the firm would face demand curve d_2, and its profit-maximizing output level would drop to 5,000 bushels. You can see that the profit-maximizing

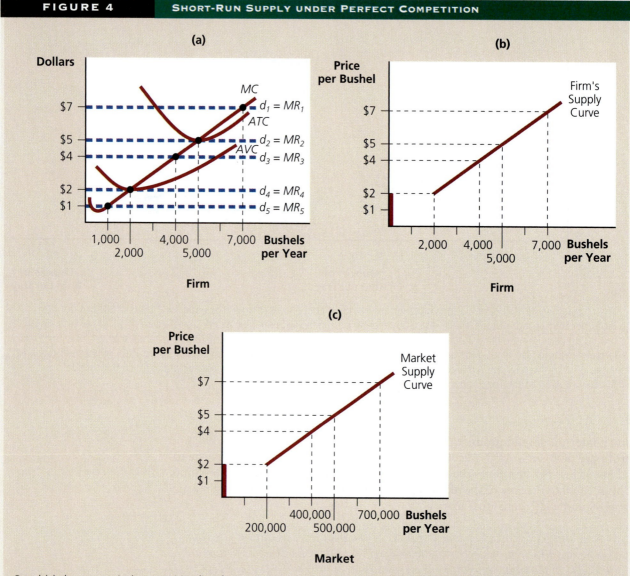

FIGURE 4   **SHORT-RUN SUPPLY UNDER PERFECT COMPETITION**

Panel (a) shows a typical competitive firm facing various market prices. For prices between $2 and $7 per bushel, the profit-maximizing quantity is found by sliding along the *MC* curve. Below $2 per bushel, the firm is better off shutting down, because *P* < *AVC*, and so *TR* < *TVC*. Panel (b) shows that the firm's supply curve consists of two segments. Above the shutdown price of $2 per bushel it follows the *MC* curve; below that price, it is coincident with the vertical axis. The market supply curve of panel (c) is obtained by adding up the quantities of output supplied by all firms in the market at each price.

output level is always found by traveling from the price, across to the firm's *MC* curve, and then down to the horizontal axis. In other words,

**MARGINAL
DECISION MAKING**

as the price of output changes, the firm will slide along its MC curve in deciding how much to produce.

But there is one problem with this: If the firm is suffering a loss—a loss large enough to justify shutting down—then it will *not* produce along its *MC* curve; it will produce zero units instead. Thus, in order to know for certain how much output the firm will produce, we must bring in the shutdown rule you learned in Chapter 6.

Suppose the price in Figure 4(a) drops down to $4 per bushel. At this price, the best output level is 4,000 bushels, and the firm suffers a loss, since $P < ATC$. Should the firm shut down? Let's see. At 4,000 bushels, it is also true that $P > AVC$, since the demand curve lies above the *AVC* curve at this output level. Multiplying both sides of the last inequality by Q gives us

$$P \times Q > AVC \times Q$$

Since $AVC \times Q$ is just *TVC*, this inequality is the same as

$$TR > TVC$$

As we know from Chapter 6, a firm should never shut down when $TR > TVC$. Thus, at a price of $4, the firm will stay open and produce 4,000 units of output.

Now, suppose the price drops all the way down to $1 per bushel. At this price, $MR = MC$ at 1,000 bushels, but notice that here $P < AVC$. Once again, we multiply both sides by Q to obtain

$$P \times Q < AVC \times Q$$

or

$$TR < TVC$$

A firm should *always* shut down when $TR < TVC$, so at a price of $1, this firm will produce *zero* units of output.

Finally, at a price of $2, $MR = MC$ at 2,000 units, and here we have $P = AVC$ or $TR = TVC$. At $2, therefore, the firm will be indifferent between staying open and shutting down. We call this price the firm's **shutdown price**, since it will shut down at any price lower and stay open at any price higher. The output level at which the firm will shut down must occur at the *minimum* of the *AVC* curve, since the best output level is found by sliding along the *MC* curve, and *MC* will always cross *AVC* at its minimum point.

Now let's recapitulate what we've found about the firm's output decision. For all prices above the minimum point on the *AVC* curve, the firm will stay open and will produce the level of output where $MR = MC$. For these prices, the firm slides along its *MC* curve in deciding how much output to produce. But for any price below the minimum *AVC*, the firm will shut down and produce zero units. We can summarize all of this information in a single curve—the **firm's supply curve**—which tells us how much output the firm will produce at any price:

> *The competitive firm's supply curve has two parts. For all prices above the minimum point on its* AVC *curve, the supply curve coincides with the* MC *curve. For all prices below the minimum point on the* AVC *curve, the firm will shut down, so its supply curve becomes a vertical line at zero units of output.*

In panel (b) of Figure 4, we have drawn the supply curve for our hypothetical soybean producer. As price declines from $7 to $2, output is determined by the firm's *MC* curve. For all prices *below* $2—the shutdown price—output is zero and the supply curve coincides with the vertical axis.

SHUTDOWN PRICE The price at which a firm is indifferent between producing and shutting down.

FIRM'S SUPPLY CURVE A curve that shows the quantity of output a competitive firm will produce at different prices.

COMPETITIVE MARKETS IN THE SHORT RUN

Recall that the short run is a time horizon too short for the firm to vary *all* of its inputs: The quantity of at least one input remains fixed. For example, in the short run, a soybean farmer will be stuck with a certain plot of land and a certain number of tractors. When we extend the concept of the short run from the firm to the market as a whole, it makes sense that if the short run is insufficient time for a firm to vary its fixed inputs, then it is also insufficient time for a *new* firm to acquire those fixed inputs and *enter* the market. Similarly, it is too short a period for firms to reduce their fixed inputs to zero and *exit* the market. We conclude that

> *In the short run, the number of firms in the industry is fixed.*

THE (SHORT-RUN) MARKET SUPPLY CURVE

MARKET SUPPLY CURVE
A curve indicating the quantity of output that all sellers in a market will produce at different prices.

Once we know how to find the supply curve of each individual firm in a market, it is a simple matter to determine the short-run **market supply curve**—showing the amount of output that all sellers in the market will offer at each price.

> *To obtain the market supply curve, simply add up the quantities of output supplied by all firms in the market at each price.*

To keep things simple, suppose there are 100 identical soybean producers and that each one has the supply curve shown in Figure 4(b). Then, at a price of $7, each firm would produce 7,000 bushels. With 100 such firms, the market quantity supplied will be $7,000 \times 100 = 700,000$ bushels. At a price of $5, each firm would supply 5,000 bushels, so market supply would be 500,000. Continuing in this way, we can trace out the market supply curve shown in panel (c) of the figure. Notice that once the price drops below $2—the shutdown price for each firm—the market supply curve jumps to zero.

The market supply curve in the figure is a *short-run* market supply curve, since it gives us the combined output level of just those firms already in the industry. As we move along this curve, we are holding two things constant: (1) the fixed inputs of each firm and (2) the number of firms in the market.

SHORT-RUN EQUILIBRIUM

Now that you see where the market supply curve comes from, we can go back to where we started our analysis of perfect competition—supply and demand—with new understanding. Figure 5 puts together the pieces we've discussed so far, including those from Chapter 4 on consumer theory, to paint a complete picture of how a competitive market arrives at a short-run equilibrium. On the right side, we add up the quantities supplied by all firms to obtain the market supply curve. On the left side, we add up the quantities demanded by all consumers to obtain the market demand curve. The market supply and demand curves show if/then relationships: *If* the price were such and such, *then* firms would supply this much and consumers would buy that much. Up to this point, the prices and quantities are purely hypothetical. But once we bring the two curves together and find their intersection point, we know the *equilibrium* price—the price at which trading will actually take place. Finally, we confront each firm and each consumer with the equilibrium price to find the actual quantity each consumer will buy and the actual quantity each firm will produce.

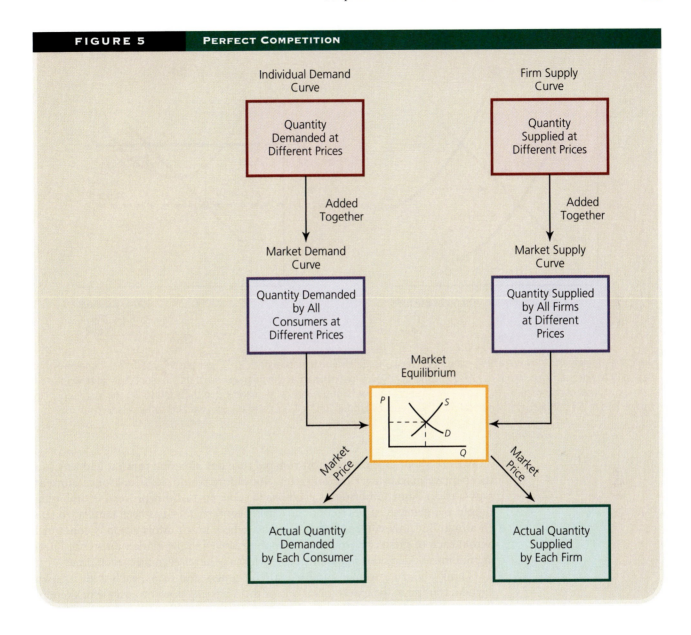

FIGURE 5 — **PERFECT COMPETITION**

Figure 6 gets more specific, illustrating two possible short-run equilibria in the soybean market. In panel (a), if the market demand curve were D_1, the short-run equilibrium price would be $7. Each firm would face the horizontal demand curve d_1 (panel b) and decide to produce 7,000 bushels. With 100 such firms, the equilibrium market quantity would be 700,000 bushels. Notice that, at a price of $7, each firm is enjoying an economic profit, since $P > ATC$.

If the market demand curve were D_2 instead, the equilibrium price would be $4. Each firm would face demand curve d_2, and produce 4,000 bushels. With 100 firms, the equilibrium market quantity would be 400,000. Here, each firm is suffering an economic loss, since $P < ATC$. These two examples show us that *in short-run equilibrium, competitive firms can earn an economic profit or suffer an economic loss.*

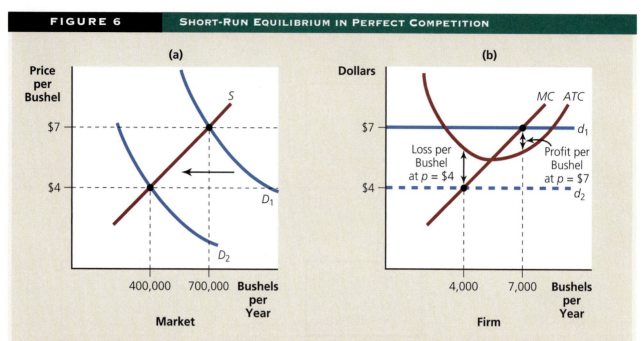

FIGURE 6	SHORT-RUN EQUILIBRIUM IN PERFECT COMPETITION

In panel (a) demand curve D_1 intersects supply curve S to determine a market price of $7 per bushel. The firm in panel (b) takes that price as given, produces 7,000 bushels per year—determined at the intersection of its marginal cost curve with the horizontal demand curve, d_1—and earns a short-run profit. If the market demand curve shifts left to D_2, the market price falls to $4 per bushel. The typical firm then reduces production to 4,000 bushels per year and suffers a short-run loss.

We are about to leave the short run and turn our attention to what happens in a competitive market over the long run. But before we do, let's look once more at how a short-run equilibrium is established. One part of this process—combining supply and demand curves to find the market equilibrium—has been familiar to you all along. But now you can better appreciate how much information is contained within each of these curves and what an impressive job the market does coordinating millions of decisions made by people who may never even meet each other.

Think about it: So many individual consumers and firms, each with its own agenda, trading in the market. Not one of them has any power to decide or even influence the market price. Rather, the price is determined by *all* of them, adjusting until *total* quantity supplied is equal to *total* quantity demanded. Then, facing this equilibrium price, each consumer buys the quantity he or she wants, each firm produces the output level that it wants, and we can be confident that all of them will be able to realize their plans. Each buyer can find willing sellers, and each seller can find willing buyers.

MARKETS AND EQUILIBRIUM

> *In perfect competition, the market sums up the buying and selling preferences of individual consumers and producers and determines the market price. Each buyer and seller then takes the market price as given, and each is able to buy or sell the desired quantity.*

This process is, from a certain perspective, a thing of beauty, and it happens each day in markets all across the world—markets for wheat, corn, barley, soybeans, apples, oranges, gold, silver, copper, and more. And something quite similar happens in other markets that do not strictly satisfy our requirements for perfect competition—markets for television sets, books, air conditioners, fast-food meals, oil, natural gas, bottled water, blue jeans. . . . The list is virtually endless.

COMPETITIVE MARKETS IN THE LONG RUN

So far, we've explored the short run only, and assumed that the number of firms in the market is fixed. But perfect competition becomes even *more* interesting in the long run, when entry and exit can occur. After all, the long run is a time horizon long enough for firms to vary *all* of their inputs. It should therefore be long enough for *new* firms to acquire fixed inputs and enter the market and for firms already in the industry to sell off their fixed inputs and *exit* from the market.

But what makes firms want to enter or exit a market? The driving force behind entry is economic profit, and the force behind exit is economic loss.

PROFIT AND LOSS AND THE LONG RUN

Recall that economic profit is the amount by which total revenue exceeds *all* costs of doing business. The costs to be deducted include implicit costs, like forgone investment income and forgone wages for an owner who devotes money and time to the business. Thus, when a firm earns positive economic profit, we know the owners are earning *more* than they could by devoting their money and time to some other activity.

A temporary episode of positive economic profit will not have much impact on a competitive industry other than the temporary pleasure it gives the owners of competitive firms. But when positive profit reflects basic conditions in the industry and is expected to continue, major changes are in the works. Outsiders, hungry for profit themselves, will want to enter the market, and—since *there are no barriers to entry*—they can do so.

Similarly, if firms are suffering economic losses, they are not earning enough revenue to cover all their costs, so there must be other opportunities that would more adequately compensate owners for their money or time. If this situation is expected to continue over the firm's long-run planning horizon—a period long enough to vary *all* inputs—there is only one thing for the firm to do: exit the industry by selling off its plant and equipment, thereby reducing its loss to zero.

> *In a competitive market, economic profit and loss are the forces driving long-run change. The expectation of continued economic profit causes outsiders to enter the market; the expectation of continued economic losses causes firms in the market to exit.*

In the real world of business, entry and exit occur literally every day. In some cases, we see entry occur through the formation of an entirely new firm. For example, in the late 1980s and early 1990s, the high profits of coffee bars led to thousands of new ones springing up all around the country. Entry can also occur when an existing firm adds a new product to its line. For example, high profits in the laptop computer industry in the early 1990s led several established firms in other industries—including Panasonic, Fujitsu, and Olivetti—to begin producing laptops. Although these were *not new firms*, they were *new participants* in the market for laptops.

Exit, too, can occur in different ways. A firm may go out of business entirely, selling off its assets and freeing itself once and for all from all costs. Every year, thousands of small businesses exit markets in this way. You may know of a local video store, grocery store, or furniture shop that decided to permanently shut its doors. Restaurants, in particular, seem especially prone to long-run economic loss: It has been reported that half of all new restaurants exit the market within two years of being established.

But exit can also occur when a firm switches out of a particular product line, even as it continues to produce other things. For example, publishing companies often decide to abandon unsuccessful magazines yet continue to thrive by publishing other magazines and books.

LONG-RUN EQUILIBRIUM

Entry and exit—however they occur—are powerful forces in real-world competitive markets. They determine how these markets change over the long run, how much output will ultimately be available to consumers, and the prices they must pay. To explore these issues, let's see how entry and exit move a market to its long-run equilibrium from different starting points.

FROM SHORT-RUN PROFIT TO LONG-RUN EQUILIBRIUM.

Suppose that the market for soybeans is initially in a short-run equilibrium like point A in Figure 7(a), with market supply curve S_1. (Ignore the other supply curves for now.) The initial equilibrium price is $9 per bushel. In panel (b), we see that a typical competitive firm—producing 9,000 bushels—is earning economic profit, since $P > ATC$ at that output level. As long as we remain in the short run—with no new firms entering the market—this situation will not change.

But as we enter the long run, much will change. First, economic profit will cause entry, increasing the number of sellers in the market and *shifting the market supply curve rightward*. (Remember, the market supply curve S_1 is drawn for a fixed number of firms; with more firms in the market, a greater quantity will be supplied at each price.) In panel (a), as the market supply curve shifts from S_1 to S_2 to S_3, several things happen:

1. The market price begins to fall—from $9 to $8 to $7 and so on.
2. As market price falls, the demand curve facing each firm begins shifting downward, from d_1 to d_2 to d_3 and so on.
3. Each firm—striving as always to maximize profit—will slide down its marginal cost curve, decreasing output. In the figure, the typical firm will move from point A to point B to point C, decreasing output from 9,000 to 8,000 to 7,000, and so on.[3]

This process of adjustment—in the market and the firm—continues until . . . until when? To answer this question, remember why these adjustments are occurring in the first place: Economic profit is attracting new entrants and shifting the market supply curve rightward. Thus, all of these changes will stop when the *reason* for entry—positive profit—no longer exists. And this, in turn, requires the market supply curve to shift rightward enough, and the price to fall enough, so that *each existing firm is earning zero economic profit*. But that will be true only when the market

---

3.   There is one other possible consequence that we ignore here: Entry into the industry—which changes the demand for the industry's inputs—may also change input prices. If this occurs, firms' *ATC* curves will shift. For now, we will assume that entry (and exit) do not affect input prices, so that the *ATC* curve does not shift.

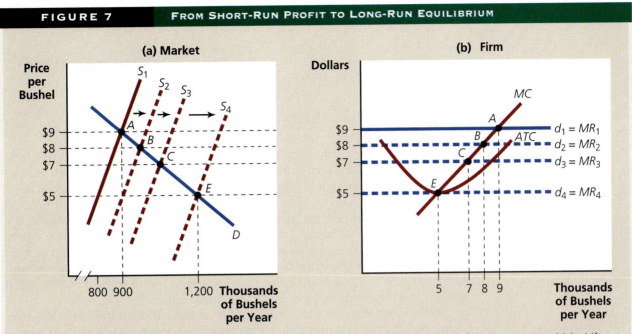

FIGURE 7 · FROM SHORT-RUN PROFIT TO LONG-RUN EQUILIBRIUM

At a price of $9 per bushel, the competitive firm of panel (b) earns an economic profit. Profit attracts entry, which shifts the market supply rightward in panel (a), reducing the market price. As the price falls, the demand curve facing each firm in panel (b) shifts downward. Each firm, trying to maximize its profit, slides down its *MC* curve, decreasing output. The process continues until economic profit is eliminated and there is no incentive for additional firms to enter the industry.

supply curve has shifted to S_4, the price has fallen to $5, and each firm is producing with *ATC* = $5. Thus, the new (and final) equilibrium is at point *E*.

> *In a competitive market, positive economic profit continues to attract new entrants until economic profit is reduced to zero.*

Before proceeding further, take a close look at Figure 7. As the market moves to its long-run equilibrium (point *E* in both panels), output at each firm *decreases* from 9,000 to 5,000 bushels. But in the market as a whole, output *increases* from 900,000 to 1,200,000 bushels. How can this be? (See if you can answer this question yourself. Hint: entry!)

FROM SHORT-RUN LOSS TO LONG-RUN EQUILIBRIUM. We have just seen how, beginning from a position of short-run profit at the typical firm, a competitive market will adjust until the profit is eliminated. But what if we begin from a position of loss? As you might guess, the same type of adjustments will occur, only in the opposite direction.

This is a good opportunity for you to test your own skill and understanding. Study Figure 7 carefully. Then see if you can draw a similar diagram that illustrates the adjustment from short-run *loss* to long-run equilibrium. Start with a market price of $2. Use the same demand curve as in Figure 7, but draw in a new, appropriate market supply curve. Then let the market work. Show what happens in the market, and at each firm, as economic loss causes some firms to exit. If you do this correctly, you'll end up once again at a market price of $5, with each firm earning zero economic profit. Your graph will illustrate the following conclusion:

> *In a competitive market, economic losses continue to cause exit until the losses are reduced to zero.*

DISTINGUISHING SHORT-RUN FROM LONG-RUN OUTCOMES

You've seen that the equilibrium in a competitive market can be very different in the short run and the long run. In short-run equilibrium, competitive firms can earn profits or suffer losses. But in long-run equilibrium, after entry or exit has occurred, economic profit is always zero. The distinction between short-run and long-run equilibrium is important and not just in competitive markets. In *any* market, the "rules of the game" depend on the time period we are considering, and the correct period depends on the question we are asking. If we want to predict what happens several years after a change in demand, we should ask what the new *long-run* equilibrium will be. If we want to know what happens a few *months* after a change in demand, we'll look for the new *short-run* equilibrium.

When economists look at a market, they automatically think of the short run versus the long run and then choose the period most appropriate for the question at hand. As you'll see, this way of thinking is applied again and again in economics. It is one of the basic principles you will learn in this book:

> ⚷ *Basic Principle #7: Short-Run versus Long-Run Outcomes*
> *Markets behave differently in the short run and the long run. In solving a problem, we must always know which of these time horizons we are analyzing.*

THE NOTION OF ZERO PROFIT IN PERFECT COMPETITION

From the preceding description, you may wonder why anyone in his or her right mind would ever want to set up shop in a competitive industry or stay there for any length of time since—in the long run—they can expect zero economic profit. Indeed, if you want to become a millionaire, you would be well advised not to buy a soybean farm. But most soybean farmers—like most other sellers in competitive markets—do not curse their fate. On the contrary, they are likely to be quite content with the performance of their businesses. How can this be?

Remember that zero *economic* profit is not the same as zero *accounting* profit. When a firm is making zero *economic* profit, it is covering all of the owner's costs—including compensation for any forgone investment income or forgone salary. Suppose, for example, that a soybean farmer paid $100,000 for land and works 40 hours per week. Suppose, too, that the money *could* have been invested in some other way and earned $6,000 per year, and the farmer *could* have worked equally pleasantly elsewhere and earned $40,000 per year. Then the farm's implicit costs will be $46,000, and zero economic profit means that the farm is earning $46,000 in *accounting profit* each year. This won't make a soybean farmer ecstatic, but it is just enough to make it worthwhile to keep at it. After all, if the farmer quits and takes up the next best alternative, he or she will do no better.

To emphasize that zero economic profit is not an unpleasant outcome, economists often replace it with the term "normal profit." Using this language, we can summarize long-run conditions at the typical firm this way:

> In the long run, every competitive firm will earn **normal profit**, that is, zero economic profit.

 **NORMAL PROFIT** Another name for zero economic profit

PERFECT COMPETITION AND PLANT SIZE

There is one more characteristic of competitive markets in the long run that we have not yet discussed: the plant size of the competitive firm. It is easy to see that the same forces—entry and exit—which ensure that all firms earn zero economic profit *also* ensure that:

> In long-run equilibrium, every competitive firm will select its plant size and output level so that it operates at the minimum point of its LRATC curve.

SHORT-RUN VERSUS LONG-RUN OUTCOMES

To see why, let's consider what would happen if this condition were violated. Figure 8(a) illustrates a firm in the competitive market for photocopy paper. The firm faces a market price of P_1 and produces quantity q_1, where $MC_1 = MR_1$. With its current plant, the firm has average costs given by ATC_1. Note that the firm is earning zero profit, since average costs are equal to P_1 at the best output level.

But panel (a) does *not* show a true long-run equilibrium. How do we know this? First, in the long run, the typical firm will want to expand. Why? Because by increasing its plant size, it could slide down its *LRATC* curve and produce more output at a lower cost per unit. Since it is a perfectly competitive firm—a small participant in the market—it can expand in this way *without* affecting market price. As a result, the firm—after expanding—could operate on a new, lower *ATC*

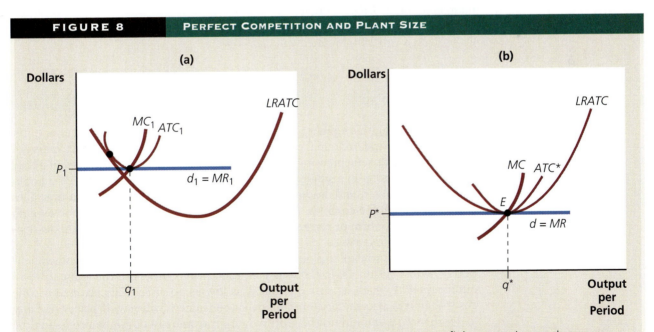

| FIGURE 8 | PERFECT COMPETITION AND PLANT SIZE |

The firm in panel (a) faces a price of P_1 and produces quantity q_1. It earns zero profit because price equals average cost. In the long run, this firm will want to expand; by sliding down *LRATC*, it could produce more output at a lower cost per unit and earn an economic profit. In turn, economic profit will attract entry, and that will reduce the market price. The firm's long-run equilibrium position is shown in panel (b). The firm earns zero profit by operating at minimum *LRATC*.

curve, so that *ATC* is less than *P*. That is, by expanding, the firm could earn an economic profit.

Second, this same opportunity to earn positive economic profit will attract new entrants that will establish larger plants from the outset. Expansion by existing firms and entry by new ones increase market output and bring down the market price. The process will stop only when there is no potential to earn positive economic profit with *any* plant size. As you can see in panel (b), this condition is satisfied only when each firm is operating at the minimum point on its *LRATC* curve, with the plant represented by the curve *ATC**, and output of *q**. Entry and expansion must continue in this market until the price falls to *P**, because only then will each firm—doing the best that it can do—earn zero economic profit. (Question: In the long run, what would happen to the firm in panel (a) if it refused to increase its plant size?)

A SUMMARY OF THE COMPETITIVE FIRM IN THE LONG RUN

Panel (b) of Figure 8 summarizes everything you have learned about the competitive firm in long-run equilibrium. The typical firm—taking the market price *P** as given—produces the profit-maximizing output level *q**, where $MR = MC$. Since this is the long run, each firm will be earning zero economic profit, so we also know that $P^* = ATC$. But since $P^* = MC$ and $P^* = ATC$, it must also be true that $MC = ATC$. As you learned in Chapter 5, *MC* and *ATC* are equal only at the minimum point of the *ATC* curve. Thus, we know that each firm must be operating at the lowest possible point on the *ATC* curve for the plant it is operating. Finally, each firm selects the plant that makes its *LRATC* as low as possible, so each operates at the minimum point on its *LRATC* curve.

As you can see, there is a lot going on in Figure 8(b). But we can put it all together with a very simple statement:

> *At each competitive firm in long-run equilibrium,* P = MC = *minimum* ATC = *minimum* LRATC.

In Figure 8(b), this equality is satisfied when the typical firm produces at point *E*, where its demand, marginal cost, *ATC*, and *LRATC* curves all intersect. This is a figure well worth remembering, since it summarizes so much information about competitive markets in a single picture. (Here is a useful self-test: Close the book, put away your notes, and draw a set of diagrams in which one curve at a time does *not* pass through the common intersection point of the other three. Then explain which principle of firm or market behavior is violated by your diagram. Do this separately for all four curves.)

Figure 8(b) also explains one of the important ways in which perfect competition benefits consumers: In the long run, each firm is driven to the plant size and output level at which its cost per unit is as low as possible. This lowest-possible cost per unit is also the price per unit that consumers will pay. If price were any lower than *P**, it would not be worthwhile for owners to continue producing the good in the long run. Thus, given the *ATC* curve faced by each firm in this industry—a curve that is determined by each firm's production function and the costs of its inputs—*P** is the lowest possible price that will ensure the continued availability of the good. In perfect competition, consumers are getting the best deal they could possibly get.

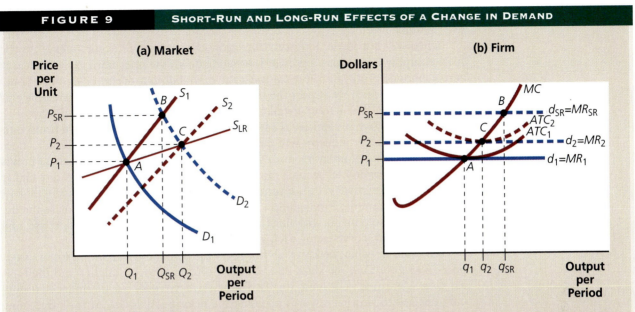

| FIGURE 9 | SHORT-RUN AND LONG-RUN EFFECTS OF A CHANGE IN DEMAND |

At point *A* in panel (a), the market is in long-run equilibrium. The typical firm in panel (b) produces q_1 and earns zero economic profit. If demand increases, market price rises to P_{SR} at point *B*. The firm increases output and earns an economic profit. But profit attracts entry, which increases market supply and drives the price back down to P_1. The typical firm once again earns zero economic profit. The long-run market supply curve is a horizontal line found by connecting points like *A* and *C* in panel (a).

WHAT HAPPENS WHEN THINGS CHANGE?

So far, you've learned how competitive firms make decisions, how these decisions lead to a short-run equilibrium in the market, and how the market moves from short- to long-run equilibrium through entry and exit. Now, we will pull all of this knowledge together to answer the following question: What happens to a competitive market in the short run and the long run when conditions change? In this section, we'll deal with a change in demand for the product and, in the process, learn some important additional features of perfect competition. In the section titled "Using the Theory," we'll look at changes in technology.

Figure 9(a) shows a competitive market that is initially in long-run equilibrium at point *A*, where the market demand curve D_1 and supply curve S_1 intersect. (Ignore the other curves for now.) Panel (b) shows conditions at the firm, which faces demand curve d_1 and produces the profit-maximizing quantity q_1.

But now suppose that the market demand curve shifts rightward to D_2 and remains there. As you learned in Chapter 3, this shift could be caused by a change in tastes for the product, an increase in income or wealth among buyers, an increase in population, a rise in the price of a substitute good, or a fall in the price of a complementary good. Regardless of the reason for the shift, its impact is the same. In the *short run*, market equilibrium moves to point *B*, with market output Q_{SR} and price P_{SR}. At the same time, each firm experiences an upward shift of its demand curve and raises output to the new profit-maximizing level q_{SR}. At this output level, $P > ATC$, so firms are earning economic profit. Thus, the short-run impact of an increase in demand is (1) a rise in market price, (2) a rise in market quantity, and (3) economic profits.

When we turn to the long run, we know that entry will occur (why?), so the market supply curve shifts rightward, bringing down the price until each firm earns zero economic profit. But how far must the price fall in order to bring this about? That is, how far can we expect the market supply curve to shift? In answering this question, we'll add one more detail to our model that we've ignored until now.

Think about what happens as entry occurs in an industry. With more firms, output increases, so the industry will demand more *inputs*—more raw materials, more labor, more capital, and more land. We can usually expect the prices of these inputs to rise.[4] But when inputs become more expensive, each firm will have to pay higher costs to produce *any* level of output. As a result, each firm's ATC curve will shift upward. For example, expansion in the artichoke industry would increase the demand for land suitable for growing this crop, cause the price of this land to rise, and force up the ATC curve facing each artichoke producer.

Let's sum up what we know so far. After the demand curve shifts, we arrive at point B (Figure 9) in the short run. At this point, the price is higher and the typical firm is earning economic profit. Profit attracts entry, so the market supply curve begins to shift rightward, bringing the price back down. At the same time, the expansion of output in the industry raises input prices and shifts the typical firm's ATC curve upward. In the figure, the ATC curve shifts upward to the dashed curve ATC_2.

Now comes our important conclusion: since the ATC curve has shifted up, zero profit will occur at a price *higher* than the initial price P_1. In the figure, the typical firm will earn zero profit when the price is P_2. Thus, entry will cease, and the market supply curve will *stop* shifting rightward, when the market price reaches P_2. In the figure, this occurs when the market supply curve reaches S_2. The final, long-run equilibrium occurs at point C, with price P_2, industry output at Q_2, and the typical firm producing q_2.

There is a lot going on in Figure 9. But we can make the story simpler if we skip over the short run equilibrium at point B, and just ask: What happens in the *long run* after the demand curve shifts rightward? The answer is: The market equilibrium will move from point A to point C. A line drawn through these two points tells us, in the long run, the market price we can expect for any quantity the market provides. In the figure, this is the thin black line, which is called the *long-run supply curve (S_{LR})*.

SHORT-RUN VERSUS LONG-RUN OUTCOMES

LONG-RUN SUPPLY CURVE A curve indicating the quantity of output that all sellers in a market will produce at different prices, after all long-run adjustments have taken place.

> The **long-run supply curve** *shows the relationship between market price and market quantity produced after all long-run adjustments have taken place.*

If input prices rise when an industry expands (as in our example), then an increase in market quantity will require an increase in the price. This is why the long-run supply curve, S_{LR}, has an *upward slope* in Figure 9.

MARKET SIGNALS AND THE ECONOMY

The previous discussion of changes in demand has included a lot of details, so let's take a moment to go over it in broad outline. You've seen that an *increase* in demand always leads to an *increase* in market output in the short run, as existing firms raise

---

4. There are other possibilities as well. Input prices could remain the same as the industry expands, or they could fall. These possibilities are explored in a Challenge Question at the end of the chapter.

their output levels, and an even *greater* increase in output in the long run, as new firms enter the market.

We could also have analyzed what happens when demand *decreases,* but you are encouraged to do this on your own instead, drawing the diagram and tracing through the logic. If you do it correctly, you'll find that the leftward shift in the demand curve will cause a drop in output in the short run and an even greater drop in the long run.

But now let's step back from these details and see what they really tell us about the economy. We can start with a simple fact: In the real world, the demand curves for different goods and services are constantly shifting. For example, over the last decade, Americans have developed an increased taste for fruit drinks. As a consequence, the production of fruit drinks has increased dramatically. This seems like magic: Consumers want more fruit drinks and—presto!—the economy provides them. What our model of perfect competition shows us are the workings behind the magic, the logical sequence of events leading from our desire to consume more fruit drinks and their appearance on store shelves.

The secret—the trick up the magician's sleeve—is this: as demand increases or decreases in a market, *prices change.* And price changes act as *signals* for firms to enter or exit an industry. How do these signals work? As you've seen, when demand increases, the price tends to initially *overshoot* its long-run equilibrium value during the adjustment process, creating sizable temporary profits for existing firms. Similarly, when demand decreases, the price falls *lower* than its long-run equilibrium value, creating sizable losses for existing firms. These exaggerated, temporary movements in price, and the profits and losses they cause, are almost irresistible forces, driving new firms into the market or driving existing firms out. In this way, the economy is driven to produce whatever collection of goods consumers prefer.

For example, as Americans shifted their tastes toward fruit drinks, the market demand curve for this good shifted rightward, and the price rose. Initially, the price rose *above* its new long-run equilibrium value, leading to high profits at fruit drink firms. High profits, in turn, attracted entry—including entirely new brands, like Snapple and Mystic, as well as new product lines by established firms, such as Minute Maid and Coca Cola—which helped match production to consumer desires. More of our land, labor, and capital are now used to produce fruit drinks. Where did these resources come from?

In large part, they were freed up from those industries that experienced a *decline* in demand. In these industries, lower prices have caused exit, freeing up land, labor, and capital to be used in other, expanding industries, such as the fruit drink industry.

> *In a market economy, price changes act as **market signals**, ensuring that the pattern of production matches the pattern of consumer demands. When demand increases, a rise in price signals firms to enter the market, increasing industry output. When demand decreases, a fall in price signals firms to exit the market, decreasing industry output.*

Importantly, in a market economy, no single person or government agency directs this process. There is no central command post where information about consumer demand is assembled, and no one tells industries how to respond. Instead, each existing firm and each new entrant—in its *own* search for higher profit—responds to market signals and helps move the overall market in the direction it needs to go. This is what Adam Smith meant when he suggested that individual decision makers act—as if guided by an *invisible hand*—for the overall benefit of society, even though, as individuals, they are merely trying to satisfy their own desires.

Adam Smith on the Internet
You can learn more about Adam Smith and the *invisible hand* by visiting Professor Brad de Long's Adam Smith Web site, at the University of California, Berkeley. For the complete text of Smith's major works online, go to Smith's page in the McMaster University Archive for the History of Economic Thought. Professor Brad de Long's Adam Smith page:
http://socserv2.socsci.mcmaster.ca/
~econ/ugcm/3ll3/smith/index.html
McMaster University Archive:
http://socserv2.socsci.mcmaster.ca/
~econ/ugcm/3113/

MARKET SIGNALS Price changes that cause firms to change their production to more closely match consumer demand.

CHANGES IN TECHNOLOGY

Perfect competition, while it does wonders for society as a whole, is hard on the individual firm. We have seen that economic profit—when it occurs—exists only fleetingly before being eliminated by the entry of other firms. Similarly, economic loss is eliminated by exit—a rather clinical term for thousands of painful business failures each year. But these features of competition make it a powerful engine for satisfying our material desires. In this section, we look at another way in which perfect competition, while rather heartless toward the individual firm, works for the overall benefit of society: the adoption of new technology.

Figure 10 illustrates the market for photocopy paper. In panel (a), the market begins at point *A*, where the price of paper is $3.00 per ream (500 sheets). In panel (b), the typical firm produces 1,000 reams per day and—with average cost given by ATC_1—earns zero economic profit. Now suppose a new technology becomes available: a new paper-cutting machine that cuts more sheets per hour than the current machinery, yet costs the same. The new machine will enable a firm to produce any level of output at lower cost.

Suppose first that only one firm uses the new technology. This firm will enjoy a downward shift in its *ATC* curve from ATC_1 to ATC_2. Since it is so small relative to the market, it can produce all it wants and continue to sell at $3.00. Although we have not drawn in the firm's *MC* curve, you can see that the firm has several output levels from which to choose where $P > ATC$ and it can earn economic profit.

But not for long. In the long run, economic profit at this firm will cause two things to happen. First, all other firms in the market will have a powerful incentive to duplicate the new technology—to buy the new paper-cutting machine themselves. Under perfect competition, they can do so; there are no barriers that prevent any firm from using the same technology as any other. As these firms adopt the new technology, their *ATC* curves, too, will drop down to ATC_2. Second, outsiders will have an incentive to enter this industry with plants utilizing the new technology, shifting the market supply curve rightward (from S_1 to S_2) and driving down the market price. The process will stop only when the market price has reached the level at which *firms using the new technology* earn zero economic profit. In the figure, this occurs at a price of $2.00 per ream.[5]

From this example, we draw two conclusions about technological change under perfect competition. First, what will happen to a firm that is reluctant to change its technology? As *other* firms make the change, and price falls from $3.00 to $2.00, the reluctant firm will find itself suffering an economic loss, since its average cost will remain at $3.00 or more along ATC_1. Its competitors will leave it to twist in the wind, and if it refuses to shape up, it will be forced to exit the industry. In the end, *all* firms in the market must use the new technology.

Second, who benefits from the new technology in the long run? Not the firms who adopt it. Some firms—the earliest adopters—may enjoy *short-run* profit before the price adjusts completely, but in the long run, all firms will be right back where they started—earning zero economic profit. The gainers are *consumers* of paper, since they benefit from the lower price.

---

5.   In this example, we assume that the price of the new technology remains the same as it is adopted throughout the industry. If the price of the new technology were to rise, then—in the long run—the typical firm's *ATC* curve could still shift downward, but not as far as ATC_2; the market supply curve would then shift rightward, but not as far as S_2; and the price would drop, but not all the way to $2.

FIGURE 10   TECHNOLOGICAL CHANGE IN PERFECT COMPETITION

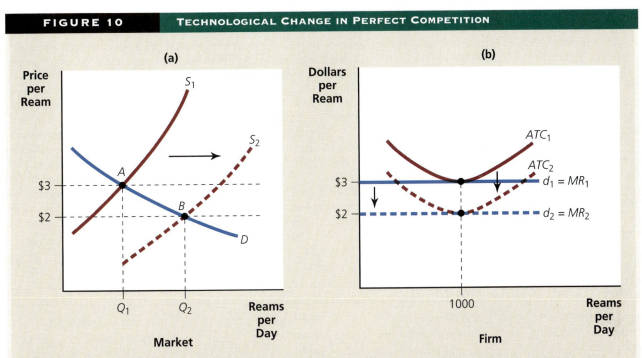

Technological change may reduce *ATC*. In panel (b), any firm that adopts new technology will earn an economic profit if it can produce at the old market price of $3 per ream. That profit will lead its competitors to adopt the same technology and will also attract new entrants. As market supply increases, price falls to $2, and each firm is again earning zero economic profit.

We can summarize the impact of technological change as follows:

> *Under perfect competition, a technological advance leads to a rightward shift of the market supply curve, decreasing market price. In the short run, early adopters may enjoy economic profit, but in the long run, all adopters will earn zero economic profit. Firms that refuse to use the new technology will not survive.*

SHORT-RUN VERSUS LONG-RUN OUTCOMES

Technological advances in many competitive industries—mining, lumber, and farming, for example—have indeed spread quickly, shifting market supply curves rapidly and steadily rightward over the past 100 years. Consumers have reaped huge rewards from these advances, but it has not always been easy on individual firms.

This may explain, at least in part, why many small farmers have lobbied for government limits on new agricultural techniques, such as genetically altered food that lowers the cost of growing, distributing, and storing crops. Small farmers know they will be the last to obtain the new technology and so will suffer losses in the short run as other, larger farmers leap ahead of them. And in the long run, the most the small farmer can hope for anyway is a return to zero economic profit. Technological change is, indeed, hard on the small farmer, but it has also enabled the industry as a whole to feed a growing world population at steadily declining prices.

S U M M A R Y

Perfect competition is a market structure in which (1) there are large numbers of buyers and sellers and each buys or sells only a tiny fraction of the total market quantity; (2) sellers offer a standardized product; and (3) sellers can easily enter or exit from the market. While few real markets satisfy these conditions precisely, the model is still useful in a wide variety of cases.

The perfectly competitive firm faces a horizontal demand curve; it can sell as much as it wishes at the market price. The firm chooses its profit-maximizing output level by setting marginal cost equal to the market price. Its *short-run supply curve* is the part of its *MC* curve that lies above average variable cost. Total profit is profit per unit ($P - ATC$) times the profit-maximizing quantity.

In the short run, market price is determined where the market supply curve—the horizontal sum of all firms' supply curves—crosses the market demand curve. In short-run equilibrium, existing firms can earn a profit (in which case new firms will enter) or suffer a loss (in which case existing firms will exit). Entry or exit will continue until, in the long run, each firm is earning zero economic profit. At each competitive firm in long-run equilibrium, price = marginal cost = minimum average total cost = minimum long-run average total cost.

When demand curves shift, prices change more in the short run than in the long run. The temporary, exaggerated price movements act as market signals, ensuring that output expands and contracts in each industry to match the pattern of consumer preferences.

K E Y   T E R M S

market structure
perfect competition
price taker

shutdown price
firm's supply curve

market supply curve
normal profit

long-run supply curve
market signals

R E V I E W   Q U E S T I O N S

1. What are the three characteristics that typify a perfectly competitive market? Explain what each characteristic means.

2. How do economists justify using the perfectly competitive model to analyze markets that clearly do not satisfy one or more of the assumptions of that model?

3. On a scale of one to five, with five being full satisfaction and one being no satisfaction at all, rank the following markets in terms of their satisfaction of the three characteristics of the perfectly competitive model. Assign a score for each characteristic and justify your assignment.
   a. Clothing stores
   b. Restaurants
   c. Book publishing
   d. Home video games
   e. Jet aircraft

4. Why is the demand curve facing a perfectly competitive firm infinitely elastic?

5. "To maximize profit, a perfectly competitive firm should set marginal cost equal to price." True, false, or ambiguous? Explain.

6. To calculate profit (loss) for a perfectly competitive firm, we look at the difference between *P* and *ATC*, but to de-

termine the profit-maximizing (loss-minimizing) level of output, we focus on *P* and *MC*. Why?

7. Discuss the following statement: "Economists need to pay more attention to the real business world. Their model of perfect competition predicts that firms in a market will end up earning no profit—nothing above costs. As any accountant can tell you, if you look at the balance sheets of most businesses in any industry, their revenue exceeds their costs; they do, in fact, make a profit."

8. True, false, or ambiguous? Explain your answer.
   a. A perfectly competitive firm is profitable when *P* exceeds minimum *AVC*.
   b. A competitive firm's supply curve is just its *MC* curve.

9. What is the fundamental characteristic that distinguishes the short run from the long run in the analysis of a competitive market?

10. In the long run, how does a competitive firm determine the optimal size of its plant?

11. True or false? In a perfectly competitive market, an increase in output requires a high price in the short run, but not in the long run. Justify your answer.

P R O B L E M S   A N D   E X E R C I S E S

1. Assume that the market for cardboard is perfectly competitive (if not very exciting). In each of the following scenarios, should a typical firm stay open or shut down in the short run? Draw a diagram that illustrates the firm's situation in each case.
   a. Minimum ATC = $2.00
      Minimum AVC = $1.50
      Market price = $1.75
   b. MR = $1.00
      Minimum AVC = $1.50
      Minimum ATC = $2.00

2. The following gives supply and demand at various prices in the perfectly competitive market for beef:

Price (per lb.)	Q_S	Q_D
	(in millions of lb.)	
$1.00	10	100
$1.25	15	90
$1.50	25	75
$1.75	40	63
$2.00	55	55
$2.25	65	40

Assume that each firm in the meat-packing industry faces the following cost structure:

Thousands of Pounds	TC
60	$110,000
61	$111,000
62	$112,000
63	$115,000

   a. What is the profit-maximizing output level for the typical firm? (Hint: Calculate MC for each change in output, then find the equilibrium price, and calculate MR for each change in output.)
   b. Is this market in long-run equilibrium? Why or why not? (Hint: Calculate ATC.)
   c. What do you expect to happen to the number of meat-packing firms over the long run? Why?

3. Consider the market for kitty litter. Assuming that this industry is perfectly competitive and is presently in long-run equilibrium:

   a. Draw diagrams for both the market as a whole and a typical firm, showing equilibrium price and quantity for the market, and MC, ATC, AVC, MR, and the demand curve for the firm.
   b. Your friend has always had a passion to get into the kitty litter business. If the market is in long-run equilibrium, will it be profitable for him to jump in (as it were) headfirst? Why or why not?
   c. Suppose people begin to prefer dogs as pets, and cat ownership declines. Show on your diagrams from part (a) what happens in the industry and the firm in the long run.
   d. Is the market supply curve more elastic in the short or long run? Why?

4. You learned in this chapter that entry and exit are powerful forces shaping industries. Check the electronic version of the Statistical Abstract of the United States by visiting http://www.census.gov/statab/www/. Go to the latest PDF files and check the index under "Business Enterprise" for tables reporting business "Failures and Starts." Study the data in these two tables on the "Mining" and "Services" industries.
   a. Over the past decade, has the mining industry tended to experience (net) entry or (net) exit? Can you identify factors affecting demand and/or supply in the mining industry that could be causing this?
   b. Over the same decade, has the services industry tended to experience (net) entry or (net) exit? Can you identify factors affecting demand and/or supply that could be causing this?
   c. Do you think that the figures reported in these tables (business starts and business failures) tend to *overstate* or *understate* the true amount of entry and exit from these two industries? Explain.

C H A L L E N G E   Q U E S T I O N

1. Figure 9 in the chapter shows the long-run adjustment process after an increase in demand. The figure assumes that input prices *rise* as industry output expands. However, in some industries, input prices might *fall* as output expands. This might occur if firms that produce inputs enjoy economies of scale (see Chapter 5). In this case, an increase in the production of inputs would actually lower their cost per unit and ultimately lower the price of inputs.

   a. Redraw Figure 9 under the assumption that input prices *fall* as industry output expands. Illustrate what happens in the short run and in the long run after the market demand curve shifts rightward.
   b. Trace out the long-run supply curve for this industry. How does it differ from the long-run supply curve in Figure 9?
   c. How might your new figure help explain why the prices of personal computers have steadily fallen over the last two decades?

CHAPTER

8

MONOPOLY AND
IMPERFECT COMPETITION

As you learned in the last chapter, we can use the perfectly competitive model to answer some important questions about markets—even markets that do not strictly satisfy its requirements. But the perfectly competitive model will not always be the best choice. In some cases, the questions we want to answer center on a market's *departures* from perfect competition, rather than its approximate fit.

Consider the question of profit. Many small businesses, and some large ones, earn high profits for their owners year after year. The perfectly competitive model is not much use if we want to explain these long-run profits, since competitive firms always earn *zero* profit in the long run.

Or think about the problem of pricing. When Braun develops a new electric toothbrush, or Toshiba develops a new laptop computer, they might spend months analyzing what price to charge before bringing their products to market. Moreover, they might consider charging *different* prices to *different* consumers. Toshiba, for example, might give a special discount to computer stores at colleges and universities. If we want to understand pricing decisions like these, the perfectly competitive model would be useless. A perfectly competitive firm is a *price taker*—it takes the market price as given. For such a firm, there is *no* price decision at all.

Or consider the way businesses interact with their rivals. Before the managers of Kellogg breakfast cereals make any important business decision, they will think very carefully about how its rivals—Post, Quaker, and General Mills—will react. If Kellogg introduces a new cereal, or increases production at one of its plants, or lowers its prices, what will these rivals do? Once again, the perfectly competitive model cannot help us answer this question. A competitive firm *never* needs to worry about its rivals, since it can sell all the output it wants at the market price, and nothing it does or doesn't do will affect that price.

Finally, there are markets for which the perfectly competitive model would be entirely inappropriate. For example, think about local markets for cable television or local telephone service. Consumers of these services can buy from only one firm—a *monopoly*—which has no competitors at all. We would never analyze such a market with the tools of Chapter 7.

As you can see, while the perfectly competitive model can be applied very widely, it is not helpful in answering *all* the important questions we might ask about *all* markets. This is why economists have identified other market structures besides perfect competition and have developed models to help us analyze them. In this chapter, you will learn about three new market structures in turn: *monopoly, oligopoly*, and *monopolistic competition*.

MONOPOLY

In most of your purchases—a haircut, a meal at a restaurant, a car, a college education—more than one seller is competing for your dollars. But in some markets, you have no choice at all. If you want to mail a letter for normal delivery, you must use the U.S. postal service. When you make a local telephone call, you must use the local phone company in your region. Many cities have only a single local newspaper. And if you live in a very small town, you may have just one doctor, one gas station, or one movie theater to select from. These are all examples of *monopolies*:

> A *monopoly firm* is the only seller of a good or service with no close substitutes. The market in which the monopoly firm operates is called a *monopoly market*.

MONOPOLY FIRM The only seller of a good or service that has no close substitutes.

MONOPOLY MARKET The market in which a monopoly firm operates.

A key concept in the definition of monopoly is the notion of *substitutability*. There is usually more than one way to satisfy a desire. A single seller of a good or service is *not* considered a monopoly if other firms sell products—close substitutes—which satisfy that same desire. For example, only one firm in the country—Kellogg—sells Kellogg's Corn Flakes. But other cereal companies sell their own brands of cornflakes, which are extremely close substitutes for Kellogg's. And many other types of flaky cereals—wheat flakes or oat flakes—are also very close substitutes for Kellogg's Corn Flakes. This is why we do not consider Kellogg to be a monopoly firm.

THE ORIGINS OF MONOPOLY

In a perfectly competitive market, there are *no* significant barriers to entry by new firms. Monopoly, by contrast, arises *because* of barriers to entry. In this section, we consider the three most common barriers responsible for creating and maintaining monopoly markets: economies of scale, control of a scarce input, and barriers created by government.

ECONOMIES OF SCALE. Recall from Chapter 5 that economies of scale in production cause a firm's long-run average-cost curve to slope downward. That is, the more output the firm produces, the lower will be its cost per unit. If economies of scale persist over even when a single firm produces for the entire market, then cost per unit will be as low as possible when the market has just one firm. In this case, we call the market a *natural monopoly:*

NATURAL MONOPOLY A market in which, due to economies of scale, one firm can operate at lower average cost than can two or more firms.

> A *natural monopoly* exists when one firm can produce at a lower cost per unit than can two or more firms.

The monopoly firm, or the market in which it operates, is called a *natural* monopoly for a good reason: Unless the government steps in, only one seller would survive—the market would *naturally* evolve into a monopoly. Why is this? Because, once a firm is already established, a new entrant would have to charge a lower price than the existing firm in order to attract customers. The existing firm would then lower *its* price in order to hang on to its customers. But in this battle of prices, the existing firm has a strong advantage: as the sole seller in the market, it already produces more output than the new entrant could hope to produce. Thus, its cost per unit is lower. If the existing firm lowers its price to just a shade above its cost per unit—still earning a small profit—it would cause the new entrant to suffer a loss. Anticipating this result, potential entrants will stay away. Small local monopolies are almost always natural monopolies. Think of the sole gas station in a small town. Since it needs a minimum of fixed inputs no matter how little gas it sells (a pump for each type of gas, space for cars to pull up, a zoning permit), each additional gallon sold will lower the station's cost per unit. By producing for the entire market, it has achieved the smallest possible cost per unit. Under these circumstances, a potential new entrant would have to think very hard about coming into this market, since it would not be able to survive a price war with the firm already in the market. The same logic can explain the monopoly position held by the sole movie theater, food market, or dentist in a small town—these are all natural monopolies.

CONTROL OF SCARCE INPUTS. Some firms maintain their monopoly status by controlling a scarce input needed to produce a good. For example, from 1893 until the 1940s, Alcoa was the sole seller of aluminum in the United States because it owned virtually all of the country's deposits of bauxite—a natural resource needed to produce aluminum. Similarly, since the 1880s, De Beers, a South African company, has enjoyed a near monopoly on the sale of finished diamonds by buying up virtually all of the world's diamond mines or the raw diamonds that come from them.

GOVERNMENT-ENFORCED BARRIERS. Sometimes, the public interest is best served by having a single seller in a market. In these cases, government usually steps in and creates barriers to entry, ensuring that the market will remain a monopoly. In the United States, monopolies have been created by all levels of government—federal, state, and local. The two main methods of creating a monopoly are (1) the protection of intellectual property through patents, trademarks, and copyrights and (2) exclusive government franchises.

Protection of Intellectual Property. The words you are reading right now are an example of *intellectual property,* which includes literary, artistic, and musical works, as well as scientific inventions. Most markets for a specific intellectual property are monopolies: One firm or individual owns the property and is the sole seller of the rights to use it. There is both good and bad in this. As you will learn in this chapter, prices tend to be higher under monopoly than under perfect competition, and monopolies often earn economic profit as a consequence. This is good for the monopoly and bad for everyone else. On the other hand, it is just this promise of monopoly profit that encourages the creation of original products and ideas, which certainly benefits the rest of us. Personal computers, cordless telephones, and surgical lasers were all launched by innovators who bore considerable costs and risks with an eye on future profits. The same is true of every compact disc you listen to, every novel you read, and every movie you see.

> *In dealing with intellectual property, government strikes a compromise: It allows the creators of intellectual property to enjoy a monopoly and earn economic profit, but only for a limited period of time. Once the time is up, other sellers are allowed to enter the market, and it is hoped that competition among them will bring down prices.*

POLICY TRADE-OFFS

The two most important kinds of legal protection for intellectual property are *patents* and *copyrights*. New scientific discoveries and the products that result from them are protected by a **patent** obtained from the federal government. The patent prevents anyone else from selling the same discovery or product for about 20 years. The Eli Lilly Company, for example, holds a patent on the chemical fluoxetine, the active ingredient in Prozac—the first antidepressant drug without serious side effects. Lilly has made an enormous profit from Prozac, selling more than $2 billion worth of the drug in 1996 alone. Other pharmaceutical companies, forced to work around Lilly's patent, took much longer to develop their own, similar drugs. In the meantime, Lilly was the sole seller of a product with no close substitutes.

PATENT A temporary grant of monopoly rights over a new product or scientific discovery.

Literary, musical, and artistic works are protected by a **copyright,** which grants exclusive rights over the material for at least 50 years. For example, the copyright on this book is owned by South-Western College Publishing. No other company or individual can print copies and sell them to the public, and no one can quote the book at length without obtaining South-Western's permission.

COPYRIGHT A grant of exclusive rights to sell a literary, musical, or artistic work.

Government Franchise. The large firms we usually think of as monopolies—such as telephone and cable television companies—are created through **government franchise**—the granting of exclusive rights over a product. Here, the barrier to entry is quite simple: Any other firm that enters the market will be prosecuted! Governments usually grant franchises when they think the market is a natural monopoly. In this case, a single large firm—enjoying economies of scale—would have a lower cost per unit than multiple smaller firms, so government tries to keep costs and prices low by *ensuring* that there are no competitors. In exchange for its monopoly status, the seller must submit to either complete government ownership and control or else government regulation over its prices and profits.

GOVERNMENT FRANCHISE A government-granted right to be the sole seller of a product or service.

This is the logic behind the monopoly status of the U.S. Postal Service. No matter how many letters it delivers, a postal firm must have enough letter carriers to reach every house every day. Two postal companies would need many more carriers to deliver the same total number of letters, raising costs and, ultimately, the price of mailing a letter. Thus, mail delivery is a natural monopoly, one that the government has chosen to own and control, rather than merely regulate. Federal law prohibits any other firm from offering normal letter-delivery service.

Local telephone service is another example of a government franchise for a natural monopoly. A company's telephone network must reach every neighborhood in the region, regardless of how many households in the neighborhood sign up with that company. Two telephone companies would have to string more wire than a single one and yet serve the same number of customers, resulting in higher costs per customer. In this case, it is *state* governments that provide the franchise: A single company is granted a monopoly over telephone service within part or all of a state and must submit to state regulation over prices and service. *Local* governments, too, create monopolies by granting exclusive franchises to water utilities, garbage collection services, and cable television companies.

MONOPOLY PROFIT MAXIMIZATION

PRICE SETTER Any firm that faces a downward-sloping demand curve and so can choose the price it charges.

In the previous chapter, we saw that perfectly competitive firms are *price takers*—they take the market price as a given. A monopoly, by contrast, is a **price setter**: it can *decide* what price to charge. Since a monopoly is the only firm in its market, the monopoly's price *will be* the market price. The monopoly will try to set that price to earn the highest possible profit. But even a monopoly faces constraints on its price-setting ability.

The chief constraint on the monopoly is the demand curve for its product. Since the monopoly is the only firm in the market, its demand curve is the same as the *market* demand curve. As you know, market demand curves slope downward—a rise in price causes a decrease in quantity demanded. Therefore,

> *A monopoly firm faces a downward sloping demand curve for its product. This demand curve tells us the maximum price the firm can charge for any level of output.*

Suppose a monopoly wants to sell more output. Then it must lower its price—not just on the additional units it wants to sell, but also on all units it was previously selling at the higher price.[1]

For example, if your local cable television company wants more subscribers, it will have to lower its rates for everyone, including those who already subscribe at the current rate. Thus, lowering price and increasing output has two competing effects on total revenue: On the one hand, more output is sold, tending to *increase* total revenue; on the other hand, *all* units now go for a lower price, tending to *decrease* total revenue. The net effect may be a rise or fall in total revenue, or—put another way—the firm's *marginal revenue* may be positive or negative.[2]

Figure 1 illustrates the demand and marginal revenue curves for Zillion-Channel Cable—a monopoly that sells cable television services to the residents of a town. We will assume that Zillion-Channel is free from government regulation. In the figure, the demand curve shows the number of subscribers at each monthly price for cable. The demand curve is both a *market* demand curve and the demand curve *facing the firm,* since Zillion-Channel is the only firm in its market.

Let's see what happens to Zillion-Channel's revenue as we move from point *A* to point *B* along its demand curve. At point *A*, the firm charges a monthly price of $25 and attracts 5,000 paid subscribers, for a total revenue of $5,000 \times \$25 = \$125,000$. If it lowers its price to $24, moving to point *B*, 6,000 people will subscribe, for a total revenue of $6,000 \times \$24 = \$144,000$. Thus, in moving from point *A* to point *B*, total revenue rises by $19,000. The marginal revenue for this move—which tells us the increase in revenue per additional unit of output—can be calculated as follows:

---

1. Price setting can be much more complex than this. Some price setting firms (monopolies and others that you will learn about in this chapter) can charge different prices to different customers. We will take up the case of multiple pricing later in the chapter. For now, we assume that the monopoly must charge the same price of every unit of output that it sells.
2. This should sound familiar to you. In Chapter 6, Ned's Beds faced a downward-sloping demand curve and had to lower its price on all of its beds in order to sell more of them. Although Ned was not necessarily the only seller in his market, his total and marginal revenue behaved in much the same way as we are describing here.

FIGURE 1	DEMAND AND MARGINAL REVENUE FOR A MONOPOLY

A monopoly faces a downward-sloping demand curve. To sell additional output, the firm must lower its price. Marginal revenue (*MR*) shows the change in total revenue that results from a one-unit increase in output. *MR* is less than price; to sell an additional unit, the monopoly must lower the price on that unit *and* on previous units.

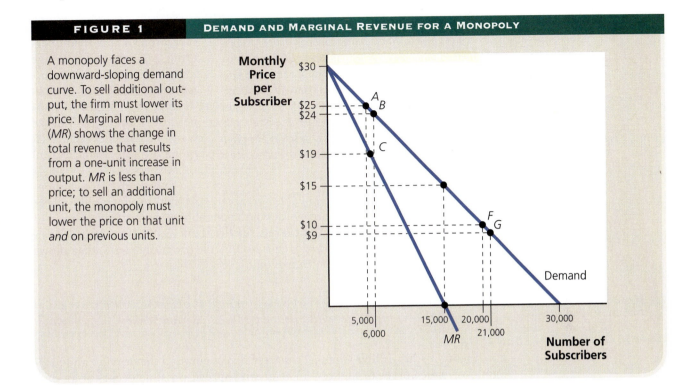

$$MR = \Delta TR/\Delta Q$$
$$= (\$144{,}000 - \$125{,}000)/(6{,}000 - 5{,}000) = \$19{,}000/1{,}000 = \$19$$

This value for marginal revenue—$19—is plotted at point *C*, which is midway between points *A* and *B*. Notice that MR is *less* than the new price of output, $24. This follows from the two competing effects just discussed: On the one hand, the monopoly is selling more output and getting $24 on each additional unit; on the other hand, it has to charge a lower price on the previous 5,000 units of output it was selling. In the move from *A* to *B*, it turns out that total revenue rises, and marginal revenue is positive, but less than $24.

> *Marginal revenue for a single-price monopoly will be less than the price of output, so the marginal revenue curve will lie below the demand curve.*

For other moves along the demand curve, total revenue may decline, so marginal revenue will be negative. (Verify this for the move from point *F* to point *G*.) In this case, the marginal revenue curve lies below the horizontal axis.

The marginal revenue curve alone tells us something about the monopoly's output decision:

> *A monopoly will never produce a level of output at which its marginal revenue is negative.*

We can be sure of this principle by simple logic. If marginal revenue is negative, then cutting back on output will *increase* the firm's total revenue. But cutting back on output will also *decrease* the firm's total cost. Since revenue will rise

DANGEROUS CURVES

A question may have occurred to you: Where is the monopoly's *supply curve*? The answer is that *there is no supply curve for a monopoly.* A firm's supply curve tells us how much the firm will want to produce and sell *when it is presented with* different prices. Thus, a supply curve implies that a firm is a *price taker*—a perfectly competitive firm. A monopoly, by contrast, is a *price setter*. It *chooses* its price in order to maximize profit. It makes no sense to ask how much a monopoly wants to sell at any given price other than the one that maximizes its profit, since that is the only price it will ever choose.

and cost will fall, profit will increase. Thus, a firm operating in a range of negative marginal revenue will *always* increase profit by producing less. Zillion-Channel, for example, will never want to charge less than $15 or have more than 15,000 subscribers.

Knowing that a monopoly will produce only where marginal revenue is positive narrows down the possibilities somewhat . . . but not enough. Which of the many output levels smaller than 15,000 units will Zillion-Channel choose? To answer this, we return to the rule (from Chapter 6) that allows *any* firm to find its profit-maximizing output level:

MARGINAL DECISION MAKING

> To maximize profit, the firm should produce the level of output where MC = MR *and the* MC *curve crosses the* MR *curve from below.*

Figure 2 adds Zillion-Channel's marginal cost curve to the demand and marginal revenue curves of Figure 1. The greatest profit possible occurs at an output level of 10,000, where the *MC* curve crosses the *MR* curve from below. In order to sell this level of output, the firm must charge a price of $20, locating at point *E* on its demand curve. You can see that for a monopoly, *price and output are not independent decisions, but different ways of expressing the same de-*

FIGURE 2	**MONOPOLY PRICE AND OUTPUT DETERMINATION**

Like any firm, the monopolist maximizes profit by producing where *MC* equals *MR*. Here, that quantity is 10,000 units. The price charged ($20) is read off the demand curve. It is the highest price at which the monopolist can sell 10,000 units of output.

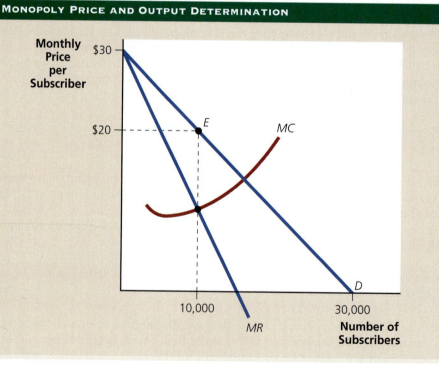

cision. Once Zillion-Channel determines its profit-maximizing output level (10,000 units), it has also determined its profit-maximizing price ($20), and vice versa.

PROFIT AND LOSS

In Figure 2, we can determine Zillion-Channel's price and output level, but we cannot see whether the firm is making an economic profit or loss. This will require one more addition to the diagram. Remember that profit at any given level of output is defined as

$$\text{Profit} = \text{Total Revenue} - \text{Total Cost}$$

Dividing both sides of this definition by the level of output (Q), we obtain the firm's *profit per unit* at any output level:

$$\text{Profit per Unit} = \frac{\text{Profit}}{Q} = \frac{\text{Total Revenue}}{Q} - \frac{\text{Total Cost}}{Q}$$

The first term on the right-hand side of the equality, Total Revenue/Q, is the firm's revenue *per unit*. As long as the firm sells all of its output at the same price, its revenue per unit is just the *price* (P) of its output. The last term, Total Cost/Q, is the firm's average total cost (ATC). Substituting P and ATC into the definition of profit per unit, we obtain

$$\text{Profit per Unit} = P - ATC$$

Now, the price at any output level is given by the demand curve facing the firm. Profit per unit, then, is just the distance between the firm's demand curve and its ATC curve.

Figure 3(a) is just like Figure 2, but adds Zillion-Channel's ATC curve. As you can see, at the profit-maximizing output level of 10,000, price is $20 and average total cost is $16, so profit per unit is $4.

Now look at the blue rectangle in the figure. The height of this rectangle is profit per unit ($4), and the width is the number of units produced (10,000). The *area* of the rectangle—height × width—equals Zillion-Channel's total profit, or $4 × 10,000 = $40,000.

> A monopoly earns a profit whenever P > ATC. *Its total profit at the best output level equals the area of a rectangle with height equal to the distance between* P *and* ATC *and width equal to the level of output.*

This should sound familiar: It is exactly how we represented the profit of a perfectly competitive firm (compare with Figure 3(a) in Chapter 7). The diagram looked different under perfect competition because the firm's demand curve was horizontal, whereas for a monopoly it is downward sloping.

Figure 3(b) illustrates the case of a monopoly suffering a loss. Here, costs are higher than in panel (a), and the ATC curve lies everywhere above the demand curve, so the firm will suffer a loss at any level of output. At the best output level—10,000—ATC is $25, so the loss per unit is $5. The total loss ($50,000) is the area of the red rectangle, whose height is the loss per unit ($5) and width is the best output level (10,000).

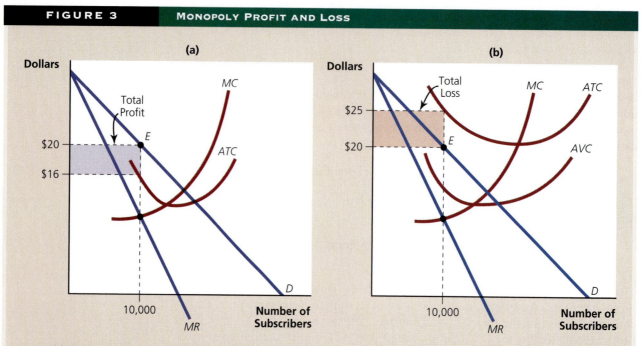

| FIGURE 3 | MONOPOLY PROFIT AND LOSS |

In panel (a), the monopolist's profit is the difference between price and average total cost (*ATC*), multiplied by the number of units sold. The blue area indicates a profit of $40,000. Panel (b) shows a monopolist suffering a loss. At the best level of output, *ATC* exceeds price. The red rectangle shows a loss of $50,000.

> *A monopoly suffers a loss whenever* P < ATC. *Its total loss at the best output level equals the area of a rectangle with height equal to the distance between* ATC *and* P *and width equal to the level of output.*[3]

MONOPOLY IN THE LONG RUN

In the short run, a monopoly may earn an economic profit or suffer an economic loss. (It may, of course, break even as well; see if you can draw this case on your own.) But what about the long run? One of the most important insights of the previous chapter was that perfectly competitive firms cannot earn a profit in the long run. Profit attracts new firms into the market, and market production increases. This, in turn, causes the market price to fall, eliminating any temporary profit earned by a competitive firm. But there is no such process at work in a monopoly market, where barriers prevent the entry of other firms into the market. Outsiders will want to enter an industry when a monopoly is earning above economic profit, but they will be unable to do so. Thus, the market provides no mechanism to eliminate monopoly profit, and

> *Unlike perfectly competitive firms, monopolies may earn economic profit in the long run.*

---

3   A monopoly facing a short-run loss would follow the shutdown rule discussed in chapters 6 and 7: shut down if *TR* < *TVC* (or, equivalently, if *P* < *AVC*); otherwise, stay open. However, if the monopoly provides a vital service under government regulation (e.g., electricity, natural gas, or phone service), the government would not allow it to shut down.

What about economic loss? If a monopoly is a government franchise, and it faces the prospect of long-term losses, the government may decide to subsidize it in order to keep it running—especially if it provides a vital service like mail delivery. But if the monopoly is privately owned and controlled, we do not expect to see

> *A privately owned monopoly suffering an economic loss in the long run will exit the industry, just as would any other business firm. In the long run, therefore, we should not find privately owned monopolies suffering economic losses.*

long-run losses. A monopoly suffering an economic loss that it expects to continue indefinitely should exit the industry, just like any other firm.

COMPARING MONOPOLY TO PERFECT COMPETITION

We have already seen one important difference between monopoly and perfectly competitive markets: In perfect competition, economic profit is relentlessly reduced to zero by the entry of other firms; in monopoly, economic profit can continue indefinitely.

But monopoly also differs from perfect competition in another way:

> *All else equal, we can expect a monopoly market to have higher prices and lower output than a perfectly competitive market.*

MARKETS AND EQUILIBRIUM

To see why this is so, let's explore what would happen if a perfectly competitive market were taken over by a single firm, changing the market to a monopoly. Figures 4(a) and (b) illustrate a competitive market consisting of 100 identical firms. In panel (a), the market is in long-run equilibrium at point *E,* with a market price of $10 and market output of 100,000 units. In panel (b), the typical firm faces a horizontal demand curve at $10, produces output of 1,000 units, and earns zero economic profit.

Now, imagine that a single company buys all 100 firms, to form a monopoly. The new monopoly market is illustrated in panel (c). Under monopoly, the horizontal demand curve facing each firm becomes irrelevant. Instead, the demand curve the monopoly cares about is the downward-sloping *market* demand curve *D,* which is the same as the market demand curve in panel (a). Since the demand curve slopes downward, marginal revenue will be less than price, and the *MR* curve will lie everywhere below the demand curve. To maximize profit, the monopoly will want to find the output level at which *MC* = *MR.* But what is the new monopoly's *MC* curve?

We'll assume that the monopoly doesn't change the way output is produced: Each previously competitive firm will continue to produce its output with the same technology as before, only now it operates as one of 100 different plants that the monopoly controls. With this assumption, *the monopoly's marginal-cost curve will be the same as the market supply curve in panel (a).* Why? The market supply curve in panel (a) tells us the marginal cost of producing one more unit of output at each of the 100 competitive firms. For example, point *A* on the market supply curve tells us that a price of $12 is needed to have a market supply of 120,000 units. This is because the marginal cost of producing the 1,200th unit at each competitive firm is $12. If a monopoly takes over all of these firms and wants to produce another unit beyond 120,000, it will do so at one of its new plants (one of the original competitive firms) where the marginal cost will be $12. The same is true at every other point along the competitive market supply curve: It will always tell us the monopoly's cost

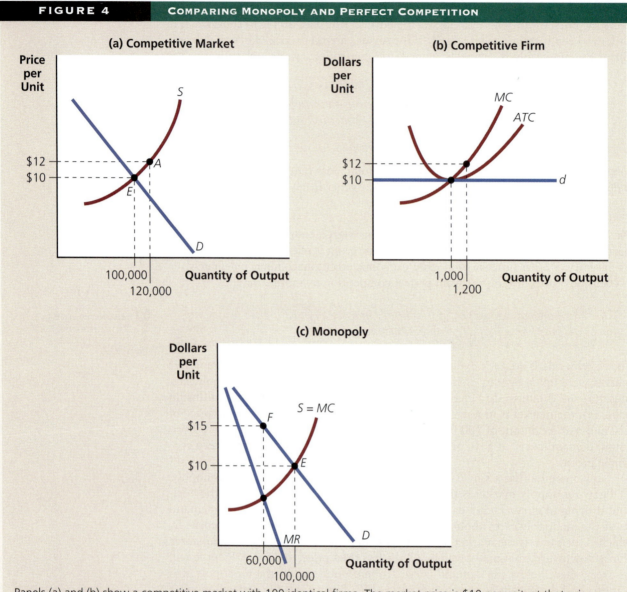

FIGURE 4   **COMPARING MONOPOLY AND PERFECT COMPETITION**

(a) Competitive Market

Price per Unit

$12 · · · · · · · · · · · A
$10 · · · · · · · E

S

D

100,000
120,000   **Quantity of Output**

(b) Competitive Firm

Dollars per Unit

MC

ATC

$12 · · · · · · · · · · ·
$10 · · · · · · · · · · · · · · · · · · *d*

1,000
1,200   **Quantity of Output**

(c) Monopoly

Dollars per Unit

S = MC

$15 · · · · · · F
$10 · · · · · · · · · · E

MR   *D*

60,000
100,000   **Quantity of Output**

Panels (a) and (b) show a competitive market with 100 identical firms. The market price is $10 per unit; at that price, each firm sells 1,000 units and earns zero economic profit. A monopolist that buys up all these firms will face the market demand curve *D* in panel (c). This is the same as the market demand curve in panel (a). The monopolist will produce 60,000 units—where *MR = MC*. The monopolist produces less than the competitive firms did and charges a higher price ($15 rather than $10).

of producing one more unit at one of the plants it now owns. In other words, the upward-sloping curve in panel (c), which is the market supply curve when the market is competitive, becomes the marginal-cost curve for a single firm when the market is monopolized. This is why the curve is labeled both *S* (market supply) and *MC* (the marginal cost of the monopolist).

Now we have all the information we need to find the monopoly's choice of price and quantity. In panel (c), the monopoly's *MC* curve crosses the *MR* curve from below at 60,000 units of output. This will be the monopoly's profit-maximizing output level. To sell this much output, the monopoly will charge $15 per unit—point *F* on its demand curve—so this is the monopoly's profit-maximizing price.

Notice what has happened in our example: After the monopoly takes over, the price rises from $10 to $15, and market quantity drops from 100,000 to 60,000. The monopoly, compared to a competitive market, would *charge more and produce less*.

Now let's see who gains and who loses from the takeover. By raising price and restricting output, the new monopoly earns economic profit. We know this because at a price of $10, each of its plants would break even, so at $15—the profit-maximizing price—it must do better than break even. Consumers, however, lose in two ways: They pay more for the output they buy, and—due to higher prices—they buy less output. The changeover from perfect competition to monopoly thus benefits the owners of the monopoly and harms consumers of the product.

Keep in mind, though, an important proviso concerning this result: Comparing monopoly and perfect competition, we see that price is higher and output is lower under monopoly *if all else is equal*. In particular, we have assumed that after the market is monopolized, the technology of production remains unchanged at each previously competitive firm.

But a monopoly may be able to *change* the technology of production, so that all else would *not* remain equal. For example, a monopoly may have each of its new plants *specialize* in some part of the production process, or it may be able to achieve efficiencies in product planning, employee supervision, bookkeeping, or customer relations. If these cost savings enable the monopoly to use a less costly input mix for any given output level, then the monopoly's marginal cost curve in panel (c) would be *lower* than the competitive market supply curve in panel (a). If you add another, lower *MC* curve to panel (c), you'll see that this tends to *decrease* the monopoly's price and *increase* its output level—exactly the reverse of the effects discussed earlier. If the cost savings are great enough, and the *MC* curve drops low enough, a profit-maximizing monopoly might even charge a lower price and produce more output than would a competitive market. (See if you can draw a diagram to demonstrate this case.) The general conclusion we can draw is this:

The monopolization of a competitive industry leads to two opposing effects. First, for any given technology of production, monopolization leads to higher prices and lower output. Second, changes in the technology of production made possible under monopoly may lead to lower prices and higher output. The ultimate effect on price and quantity depends on the relative strengths of these two effects.

THE DECLINE OF MONOPOLY

The twentieth century has not been kind to monopolies. In the first half of the century, vigorous antitrust legislation and enforcement broke up many long-standing monopolies, such as Standard Oil in 1911, and Alcoa in 1945. Today, monopolies face a different threat: the relentless advance of technology.

Consider, for example, the natural monopolies of cable television and local phone service. Production in both services is characterized by economies of scale: A single company can produce at a lower cost per unit than could several competitors. But soon, cable television companies will have the technology to offer local telephone service, and local phone companies will be able to offer entertainment services through your home television. Most homes in the United States already have both types of wires—phone and cable—so the separate franchises granted to phone and cable companies are beginning to make less and less sense. And wireless technologies (cellular and satellite) threaten to break open the competition still further: With no need to hardwire homes, there is no reason why hundreds of different companies could not compete to offer phone and entertainment services in any given city. Any way you look at it, the monopolies enjoyed by local telephone and cable companies are threatened.

Even the old standard of monopolies—the post office—is being threatened by technology. Computerized inventory tracking and fuel-efficient jets have enabled companies such as Federal Express and DHL to offer low-cost overnight letter delivery services, while e-mail and bill paying by computer are cutting into the volume of old-fashioned letters. It is not hard to imagine a time in the future when you will receive all your mail on the Internet, and the notion of *hand-delivered* letters will become a thing of the past, a quaint idea you can explain to your children.

This is not to say that all monopolies are taking their last breaths. Some monopolies—like those created by patents and copyrights—will continue to make sense, because they are needed to reward those who bear the costs and risks of innovation. And many small-town monopolies—especially those that provide hands-on personal services, such as medical care or haircuts—may remain immune to the technological threat. But it is safe to say that the world of monopoly, as we know it, is shrinking.

MONOPOLISTIC COMPETITION

In perfect competition, there are so many firms selling the same product, that none of them can affect the market price. In monopoly, there is just *one* seller in the market, so it sets the price as it wishes. Most markets for goods and services, however, are neither perfectly competitive nor purely monopolistic. Instead, they lie somewhere *between* these two extremes, with more than one firm, but not enough firms to qualify for perfect competition. We call such markets *imperfectly competitive*:

IMPERFECT COMPETITION
A market structure with more than one firm, but in which one or more of the requirements of perfect competition are violated.

> *Imperfect competition refers to market structures between perfect competition and monopoly. In imperfectly competitive markets, there is more than one seller, but still too few to create a perfectly competitive market. In addition, imperfectly competitive markets often violate other conditions of perfect competition, such as the requirement of a standardized product or free entry and exit.*

There are two different types of imperfect competition. *Monopolistic competition*—the subject of this section—and *oligopoly*, which we take up in the next section.

MONOPOLISTIC COMPETITION A market structure in which there are many firms selling products that are differentiated, yet are still close substitutes, and in which there is free entry and exit.

> *Monopolistic competition is a market structure with three fundamental characteristics:*
>
> 1. *many buyers and sellers;*
> 2. *no significant barriers to entry or exit; and*
> 3. *a differentiated product.*

Note that monopolistic competition combines features of both perfect competition and monopoly—hence its name. Like perfect competition, there are many buyers and sellers and easy entry and exit. Restaurants, photocopy shops, dry cleaners, and virtually all retail stores, such as clothing stores or food markets, are almost always monopolistic competitors. In each case, there are many sellers in the market, and it is easy to set up a business or to exit if things don't go well. But unlike perfect competitors, each seller produces a somewhat different product from the others. No two coffeehouses, photocopy shops, or food markets are exactly the same. For this reason, a monopolistic competitor can raise its price (up to a point) and lose only *some* of its customers. The others will stay with the firm because they like its product, even when it charges somewhat more than its competitors. Thus, a monopolistic competitor faces a *downward-sloping demand curve* and, in this sense, is more like a monopolist than a perfect competitor:

> *Because it produces a differentiated product, a monopolistic competitor faces a downward-sloping demand curve: When it raises its price a modest amount, quantity demanded will decline (but not all the way to zero).*

What makes a product differentiated? Sometimes, it is the *quality* of the product. By many objective standards—room size, service, and other amenities—the Hilton has better hotel rooms than Motel 6. In other cases, the difference is a matter of taste, rather than quality. In terms of measurable characteristics, Colgate toothpaste is probably neither better nor worse than Crest, but each has its own flavor and texture, and each appeals to different people.

Another type of differentiation arises from differences in *location*. Two bookstores may be identical in every respect—range of selection, atmosphere, service—but you will prefer the one closer to your home or office.

Ultimately, product differentiation is a subjective matter: A product is different whenever people *think* that it is, whether their perception is accurate or not. You may know, for example, that all bottles of bleach have identical ingredients—5.25 percent sodium hypochlorite and 94.75 percent water. But if some buyers think that Clorox bleach is different and would pay a bit more for it, then Clorox bleach is a differentiated product. Thus, whenever a firm faces a downward-sloping demand curve, we can assume that it produces a differentiated product. The reason for the downward slope may be a difference in product quality, consumer tastes, or location, or it may be entirely illusory, but the economic implications are always the same: The firm can raise its price without losing all of its business.

MONOPOLISTIC COMPETITION IN THE SHORT RUN

The individual monopolistic competitor behaves very much like a monopoly: It faces a downward-sloping demand curve, it maximizes profit by producing where $MR = MC$, and the result may be economic profit or loss in the short run. The only difference is this: While a monopoly is the *only* seller in its market, a monopolistic competitor is one of many sellers. When a *monopoly* raises its price, its customers must pay up or consume less of the good. When a *monopolistic competitor* raises its price, its customers have one additional option: They can buy a similar good from some other firm.

Figure 5 illustrates the situation of a monopolistic competitor—Kafka Exterminators. The figure shows the demand curve—d_1—that the firm faces, as well as the marginal revenue, marginal cost, and average total cost curves. As a monopolistic competitor, Kafka Exterminators competes with many other extermination services in its local area. Thus, if it raises its price, it will lose some of its customers to the competition.

Like any other firm, Kafka Exterminators will produce where $MR = MC$. As you can see in Figure 5, when Kafka faces demand curve d_1 and the associated marginal

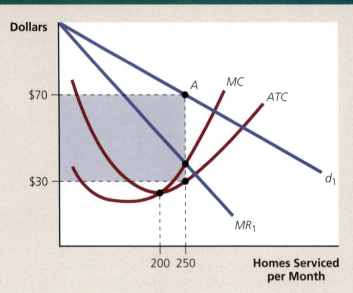

FIGURE 5   **A MONOPOLISTICALLY COMPETITIVE FIRM IN THE SHORT RUN**

Kafka Exterminators, a monopolistic competitor, faces downward-sloping demand curve d_1 and marginal revenue curve MR_1. It services 250 homes per month (where $MR = MC$), charges $70 per home, and earns a short-run profit of $10,000, shown by the blue rectangle.

revenue curve MR_1, its profit-maximizing output level is 250 homes served per month, and its profit-maximizing price is $70 per home. In the short run, the firm may earn an economic profit or an economic loss, or it may break even. In the figure, Kafka is earning an economic profit: Profit per unit is $P - ATC = \$70 - \$30 = \$40$, and total monthly profit—the area of the shaded rectangle—is $\$40 \times 250 = \$10,000$.

MONOPOLISTIC COMPETITION IN THE LONG RUN

If Kafka Exterminators were a monopoly, Figure 5 might be the end of our story. The firm would continue to earn economic profit forever, since barriers to entry would keep out any potential competitors. But under monopolistic competition—in which there are no barriers to entry and exit—the firm will not enjoy its profit for long. New sellers enter the market, attracted by the profits that can be earned there. Some of Kafka's customers will switch to these new entrants. Then, at any given price, Kafka will find itself servicing fewer and fewer homes than before, and the demand curve it faces will shift leftward. Entry will continue to occur, and the demand curve will continue to shift leftward until Kafka and other firms are earning zero economic profit.[4]

This is shown in Figure 6. Notice that the new demand curve, d_2, lies to the left of the original demand curve d_1 from Figure 5. The slope of the demand curve may have changed as well. Since the demand curve has shifted leftward, so has the MR curve, to MR_2. Producing one more unit of output will add less to total revenue than it did before the shift, since the price consumers are willing to pay at each output level is now lower. The new profit-maximizing output level—where $MR = MC$—is 100 units, and the profit-maximizing price is $40 per unit. Since ATC is also $40, the firm is earning zero economic profit. Notice that, in long-run

---

4. Other things may also happen as the industry expands. For example, the increased demand for inputs may raise or lower the typical firm's ATC or MC curves. This does not change our result, however: Entry into the market will continue until the typical firm earns zero economic profit, even if its MC and ATC curves have shifted.

FIGURE 6   A MONOPOLISTICALLY COMPETITIVE FIRM IN THE LONG RUN

If existing firms are earning short-run profits, entry will occur. The demand curve facing Kafka Exterminators will shift left. Long-run equilibrium occurs at an output level of 100, where the new marginal revenue curve, MR_2, intersects MC. The price of $40 equals ATC, so the firm earns zero economic profit.

Entry changes costs and divides the market

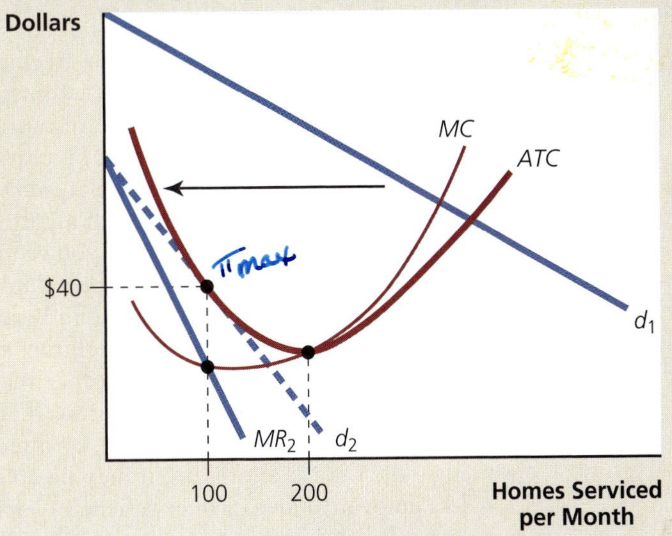

equilibrium, the demand curve just touches the ATC curve at a single point. (Question: Why can't the demand curve actually *cross* the ATC curve? Hint: This would mean that $P > ATC$ at some output levels.)

We can also reverse these steps. If the typical firm is suffering an economic loss (draw this diagram on your own), *exit* will occur. With fewer competitors, those firms that remain in the market will gain customers, so their demand curves will shift *rightward*. Exit will cease only when the typical firm is earning zero economic profit—as in Figure 6. Thus, the dashed demand curve d_2 in Figure 6, which touches but does not cross the ATC curve, represents the long-run equilibrium of the typical firm whether we start from a position of economic profit or economic loss:

> *Under monopolistic competition, firms can earn positive or negative economic profit in the short run. But in the long run, free entry and exit will ensure that each firm earns zero economic profit, just as under perfect competition.*

SHORT-RUN VERSUS LONG-RUN OUTCOMES

Is this prediction of our model realistic? Indeed it is: In the real world, monopolistic competitors often earn economic profit or loss in the short run, but—given enough time—profits attract new entrants, and losses result in an industry shakeout until firms are earning zero profit. In the long run, restaurants, retail stores, hair salons, and other monopolistically competitive firms earn zero economic profit for their owners—just enough to keep them from shifting their time and money to some alternative enterprise.

NONPRICE COMPETITION

If a monopolistic competitor wants to increase its output, one way is to cut its price—that is, it can move *along* its demand curve. But a price cut is not the only way to increase output. Since the firm produces a differentiated product, it can sell more by convincing people that its own output is better than that of other firms. Such efforts, if successful, will *shift* the firm's demand curve rightward.

NONPRICE COMPETITION
Any action a firm takes to increase the demand for its product, other than cutting its price.

> *Any action a firm takes to increase the demand for its output—other than cutting its price—is called* **nonprice competition.**

Better service, product guarantees, free home delivery, more attractive packaging—as well as advertising to inform customers about these things—are all examples of nonprice competition. Fast-food restaurants are notorious for nonprice competition. When Burger King says, "Have it your way," the company is saying, "Our hamburgers are better than those at McDonald's, because we make them to order." When McDonald's responds with an attractive, fresh-faced young woman behind the counter, smiling broadly as if you've made her day by "Super-Sizing" your meal, it is saying, in effect, "So what if we don't make your burgers to order; our staff is better looking and more upbeat than Burger King's, and you won't just get a burger at McDonald's—you'll have an uplifting *experience.*"

Nonprice competition is another reason that monopolistic competitors earn zero economic profit in the long run. If an innovative firm discovers a way to shift its demand curve rightward—say, by offering better service or more clever advertising—then in the short run, it may be able to earn a profit. This means that other, less innovative firms will experience a leftward shift in *their* demand curves, as they lose sales to their more innovative rival.

But not for long. Eventually, *all* firms will imitate the actions of the most successful among them. If product guarantees are enabling some firms to earn economic profit, then all firms will offer product guarantees. If advertising is doing the trick, then all firms will start ad campaigns. In the long run, we can expect *all* monopolistic competitors to run advertisements, to be concerned about service, and to take whatever actions have proven profitable for other firms in the industry. All this nonprice competition is costly—one must *pay* for advertising, for product guarantees, for better staff training—and these costs must be included in each firm's *ATC* curve, shifting it upward. But this does not change any of our conclusions about monopolistic competition in the long run.

Indeed, nonprice competition strengthens our conclusions. In the short run, a firm may earn profit because it has relatively few competitors or because it has discovered a new way to attract customers. But in the long run, the profitable firm will find its demand curve shifting leftward due to the entry of new firms, or the imitation of its successful nonprice competition, or both. In the end, each firm will find itself back in the situation depicted by demand curve d_2 in Figure 6. Because of the costs of nonprice competition, each firm's *ATC* curve will be higher than it would otherwise be. However, it will still touch, but not cross, the demand curve, and the firm will still earn zero economic profit.

OLIGOPOLY

A monopolistic competitor enjoys a certain amount of independence. There are so many *other* firms selling in the market—each one such a small fish in such a large pond—that each of them can make decisions about price and quantity without worrying about how the others will react. For example, if a single pharmacy in a large city cuts its prices, it can safely assume that any other pharmacy that could benefit from price cutting has already done so, or will shortly do so, regardless of its own actions. Thus, there is no reason for the price-cutting pharmacy to take the reactions of other pharmacies into account in making its own pricing decisions.

But in some markets, a large share of the output is sold by just a few firms. These markets are not monopolies (there is more than one seller), but they are not monopolistically competitive either. There are so few firms, that the actions taken by any one will *very much* affect the others and will likely generate a response. For example, more than 60 percent of the automobiles sold in the United States are made by one of the "Big Three": General Motors, Ford, and Chrysler. If GM were to lower its price in order to sell more cars, then Ford and Chrysler would suffer a significant drop in their own sales. They would not be happy about this and would probably respond with price cuts of their own. GM's output, in turn, would be affected by the price cuts at Ford and Chrysler.

When just a few large firms dominate a market, so that the actions of each one have an important impact on the others, it would be foolish for any one firm to ignore its competitors' reactions. On the contrary, in such a market, each firm recognizes its *strategic interdependence* with the others. Before the management team makes a decision, it must reason as follows: "If we take action *A,* our competitors will do *B,* and then we would do *C,* and they would respond with *D . . . ,*" and so on. This kind of thinking is the hallmark of the market structure we call *oligopoly:*

> An **oligopoly** *is a type of imperfect competition in which the market is dominated by a small number of strategically interdependent firms.*

OLIGOPOLY A market structure in which a small number of firms are strategically interdependent.

There are many different types of oligopolies. The output may be more or less identical among firms—such as copper wire—or differentiated—such as laptop computers. An oligopoly market may be international, as in the market for automobile tires; national, as in the market for breakfast cereals; or local, as in the market for daily newspapers. There may be one dominant firm whose share of the market far exceeds all the others, such as Microsoft in the market for personal computer software. Or there may be several large firms of roughly similar size, like General Motors, Chrysler, and Ford in the U.S. automobile market. You can see that oligopoly markets can have different characteristics, but in all cases, *a small number of strategically interdependent firms produce the dominant share of output in the market.*

How Oligopolies Arise

If a few large firms continue to dominate an industry, there must be some reason why additional firms do not enter. More specifically, there must be some *barriers to entry* that keeps out competitors. What are these barriers?

ECONOMIES OF SCALE: NATURAL OLIGOPOLIES. Economies of scale (see Chapter 5) can explain why some industries remain oligopolies. The output level at which economies of scale are exhausted—and the firm's *LRATC* curve bottoms out—is called the firm's **minimum efficient scale (MES)**. In general, a firm's MES will depend on its production technology and the prices it must pay for its inputs. Figure 7 illustrates three different possibilities for the MES of a typical firm in an industry. In all three cases, the minimum long-run average cost is assumed to be $50, so this is the lowest price firms could charge without suffering a long-run loss. The demand curve in such a market tells us that, if price *were* $50, quantity demanded would be 100,000 units. Since $50 is the lowest price firms could charge in the long run, 100,000 units is the greatest possible long-run quantity sold in this market.

In panel (a), the MES occurs at 1,000 units. A small firm producing 1,000 units would have a cost advantage over a large firm producing, say, 10,000 units. If there

MINIMUM EFFICIENT SCALE (MES) The level of output at which economies of scale are exhausted and minimum *LRATC* is achieved.

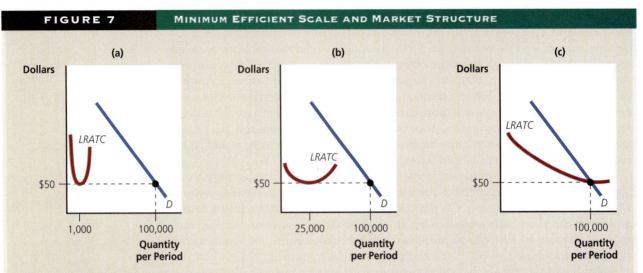

| FIGURE 7 | MINIMUM EFFICIENT SCALE AND MARKET STRUCTURE |

In all three panels, the minimum *LRATC* is $50, so the lowest price that could be charged in the long run is $50. Given the demand curve *D,* 100,000 units is the maximum long-run quantity that could be sold. In panel (a), MES occurs at 1,000 units. With no barriers to entry, a large number of small firms should populate the market. Panel (c) illustrates a natural monopoly; the lowest average cost is achieved when a single firm supplies the entire market. Panel (b) shows a natural oligopoly. MES occurs at 25,000 units, so there should be no more than four firms.

are no barriers to entry, we would expect to see many small firms in this market (but no more than 100 firms—can you explain why?). Thus, we would expect the market to be either purely competitive or monopolistically competitive, depending on whether the output is standardized or differentiated.

Panel (c) illustrates the case of *natural monopoly,* discussed earlier in this chapter. Here, economies of scale continue over such a wide range of output that the lowest cost per unit is achieved when a single firm produces for the entire market. Once a single firm is established in this industry, it could prevent entry by underpricing any potential competitor, since—by producing for the entire market—it achieves the lowest possible average cost.

Finally, panel (b) illustrates the intermediate case, where economies of scale extend over a large range of output, but there is still room for more than one competitor. This is the case of *natural oligopoly.* In the figure, the MES is achieved at 25,000 units, and we would expect this industry to have no more than 4 firms. Why? Because once 4 firms are established, they could easily underprice any new entrant by temporarily producing 25,000 units each, achieving the lowest possible cost per unit, and charging a price of $50. (Why couldn't 5 firms each produce 25,000 units in this market?) Moreover, a new entrant must often start out small and then attempt to gradually gain customers from the preexisting firms. But by starting small, the new entrant will have higher costs per unit than any of those firms and will have a hard time gaining customers from them.

REPUTATION AS A BARRIER. A new entrant may suffer just from being new. Established oligopolists are likely to have favorable reputations. In many oligopolies—like the markets for soft drinks and breakfast cereals—favorable reputations are solidified by heavy advertising expenditure. A new entrant *might* be able to catch up to those already in the industry, but only after a long period of high advertising costs and low revenues. In some cases, where the potential profits are great, investors may decide it is worth the risk and accept the initial losses in order to enter the industry. Ted Turner took such a risk and sustained several years of losses before his cable ventures (Cable News Network, Turner Network Television, and Turner Broadcasting System) earned a profit. But in other industries, the initial losses may be too great and the probability of success too low for investors to risk their money starting a new firm.

STRATEGIC BARRIERS. Oligopoly firms often pursue strategies *designed* to keep out potential competitors. They can maintain excess production capacity as a signal to a potential entrant that, with little advance notice, they could easily saturate the market and leave the new entrant with little or no revenue. They can make special deals with distributors to get the best shelf space in retail stores or make long-term arrangements with customers to ensure that their products are not displaced quickly by those of a new entrant. And they can spend large amounts on advertising to make it difficult for a new entrant to differentiate its product.

GOVERNMENT-CREATED BARRIERS. Oligopolies often lobby the government to preserve their market domination. One of the easiest targets is foreign competition. The big three U.S. automobile companies are relentless in their efforts to limit the number of foreign—especially, Japanese—automobiles sold in the U.S. market. In the past, they have succeeded in getting special taxes on imported cars, quotas that set a maximum quantity of imports, and financial penalties imposed upon successful foreign companies. Other U.S. industries—including textiles, steel, and computer memory chips—have had similar successes.

Government barriers can operate against domestic entrants, too. Zoning regulations may prohibit the building of a new supermarket, movie theater, or auto repair shop in a local market, preserving the oligopoly status of the few firms already established there. Lobbying by established firms is often the source of these restrictive practices.[5]

OLIGOPOLY BEHAVIOR

Of the market structures you have studied in this book, oligopoly presents the greatest challenge to economists. In the other types of markets—pure competition, monopoly, and monopolistic competition—each firm acts independently, without worrying about the reactions of other firms. Its task is a simple one: to select the output level along its demand curve that gives it maximum profit.

But this approach doesn't describe an oligopolist. The essence of oligopoly, remember, is *strategic interdependence*, wherein each firm anticipates the actions of its rivals when making decisions. Thus, we cannot analyze one firm's decisions in isolation from other firms. In order to understand and predict behavior in oligopoly markets, economists have had to modify the tools used to analyze the other market structures and to develop entirely new tools as well.

Let's look at this idea of strategic interdependence more closely and see why the simple approach used in other markets will not work in an oligopoly. Imagine that

---

5.   This kind of lobbying is often disguised. In 1995, Home Depot, Inc., sued Rickel Home Centers for secretly forming an organization called "Concerned Citizens for Community Preservation." The sole purpose of the organization was to prevent Home Depot from opening new stores in towns where Rickel already had its own outlets. (*Wall Street Journal*, August 19, 1995.)

Kafka Exterminators, instead of being a monopolistic competitor, was one of just three exterminators in town—an oligopolist. In order to draw Kafka's demand curve—like the one in Figure 6—we must hold constant the prices charged by its competitors.

To see why, imagine that Kafka's demand curve is initially the one in Figure 5, and then one or both competitors *lowered* their prices. The competitors would lure some of Kafka's customers away, and Kafka's demand curve would shift leftward— it would have fewer customers at any given price. Similarly, if one or both rivals *raised* their price, Kafka's demand curve would shift rightward. Thus, the position of Kafka's demand curve will depend on the prices set by its rivals.

This complicates the firm's decision making. Each time Kafka considers moving along its demand curve by changing its own price, it knows its competitors will re-act by changing *their* prices, causing Kafka's own demand curve to shift. Thus, Kafka does not face a stable demand curve. Our simple $MC = MR$ rule for profit maximization, which works in other types of markets, will not work under condi-tions of strategic interaction. You can see why oligopoly presents such a challenge, not only to the firms themselves, but also to economists studying them.

Although great progress has been made, there is not yet a single, unified theory of oligopoly. Rather, there have been a variety of approaches, with important new discoveries continuing to deepen our understanding. The approaches that have of-fered the richest insights into oligopoly behavior make use of **game theory.**

GAME THEORY An approach to modeling the strategic interac-tion of oligopolists in terms of moves and countermoves.

THE GAME THEORY APPROACH. The word "game" applied to oligopoly deci-sion making might seem out of place. Games—like poker, basketball, or chess—are usually played for fun, and even when money is at stake, the sums are usually small. What do games have in common with important business decisions, where hun-dreds of millions of dollars and thousands of jobs may be at stake?

In fact, quite a bit. In all games—except those of pure chance, such as roulette— a player's strategy must take account of the strategies followed by other players. This is precisely the situation of the oligopolist. Game theory analyzes oligopoly de-cisions as if they were games by looking at the rules players must follow, the pay-offs they are trying to achieve, and the strategies they can use to achieve them.

SIMPLE OLIGOPOLY GAMES. Imagine a town with just two gas stations: Gus's Gas and Filip's Fillup. This is an example of an oligopoly with just two firms, called a **duopoly.** We will regard Gus and Filip as *players* in a *game* in which they must make their decisions independently, without knowing in advance what the other will do.

DUOPOLY An oligopoly market with only two sellers.

Figure 8 shows the **payoff matrix** for this game—a listing of the payoffs that each player will receive for each possible combination of strategies that might be se-lected. The payoff matrix presents a lot of information at once, so let's take it step-by-step.

PAYOFF MATRIX A table showing the payoffs to each of two firms for each pair of strate-gies they choose.

First, notice that each *column* represents a strategy that Gus might choose: to charge a low price for his gas, or a high price.[6] Second, each *row* represents a strat-egy that Filip might select: a low price, or a high price. Thus, each of the four boxes in the payoff matrix represents one of four possible strategy combinations that might be selected by the two players in this game:

6. In a real-world market for gasoline—even one with just two gas stations—there would be many prices from which to choose. Our assumption of just two prices is a "simplifying assumption" that makes it easier to see what is going on.

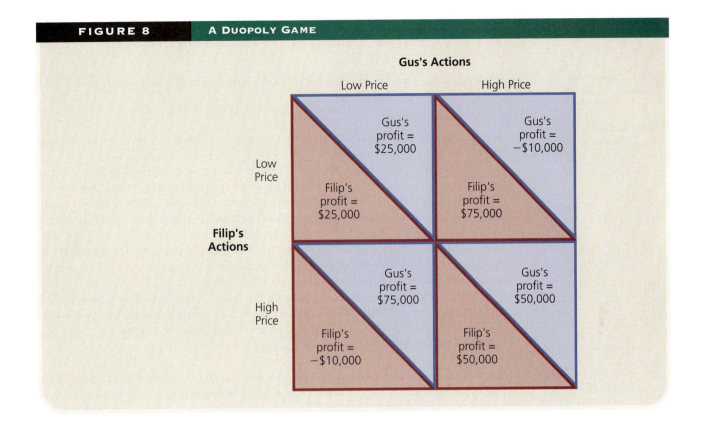

FIGURE 8   **A DUOPOLY GAME**

1. Upper left box: Both Gus and Filip charge a low price.
2. Lower left box: Gus charges a low price and Filip charges a high price.
3. Upper right box: Gus charges a high price and Filip charges a low price.
4. Lower right box: Both Gus and Filip charge a high price.

Let's make two additional (temporary) assumptions: First, each player must decide on his strategy without knowing what the other will do. Second, once the strategy is selected, the player is stuck with it for some time. (These assumptions are actually realistic in some oligopoly markets, especially those in which prices are negotiated with customers privately and in which it is costly to change prices after they are set.)

Let's now look at the game from Gus's point of view. The entries shown in *blue* in each box are Gus's possible *payoffs*—the yearly profit he will earn in each case. (Ignore the red entries for now.) For example, the lower left square shows that when Gus charges a low price and Filip charges a high price, Gus's yearly profit will be $75,000.

Gus wants the best possible profit for himself, but he is not sure what Filip will do. So Gus asks himself which strategy would be best *if* Filip were to charge a low price. The *top row* of the matrix guides us through his reasoning. "If Filip decides to charge a low price, my best choice would be to charge a low price too, because then I'd earn $25,000 in profit, rather than a loss of $10,000." Next, Gus determines the best strategy if Filip were to charge a *high* price. As the *bottom row* shows, he'll reason as follows: "If Filip charges a high price, my best choice would be to charge a low price, because then I'd earn $75,000 in profit, rather than $50,000."

Let's recap: If Filip charges a low price, Gus's best choice is a low price. If Filip charges a high price, Gus's best choice is—once again—to charge a low price. Thus, regardless of Filip's strategy, Gus's best choice is to charge a low price. In this game, the strategy "low price" is an example of a *dominant strategy* for Gus.

DOMINANT STRATEGY A strategy that is best for a firm no matter what strategy its competitor chooses.

> A **dominant strategy** is a strategy that is best for a player regardless of the strategy of the other player.

If a player has a dominant strategy in a game, we can safely assume that he will follow it.

What about Filip? He is presented with the same set of options and payoffs as his partner—as shown by the red entries in the payoff matrix. When Filip looks down each *column*, he can see his possible payoffs for each strategy that Gus might follow. As you can see (and make sure that you can, by going through all the possibilities), Filip also has a dominant strategy—charge the low price. We can now predict that *both* players will follow the strategy of charging a low price, and that the outcome of the game—the upper left-hand corner—is a low price for each player, with each earning $25,000 in profit.

When each decision maker is charging the lower price, he is doing the best that he can do, given the actions of the other. Therefore, once they reach the upper left-hand corner, neither Gus nor Filip will have any incentive to change his price. The *market equilibrium* price, in this case, is the low price.

OLIGOPOLY GAMES IN THE REAL WORLD. While our simple example helps us understand the basic ideas of game theory, real-world oligopoly situations are seldom so simple. First, there will typically be more than two strategies from which to choose (for example, a variety of different prices or several different amounts to spend on *non*price competition such as advertising). Also, there will usually be more than two players, so a two-dimensional payoff matrix like the one in Figure 8 would not suffice. Still, as long as each firm has a dominant strategy, we can predict the outcome of the game—the market equilibrium—although we might need the help of a computer in the more complex cases.

Second, in some games, one or more players may *not* have a dominant strategy. For example, if we alter just one entry in the figure—changing Gus's payoff of $75,000 (lower left-hand box) to $40,000—Gus would no longer have a dominant strategy. As you can verify on your own, if Filip charges a low price, Gus should charge a low price; but if Filip charges a high price, Gus should charge a high price too. Thus, Gus's choice depends on Filip's choice. However, since we have not changed any of Filip's payoffs, he still has a dominant strategy—to charge a low price. Since Gus knows that Filip will select a low price, Gus will always select a low price, too. Thus, we can still predict the market equilibrium: a low price for both firms. This example shows us that, *when one player has a dominant strategy, we can still predict the game's outcome, whether the other player has a dominant strategy or not.*

But what if we also change Filip's payoff of $75,000 (upper right-hand corner) to $40,000? Then, as you can verify, *neither* player will have a dominant strategy, so neither can predict what the other will do. Moreover, we—as outside observers—will be unable to predict the outcome. *When neither player has a dominant strategy, we will need a more sophisticated analysis to predict an outcome to the game.*

Third, in our example, we've limited the players to *one* play of the game. This would make sense if firms' prices had to be set in advance and could not be changed very easily, but it is not realistic for most oligopoly markets. In reality, for gas stations and almost all other oligopolies, there is **repeated play,** where both players select a strategy, observe the outcome of that trial, and play the game again and again, as long as they remain rivals. Repeated play can fundamentally change the way players view a game and lead to new strategies based on long-run considerations. One possible result of repeated trials is *cooperative behavior,* to which we now turn.

COOPERATIVE BEHAVIOR IN OLIGOPOLY

In the real world, oligopolists will usually get more than one chance to choose their prices. Pepsi and Coca-Cola have been rivals in the soft-drink market for most of this century, as have Ford, Chrysler, and GM in the automobile market and Kellogg, Post (Kraft Foods), Quaker, and General Mills in the breakfast cereal market. These firms can change their prices based on the past responses of their rivals.

The equilibrium in a game with repeated plays may be very different from the equilibrium in a game played only once. Often, firms will evolve some form of *cooperation* in the long run.

For example, look again at Figure 8. If this game were played only once, we would expect each player to pursue its dominant strategy, select a low price, and end up with $25,000 in yearly profit. But there is a better outcome for both players. If each were to charge a high price, each would make a profit of $50,000 per year. If Gus and Filip remain competitors year after year, we would expect them to realize that by cooperating, they would both be better off. And there are many ways for the two to cooperate.

EXPLICIT COLLUSION. The simplest form of cooperation is **explicit collusion,** in which managers meet face to face to decide how to set prices. In our example, Gus and Filip might strike an agreement that each will charge a high price, moving the outcome of the game to the lower right-hand corner in Figure 8, where each earns $50,000 in yearly profit instead of $25,000.

One form of explicit collusion is a **cartel,** wherein the parties select a price along the market demand curve that maximizes total profits in the industry. They do this by choosing the price and quantity of output that a monopoly would charge if it owned all of the firms in the market. To maintain its monopoly profit, the cartel must ensure that the combined output of all firms equals the profit-maximizing quantity. It accomplishes this by allocating a share of the market output to each member of the cartel.

The most famous cartel in recent years has been OPEC—the Organization of Petroleum Exporting Countries—which meets periodically to set the price of oil and the amount of oil that each of its members can produce. In the mid-1970s, OPEC quadrupled its price per barrel in just two years, leading to a huge increase in profits for the cartel's members.

If explicit collusion to raise prices is such a good thing for oligopolists, why don't all oligopolists do it? For two reasons. First, it is illegal in many countries, including the United States, and the penalties, if the oligopolists are caught, can be severe. OPEC was not considered illegal by any of the participating nations. But in most cases, explicit collusion *is* illegal and must be conducted with the utmost secrecy.

Second, it takes a lot of effort to maintain explicit collusion. In a cartel, each member can make more profit by selling more than its allocated share. The cartel needs to have some enforcement mechanism—some way to punish firms that produce more than their agreed-upon shares. Of course, because of its illegal status, the cartel cannot bring offenders to court. But alternative enforcement mechanisms may

REPEATED PLAY A situation in which strategically interdependent sellers compete over many time periods.

EXPLICIT COLLUSION Cooperation involving direct communication between competing firms about setting prices.

CARTEL A group of firms that selects a common price that maximizes total industry profits.

not work. For example, threatening to allow other members to increase their output may lack credibility at best or destroy the cartel at worst.

TACIT COLLUSION. Since explicit collusion is illegal, it is rare in the United States. But other ways of cooperating have evolved among oligopolists. Any time firms cooperate *without* an explicit agreement, they are engaging in **tacit collusion.** Typically, players adopt strategies along the following lines: "In general, I will set a high price. If my rival also sets a high price, I will go on setting a high price. If my rival sets a low price this time, I will punish him by setting a low price next time." You can see that if both players stick to this strategy, they will both always set the high price. Each is waiting for the other to go first in setting a low price, so it never happens.

An example of this type of strategy is **tit for tat,** defined as doing to the other player what he has just done to you. In our gas station duopoly, for example, Gus will pick the high price whenever Filip has set the high price in the previous play, and Gus will pick the low price if that is what Filip did in the previous play. With enough plays of the game, Filip may eventually catch on that he can get Gus to set the desired high price by setting the high price himself and that he should not exploit the situation by setting the low price, because that will cause Gus to set the low price next time. The outcome in every play will then be in the lower right-hand corner of Figure 8, with each firm earning the higher $50,000 in profit.

Tit-for-tat strategies are prominent in the airline industry. When one major airline announces special fares, its rivals almost always announce identical fares the next day. Often, as well, one airline's fare increase is copied by rivals. However, tit for tat is not always effective, and the airline industry has had periods of instability. In 1992, when several airlines announced special restricted summer fares, American Airlines responded with even lower fares, cutting the price of many tickets in half. Most other airlines copied American's move, resulting in fares that were way below the profit-maximizing level for most of the summer. Continental and Northwest, two of the airlines hit hardest by American's fare cut, sued American on the theory that American was trying to teach them a lesson not to deviate from normal fares. The jury rejected Continental and Northwest's claims and concluded that this type of conduct was not a violation of antitrust laws. Airline fares have been much more stable since the jury's verdict. It is possible that American's rivals now respect American's strong tit-for-tat strategy and are reluctant to make fare cuts that would attract a similar reaction.

Another form of tacit collusion is **price leadership,** in which one firm—the *price leader*—sets its price, and other sellers copy that price. The leader may be the dominant firm in the industry (the one with the greatest market share, for example), or the position of leader may rotate from firm to firm. During the first half of this century, U.S. Steel typically acted as the price leader in the steel industry: When it changed its prices, other firms would automatically follow. More recently, Goodyear has been the acknowledged leader in the tire industry; its price increases are virtually always matched within days by Michelin, Bridgestone, and most other firms in the industry.

With price leadership, there is no formal agreement. Rather, the choice of the leader, the criteria it uses to set its price, and the willingness of other firms to follow come about because the firms realize—without formal discussion—that the system benefits all of them.

THE LIMITS TO OLIGOPOLY

Some people think that the U.S. and other Western economies are moving relentlessly toward oligopoly as the dominant market structure. Technological change is often cited as the reason. For example, in the early part of the century, several dozen

TACIT COLLUSION Any form of oligopolistic cooperation that does not involve an explicit agreement.

TIT FOR TAT A game-theoretic strategy of doing to another player this period what he has done to you in the previous period.

PRICE LEADERSHIP A form of tacit collusion in which one firm sets a price that other firms copy.

U.S. firms manufactured passenger cars. With the development of mass-production technology, the number has steadily fallen to three. Stories like this suggest an economy in which markets are increasingly controlled and manipulated by a few players who—by colluding—exploit the public for their own gain. In 1932, economists Adolf Berle and Gardiner Means noted the trend toward big business and predicted that, unless something were done to stop it, the 200 largest U.S. firms would control the nation's entire economy by 1970.

These fears have proven to be unfounded. Today, there are hundreds of thousands of business firms in the United States. Moreover, the evidence shows no strong trend toward increasing concentration in U.S. industries.

We have already noted one reason why: In many industries, the minimum efficient scale of production is so small relative to the size of the market that a small firm can produce at the same—or even lower—cost per unit as a large firm that controls a significant share of the market. And there are other, powerful forces operating to restrict and even reduce the extent of oligopoly in the economy.

ANTITRUST LEGISLATION AND ENFORCEMENT. Antitrust policies in the United States and many other countries are designed to protect the interests of consumers by ensuring adequate competition in the marketplace. In practice, antitrust enforcement has focused on three types of actions: (1) preventing collusive agreements among firms, such as price-fixing agreements; (2) breaking up or limiting the activities of large firms whose market dominance harms consumers; and (3) preventing mergers that would lead to harmful market domination.

Microsoft, giant of the software industry, has come under antitrust challenge repeatedly. In 1994, the government negotiated restrictions on its dealings with computer makers in order to keep the market open to other companies. In 1998, the government went to court to prove that Microsoft had obtained monopoly power by illegal means.

The impact of antitrust actions goes far beyond the specific companies called into the courtroom. Managers of other firms, considering anticompetitive moves, have to think long and hard about the consequences of acts that might violate the antitrust laws. For example, many economists believe that in the late 1940s and early 1950s, General Motors would have driven its two competitors out of business or bought them out were it not for fear of antitrust action. (Antitrust law is discussed in more detail in Chapter 10.)

THE GLOBALIZATION OF MARKETS. Although oligopolists often try to prevent it, they face increasingly stiff competition from foreign producers. Some have argued, for example, that the U.S. market for automobiles now has so many foreign sellers that it resembles monopolistic competition more than oligopoly. Similar changes have occurred in the U.S. markets for color televisions, stereo equipment, computers, beer, and wine. At the same time, the entry of U.S. producers has helped to increase competition in foreign markets for movies, television shows, clothing, household cleaning products, and prepared foods.

TECHNOLOGICAL CHANGE. You may think that technological change invariably favors bigness and domination by a few firms. But many new technologies serve to *increase* competition by eliminating barriers to entry. The oligopoly of the three major television networks (CBS, ABC, and NBC) was due in part to the limited television broadcast spectrum. Cable television has broken through that barrier and significantly reduced the domination of the networks.

**Antitrust Division,
U.S. Department of Justice**
Federal agency enforcing U.S. antitrust laws. Browse the site for information on enforcement activities and recent antitrust cases. You will also find guidelines the agency uses in evaluating the competitive impact of mergers.
http://www.usdoj.gov/atr/index.html

New technology can also destroy a natural oligopoly by eroding economies of scale. Recall (see Figure 7) that in a natural oligopoly, the minimum efficient scale (MES) is large relative to the size of the market. Thus, anything that decreases the MES, or increases the size of the market, may increase the number of firms that can effectively compete in the industry. In the home entertainment industry, both of these changes are about to occur. Wireless technology will eliminate the need to string expensive cable and thus reduce the number of subscribers needed to minimize cost per unit (the MES). At the same time, this technology will enable firms to sell in more than one locality, thus changing the home entertainment market from a local one to a national one, where dozens or even hundreds of firms will compete.

PRICE DISCRIMINATION

So far in this text, we've analyzed the decisions of *single-price firms*—those that charge the same price on every unit that they sell. But not all firms operate this way. For example, local utilities typically charge different rates per kilowatt-hour, depending on whether the energy is used in a home or business. Telephone companies charge different rates for calls made by people on different calling plans. Movie theaters charge lower prices to students and senior citizens. And airlines charge lower prices to those who book their flights in advance.

In some cases, the different prices are due to differences in the firm's costs of production. For example, it may be more expensive to deliver a product a great distance from the factory, so a firm may charge a higher price to customers in outlying areas. But in other cases, the different prices arise not from cost differences, but from the firm's recognition that *some customers are willing to pay more than others:*

PRICE DISCRIMINATION
Charging different prices to different customers for reasons other than production costs.

> *Price discrimination* occurs when a firm charges different prices to different customers for reasons other than differences in production costs.

The term "discrimination" in this context requires some getting used to. In everyday language, "discrimination" carries a negative connotation: We think immediately of discrimination against someone because of his or her race, sex, or age. But a price-discriminating firm does not discriminate based on prejudice, stereotypes, or ill will toward any person or group; rather, it divides its customers into different categories based on their *willingness to pay* for the good—nothing more and nothing less. By doing so, a firm may be able to squeeze even more profit out of the market. Why, then, doesn't *every* firm practice price discrimination?

REQUIREMENTS FOR PRICE DISCRIMINATION

Although every firm would like to practice price discrimination, not all of them can. To successfully price discriminate, three conditions must be satisfied:

1. *There must be a downward-sloping demand curve for the firm's output.* In order to price discriminate, a firm must be able to raise its price to at least *some* customers without losing their business. A perfectly competitive firm cannot price discriminate: If it were to raise its price even slightly to some customers, they would simply buy the identical output from some other firm that is selling at the market price. This is why buyers of wheat, soybeans, silver, and other competitively produced goods generally pay the same price, even though some of them would be *willing* to pay more if they had to.

When a firm faces a downward-sloping demand curve, however, we know that some customers will continue to buy even when the price increases. Monopolies and monopolistic competitors—which face downward-sloping demand curves—always satisfy this requirement. Oligopoly pricing, as you've learned, is more complicated. Nevertheless, an oligopoly may be able to price discriminate as well. As long as other firms will not react—say, because some form of tacit collusion permits price discrimination—an oligopolist can raise its price to some customers and only lose a portion of them.

2. *The firm must be able to identify consumers willing to pay more.* In order to determine which prices to charge to which customers, a firm must identify how much different customers are willing to pay. But this is often difficult. Suppose your barber or hair stylist wanted to price discriminate. How would he determine how much you are willing to pay for a haircut? He could ask you, but . . . let's be real: You wouldn't tell him the truth, since you know he would only use the information to charge you more than you've been paying. Price-discriminating firms must be a bit sneaky, relying on more indirect methods to gauge their customers' willingness to pay.

For example, airlines know that business travelers, who must get to their destination quickly, are willing to pay a higher price for air travel than are tourists or vacationers, who can more easily travel by train, bus, or car. Of course, if airlines merely *announced* a higher price for business travel, then no one would admit to being a business traveler when buying a ticket. So the airlines must find some way to identify business travelers without actually asking. Their method is crude, but reasonably effective: Business travelers typically plan their trips at the last minute and don't stay over Saturday night, while tourists and vacationers generally plan long in advance and do stay over Saturday. Thus, the airlines give a discount to any customer who books a flight several weeks in advance and stays over, and they charge a higher price to those who book at the last minute and don't stay over. In this way, the airlines are able to charge a higher price to a group of people—business travelers—who are willing to pay more.[7]

3. *The firm must be able to prevent low-price customers from reselling to high-price customers.* Unless this condition is satisfied, high-price customers will only buy from low-price customers, and the firm will never collect the high price.

Preventing a product from being resold by low-price customers can be a vexing problem for a would-be discriminator. For example, when airlines began price discriminating, an active resale market developed: Business travelers would buy tickets at the last minute from intermediaries, who had booked in advance at the lower price and then advertised their tickets for sale. To counter this, the airlines imposed an additional requirement for a discount: the Saturday-night stay-over. The airlines reasoned, quite properly, that business travelers generally conduct their business on weekdays and are anxious to fly home when they are done; tourists and vacationers, by contrast, generally *want* to stay over on a Saturday night. By adding this restriction to the discount, they were able to substantially reduce the loss of revenue from the resale market.

---

7.   It is sometimes argued that airlines' pricing behavior is based entirely on a cost difference to the airline. For example, it is probably more costly for an airline to keep seats available until the last minute, because there is a risk that they will go unsold. The higher price for last-minute bookings would then compensate the airline for the unsold seats. (See, for example, the article by John R. Lott, Jr., and Russell D. Roberts in *Economic Inquiry,* January, 1991.) But we know that cost differences are not the only reason for the price differential, or else the airlines would not have added the Saturday stay-over requirement, which has nothing to do with their costs.

EFFECTS OF PRICE DISCRIMINATION

Price discrimination always benefits the owners of a firm: When the firm can charge different prices to different consumers, it can use this ability to increase its profit. But the effects on consumers can vary. To understand how price discrimination affects the firm and the consumers of its product, let's take a simple example. Imagine that only one company—No-Choice Airlines—offers direct, small-plane flights between Omaha and Salina, Kansas. (What barrier to entry might explain No-Choice's monopoly on this route?)

Figure 9(a) illustrates what No-Choice would do if it could *not* price discriminate and had to operate as a single-price monopoly. Since $MR = MC$ at 30 round-trip tickets per day, No-Choice's profit-maximizing price would be $120 per ticket. The firm's average total cost for 30 round trips is $80, so its profit per ticket would be $120 − $80 = $40. Total profit is $40 × 30 = $1,200, equal to the area of the shaded rectangle.

PRICE DISCRIMINATION THAT HARMS CONSUMERS. Now suppose that No-Choice discovers that on an average day, 10 of the 30 people buying tickets are business travelers who are willing to pay more, and it can identify them by their *un*willingness to book in advance and stay over on Saturday night. No-Choice could price discriminate by offering two prices: $120 for those who book in advance and stay over on Saturday, and $160 to all others. In effect, No-Choice is raising the price from $120 to $160 for its 10 business customers.

Let's calculate the impact on No-Choice's profit. Since it continues to sell the same 30 round-trip tickets, there is no impact on its costs. Its revenue, however, will rise: It charges $40 more than before on 10 of its round-trip tickets. Thus, No-Choice will earn an additional daily profit of $40 × 10 = $400. This *increase* in profit is identified as the shaded rectangle in Figure 9(b). Total profit is now the sum of two numbers: the profit No-Choice earned *before* price discrimination ($1,200, the area of the shaded rectangle in panel [a]) and the *increase* in profit due to price discrimination ($400, the area of the shaded rectangle in panel [b]). By price discriminating, No-Choice has raised its total profit from $1,200 to $1,600 per day.

What about consumers? Since 10 customers each pay $40 more than before, they lose 10 × $40 = $400 from paying the higher price. Other travelers, who continue to pay $120 for their tickets, are unaffected by the higher price.

Summing up, in this case the impact of price discrimination—compared to a single-price policy—is a direct transfer of funds from consumers to the firm. The increase in the firm's profit is equal to the additional payments by consumers. This conclusion applies more generally as well:

When price discrimination raises the price for some consumers above the price they would pay under a single-price policy, it harms consumers. The additional profit for the firm is equal to the monetary loss of consumers.

PRICE DISCRIMINATION THAT BENEFITS CONSUMERS. Let's go back to the initial situation facing No-Choice and suppose that, instead of charging a higher price to business travelers, it decides to price discriminate in a different way. No-Choice discovers that students who travel to college in Salina are going by train, because it is cheaper. However, at a price of $100, the airline could sell an average of 10 round-trip tickets per day to the students. No-Choice's new policy is this: $120 for a round-trip ticket, but a special price of $100 for students who show their ID cards. The result is shown in panel (c). Although the decision to sell an additional

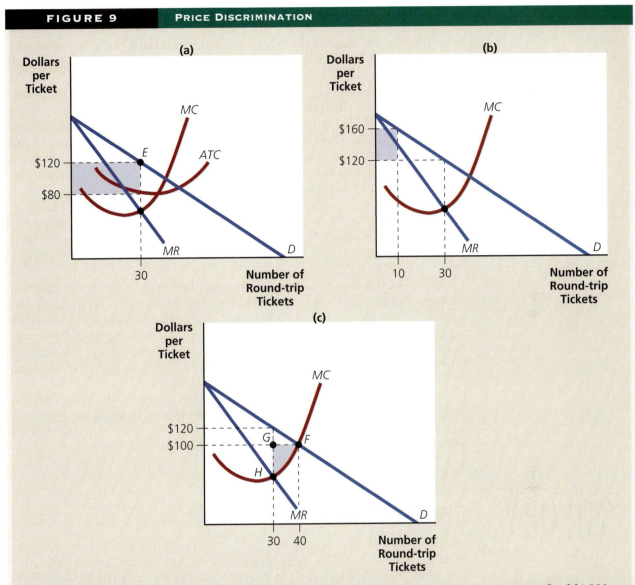

FIGURE 9 **PRICE DISCRIMINATION**

Panel (a) shows a single-price monopoly airline selling 30 round-trip tickets at $120 each and earning a profit of $1,200. Panel (b) shows the same airline if it can charge a higher price to its business travelers. The shaded rectangle shows the *additional* profit the airline earns by price discriminating; total profit is now $1,600. Panel (c) shows an alternative strategy. In addition to selling 30 regular tickets at $120 each, the airline attracts an additional 10 passengers at a lower student fare of $100. *MR* exceeds *MC*, so profit rises by the area of the shaded region.

10 tickets pushes No-Choice beyond the output level at which $MC = MR$, this is no problem. The *MR* curve was drawn under the assumption that No-Choice charges a single price and must lower the price on all tickets in order to sell more. But this is no longer the case. With price discrimination, the *MR* curve no longer tells us what will happen to No-Choice's revenue when output increases. As you are about to see, the firm will be able to increase its profit by selling the additional tickets.

The reasoning is as follows: No-Choice is now selling 10 *additional* round-trip tickets, so in this case both its cost and its revenue will change. Each additional ticket adds $100 to the firm's revenue—this is the new marginal revenue. Each additional ticket adds an amount to costs given by the firm's *MC* curve. Thus, the distance between $100 and the *MC* curve gives the *additional profit* earned on each additional ticket, and the total additional profit is the area of the shaded triangle *HGF* in panel (c).

What about consumers? The original 30 consumers are unaffected, since their ticket price has not changed. But the new customers—the 10 students—come out ahead: Each is able to take the flight rather than the longer train trip. In this case, price discrimination benefits the firm at the same time as it benefits a group of consumers—the students who were not buying the service before, but who *will* buy it at a lower price and gain some benefits by doing so. Since no one's price is raised, no one is harmed by this policy:

> *When price discrimination lowers the price for some consumers below what they would pay under a single-price policy, it benefits consumers as well as the firm.*

Of course, it is possible for a firm to combine both types of price discrimination, raising the price above what it would charge as a single-price firm for some consumers and lowering it for others. This kind of price discrimination would increase the firm's profit, while benefiting some consumers and harming others. (For practice, draw a diagram showing the change in total profit if No-Choice were to charge three prices: a basic price of $120, a price of $160 for business travelers, and a price of $100 for students. Who would gain and who would lose?)

As you can see, price discrimination can become quite complex. Some firms can even divide their consumers into *several* different groups, charging each one a different price. The following "Using the Theory" section gives an example that will prove close to home: price discrimination by colleges and universities.

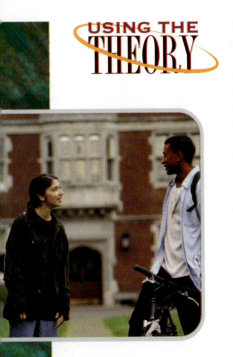

USING THE THEORY

PRICE DISCRIMINATION BY COLLEGES AND UNIVERSITIES

Most colleges and universities give some kind of financial aid to a large proportion of their students. A typical aid package might include outright grants to help pay tuition and room and board, a low-interest loan, and a work-study job on campus. Colleges have many motives for this policy, such as having a more socially diverse student body and helping to create a better society by making educational services accessible to many who might not otherwise afford them. But increasingly, financial aid has been used as an effective method of price discrimination, designed to increase the revenue of the college.

How does a college price discriminate? By offering different levels of assistance to different students, financial aid permits the college to charge *different prices* to different groups. For example, if full tuition is $12,000 per year, then a student who receives a yearly $5,000 grant pays only $7,000 per year, a student who receives an $8,000 grant pays only $4,000 per year, and so on.

Colleges have long been in an especially good position to benefit from price discrimination, because they satisfy all three requirements:

1. *Colleges face downward-sloping demand curves.* Although colleges are not monopolies (other, similar institutions are close substitutes), they are not perfect

competitors either. Each college is unique in some ways—location, reputation, living conditions, social life, and more. For this reason, colleges face downward-sloping demand curves for their services. A college can raise its price and lose only *some*—rather than all—of its enrollment applicants. Similarly, any college that wants to increase enrollment can do so by lowering its price and attracting applications from those who would not attend at the higher price.

2. *Colleges are able to identify consumers willing to pay more.* Colleges have long been in an excellent position to discover how much their customers would be willing to pay for their product. Applicants for financial aid have had to submit data on their families' income and wealth. Admissions officials know that students from poor families are less likely to attend their institutions unless they are offered a relatively low price, while students from wealthier families are likely to attend at higher prices. In recent years, however, colleges have gone even further in their attempts to identify willingness to pay. (See below.)

3. *Colleges are able to prevent low-price customers from reselling to high-price customers.* Once you pay for it, you cannot resell your college education to someone else.

While most colleges have been active price discriminators for decades, many have stepped up their efforts since 1992. That year, Congress changed the formula used to determine financial need, making most students eligible for assistance. This allowed colleges to allocate financial aid dollars among a wider pool of students. Suddenly, price discrimination could be used even more extensively. But this required new methods of identifying willingness to pay among different students.

The market responded. Specialized consultants, using computer models to predict the likelihood that students would attend college at different prices, began offering their services. One consultant's pamphlet asked admissions officials, "Did you overspend to get students who would have matriculated with lesser aid? Did you underspend and lose students who would have come with more support?"[8]

As a result, the traditional role of financial aid as assistance for those in need has changed. Some colleges have shifted aid dollars toward top-ranked applicants—regardless of financial need—because those students have more options and are less likely to attend any college without financial aid. Drexel University in Philadelphia shifted aid toward those who applied as business majors after a computer model predicted that these students' enrollment decisions were more sensitive to price. Johns Hopkins University shifted aid dollars to humanities majors with SAT scores above 1,200 and relatively low financial need, based on a similar model.

Many financial aid consultants have even recommended that colleges shift aid money away from students who come for on-campus interviews, since by doing so, those students reveal a strong desire to attend college. There are rumors that some institutions have begun following this advice, but no college has admitted to the practice.

More effective price discrimination at colleges and universities is certainly changing the traditional view of financial assistance as a program designed primarily to help those in need. And while it has benefited some groups of students, it has harmed others. Under the newer systems, those who can signal a lower willingness to pay have benefited from reduced prices, while those signaling greater willingness to pay have suffered a price increase.

---

8. "Colleges Manipulate Financial-Aid Offers, Shortchanging Many," *Wall Street Journal*, April 1, 1996, p. 1. The specific examples of price discrimination in the discussion also come from this article.

But fully assessing the effects of price discrimination at colleges is complicated by one important fact: Most educational institutions are not private firms striving to maximize profits for their owners. Rather, they are *nonprofit* institutions, *without* private owners. Thus, any additional revenue they gain through price discrimination is likely to be used for educational purposes: to attract better faculty by raising salaries, to improve living conditions for students, to keep tuition lower than it otherwise would be, and even to provide increased aid for more students in the future. Each of these alternatives has value to the college and its students, suggesting that increased price discrimination at colleges, like so many other economic issues, is a matter of trade-offs.

THE FOUR MARKET STRUCTURES: A POSTSCRIPT

You have now been introduced to the four different market structures: pure competition, monopoly, monopolistic competition, and oligopoly. Each has different characteristics, and each leads to different predictions about pricing, profit, and firms' responses to changes in their environments.

Table 1 summarizes some of the assumptions and predictions associated with each of the four market structures. While the table is a useful review of the *models* we have studied, care must be exercised in applying it to the real world. We cannot simply look at the array of markets we see around us and say, "This one is purely competitive," "That one is an oligopoly," and so on. Why not? Because markets in the real world will typically have characteristics of more than one kind of market structure. A barbecue restaurant, for example, may be viewed as a monopolistic competitor in the market for restaurants in Memphis, or an oligopolist in the market for *barbecue* restaurants in Memphis (if there are only a few), or a monopolist in the market for barbecue restaurants within walking distance of Graceland (if it is the only one).

You can see how market structure models help us organize and understand the apparent chaos of real-world markets. Now, it seems, we've ended up with a different type of chaos: We can usually choose among several different models when studying a particular market.

But, as we've seen several times in this text, our choice of model is not really arbitrary; rather, it depends on the *questions we are trying to answer*. To explain why

TABLE 1	A SUMMARY OF MARKET STRUCTURES			
	Perfect Competition	**Monopolistic Competition**	**Oligopoly**	**Monopoly**
ASSUMPTIONS:				
Number of Firms	Very Many	Many	Few	One
Output of Different Firms	Identical	Differentiated	Identical or differentiated	—
View of Pricing	Price taker	Price setter	Price setter	Price setter
Barriers to Entry or Exit?	No	No	Yes	Yes
Strategic Interdependence?	No	No	Yes	—
PREDICTIONS:				
Price and Output Decisions	$MC = MR$	$MC = MR$	Through strategic interdependence	$MC = MR$
Short-Run Profit	Positive, zero, or negative	Positive, zero, or negative	Positive, zero, or negative	Positive, zero, or negative
Long-Run Profit	Zero	Zero	Positive or zero	Positive or zero

a *particular* barbecue restaurant with no competitors very close by earns economic profit year after year, we might use the monopoly model. If we want to explain why *most* barbecue restaurants do *not* earn much economic profit, or why they pay for advertisements in the yellow pages and the local newspapers, we would use the model of monopolistic competition. To explain a price war among the few restaurants in a neighborhood, or to explore the possibility of explicit or tacit collusion in pricing or advertising, we would use the oligopoly model. And if we want the *simplest* possible explanations about prices, entry and exit, and profit over the short run and the long run, we would use the purely competitive model, which ignores the distinctions between meals at different restaurants and any barriers to entry that might exist. This example should convince you that economics is as much art as science, and this, in part, is what keeps it interesting and intellectually challenging.

S U M M A R Y

A *monopoly firm* is the only seller of a good or service with no close substitutes. Monopoly arises because of some barrier to entry: economies of scale, control of a scarce input, or a government-created barrier. As the only seller, the monopoly faces the demand curve for the entire market, and must decide what price to charge in order to maximize profit.

Like other firms, a monopolist will produce where $MR = MC$ and set that maximum price consumers are willing to pay for that quantity. Monopoly profit ($P - ATC$ multiplied by the quantity produced) can persist in the long run because of barriers to entry.

Imperfect competition refers to market structures with more than one firm, but in which one or more of the requirements of pure competition are violated. Monopolistic competition is one type of imperfect competition. In this type of market, there are many small buyers and sellers, no significant barriers to entry or exit, and firms sell differentiated profits. As in monopoly, each firm faces a downward-sloping demand curve, chooses the profit-maximizing quantity where $MR = MC$, and charges the maximum price it can for that quantity. As in perfect competition, short-run profit attracts new entrants. As firms enter the industry, the demand curves facing existing firms shift left. Eventually, each firm earns zero economic profit and produces a level of output above minimum average cost.

Oligopoly is another type of imperfect competition. The market is dominated by a small number of strategically interdependent firms. New entry is deterred by economies of scale, reputational barriers, strategic barriers, and government-created barriers to entry. Because each firm, when making decisions, must anticipate its rivals' reactions, oligopoly behavior is hard to predict. However, one approach—*game theory*—has offered rich insights.

In game theory, a *payoff matrix* indicates the payoff to each firm for each combination of strategies adopted by that firm and by its rivals. A *dominant strategy* is a strategy that is best for a particular firm regardless of what its rival does. If a firm has a dominant strategy, it will always play it, and that helps predict the outcome of the game. If no firm has a dominant strategy, it is much harder to predict what will happen—especially for games that are played only once.

Sometimes oligopolists will wish to cooperate in an effort to increase profits. *Explicit collusion,* where managers meet to set prices, is illegal in the United States. As a result, other forms of *tacit collusion* have evolved. Still, collusion is limited by a number of factors: cheating by firms, government antitrust enforcement, market globalization, and technological change.

Some monopolies and imperfectly competitive firms can practice *price discrimination* by charging different prices to different customers. Doing so requires the ability to identify customers who are willing to pay more and to prevent low-price customers from reselling to high-price customers. Price discrimination always benefits the firm (otherwise, it would charge a single price), and it *may* sometimes benefit some consumers.

K E Y   T E R M S

monopoly firm	price setter	game theory	cartel
monopoly market	imperfect competition	duopoly	tacit collusion
natural monopoly	monopolistic competition	payoff matrix	tit for tat
patent	nonprice competition	dominant strategy	price leadership
copyright	oligopoly	repeated play	price discrimination
government franchise	minimum efficient scale (MES)	explicit collusion	

R E V I E W   Q U E S T I O N S

1. Why do monopolies arise? Discuss the most common factors that explain the existence of a monopoly.

2. How can the government create a monopoly? Why might the government want to do this?

3. Drunk with power, the CEO of Monolith, Inc., a monopoly, assumes that he can set any price he wants and sell as many units as he wants at that price. Is he correct? Why or why not?

4. True or False? "A firm's marginal cost curve is always its supply curve." Explain.

5. Why might a monopoly earn an economic profit in the long run? How does this differ from the situation faced by a perfectly competitive firm?

6. Explain why, if a monopoly takes over all the firms in a perfectly competitive industry, its marginal cost curve will be the same as a perfectly competitive market supply curve.

7. Firm *A* maximizes profit at an output of 1,000 units, where price = 50 and *MC* = 50. Firm *B* maximizes profit at an output of 2,000 units, where price = 5 and *MC* = 3. Which firm is likely to be a monopoly and which perfectly competitive? Explain your reasoning.

8. How do output and price for a monopoly compare with output and price if the same market were perfectly competitive?

9. What features does a monopolistically competitive market share with a perfectly competitive market? With monopoly?

10. How does oligopoly differ from monopolistic competition, perfect competition, and monopoly?

11. What is the difference between a natural oligopoly and a natural monopoly?

12. Discuss some factors that might keep new entrants out of an oligopolistic market.

13. The minimum efficient scale (MES) in a certain industry is 2,300 units. Exactly what additional information do you need in order to determine which of the four market structures the industry will most closely resemble?

14. What conditions must be present in order for a firm to be able to price discriminate? Explain why each is necessary.

15. True or False? "Price discrimination by a firm always harms consumers." Explain.

P R O B L E M S   A N D   E X E R C I S E S

1. Draw the demand curve for a perfectly competitive firm and for a monopoly, showing the *MR* curve, as well as the demand curve on both graphs.
   a. In each case, what is the relationship between demand in the market as a whole and demand for an individual firm's output?
   b. For both graphs, explain the position of the *MR* curve in relation to the demand curve.

2. Draw demand, *MR,* and *ATC* curves that illustrate each of the following three cases: (a) a monopoly just breaking even; (b) a monopoly with a loss that should stay open in the short run; and (c) a monopoly with a loss that will cause it to shut down in the short run.

3. Below is demand and cost information for Warmfuzzy Press, which holds the copyright on the new best-seller, *Burping Your Inner Child.*

Q	P	ATC
(no. of copies)	**(per book)**	**(per book)**
100,000	$100	$20
200,000	$ 80	$15
300,000	$ 60	$16.66
400,000	$ 40	$22.50
500,000	$ 20	$31

a. Determine what quantity of the book Warmfuzzy should print, and what price it should charge, in order to maximize profit.
b. What is Warmfuzzy's maximum profit?
c. Prior to publication, the book's author renegotiates his contract with Warmfuzzy. He will receive a great big hug from the CEO, along with a one-time bonus of $1,000,000, payable when the book is published. This payment was not part of Warmfuzzy's original cost calculations. How many copies should Warmfuzzy publish now? Explain your reasoning.

4. Draw the relevant curves showing a monopolistic competitor suffering a loss in the short run. What will this firm do in the long run if things don't improve? How will its action in this case affect producers of similar goods in the long run?

5. Assume that the plastics industry is monopolistically competitive.
   a. Draw a graph showing the long-run equilibrium situation for a typical firm in the industry. Clearly label the demand, *MR, MC,* and *ATC* curves.
   b. One of the major inputs into plastics is oil. Draw a new graph illustrating the likely short-run position of a plastics company in 1979, after oil prices had more than quadrupled. Again, show all relevant curves.

c. If oil prices had remained high, what would have happened over time to get firms in the plastics industry back to a long-run equilibrium?

6. In a small Nevada town, Ptomaine Flats, there are only two restaurants—the Road Kill Cafe and Sal Monella's. Each restaurant has to decide whether to clean up its act or to continue to ignore health code violations.

   Each restaurant currently makes $7,000 a year in profit. If they both clean up, they will attract more patrons, but must bear the cost of the clean-up; leaving each with a profit of $5,000. However, if one cleans up and the other doesn't, the influx of diners to the cleaner joint will more than cover the costs of the scrubbing; the cleaner place ends up with $12,000, and the grubbier one loses $3,000.

   a. Write out the payoff matrix for this "game," clearly labeling strategies and payoffs to each player.
   b. What is each player's dominant strategy?
   c. What will be the outcome of the game? Explain your answer.
   d. Suppose the two restaurants believe they will face the same decision repeatedly. How might the outcome differ? Why?
   e. Assume that if one cleans up and one stays dirty, the cleaner restaurant makes only $6,000 in profit. All other payoffs are the same as before. What will the outcome of the game be now without collusion? With collusion?

7. Assume that Nike and Adidas are the only sellers of athletic footwear in the United States. They are deciding how much to charge for similar shoes. The two choices are "High" (H) and "Outrageously High" (OH). The payoff matrix is as follows (Nike's payoffs are in the lower left of each cell):

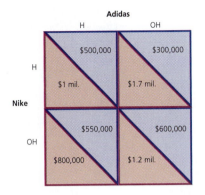

a. Do both companies have dominant strategies? What are they?
b. What will be the outcome of the game?
c. If Nike becomes the acknowledged price leader in the industry, what will be its dominant strategy? What will be the outcome of the game? Why?

8. The Antitrust Division often uses *simulation techniques* to assess the anticompetitive impact of mergers between firms in monopolistically competitive markets. (See, for example, the speech by economist and former DOJ official Carl Shapiro at http://www.antitrust.org/law/shapSpeech.html. To get a feel for how these analyses are done, go to the interactive on-line merger games developed jointly by the Mathematics Department and the Owen Graduate School of Management at Vanderbilt University (http://mss.math.vanderbilt.edu/~pscrooke/MSS/sg.html). Start with the "Student Edition" of the "Unilateral Effects Merger Simulation" and do the Exercise at the bottom of the page. Then graduate to the "Attorney Edition." For something different, try your hand at the "Spatial Merger Simulation," too.

C H A L L E N G E   Q U E S T I O N S

1. Are there any circumstances under which a monopoly will sell at the same price as would a perfectly competitive firm selling the same product? Explain.

2. The demand curve for a monopoly that must sell all its output at a single price is given by $P = 20 - 4Q$, where P is price and Q is quantity demanded. Marginal revenue is $MR = 20 - 8Q$. Marginal cost is $MC = Q^2$. How much should this firm produce in order to maximize profit?

3. a. Draw a demand curve for an oligopolistic firm whose competitors do *not* change their prices when the firm does.

   b. On the same graph, draw the demand curve for the firm, assuming that its competitors respond to its price changes by lowering their prices when the firm lowers its prices and raising their prices when the firm raises its prices.

   c. Which curve is flatter? Why?

   d. The firm's CEO, a real pessimist, reasons as follows: "If we raise our price, none of our competitors will follow. But if we lower our prices, all of our competitors will follow suit." Assume that the firm is presently operating where the two curves you drew in (a) and (b) intersect. If the gloomy CEO is right, trace out the demand curve the firm actually faces.

CHAPTER 9

LABOR MARKETS AND WAGES

You sit down at a meeting with your video people and your international people and you crunch the numbers. With, say, Nicholas Cage and Ed Harris . . . you get one set of numbers. You put in [Sean] Connery's name, the numbers go way up.
—**A high ranking Disney executive, explaining why Sean Connery was paid $12 million to star opposite Nicholas Cage in The Rock.**[1]

Imagine, for a pleasant moment, that you are Sean Connery. Your typical workday begins in a limousine, escorting you to the site of the day's shooting, where you are fussed over by makeup artists and wardrobe staff. You memorize a few lines of dialogue, and then you stand around for several hours while the inevitable technical problems are resolved. During this time, you are doted on by assistants whose sole job is to keep you happy, who look at you respectfully, even worshipfully, and call you "Mr. Connery." Finally, you perform the day's work: maybe 10 minutes' worth of dialogue. If you make a mistake, you get another chance to get it right, as many chances as you need. And after doing this each day for 8 or 10 months, you pick up a check for $12 million.

Now, switch gears and imagine that you have a somewhat less rewarding job, say, a short-order cook at a coffeehouse. You spend the day sweating over a hot grill, spinning a little metal wheel with an endless supply of orders, each one telling you what you must do for the next three minutes. You cook several hundred meals that day, all the while suffering the short tempers of waiters and waitresses who

---

1. *New York Times,* September 18, 1995, p. D11.

want you to do it faster, who glare at you if you forget that a customer wanted french fries instead of home fries, and who call you everything but your proper name. At the end of the day, your face is covered with grease, your eyes are red from smoke, and your feet are sore from standing. It's hard work. But for toiling in this way day after day, for an entire year, you earn $15,000.

Why does Sean Connery earn so much more for his work than a short order cook? Indeed, why do most lawyers, doctors, and corporate managers earn more than most teachers, truck drivers, and assembly-line workers? And why do these workers, in turn, earn more than farmworkers, store clerks, and waiters? As you'll learn in this chapter, we can explain much about wage differences once we understand how labor markets work.

LABOR MARKETS IN PERSPECTIVE

Labor markets differ in an important way from the other markets we've considered so far in this book. When we analyzed the markets for soybeans, bed frames, TV cable service, gasoline and more, we were studying *output markets*, in which firms sell goods and services to households or other firms. Of course, output isn't produced out of thin air. Firms need *resources*—labor, capital, land, and natural resources—to make goods and services. Firms obtain these resources by purchasing them from their owners in **resource markets**.

Figure 1 illustrates the essential difference between output markets and resource markets. Notice that, in output markets, households demand goods and services, and firms supply them. In resource markets, these roles are typically reversed: Firms demand resources, and households—which own the resources—are the suppliers.

We can identify three general categories of resource markets. Firms purchase factory buildings, office buildings, computers, cash registers, and other plant and equipment in *markets for capital*. They buy or rent real estate for their operations in *various markets for land*. When they purchase oil, coal, and lumber, they are buying in *natural resource markets*. And finally, when firms hire workers, they act as buyers in *markets for labor*.

The basic approach we will take in studying labor markets may initially strike you as a bit heartless: We will treat labor as a commodity—something that is bought and sold in the marketplace. We'll regard the *wage rate*—what a firm pays for an hour of labor—as the price of that commodity. In other words, we explain how a wage rate is determined in much the same way we'd explain how the price of a bushel of soybeans is determined. We do this for one simple reason: It works.

Of course, labor *is* different from other things that are traded. First, sellers of soybeans do not care who buys their product, as long as they get the market price. Sellers of labor, on the other hand, care very much who buys their labor, because that firm becomes their employer. This gives sellers of labor an interest in working conditions, friendly coworkers, commuting distance, possibilities for advancement, prestige, a sense of fulfillment, and more.

A second distinct feature of labor is the special meaning of the price in this market: the wage rate. Most of the income people earn over their lifetimes will come from their jobs—from selling their labor—so their wage rate will determine how well they can feed, clothe, house, and otherwise provide for themselves and their families. Differences in wages thus bring up vital issues of *equity* and *fairness* in the economy. Economics has much to say about how and why wages differ, as you will see in this chapter.

RESOURCE MARKETS Markets in which households sell resources—land, labor, and natural resources—to firms.

FIGURE 1   OUTPUT MARKETS AND RESOURCE MARKETS

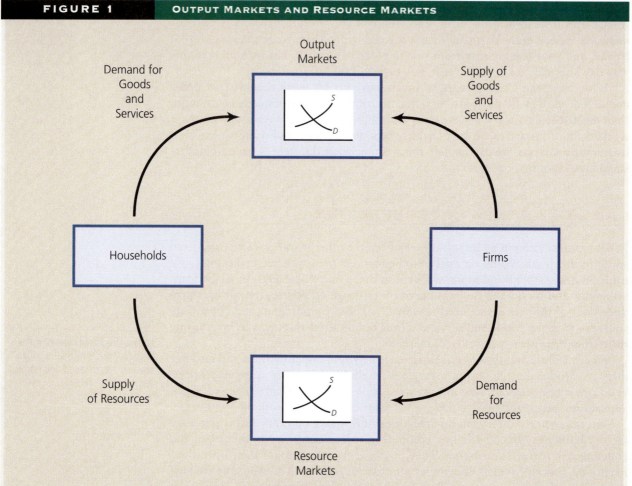

In output markets, households demand goods and services and firms supply them. In resource markets, the roles are reversed: Firms demand resources and households supply them.

DEFINING A LABOR MARKET

If you are like most college students, you will be looking for a full-time job shortly after you graduate. From the economic point of view, you will become a seller in a labor market. But which labor market? Most broadly, you will be selling in the market for college graduates. But we could also define your labor market more narrowly—perhaps the market for economics B.A.s, or even the market for economics B.A.s in Scranton.

How broadly or narrowly we define a labor market depends on the specific questions we wish to answer.

For example, suppose we are interested in explaining why college graduates, on average, earn more than those with just high school diplomas. Then we would want to analyze two very broadly defined labor markets: the national market for college-educated labor and the national market for high-school educated labor. In either of

FIGURE 2   **A COMPETITIVE LABOR MARKET**

The diagram shows the labor market for factory workers in Orlando, Florida. The demand for labor curve (L^D) slopes downward, and the supply of labor curve (L^S) slopes upward. The intersection of the two curves determines the equilibrium wage ($8), and the equilibrium number of factory workers is 50,000.

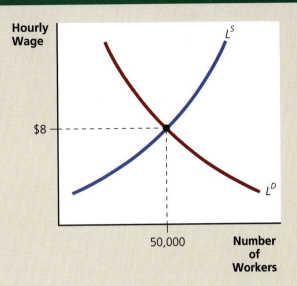

lions of others have similar criteria for working: there is some critical wage rate beyond which they would choose to work, and below which they would *not* want to work. As the wage rate rises, it reaches more and more individuals' critical wage rate, and so more and more people decide to offer their labor services for sale.

There is a second reason that an increase in the wage rate causes an increase in the quantity of labor supplied to a market. As the wage rate rises, some people will *switch into* the now, more lucrative labor market from other labor markets. For example, a rise in factory wage rates in Orlando would attract factory workers from other areas, such as Miami. It might also induce other workers in Orlando—cab drivers, store clerks, and waiters—to switch to factory work.

> *The labor supply curve in any labor market slopes upward because a rise in the wage rate (1) induces some of those not currently working to seek work; and (2) attracts some of those who are currently working in other labor markets.*

Now let's return to the question that brought us to Figure 2 in the first place: How is the wage rate determined in a competitive labor market? As you have no doubt guessed by now: the equilibrium wage will be determined by the intersection of the labor supply curve (L^S) and the labor demand curve (L^D). At any other wage rate, there would be either an excess demand for labor or an excess supply of labor, forcing the wage rate to move to its equilibrium value. In Figure 2, the equilibrium wage is $8 per hour. At this wage, firms will want to hire 50,000 factory workers— the same number of people who want jobs as factory workers. Thus, the equilibrium level of employment is 50,000.

> *The forces of supply and demand will drive a competitive labor market to its equilibrium point—the point where the labor supply and labor demand curves intersect.*

MARKETS AND EQUILIBRIUM

TABLE 1	AVERAGE HOURLY WAGES		
Industry	**1978**	**1988**	**1998**
Petroleum and Coal	$8.63	$14.97	$20.90
Transportation Equipment	$7.91	$13.29	$17.56
Mining	$7.67	$12.80	$16.95
Retail Trade	$4.20	$ 6.31	$ 8.75
Apparel	$3.94	$ 6.12	$ 8.52
Average for Private Sector	$5.69	$ 9.28	$12.77

Source: "National Current Employment Statistics," Bureau of Labor Statistics Web site (www.bls.gov).

WHY DO WAGES DIFFER?

Table 1 shows average hourly earnings in several industries in 1978, 1988, and 1998. Notice the substantial differences in wages that have persisted over the last two decades. For example, the average workers in the petroleum and coal industries have consistently earned between two and three times more than the average worker in the apparel industry. And inequality in labor incomes among *individuals* is much greater than the table shows. First, the figures are average figures; they ignore substantial differences in wages *within* each industry. In 1998, the highest paid hourly workers in petroleum and coal earned substantially *more* than $20.90 per hour, and the lowest paid in apparel earned *less* than $8.52. Second, the table ignores fringe benefits like health insurance and retirement benefits. This hidden income tends to be larger at the high end of the scale, increasing the degree of inequality still further. Third, the table includes payments to *hourly* workers only and excludes the (usually higher) labor incomes of supervisors and executives on a monthly salary. More accurate data—if it could be obtained—would reveal an even greater disparity in wages among U.S. workers. How can an hour of human labor have such different values in the market, and why do these differences persist year after year?

AN IMAGINARY WORLD

To understand why wages differ in the real world, let's start by imagining an *un*real world, with three features:

1. Except for differences in wages, all jobs are equally attractive to all workers.
2. All workers are equally able to do any job.
3. All labor markets are perfectly competitive.

In such a world, we would expect every worker to earn an identical wage in the long run. Let's see why.

Figure 3 shows two different labor markets that, initially, have different wages. Panel (a) shows a local market for word processors, who earn $10 per hour. Panel (b) shows the market for carpenters, who earn $15 per hour. In our imaginary world, could this situation persist for very long? Absolutely not.

Imagine that you are a word processor. By our first assumption, carpentry is just as attractive to you as word processing. But since carpentry pays more, you would prefer to be a carpenter. By our second assumption, you are *qualified* to be a carpenter, and by our third assumption, there are no barriers to prevent you from becoming one. Thus, once you find out that jobs in carpentry pay $15, you will begin to look for a job as a carpenter.

FIGURE 3	DISAPPEARING WAGE DIFFERENTIALS

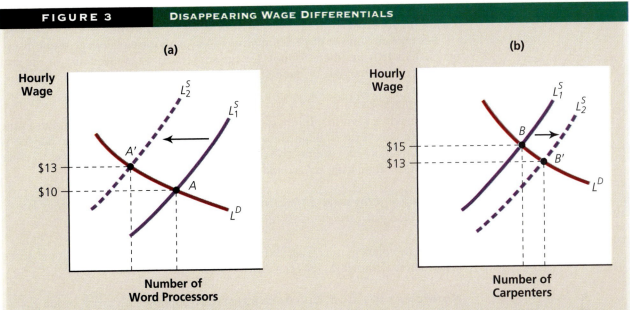

Initially, the supply and demand for word processors, in panel (a), determines an equilibrium wage of $10 per hour—at point *A*. In panel (b), the initial wage for carpenters is $15 per hour. If these markets are competitive, if the two jobs are equally attractive, and if all workers are equally able to do both jobs, this wage differential cannot persist. Some word processors give up that occupation—reducing supply in panel (a)—and become carpenters—increasing supply in panel (b). This migration will continue until the wage in both markets is $13.

Once you make your decision—and once other workers like you make similar decisions—changes will occur in Figure 3. In panel (a), the labor supply curve will shift leftward: Fewer people would want to be word processors at *any* wage once they realize carpentry pays more. In panel (b), the labor supply curve will shift rightward: More people will want to be carpenters at any wage. As these shifts occur, the market wage of word processors will rise, and that of carpenters will fall.

When will the entry and exit stop? When there is no longer any reason for a word processor to want to be a carpenter—that is, when both labor markets are paying the same wage—$13 in our example. In the long run, the market for word processors reaches equilibrium at point *A'* and the market for carpenters at *B'*.

In our story, word processors actually switch jobs to become carpenters. But wages would eventually equalize even if no one were to switch jobs. Why? If carpentry pays more, then new entrants into the labor force, choosing their trade for the first time, will pick carpentry over word processing. Then, since the number of retiring word processors will exceed the number entering the profession, the total number of word processors will shrink. In carpentry, by contrast, there will be more new entrants than retirees, and the number of carpenters will grow. These changes will continue until wages are equal in both markets.

What is true of word processors and carpenters is true of any pair of labor markets we might choose: Doctors and construction workers, teachers and farmworkers—all would earn the same wage under the assumptions of our imaginary world. In this world, different labor markets are like water in the same pool—if the level rises at one end, water will flow into the other end until the level is the same everywhere. In the same way, workers will flow into labor markets with higher wages, evening out the wages in different jobs . . . *if* our three critical assumptions are satisfied.

But take any one of these assumptions away, and the equal-wage result disappears. This tells us where to look for the sources of wage inequality in the real world: a *violation* of one or more of our three assumptions.

COMPENSATING DIFFERENTIALS

In our imaginary world, all jobs were equally attractive to all workers. But in the real world, jobs differ in hundreds of ways that matter to workers. When one job is intrinsically more or less attractive than another, we can expect their wages to differ by a *compensating wage differential:*

> *A **compensating wage differential** is the difference in wages that makes two jobs equally attractive to a worker.*

COMPENSATING WAGE DIFFERENTIAL A difference in wages that makes two jobs equally attractive to workers.

To see how compensating wage differentials come about, let's consider some of the important ways in which jobs can differ.

NONMONETARY JOB CHARACTERISTICS. Suppose you work inside a sky-scraper, and you find you could earn $1 more per hour washing the building's windows . . . from the outside. Would you flow to the window washer's labor market, like water in a pool? Probably not. The higher risk of death just wouldn't be worth it.

NONMONETARY JOB CHARACTERISTIC Any aspect of a job—other than the wage—that matters to a potential or current employee.

Danger is an example of a **nonmonetary job characteristic**—an aspect of a job, good or bad, that is not easily measured in dollars. When you think about a career, whether you are aware of it or not, you are evaluating hundreds of nonmonetary job characteristics: the risk of death or injury, the cleanliness of the work environment, the prestige you can expect in your community, the amount of physical exertion required, the degree of intellectual stimulation, the potential for advancement . . . the list goes on and on. You will also think about the geographic location of the job and the characteristics of the community in which you would live and work: weather, crime rates, pollution levels, the transportation system, cultural amenities, and so on. What does all this suggest about wage difference? Remember that in equilibrium, the wage has no automatic tendency to change. This, in turn, means that decision makers have no incentive to leave one labor market and enter another, for such changes would shift labor supply curves and change the wage in each market. But workers will be satisfied to stay in a job they consider less desirable only if it pays a compensating wage differential. The compensating differential will be just enough to keep workers from migrating from one labor market to another.

Let's see how compensating differentials figure into our example of word processors and carpenters. Look back at Figure 3. Earlier, we saw that if both jobs are equally attractive, both will eventually pay the same wage. But now suppose that everyone prefers sedentary jobs such as word processing to physical labor such as carpentry, and it takes a $5 wage differential in favor of carpentry to make the two jobs equally desirable. Then the two markets would settle at points *A* and *B*, where carpenters are paid a compensating wage differential of $5 per hour, to make up for the less desirable features of their jobs.

> *The nonmonetary characteristics of different jobs give rise to compensating wage differentials. Jobs considered intrinsically less attractive will tend to pay higher wages, other things equal.*

TABLE 2	COMPENSATING WAGE DIFFERENTIALS FOR DANGEROUS JOBS	
Occupation	**Occupational Deaths in 1967 (per 100,000 workers per year)**	**Additional Wage in 1967 (dollars per year)**
Police Officers	78	$137
Electricians	93	$164
Mine Operators	176	$310
Taxi Drivers	182	$320
Lumberjacks	256	$451
Guards	267	$470

If the theory of compensating wage differentials is valid, we would expect jobs with a relatively high risk of death or injury to pay more than otherwise similar jobs. A number of researchers have found that this is, indeed, the case. Table 2 shows the results of one of the more famous studies, published in 1973, by economists Richard Thaler and Sherwin Rosen.[2] Notice, for example, that security guards have an unusually high risk of death on the job. As a result, they earned, on average, about $470 more each year than those in occupations requiring similar skills, but without any significant risk of death.

What about unusually *attractive* jobs? These jobs will generally pay *negative* compensating differentials. For example, many new college graduates are highly attracted to careers in the arts or the media. Since entry-level jobs in these industries are so desirable for nonmonetary reasons, they tend, on average, to pay lower wages than similar jobs in other industries. For the same reason, people will accept lower wages when they have a high probability of advancement—and a higher salary—in the *future*. It comes as no surprise, then, that management trainees at large corporations are often paid relatively low salaries.

Of course, different people have different tastes for working and living conditions. While some prefer a quiet, laid-back work environment like a library or laboratory, others like the commotion of a loading dock or a trading floor. While most people are extremely averse to risking their lives, some actually prefer to live dangerously, as in police work or rescue operations. Therefore, we cannot use our own preferences to declare a job as less attractive or more attractive, or to decide which jobs should pay a positive or negative compensating differential. Rather, when labor markets are perfectly competitive, the entry and exit of workers automatically determines the compensating wage differential in each labor market.

This is one reason most economists are skeptical about the idea of *comparable worth,* which holds that jobs with similar skill requirements should pay similar wage rates, and that the government should intervene in labor markets to ensure this result. Although this policy could correct some inequities when labor markets are imperfectly competitive, it could also introduce serious inequities of its own. First, comparable worth disallows compensating differentials for jobs with similar skill requirements. They would make labor markets less equitable. Second, even if a government agency tried to set compensating differentials in wage rates, it could never know how different workers would value the hundreds of nonmonetary characteristics of each job. Economists generally prefer policies

2.   Richard Thaler and Sherwin Rosen, *The Value of Saving a Life: Evidence from the Labor Market* (Rochester, NY: University of Rochester, 1973).

to increase competition and eliminate discrimination, so that the market itself can determine comparable worth.

A Digression: It Pays to Be Unusual. One implication of compensating wage differentials is that workers with unusual tastes often have a monetary advantage in the labor market. For example, only a small fraction of workers *like* dangerous jobs, such as police work. As long as the labor market is competitive, and there is relatively high demand for workers in dangerous jobs, police officers will earn more than those in other, similar jobs that have a lower risk of death or injury. But if you are one of those unusual people who *like* danger, you will earn the same compensating wage differential as all other police officers, even though you would have chosen to be a police officer anyway.

Similarly, if you like the frigid winter weather in Alaska, if you like washing windows on the 90th floor, or if you think it would be fun to defend the cigarette industry in the media, you can earn a higher wage by putting your somewhat unusual tastes to work.

COST-OF-LIVING DIFFERENCES. Many people would find living in Cleveland and living in Philadelphia about equally attractive. Yet wage rates in Philadelphia are about 10 percent higher than in Cleveland. Why? One major reason is that prices in Philadelphia are about 10 percent higher than in Cleveland. If wage rates were equal in the two cities, many people deciding where to live would prefer Cleveland, where their earnings would have greater purchasing power. The supply of labor in Philadelphia's labor markets would shrink, increasing the wage there, while the supply in Cleveland's labor markets would rise, driving down the wage in Cleveland. In the end, the wage difference would be sufficient to compensate Philadelphians for the higher cost of living in their city.

> *Differences in living costs can cause compensating wage differentials. Areas where living costs are higher than average will tend to have higher-than-average wages.*

DIFFERENCES IN HUMAN CAPITAL. Suppose that you are interested in becoming an ontological prognosticator (no need to look it up—its a hypothetical job). You've been informed that the job requires a Ph.D. degree and that it pays $60,000 per year—just enough to make this career worth it for you. As you are applying for graduate school, you suddenly discover that ontological prognosticators must have *two* Ph.D. degrees, not one. Would you still want the job if it paid $60,000 per year? Absolutely not. A second Ph.D. would mean at least another four years of schooling, and additional opportunity costs for tuition, books, and forgone income. If a salary of $60,000 was *just enough* when only one Ph.D. was required, then it will *not* be enough when *two* Ph.D.s are required.

This hypothetical story should convince you that higher training costs—like those facing doctors, attorneys, engineers, and research scientists—make a job less attractive. In order to attract workers, these professions must pay a wage greater than other professions that are similar in other ways, but require less training.

In terms of Figure 3, let's go back to our starting points, A and B, where carpenters earn a higher wage than word processors. In our imaginary world, this wage difference attracted workers to carpentry and repelled them from word processing, until wages were equal in the two markets. But now suppose that carpentry required more training than word processing. Then we would expect job shifting—and shifts in labor supply curves—to stop *before* wages were equalized. In the end, carpenters would earn more to compensate them for bearing higher training costs.

> *Differences in human capital requirements can give rise to compensating wage differentials. Jobs that require more costly training will tend to pay higher wages, other things equal.*

Compensating differentials explain much of the wage differential between jobs requiring college degrees and those that require only a high school diploma. In 1992, the median college graduate earned an annual salary of $37,400, while the median high school graduate earned only $21,241. The especially high median earnings of dentists ($71,300), lawyers ($73,600), and physicians ($88,300) reflect, at least in part, a compensating differential for the high human capital requirements—and human capital costs—of entering their professions.

The idea of compensating wage differentials dates back to Adam Smith, who first observed that unpleasant jobs seem to pay more than other jobs that require similar skills and qualifications. It is a powerful concept, and it can explain many of the differences we observe in wages . . . but not all of them.

DIFFERENCES IN ABILITY. In 1995, at the age of 23, Shaquille O'Neal earned $16 million—$4.8 million playing basketball for the Orlando Magic, and the rest for endorsing products such as Pepsi and Reebok shoes. Was this a compensating differential for the unpleasantness of playing professional basketball? For an unusually high risk of death on the job? Was the cost of living in Orlando hundreds of times greater than in other cities? Had O'Neal, at the age of 23, spent more years honing his skills than the average attorney, doctor, architect, or engineer—or even more than the average basketball player?

The answer to all of these questions is no. We have overlooked the obvious explanation: O'Neal is an *outstanding* basketball player, better than 99.999 percent of the population could ever hope to be with *any* amount of practice, mostly because of his *endowments*—the valuable characteristics he possesses due to birth or childhood experiences, but that did not require any opportunity cost on his part. In O'Neal's case, these would include his size (7'1" tall, 300 pounds), his coordination, his personality, and his perseverance in exploiting his talent.

While Shaquille O'Neal may be an extreme case, the principle applies across the board. Not everyone has the intelligence needed to be a research scientist, the steady hand to be a neurosurgeon, the quick-thinking ability to be a commodities trader, the well-organized mind to be a business manager, or the talent to be an artist or a ballet dancer. This violates our imaginary-world principle that all workers have equal ability in all jobs and explains much of the wage inequality we observe in the real world.

We can understand this in terms of Figure 3. A wage differential between two otherwise equal jobs could persist if those working for lower wages (point *A* in panel [a]) cannot enter the high-wage market (point *B* in panel [b]) because—regardless of how much human capital they acquire—they can never perform well enough.

Many economists believe that income inequality has worsened in the 1990s. If this is true, differences in abilities may be playing an important role. Scientific discoveries and technological advances may have increased not only the skill requirements of many jobs, but also the abilities needed to acquire those skills. (For example, greater perseverance and intelligence are needed to master a word-processing program than to learn how to type.)

But Figure 3 only tells part of the story: Wages differ not only *between* different types of jobs, but also *within* job categories. And this is largely because, in any trade or profession, workers' talent, intelligence, and physical ability—and their value to firms—vary considerably.

For example, suppose two architects have equal education and training, but architect *A*—being more talented—can design more innovative projects and attract twice as many high-paying clients than can architect *B*. Then a firm should be willing to pay architect *A* twice as much as architect *B*.

> *In general, those with greater endowments of talent, intelligence, or persever-ance will be more productive on the job and generate more revenue for firms. Thus, firms will be willing to pay them a higher wage.*

Take another look at the quote at the beginning of this chapter. Why was Disney willing to pay Sean Connery $12 million to star in *The Rock*? The high-ranking executive explains it: "When you plug in Connery's name, the numbers go way up." The numbers he is referring to are *box office revenue*, about half of which flows to Disney. In large part because of his endowments of talent and looks, Sean Connery can earn more revenue for Disney than Ed Harris can—enough revenue to justify a salary of $12 million, when Harris might have been hired for, say, $1 million.

THE ECONOMICS OF SUPERSTARS. Sean Connery and Shaquille O'Neal are ex-amples of superstars—individuals who are almost universally regarded as the best, or among the top few, in their professions. In recent years, these individuals have in-cluded model Claudia Schiffer, attorney Johnny Cochran, singer Courtney Love, talk show host David Letterman, and writer John Grisham. (Whatever your own feelings about any of these people, the market—where people vote with their dollars—con-siders them at the very top of their professions.) Still, does outstanding ability fully explain the extremely high earnings of these superstars? Not completely.

In Figure 4, the curve labeled "ability" shows the distribution of intelligence, skill, or general ability (I.Q.) in a field. It is bell shaped, so that deviations in either a positive or negative direction from the average are about equally likely to occur. For example, a person picked at random is equally likely to have an I.Q. 10 points above as 10 points below the average. But the distribution of labor *earnings* is skewed rather than bell shaped. Most people are concentrated toward the lower end, while a few have staggeringly high earnings, so that the right-hand tail extends out farther than the left-hand tail. This suggests that earnings are not proportional to ability. For example, most actors earn less than $12,000 per year. No doubt, Sean Connery is substantially better than aver-age, maybe even among the best. But, by any measure, is

DANGEROUS CURVES

It is tempting to think that jobs which require greater abilities or talents will *automatically* pay more than jobs that are easier and that more people can do. But this is not necessarily true. Fewer people can write good poetry than can write a good newspaper article, yet journalists earn sub-stantially more than poets. Why? Very few people *read* poetry, so the demand for poets is very low relative to their supply. On the other hand, large numbers of people read newspapers. Compared to the market for po-ets, the demand for journalists is considerably higher relative to the supply. You will avoid much confusion if you remember that the equilibrium wage is deter-mined by *both* sides of the market—supply *and* demand—rather than just one or the other.

| **FIGURE 4** | **THE DISTRIBUTIONS OF EARNINGS AND ABILITY** |

In most populations, the distribution of intelligence, skills, or general ability is bell shaped. Deviations in a positive or negative direction from the average are equally likely. The distribution of labor earnings, however, is skewed. Many people are concentrated at the lower end, while only a few have extremely large incomes.

he *1,000 times better* than the average? NBC news anchor Tom Brokaw may be better at delivering the news than most local news anchors, but better enough to justify a salary hundreds of times greater than the highest paid local broadcaster? The same is observed among the top singers, doctors, attorneys, and so on: The additional earnings garnered by those at the very top go far beyond their additional abilities. Why is this?

The reasons vary by profession, but center around the exaggerated rewards we bestow on those deemed the best or one of the best in many fields.[3] Say you like to read one mystery novel a month for entertainment. If you can choose between the best novel published that month or one that is almost—but not quite—as good, you will naturally choose the one you think is best. Only people who read two novels each month would choose the best and the second best, and only those who read three will choose the top three. If most people rank recent mystery novels in the same order, then the best will sell millions of copies, the second best might sell hundreds of thousands, and the third best might sell only thousands. Even though all three novels might be very close in quality, the authors' earnings will be vastly different.

The same thing happens in the markets for rock concerts, action movies, and news broadcasts. In all these cases, where those at the top can sell their services to millions of people simultaneously, the reward for being the best can be astronomical.

But this phenomenon is not limited to media stars. Suppose you needed a heart transplant, and the best surgeon is 10 percent better than the second-best surgeon. Wouldn't you be willing to pay more than a 10-percent premium to have the best, rather than the second best? The same applies to corporate executives. If Dell Computer Corporation's chief executive officer can make decisions that are just slightly better than Compaq's, then Dell may gain significant market share over Compaq and its earnings could increase manyfold. This is one reason that, in the business world, small differences in perceived abilities of executives can justify huge differences in salaries.

---

3. See, for example, Robert H. Frank and Philip J. Cook, *The Winner Take All Society* (The Free Press: New York, 1995).

BARRIERS TO ENTRY

In our imaginary world, there were no barriers to entering any trade or profession. The absence of barriers is an important element of our assumption that the labor market is competitive. But in some labor markets, barriers keep out would-be entrants, resulting in higher wages in those markets.

In Figure 3, we saw that if carpenters were paid higher wages than word processors, entry into the market for carpenters would equalize wages in the two jobs. But what if carpenters were protected from competition by a barrier to entry, one that kept newcomers from becoming carpenters? Then the labor supply curve in panel (b) would *not* shift rightward, and the higher wage for carpenters could persist. Going back to our pool analogy, a barrier to entry is like a wall in the middle of the pool, blocking the flow, allowing one end to have a higher water level than the other.

Barriers to entry help maintain high wages for those who already have jobs in the protected market. So we should not be surprised to find that in almost all cases, it is those already employed who are responsible for erecting the barriers. But it is not enough to simply put up a sign, "Newcomers, stay out!" The pull of higher wages is a powerful force, and to prevent entry requires a force at least as powerful. What are the barriers that keep newcomers out of a market, thus maintaining a higher-than-competitive wage for those already working there?

In many labor markets, the barriers are occupational licensing laws. Highly paid professionals such as doctors, lawyers, and dentists, as well as those who practice a trade, like barbers, beauticians, and plumbers, must obtain a license to sell their services. In many states you cannot even sell the service of braiding hair without a license. In order to get the license, you must complete a long course in cosmetology and pass an exam.

The American Medical Association (AMA)—a professional organization to which almost half of American physicians belong—is perhaps the strongest example of occupational licensing as a barrier to entry. The AMA portrays itself as a vigilant defender of high standards in health care, through its regulation of medical schools, its certification of specialists, and its government lobbying. Economists tend to have a much different view of the AMA: While not denying that some of its efforts do raise the quality of physicians, they see the association primarily as an instrument to maintain high incomes for doctors.

Figure 5 shows the market for physicians in the United States. In the absence of any income-raising activity, labor supply curve L_1^S would intersect labor demand curve L_1^D at point A, resulting in equilibrium wage W_1. Whether this wage would be relatively high or low is not known; since 1847—when the AMA was founded—this competitive equilibrium has never been attained.

Much of the AMA's activity has been designed to decrease the *supply* of doctors. Immediately after its founding, it imposed strict licensing procedures that increased entry costs for *new* doctors. Significantly, existing practitioners were exempted from the new requirements. In spite of these restrictions, there was a rapid increase in the number of physicians toward the end of the century. In response, between 1900 and 1920, the AMA closed down almost half of the nation's medical schools.[4] These and other efforts to restrict the supply of doctors have resulted in a supply curve for physicians like L_2^S, lying to the left of L_1^S, moving the equilibrium to point B, and raising salaries to W_2.

---

4.   "Doctors Operate to Cut Out Competition," *Business and Society Review,* Summer 1986, pp. 4–9.

FIGURE 5   THE MARKET FOR PHYSICIANS

Without the AMA, the labor supply and demand curves for physicians would intersect at point *A* to determine wage W_1. AMA actions to restrict the supply of physicians have caused the supply curve to be L_2^S, which lies to the left of L_1^S. This implies a higher wage, W_2. In addition, the AMA has sought to increase the demand for physicians' services by preventing non-physicians from competing. This shifts the demand curve to the right—to L_2^D—further increasing the wage to W_3.

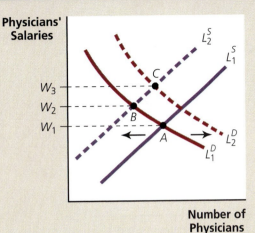

But this is not the end of the story. The AMA has also increased the *demand* for physicians' services by preventing competition from nonphysicians. Throughout its history, the association has moved aggressively to limit competition from midwives, chiropractors, homeopathists, and other health professionals. By limiting access to these alternative health professionals, the AMA increases the demand for the services of its own members. The impact of these policies has been a rightward shift in the demand curve for doctors, to L_2^D, moving the equilibrium to a point like *C* and raising salaries further, to W_3.

(If you think maintaining high standards is the main motivation for these policies, consider this: AMA policy allows a physician to practice in *any* area of medicine, even one in which he has no specialized training. For example, a dermatologist with no training or experience in obstetrics can legally deliver a baby. By contrast, a midwife with extensive experience might be arrested if she delivers a baby without the supervision of an M.D.)

In the 1980s, rising health-care costs led to increased public scrutiny of the AMA, and its anticompetitive practices came under heavy attack. Some restrictions were eased, and the number of doctors per 100,000 people increased from 169 in 1975 to 233 in 1990. At the same time, the Federal Trade Commission and the courts pressured the AMA to remove its ban on physician advertising. For the first time, new entrants could compete with established physicians by advertising their prices and services. Not surprisingly, many physicians began to complain about falling incomes.

UNION WAGE SETTING

A labor union represents the collective interests of its members. Unions have many functions, including pressing for better and safer working conditions, operating apprenticeship programs, and administering pension programs. But the foremost objective of a union is to raise its members' pay. Federal law prohibits a union from

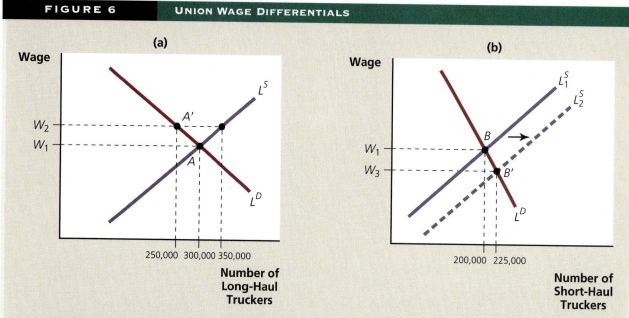

FIGURE 6   **UNION WAGE DIFFERENTIALS**

In the absence of a union, the markets for short-haul and long-haul truck drivers would be in equilibrium at the same wage, W_1. If long-haul truckers organize into a union, they can negotiate a higher wage—W_2. At this wage, there is an excess supply of 100,000 long-haul truckers. With fewer jobs available in the unionized sector, displaced truckers seek work in the short-haul trucking industry, increasing supply there, and driving the wage down to W_3.

creating an overt barrier to entry—it is illegal for a firm to agree to hire only union members. Instead, the union negotiates a higher-than-competitive wage with the firm. But, as we know from the last chapter, at a higher wage, the firm will want to employ fewer workers. Thus, many potential workers are kept out of union jobs because the firm will not hire them at the union wage.

A higher union wage reduces an employer's profits. So why does the employer agree? In large part, because the union has the power to strike. During a strike—when the firms' workers refuse to come to work—the firm may suffer an even more serious loss of profits. Rather than take the risk of a strike, employers will often agree to the higher wage demanded by the union.

Figure 6 illustrates how unions can create wage differences. We assume that jobs in two industries—long-haul trucking and short-haul trucking—are equally attractive in all respects other than the wage rate. With no labor union, these two markets would reach equilibrium at points A and B, respectively, where both pay the same wage, W_1.

Now suppose instead that long-haul truckers are organized into a union, which has negotiated a higher wage, W_2, with employers. At this wage, there is an excess supply of long-haul truckers equal to 350,000 − 250,000 = 100,000. Ordinarily, we would expect an excess supply of labor to force the wage down, but the union wage agreement prevents this. With fewer jobs available in the unionized sector, some former long-haul truckers will look for work as *non*union, short-haul truckers. Thus, in panel (b), the labor supply curve shifts rightward. In equilibrium, the number of short-haul truckers rises from 200,000 to 225,000, and the wage of short-haul truckers drops to W_3. The end result is a union–nonunion wage differential of $W_2 - W_3$. Notice that only *part* of the differential $(W_2 - W_1)$ represents an *increase* in union wages; the other part $(W_1 - W_3)$ comes from a *decrease* in *nonunion wages*.

> *Through an increase in member wages and a decrease in nonmember wages, unions create a wage differential between union and nonunion labor markets.*

In the end, how big is the union–nonunion wage differential? H. Gregg Lewis[5] reviewed more than 200 studies that asked precisely this question and determined that between 1967 and 1979, union members earned, on average, about 15 percent more than otherwise similar nonunion workers.

Given the conflict surrounding many union–management wage negotiations, and the media attention devoted to them, this difference may seem rather small. But keep in mind that a 15 percent differential—about $1.75 per hour at today's average wage—amounts to $3,640 per year, and it continues year after year. After 40 years on the job, the average union member could expect to have earned about $145,000 more than the average nonunion member, enough to put a down payment on a house *and* put a child through college with no student loans. And if each year's differential were put in the bank at 5 percent interest, it would amount to about $465,000 after 40 years. A 15 percent wage differential is nothing to sneeze at.

The differential has most likely declined since 1979, as unions' bargaining power has weakened. This is partly reflected in a decline in union membership: In the mid-1950s, 25 percent of the U.S. labor force was unionized; today, it is less than 13 percent. Nevertheless, unions still maintain a significant presence in many industries, such as automobiles, steel, coal, construction, mining, and trucking, and they are certainly responsible for at least *some* of the higher wages earned in those industries.

DISCRIMINATION AND WAGES

Discrimination occurs when the members of a group of people have different opportunities because of characteristics that have nothing to do with their abilities. Throughout American history, discrimination against women and minorities has been widespread in housing, business loans, consumer services, and jobs. The last arena—jobs—is our focus here. Tough laws and government incentive programs have lessened overt job discrimination—such as help-wanted ads that as recently as the 1950s asked for white males. But less obvious forms of discrimination remain.

Our first step in understanding the economics of discrimination is to distinguish two words that are often confused. *Prejudice* is an emotional dislike for members of a certain group; *discrimination* refers to the restricted opportunities offered to such a group. As you will see, although prejudice sometimes causes discrimination, it doesn't always do so.

EMPLOYER PREJUDICE

When you think of job discrimination, your first image might be a manager who refuses to hire members of some group, such as African Americans or women, because

DISCRIMINATION When a group of people have different opportunities because of personal characteristics that have nothing to do with their abilities.

---

5. H.G. Lewis, *Union Relative Wage Effects: A Survey* (Chicago: University of Chicago Press, 1986).

FIGURE 7   **EMPLOYER DISCRIMINATION AND WAGE RATES**

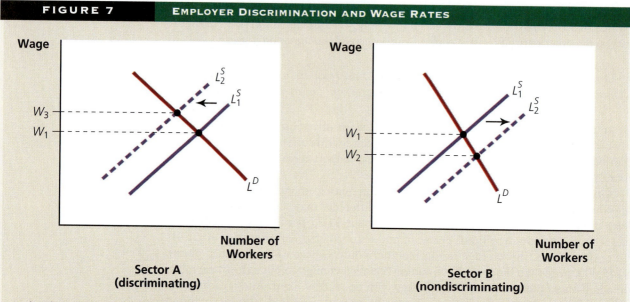

In the absence of discrimination, the wage rate would be W_1 in both sector A and sector B. If firms in sector A discriminate against some group—such as women—the group would seek work in nondiscriminating sector B. The increased labor supply in sector B causes the wage there to fall to W_2, while the decreased supply in sector A causes the wage there to rise to W_3.

---

of pure prejudice. As a result, the victims of prejudice, prevented from working at high-paying jobs, must accept lower wages elsewhere. No doubt, many employers hire according to their personal prejudices. But it may surprise you to learn that economists generally consider employer prejudice one of the *least* important sources of labor market discrimination.

To see why, look at Figure 7, which shows the labor market divided into two broad sectors, A and B. To keep things simple, we'll assume that all workers have the same qualifications, and they find jobs in either sector equally attractive. Under these conditions, if there were *no* discrimination, both sectors would pay the same wage, W_1. (Can you explain why?)

Now suppose the firms in sector A decide they no longer wish to employ members of some group, say, women. What would happen? Women would begin looking for jobs in the *non*discriminating sector B, and the labor supply curve there would shift rightward, decreasing the wage to W_2. At the same time, with women no longer welcome in sector A, the labor supply curve there would shift leftward, driving the wage up to W_3. It appears that employer discrimination would create a gender wage differential equal to $W_3 - W_2$.

But the differential would be only temporary. Why? With wages in sector B now lower, *men* would exit that market and seek jobs in the higher paying sector A. These movements would reverse the changes in labor supply, and, in the end, both sectors would pay the same wage again. Employer prejudice against women might lead to a permanent change in the *composition* of labor in each sector—with only men working in sector A and both sexes working in sector B—but *no change in wages.*

But employer prejudice might not even change the composition of labor in either sector, because there is another force working to eliminate this form of discrimination altogether: the output market. Since biased employers must pay higher wages to employ men, they will have higher average costs than unbiased employers. If biased firms sell their output in a competitive market, they will suffer losses and ultimately be forced to exit their industries. Over the long run, prejudiced employers should be replaced with unprejudiced ones. Even if the output market is *imperfectly competitive,* the firm will still have its stockholders or owners to contend with. Unless *their* prejudice is so strong that they are willing to forgo profit, management will be under pressure to hire qualified women at a lower wage. In either case,

> *When prejudice originates with employers, market forces work to discourage discrimination and reduce or eliminate any wage gap between the favored and the unfavored group.*

EMPLOYEE AND CUSTOMER PREJUDICE

What if *workers*—rather than employers—are prejudiced? Then our conclusions are very different. If, for example, a significant number of male assembly-line workers dislike supervision by women, then hiring female supervisors might cause conflict. The result might be lower productivity, higher costs, and therefore lower profit. In a competitive output market, the *non*discriminating firm would be forced out of business. And even in imperfectly competitive output markets, stockholders would *want* the firm to discriminate against female supervisors, even if they themselves are not prejudiced. In this case, we cannot count on the market to solve the problem at all.

The same argument applies if the prejudice originates with the firm's *customers.* For example, if many automobile owners distrust female mechanics, then an auto-repair shop that hires them would lose some customers and sacrifice profit. True, excluding qualified female mechanics is costly—it means paying higher wages to men and charging higher prices. But customers will be willing to *pay* a higher price, since they prefer male mechanics. Even in the long run, then, women might be excluded from the auto-mechanics trade, or earn lower wages when they manage to find a job.

More generally, if worker or customer prejudice is common in high-wage industries, then women would be forced into low wage jobs.

> *When prejudice originates with the firm's employees or its customers, market forces encourage, rather than discourage, discrimination and can lead to a permanent wage gap between the favored and unfavored group.*

STATISTICAL DISCRIMINATION

Suppose you are in charge of hiring 10 new employees at your firm. Suppose, too, that young, married women in your industry are twice as likely to quit their jobs within 2 years than men (say, because they decide to have children) and that quits are very costly to your firm: Let us say that 20 people apply for the 10 positions—half men and half women. All are equally qualified, and you have no way of knowing which individuals among them are more likely to quit within 2 years. Whom will you hire?

If your sole goal is to maximize the firm's profit, there is no question: You will hire the men. (If you have other goals, you may not last very long as a manager at

STATISTICAL DISCRIMINA-TION When individuals are excluded from an activity based on the statistical probability of behavior in their group, rather than their personal characteristics.

that firm.) Notice that in this example, there was no mention of prejudice. Indeed, even if there isn't a trace of prejudice in you, in the firm's employees, or in its customers, profit maximization may still dictate hiring the men.

Statistical discrimination—so called because individuals are excluded based on the statistical probability of behavior in their group, rather than their own personal traits—is a case of discrimination without prejudice. It can lead an unbiased profit-maximizing employer to discriminate against an individual member of a group, even though that particular individual might never engage in the feared behavior.

However, statistical discrimination can often be a cover for prejudice. For example, consider statistical discrimination against women. True, women are more likely to leave work to care for their children. But men are more likely to develop alcohol and drug problems, which can lead to poor judgment and costly accidents on the job. If there were no prejudice, then the risks associated with hiring men would be thrown into the equation—not just the risks of hiring women. According to critics of the statistical discrimination theory, the negative behavior of a favored group (such as men) is rarely considered by employers.

DEALING WITH DISCRIMINATION

As you've seen, discrimination due to pure employer prejudice is unlikely to have much of an impact on labor markets. As long as other employers are *not* prejudiced, those who *are* prejudiced will be at a competitive disadvantage. In the long run, the market helps to eliminate this type of discrimination.

But for other types of discrimination—such as statistical discrimination or discrimination due to worker or consumer prejudice—market incentives work in the opposite way, leading to a permanent and stubborn problem. In these cases, many economists and other policy makers believe that government action is needed. This is especially so when the groups discriminated against are already poor or disadvantaged in some way.

Some favor affirmative action programs, which actively encourage firms to expand opportunities for women and minorities; others favor stricter enforcement of existing antidiscrimination laws and stiffer penalties when discriminatory hiring occurs. Both approaches to policy force *all* firms to bear the costs of nondiscriminatory hiring, so that no single firm is at a disadvantage. For example, by forcing all firms in an industry that discriminates against women to hire them—so all firms bear the costs of greater quit rates or of alienating workers or customers who might be prejudiced—no single firm will lose out to competitors.

DISCRIMINATION AND WAGE DIFFERENTIALS

How much have the wages of victimized groups been reduced because of discrimination? As you are about to see, this is a very difficult question to answer.

A starting point—but *only* a starting point—is Table 3, which shows median earnings for different groups in the population in 1997. Notice the substantial earnings gap between men and women of either race and between whites and blacks of either sex. Doesn't this prove that the impact of discrimination on wages is substantial? Not necessarily.

Consider the black–white differential for men. In 1997, black men earned 31 percent less than white men, on average. But some of the difference in earnings is

TABLE 3	**MEDIAN ANNUAL INCOME (OF THOSE WITH INCOME), 1997**	
	Median Income	**Percent of White Male Income**
White Males	$26,115	100%
Black Males	$18,096	69%
Hispanic Males*	$16,216	62%
White Females	$13,792	53%
Black Females	$13,048	50%
Hispanic Females*	$10,260	39%

*Persons of Hispanic origin may be of any race.
Source: U.S. Census Bureau Web site, "Historical Income Tables—People," 1999 Table P-02.

due to differences in education, job experience, job choice, and geographic location between whites and blacks. For example, the proportion of black adults with college degrees is about half that of white adults. Even if all firms were completely color blind in their hiring and wage payments, disproportionately fewer blacks would have higher paying jobs because they require college degrees, and this would produce an earnings differential in favor of whites. The same would apply if blacks were more likely to live in low-wage areas or, on average, had fewer years of prior experience when applying for jobs.

Several studies suggest that if we limit comparisons to whites and blacks with the same educational background, geographic location, and, in some cases, the same ability (measured by a variety of different tests), 50 percent or more of the earnings difference disappears.[6]

Does this mean that discrimination accounts for half or less of the earnings differential? Not at all: Many of the observed differences in education, geographic location, and ability are themselves the *result* of job-market discrimination. Figure 8 illustrates a vicious cycle of discrimination in the labor market. First, job discrimination causes a wage differential between equally qualified whites and blacks. With a lower wage, blacks have less incentive to remain in the labor force or to invest in human capital, since they reap smaller rewards for these activities. The result is that blacks, on average, have less education and less job experience than whites, and even color-blind employers will hire disproportionately fewer blacks in high-paying jobs, perpetuating their lower wages.

In addition to job-market discrimination, there is *premarket* discrimination—unequal treatment in education and housing—that occurs before an individual enters the labor market. For example, regardless of black families' incomes, housing discrimination may exclude them from neighborhoods with better public schools, resulting in fewer blacks being admitted to college. Discriminatory treatment by teachers within a school may contribute to lowered aspirations and diminished job-market expectations. All of these contribute to the low-wage syndrome.

Similar reasoning applies to the earnings gap between women and men. On the one hand, we have a large earnings gap. In 1997, for example, the median earnings of white, female workers were only 53 percent of those of white men. Table 4,

---

6. See, for example, June O'Neill, "The Role of Human Capital in Earnings Differences between Black and White Men," *Journal of Economic Perspectives* (Fall 1990), pp. 25–45.

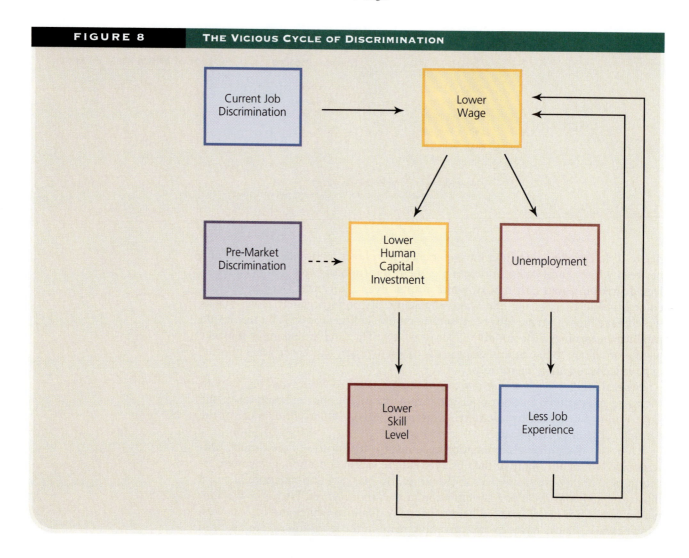

FIGURE 8   **THE VICIOUS CYCLE OF DISCRIMINATION**

based on data for the mid-1980s, shows that the gap in earnings is an international phenomenon. The data show a substantial earnings gap, even when only those with full-time jobs are considered.

On the other hand, studies suggest that a third or more of the male–female earnings gap is due to differences in skills and job experience. But when we think deeper, we realize that for women, as well as blacks and other minorities, differences in skills and experience can be the *result* of lower wages, not just the cause of them: If women know they will earn less than men and will have more trouble advancing on the job, they have less incentive to invest in human capital and to stay in the labor force. Premarket discrimination plays a role, too. Several studies have suggested that different treatment of girls in secondary school may lower their job-market aspirations. And even before school, girls may be socialized to prefer different (and lower paying) career paths than boys, such as nursing rather than medicine.

In the end, we do not know nearly as much about the impact of discrimination on wages as we would like to know, but research is proceeding at a rapid pace. As we've seen, the data must always be interpreted with care:

TABLE 4	THE MALE–FEMALE GAP IN DIFFERENT COUNTRIES	
Country	**Female Earnings as Percent of Male Earnings (full-time workers only)**	
Sweden	77%	
Australia	75%	
Norway	73%	
Austria	73%	
Germany	69%	
United States	68%	
United Kingdom	63%	
Switzerland	62%	

Source: Ronald Ehrenberg and Robert Smith, *Modern Labor Economics,* 5th edition (New York: HarperCollins, 1994), 406.

In measuring the impact of job-market discrimination on earnings, the wage gap between two groups gives an overestimate, since it fails to account for differences in skills and experience. However, comparing only workers with similar skills and experience leads to an underestimate, since some of the differences are themselves caused by discrimination—both in the job market and outside of it.

THE MINIMUM WAGE

The federal minimum wage law is motivated by a desire to raise the wages of the lowest paid American workers. When it was first established in 1938, the minimum wage was 25 cents per hour and applied to industries employing only 43 percent of the workforce. In 1997, the minimum wage was $5.15 per hour and covered almost 90 percent of the workforce. Does the minimum wage create greater wage equality among our citizens? Let's see.

To understand the effect of the minimum wage, we'll divide the U.S. labor market into three parts: (1) the market for skilled labor; (2) the market for unskilled labor in industries covered by the minimum-wage law; and (3) the market for unskilled labor in industries not covered by the law, either because it does not apply (waiters, house-cleaners, and nannies) or because firms routinely violate it (typically, very small firms that are difficult to monitor).

Figure 9 shows the initial equilibrium in all three markets if there were no minimum wage. Initially, wages in the skilled-labor market, where demand is high relative to supply, are $15.00. In the unskilled-labor markets, where demand is lower relative to supply, we assume that the wage would initially be $3.00.

Notice that wages in both unskilled-labor markets are equal. Why? If the wage in one of those unskilled sectors were higher than in the other, then workers would migrate from the lower- to the higher-wage sector. This would shift the labor supply curve leftward in the lower-wage sector, causing the wage there to rise. It would also shift the labor supply curve rightward in the higher-wage sector, causing the wage there to fall. The migration would continue until the wages were equal—say at $3—in both sectors.

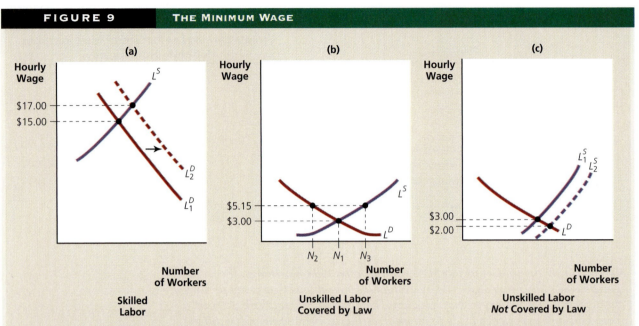

FIGURE 9   **THE MINIMUM WAGE**

In the absence of a minimum-wage law, the wage in the market for skilled labor is high—say, $15.00 per hour. In the unskilled labor market, the wage is low—$3.00 per hour. If a minimum wage of $5.15 per hour is imposed, employment in the covered unskilled sector—panel (b)—falls from N_1 to N_2. With a higher wage for unskilled labor, some firms will substitute skilled workers and capital equipment. This increases the demand for skilled labor and increases the hourly wage in panel (a) to $17.00. At the same time, some individuals who lose their jobs in the covered, unskilled market of panel (b) will move to the uncovered labor market—panel (c)—further depressing the wage there.

Now let us impose a minimum wage of $5.15 in the covered unskilled sector and trace through the effects in the figure. First, employment in the covered unskilled sector falls, from N_1 to N_2 in panel (b). Since quantity demanded is less than quantity supplied at a wage of $5.15, and since no firm can be forced to hire more workers than it desires, there will be an excess supply of labor equal to $N_3 - N_1$. Part of this excess is due to an increase in quantity supplied from N_1 to N_3; with a higher wage, more people want to work. But part of it is also due to a decrease in quantity demanded from N_1 to N_2. You can already see that while some unskilled workers have benefited—they are earning a higher wage—others have been hurt—they have lost their jobs. But this is just the beginning.

Some of those who have lost their jobs in the covered sector will move to the only sector where jobs are still available—the uncovered sector. There, the labor supply curve will shift rightward, from L_1^S to L_2^S in panel (c), and the market wage will fall below its initial value—to $2.00 in our example. Thus, the impact of the minimum wage spills over into the sector not covered by it. Increased competition for jobs drives down the wages of *all* workers there, even those who were already employed before the minimum wage was imposed. More specifically, we would expect a decline in the wages of waiters, housecleaners, and unskilled workers who work in firms that ignore the minimum wage law.

What about skilled workers? Are they affected by minimum-wage legislation? You might think not, since they are already earning more than the minimum. But when the wage of unskilled labor rises in the covered sector, employers there will, to some degree, substitute skilled workers and capital equipment for unskilled labor.

For example, an unskilled dishwasher might be replaced by a sophisticated dishwashing machine that requires maintenance and repair by skilled workers. An unskilled floorwasher with a mop might be replaced by a cleaning service that uses skilled workers operating high-tech equipment to clean and wax floors. Substitution toward skilled labor will shift the labor demand curve in panel (a) rightward, from L_1^D to L_2^D. Further, skilled labor is needed to design, produce, and market the new capital equipment, contributing to a further increase in demand. As a result, wages in the skilled sector will increase, from $15 to $17 in our example.

You can see that the minimum wage sets off a chain of events. In the end, some unskilled workers benefit in the form of higher pay. Other unskilled workers are harmed by lower pay or unemployment. There is only one group of workers in which everyone benefits: skilled workers. It should come as no surprise, then, that the most vocal advocates of raising the minimum wage are labor unions, whose membership consists almost entirely of skilled workers. For these reasons, most economists regard the minimum wage with some skepticism, especially when it is touted as a policy to reduce wage inequality.

SUMMARY

Firms need *resources*—land, labor, and capital—in order to produce output. These resources are traded in *resource markets* in which firms are demanders and households are suppliers. *Labor markets* are key resource markets. A *perfectly competitive labor market*—the type of labor market explored in this chapter—is one in which there are many buyers and sellers, all workers appear the same to firms, and there are no barriers to entry or exit.

The labor demand curve in any labor market slopes downward for two reasons. First, a higher wage rate raises firms' marginal costs, causing a decrease in output and employment. Second, a higher wage rate raises the *relative* cost of labor from a particular market, causing firms to substitute other inputs, such as capital or other types of labor.

The labor supply curve in any labor market slopes upward for two reasons. First, a higher wage rate induces some of those not currently working to seek work. Second, a higher wage rate attracts those who are currently working in *other* labor markets.

Labor supply and demand curves can help us understand why wages vary so widely among the population. For a given category of labor, the intersection of the supply and demand curves determines the market wage and employment. In an imaginary world that satisfied three conditions—(1) all jobs are equally attractive to all workers (except for wage differences); (2) all workers are equally able to do any job; and (3) all labor markets are perfectly competitive—the wages of all workers would be identical. Thus, differences in wages must arise from a violation of one or more of these conditions.

When the attractiveness of two jobs differs, *compensating wage differentials* will emerge to offset those differences. When the productivity of workers differs, the more productive workers will earn higher wages. And in some cases, barriers to entry—violating the conditions of perfect competition—contribute to higher wages for protected workers.

Another reason for wage differentials is prejudice, which creates barriers to entry for unfavored groups of workers. When employer prejudice exists, market forces work to discourage discrimination and reduce wage gaps between groups. However, employee and customer prejudice encourage discrimination and can lead to permanent wage gaps.

The federal minimum wage law is designed to address some of the disparity in wages among the population. In particular, it is designed to help those who earn the lowest wages by increasing their wage rate above the equilibrium value. While many low-wage workers are helped by the minimum wage, it also has side effects that undermine its purpose. These include higher unemployment in labor markets covered by the minimum wage and lower wages for unskilled workers in the uncovered sector. Another unintentional side effect is to raise the wages of skilled workers who end up replacing the now-more-expensive unskilled workers.

KEY TERMS

resource markets
perfectly competitive labor
  market

compensating wage
  differential

nonmonetary job
  characteristic

discrimination
statistical discrimination

R E V I E W   Q U E S T I O N S

1. Using "teacher in a private prep school" as the basis for comparison, would you expect the compensating wage differential to be positive or negative for each of the following jobs? Describe what nonmonetary job characteristics might be at work in each case.
   a. Teacher at a tough inner-city school
   b. Worker in a slaughterhouse
   c. Computer programmer
   d. Attorney
   e. Bartender at a tropical resort

2. What might account for each of the following?
   a. A paralegal (a legal professional without a law degree) in New York earns more than a paralegal doing the same work in Keokuk, Iowa.
   b. Although they work on the same cases and do many of the same things, an attorney's salary is many times that of a paralegal.
   c. Larry King earns more as a talk show host than "Goofey Gary," the morning man on a New York radio show.
   d. A professor of philosophy with a Ph.D. earns less than an accountant with only a B.A.
   e. Construction workers who are American citizens or legal residents of the United States are paid a higher wage than illegal immigrants doing the same work.

3. Why are earnings not always proportional to ability?

4. How might the AMA have contributed to the high cost of health care?

5. True or False. Explain. "Discrimination does not always arise from prejudice."

6. Explain how market forces tend to:
   a. encourage discrimination when the prejudice comes from a firm's employees or customers;
   b. discourage discrimination when the prejudice comes from employers.

7. What is "statistical discrimination"? What are some possible remedies for it?

8. How may technological advances be indirectly responsible for increased income inequality in the 1990s?

9. Explain how the union–nonunion wage differential can arise. Illustrate with relevant graphs.

P R O B L E M S   A N D   E X E R C I S E S

1. This problem illustrates why the labor demand curve in a labor market slopes downward.
   a. Graph the marginal cost and marginal revenue curve for a typical perfectly competitive firm. Identify the profit-maximizing level of output.
   b. Now suppose that the wage rate the firm must pay rises. How will the diagram change? How will the profit-maximizing level of output change? Indicate on your graph.
   c. Since lower levels of output can be produced with fewer workers, what happens to employment at this firm when the wage rate rises? Explain briefly.
   d. If all firms in a labor market respond this way to an increase in the wage rate, what will happen to the demand for labor in that market as the wage rate rises? Explain briefly.

2. The labor markets for factory workers and construction workers are in equilibrium: The wage in both is W_0, and the number employed is n_0. Assume the labor market in each industry is perfectly competitive, there are no barriers to entry or exit of workers, and factory skills are very similar to construction skills.
   a. Unexpectedly, the demand for factory workers rises. Using graphs, show the effect on the equilibrium wage and number employed in factories *before* workers move from one labor market to another.
   b. Draw graphs that illustrate the final equilibrium position in the two industries, after workers have had an opportunity to move from one labor market to another.
   c. Now assume that, at the same time as the demand for factory workers increases, factory workers become unionized. How would this change the final equilibrium in the two industries?

3. The Occupational Safety and Health Administration (OSHA) is an agency of the Department of Labor. Visit OSHA's Web site at http://www.osha.gov/index.html and familiarize yourself with the range of tasks undertaken by the agency in its mission "to save lives, prevent injuries, and protect the health of America's workers." Do the regulations imposed by OSHA improve the wellbeing of workers in "safe" jobs? What effect do the regulations have on the wellbeing of workers who prefer dangerous, high paying jobs? What arguments can you think of for the existence of OSHA?

C H A L L E N G E   Q U E S T I O N

1. a. Assume the equilibrium wage for unskilled workers is $5 per hour. The government imposes a minimum wage of $6. Using graphs, discuss the effect of the policy on the level of employment of unskilled workers.

    b. Advocates of the minimum wage argue that any effect on employment will be slight. Furthermore, they assert that any increase in the minimum wage will actually increase the total amount paid to all unskilled workers. Discuss what assumptions they are making about the wage elasticity of labor demand.

CHAPTER

10

ECONOMIC EFFICIENCY AND THE
ROLE OF GOVERNMENT

In December 1991, the Soviet Union—the world's second most powerful country—ceased to exist. At the same time, its economic system—centrally planned socialism—was thoroughly discredited.

Many powerful forces combined to destroy the Soviet system. These included corruption within the highest levels of government, alienation and cynicism among the population, the universal desire for democracy and individual freedom, and strong nationalism within the Soviet republics. But there was an additional reason for the Soviet Union's demise—a purely *economic* reason: The Soviet economic system was deeply inefficient.

In this chapter, we take a close look at the concept of efficiency. You will learn that there is more to this concept than appears at first glance. You will also learn why economists believe that the market system is able to achieve a higher level of efficiency than any other economic system devised so far.

In many situations, however, the market does not work properly. Thus, in order to achieve the highest possible level of efficiency, the government must play an active role in the economy. Economics has much to say about the need for government intervention and the type of intervention needed to remedy different types of problems in the private economy. In the second part of this chapter, we focus on the role of government in bringing about economic efficiency.

THE MEANING OF EFFICIENCY

What, exactly, do we mean by the word *efficiency*? We all use this word, or its opposite, in our everyday conversation: "I wish I could organize my time more efficiently," "He's such an inefficient worker," "Our office is organized very efficiently," and so on. In each of these cases, we are using the word "inefficient" to mean "wasteful" and "efficient" to mean "the absence of waste."

In economics, too, efficiency means the absence of waste—although a very specific kind of waste: *the waste of an opportunity to make one person better off without making anyone else worse off.* More specifically,

> Economic efficiency *is achieved when there is no way to rearrange the production or allocation of goods in a way that makes one person better off without making anybody else worse off.*

Notice that economic efficiency is a somewhat limited concept. While it is an important goal for a society, it is not the only goal. Most of us would list "fairness" as another important goal of our society. But an economy can be efficient even if most people are poor and a few are extraordinarily rich—a situation that many of us would regard as unfair.

> *An efficient economy is not necessarily a fair economy.*

Why, then, do economists put so much stress on efficiency, rather than on issues of fairness? Largely because one's position on issues of fairness depends on ethical and moral values, about which there is considerable disagreement in our society. Issues of fairness must therefore be resolved politically.

But virtually all of us would agree that if we fail to take actions that would make some people in our society better off *without harming anyone*—that is, if we fail to achieve economic efficiency—we have wasted a valuable opportunity. Economics—by helping us understand the preconditions for economic efficiency, and teaching us how we can bring about those preconditions—can make a major contribution to our material well-being.

PARETO IMPROVEMENTS

Imagine the following scenario: A boy and a girl are having lunch in elementary school. The boy frowns at a peanut butter and jelly sandwich, which, on this particular day, makes the girl's mouth water. She says, "Wanna trade?" The boy looks at her tuna sandwich, considers a moment, and says, "Okay."

This little scene, which is played out thousands of times every day in schools around the country, is an example of a trade in which both parties are made better off, and no one is harmed. And as simple as it seems, such trading is at the core of the concept of economic efficiency. It is an example of a *Pareto* (pronounced puh-RAY-toe) *improvement,* named after the Italian economist, Vilfredo Pareto (1848–1923), who first systematically explored the issue of economic efficiency.

> A ***Pareto** improvement is any action that makes at least one person better off, and harms no one.*

PARETO IMPROVEMENT An action that makes at least one person better off, and harms no one.

In a market economy such as that in the United States where trading is voluntary, literally hundreds of millions of Pareto improvements take place every day. Indeed, every purchase is an example of a Pareto improvement. If you pay $18 for

DANGEROUS CURVES

Deciding what is and what is not a Pareto improvement can often be confusing. For example, suppose you are in the desert, about to die of thirst, and you come upon a stand that sells bottled water. "How much for the bottle?" you ask. "Let me see your wallet," says the owner of the stand. You hand over your wallet, and the owner quickly assesses its contents: $200. "That'll be $200 per bottle." You are so desperate for the water that you agree.

Was this a Pareto improvement? Absolutely. The water was worth much more than $200 to you (without it, you would have died), so you are definitely better off. The seller benefited as well, since he has presumably realized quite a large profit. And no one was harmed by this transaction.

But wait . . . didn't the seller of the water take advantage of you? How can such a clear example of exploitation be considered a desirable Pareto improvement? To understand why it is desirable, remember that characterizing an action as a Pareto improvement only means that both sides benefit from the action; it doesn't tell us whether the total benefit is *distributed* between the two parties in a manner we would consider *fair*. In this example, both parties are better off if they trade, rather than not trade. Thus, it is a Pareto improvement. The lesson to remember is that a Pareto improvement is not necessarily fair or equitable, but both parties are always better off for making it.

a pair of jeans, then the jeans must be worth more to you than the $18 that you parted with, or you wouldn't have bought them. Thus, you are better off after making the purchase. On the other side, the owner of the store must have valued your $18 more than the jeans he parted with, or he wouldn't have sold them to you. So he is better off, too. Your purchase of the jeans, like virtually every purchase made by every consumer every day, is an example of a Pareto improvement.

The notion of a Pareto improvement helps us arrive at a formal definition of economic efficiency:

ECONOMIC EFFICIENCY A situation in which every Pareto improvement has occurred.

> *Economic efficiency is achieved after every Pareto improvement has occurred.*

This definition can be applied to an individual market or to the economy as a whole. For example, suppose we look at the market for laser printers and cannot identify a single Pareto improvement in that market that has not already been exploited. No matter how hard we look, we cannot find a change in price or output level, or any other change for that matter, that would make some producer or some consumer better off without harming anyone. Then we would say that the market for laser printers is economically efficient.

Alternatively, we can look at the economy as a whole. If we discover remaining Pareto improvements that have not yet occurred—say, a change in the price of some good or a change in the quantity of a good produced—then we would deem the economy economically *in*efficient.

Of course, no economy can exploit *every* Pareto improvement, so no society can ever be completely economically efficient according to our definition. But achieving something close to economic efficiency is an important goal. When we look at real-world markets and real-world economies, it is best to view economic efficiency as a continuum. At one end of the continuum are economies in which, in most markets, most opportunities for Pareto improvements are exploited. At the other end of the continuum are economies in which many markets are economically inefficient— where many opportunities for mutual gain remain unexploited. As you will see in this chapter, perfectly competitive markets tend to be economically efficient, and market economies tend to lie closer to the economically efficient end of the spectrum than other types of economies.

SIDE PAYMENTS AND PARETO IMPROVEMENTS

The examples of Pareto improvements we have considered so far involve normal transactions, in which one person trades with another and both come out ahead.

These transactions typically occur rather easily and automatically: Since both parties benefit, they have every incentive to find each other and trade.

But there are more complicated situations, involving groups of people, in which a Pareto improvement will come about only if one side makes a special kind of payment to the other, which we call a *side payment*. Here's an example: Suppose a dry-cleaning shop sets up on the ground floor of an apartment building. Everyone who lives in the building suffers from fumes and loud noise, and they want the dry cleaner to move. But because of a zoning law that prevents the entry of additional dry cleaners into the area, the dry cleaner is making an economic profit and does not want to move. Thus, we seem to be at an impasse: If the dry cleaner moves to another location (say, in the competitive business district of the city), the tenants would gain, but the dry cleaner would be harmed—she would lose her economic profit. Is it possible to make at least one party—the dry cleaner or the tenants or both—better off without simultaneously harming someone? Let's see.

Suppose there are 100 tenants, and each would gladly pay an extra $50 per month—a total of $100 \times \$50 = \$5,000$—to get the dry cleaner out. Suppose, too, that the dry cleaner's economic profit is $3,000 per month. The tenants might get together and agree to pay the dry cleaner $4,000 per month to move from the building. If the deal is struck, the tenants are better off, since they gain benefits that are worth at least $5,000 per month to them, but actually pay only $4,000 per month. The dry cleaner is better off, since she loses $3,000 in monthly profit, but gains $4,000 in monthly payments from the tenants. In other words, by arranging a proper side payment from the tenants to the dry cleaner—compensation to leave the building—everyone can be made better off. As you can see, there are many side payments that would do the trick: Tenants could pay any amount between $3,000 and $5,000 per month, and both parties would still gain.

We'll be looking at quite a number of Pareto improvements in this chapter and the next one. To help keep track, we'll illustrate each of them with a scorecard, to show that nobody involved in the deal comes out behind. For our apartment tenants and dry cleaner, the scorecard looks like this:

Action: Tenants Pay Dry Cleaner $4,000 per Month to Move Out of Building

Dry cleaner	Gains payment of:	$4,000 per month
	Loses profit of:	$3,000 per month
	Comes out ahead by:	$1,000 per month
Tenants	Gain benefits worth:	$5,000 per month
	Pay:	$4,000 per month
	Come out ahead by:	$1,000 per month

Notice that, without the side payment, making the dry cleaner leave the building would *not* be a Pareto improvement, since the dry cleaner would be harmed. But the side payment converts an action that would harm someone into an action that harms no one—a Pareto improvement.

> *Some actions that—by themselves—would not be Pareto improvements can be converted into Pareto improvements if accompanied by an appropriate side payment.*

POTENTIAL PARETO IMPROVEMENTS

Another Pareto concept—related to, but not the same as, a Pareto improvement—is a *potential* Pareto improvement:

POTENTIAL PARETO IMPROVEMENT An action in which the gains to the gainers would exceed the losses to the losers.

> A *potential Pareto improvement* is any action in which the gains to the gainers are greater than the losses to the losers.

Notice the key difference when we include the word "potential." In a simple Pareto improvement, there are no losers. In a *potential* Pareto improvement, there *can* be losers. However, the total losses are smaller than the total gains to the gainers.

For example, in our previous example, suppose the dry cleaner is forced out of the building with no side payment. This action would *not* be a Pareto improvement, since the dry cleaner would be worse off. However, it would be a *potential* Pareto improvement, since the gains to the apartment dwellers ($5,000 per month) would be greater than the losses to the dry cleaner ($3,000 per month).

Although these two types of actions we've been discussing are not the same thing, there is an important relationship between them.

> Any potential Pareto improvement could become *a Pareto improvement if an appropriate side payment is made.*

How can we be sure of this? In a potential Pareto improvement, the total gains exceed the total losses. Thus, we could always take some of the gains away from the gainers, transfer them to the losers, and make everyone come out ahead. In our dry-cleaning story, a side payment of $4,000 did the trick.

Now, why have we bothered so much about potential Pareto improvements? Because they tell us something important about the requirements for economic efficiency:

> Economic efficiency, which requires that all Pareto improvements have taken place, also requires that all potential *Pareto improvements have taken place.*

To understand the logic of this, suppose that there is some potential Pareto improvement that has not taken place. That is, there is some action—not yet taken—wherein the gains to the gainers are greater than the losses to the losers. Since the appropriate side payment would convert this move into a Pareto improvement, we know that some Pareto improvement has not occurred either—a violation of economic efficiency.

ECONOMIC EFFICIENCY AND PERFECT COMPETITION

In a market system, where firms and consumers are free to produce and consume as they wish, without anyone organizing the whole process from above, will markets for goods and services be economically efficient? That is, will the quantities of goods that firms produce, and consumers consume, exploit all Pareto improvements and potential Pareto improvements? In this section, you'll see that the answer is a *conditional* yes. A market economy will, indeed, produce efficient quantities of goods . . . *as long as the goods are traded in perfectly competitive markets.* To demonstrate this important insight, let's return to the familiar tools we've used to analyze perfectly competitive markets: demand and supply curves.

FIGURE 1	ANGELA'S MARGINAL BENEFIT FROM CONSUMING ORANGES

Angela's demand curve shows the marginal benefit she receives from each additional orange. At $0.28 each, she consumes 5 oranges. If the price falls to $0.27, she consumes a 6th. Her marginal benefit from that 6th orange must be $0.27. In a similar way, the height of the demand curve at point *B* shows her marginal benefit from the 16th orange—$0.17.

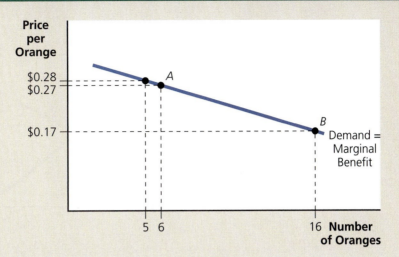

ANOTHER VIEW OF DEMAND AND SUPPLY CURVES

Figure 1 shows Angela's demand curve for oranges. This demand curve shows us the quantity demanded at each price. For example, at $0.28 per orange, Angela buys 5 oranges per week.

But we can also view this demand curve in a different way: it tells us how much each additional orange is *worth* to Angela. For example, suppose we want to know the value, to Angela, of the 6th orange. We know that when the price of oranges is $0.28, Angela chooses *not* to buy the 6th orange. But if the price falls to $0.27, she *does* buy the 6th orange. Therefore, the 6th orange must be worth $0.27 to her.

We can conclude that the height of the demand curve at each quantity indicates the additional value or extra benefit a consumer would obtain by consuming that last orange. The *marginal benefit* of the 6th orange to Angela (at Point *A*) is $0.27. Similarly, the marginal benefit of the 16th orange (at point *B*) is $0.17. This is why, in the figure, the demand curve is also labeled the *marginal benefit curve*.

What's true for Angela will also be true for every other consumer of oranges, so when we turn our attention to the *market* demand curve for oranges—like the one in Figure 2—the height of the curve tells us the value that *some* consumer will get from the last orange consumed. More generally,

> *the height of the market demand curve at any quantity shows us the marginal benefit—to someone—of the last unit of the good consumed.*

Now that we've reinterpreted the market demand curve as the marginal benefit curve, let's take another look at its counterpart: the market supply curve. In Chapter 7, you learned that a competitive firm's supply curve is also its marginal cost curve. And in Chapter 8—in the section entitled, "Comparing Monopoly to Perfect Competition"—you learned that the market supply curve tells us the marginal cost of producing an additional unit of output at *some* firm. That is,

> *the height of the market supply curve at any quantity measures the marginal cost—to some firm—of the last unit produced.*

FIGURE 2	**EFFICIENCY IN THE MARKET FOR ORANGES**

Quantity Q^*, where the demand and supply curves cross, is the economically efficient quantity. The marginal benefit to some consumer from the last orange consumed just equals the marginal cost of producing it—$0.15. At a lower quantity, such as Q_L, the marginal benefit ($0.25) exceeds the marginal cost ($0.08). Q_L is an inefficient quantity.

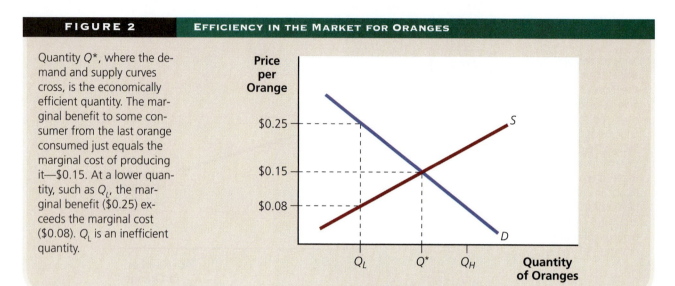

WHY PERFECTLY COMPETITIVE MARKETS ARE EFFICIENT

In a perfectly competitive market, the equilibrium quantity is determined at the intersection of the supply and demand curves. In Figure 2, for example, the equilibrium quantity of oranges is Q^*. Now, by using our new interpretations of these curves, we can demonstrate that Q^*— the equilibrium quantity—is also the *efficient* quantity of output.

Our first step is to show that, if output is at any level *other* than Q^*, then a Pareto improvement occurs as we move closer to Q^*. For example, at Q_L, a level below the efficient level, the demand (marginal benefit) curve lies above the supply (marginal cost) curve. From the marginal benefit curve, we know that some consumer would be willing to pay as much as $0.25 for an additional orange. The marginal cost curve tells us that some firm would be willing to supply that orange for $0.08. Both parties would be better off if the orange were produced and sold at any price between $0.08 and $0.25. For example, a Pareto improvement occurs if the orange is produced and sold for $0.15, as you can see in the following scorecard:

Action: One More Orange Is Produced and Sold for $0.15

Some consumer	Gains benefits worth:	$0.25
	Pays:	$0.15
	Comes out ahead by:	$0.10
Some producer	Gains revenue of:	$0.15
	Cost:	$0.08
	Comes out ahead by:	$0.07

In a similar way, you should be able to show that consumption level Q_H is too high to be efficient. (Describe a Pareto improvement that involves producing one less orange.) The only level of output at which no further Pareto improvements are possible is Q^*—the efficient level. At Q^*, the marginal benefit to some consumer from the last orange consumed—$0.15—is exactly equal to the marginal cost to some firm of picking, shipping, and selling that orange.

> *The efficient level of production of any good is where the marginal benefit and marginal cost of the good are equal. Graphically, this is where the marginal benefit and marginal cost curves intersect.*

Now we can pull together everything we've learned about the efficiency and equilibrium under perfect competition:

MARKETS AND EQUILIBRIUM

> *In a perfectly competitive market, the marginal cost of a good is given by the market supply curve, and the marginal benefit of the good is given by the market demand curve. Thus, the efficient quantity—where marginal benefit and marginal cost are equal—is also the equilibrium quantity—where the supply and demand curves intersect.*

Let's consider this last statement carefully. It tells us that, if we leave producers and consumers alone to trade with each other as they wish, then—as long as the market is perfectly competitive—the quantity bought and sold will automatically be the economically efficient quantity.

How does the market achieve this remarkable result? The market's job is to establish the equilibrium price of the good—the price at which quantity demanded and quantity supplied are equal. Once that price is determined, each consumer adjusts consumption until his *marginal benefit just equals the price.* Each firm continues to adjust its production until its *marginal cost equals the price.* Thus, each consumer will end up consuming until his *marginal benefit is equal to the marginal cost* to some firm. Thus, in the market as a whole, the last unit produced will provide a marginal benefit to some consumer equal to its marginal cost to some firm.

Notice that this result comes about automatically. Consumers don't have to approach firms and ask them to produce the economically efficient quantity of each good. Rather, firms maximize profit and consumers maximize their well-being, and—as a consequence—the economy produces the efficient amount of the good. There are no remaining opportunities for Pareto improvement in the market.

The notion that perfect competition—where many buyers and sellers each try to do the best for themselves—actually delivers an efficient economy is one of the most important ideas in economics. The great British economist of the eighteenth century,

DANGEROUS CURVES

Here is an important reminder: Don't confuse efficiency with fairness. Producing the quantity of a good where the demand and supply curves intersect will be *efficient,* but it may not be *fair.*

To see why, remember that the demand—or marginal benefit—curve tells us how much income or wealth some consumer would give up to buy another unit of a good. But this, in turn, depends on how much income or wealth the consumer *has.* A very poor person might want food very badly, but if she has no income or wealth, her desire would not register at all on the demand curve in Figure 2. Thus, in principle, an efficient level of food production could be one in which many people starve, and just a few—those with income—have food.

More generally, the market demand curve for any good will depend on the distribution of income and wealth in the society. If that distribution is regarded as unfair, then the quantities of goods produced and consumed will be unfair as well, even though they may be efficient.

Adam Smith, coined the term "invisible hand" to describe the force that leads a competitive economy relentlessly and automatically toward economic efficiency:

> [The individual] neither intends to promote the public interest, nor knows how much he is promoting it. . . . [H]e intends only his own gain, and he is in this, as in many other cases, led by an invisible hand to promote an end which was not part of his intention. Nor is it always the worse for the society that it was no part of it. By pursuing his own interest, he frequently promotes that of society more effectually than when he really intends to promote it. [Emphasis added][1]

One implication of Smith's insight is that in many cases the results we get from the invisible hand of competition are better than we would get from the *visible* hand of regulation or government operation of the economy. But remember that the invisible hand works best in an economy in which markets are working well and where they are perfectly competitive. As we will see in the rest of this chapter, when there is imperfect competition or when markets fail to function in other ways, then the invisible hand may not work. In those cases, government action may be needed to bring about economic efficiency.

THE INEFFICIENCY OF IMPERFECT COMPETITION

We've seen that perfect competition delivers the efficient quantities of goods to consumers. What about other market structures? In this section we'll show that when firms face downward sloping demand curves for their products—that is, when they sell in markets that are *not* perfectly competitive—the market output level is *in*efficient.

Consider the market for cornflakes. The situation of the typical firm—Kellogg, for example—is shown in Figure 3, where Kellogg faces a downward-sloping demand curve for its product. As you first learned in Chapter 6, when the demand curve facing the firm slopes downward, marginal revenue at each output level will be less than the price. This is why, in the figure, the marginal revenue curve is drawn *below* the demand curve. Finally, you've learned that the firm will maximize profit by equating marginal revenue to marginal cost. In the figure, this occurs when the firm produces the output level q^*. Now consider a crucial feature of this market:

> *In monopoly or imperfectly competitive markets, in which each firm faces a downward sloping demand curve, each firm will set its price* above *its marginal cost of production.*

The fact that firms charge a price greater than marginal cost has a surprising implication. Remember that each consumer will continue to adjust his or her quantity demanded until their marginal benefit from the product is equal to its price. So, even when the market is *not* imperfectly competitive, we can still be sure that the marginal benefit from a good will be equal to the price. But now, since the price exceeds marginal cost, it must be that marginal benefit, too, exceeds marginal cost. Thus, the market cannot be efficient.

The inefficiency can be seen more concretely in Figure 3. The firm is maximizing profit at output level q^*, where the price—and the marginal benefit to some

1. Adam Smith, *An Inquiry into the Nature and Causes of the Wealth of Nations* (1776), ed. Edwin Cannan (Chicago: University of Chicago Press, 1976), p. 477.

FIGURE 3	**THE INEFFICIENCY OF IMPERFECT COMPETITION**

An imperfectly competitive firm, such as Kellogg, faces a downward-sloping demand curve and maximizes profit by producing q^* boxes of cornflakes. At that output, the benefit of another box to some consumer ($3) exceeds the marginal cost of producing it ($1). That is economically inefficient.

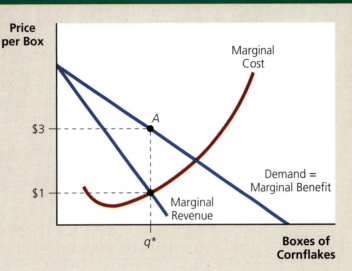

consumer—is $3.00 per box of cornflakes, while marginal cost is just $1.00. This output level is inefficient, since we can find a potential Pareto improvement—a change such that the gains to the gainers are greater than the losses to the losers. For example, a consumer could buy one more box of cornflakes and pay $2.00. Here is a scorecard for that transaction, showing that it would yield a Pareto improvement:

Action: One More Box of Cornflakes Is Produced and Sold

Some consumer	Gains benefits worth:	$3.00
	Pays:	$2.00
	Comes out ahead by:	$1.00
Cornflakes producer	Gains revenue of:	$2.00
	Marginal cost:	$1.00
	Comes out ahead by:	$1.00

The additional consumption is beneficial, because the marginal benefit to the consumer exceeds the marginal cost to the producer. If Kellogg does *not* produce this additional box, then the market for cornflakes will be inefficient.

As you can see, in monopoly or imperfectly competitive markets, the profit-maximizing quantity for firms—and the equilibrium quantity in the market—is inefficient. It is possible to produce more of the good and make both producers and consumers better off—a Pareto improvement. However, this will not happen as long as firms continue to charge a price greater than marginal cost. Thus, from the point of view of efficiency,

monopoly and imperfectly competitive markets, in which firms charge a price greater than marginal cost, produce too little output at too high a price.

This conclusion applies to any market structure in which we expect price to exceed marginal cost—monopolistic competition, monopoly, or oligopoly.

But wait, you might object, if both sides gain from the kind of transaction we've just described, what stops them from carrying it out? The answer can be found in Figure 3. The demand curve for cornflakes slopes downward. To sell additional boxes, Kellogg must charge a lower price—on *all* boxes. If the firm could sell an additional box at $2.00—*and keep charging $3.00 on all other boxes—then it would, indeed, make the transaction.* As you learned in Chapter 8, a *price-discriminating* firm can do just that. But you also learned that not every firm can price discriminate, and even a price-discriminating firm may not be able to charge enough different prices to take advantage of *every* Pareto improvement.

> *In monopoly and imperfect competition, it is the inability of firms to make separate side deals through price discrimination that prevents potential Pareto improvements from being carried out.*

THE ROLE OF GOVERNMENT IN ECONOMIC EFFICIENCY

In the last section, you learned that an important requirement for economic efficiency is that markets are perfectly competitive. Once could argue—and many economists do—that most markets in the United States come reasonably close to satisfying this requirement. That helps us understand why the U.S. economy relies so heavily on markets. Indeed, in most markets, the government seems to recognize that Adam Smith's invisible hand will give us close-to-efficient quantities of goods and services, and that government can serve the public interest largely by leaving the public alone.

But not *entirely* alone. Even in the United States, market activity is supported by government in two crucial ways. First, the government provides the infrastructure that permits markets to function. Part of the infrastructure is physical—roads, bridges, airports, waterways, and buildings. But an equally important part is the market system's *institutional infrastructure*—laws, courts, and regulatory agencies. Although maintenance of the institutional infrastructure accounts for only a small fraction of the government's budget, a market economy would collapse without it.

The second way government supports market activity is by stepping in when markets are not working properly—when they leave Pareto improvements unexploited and therefore fail to achieve economic efficiency. The government's tools for making markets more efficient include regulation, antitrust law, and taxation. In this chapter, you will see how these tools work.

This is not the first time we've discussed government involvement in markets. But our earlier discussions focused on situations in which government *interfered* with the workings of a market economy. These situations included price ceilings and price floors, as well as government-created barriers to entry in product and labor markets. In many cases, the result was problems for the economy that could have been avoided by better policies. In this chapter, our focus is entirely different: We will look at how government *contributes* to economic efficiency by helping us achieve Pareto improvements that would not otherwise occur.

We begin by examining the institutional infrastructure of a market economy and then—in more detail—two important parts of that infrastructure: the legal and regulatory systems. Then we'll turn our attention to markets that fail to work efficiently and what the government can do about them.

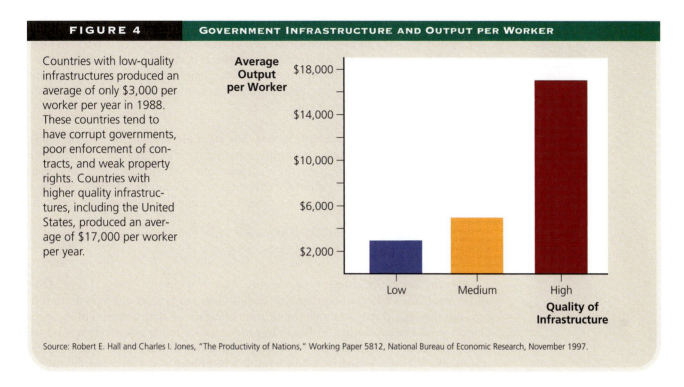

FIGURE 4 | **GOVERNMENT INFRASTRUCTURE AND OUTPUT PER WORKER**

Countries with low-quality infrastructures produced an average of only $3,000 per worker per year in 1988. These countries tend to have corrupt governments, poor enforcement of contracts, and weak property rights. Countries with higher quality infrastructures, including the United States, produced an average of $17,000 per worker per year.

Source: Robert E. Hall and Charles I. Jones, "The Productivity of Nations," Working Paper 5812, National Bureau of Economic Research, November 1997.

THE INSTITUTIONAL INFRASTRUCTURE OF A MARKET ECONOMY

Americans take their institutional infrastructure almost completely for granted. The best way to appreciate the infrastructure of the United States is to visit another country that has a poor one. In many countries, the police are more likely to *steal* from citizens than to protect them from thievery. In some nations, the people have no effective rights to their own property—somebody can start building a shack on their land, and the government won't stop him. If a person is injured by a drunk driver, there may be no system for compensating her or punishing the driver. Many nations suffer from powerful mafias that extort protection money by threatening to shut down businesses or physically harm their owners.

All too many nations suffer from problems such as these. Figure 4 illustrates one important result: When countries are divided into three groups, according to the quality of their institutional infrastructure, there is a strong relation between infrastructure and output per worker. The countries on the left—the third with the lowest quality infrastructures—were able to produce only about $3,000 in output per worker per year in 1988. These are the nations where property rights are weak, contracts are not enforced, and the government is more often predator than protector of economic activity. In the middle of the figure are countries with medium-quality infrastructures, and these countries average about $5,500 in output per worker per year. On the right are the best organized countries, averaging $17,000 in output per worker, and those countries with the very best infrastructures—such as the United States—achieved levels of output more than double that average.

THE LEGAL SYSTEM

The legal system is the backbone of the institutional infrastructure that supports market activity. Of course, the legal system is also important for noneconomic reasons.

The law protects us from physical and emotional harm. And it protects our democracy by guaranteeing freedom of speech and other vital civil liberties. We won't discuss these here. Instead, we will focus on the purely economic role of the legal system—that is, on the ways that it supports markets and helps us achieve economic efficiency. We'll look at five very broad categories: criminal law, property law, contract law, tort law, and antitrust law.

CRIMINAL LAW. While criminal law has important moral and ethical dimensions, its central economic function is to limit exchanges to *voluntary* ones. When both parties agree to an exchange, they must each benefit from it. Therefore, as long as no third party is harmed, a voluntary exchange will always be a Pareto improvement. But an involuntary exchange—robbery, for example—always harms one side.

> *By limiting exchanges to those that benefit both sides, criminal law channels our energies into activities that increase economic efficiency.*

But why is it more efficient for the *government* to enforce criminal law? After all, we could each have our own *private* security force to protect our lives and property. But this would require much duplication of effort—a large fraction of the population would be protectors, rather than producers, of goods and services. And we would not be able to anticipate when another person, with a better security force, would take over our property. So we wouldn't be able to make long-term plans for using our resources—they could be taken away at any time. Government-enforced criminal law protects us from involuntary transactions, at relatively low cost.

PROPERTY LAW. Property law gives people precisely defined, enforceable rights over the things they own. Without property law, you would spend a good part of your time dealing with people who claimed to own your house, your farm, or your factory. In the United States and other advanced countries, highly secure systems keep track of who owns land, cars, shares of stock, airplanes, and other important pieces of property. Disputes about property ownership are rare because the system works so well.

When property rights are poorly defined, much time and energy are wasted in disputes about ownership, and people spend time trying to capture resources from others, time that could have been spent producing valuable goods and services. As a result,

> *countries with poorly defined property rights do not produce as much output from their resources as they could with better defined property rights. Greater output could make some people better off without harming anyone—a Pareto improvement. Thus, countries with poorly defined property rights are economically inefficient.*

CONTRACT LAW. In 1991, a lawyer named John Mackall had a great idea—to start a mail-order company to sell batteries for laptop computers. He had the money to start the business, but not the time. So he made a deal with a (very lucky) business school student, Ken Hawk, to start 1-800-BATTERIES.

As part of their deal, Mackall and Hawk signed a contract that gave Hawk a 75 percent interest in the company. Mackall invested $50,000 and received the remaining 25 percent of the company. It turned out that the company was a success: In

1996, it sold about $5 million worth of batteries. But what guaranteed that Hawk would give Mackall his 25 percent share of the profits? In Russia or Bosnia, somebody in Mackall's position would worry that he would not be able to collect his share later. In the United States, that worry would not arise, because contracts can be enforced.

A contract is a mutual promise. Often, as in the example of the battery business, one person does something first (Mackall provided his idea and $50,000 in cash) and the other person promises to do something later (Hawk promised to run the business and pay Mackall 25 percent of the profit). As long as no third parties are harmed, the exchange that occurs under a contract is always a Pareto improvement—it's a voluntary deal that won't happen unless both sides are made better off.

Contracts play a special role in a market economy. Without them, the only Pareto improvements that could take place would be those involving simultaneous exchange. But contracts enable us to make exchanges in which one person goes first. That person has to be able to rely on the other person to make good on the promise later. Without this assurance, whoever goes first would not be willing to make the deal in the first place. Thus, contracts make it possible to form new companies and to hire the services of experts who specialize in such things as auto repair, plumbing, roof repair, dentistry, and legal services—all cases in which someone goes first:

> *Contracts enable us to make exchanges that take place over time and in which one person must act first. In this way, contracts help society enjoy the full benefits of specialization and exchange.*

SPECIALIZATION AND EXCHANGE

It is important to note that legal enforcement of contracts is not the only force that makes people keep promises. First, parents, religious organizations, and schools teach people that keeping promises is a moral obligation. Second, a reputation for failing to keep promises would be harmful to a business or a person. Nonetheless, contracts and the infrastructure for enforcing them are important for economic efficiency. For example, contracts help new businesses get started, before they have developed reputations for making good on their promises. And we know that despite the efforts of parents, religious leaders, and schools, there are enough would-be cheaters that we need an effective way to deal with them.

TORT LAW. Contract law deals with people or businesses that are economically involved with each other, such as suppliers and their customers, or partners in a business deal. Tort law, on the other hand, deals with interactions among strangers or people not linked by contracts. Tort law sets up incentives against injuries that result from accidents, fraud, and other events. Someone who injures another must compensate the victim. A careless driver who causes an accident must pay to fix the car he has damaged.

When people and businesses are held responsible for injuries they cause, they act more carefully. Tort law in the United States provides incentives for drivers to drive carefully, for lawyers to represent their clients competently, and for manufacturers of products such as power mowers to control hazards through proper design.

Tort law also protects against *fraud,* in which a seller of something—a product, a business, shares of stock—lies to the buyer in order to make the sale. In some countries, fraud is such a pervasive problem that you can't trust the claims made by the sellers of anything. In the United States, by contrast, sellers are extraordinarily careful about their claims. You would be extremely surprised if you bought a down vest and found later that it was stuffed with polyester. Similarly, the information that is released by a company when it sells stock to the public is scrutinized minutely by the company's lawyers, to be absolutely sure of its accuracy. If a firm says it owns 17 million barrels of proven oil reserves or 125 multiplex movie theaters, you can be almost completely confident that it does. The penalties for lying about a subject like that are severe.

ANTITRUST LAW. Antitrust law is designed to prevent businesses from making agreements or engaging in other behavior that limits competition and harms consumers. More specifically, antitrust law operates in three areas:

Agreements among Competitors. U.S. antitrust law—outlined in Section 1 of the Sherman Act—prohibits "contracts, combinations, or conspiracies" among competing firms that would harm consumers by raising prices. The most flagrant agreements prohibited by this law are those that directly fix prices. But the law also prohibits agreements that raise prices *indirectly*, by limiting competition among sellers. An agreement by firms to allocate markets among them—so that one seller serves one group of customers exclusively, while other sellers are assigned their own groups of exclusive customers, may violate the law. For example, in the mid-1990s, the only two important sellers of review courses for the bar exam taken by prospective lawyers divided up their territory to avoid competition. The courts outlawed their agreement, because it reduced competition.

Monopolization. Section 2 of the Sherman Act makes it illegal to monopolize or attempt to monopolize a market. As the law is now interpreted, it is illegal for one seller to harm a rival by interfering with its operations or hobbling the rival in certain ways. For example, it is illegal for a company to spread false information about a rival's product as part of an attempt to drive that rival out of the market. But the law does not prohibit monopoly or harm to competitors. Rather, it prohibits *certain steps* to acquire or maintain a monopoly or to harm competitors. A firm that harms its rivals by selling a better product, thus taking business away from them, is not in violation of the law.

Mergers. In a merger, two firms combine to form one new firm. The result is to increase the danger of higher prices from oligopoly or monopoly. For example, if the largest firm in a market has a 40 percent share of total sales, and the second largest has a 30 percent share, we can expect that the rivalry between them will benefit consumers. But if they merge to form a single firm with a 70 percent share, the rivalry would disappear, and prices would rise. Mergers of this type are often blocked by the U.S. government based on Section 7 of the Clayton Act.

REGULATION

Regulation is another important part of the institutional infrastructure that supports a market economy. Under regulation, a government agency—such as the Food and Drug Administration (FDA), the Environmental Protection Agency (EPA), or a state public utilities commission—has the power to direct businesses to take specific actions. The EPA has detailed control over what substances a business can release into the atmosphere or into the water. Public utilities commissions set the prices for electricity, gas, and telephone service. Often, regulators must approve business actions before they are undertaken, as in the case of the FDA's approval of new drugs. In addition to protecting public safety and health, regulation is also used to help markets function more efficiently, as we will discuss more thoroughly later in the chapter.

Federal Trade Commission (FTC)
Federal agency enforcing consumer protection laws and (along with the Antitrust Division of the Department of Justice) antitrust laws, as well. The Bureau of Economics at the FTC offers professional advice for enforcement and analyzes issues before the Commission. Browse the site to learn about recent actions and rulings.
http://www.ftc.gov/

Regulation differs from the use of legal procedures in a fundamental way: Regulators reach deep into the operations of businesses to tell them what to do, while legal procedures typically result in fines or other penalties if businesses do something wrong. To help see the distinction, consider the different ways in which regional and long-distance telephone companies are treated. Because they are regulated, regional telephone companies (such as Bell Atlantic or Cincinnati Bell) are *told* what price to charge. Long-distance phone companies, by contrast, are largely unregulated, so they can charge whatever price they wish. But if long distance companies are caught breaking the law in setting prices (such as, by entering into illegal agreements to restrict competition), they will have to pay fines and their managers may even have to go to jail.

LAW AND REGULATION IN PERSPECTIVE

The invisible hand of the market system cannot operate on its own. The legal system, along with our regulatory agencies, creates an environment in which the invisible hand can do its job. Almost every Pareto improvement that we can think of relies on the legal and regulatory infrastructure. Think of the last time you bought a meal in a restaurant. If you paid cash, the law against counterfeiting enabled the restaurant to more readily accept your paper currency. If you paid by credit card, contract law assured the restaurant that it would eventually be paid by the credit card company. The restaurant itself couldn't function without contracts with its suppliers, landlord, and employees. You could be reasonably confident that the food was not contaminated, in part because of inspections by local regulatory agencies and also because of legal disincentives for harmful products.

But what about cases where law and regulation don't seem to be working perfectly? After all, we still have crimes against people and property. Unsafe products like poorly designed automobiles or tainted frozen dinners *are* produced and only sometimes recalled before someone is harmed. Businesses *do* fix prices and are only sometimes caught. Do these and countless other examples mean that our institutional infrastructure is failing us?

Yes . . . and no. While instances like these are never welcome, our society has *chosen* not to eliminate them entirely. We could, if we wanted to, eliminate all crime, all unsafe products, and all other detriments to economic life by enacting more stringent laws and regulations and enforcing them to the hilt. But doing so would require even larger expenditures on legal and regulatory enforcement than we currently make. In deciding whether to make these expenditures, we must balance the benefits—safer products, reduced crime, and so on—against the costs.

For example, in part because of our strong tort law, the United States is one of the safest countries of the world. But even the United States has chosen not to *completely eliminate* safety hazards: Each year, 20 people out of every 100,000 die from accidents. Why do we accept this? Because the complete (or almost complete) elimination of fatal accidents would require so many of our resources to be diverted from other uses that most of us would think it is simply not worth it. For example, to eliminate all fatal accidents, we would have to require that every passenger aircraft be inspected dozens—perhaps even hundreds—of times after each flight; that drivers enroll in a refresher course each year, perhaps each month, updating and reinforcing their driving skills and safety consciousness; that all restaurants inspect every meal for *E. coli* contamination before serving it; and that all floors and shoes be manufactured out of special materials to make slipping impossible. Moreover, all of these requirements would have to be strictly enforced, requiring more police and inspectors to catch violators and more courts and jails to prosecute and penalize them. Our standard of living would plummet in such a world, and we could all be made better off by taking on some additional risk of accidents in order to free up resources for increased production.

POLICY TRADEOFFS

> *A legal and regulatory system that ensured the* complete elimination *of crime, unsafe products, and other unwelcome activities would be less efficient than a system that tolerated some amount of these activities. An efficient infrastructure must consider the costs, as well as the benefits, of achieving our legal and regulatory goals.*

MARKET FAILURES

MARKET FAILURE A market equilibrium that fails to take advantage of every Pareto improvement.

A **market failure** occurs whenever a market is inefficient—whenever it fails to take advantage of every Pareto improvement. As you'll see, government involvement can often help deal with, and even cure, a market failure. But government involvement has costs as well as benefits, and dealing with market failures remains one of the more controversial aspects of economic policy. In this section, we'll look at three different types of market failures: imperfect competition, externalities, and public goods.

IMPERFECT COMPETITION

Earlier in this chapter, you learned that a perfectly competitive market will produce the economically efficient level of output—all Pareto improvements will be made. But you also saw that under *imperfect* competition, firms produce too little output and leave opportunities for mutual gain unexploited. The inefficiency arises because the marginal value of a good to a consumer is the price she pays. But in an imperfectly competitive market, price is greater than marginal cost. Therefore, producing another unit would benefit some consumer more than it would cost some firm. In our earlier example, the equilibrium price of cornflakes was $3.00 per box, while the marginal cost was $1.00 per box. Thus, producing an extra box of cornflakes would benefit some consumer by $3.00, but would cost some firm only $1.00 to produce. Both could come out ahead if the additional box was produced and sold for any price between $1.00 and $3.00.

Will this mutual gain occur? Probably not. Unless breakfast cereal companies can price discriminate in a major way (which is doubtful—see Chapter 8), lowering the price on one box of cornflakes would require lowering the price on *all* boxes. And this would make the company's overall profit decrease. Therefore, the additional cereal will not be produced—the Pareto improvement will not take place.

Can the government change an imperfectly competitive market—like the market for cornflakes—into a competitive one? Is there some other correction that would prevent the inefficiency of overpricing? The answers to both questions are unqualified maybes. Antitrust law provides some tools for increasing the amount of competition in a market. And regulation can lower a price to the level of marginal cost, by replacing the market price with a price set by a regulator.

But for most goods and services, it is unlikely that either antitrust law or regulation would ever be used to correct the inefficiency. To bring antitrust law into play, a company must be suspected of specific illegal acts, and these must be provable in court. But the most common violations of antitrust law involve *tacit* collusion, which is notoriously difficult to prove. Moreover, charging a price greater than marginal cost does not necessarily imply collusion or anti-competitive activities. We expect this result whenever a firm faces a downward-sloping demand curve for its output—say, because it produces a differentiating product (Kellogg's cornflakes are viewed differently than similar products produced by Post or Quaker).

What about *regulation?* We could imagine a state breakfast cereal commission. It would have a staff to gather data on the costs of making cornflakes and other cereals and determine, say, once a year, the maximum price that companies could charge. Would we want our government to set up such a commission for breakfast cereals and most other goods? Probably not. The costs of a government bureaucracy to regulate the price of cereal and most other consumer goods would probably exceed the benefits. But for products that account for larger fractions of most families' budgets—and where it is likely that an unregulated price would be far above marginal cost—we often do make use of regulation. This has long been the case for local telephone service and electricity.

EXTERNALITIES

If you live in a dormitory, you have no doubt had the unpleasant experience of trying to study while the stereo in the next room is blasting through your walls—and usually not your choice of music. This may not sound like an economic problem, but it *is* one. The problem is that your neighbor, in deciding to listen to loud music, is considering only the *private* costs (the sacrifice of his own time) and *private* benefits (the enjoyment of music) of his action. He is not considering the harm it causes to you. Indeed, the harm you suffer from not being able to study might be greater than the cost to him of turning down the volume. In this case, his turning down the volume would be a *potential* Pareto improvement, which could be turned into a Pareto improvement by an appropriate side payment. But unless he does turn down the volume, the situation remains inefficient.

When a private action has side effects that affect other people in important ways, we have the problem of *externalities:*

> An **externality** is a by-product of a good or activity that affects someone not *immediately involved in the transaction.*

EXTERNALITY A by-product of a good or activity that affects someone not immediately involved in the transaction.

For example, the by-product of your neighbor blasting his stereo is the noise coming into your room. We call this a *negative* externality, because the by-product is harmful. But notice that the definition of externality is not limited to harmful effects. When the by-product is *beneficial* to a third party, it is a *positive* externality. We'll consider examples of positive externalities a bit later.

Negative externalities often arise in social situations. If you are doing a group project, someone who likes to hear himself talk may dominate the conversation and prevent others in the group from making progress. The talker is considering the private costs and benefits of his action (to continue speaking), but not the extra time costs imposed on the group as a whole. In cases like these, rules, social conventions of politeness, or side payments can often solve the problem. In the group project, a reminder might be enough to keep everyone's comments short and to the point. In the case of the loud stereo, a request to turn down the volume might be sufficient, or the dorm might establish a rule forbidding the blasting of a stereo between certain hours. If all else fails, you might offer an implicit side payment: telling your neighbor that you'd be happy to lend him some of your CDs if he would just keep the volume down.

But when negative externalities arise in *markets* with large numbers of affected people, the problem can rarely be solved with social conventions, simple rules, or side payments. Earlier in this chapter, we saw an example of an externality—the dry cleaner whose fumes annoyed the tenants in an apartment building. We showed that getting the dry cleaner to move would be a *potential* Pareto improvement, and could be a Pareto improvement with the appropriate side payment. But chances are, where business is concerned, no social convention or universally accepted rule will get the dry cleaner out. And side payments to the dry cleaner may be problematic. Just because the apartment dwellers would be *willing* to compensate the dry cleaner for his loss doesn't mean that they can actually arrange the necessary side payment. On order for this to happen, somebody must have the idea of collective action, negotiate with the parties involved, and then collect money from each tenant. With 100 tenants, that will be quite a difficult undertaking. Some tenants may try to get a free ride—refusing to pay, reasoning that if most others pay up, the dry cleaner will move anyway, and the nonpaying tenants get the benefit for free. This *free rider problem* stands in the way of many Pareto improvements. This is why we typically turn to government to deal with externalities that are important and affect many people.

DEALING WITH A NEGATIVE EXTERNALITY. Many negative externalities result from some kind of *pollution*. The blaring stereo is noise pollution—the addition of undesirable noise to your environment. Cities pollute rivers and lakes with sewage, and industries pollute them with chemicals. Cars and power plants pollute the atmosphere. As you are about to see, pollution—like other negative externalities—creates inefficiency.

Let's consider one of the biggest issues in pollution. Evidence has accumulated that burning any product containing carbon—coal, oil, or even wood—pollutes the world's atmosphere. Carbon dioxide, the pollutant, is harmful because of the greenhouse effect. Extra carbon dioxide in the atmosphere traps the sun's heat and increases the average temperature of the earth.

Figure 5 illustrates the inefficiency that results from uncontrolled burning of coal to generate electricity (by far the main use of coal in the United States). In the figure, we assume that the market for coal-generated electricity is perfectly competitive. The supply curve reflects the marginal costs of producing electricity *to some firm*. We can call this the *marginal private cost*, since it ignores any costs to the general public, such as the health and environmental damage caused by pollution.

The demand curve, *D*, reflects the *marginal private benefit* of the good. It tells us the value that consumers place on the good when they consider the benefits to themselves only. Without any control of carbon dioxide pollution, competitive market equilibrium occurs at point *A,* where the supply curve *S* and the demand curve intersect. At this point, the private benefit of the last unit produced is equal to its private cost of production. If there were no externality, this point would be efficient, as we discussed earlier in this chapter.

But this is not the economically efficient output level. Why? Because each unit produced causes harm in the form of carbon dioxide pollution, and that is not being considered in the market. Let's suppose that each kilowatt-hour (kwh) of electricity imposes a cost on the world economy of \$0.05. The curve labeled *MSC* tells us the *marginal social cost* of electricity, which is equal to marginal private cost plus

FIGURE 5   A NEGATIVE EXTERNALITY

At point *A*, the market for electricity is in equilibrium. However, the generation of electricity creates pollution, imposing a cost on society of $0.05 per kilowatt-hour. The equilibrium at point *A* is inefficient because the marginal social cost (*MSC*) of $0.15 per kilowatt-hour exceeds the marginal private (and social) benefit of $0.10. The government could remedy this externality by imposing a tax equal to the cost of the pollution created. This would shift the supply curve to *MSC* = *S* + tax. In the new equilibrium at point *B*, marginal social cost equals marginal social benefit; that is efficient.

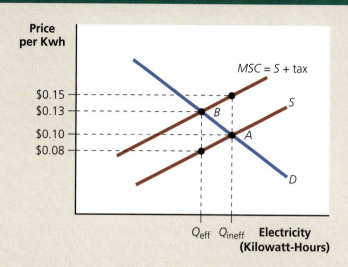

$0.05. Notice that the *MSC* curve lies *above* the market supply curve. Since there are no important benefits to the public other than those enjoyed by consumers of electricity, we can assume that the *marginal social benefit*—the marginal private benefit plus the marginal benefits to the general public—is the same as the marginal private benefit curve to consumers—the market demand curve.

Once we draw the separate *MSC* curve in Figure 5, we discover a problem: At the equilibrium output level (point *A*), the marginal social cost of $0.15 is greater than the marginal social benefit (and marginal private benefit) of $0.10. That is, the last unit of electricity produced in this market costs society more than it benefits society. As you are about to see, this is inefficient.

> *A market with a negative externality associated with producing or consuming a good will be inefficient. In market equilibrium, the marginal costs to all parties exceeds the marginal benefit to all parties.*

Let's demonstrate this general conclusion in the market for electricity. We'll do this by coming up with a potential Pareto improvement—a change in output away from point A—that does not occur. Suppose the electric utility were to produce one less kwh. The consumer who gives up this kwh would lose a marginal benefit of $0.10. But now suppose he receives a side payment of $0.08 from the utility and $0.04 from society at large, for a total of $0.12. The electric utility pays $0.08 of the side payment, but avoids a marginal production cost of $0.10. And the people of the world pay the remaining $0.04 of the side payment, while gaining a marginal benefit of $0.05 from the reduced carbon dioxide pollution. We can fill out our usual Pareto improvement scorecard as follows:

Action: A Consumer Uses One Less kwh and Is Given a Side Payment of $0.08 from the Utility and $0.04 from Society in General

Electric utility	Gains cost saving from producing 1 less kwh:	$0.10
	Pays share of side payment:	0.08
	Comes out ahead by:	$0.02
Electricity customer	Receives side payment of:	$0.12
	Loses electricity benefits worth:	0.10
	Comes out ahead by:	$0.02
Humankind	Gains benefits from less pollution worth:	$0.05
	Pays share of side payment:	0.04
	Comes out ahead by:	$0.01

We've just demonstrated that, in the market for electricity, point *A* is inefficient. Now consider point *B*. At this point, the marginal *social* cost of generating electricity equals the marginal benefit of $0.13 per kwh. The marginal private cost is $0.08 per kwh, and the negative externality still costs society $0.05 per kwh. This point is efficient. A reduction of another kwh of electricity production would deprive a consumer of electricity he valued at $0.13. It would release resources at the electric utility worth only $0.08, so that is the maximum side payment the utility could make without being harmed. Finally, the maximum side payment that could come from the general public—without causing them a loss—would be $0.05. Thus, the maximum possible side payment that could be paid to the consumer is $0.08 + $0.05 = $0.13, which is just enough to compensate the consumer for the loss of the electricity. No one comes out ahead in this move, so there is no reason to make it! At point *B*, all potential Pareto improvements have been exploited—the market has reached its efficient point.

Now, how can we get this efficient result? If we thought it was unlikely that 100 tenants could get together to make a side payment, how could the 6 billion members of humankind bring it off? Only through government action. Indeed, governments of the world are now turning their attention to carbon dioxide pollution.

One method government could use to move the electricity market to point *B* would be a tax. In Figure 5, suppose the government imposed a tax equal to $0.05—the harm caused by each additional kwh of electricity. Then, in addition to paying for its other inputs, each firm in this market would have to pay an additional $0.05 to the government. This would raise each firm's marginal cost of production by $0.05—that is, it would make the marginal *private* cost equal to the marginal *social* cost. As a result, the market supply curve would shift upward from the curve labeled *S* in the figure to the curve labeled *MSC = S + tax*. Notice that, as a result of the tax, the new market supply curve intersects the demand curve at the efficient point *B*. Once the tax is imposed, the market will *automatically* reach the economically efficient output level—point *B*.

> *A tax equal to the difference between marginal social cost and marginal private cost can correct a negative externality and make a market efficient.*

A tax is not the only way to correct a negative externality. The government could instead use regulation to move the electricity market to the efficient point. Regulators could tell coal-burning utilities how much electricity they could make with coal and require them to meet the other needs of their customers with hydroelectric power. (One of the end-of-chapter problems asks you to explore this kind of regulation further.) But whether taxes, regulation, or some other government policy is used, the conclusion remains the same: In the presence of a negative externality, the market, by itself, will produce "too much" output—too much to be efficient. Government interference with the market is needed to decrease output to the efficient level.

DEALING WITH A POSITIVE EXTERNALITY. What about the case of a positive externality, in which the by-product of an activity or a service *benefits* other parties, rather than harms them? Once again, the market will not arrive at the economically efficient output level—but in this case, output will be too *low*. To see why, consider the market for a college education. Each of us, in deciding whether to go to college, takes account of the private costs (tuition, room and board, what we could have earned instead of going to college) and the private benefits (a higher paying and more interesting job in the future, the enjoyment of learning). But by becoming educated, you also benefit other members of society in many ways. For example, you will be a more informed voter and thereby help to steer the government in directions that benefit many people. If you major in chemistry, biology, or mechanical engineering, you may invent something that benefits society at large more than it benefits you. Or you may learn concepts and skills that make you a more responsible member of your community. At a minimum, because you'll earn a higher income, you'll end up paying more in taxes, which benefits society at large. Thus, the market for college education involves a positive externality.

Let's see why a competitive market in college education—with no government interference—would not produce the economically efficient amount of education.

Figure 6 shows the market for bachelor's degrees. Without a policy to correct for the externality, the market will be in equilibrium at point *A*, where the marginal private benefit curve (demand curve) intersects the marginal private cost curve (supply curve). In this equilibrium, the demand curve tells us that the last student who buys a college education values it at $50,000.

But this is not the economically efficient output level. Why? Because each time a student goes to college, the general public benefits in ways that are not being considered in the market. Let's suppose that we can measure these benefits to the general public, and that they amount to $15,000 per additional bachelor's degree. In Figure 6, the curve labeled *MSB* tells us the *marginal social benefit* of another bachelor's degree, which is equal to the marginal private benefit plus $15,000. We'll assume that the marginal social cost of an additional bachelor's degree is the same as the marginal private cost. That is, there are no negative externalities in this market—only positive externalities. Thus, the market supply curve is also the marginal social cost curve.

Now you can see the problem: At the equilibrium (point *A*), the marginal social benefit is greater than the marginal social cost. At point *A*, there are additional students who—if they went to college—would provide additional benefits (to themselves and society) greater than the additional costs. Unless these students go to college, we are not taking advantage of a potential Pareto improvement. Point *A* is not efficient.

More generally,

A market with a positive externality associated with producing or consuming a good will be inefficient. In market equilibrium, the marginal benefit to all parties exceeds the marginal cost to all parties.

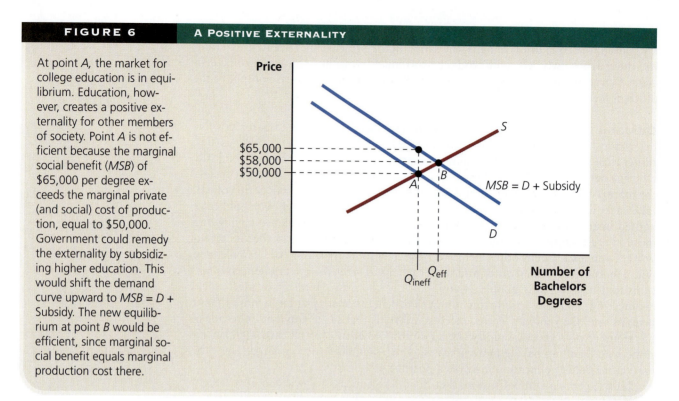

FIGURE 6   **A POSITIVE EXTERNALITY**

At point *A*, the market for college education is in equilibrium. Education, however, creates a positive externality for other members of society. Point *A* is not efficient because the marginal social benefit (*MSB*) of $65,000 per degree exceeds the marginal private (and social) cost of production, equal to $50,000. Government could remedy the externality by subsidizing higher education. This would shift the demand curve upward to *MSB* = *D* + Subsidy. The new equilibrium at point *B* would be efficient, since marginal social benefit equals marginal production cost there.

If you are still not convinced, here is just one example of a Pareto improvement that is not occurring when we are at point *A:* One more student goes to college accompanied by a $10,000 side payment from the people of the United States. The side payment is made to the college, which passes half of it on to the student in the form of a reduction in tuition from $50,000 to $45,000. The following scorecard shows how everyone could gain in this example.

Action: One More Student Goes to College with a $10,000 Side Payment from Society to the College

College student	Gains benefits worth:	$50,000
	Pays:	45,000
	Comes out ahead by:	$ 5,000
College	Receives tuition from student of:	$45,000
	Receives side payment of:	10,000
	Incurs cost of:	50,000
	Comes out ahead by:	$ 5,000
Citizens of the United States	Gain benefits worth:	$15,000
	Pay side payment of:	10,000
	Come out ahead by:	$ 5,000

Now that we know that the market equilibrium at point *A* is inefficient, what point represents the *efficient* output level? The answer is point *B*, where the marginal social benefit of a college education and the marginal social (and private) cost are equal. From point *B*, there are no potential Pareto improvements left to make—no changes in output for which we could find a side payment that would make one person better off and harm no one.

How can we move a market with a positive externality to a more efficient outcome, such as at point *B*?

One answer: the government could subsidize college education by $15,000 per bachelor's degree. The subsidy could be provided to the student or the school; the effect will be the same in either case. In our diagram, we suppose that the subsidy goes to the student. (As an exercise, see if you can draw the diagram for the case where the subsidy goes to the college. Hint: in this case, it will affect the market supply curve, not the market demand curve.)

Once students receive a subsidy of $15,000, the market demand curve will shift upward by $15,000. Whatever price led to a certain number of degrees *before* the subsidy, now that price will be $15,000 higher. That is, if 2 million bachelor's degrees per year were demanded without the subsidy at a price of $50,000 each, then, after the subsidy, the same 2 million degrees would be demanded at a price of $65,000. Of that price, buyers would only be paying $50,000 out of their own pockets, and the rest would be paid by the government. Notice that, as a result of the subsidy, the new market demand curve intersects the supply curve at the efficient point *B*.

> *A subsidy equal to the difference between marginal social benefit and marginal private benefit can correct a positive externality and make a market efficient.*

PUBLIC GOODS

One of the major roles of government in the economy is to provide **public goods.** These are goods that the market *cannot* provide, and *should not* provide, because of their unique characteristics. It is left to the *government* to provide public goods in the efficient quantities, usually free of charge.

To understand what makes a good public, rather than private, let's begin by noting two features of **private goods,** those supplied by private firms in the marketplace. First, a private good is characterized by **rivalry** in consumption—if one person consumes it, someone else cannot. If you rent an apartment, then someone else will *not* be able to rent that apartment. The same applies to virtually all goods that you buy in the marketplace: food, computers, furniture, and so on. Rivalry also applies to privately provided services. For example, the time you spend with your doctor, lawyer, or therapist is time that someone else will *not* spend with that professional.

Most of the goods and services we've considered so far in this text are rival goods. By allowing the market to provide rival goods at a price, we ensure that people will properly take account of the costs of their decisions. If these goods were provided free of charge, people would tend to overconsume them, depriving others who might value the goods even more. Thus, leaving such goods to the market—which will charge a price reflecting their cost—tends to promote economic efficiency. If there are externalities associated with rival goods, they should be corrected by taxes, subsidies, or other government tools. We conclude:

> *If there is rivalry in consumption of a good, the private market should provide it.*

A second feature of a private good is **excludability,** the ability to exclude those who do not pay for a good from consuming it. When you go to the supermarket, you are not permitted to eat raspberries unless you pay for them. The same is true when you go to the movies, purchase a car, or attend college. But imagine a

PUBLIC GOOD A good that private firms cannot, and should not, provide.

PRIVATE GOOD A good that can be, and should be, provided by private firms.

RIVALRY A situation in which one person's consumption of a good or service means that no one else can consume it.

EXCLUDABILITY The ability to exclude those who do not pay for a good from consuming it.

situation in which firms could not prevent nonpayers from consuming a good. Then the market would be *unable* to provide the good, because no firm will willingly offer it for sale. Without excludability, no customer would pay for the good, since it can be consumed with or without paying.

> *Private goods have two characteristics: rivalry and excludability. Rivalry suggests that the market* should *provide the good, and excludability suggests that the market* will *provide the good.*

But not all goods have these two characteristics. Consider, for example, information about the weather. To gather this information requires many resources: satellites, meteorologists, communication facilities, and so on. However, information about the weather is *nonexcludable.* If a private firm supplied weather information, the firm could not limit consumption to those who paid for it. The media would report the information, and people would talk about it. For this reason, a private weather forecasting firm would have difficulty surviving.

"But wait," you may think. "Couldn't the firm *ask* people to contribute according to the importance they place on weather reports?" Yes, but then each individual would have an incentive to downplay its importance and pay nothing. This is the *free rider problem* mentioned earlier in this chapter:

> *When a good is nonexcludable, people have an incentive to become* free riders—*to let* others *pay for the good, so they can enjoy it without paying.*

Privately provided weather reports would face an extremely serious free-rider problem. People would reason that their own contribution would make such a small difference to the information available that, other than moral obligation or a sense of social responsibility, they would have no reason to pay at all. There would be so many free riders, that those who did pay would share a very heavy burden—too heavy to bear. Thus, a private firm would be unable to provide this service at all—it would not be able to stay in business.

> *When a good is nonexcludable, the private sector* will not *provide it. If we want such a good, government must provide it.*

In addition to being nonexcludable, information about the weather—like all information—is *nonrival:* One person can consume or enjoy the good without anyone else consuming or enjoying less of it. If I hear that it will rain tomorrow, that has no effect on your ability to obtain the same information. Moreover, it uses up *no more of society's resources* when an additional person obtains information about the weather. For this reason, even if the private sector *could* somehow charge us according to our consumption of weather reports, it *should not* charge us. Why not? Because by charging a price each time we hear about the weather, it would force each of us to consider a personal cost that does *not* correspond to any opportunity cost for society. Each time an additional person finds out about the weather, a Pareto improvement takes place: The person gains and no one loses. Thus, to be economically efficient, once anyone knows about the weather, *everyone* else who places *any value at all* on this information should get it. But this will only happen if the price of weather reports is *zero.*

This leads us to an important conclusion: Since the economically efficient price for weather reports is zero, private firms—which would have to charge a positive price—should not be the ones to provide it. By charging a positive price, information about the weather would be restricted below the economically efficient level.

> *When a good or service is nonrival, the market cannot provide it efficiently. Rather, to achieve economic efficiency, the good or service should be provided by government—free of charge.*

We've now seen that goods can be either rival or nonrival, and either excludable or nonexcludable. This leads to four possible combinations of characteristics, as shown in the following table:

	Excludability	**Nonexcludability**
Rivalry	**Private good:** Market should and will provide.	Mixed good: Market will not provide at all.
Nonrivalry	Mixed good: Market will provide too little.	**Public good:** Market should not and will not provide.

At the upper left are private goods—the types of goods we've been discussing in earlier chapters. These include bed frames, car washes, soybeans, extermination services, electricity, and so on. The market, possibly assisted by corrections for externalities, will provide them efficiently.

The lower left is a mixed category—a good that is neither purely private nor purely public. This type of good is becoming increasingly important, because it includes most information products. Consider the software produced by Microsoft. The firm has the power to exclude you from using its software, at least in principle. Yet, your use of that software costs Microsoft hardly anything at all—software is so easy to copy that it is effectively a nonrivalrous good. The same reasoning that has led us to make weather reports freely available argues for allowing unlimited free copying of software. But in fact, copying software is a violation of federal copyright law. And we do not generally subsidize the writing of software. Thus, public policy deliberately fails to distribute software efficiently among computer users. Why?

The answer concerns incentives. Unless Microsoft can charge for the use of its software, it would have no incentive to develop new products. The same principle applies to many other information products, such as patented ideas, paintings, books, movies, and trademarks. In the absence of patent protection, no new products would be developed by private firms.

In the upper-right quadrant is another mixed category—a good that is neither purely public nor purely private. In this category, goods are rivalrous—so they *should* be sold for a price—but excludability is difficult or impossible, so the market *will not* provide them. City streets, urban parks, and some important natural resources fall into this category. Economists use the term *tragedy of the commons* to describe the problem that develops when people can't be excluded from using rivalrous goods. In a traditional English village, the commons was an area freely available to all families for grazing their animals. Grazing rights are a rivalrous good—if one cow eats the grass, another cannot. But the commons had no method of exclusion, so it was overgrazed, causing harm to all families.

In modern life, the most important example of the tragedy of the commons is in the use of roads. With few exceptions, government provides us with roads, and we can use them as much as we want, free of charge—they are regarded as largely nonexcludable. Yet space on the road is completely rivalrous—two cars can't use the same place on the road at the same time. As a result, we have the tragedy of the commons: traffic jams at peak times, as commuters overuse roads because they are not taking into account the delays they cause other drivers. On some roads, government or private firms have excluded some users by charging tolls, but these are the exceptions to the rule.

Finally, at the lower right, we find public goods: those that are nonrival—so the private market *should not* provide them—and nonexcludable—so the private market *will not* provide them. Most of us agree that public goods should be provided by government, and governments around the world do so. In addition to the weather service, public goods include national defense, police and fire protection, and the legal and regulatory infrastructure we discussed earlier in this chapter. (See if you can explain why this infrastructure is both nonexcludable and nonrival.)

Keep in mind, though, that just because government provides a good does not automatically make it a "public good" in the economic sense. Some governments in other countries own banks, manufacturing firms, and media companies. These governments provide goods and services, but economists would call them private goods because they are rivalrous and excludable. We categorize goods into public and private based on their *characteristics*, not which sector ends up providing them.

EFFICIENCY AND GOVERNMENT IN PERSPECTIVE

In this chapter, you've seen that an economy with *well-functioning, perfectly competitive markets* tends to be economically efficient. But notice the italicized words. As you've seen in this chapter, many types of government involvement are needed to ensure that markets function well and to deal with market failures. The government helps markets to function by providing a legal and regulatory infrastructure. In extreme cases of imperfect competition, government antitrust action or regulation may be needed. The government imposes taxes and subsidies to deal with externalities. And the government itself steps in to provide goods and services that are nonrival, nonexcludable, or both.

These cases of government involvement are not without controversy. In fact, most of the controversies that pit Democrats against Republicans in the United States (or Conservatives against Labourites in Britain, or Social Democrats against Christian Democrats in Germany) relate to when, and to what extent, the government should be involved in the economy. Debates about public education, social security, international trade, and immigration center on questions of the proper role for government. Some of the disagreement is over the government's role in bringing about a more *fair* economy, but there is also debate about the government's role in bringing about economic efficiency.

These controversies are so heated, and so varied, that it is easy to forget how much *agreement* there is about the role of government. Anyone studying the role of government in the economies of the United States, Canada, Mexico, France, Germany, Britain, Japan, and the vast majority of other developed economies, is struck by one glaring fact: Most economic activity is carried out among private individuals. In all of these countries, there is widespread agreement that—while government intervention is often necessary—the most powerful force that exploits Pareto improvements and drives the economy toward efficiency is the actions of individual producers and consumers.

Until recently, a large part of the world's population—those in communist countries—lived under a different kind of system. The government was involved in almost every aspect of economic activity—telling producers what to produce and how to produce it, and how much to pay for their labor and other resources. And here, too, there is a strong consensus: Government played *too large* a role in the communist countries' economies. In the "Using the Theory" section that follows, you will learn why so many observers have come to this conclusion.

THE COLLAPSE OF COMMUNISM

The economic system of the former Soviet Union—and the system it imposed on many Eastern European nations—was centrally planned socialism. As you learned in Chapter 2, this is a system in which resources are allocated by command and owned by the state. The system was called "communism" because of an official belief in these countries: that one day, their economic system would generate such a wealth of goods and services that scarcity would be eliminated, and all resources would be owned by everyone—communally.

It is true that centrally planned socialism enabled the Soviet Union to marshal the resources necessary to become a superpower. But the system was plagued by so much inefficiency that—far from achieving true communism—it collapsed. While the Soviet Union was rich in natural resources, physical capital and human capital, production per worker was only about a third of its level in the United States. How did the Soviet economy actually work? Here were some of its key features:

- *Resource ownership:* With few exceptions, the state owned all factories, land, and capital equipment.
- *Resource allocation:* By command. Planners in Moscow set thousands of output targets and allocated the resources that the state felt were needed to achieve them. Since the output of one firm was the input of another, firms were heavily interdependent, and state planners took their output targets very seriously.
- *Prices of consumer goods:* Set by the state. In part, planners attempted to equate the demand for each good with the supply (the state's output target). But in practice, this usually proved impossible. Shortages and surpluses were regular occurrences.
- *Price of raw materials and resources:* Set by the state; often deviating widely above and below marginal cost.
- *Wages:* Set by the state, with heavy emphasis on equity.

Running the economy from Moscow never worked the way the authorities wanted it to. One reason was sheer complexity: Tens of thousands of plants needed to be told what to produce, how to produce it, in what quantities, with how much of each input, and which firms and stores to deliver the output to. When one plant failed to meet its output target, shortages cascaded throughout the economy, paralyzing sectors dependent on that plant.

A famous example occurred in 1989, when the plant that produced locomotives for the entire Soviet economy reached only 75 percent of its target. When Moscow planners investigated, they found out why: The plant that made *engines* for locomotives had reached only 75 percent of *its* target. Why? Because the engine plant couldn't get enough raw materials to meet *its* target. Why? Because the train system was running so poorly, in part because of a shortage of locomotives!

To prevent gridlock like this, Moscow did everything it could to ensure that output targets were satisfied, often regardless of cost. Managers faced serious consequences if they fell short of their output target—at some times in Soviet history, they faced long prison terms—but they incurred little penalty for any other poor management practices, since the state was so heavily focused on the output targets.

As a result, firms wasted many inputs. The system did not harness the powerful incentive of profit maximization. If a manager ran out of inputs, he just asked the state planning agency to give him more. There was no way for the planning agency to verify whether the manager of, say, a radio factory truly *needed* more copper wire, whether he was doing a poor job of managing, or even whether he was selling copper wire on the side.

Further, if a manager actually was able to produce his target output one year by using *less* than his allocated amounts of inputs, the planning agency had a habit of "ratcheting" his input allocation down the next year. For example, if an automobile factory was able to produce its target number of cars with 10 percent less steel than it was allocated, it would likely find that its steel allocation was 10 percent lower the next year. This gave the manager of the auto factory an incentive to make sure all allocated steel was used up, even if it meant wasting some steel to do so. Hotels would burn off heating fuel on hot days to make sure that they weren't caught with extra gas or coal at the end of the year.

In other words, compared to market economies, the Soviet economy did a poor job of solving the principal-agent problem discussed in Chapter 6. The backup systems that help in the U.S. economy if managers perform poorly—shareholder revolts and takeovers—had no counterparts under communism. Soviet managers—as agents of the planners—could continue to do whatever they wanted, as long as they satisfied their output targets and made it seem to the distant central planners that they were doing a good job.

In addition to not making the best use of inputs within firms, inputs were allocated *among* firms in an inefficient manner. For example, every plant manager had an incentive to *hoard labor*—to keep more on hand than was needed. Since firms had no private owners, there was no one to complain about the extra cost of the unneeded labor. But having extra workers made it easier to take care of emergency production—such as when the state suddenly asked the firm to increase its production because some other firm needed more inputs. As a result, some plants had excess labor, while others suffered a severe shortage. Shifting workers from one firm to another could have increased the production of some goods, without decreasing the production of any other. But such shifts rarely took place, because managers with excess labor had no incentive to give it up to some other firm.

Finally, while households were free to buy whatever goods they wished with their state-determined incomes, many goods were unavailable. When anything went wrong in the plan—say, the electricity industry fell short of its monthly output target—it was always the consumer who suffered. The state would ensure that all *industries* that needed electricity got it—if those industries didn't get it, the shortage could threaten the entire structure of the plan. So instead, the state would simply make less available to *households*. The same occurred with other products that served as both consumer goods and inputs for other firms—pencils, paper, wood, gasoline, cooking oil, sugar, and more. In a market economy, if the supply of some good decreases, its price will rise, and consumers will economize on its use, trying to find substitutes instead. But in the Soviet economy, all prices were set by the state. A decrease in supply simply meant a shortage. Most Soviets carried collapsible shopping bags all of the time just in case something to buy became available.

While the Soviet system suffered shortages of many consumer goods, it also had surpluses of others, especially shoes, shirts, suits, and dresses that no one wanted because they were shabby or out of style. Central planners had enough trouble coming up with a *consistent* plan—one where some firms produced enough inputs to enable other firms to produce enough outputs. They spent little time trying to make their plan coincide with consumer preferences.

In sum, the Soviets tried to rely on a *visible* hand, rather than relying on the automatic mechanisms of the *invisible* hand. In the end, this proved too daunting a task, and the system was extremely inefficient. Many important Pareto improvements that would have taken place in a market economy did not—or could not—take place in the Soviet economy. Since resources were scarce (as in *any* country), forgoing so many opportunities to make people better off led to a much lower standard of living than the Soviet Union should have had. The standard of living was not only low relative to the West, but—beginning in the 1980s—it began to *grow* much more slowly than the West's as well. It became clear to Soviet leaders that their country was falling further and further behind with each passing year. As fax and copying machines, videotapes, and other modern methods of communication made it possible to learn about life in other, better-organized countries, Soviet citizens became more and more disaffected and cynical about their own system.

Now Russia and the other countries that made up the Soviet Union are trying to convert to market economies. This task, as well, is proving difficult. One of the reasons for the difficulty was discussed in Chapter 5's "Using the Theory" section: Under communism, it made sense to build huge factories that could produce enough to satisfy the entire Soviet Union's need for particular products. But now, with the transition to a market system, the owners of these plants are monopolists, charging inefficiently high prices.

Moreover, in market economies, the invisible hand operates within an infrastructure of laws and institutions provided by the government. While many Eastern European nations have had great success building this infrastructure, the nations of the former Soviet Union—which have been communist the longest—are having great difficulty. For example, Russia lacks systems for enforcing contracts that are taken for granted in market economies. In some cases, the inability to enforce contracts prevents deals from being reached—and valuable production does not take place. It is a sad fact that eight years after the demise of communism, output in Russia was still below the level it had attained under central planning.

SUMMARY

A market or an economy is economically efficient when it does not waste any opportunities to make people better off. A more specific definition of economic efficiency follows from two related concepts. A Pareto improvement is any change in the economy that makes at least one person better off without making anyone else worse off. A *potential* Pareto improvement is any change in the economy in which the benefits to the gainers are greater than the losses to those harmed. Any potential Pareto improvement—if accompanied by an appropriate side payment—can be converted into a Pareto improvement. Economic efficiency is achieved when all Pareto improvements and potential Pareto improvements have been made. Unless this condition is met, there are wasted opportunities to make some people better off without harming anyone.

Under certain conditions, we can expect markets to give us the efficient level of output of a good. These conditions include: (1) a proper legal and regulatory infrastructure to enable trading to take place, (2) perfect competition, (3) no significant impacts on third parties, and (4) a rivalrous and excludable good. If any of these conditions are violated, government can often step in and make the economy more efficient.

The legal system run by governments is a key element of institutional infrastructure. Criminal law limits exchanges to voluntary ones. Property law contributes to enforceable property rights. Contract law helps improve the efficiency of exchange when one party must go first, while tort law affects interactions among strangers. Finally, antitrust law attempts to prevent harm to consumers from limited competition. In addition to the legal system, the government's regulatory system affects many aspects of economic life.

A market failure occurs when a market, left to itself, fails to achieve economic efficiency. Imperfect competition, externalities, and public goods are examples of market failures. Governments have a variety of tools to correct these failures. Through antitrust action and regulation, governments can sometimes narrow the gap between price and marginal cost in imperfectly competitive markets. Externalities—by-products of economic transactions that affect outsiders—can be corrected through taxes or subsidies. And public goods—those that are nonrival and nonexcludable—can be provided by government itself.

K E Y   T E R M S

Pareto improvement
economic efficiency
potential Pareto improvement

market failure
externality

public good
private good

rivalry
excludability

R E V I E W   Q U E S T I O N S

1. Which of the following actions would be a Pareto improvement? A potential Pareto improvement? Both a Pareto improvement *and* a potential Pareto improvement?
   a. You buy a Coke at the airport restaurant, where it costs $4.00.
   b. You and a friend go to a movie and compromise on which one to see.
   c. An acquaintance who values your tennis racket more than you do borrows it and never returns it.

2. Explain why imperfect competition leads to inefficient outcomes.

3. Explain how each of the following enhances economic efficiency:
   a. Criminal law
   b. Property law
   c. Contract law
   d. Tort law
   e. Antitrust law

4. What specific actions are forbidden by antitrust law?

5. How does regulation differ from court decisions in its effect upon business?

6. What is a market failure? What are some main causes of market failure?

7. What is an externality? Give one example each of a positive and a negative externality not mentioned in the chapter. What are the effects of positive and negative externalities in the absence of government intervention?

8. What is a public good? How is a public good different from a private good?

9. What is the free rider problem?

P R O B L E M S   A N D   E X E R C I S E S

1. In each of the following situations, identify a potential Pareto improvement that is unexploited. Explain what can be done to permit the potential Pareto improvement to be realized. In each case, would your solution be a Pareto improvement? Why might governments want to prevent such Pareto improvements?
   a. You are a low-income individual who receives food stamps from the government. Food stamps cannot be used to purchase nonfood items (e.g., paper towels). You wish to buy some paper towels.
   b. In some cities, the government limits the rent that can be charged for apartments. You wish to rent a rent-controlled apartment. The controlled rent is below the equilibrium rent, and many other people also desire to rent this apartment. You have an appointment with the superintendent of the building to see the apartment.

2. There are 30 students in an economics class. Each student likes doughnuts—all types, and the more the better. But

they differ in their preferences. Half of the students prefer chocolate doughnuts to plain. The other half of the students prefer plain to chocolate. The instructor wishes to give away all the doughnuts he has. Explain whether the actions in parts (a) through (c) result in a situation that is economically efficient.
   a. The instructor brings in 60 doughnuts (all plain) and gives them to a single student; no other student receives any doughnuts.
   b. The instructor brings in 60 doughnuts (all plain) and gives two to each student.
   c. The instructor brings in 60 doughnuts (half plain, half chocolate) and gives two (one of each kind) to each student.

   For any allocation of donuts you identify as inefficient, describe a Pareto-improving trade.

3. Look back at Figure 2—the market for oranges. Suppose the government imposes a price floor of $0.25 per or-

ange. What would the new price and quantity be? Is that result efficient? If not, describe the nature of the inefficiency by identifying a Pareto improvement that is not being exploited.

4. Suppose Douglas and Ziffel have properties that adjoin the farm of Mr. Haney. The current zoning law permits Haney to use the farm for any purpose. Haney has decided to raise pigs (the best use of the land). A pig farm will earn $50,000 per year, forever. Douglas and Ziffel, however, do not like pigs: not the sight of them, not the smell of them, and certainly not the constant squealing.
   a. Suppose the next best use of Haney's property is residential, where it could earn $20,000 per year. What is the minimum yearly payment Haney would accept to agree to restrict his land for residential use forever?
   b. Suppose Douglas is willing to pay $20,000 per year for an end to pig farming on Haney's land, while Ziffel is willing to pay no more than $15,000 per year. (For some reason, Ziffel does not mind pig farming as much as Douglas does.) If Douglas pays Haney $20,000 and Ziffel pays Haney $15,000 per year, is this a Pareto improvement? Who benefits, who loses, and by how much?
   c. If Douglas pays $15,000 and Ziffel pays $15,000 per year, is this move a Pareto improvement? Who benefits, who loses, and by how much?

5. When a negative externality creates an inefficiency, the government can sometimes correct the inefficiency by imposing a tax, as shown in Figure 5. An alternative approach is regulation. Suppose the electricity market in Figure 5 is in equilibrium at point A. The government wishes to correct the externality by imposing an upper limit on each firm, in order to limit the total electricity generated in the market.
   a. What total quantity should it choose as the upper limit in this market?
   b. How would imposing that limit change the diagram?
   c. Would regulating firms in this way (giving each an upper limit on production) correct the inefficiency?

6. Classify each of the following goods, using your best judgment as to whether it is (a) rival or nonrival, and (b) excludable or nonexcludable.

a. Parks in a residential neighborhood
b. Military defense
c. Food
d. Clothing
e. Shelter
f. Health care

7. Give an example of a public good that is not provided by the government. Give an example of a good that is provided by government but is not a public good.

8. Last year, Pat and Chris occupied separate apartments. Each consumed 400 gallons of hot water monthly. This year, they are sharing an apartment. To their surprise, they find that they are using a total of 1,000 gallons per month between them. Why?

9. Many universities subsidize their football teams. That is, if ticket sales are insufficient to cover the cost of the football program, the university makes up the difference. Are there positive externalities that justify the use of a subsidy? If so, what are those externalities, and who are the third parties who benefit from them?

10. In this chapter, you learned that the Environmental Protection Agency (EPA) plays an important regulatory role in the economy. Go to the EPA Web site, at http://www.epa.gov, and click on "Laws and Regulations." Browse the page, then, at the bottom, click on the "dozen major laws" forming the legal basis of EPA programs. Pick one of the dozen that interests you most, and read the summary provided.
   a. What kind of market failure is the law intended to address? If it is intended to remedy an externality, is it a positive or a negative externality? Is the externality associated with production, consumption, or both?
   b. As it is formulated, do you see the law providing an appropriate remedy to the problem it is intended to address? Explain why or why not.

CHALLENGE QUESTIONS

1. A monopoly supplier of electricity faces a demand curve given by $P = 15 - Q$ where P is price in cents per kilowatt-hour of electricity and Q is thousands of kilowatt-hours produced and sold. The marginal revenue (MR) curve is $MR = 15 - 2Q$, and the marginal cost of producing a kilowatt-hour of electricity is constant at $MC = 5$ (i.e., $0.05 per kilowatt-hour).

a. What are the equilibrium price and quantity?
b. The government wishes to negotiate a special price at which an additional 2,000 kilowatt-hours of electricity will be sold to low-income households. The special price will have no effect on the price charged to existing customers. What is the maximum price per kilowatt-hour the utility can charge and still expect to

sell the extra electricity? What is the minimum price it would be willing to accept?

c.   Would moving to this two-tiered pricing system be a Pareto improvement? Explain why or why not. Develop a scorecard to illustrate your conclusion.

2.   In class, one student frequently asks questions, engages the instructor in long discussions, and so on.

a.   Does his behavior involve positive externalities? Negative externalities? Both? Neither? (Be clear about the assumptions you are making to arrive at your answers.)

b.   Is the result efficient? If not, what kinds of "solutions" can you suggest?

3.   Figure 3 shows an inefficient level of output produced by a monopolistically competitive supplier of cornflakes. Suppose the government imposed a tax of $2 per box of cornflakes. Would the tax affect the level of output produced by that firm? Would the result still be inefficient?

CHAPTER
11

INTRODUCTION TO MACROECONOMICS

You have no doubt seen images of the Earth taken from satellites thousands of miles away. Viewed from that great distance, the world's vast oceans look like mere puddles, its continents like mounds of dirt, and its mountain ranges like wrinkles on a bedspread. In contrast to our customary view from the Earth's surface—of a car, a tree, a building—this is a view of the big picture.

What, you may be wondering, could this possibly have to do with economics? Actually, quite a bit: These two different ways of viewing the Earth—from up close or from thousands of miles away—are analogous to two different ways of viewing the economy. When we look through the *micro*economic lens—from up close—we see the behavior of *individual decision makers* and *individual markets*. When we look through the *macro*economic lens—from a distance—these smaller features fade away, and we see only the broad outlines of the economy.

Which view is better? That depends on what we're trying to do. If we want to know why rents are so high in big cities, why computers are getting better and cheaper each year, or why the earnings of anesthesiologists are falling, we need the close-up view of microeconomics. But to answer questions about the *overall* economy—What determines the amount of unemployment? How fast will the average standard of living rise over the next decade? How fast will prices rise?—we need the more comprehensive view of *macro*economics.

MACROECONOMIC CONCERNS

While there is some disagreement among economists about *how* to make the macroeconomy perform well, there is widespread agreement about the goals we are trying to achieve:

> *Economists—and society at large—agree on three important macroeconomic goals: rapid economic growth, full employment, and stable prices.*

Why is there such universal agreement on these three goals? Because achieving them gives us the opportunity to make *all* of our citizens better off. Let's take a closer look at each of these goals and see why they are so important.

RAPID ECONOMIC GROWTH

Imagine that you were a typical American worker living at the beginning of this century. You would work about 60 hours every week, and your yearly salary—about $450—would buy a bit less than $8,000 would buy today. You could expect to die at the age of 47. If you fell seriously ill before then, your doctor wouldn't be able to help much: There were no x-ray machines or blood tests and little effective medicine for the few diseases that could be diagnosed. You would probably never hear the sounds produced by the best musicians of the day, or see the performances of the best actors, dancers, or singers. And the most exotic travel you'd enjoy would likely be a trip to a nearby state.

Today, the typical worker has it considerably better. He or she works about 35 hours per week, for an average yearly income of about $25,000, not to mention fringe benefits like health insurance, retirement benefits, and paid vacation. Thanks to advances in medicine, nutrition, and hygiene, the average man can expect to live to 73, and the average woman to 80. And more of a worker's free time today is really free: There are machines to do laundry and dishes, cars to get to and from work, telephones for quick communication, and—increasingly—personal computers to keep track of finances, appointments, and correspondence. Finally, during their lifetimes, most Americans will have traveled—for enjoyment—to many locations in the United States and abroad.

What is responsible for these dramatic changes in economic well-being? The answer is three words: *Rapid economic growth*. In the United States—as in most developed economies—our output of goods and services has risen faster than the population. As a result, the average person can consume much more today—more food, clothing, housing, medical care, entertainment, and travel—than at the turn of the century.

Economists monitor economic growth by keeping track of *real gross domestic product (real GDP)*—the total quantity of goods and services produced in a country over a year. When real GDP rises faster than the population, output per person rises and so does the average standard of living.

Figure 1 shows real GDP in the United States from 1920 to 1998. As you can see, real GDP has increased dramatically over the greater part of this century. Part of the reason for the rise is an increase in population: More workers can produce more output. But real GDP has actually increased *faster* than the population: During this period, while the U.S. population has not quite tripled, the quantity of goods and services we produce each year has increased more than tenfold, hence, the remarkable rise in the average American's living standard.

But when we look closer, we see something disturbing: Although output per person continues to grow, its *rate* of growth has decreased since the 1970s. From 1950 to 1973, output per person grew, on average, by 2.6 percent per year. But from 1973 to 1998, growth slowed to 1.6 percent annually. This may seem like a very slight difference, hardly worthy of the term "slowdown." But over long peri-

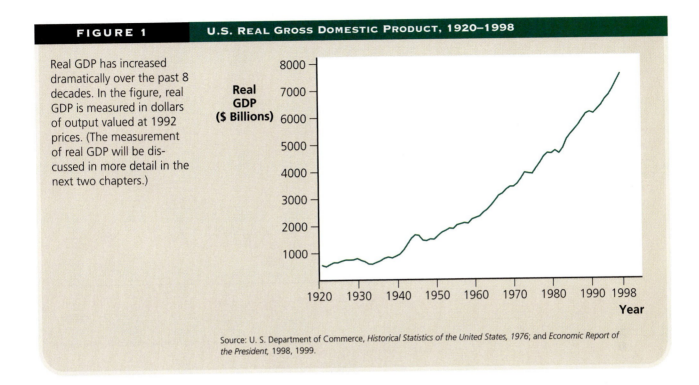

FIGURE 1   **U.S. REAL GROSS DOMESTIC PRODUCT, 1920–1998**

Real GDP has increased dramatically over the past 8 decades. In the figure, real GDP is measured in dollars of output valued at 1992 prices. (The measurement of real GDP will be discussed in more detail in the next two chapters.)

Source: U. S. Department of Commerce, *Historical Statistics of the United States, 1976*; and *Economic Report of the President*, 1998, 1999.

ods of time, such small differences in growth rates can cause huge differences in living standards. For example, suppose that from 1973 to 1998, output per person had grown at its previous pace of 2.6 percent per year instead of its actual rate of 1.6 percent. Then—over those 24 years—every man, woman, and child would have been able to consume an additional $23,000 in goods and services, valued at today's prices. (Think what you could do with an additional $23,000.) Economists and government officials are very concerned with the slowdown in growth.

Because growth increases the size of the economic pie, it becomes possible—at least in principle—for every citizen to have a larger slice. This is why economists agree that growth is a good thing. But in practice, growth does *not* benefit everyone. Living standards will always rise more rapidly for some groups than for others, and some may even find their slice of the pie shrinking. For example, since the late 1980s, economic growth has improved the living standards of the highly skilled, while less-skilled workers have actually become worse off. Partly, this is due to improvements in technology that have lowered the earnings of workers whose roles can be taken by computers and machines. But very few economists would advocate a halt to growth as a solution to the problems of unskilled workers. Some believe that, in the long run, everyone will indeed benefit from growth. Others see a role for the government in taxing successful people and providing benefits to those left behind by growth. But in either case, economic growth—by increasing the size of the overall pie—is seen as an important part of the solution.

HIGH EMPLOYMENT

Economic growth is one of our most important goals, but not the only one. Suppose our real GDP were growing at, say, a 3 percent annual rate, but 10 percent

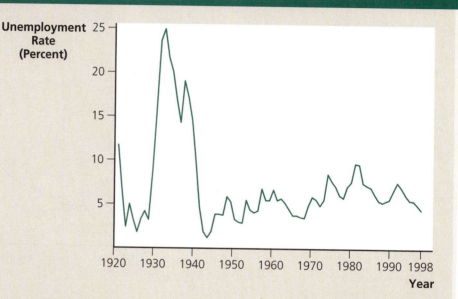

FIGURE 2   **U.S. UNEMPLOYMENT RATE, 1920–1998**

The unemployment rate fluctuates over time. During the Great Depression of the 1930s, it was extremely high, reaching 25 percent in 1933. In the early 1980s, the rate reached around 10 percent, but by the late 1990s, it had declined to just above 4 percent.

Source: Stanley Lebergott, *Manpower in Economic Growth: An American Record Since 1800* (New York, N.Y.: McGraw Hill Book Co., 1964), and *Economic Report of the President,* 1998, 1999.

of the workforce was unable to find work. Although the economy would be growing at a healthy pace, we would not be achieving our full economic potential—our average standard of living would not be as high as it *could be.* There would be millions of people who wanted jobs, who *could* be producing output we could all use, but who would not be producing anything. This is one reason why consistently *high employment*—or consistently *low unemployment*—is an important macroeconomic goal.

But there is another reason, too. In addition to its impact on our average standard of living, unemployment also affects the distribution of economic well-being among our citizens. People who cannot find jobs suffer. Their incomes—and their ability to buy goods and services—decrease. And even though many of the jobless receive unemployment benefits and other assistance from the government, the unemployed typically have lower living standards than the employed.

One measure economists use to keep track of employment is the *unemployment rate*—the percentage of the workforce that would like to work, but cannot find jobs. Figure 2 shows the average unemployment rate during each of the past 79 years. Notice that the unemployment rate is never zero—there are always some people looking for work, even when the economy is doing well. But in some years, unemployment is unusually high. The worst example occurred during the Great Depression of the 1930s, when millions of workers lost their jobs and the unemployment rate reached 25 percent: One in four potential workers could not find a job. More recently, in 1981 and 1982, the average unemployment rate reached almost 10 percent.

The nation's commitment to high employment has twice been written into law. With the memory of the Great Depression still fresh, Congress passed the Employment Act of 1946, which required the federal government to "promote maximum

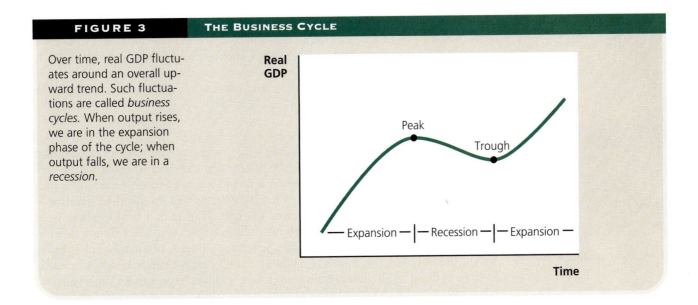

| FIGURE 3 | THE BUSINESS CYCLE |

Over time, real GDP fluctuates around an overall upward trend. Such fluctuations are called *business cycles*. When output rises, we are in the expansion phase of the cycle; when output falls, we are in a *recession*.

Real GDP

Peak

Trough

— Expansion —│— Recession —│— Expansion —

Time

employment, production, and purchasing power." It did not, however, dictate a target rate of unemployment the government should aim for. A numerical target was added in 1978, when Congress passed the Full Employment and Balanced Growth Act, which called for an unemployment rate of 4 percent.

A glance at Figure 2 shows how seldom we have hit this target over the last few decades. In fact, we did not hit it at all through the 1970s and 1980s, although we came close in the late 1990s. In future chapters, you will learn why the unemployment rate has often been higher than its target, and what the government can and cannot do to achieve its goal of low unemployment.

EMPLOYMENT AND THE BUSINESS CYCLE. When firms produce more output, they hire more workers; when they produce less output, they tend to lay off workers. We would thus expect real GDP and employment to be closely related, and indeed they are. In recent years, each 1 percent drop in output has been associated with the loss of about half a million jobs. Consistently high employment, then, requires a high, stable level of output. Unfortunately, output has *not* been very stable. If you look back at Figure 1, you will see that while real GDP has climbed upward over time, it has been a bumpy ride. The periodic fluctuations in GDP—the bumps in the figure—are called **business cycles.**

Figure 3 shows a close-up view of a hypothetical business cycle. When output rises, we are in the **expansion** phase, which continues until we reach a **peak.** Then, as output falls, we enter a **recession**—a period of declining or abnormally low output. When output hits bottom, we are in the **trough** of the recession.

Of course, real-world business cycles never look quite like the smooth, symmetrical cycle in Figure 3, but rather like the jagged, irregular cycles of Figure 1. Recessions can be severe or mild, and they can last several years or less than a single year. When a recession is particularly severe and long lasting, it is called a **depression.** In the twentieth century, the United States experienced just one decline in output serious enough to be considered a depression—the worldwide Great Depression of the 1930s. From 1929 to 1933, the first four years of the Great Depression, U.S. output dropped by almost half.

BUSINESS CYCLES Fluctuations in real GDP around its long-term growth trend.

EXPANSION A period of increasing real GDP.

PEAK The point at which real GDP reaches its highest level during an expansion.

RECESSION A period of declining or abnormally low real GDP.

TROUGH The point at which real GDP reaches its lowest level during a recession.

DEPRESSION An unusually severe recession.

Economic Statistics Briefing Room
Links to a wealth of macroeconomic information produced by Federal agencies.
http://www.whitehouse.gov/fsbr/esbr.html

But even during more normal times, the economy has gone through many recessions. Since 1959, we have suffered through two severe recessions (in 1974–1975 and 1981–1982) and several less severe ones, such as the recession of 1990 to 1991. Later in this book, you will learn about some of the causes of recessions, why we cannot seem to eliminate them entirely, and what we *may* be able to do to make them milder in the future.

STABLE PRICES

Figure 4 shows the annual inflation rate—the percentage increase in the average level of prices—from 1922 to 1998.[1] With very few exceptions, the inflation rate has been positive—on average, prices have risen in each of those years. But notice the wide variations in inflation: In 1979 and 1980, we had double-digit inflation—prices were rising by 10 percent or more per year. During that time, polls showed that people were more concerned about inflation than any other national problem—more than unemployment, crime, poverty, pollution, or anything else. In the 1990s, the inflation rate has averaged less than 3 percent per year, and we hardly seem to notice it at all. Pollsters no longer even include "rising prices" as a category when asking about the most important problems facing the country.

Other countries have not been so lucky. In the 1980s, several Latin American nations experienced inflation rates of thousands of percent per year. In the early 1990s, some of the newly emerging nations of Central Europe and the former Soviet Union suffered annual inflation rates in the triple digits. An extreme case was the new nation of Serbia, where prices rose by 1,880 percent in the single month of August 1993. If prices had continued to rise at that rate all year, the annual inflation rate would have been 363,000,000,000,000,000 percent.

Why are stable prices—a low inflation rate—an important macroeconomic goal? Because inflation is *costly* to society. With annual inflation rates in the thousands of percent, the costs are easy to see: A nation's monetary system breaks down entirely, and people must waste valuable time and resources bartering with each other—for example, trading plumbing services for dentistry services. With so much time spent trying to find trading partners, there is little time left for producing goods and services. As a result, the average standard of living falls.

With more modest inflation—like the double-digit rates the United States experienced in the late 1970s—the costs to society are less obvious and less severe. But they are still significant. And when it comes time to bring down even a modest inflation rate, painful corrective actions by government are required. These actions cause output to decline and unemployment to rise. For example, in order to bring the inflation rate down from the high levels of the early 1980s (see Figure 4), government policy purposely caused a severe recession in 1981–1982, reducing output (Figure 1) and increasing unemployment (Figure 2).

The previous paragraph raises a number of questions. How, precisely, does a modest inflation harm society? Why would a recession reduce inflation? And how does the government create a recession? If you're a bit confused, don't worry. You are just beginning your study of macroeconomics, and we have a lot of ground to cover.

---

1. The figure is based on the Consumer Price Index, the most popular measure of the price level, as well as historical estimates of what this index *would* have been in the early part of the century, before the index existed. We'll discuss the Consumer Price Index and other measures of inflation in more detail in later chapters.

FIGURE 4   U.S. ANNUAL INFLATION RATE, 1922–1998

In most years, the inflation rate has been positive. The overall price level increased during those years.

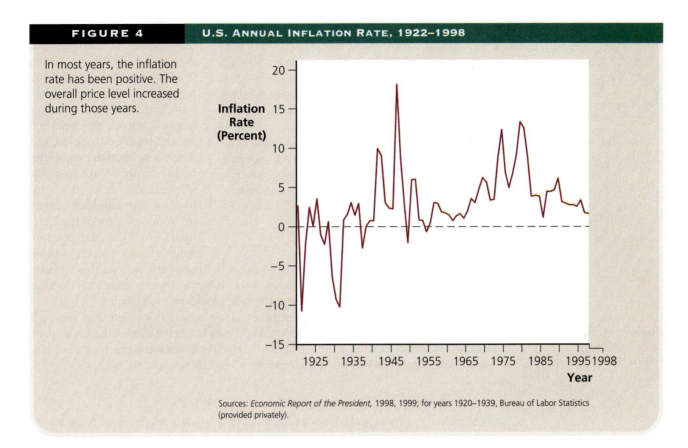

Sources: *Economic Report of the President*, 1998, 1999; for years 1920–1939, Bureau of Labor Statistics (provided privately).

THE MACROECONOMIC APPROACH

Because you have already studied *micro*economics, you will notice much that is familiar in *macro*economics. The *basic principles of economics* play an important role in both branches of the field. But the macroeconomic approach is different from the microeconomic approach in significant ways. Most importantly, in *micro*economics, we typically apply the basic principle of *markets and equilibrium* to *one market at a time*—the market for soybeans, for neurosurgeons, or for car washes. In *macro*economics, by contrast, we want to understand how the entire economy behaves. Thus, we apply the principle of markets and equilibrium to *all markets simultaneously*. This includes not only markets for goods and services, but also markets for labor and for financial assets like bonds and foreign currency.

How can we possibly hope to deal with all of these markets at the same time? One way would be to build a gigantic model that included every individual market in the economy. The model would have tens of thousands of supply and demand curves, which could be used to determine tens of thousands of prices and quantities. And with today's fast, powerful computers, we could, in principle, build this kind of model.

But it would not be easy. We would need to gather data on every good and service in the economy, every type of labor, every type of financial asset, and so on. As you might guess, this would be a formidable task, requiring thousands of

In many English words, the prefix *macro* means "large" and *micro* means "small." As a result, you might think that in microeconomics, we study economic units in which small sums of money are involved, while in macroeconomics we study units involving greater sums. But this is not correct: The annual output of General Motors is considerably greater than the total annual output of many small countries, such as Estonia or Guatemala. Yet when we study the behavior of General Motors, we are practicing *micro*economics, and when we study the causes of unemployment in Estonia, we are practicing *macro*economics. Why? Microeconomics is concerned with the behavior and interaction of *individual* firms and markets, even if they are very large; macroeconomics is concerned with the behavior of *entire economies,* even if they are very small.

DANGEROUS CURVES

workers just to gather the data alone. And in the end, the model would not prove very useful. We would not learn much about the economy from it: With so many individual trees, we could not see the forest. Moreover, the model's predictions would be highly suspect: With so much information and so many moving parts, high standards of accuracy are difficult to maintain. Even the government of the former Soviet Union, which directed production throughout the economy, was unable to keep track of all the markets under its control. In a market economy, where production decisions are made by individual firms, the task would be even harder.

What, then, is a macroeconomist to do? The answer is a word that you will become very familiar with in the chapters to come: **aggregation**—the process of combining different things into a single category and treating them as a whole. Let's take a closer look at how aggregation is used in macroeconomics.

AGGREGATION The process of combining different things into a single category.

AGGREGATION IN MACROECONOMICS

Aggregation is a basic tool of reasoning, one that you often use without being aware of it. If you say, "I applied for 15 jobs last month," you are aggregating 15 very different workplaces into the single category, *jobs*. Whenever you say "I'm going out with my friends," you are combining several different people into a single category: people you consider *friends*.

Aggregation plays a key role in both micro- and macroeconomics. Microeconomists will speak of the market for automobiles, lumping Toyotas, Fords, BMWs, and other types of cars into a single category. But in macroeconomics, we take aggregation to the extreme. Because we want to consider the entire economy at once, and yet keep our model as simple as possible, we must aggregate all markets into the broadest possible categories. For example, we lump together all the millions of different goods and services—computers, coffee tables, egg rolls, newspapers—into the single category, *output*. Similarly, we combine the thousands of different types of workers in the economy—doctors, construction workers, plumbers, college professors—into the category, *labor*. By aggregating in this way, we can create workable—and reasonably accurate—models that teach us a great deal about how the overall economy operates.

MACROECONOMIC CONTROVERSIES

Macroeconomics is full of disputes and disagreements. Indeed, modern macroeconomics—which began with the publication of *The General Theory of Employment, Interest, and Money,* by British economist John Maynard Keynes in 1936—originated in controversy. Keynes was taking on the conventional wisdom of his time—*classical economics*—which held that the macroeconomy worked very well on its own, and the best policy for the government to follow was laissez faire—"leave it alone." As he was working on *The General Theory,* Keynes wrote to his friend, the playwright George Bernard Shaw: "I believe myself to be writing a book on economic theory which will largely revolutionize—not, I suppose, at once but in the course of the next ten years—the way the world thinks about economic problems." Keynes's prediction was on the money: After the publication of his book, economists argued about its merits, but 10 years later, the majority of the profession was won over; they had become Keynesians. This new school of thought held that the economy does *not* do well on its own (one needed only to look at the Great Depression for evidence) and requires continual guidance from an activist and well-intentioned government.

From the late 1940s until the early 1960s, events seemed to prove the Keynesians correct. Then, beginning in the 1960s, several distinguished economists began to challenge Keynesian ideas. Their counterrevolutionary views—which in many ways mirrored those of the classical economists—were strengthened by events in the 1970s, when the economy's behavior began to contradict the most important Keynesian ideas. While some of the early disagreements have been resolved, others have arisen to take their place.

Some of today's controversies are purely *positive* in nature. For example, in Chapter 16 you will learn about the Federal Reserve System—the central bank in the United States—which can influence many important macroeconomic aggregates, such as output, employment, and the inflation rate. As this is being written (early 1999), most economists believe that the Federal Reserve (or "Fed") is doing an excellent job managing these aggregates. They point out that the Fed has successfully engineered high employment and rapid economic growth for almost a decade, without overheating the economy and risking future inflation. A few economists, however, think that the Fed has made a mistake. They believe that it is indeed overheating the economy, which will lead to higher inflation in the future. (Are you confused about the connections between rapid economic growth, overheating the economy, and future inflation? Don't worry: All of this will be explained in future chapters.)

To some extent, this is a *positive* disagreement: The two sides might have different views about how the economy is performing now and what that performance implies about the future. That is, it's in part a disagreement about *how the economy works*. But for some, the controversy is also *normative*. We might find two economists who agree about the extent that the Fed's current policies are risking future inflation. But they might disagree strongly about the wisdom of the gamble because of differences in *values*. One economist may place more weight on high employment and rapid growth and is willing to risk future inflation to achieve them. The other might put more weight on avoiding future inflation, even if it means lower employment and slower growth now.

Economists, like all other human beings, hold different values, and often hold them strongly. Not surprisingly, disagreements among economists are often emotionally charged. But there is also more agreement than meets the eye. Macroeconomists agree on many basic principles, and we will stress these as we go. And even when there are strong disagreements, there is surprising consensus on the approach that should be taken to resolve them.

AS YOU STUDY MACROECONOMICS...

Macroeconomics is a fascinating and wide-ranging subject. You will find that each piece of the macroeconomic puzzle connects to all of the others in many different ways. Each time one of your questions is answered, 10 more will spring up in your mind, each demanding immediate attention. This presents a problem for a textbook writer and for your instructor as well: What is the best order to present the principles of macroeconomics? We could follow the line of questions that occur to the curious reader, but this would be an organizational disaster. For example, learning about unemployment raises questions about international trade, but it also raises questions about government spending, government regulations, economic growth, wages, banking, and much, much more. And each of these topics raises questions about still others. Organizing the material in this way would make you feel like a ball in a pinball machine, bouncing from bumper to bumper. Still, the pinball approach—bouncing from topic to topic—is the one taken by the media when reporting on the economy. If you have ever tried to learn economics from a newspaper, you know how frustrating this approach can be.

In our study of macroeconomics, we will follow a different approach: presenting material as it is *needed* for what follows. In this way, what you learn in one chapter will form the foundation for the material in the next, and your understanding of macroeconomics will deepen as you go.

But be forewarned: This approach requires considerable patience on your part. Many of the questions that will pop into your head will have to be postponed until the proper foundations for answering them have been laid. It might help, though, to give you a brief indication of what is to come.

In the next two chapters, we will discuss three of the most important aggregates in macroeconomics: output, employment, and the price level. You will see why each of these is important to our economic well-being, how we keep track of them with government statistics, and how to interpret these statistics with a critical eye.

Then, in the remainder of the book, we study how the macro-economy operates, starting with its behavior in the long run. Here, you will learn what makes an economy grow over long periods of time, and which government policies are likely to help or hinder that growth.

Then, we turn our attention to the short run. You will learn why the economy behaves differently in the short run than in the long run, why we have business cycles, and how these cycles may be affected by government policies. Then we'll expand our analysis to include the banking system and the money supply, and the special challenges they pose for government policy makers.

Finally, we'll turn our attention to the special problems of a global economy. You'll learn how trade with other nations constrains and expands our options at home and how economic events abroad influence our own economy. You will also learn why the United States has run persistent trade deficits with the rest of the world and what that means for our citizens.

This sounds like quite a lot of ground to cover, and indeed, it is. But it's not as daunting as it might sound. Remember that the study of macroeconomics—like the macro-economy itself—is not a series of separate units, but an integrated whole. As you go from chapter to chapter, each principle you learn is a stepping-stone to the next one. Little by little, your knowledge and understanding will accumulate and deepen. Most students are genuinely surprised at how well they understand the macroeconomy after a single introductory course, and find the reward well worth the effort.

S U M M A R Y

Macroeconomics is the study of the economy as a whole. It deals with issues such as economic growth, unemployment, inflation, and government policies that might influence the overall level of economic activity.

Economists generally agree about the importance of three main macroeconomic goals. The first of these is rapid economic growth. If output—real gross domestic product—grows faster than population, the average person can enjoy an improved standard of living.

High employment is another important goal. In the U.S. and other market economies, the main source of households' incomes is labor earnings. When unemployment is high, many people are without jobs and must cut back their purchases of goods and services.

The third macroeconomic goal is stable prices. This goal is important because inflation imposes costs on society. Keeping the rate of inflation low helps to reduce these costs.

In this text, we will study macroeconomics using models—simplified representations of reality. Because an economy like that of the United States is so large and complex, the models we use must be highly aggregated. For example, we will lump together millions of different goods to create an aggregate called "output" and combine all their prices into a single "price index."

K E Y   T E R M S

business cycles	peak	trough	aggregation
expansion	recession	depression	

R E V I E W   Q U E S T I O N S

1. Discuss the similarities and differences between macroeconomics and microeconomics.

2. What is the basic tool macroeconomists use to deal with the complexity and variety of economic markets and institutions? Give some examples of how they use this tool.

3. List the nation's macroeconomic goals and explain why each is important.

4. Consider an economy whose real GDP is growing at 4 percent per year. What else would you need to know in order to say whether the average standard of living is improving or deteriorating?

5. The Business Cycle Dating Committee of the National Bureau of Economic Research (NBER) has determined peaks and troughs for business cycles in the United States since 1854. A complete chronology is given at http://www.nber.org/cycles.html. After visiting this site, answer the following questions:

   a. What is the NBER's definition of a recession? According to the NBER, when did the most recently completed recession end? What was the duration of that recession? How did the duration of that recession compare to the average duration of peacetime recessions since 1945?

   b. According to the NBER, when did the most recently completed expansion end? What was the duration of that expansion? How did that compare to the average duration of peacetime expansions since 1945?

C H A L L E N G E   Q U E S T I O N

1. Speculate about some factors that might help explain the post-1973 growth slowdown. What changes in the economy or in society as a whole may have contributed to this phenomenon? Why might growth have speeded up again in the late 1990s?

   Economists often argue that the state of the macroeconomy is an important factor in determining the outcome of national elections. Some believe that the "misery index," the sum of the inflation rate and the unemployment rate, can be used to predict the fate of the incumbent. That is, if the misery index is high or increasing, the incumbent will face trouble; if the index is low or decreasing, however, the incumbent stands a good chance of reelection.

CHAPTER 12

PRODUCTION, INCOME, AND EMPLOYMENT

On the first Friday of every month, at 8:00 A.M., dozens of journalists mill about in a room in the Department of Labor. They are waiting for the arrival of the press officer from the government's Bureau of Labor Statistics. When she enters the room, carrying a stack of papers, the buzz of conversation stops. The papers—which she passes out to the waiting journalists—contain the monthly report on the experience of the American workforce. They summarize everything the government knows about hiring and firing at businesses across the country; about the number of people working, the hours they worked, and the incomes they earned; and about the number of people *not* working and what they did instead. All of this information is broken down by industry, state, city, race, sex, and age. But one number looms large in the journalists' minds as they scan the report and compose their stories: the percentage of the labor force that could not find jobs, or the nation's *unemployment rate*.

Once every three months, a similar scene takes place at the Department of Commerce, as reporters wait for the release of the quarterly report on the nation's output of goods and services and the incomes we have earned from producing it. Once again, the report includes tremendous detail. Output is broken down by industry and by the sector that purchased it (ordinary households, businesses, government agencies, and foreigners), and income is broken down into the different types of earners—wage earners, property owners, and owners of small businesses. And once again, the reporters' eyes will focus on a single number, a number that will dominate their stories and create headlines in newspapers across the country: the nation's *gross domestic product*.

The government knows that its reports on employment and production will have a major impact on the American political scene and on financial markets in the United States and around the world. So the government takes great pains to ensure fair and equal access to the information. For example, the Bureau of Labor Statistics allows journalists to look at the employment report at 8:00 A.M. on the day of the release (the first Friday of every month). But all who see the report must stay inside a room—appropriately called the "lockup room"—and cannot contact the outside world until the official release time of 8:30 A.M. At precisely 8:29 A.M., the reporters are permitted to hook up their laptop modems, and then a countdown begins, ending at precisely 8:30 A.M. At that moment—and not a second before—the reporters are permitted to transmit their stories. At the same instant, the Bureau posts its report on an Internet Web site. (The URL is http://stats.bls.gov/blshome.html.)

The reactions to the government's reports come almost immediately. Within seconds, wire-service headlines appear on computer screens across the country—"Unemployment Rate Up Two-Tenths of a Percent" or "Nation's Production Steady." Within minutes, financial traders, regarding these news flashes as clues about the economy's future, make snap decisions to buy or sell, and prices move in the stock and bond markets. This creates further headlines—"Stock Market Plunges on Unemployment Data" or "Bonds Rally on Output Report." Within the hour, politicians and pundits will respond with sound bites, attacking or defending the administration's economic policies.

Why is so much attention given to the government's reports on production and employment, and—in particular—to those two numbers: gross domestic product and the unemployment rate? Because they describe aspects of the economy that dramatically affect each of us individually and our society as a whole. In this chapter, we will take our first look at production and employment in the economy. The purpose here is not to explain what causes these variables to rise or fall—that will come a few chapters later when we begin to study macroeconomic models. Here, we will focus on the reality behind the numbers: what the statistics tell us about the economy, how the government obtains them, and how they are sometimes misused.

PRODUCTION AND GROSS DOMESTIC PRODUCT

You have probably heard the phrase *gross domestic product*—or its more familiar abbreviation, GDP—more than once. It is one of those economic terms that are frequently used by the media and by politicians. In the first part of this chapter, we take a close look at GDP, starting with a careful definition.

GDP: A DEFINITION

The U.S. government has been measuring the nation's total production since the 1930s. You might think that this is an easy number to calculate, at least in theory: Simply add up the output of every firm in the country during the year. Unfortunately, measuring total production is not so straightforward, and there are many conceptual traps and pitfalls. This is why economists have come up with a very precise definition of GDP.

*The nation's **gross domestic product** (GDP) is the total value of all final goods and services produced for the marketplace during a given year, within the nation's borders.*

GROSS DOMESTIC PRODUCT (GDP) The total value of all final goods and services produced for the marketplace during a given year, within the nation's borders.

Quite a mouthful. Is everything in this definition really necessary? Absolutely. To see why, let's break the definition down into pieces and look more closely at each one.

The total value . . .

An old expression tells us that "you can't add apples and oranges." But that is just what government statisticians must do when they measure our total output. In a typical day, American firms produce millions of loaves of bread, thousands of pounds of peanut butter, millions of yards of VCR tape, hundreds of hours of television programming, and so on. These are *different* products, and each is measured in its own type of units. Yet somehow, we must combine all of them into a single number. But how?

The approach of GDP is to add up the *dollar value* of every good or service—the number of dollars each product is *sold* for. As a result, GDP is measured in dollar units. For example, in 1998, the GDP of the United States was about $8,511,000,000,000:—give or take a few billion dollars.

Using dollar values has two important advantages. First, it gives us a common unit of measurement for very different things, thus allowing us to add up "apples and oranges." Second, it ensures that more valuable goods (like 100 computer chips) will count more in our GDP than less valuable ones (100 tortilla chips).

. . . of all final . . .

When measuring production, we do not count *every* good or service produced in the economy, but only those that are sold to their *final users*. An example will illustrate why.

Figure 1 shows a simplified version of the stages of production needed to produce a ream (500 sheets) of notebook paper: A lumber company cuts down trees and produces wood chips, which it sells to a paper mill for $1.00. The mill cooks, bleaches, and refines the wood chips, turning them into paper rolls, which it sells to an office supplies manufacturer for $1.50. This manufacturer cuts the paper, prints lines and margins on it, and sells its to a wholesaler for $2.25, which sells it to a retail store for $3.50, and then—finally—it is sold to a consumer—perhaps you—for $5.00.

Should we add the value of *all* of this production and include $1.00 + $1.50 + $2.25 + $3.50 + $5.00 = $13.25 in GDP each time a ream of notebook paper is produced? No, this would clearly be a mistake, since all of this production ends up creating a good worth only $5 in the end. In fact, the $5 you pay for this good already

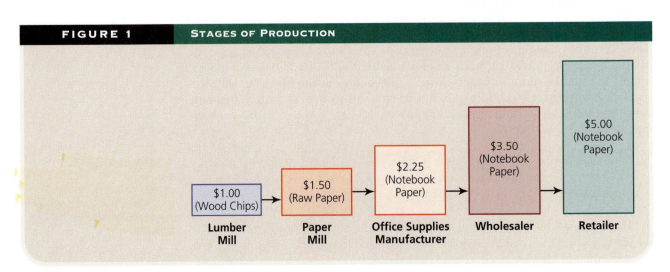

| FIGURE 1 | STAGES OF PRODUCTION |

includes the value of all the other production in the process.

In our example, the goods sold by the lumber company, paper mill, notebook paper manufacturer, and wholesaler are all **intermediate goods**— goods used up in the current period to produce something else. But the retailer (say, your local stationery store) sells a **final good**—a product sold to its *final user* (you). If we separately added in the production of intermediate goods when calculating GDP, we would be counting them more than once, since they are already included in the value of the final good.

> You've learned that GDP excludes the value of many things that are bought and sold—such as land, financial assets, and used goods—because they are not *currently produced goods and services*. But all of this buying and selling *can* contribute to GDP indirectly. How? If a dealer or broker is involved in the transaction, then that dealer or broker is producing a current service: bringing buyer and seller together. The value of this service is part of current GDP.
>
> For example, suppose you bought a secondhand book at your college bookstore for $25. Suppose, too, that the store had bought the book from another student for $15. Then the purchase of the used book will contribute $10 to this year's GDP. Why? Because $10 is the value of the bookstore's services; it's the premium you pay to buy the book in the store, rather than going through the trouble to find the original seller yourself. The remainder of your purchase—$15—represents the value of the used book itself and is *not* counted in GDP. The book was already counted when it was newly produced—in this or a previous year.

DANGEROUS CURVES

> *To avoid overcounting intermediate products when measuring GDP, we add up the value of final goods and services only. The value of all intermediate products is automatically included in the value of the final products they are used to create.*

INTERMEDIATE GOODS
Goods used up in producing final goods.

FINAL GOOD A good sold to its final user.

. . . goods and services . . .

We all know a "good" when we see one: We can look at it, feel it, weigh it, and, in some cases, eat it, strum it, or swing a bat at it. Not so with a service: When you get a medical checkup, a haircut, or a car wash, the *effects* of the service may linger, but the service itself is used up the moment it is produced. Nonetheless, final services are as much a part of our GDP as are final goods.

Services have become an increasingly important part of our total output in recent decades. The service sector has grown from 31 percent of total output in 1950 to 53 percent of total output in 1997.

. . . produced . . .

In order to contribute to GDP, something must be *produced*. This may sound obvious, but it is easy to forget. Every day, Americans buy billions of dollars worth of things that are *not* produced, or at least not produced this year, and so are not counted in this year's GDP. For example, people may buy land, or they may buy financial assets such as stocks or bonds. While these things cost money, they are not counted in GDP because they are not "goods and services *produced*." Land (and the natural resources on it or under it) is not produced at all. Stocks and bonds represent a claim to ownership or to receive future payments, but they are not themselves goods or services.

In addition, people and businesses buy billions of dollars in *used* goods during the year, such as secondhand cars, previously occupied homes, used furniture, or an old photo of Elvis talking to an extraterrestrial. These goods were all produced, but not in the current period. We include only *currently produced* output when figuring this year's GDP.

> **DANGEROUS CURVES**
>
> GDP is measured and reported each *quarter*. But be careful: Quarterly GDP is almost always reported at an *annual rate*. For example, in the first quarter of 1998, we produced $2,096 billion in final goods and services; but the GDP was reported at the *annual* rate of 4 × $2,096 = $8,384 billion. This is what we *would* have produced in 1998 if production had continued at the first quarter's rate for the entire year.

. . . for the marketplace . . .

GDP does not include *all* final goods and services produced in the economy. Rather, it includes only the ones produced for the marketplace—that is, with the intention of being *sold*. Because of this restriction, we exclude many important goods and services from our measure. For example, when you clean your own home, you have produced a final service—housecleaning—but it is *not* counted in GDP, because you are doing it for yourself, not for the marketplace. If you *hire* a housecleaner to clean your home, however, this final service *is* included in GDP; it has become a market transaction.

The same is true for many services produced in the economy. Taking care of your children, washing your car, mowing your lawn, walking your dog—none of these services are included in GDP if you do them for yourself, but all *are* included if you pay someone else to do them for you.

. . . during a given year . . .

FLOW VARIABLE A measure of a process that takes place over a period of time.

This part of the definition of GDP tells us that GDP is an example of a **flow variable**—a measure of a *process* that takes place over a period of time:

> *Gross domestic product is a flow variable: It measures a process—production—over a period of time.*

The value of a flow depends on the length of the period over which we choose to measure it. For example, if you are asked, "What is your *income*?" (another flow variable), your answer will be different depending on whether the question refers to your hourly, weekly, monthly, or yearly income. The same is true of GDP: We can measure it per day, per month, or per year. (For example, in 1998, the U.S. produced $23 billion worth of output on a typical day, $709 billion in a typical month, and $8,511 billion for the year as a whole. By tradition, the basic period for reporting GDP is a year.)

STOCK VARIABLE A measure of an amount that exists at a moment in time.

Not all macroeconomic variables are flow variables; some are **stock variables**—measures of things that exist at a moment in time. The U.S. population, the number of homes in the nation, the current value of your wealth—all these are stock variables, because they are values measured at a particular instant. In this case, we never need to add the phrase per week or per month, since there is no *period* attached to the variable. (For example, it makes no sense to ask "What is your wealth per month?" Instead, we would ask, "What is your wealth *right now*?")

. . . within the nation's borders.

Finally, we come to the last part of the definition: GDP measures output produced *within U.S. borders*—regardless of whether it was produced by Americans. This means we include output produced by *foreign-owned* resources and foreign citizens located in the United States, and we exclude output produced by Americans located in other countries. For example, when Paul McCartney, a resident of Britain, gives a concert tour in the United States, the value of his services are counted in U.S. GDP and not in British GDP. Similarly, the output produced by an

American nurse working temporarily in an Ethiopian hospital is part of Ethiopian GDP and not U.S. GDP.

THE EXPENDITURE APPROACH TO GDP

The Commerce Department's Bureau of Economic Analysis (BEA)—the agency responsible for gathering, reporting, and analyzing movements in the nation's output—calculates GDP in several different ways. The most important of these is the *expenditure approach*. Because this method of measuring GDP tells us so much about the structure of our economy, we'll spend the next several pages on it.

In the expenditure approach, we divide output into four categories according to which group in the economy purchases it. The four categories are:

1. *consumption goods and services (C)*, purchased by households;
2. *private investment goods and services (I^a)*, purchased by businesses;[1]
3. *government goods and services (G)*, purchased by government agencies; and
4. *net exports (NX)*, purchased by foreigners.[2]

This is an exhaustive list: Every buyer of U.S. output belongs to one of these four sectors. Thus, when we add up the purchases of the four sectors, we must get GDP:

> *In the **expenditure approach** to measuring GDP, we add up the value of the goods and services purchased by each type of final user:*
>
> $$GDP = C + I^a + G + NX.$$

EXPENDITURE APPROACH Measuring GDP by adding the value of goods and services purchased by each type of final user.

As you can see in Table 1, applying the expenditure approach to GDP in 1998 gives us $GDP = C + I^a + G + NX = \$5,808 + \$1,367 + \$1,487 + (-\$151) = \$8,511$ billion.

Now let's take a closer look at each of the four components of GDP.

CONSUMPTION SPENDING. Consumption (C) is both the largest component of GDP—making up about three-quarters of total production in recent years—and the easiest to understand:

> *Consumption is the part of GDP purchased by households as final users.*

CONSUMPTION The part of GDP purchased by households as final users.

Almost everything that households buy during the year—restaurant meals, gasoline, new clothes, doctors' visits, movies, electricity, and more—is included as part of consumption spending when we calculate GDP.

But notice the word "almost." Some of the things households buy during the year are *not* part of consumption, because they are not part of GDP at all. (Can you identify what they are? Hint: Flip back a few pages to the discussion of the word "production" in the definition of GDP.)

There are also some quirky exceptions to the definition of consumption. For example, two things are included even though households do not actually buy them: (1) the total value of all food products that farm families produce and consume themselves (meat, dairy products, fruit, and vegetables) and (2) the total value of the shelter provided by homes that are owned by the families living in them. The

---

1. The reason for the superscript "*a*" on investment will be explained shortly.
2. The meaning and importance of the term "net" will become clear shortly.

TABLE 1	GDP IN 1998: THE EXPENDITURE APPROACH (BILLIONS OF DOLLARS)		
Consumption Purchases	**Private-Investment Purchases**	**Government Purchases**	**Net Exports**
Services $3,421	Plant and equipment $938	Government consumption $1,250	Exports $959
Nondurable goods $1,662	New home construction $370	Government investment $237	Imports $1,110
Durable goods $725	Changes in business inventories $59		
Consumption = $5,808	**Private investment = $1,367**	**Government purchases = 1,487**	**Net exports = –$151**

$$GDP = C + I^p + G + NX$$
$$= \$5,808 + \$1,367 + \$1,487 + (-\$151)$$
$$= \$8,511$$

Source: Bureau of Economic Analysis, U.S. Dept. of Commerce.

government estimates (and adds to GDP) what farm families *would* pay if they had to buy all of their farm products in the marketplace like everyone else. It also estimates the rent that homeowners *would* pay for their homes if they were renting from someone else. Another exception is that the construction of new homes—even when households buy them—is not counted as consumption, but rather as private investment.

PRIVATE INVESTMENT SPENDING. What do oil-drilling rigs, cash registers, office telephones, and the house you grew up in all have in common? They are all examples of *capital goods*—goods that will provide useful services in future years. When we sum the value of all of the capital goods in the country, we get our **capital stock.** As the name suggests, this is a *stock* variable—a value that exists at a moment in time.

Understanding the concept of capital stock helps us understand and define the concept of investment. A rough definition of **private investment spending** is *capital formation*—the *increase in the nation's capital stock* during the year. Investment, like the other components of GDP, is a *flow* variable—a process (capital formation) that takes place over a period of time.

More specifically,

> *private investment has three components: (1) business purchases of plant and equipment; (2) new home construction; and (3) changes in business firms' inventory stocks (stocks of unsold goods).*

Each of these components requires some explanation.

Business Purchases of Plant and Equipment. This category might seem confusing at first glance. Why aren't plant and equipment considered intermediate goods? After all, business firms buy these things in order to produce other things. Doesn't the value of their final goods include the value of their plant and equipment as well?

Actually, no, and if you go back to the definition of intermediate goods, you will see why. Intermediate goods are *used up* with the current year's production. But a firm's plant and equipment are intended to last for many years; only a small part of

CAPITAL STOCK The total value of all goods that will provide useful services in future years.

PRIVATE INVESTMENT SPENDING The sum of business plant and equipment purchases, new home construction, and inventory changes.

it is used up to make the current year's output. Thus, we regard plant and equipment as final goods, and the firms that buy them as the final users of those goods.

For example, suppose our paper mill—the firm that turns wood chips into raw paper—buys a new factory building that is expected to last for 50 years. Then only a small fraction of that factory building—1/50—is used up in any one year's production of raw paper, and only a small part of the factory building's value will be reflected in the value of the firm's current output. But since the factory is produced during the year, we must include its value *somewhere* in our measure of total production. In calculating GDP, we therefore count the factory building as an investment good.

Plant and equipment purchases are always the largest component of private investment. In 1998, businesses purchased and installed $938 billion worth of plant and equipment, which was about two-thirds of total private investment spending that year (see Table 1).

New Home Construction. As you can see in Table 1, new home construction made up a significant part of total private investment in 1998. But it may strike you as odd that this category is part of investment spending at all, since most new homes are purchased by households and could reasonably be considered consumption spending instead. Why do we treat new home construction as investment spending in GDP?

Largely because residential housing is an important part of the nation's *capital stock*. Just as an oil-drilling rig will continue to provide oil-drilling services for many decades, so, too, a home will continue to provide shelter services into the future. If we want our measure of private investment spending to roughly correspond to the increase in the nation's capital stock, we must include this important category of capital formation in investment spending.

Changes in Inventories. Inventories are goods that have been produced, but not yet sold. They include goods on store shelves, goods making their way through the production process in factories, and raw materials waiting to be used. We count the *change* in firms' inventories as part of investment spending in measuring GDP. Why? When goods are produced but not sold during the year, they end up in some firm's inventory stocks. If we did *not* count changes in inventories, we would be missing this important part of current production. Remember that GDP is designed to measure total *production*, not just the part of production that is sold during the year.

To understand this more clearly, suppose that in some year, the automobile industry produced $100 billion worth of automobiles, and that $80 billion worth were sold to consumers. Then the other $20 billion remained unsold and was added to the auto company's inventories. If we counted consumption spending alone ($80 billion), we would underestimate automobile production in GDP. To ensure a proper measure, we must include not only the $80 billion in cars sold (consumption spending), but also the $20 billion change in inventories (private investment spending). In the end, the contribution to GDP would be $80 billion (consumption) + $20 billion (private investment) = $100 billion, which is, indeed, the total value of automobile production during the year.

What if inventory stocks *decline* during the year, so that the change in inventories is negative? Our rule still holds: We include the change in inventories in our measure of GDP—but in this case, we must add a *negative* number. For example, if the automobile industry produced $100 billion worth of cars, but consumers bought $120 billion, then $20 billion worth of cars must have come from inventory stocks—cars that were produced (and counted) in previous years, but that remained unsold until this year. In this case, the consumption spending of $120 billion will *overestimate* automobile production during the year, and subtracting $20 billion corrects for this overcount. In the end, GDP would rise by $120 billion (consumption) – $20 billion (private investment) = $100 billion.

Inventory changes are included in investment spending, rather than some other component of GDP, because unsold goods are part of the nation's capital stock. They will provide services in the future when they are finally sold and used. An increase in inventories represents capital formation; a decrease in inventories—negative investment—is a decrease in the nation's capital.

Inventory changes are generally the smallest component of private investment spending, but the most highly volatile in percentage terms. In 1998, for example, inventories increased by about $59 billion; two years earlier, they increased by only a third as much, and a few years before that, inventory stocks *decreased*. Part of the reason for this volatility is that, while some inventory investment is intended, much of it is *unintended*. During recessions, for example, businesses are often unable to sell all of the goods they have produced and had planned to sell. The unsold output will be added to inventory stocks—an unintended increase in inventories. During rapid expansions, the opposite may happen: Businesses find themselves selling more than they produced—an unintended decrease in inventories.

In later chapters, it will be important to distinguish *actual* private investment spending (I^a)—which includes any unintended changes in inventories—from *planned* private investment spending (I), which excludes them. Thus, we can write:

Actual private investment spending =

Planned private investment spending + Unintended inventory changes

or

$$I^a = I + \text{Unintended inventory changes}$$

The superscript "*a*" stands for "actual," and tells us that we're including unintended inventory changes in our measure of investment.

PRIVATE INVESTMENT AND THE CAPITAL STOCK: SOME IMPORTANT PROVISOS. A few pages ago, it was pointed out that private investment spending corresponds only *roughly* to the increase in the nation's capital stock. Why this cautious language? Because changes in the nation's capital stock are a bit more complicated than we are able to capture with our measure of private investment spending alone.

First, an important part of the nation's capital stock is owned and operated not by businesses, but by government—federal, state, and local. Courthouses, police cars, fire stations, weather satellites, military aircraft, highways, and bridges are all examples of government capital. In any given year, some of the nation's capital formation consists of an increase in government capital, which is not included in our measure of private investment spending. Thus, private investment spending alone tends to *underestimate* the increase in the nation's capital stock. A better measure of capital formation would include both private and government investment spending:

Total investment spending during the year is the sum of private investment spending and government investment spending.

In 1998, for example, the government estimated that $237 billion of its spending was devoted to capital formation, so that total investment spending in that year was

$$\text{Total investment} = \text{Private investment} + \text{Government investment}$$
$$= \$1,367 \text{ billion} + \$237 \text{ billion}$$
$$= \$1,604 \text{ billion}$$

Second, in any given year, some of the nation's existing capital stock will wear out, or *depreciate*. Total investment spending, because it ignores depreciation, tends to *overestimate* the increase in the nation's capital stock. We can fix this, however, by subtracting depreciation from total investment spending, to obtain *net investment spending*. This is the amount by which private and government investment actually causes the capital stock to increase:

$$\text{Net investment spending} = \text{Total investment spending} - \text{Depreciation}$$

NET INVESTMENT SPENDING Total investment spending minus depreciation.

For example, the government estimates that in 1998, $908 billion of private and governemnt capital depreciated so that net investment spending for the year was

$$\text{Net investment spending} = \$1,604 \text{ billion} - \$908 \text{ billion} = \$696 \text{ billion}$$

Net investment spending comes close to being a true measure of the increase in the capital stock during the year. But in the minds of many economists, we are still not completely there, because we are still ignoring two kinds of capital formation. One is the purchase of *consumer durables*—goods such as furniture, automobiles, washing machines, and personal computers for home use. All of these goods can be considered capital goods, since they will continue to provide services for many years. In 1998, households purchased $725 billion in durables. If we deduct from this an estimate of depreciation on the existing stock of durables (say, $100 billion), we would get the increase in the stock of durables: $725 billion – $100 billion = $625 billion. Some economists would argue that *if* we included this $625 billion or so as part of investment spending, we would have an even better measure of the increase in the capital stock.

Finally, our typical measures of capital formation ignore *human capital*—the skills and training of the labor force. Think about a surgeon's skills in performing a heart bypass operation, or a police detective's ability to find clues and solve a murder, or a Web page designer's mastery of HTML and Java. These types of knowledge will continue to provide valuable services well into the future, just like plant and equipment or new housing. To measure the increase in the capital stock most broadly, then, we *should* include the additional skills and training acquired by the workforce during the year. But human capital growth—like growth in consumer durables—is *not* included in the official measure of investment spending by the BEA.

GOVERNMENT PURCHASES. In 1998, the government bought $1,487 billion worth of goods and services that were part of GDP—about a fifth of the total. This component of GDP is called **government purchases**, although in recent years the Department of Commerce has begun to use the phrase *government consumption and investment purchases*. Government *investment*, as discussed earlier, refers to capital goods

GOVERNMENT PURCHASES Spending by federal, state, and local governments on goods and services.

> **DANGEROUS CURVES**
>
> Be *extremely* careful when using the term "investment" in your economics course. In economics, "investment" refers to capital formation, such as the building of a new factory, home, or hospital, or the production and installation of new capital equipment, or the accumulation of inventories by business firms. In everyday language, however, "investment" has a very different meaning: a place to put your wealth. Thus, in ordinary English, you invest whenever you buy stocks or bonds or certificates of deposit or when you lend money to a friend who is starting up a business. But in the language of economics, you have not invested, but merely changed the form in which you are holding your wealth (say, from checking account balances to stocks or bonds). To avoid confusion, remember that investment takes place only when there is new production of capital goods, that is, only when there is *capital formation*.

purchased by government agencies. The rest of government purchases is considered government *consumption*—spending on goods and services that are used up during the year. This would include the salaries of government workers and military personnel and raw materials, such as computer paper for government offices, gasoline for government vehicles, and the electricity used in government buildings.

There are a few things to keep in mind about government purchases in GDP. First, we include purchases by state and local governments as well as the federal government. In macroeconomics, it makes little difference whether the purchases are made by a local government agency like the parks department of Kalamazoo, Michigan, or a huge federal agency such as the U.S. Department of Defense.

Second, government purchases include goods—like fighter jets, police cars, schools buildings, and spy satellites—and services—such as those performed by police, legislators, and military personnel. The government is considered to be a purchaser even if it actually produces the goods or services itself. For example, if you are taking your economics course at a public college or university—like Western Illinois University or the City University of New York—then your professor is selling teaching services to a state or city government, and his or her salary enters into GDP as part of government purchases.

Finally, it's important to distinguish between government *purchases*—which are counted in GDP—and government *spending*, as measured by local, state, and federal budgets and reported in the media. What's the difference? In addition to their purchases of goods and services, government agencies also disburse money for transfer payments. These funds are *given* to people or organizations—*not* to buy goods or services from them, but rather to fulfill some social obligation or goal. For example, Social Security payments by the federal government, unemployment insurance and welfare payments by state governments, and money disbursed to homeless shelters and soup kitchens by city governments are all examples of transfer payments. The important thing to remember about transfer payments is this:

TRANSFER PAYMENTS Funds the government gives to people or organizations, but *not* as payment for goods or services.

> *Transfer payments represent money redistributed from one group of citizens (taxpayers) to another (the poor, the unemployed, the elderly). While transfers are included in government budgets as spending, they are not purchases of currently produced goods and services, and so are* not *included in government purchases or in GDP.*

NET EXPORTS. There is one more category of buyer for output produced in the United States: *the foreign sector.* In 1998, for example, purchasers *outside* the nation bought approximately $959 billion of U.S. goods and services—about 11 percent of our GDP. These exports are part of U.S. production of goods and services and so are included in GDP.

However, once we recognize dealings with the rest of the world, we must correct an inaccuracy in our measure of GDP the way we've reported it so far. Americans buy many goods and services every year that were produced *outside* of the United States (Chinese shoes, Japanese cars, Mexican beer, Costa Rican coffee). When we add up the final purchases of households, businesses, and government agencies, we *overcount* U.S. production, because we include goods and services produced abroad, which are *not* part of U.S. output. To correct for this overcount, we deduct all *imports* into the United States during the year, leaving us with just output produced in the United States. In 1998, these imports amounted to $1,110 billion—about 13 percent of our GDP.

Let's recap: To obtain an accurate measure of GDP, we must add the part of U.S. production that is purchased by foreigners—total exports. But to correct for including the goods produced abroad, we must subtract Americans' purchases of goods produced outside of the United States—total imports. In practice, we take both of these steps together by adding **net exports (NX)**—total exports minus total imports. In 1998, when total exports were $959 billion and total imports were $1,110 billion, net exports—as you can see in Table 1—were $959 – $1,110 = –$151 billion. The negative number indicates that the imports we're subtracting from GDP are greater than the exports we're adding.

NET EXPORTS (NX) Total exports minus total imports.

OTHER APPROACHES TO GDP

In addition to the expenditure approach, where we calculate GDP as $C + I^a + G + NX$, there are other ways of measuring GDP. You may be wondering: Why bother? Why not just use one method—whichever is best—and stick to it? Is the Bureau of Economic Analysis just trying to make life difficult for introductory economics students?

Actually, there are two good reasons for measuring GDP in different ways. The first is practical. Each method of measuring GDP is subject to measurement errors. By calculating total output in several different ways and then trying to resolve the differences, the BEA gets a more accurate measure than would be possible with one method alone. The second reason is that the different ways of measuring total output give us different insights into the structure of our economy. Let's take a look at two more ways of measuring—and thinking about—GDP.

THE VALUE-ADDED APPROACH. In the expenditure approach, we record goods and services only when they are sold to their final users—at the end of the production process. But we can also measure GDP by adding up each *firm's* contribution to the product *as it is produced.*

A firm's contribution to a product is called its *value added*. More formally,

> A firm's **value added** is the revenue it receives for its output, minus the cost of all the intermediate goods that it buys.

VALUE ADDED The revenue a firm receives minus the cost of the intermediate goods it buys.

Look back at Figure 1, which traces the production of a ream of notebook paper. The paper mill, for example, buys $1.00 worth of wood chips (an intermediate good) from the lumber company and turns it into raw paper, which it sells for $1.50. The value added by the paper mill is $1.50 – $1.00 = $0.50. Similarly, the office-supplies maker buys $1.50 worth of paper (an intermediate good) from the paper mill and sells it for $2.25, so its value added is $2.25 – $1.50 = $0.75. If we total the value added by each firm, we should get the final value of the notebook paper, as in

TABLE 2	VALUE ADDED AT DIFFERENT STAGES OF PRODUCTION		
Firm	**Cost of Intermediate Goods**	**Revenue**	**Value Added**
Lumber Company	$0	$1.00	$1.00
Paper Mill	$1.00	$1.50	$0.50
Office Supplies Manufacturer	$1.50	$2.25	$0.75
Wholesaler	$2.25	$3.50	$1.25
Retailer	$3.50	$5.00	$1.50
			Total: $5.00

Table 2.[3] The total value added is $1.00 + $0.50 + $0.75 + $1.25 + $1.50 = $5.00, which is equal to the final sales price of the ream of paper. For any good or service, it will always be the case that the sum of the values added by all firms equals the final sales price. This leads to our second method of measuring GDP:

> In the **value-added approach,** GDP is the sum of the values added by all firms in the economy.

VALUE-ADDED APPROACH
Measuring GDP by summing the value added by all firms in the economy.

THE FACTOR PAYMENTS APPROACH. If a bakery sells $200,000 worth of bread during the year and buys $25,000 in intermediate goods (flour, eggs, yeast), then its value added—its revenue minus the cost of its intermediate goods—is $200,000 – $25,000 = $175,000. This is also the sum that will be left over from its revenue after the bakery pays for its intermediate goods.

Where does this $175,000 go? Is the entire sum kept by the owner of the bakery as profit? Unfortunately for the owner, no. In addition to its intermediate goods, the bakery must pay for the *resources* it used during the year—the land, labor, and capital that enabled it to add value to its intermediate goods.

FACTOR PAYMENTS Payments to the owners of resources that are used in production.

Payments to owners of resources are called **factor payments,** because resources are also called the "factors of production." Owners of capital (the owners of the firm's buildings or machinery, or those who lend funds to the firm so that *it* can buy buildings and machinery) receive *interest payments;* owners of land and natural resources receive *rent;* and those who provide labor to the firm receive *wages and salaries.* Finally, there is one additional resource used by the firm: *entrepreneurship.* In every capitalist economy, the entrepreneurs are those who visualize society's needs, mobilize and coordinate the other resources so that production can take place, and gamble that the enterprise will succeed. The people who provide this entrepreneurship (often the owners of the firms) receive a fourth type of factor payment—*profit.*

Now let's go back to our bakery, which received $200,000 in revenue during the year. We've seen that $25,000 of this went to pay for intermediate goods, leaving $175,000 in value added earned by the factors of production. Let's suppose that $110,000 went to pay the wages of the bakery's employees, $10,000 was paid out as interest on loans, and $15,000 was paid in rent for the land under the bakery. That leaves $175,000 – $110,000 – $10,000 – $15,000 = $40,000. This last sum—since it doesn't go to anyone else—stays with the owner of the bakery. It, too, is a

---

3.   To keep our example simple, we assume that the lumber company simply cuts down trees and slices up lumber, using just land, labor, and capital. We thus assume it uses no intermediate goods.

factor payment—profit—for the entrepreneurship she provides. Thus, when all of the factor payments—including profit—are added together, the total will be $110,000 + $10,000 + $15,000 + $40,000 = $175,000—precisely equal to the value added at the bakery. More generally,

in any year, the value added by a firm is equal to the total factor payments made by that firm.

Earlier, we learned that GDP equals the sum of all firms' value added; now we've learned that each firm's value added is equal to its factor payments. Thus, GDP must equal the total factor payments made by all firms in the economy. This gives us our *third* method of measuring GDP:

*In the **factor payments approach**, GDP can be measured by summing all of the factor payments made by all firms in the economy. Equivalently, it can be measured by adding up all of the income—wages and salaries, rent, interest, and profit—earned by all households in the economy.[4]*

FACTOR PAYMENTS AP-PROACH Measuring GDP by summing the factor payments made by all firms in the economy.

The factor payments approach to GDP gives us one of our most important insights into the macro-economy:

GDP—the total output of the economy—is equal to the total income earned in the economy.

This simple idea—output equals income—follows directly from the factor payments approach to GDP. And it explains why macro-economists often use the terms "output" and "income" interchangeably: They are one and the same. If output rises, income rises by the same amount; if output falls, income must drop by an equal amount.

Measuring GDP: A Summary
You've now learned three different ways to calculate GDP:

Expenditure Approach: GDP = $C + I^a + G + NX$

Value-Added Approach: GDP = Sum of value added by all firms

Factor Payments Approach: GDP = Sum of factor payments made by all firms
= Wages and salaries + interest + rent + profit
= Total household income

We will use these three approaches to GDP again and again as we study what makes the economy tick. Make sure you understand why each one of them should, in theory, give us the same number for GDP.

Real versus Nominal GDP
Since GDP is measured in dollars, we have a serious problem when we want to track the change in output over time. The problem is that the value of the dollar—

---

4. Actually, this is just an approximation. Before a firm divides up its value added among the different factors of production, it first deducts a small amount for depreciation of its plant and equipment, and another small amount for the sales taxes it must pay to the government. Thus, there is actually some difference between the value of GDP and the value of total factor payments. We ignore this difference in the text.

its purchasing power—is itself changing. As prices have risen over the past 100 years, the value of the dollar has steadily fallen. Trying to keep track of GDP using dollars in different years is like trying to keep track of a child's height using a ruler whose length changes each year. If we find that the child is three rulers tall in one year and four rulers tall in the next, we cannot know whether the child is really growing taller—or, if so, by how much—until we adjust for the effects of a changing ruler. The same is true for GDP and for any other economic variable measured in dollars: We usually need to adjust our measurements to reflect changes in the value of the dollar.

NOMINAL VARIABLE A variable measured without adjustment for the dollar's changing value.

> *When a variable is measured over time with no adjustment for the dollar's changing value, it is called a **nominal variable**. When a variable is adjusted for the dollar's changing value, it is called a **real variable**.*

REAL VARIABLE A variable adjusted for changes in the dollar's value.

   Most government statistics are reported in both nominal and real terms, but economists focus almost exclusively on real variables. This is because changes in nominal variables don't really tell us much. For example, from 1990 to 1991, nominal GDP increased from $5,744 billion to $5,917 billion. But production actually decreased during those years—the increase in nominal GDP was due entirely to a rise in prices.

THE IMPORTANCE OF REAL VALUES: A BASIC PRINCIPLE

The distinction between nominal and real values is crucial in macroeconomics. The public, the media, and sometimes even government officials have been confused by a failure to make this distinction. Whenever we want to track changes in key macroeconomic variables—such as the average wage rate, wealth, income, or GDP or any of its components—we always use *real* variables. This is why the importance of real variables is one of the basic principles of economics:

> *Basic Principle #8: The Importance of Real Values:*
> *Since our economic well-being depends, in part, on the goods and services we can buy, it is important to translate nominal values—which are measured in current dollars—to real values—which are measured in purchasing power.*

In the next chapter, you'll learn how economists translate nominal variables into real variables.

HOW GDP IS USED

We've come a long way since 1931. In that year—as the United States plummeted into the worst depression in our history—Congress summoned economists from government agencies, from academia, and from the private sector to testify about the state of the economy. They were asked the most basic questions: How much output was the nation producing, and how much had production fallen since 1929? How much income were Americans earning, how much were they spending on goods and services, and how much were they saving? How much profit were businesses earning, and what were they doing with their profits? Had the economy continued to deteriorate in the previous year, or had it finally hit bottom? To the surprise of the members of Congress, no one could answer any of these questions, because *no one was keeping track of our national income and output!* The last measurement—which was rather incomplete—had been made in 1929.

FIGURE 2	REAL GDP GROWTH (PERCENT): 1960–1998

Although the growth rate of real GDP has fluctuated over time, it has almost always exceeded the 1% rate needed to maintain output per capita. On the average, it has also exceeded the 2.5% rate needed to keep the unemployment rate from rising.

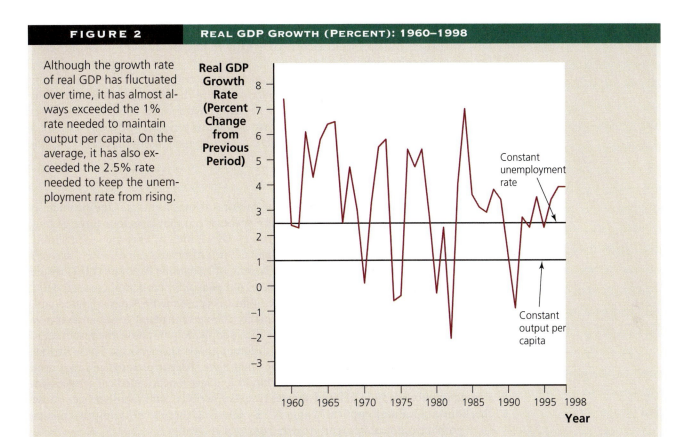

Source: *Economic Report of the President,* 1998 and 1999, and *Survey of Current Business,* various issues.

Thus began the U.S. system of national income accounts—a system whose value was instantly recognized around the world and was rapidly copied by other countries. Today, the government's reports on GDP are used to steer the economy over both the short run and the long run. In the short run, sudden changes in real GDP can alert us to the onset of a recession or a too-rapid expansion that can overheat the economy. Many (but not all) economists believe that, if alerted in time, the government can design policies to help keep the economy on a more balanced course.

GDP is also used to measure the long-run growth rate of the economy's output. Indeed, we typically define the average *standard of living* as *output per capita*—real GDP divided by the population. In order for output per capita to rise, real GDP must grow faster than the population. Since the U.S. population tends to grow by about 1 percent per year, a real GDP growth rate of 1 percent per year is needed just to *maintain* our output per capita; higher growth rates are needed to increase it.

Look at Figure 2, which shows the annual percentage change in real GDP from 1960 to 1998. The lower horizontal line indicates the one-percent growth needed to just maintain output per capita. You can see that, on average, real GDP has grown by more than this, so that output per capita has steadily increased over time.

Long-run growth in GDP is also important for another reason: to ensure that the economy generates enough additional jobs for a growing population. In order to prevent the unemployment rate from rising, real GDP must increase even faster than the population. In practice, a growth rate of about 2.5 percent per year—the upper horizontal line in the figure—seems to generate the required number of new jobs each year. You can see that real GDP growth has, on average, been sufficient for this purpose as well.

To sum up, we use GDP to guide the economy in two ways: in the short run, to alert us to recessions and give us a chance to stabilize the economy; and in the long run, to tell us whether our economy is growing fast enough to raise output per capita and our standard of living, and fast enough to generate sufficient jobs for a growing population. You can see that GDP is an extremely useful measure. But it is not without its problems.

PROBLEMS WITH GDP

Our GDP statistics are plagued by some important inaccuracies. One problem is *quality changes*. Suppose a new ballpoint pen comes out that lasts four times as long as previous versions. What *should* happen to GDP? Ideally, each new pen should count the same as four old pens, since one new pen offers the same *writing services* as four old ones. But the analysts at the Bureau of Economic Analysis (BEA) would most likely treat this new pen the same as an old pen and record an increase in GDP only if the total number of pens increased. Why? Because the BEA has a limited budget. While it does include the impact of quality changes for many goods and services (such as automobiles and computers), the BEA simply does not have the resources to estimate quality changes for millions of different goods and services. These include many consumer goods (such as televisions that have sharper pictures and that need fewer repairs, or razor blades that shave closer and last longer), medical services (increased surgery success rates and shorter recovery periods), and retail services (faster checkout times due to optical scanners). By ignoring these quality improvements, GDP probably understates true growth from year to year.

A second problem arises from the *underground economy*, which contains hidden economic activity, either because it is illegal (drugs, prostitution, most gambling) or because those engaged in it are avoiding taxes. These activities cannot be measured accurately, so the BEA must estimate them. Many economists believe that the BEA's estimates are too low. As a result, GDP may understate total output. However, since the *relative* importance of the underground economy does not change rapidly, the BEA's estimates of *changes* in GDP from year to year should not be seriously affected.

NONMARKET PRODUCTION
Goods and services that are produced, but not sold in a market.

Finally, except for food grown and consumed by farmers and for housing services, GDP does not include **nonmarket production**—goods and services that are produced, but not sold in the marketplace. All of the housecleaning, typing, sewing, lawn mowing, and child rearing that people do themselves, rather than hiring someone else, are excluded from GDP. Whenever a nonmarket transaction (say, cleaning your apartment) becomes a market transaction (hiring a housecleaner to do it for you), GDP will rise, even though total production (cleaning one apartment) has remained the same. This can exaggerate the growth in GDP over long periods of time. Over the last half-century, much production has, indeed, shifted away from the home and to the market. Parenting, which was not counted in past years' GDP, has become day care, which *does* count, currently contributing more than $4 billion annually to GDP. Similarly, home-cooked food has been replaced by takeout, talking to a friend has been replaced by therapy, and the neighbor who watches your house while you're away has been replaced by a store-bought alarm system or an increase in police protection. In all of these cases, real GDP increases, even though production has not.

What do these problems tell us about the value of GDP? That for certain purposes—especially interpreting *long-run* changes in GDP—we must exercise extreme caution. For example, suppose that, over the next 20 years, the growth rate of GDP slows down. Would this mean that something is going wrong with the economy? Would it suggest a need to change course? Not necessarily. It *could* be that the underground economy or unrecorded quality changes are becoming more important. Similarly, if GDP growth accelerates, it could mean that our living standards are rising more rapidly. But it might instead mean that economic activity is shifting out of the home and into the market even more rapidly than in the past.

When it comes to *short-term* changes in the economy, however, we can have much more confidence in using GDP. Look back at our discussion of problems with GDP in this section. The distortions we've discussed tend to remain roughly constant over the short run. If GDP suddenly drops, it is extremely unlikely that the underground economy has suddenly become more important, or that there has been a sudden shift from market to nonmarket activities, or that we are suddenly missing more quality changes than usual. Rather, we can be reasonably certain that output and economic activity are slowing down.

> *Short-term changes in real GDP are fairly accurate reflections of the state of the economy. A significant short-term drop in real GDP virtually always indicates a decrease in production, rather than a measurement problem.*

This is why policy makers, business people, and the media pay such close attention to GDP as a guide to the economy from quarter to quarter.

EMPLOYMENT AND UNEMPLOYMENT

When you think of unemployment, you may have an image in your mind that goes something like this: As the economy slides into recession, an anxious employee is called into an office and handed a pink slip by a grim-faced manager. "Sorry," the manager says, "I wish there were some other way. . . ." Perhaps, in your mind, the worker spends the next few months checking the classified ads, pounding the pavement, and sending out resumes in a desperate search for work. And perhaps, after months of trying, the laid-off worker gives up, spending days at the neighborhood bar, drinking away the shame and frustration, and sinking lower and lower into despair and inertia.

For some people, joblessness begins and ends very much like this—a human tragedy, and a needless one. On one side, we have people who want to work and support themselves by producing something; on the other side is the rest of society, which could certainly use more goods and services. Yet somehow, the system isn't working, and the jobless cannot find work. The result is often hardship for the unemployed and their families, and a loss to society in general.

But this is just one face of unemployment, and there are others. Some instances of unemployment, for example, have little to do with macroeconomic conditions. And frequently, unemployment causes a lot less suffering than in our grim story.

TYPES OF UNEMPLOYMENT

Economists have found it useful to classify unemployment into four different categories, each arising from a different cause and each having different consequences.

FRICTIONAL UNEMPLOYMENT. **Frictional unemployment** is short-term joblessness experienced by people who are between jobs or who are entering the labor

FRICTIONAL UNEMPLOYMENT Joblessness experienced by people who are between jobs or who are just entering or re-entering the labor market.

market for the first time or after a long absence. For example, imagine that you have a job, but that you think you'd be happier at some other firm. Since you can't search for a new job while working full-time, you may decide to quit your job and begin looking elsewhere. In an ideal frictionless world, every potential employer would immediately know that you were available, and you would immediately know which job you'd prefer most, so you would become reemployed the instant you quit; you would not be unemployed between jobs. Of course, in the real world, it takes time to find a job—time to prepare your resume, to decide where to send it, to wait for responses, and then to investigate job offers so you can make a wise choice. It also takes time for employers to consider your skills and qualifications and to decide whether you are right for their firms. During all that time, you will be unemployed: willing and able to work, but not working.

There are other examples of this type of unemployment. A parent reenters the labor force after several years spent raising the children. A 22-year-old searches for a job after graduating from college. In both of these cases, it may take some time to find a job, and during that time, the job seeker is *frictionally* unemployed.

Because frictional unemployment is, by definition, short term, it causes little hardship to those affected by it. In most cases, people have enough savings to support themselves through a short spell of joblessness, or else they can borrow on their credit card or from friends or family to tide them over. Moreover, this kind of unemployment has important benefits: By spending time searching rather than jumping at the first opening that comes their way, people find jobs for which they are better suited and in which they will ultimately be more productive. As a result, workers earn higher incomes, firms have more productive employees, and society has more goods and services.

SEASONAL UNEMPLOYMENT. **Seasonal unemployment** is joblessness related to changes in weather, tourist patterns, or other seasonal factors. For example, most ski instructors lose their jobs every April or May, and many construction workers are laid off each winter.

Seasonal unemployment, like frictional unemployment, is rather benign: It is short term, and, because it is entirely predictable, workers are often compensated in advance for the unemployment they experience in the off-season. Construction workers, for example, are paid higher-than-average hourly wages, in part to compensate them for their high probability of joblessness in the winter.

Seasonal unemployment complicates the interpretation of unemployment data. Seasonal factors push the unemployment rate up in certain months of the year and pull it down in others, even when overall conditions in the economy remain unchanged. For example, each June, unemployment rises as millions of high school and college students—who do not want to work during the school year—begin looking for summer jobs. If the government reported the actual rise in unemployment in June, it would *seem* as if labor market conditions were deteriorating, when in fact, the rise is just a predictable and temporary seasonal change. To prevent any misunderstandings, the government usually reports the *seasonally adjusted* rate of unemployment, a rate that reflects only those changes beyond normal for the month. For example, if the unemployment rate in June is typically one percentage point higher than during the rest of the year, then the seasonally adjusted rate for June will be the actual rate minus one percentage point.

STRUCTURAL UNEMPLOYMENT. Sometimes, there are jobs available and workers who would be delighted to have them, but job seekers and employers are

SEASONAL UNEMPLOYMENT Joblessness related to changes in weather, tourist patterns, or other seasonal factors.

mismatched in some way. For example, in the 1990s, there have been plenty of job openings in high-tech industries such as computer hardware and software design, satellite technology, and communications. Many of the unemployed, however, do not have the skills and training to work in these industries—there is a mismatch between the skills they have and those that are needed. The mismatch can also be geographic, as when construction jobs go begging in Northern California, Oregon, and Washington, but unemployed construction workers live in other states.

Unemployment that results from these kinds of mismatches is called **structural unemployment,** because it arises from *structural change* in the economy: when old, dying industries are replaced with new ones that require different skills and are located in different areas of the country. Structural unemployment is generally a stubborn, *long-term* problem, often lasting several years or more. Why? Because it can take considerable time for the structurally unemployed to find jobs—time to relocate to another part of the country or time to acquire new skills. To make matters worse, the structurally unemployed often need financial assistance for job training or relocation, but—because they don't have jobs—they are unable to get loans.

Structural unemployment is a much bigger problem in other countries, especially in Europe, than it is in the United States. At the end of 1998, when the U.S. unemployment rate was 4.3 percent, the rate in France was 11.5 percent; in Italy, 12.3 percent; and in Spain, 18.2 percent. All three countries have large groups of less-skilled workers who are unqualified for the jobs that are available. Even Canada suffers from much more structural unemployment than does the United States—its unemployment rate at the end of 1998 was 8.0 percent, much of it concentrated in the maritime provinces.

STRUCTURAL UNEMPLOYMENT Joblessness arising from mismatches between workers' skills and employers' requirements or between workers' locations and employers' locations.

The types of unemployment we've considered so far—frictional, structural, and seasonal—arise from *microeconomic* causes; that is, they are attributable to changes in specific industries and specific labor markets, rather than to conditions in the overall economy. This kind of unemployment cannot be eliminated, as people will always spend some time searching for new jobs, there will always be seasonal industries in the economy, and structural changes will, from time to time, require workers to move to new locations or gain new job skills. Some amount of microeconomic employment is a sign of a dynamic economy. It allows workers to sort themselves into the best possible jobs, enables us to enjoy seasonal goods and services like winter skiing and summers at the beach, and permits the economy to go through structural changes when needed.

Nevertheless, many economists feel that the levels of microeconomic unemployment in the United States are too high and that we can continue to enjoy the benefits of a fast-changing and flexible economy with a lower unemployment rate. To achieve this goal, they advocate government programs to help match the unemployed with employers and to help the jobless relocate and learn new skills. Note, however, that these are *microeconomic* policies—government intervention in particular labor markets or to help particular kinds of workers. Since frictional, seasonal, and structural unemployment have microeconomic causes, they need *micro*economic cures.

Our fourth and last type of unemployment, however, has an entirely *macro*economic cause.

CYCLICAL UNEMPLOYMENT. When the economy goes into a recession and total output falls, the unemployment rate rises. Many previously employed workers

| FIGURE 3 | U.S. QUARTERLY UNEMPLOYMENT RATE, 1960–1998 |

The unemployment rate rises during recessions (shaded) and falls during expansions.

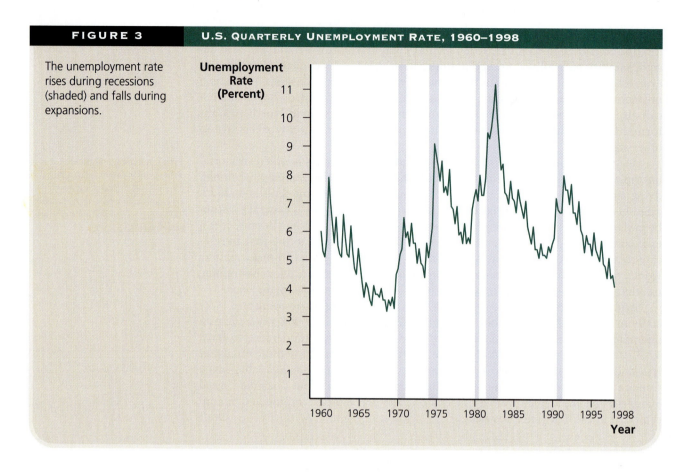

CYCLICAL UNEMPLOY-MENT Joblessness arising from changes in production over the business cycle.

lose their jobs and have difficulty finding new ones. At the same time, there are fewer openings, so new entrants to the labor force must spend more than the usual "frictional" time searching before they are hired. This type of unemployment—because it is caused by the business cycle—is called **cyclical unemployment.**

Look at Figure 3, which shows the unemployment rate in the United States for each quarter since 1960, and notice the rises that occurred during periods of recession (shaded). For example, in the recessions of the early 1980s, the unemployment rate rose from about 6 percent to more than 10 percent; in the more recent recession of 1990–1991, it rose from 5.3 percent to more than 7 percent. These were rises in cyclical unemployment.

Since it arises from conditions in the overall economy, cyclical unemployment is a problem for *macro*economic policy. This is why macroeconomists focus almost exclusively on cyclical unemployment, rather than the other types of joblessness. Reflecting this emphasis, macroeconomists say we have reached **full employment** when we come out of a recession and *cyclical unemployment is reduced to zero,* even though substantial amounts of frictional, seasonal, and structural unemployment may remain:

FULL EMPLOYMENT A situation in which there is no cyclical unemployment.

> *In macroeconomics, full employment is achieved when cyclical unemployment has been reduced to zero. But the overall unemployment rate at full employment is greater than zero, because there are still positive levels of frictional, seasonal, and structural unemployment.*

How do we tell how much of our unemployment is cyclical? Many economists believe that today, normal amounts of frictional, seasonal, and structural unemployment account for an unemployment rate of about 4.5 percent in the United States. Therefore, any unemployment beyond this is considered cyclical unemployment. For example, if the actual unemployment rate were 7 percent, we would identify 7 – 4.5 = 3.5 percent of the labor force as cyclically unemployed.

THE COSTS OF UNEMPLOYMENT

Why are we so concerned about achieving a low rate of unemployment? What are the *costs* of unemployment to our society? We can identify two different types of costs: economic costs—those that can be readily measured in dollar terms—and noneconomic costs—those that are difficult or impossible to measure in dollars, but still affect us in important ways.

ECONOMIC COSTS. The chief economic cost of unemployment is the *opportunity cost* of lost output—the goods and services the jobless would produce if they were working, but do not produce because they cannot find work. This cost must be borne by our society, although the burden may fall more on one group than another. If, for example, the unemployed were simply left to fend for themselves, then *they* would bear most of the cost. If they turned to crime in order to survive, then crime victims would share the burden. In fact, the unemployed are often given government assistance, so that the costs are spread among citizens in general. But there is no escaping this central fact:

> *When there is cyclical unemployment, the nation produces less output, and so some group or groups within society must consume less output.*

OPPORTUNITY COST

One way of viewing the economic cost of cyclical unemployment is illustrated in Figure 4. The blue line shows real GDP over time, while the red line shows the path of our **potential output**—the output we *could* have produced if the economy were operating at full employment.

Notice that actual output is sometimes *above* potential output. At these times, unemployment is *below* the full-employment rate. For example, during the expansion in the late 1960s, cyclical unemployment was eliminated, and the sum of frictional, seasonal, and structural unemployment dropped below 4.5 percent, its normal level for those years. At other times, real GDP is *below* potential output, most often during and immediately following a recession. At these times, unemployment rises above the full-employment rate. In the 1982–83 recession, the unemployment rate remained above 9.5 percent for more than a year.

In the figure, you can see that we have spent more of the last 35 years operating *below* our potential than above it. That is, the cyclical ups and downs of the economy have, on balance, led to lower living standards than we would have had if the economy had always operated just at potential output.

BROADER COSTS. There are also costs of unemployment that go beyond lost output—the *human* costs that we do not measure in dollars, but are significant nonetheless. Unemployment—especially when it lasts for many months or years—can have serious psychological and physical effects. Some studies have found that increases in unemployment cause noticeable rises in the number of heart attack deaths, suicides, and admissions to state prisons and psychiatric hospitals. The jobless are more likely to suffer a variety of health problems, including high blood pressure, heart disorders,

POTENTIAL OUTPUT
The level of output the economy could produce if it were operating at full employment.

FIGURE 4	ACTUAL AND POTENTIAL REAL GDP, 1960–1998

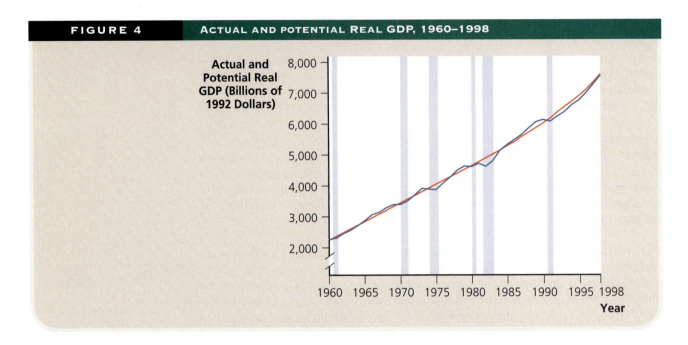

Actual and Potential Real GDP (Billions of 1992 Dollars)

troubled sleep, and back pain. There may be other problems—such as domestic violence, depression, and alcoholism—that are more difficult to document. And, tragically, most of those who lose their jobs also lose their health insurance, increasing the likelihood that these problems will have serious consequences.

Unemployment also causes setbacks in achieving important social goals. For example, most of us want a fair and just society where all people have an equal chance to better themselves. But our citizens do not bear the burden of unemployment equally. In a recession, we do not all suffer a reduction in our work hours; instead, some people are laid off entirely, while others continue to work roughly the same hours.

Moreover, the burden of unemployment is not shared equally among different groups in the population, but tends to fall most heavily on minorities, especially minority youth. As a rough rule of thumb, the unemployment rate for blacks is twice that for whites; and the rate for *teenage* blacks is triple the rate for blacks overall. Table 3 shows that the unemployment rates for December 1998 are consistent with this general experience. Notice the extremely high unemployment rate for black teenagers: 19.8 percent. Two years earlier—when the overall unemployment rate was 5.3 percent, the rate for black teenagers was even higher: 34.7 percent. This contributes to a vicious cycle of poverty and discrimination: When minority youths

TABLE 3	UNEMPLOYMENT RATES FOR VARIOUS GROUPS, DECEMBER 1998

Group	Rate
Whites	3.6%
Hispanics	7.5%
Blacks	7.1%
White Teenagers	11.1%
Black Teenagers	19.8%

Source: *The Employment Situation: December 1998*, Bureau of Labor Statistics News Release, January 7, 1999.

are deprived of that all-important first job, they remain at a disadvantage in the labor market for years to come.

How Unemployment Is Measured

In December 1998, about 140 million Americans did not have jobs at the time. Were all of these people unemployed? Absolutely not. The unemployed are those *willing and able* to work, but who do not have jobs. Most of the 140 million nonworking Americans were either *un*able or *un*willing to work. For example, the very old, the very young, and the very ill were unable to work, as were those serving prison terms. Others were able to work, but preferred not to, including millions of college students, homemakers, and retired people.

But how, in practice, can we determine who is willing and able? This is a thorny problem, and there is no perfect solution to it. In the United States, we determine whether a person is willing and able to work by his or her *behavior*. More specifically, to be counted as unemployed, you must have recently *searched* for work. But how can we tell who has, and who has not, recently searched for work?

The Census Bureau's Household Survey. Every month, thousands of interviewers from the United States Census Bureau—acting on behalf of the U.S. Bureau of Labor Statistics (BLS)—knock on the doors of 50,000 households across America. This sample of households is carefully selected to give information about the entire population. Household members who are under 16, in the military, or currently residing in an institution like a prison or hospital are excluded. The interviewer will then ask questions to determine what the remaining household members did during the *previous week*.

Figure 5 shows roughly how this works. First, the interviewer asks whether the household member has worked one or more hours for pay or profit. If the answer

The Economy at a Glance
The Bureau of Labor Statistics' latest data on employment, unemployment, earnings, and productivity with charts showing the recent history of each data series.
http://www.bls.gov/eag.table.html

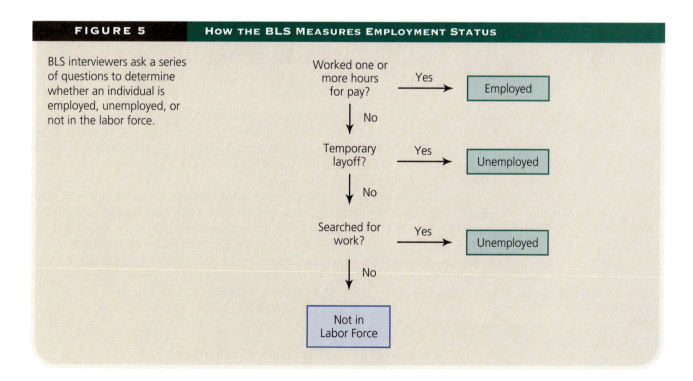

| FIGURE 5 | HOW THE BLS MEASURES EMPLOYMENT STATUS |

BLS interviewers ask a series of questions to determine whether an individual is employed, unemployed, or not in the labor force.

Worked one or more hours for pay? — Yes → Employed
↓ No
Temporary layoff? — Yes → Unemployed
↓ No
Searched for work? — Yes → Unemployed
↓ No
Not in Labor Force

| FIGURE 6 | EMPLOYMENT STATUS OF THE U.S. POPULATION (DECEMBER 1998) |

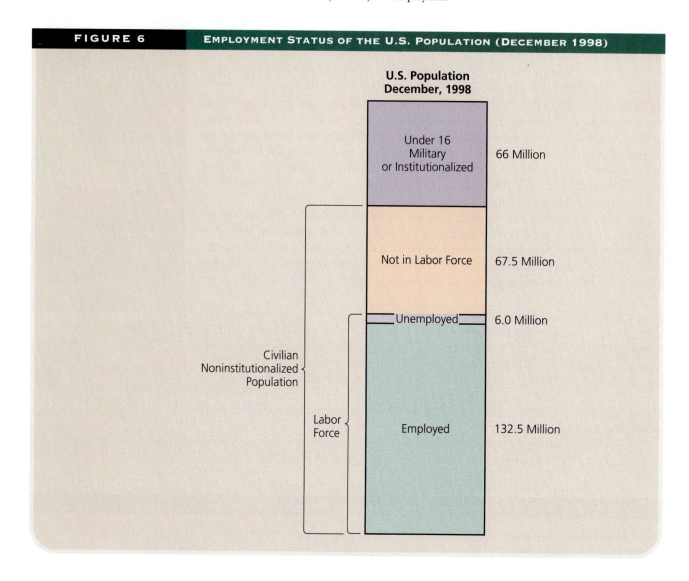

is yes, the person is considered employed; if no, another question is asked: Has she been *temporarily* laid off from a job from which she is waiting to be recalled? A yes means the person is unemployed; a no leads to one more question: Did the person actively search for work during the previous four weeks? If yes, the person is unemployed; if no, she is not in the labor force.

Figure 6 illustrates how the BLS, extrapolating from its 50,000-household sample, classified the U.S. population in December 1998. First, note that 66 million people were ruled out from consideration because they were under 16 years of age, living in institutions, or in the military. The remaining 206 million people made up the civilian, noninstitutional population, and of these, 132.5 million were employed, and 6.0 million were unemployed. Adding the employed and unemployed together gives us the **labor force**, equal to 132.5 million + 6.0 million = 138.5 million.

Finally, we come to the official **unemployment rate**, which is defined as the percentage of the labor force that is unemployed:

$$\text{Unemployment rate} = \text{Unemployed/Labor force}$$
$$= \text{Unemployed/(Unemployed + Employed)}$$

LABOR FORCE Those people who have a job or who are looking for one.

UNEMPLOYMENT RATE The fraction of the labor force that is without a job.

Using the numbers in Figure 6, the unemployment rate in December 1998 was 6.0 / (6.0 + 132.5) = 0.043 or 4.3 percent. This was the number released to journalists at 8:00 A.M. on the first Friday of January 1999, and the number that appeared in the headlines of your local newspaper the next day.

PROBLEMS IN MEASURING UNEMPLOYMENT

The Bureau of the Census earns very high marks from economists for both its sample size—65,000 households—and the characteristics of its sample, which very closely match the characteristics of the U.S. population. Still, the official unemployment rate suffers from some important measurement problems.

Many economists believe that our official measure seriously underestimates the extent of unemployment in our society. There are two reasons for this belief: the treatment of *involuntary part-time workers,* and the treatment of *discouraged workers.* As you can see in Figure 5, anyone working one hour or more for pay during the survey week is treated as employed. This includes many people who would like a full-time job—and may even be searching for one—but who did some part-time work during the week. Some economists have suggested that these people—called **involuntary part-time workers**—should be regarded as partially employed and partially unemployed.

INVOLUNTARY PART-TIME WORKERS Individuals who would like a full-time job, but who are working only part time.

How many involuntary part-time workers are there? At the end of 1998, the BLS estimated that there were about 3.5 million.[5] If each of these workers were considered half employed and half unemployed, the unemployment rate at the end of 1998 would have been 5.5 percent, instead of the officially reported 4.3 percent.

Another problem is the treatment of **discouraged workers**—individuals who would like to work but, because they feel little hope of finding a job, have given up searching. Because they are not taking active steps to find work, they are considered "not in the labor force" (see Figures 5 and 6). Some observers feel that discouraged workers should be counted as unemployed. After all, these people are telling us that they are willing and able to work, but they are not working. It seems wrong to exclude them just because they are not actively seeking work. Others argue that counting discouraged workers as unemployed would reduce the objectivity of our unemployment measure. Talk is cheap, they believe, and people may *say* anything when asked whether they would like a job; the real test is what people *do.* Yet even the staunchest defenders of the current method of measuring employment would agree that *some* discouraged workers are, in fact, willing and able to work and should be considered unemployed. The problem, in their view, is determining which ones.

DISCOURAGED WORKERS Individuals who would like a job, but have given up searching for one.

How many discouraged workers are there? No one knows for sure. The BLS tries to count them periodically, but defining who is genuinely discouraged is a thorny problem. Using the BLS's rather strict criteria, there were 358,000 discouraged workers at the end of 1998. But with a looser, unofficial definition of "discouraged worker"—people who are not working but say they want a job—the count rises to 4.2 million. Including some or all of these people among the unemployed would raise the unemployment rate significantly.

There are also reasons to believe that the unemployment rate overstates the amount of joblessness as we usually think of it. Remember that a person is counted as unemployed if he or she did not work in the past week, but took some active steps to look for work in the past month. Some of those counted as unemployed did work earlier in the month, even though they were not at work in the survey week.

---

5.   This and other information about unemployment in December 1998 comes from *The Employment Situation: December 1998,* Bureau of Labor Statistics News Release, January 7, 1999.

Others whose principal activities are outside the labor market—going to school, keeping house, or being retired—are counted as unemployed because they checked the help-wanted ads in the past month or talked to friends about what jobs might be available.

Still, the unemployment rate—as currently measured—tells us something important: the number of people who are *searching* for jobs, but have not yet found them. It is not exactly the same as the percentage of the labor force that is jobless even though willing and able to work. But if we could obtain a perfect measure of the latter, the unemployment rate—as currently measured—would be highly correlated with it.

Moreover, the unemployment rate tells us something unique about conditions in the macro-economy. When the unemployment rate is relatively low—so that few people are actively seeking work—a firm that wants to hire more workers may be forced to lure them from other firms by offering a higher wage rate. This puts upward pressure on wages and can lead to future inflation. A high unemployment rate, by contrast, tells us that firms can more easily expand by hiring those who are actively seeking work, without having to lure new workers from another firm and without having to offer higher wages. This suggests little inflationary danger. Later in the book, we will discuss the connection between unemployment and inflation more fully.

USING THE THEORY

SOCIETY'S CHOICE OF GDP

The title of this section might seem absurd: How can we say that society chooses its level of GDP? Wouldn't the citizens of any nation want their GDP to be as large as possible—and certainly larger than it currently is? The answer is yes. After all, GDP is certainly important to our economic well-being. Few of us would want to live at the levels of output per capita that prevailed 100, 50, or even 25 years ago. Increased output of medical care, restaurant meals, entertainment, transportation services, and education have all contributed to a higher standard of living and an overall improvement in our economic well-being.

But there is more to economic well-being than *just* GDP. Suppose that, over the next 10 years, real GDP per capita were to double. Further, suppose that our measure is entirely accurate (not plagued by the measurement problems discussed in the previous section). Would the average person be better off in 10 years? Maybe. But maybe not. We cannot say, because our GDP statistic ignores so many *other* things that are important to our economic well-being besides the quantity of goods and services at our disposal, and these things may be changing at the same time that GDP is changing.

What are these other things that affect our economic well-being? They include the leisure time we have to spend with family and friends; the cleanliness of our environment; the safety of our workplaces, homes, and streets; the fairness of our society; and more. None of these are included in GDP, which is, after all, just a measure of our output of goods and services.

But what does this have to do with society's choice of GDP? Remember that economics is the study of choice under conditions of scarcity, and just as individuals are constrained by a scarcity of time or income or wealth, society as a whole is constrained by the resources at its disposal. In many cases, we must choose between using our resources to have more of the output that is included in GDP or more of *other* things we care about that are *not* part of GDP.

FIGURE 7	THE TRADEOFF BETWEEN REAL GDP AND LEISURE

The production possibilities frontier shows that, for a given population and state of technology, a fully employed economy must choose between the level of real GDP and the time available for leisure. At point *A*, people devote all their time to leisure, so GDP is zero. Point *D*, by contrast, represents the maximum GDP attainable if everyone works the maximum hours, year-round. *B* and *C* represent intermediate possibilities.

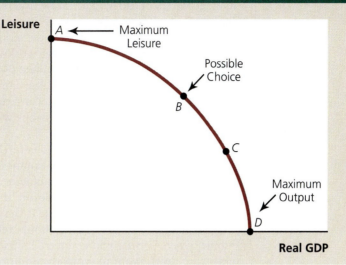

For example, look at Figure 7, which shows the familiar production possibility frontier, or PPF, from Chapter 2, but with a new twist. Instead of looking at the tradeoff between two different *goods*—such as movies and medical care—we explore the tradeoff between real GDP on the horizontal axis and some other thing that we care about—in this example, leisure time—on the vertical axis.

Why is there a tradeoff between real GDP and leisure? Because with a given state of technology for producing output, a given population, and given quantities of other resources, the more labor time we devote to production, the more goods and services we will have. But more labor time means less leisure time: Either more people must become employed, or the employed must work longer hours. In either case, the total amount of leisure time enjoyed by the population will decrease.

Let's first identify the two extremes of the PPF in the figure. The maximum leisure time achievable would occur at point *A*—zero output. Here, people would have to survive by eating fruit and nuts that fell to the ground, since even climbing trees or hunting animals would involve "work." On the other hand, the maximum GDP achievable would require the lowest possible level of leisure—every able-bodied person working 16 hours per day, 365 days per year. This is indicated by point *D* in the figure. The curve which connects points *A* and *D* is the PPF that shows the maximum combinations of output and leisure achievable. (Why does the curve bow out from the origin? Review the material on PPFs in Chapter 2 if you need to.)

The PPF in the figure makes it clear that society faces a tradeoff and that, in any year, we choose our level of GDP subject to the constraints of this tradeoff. We could draw a similar PPF illustrating the tradeoff between a high GDP on the one hand and a clean environment or workplace safety on the other.

How does society choose its location on this kind of PPF?

In a market economy, the choice is made partly by individual households and firms. Suppose that most workers' tastes began to shift toward having more leisure and that they were willing to sacrifice income in order to have it. For example, workers might prefer a 20 percent cut in work hours, with a 20 percent cut in total compensation. Suppose, too, that there were no loss of efficiency from having people work shorter hours. Then any firm that refused to match these new worker preferences—cutting pay and work hours by 20 percent—would have to pay above-average wages in order to attract workers. With higher labor costs, the firm would have to charge a higher price for its output. Such a firm would not be able to compete with other firms that were offering the more desired, shorter workweek. As more and more firms moved toward a shorter workweek, society as a whole would move from a point like C in Figure 7 to a point like B—more leisure and a lower GDP.

Thus, at least to some extent, we can expect market pressures to adjust work hours to worker preferences for leisure on the one hand and income on the other. The result of these individual decisions will determine, in large measure, where we will be on the PPF in Figure 7.

Interestingly, the United States is farther down and to the right on this PPF (a point like C) than most European countries (which are at points like B). For example, the average workweek in manufacturing is 37.7 hours in the United States, but only 30 hours in Germany. In addition, the typical U.S. worker takes two weeks of vacation each year, while the typical German worker takes five weeks. To a great extent, these differences in labor hours reflect differences in worker tastes. For example, when Germany introduced Thursday night shopping in 1989, retail workers—who didn't want to work the additional two hours even for additional pay—went on strike. As a result of his greater taste for leisure, the typical German—and the typical French person, Italian, and Spaniard—enjoys more leisure each year than the typical American does. But Europeans pay a cost: a lower GDP, and therefore fewer goods and services per person than they would otherwise have.

Our location on the PPF is also determined by society as a whole, as a matter of public policy. We vote for our representatives, who make rules and regulations under which our firms must operate. If, for example, the majority prefers a higher GDP and less leisure, it can vote for representatives who promise to change work rules. In Germany, for example, it is *illegal* for workers to take another job during their five-weeks of annual vacation.[6]

There are also other dimensions to our choice of GDP. For example, with economic growth, a nation can enjoy a greater GDP in the future *and* more of other things—say, workplace safety or leisure. But economic growth comes at a cost as well. We'll examine that cost—and society's choices concerning the rate of economic growth—in Chapter 14.

---

6. Benjamin, Daniel and Tony Horwitz, "German View: You Americans Work Too Hard—And For What?" *Wall Street Journal*, July 14, 1994, p. B1.

S U M M A R Y

This chapter discusses how some key macroeconomic aggregates are measured and reported. One important economic aggregate is *gross domestic product*—the total value of all final goods and services produced for the marketplace during a given year, within a nation's borders. GDP is a measure of an economy's total production. It is a flow variable that measures sales, to final users, of newly produced output.

In the *expenditure approach,* GDP is calculated as the sum of spending by households, businesses, governments, and foreigners on domestically produced goods and services. The *value-added approach* computes GDP by adding up each firm's contributions to total product as it is being produced. Value added at each stage of production is the revenue a firm receives minus the cost of the intermediate inputs it uses. Finally, the *factor payments approach* sums the payments to all resource owners. The three approaches reflect three different ways of viewing GDP.

Since nominal GDP is measured in current dollars, it changes when either production or prices change. *Real GDP* is nominal GDP adjusted for price changes; it rises only when production rises.

Real GDP is useful in the short run for giving warnings about impending recessions, and in the long run for indicating how fast the economy is growing. Unfortunately, it is plagued by important inaccuracies. It does not fully reflect quality changes or production in the underground economy, and it does not include many types of nonmarket production.

When real GDP grows, employment tends to rise and unemployment tends to fall. In the United States, a person is considered unemployed if he or she does not have a job but is actively seeking one. Economists have found it useful to classify unemployment into four different categories. *Frictional unemployment* is short-term unemployment experienced by people between jobs or by those who are just entering the job market. *Seasonal unemployment* is related to changes in the weather, tourist patterns, or other predictable seasonal changes. *Structural unemployment* results from mismatches—in skills or location—between jobs and workers. Finally, *cyclical unemployment* occurs because of the business cycle. Unemployment, particularly the structural and cyclical forms, involves costs. From a social perspective, unemployment means lost production. From the individual viewpoint, unemployment often involves financial, psychological, and physical harm.

K E Y   T E R M S

gross domestic product (GDP)	private-investment spending	factor payments approach	cyclical unemployment
intermediate goods	net investment spending	nominal variable	full employment
final good	government purchases	real variable	potential output
flow variable	transfer payments	nonmarket production	labor force
stock variable	net exports	frictional unemployment	unemployment rate
expenditure approach	value added	seasonal unemployment	involuntary part-time workers
consumption	value-added approach	structural unemployment	discouraged workers
capital stock	factor payments		

R E V I E W   Q U E S T I O N S

1. What is the difference between final goods and intermediate goods? Why is it that only the value of final goods and services is counted in GDP?

2. Which of the following are stock variables, and which are flow variables?
   a. Microsoft's revenues
   b. Microsoft's market value (the total value of shares held by its stockholders)
   c. A household's spending
   d. The value of a household's stock portfolio

3. Using the expenditure approach, which of the following would be directly counted as part of 1999 U.S. GDP? In each case, state whether the action causes an increase in C, I^a, G, or NX.
   a. A new personal computer produced by IBM, which remained unsold at the year's end
   b. A physician's services to a household
   c. Produce bought by a restaurant to serve to customers
   d. The purchase of 1,000 shares of Disney stock
   e. The sale of 50 acres of commercial property
   f. A real estate agent's commission from the sale of property
   g. A transaction in which you clean your roommate's apartment in exchange for his working on your car
   h. An Apple Imac computer produced in the United States and purchased by a French citizen.
   i. The government's Social Security payments to retired people

4. How is the word "investment" used differently in economics than in ordinary language? Explain each of the three categories of investment.

5. Describe the different kinds of factor payments.

6. What is the difference between nominal and real variables? What is the main problem with using nominal variables to track the economy?

7. Discuss the value and reliability of GDP statistics in both short-run and long-run analyses of the economy.

8. GDP was measured at around $7.2 trillion in 1995. Was the actual value of goods and services produced in the United States in 1995 likely to have been higher or lower than that? Why?

9. In later chapters, you will learn about policies the government can pursue to reduce cyclical unemployment. What, if anything, could the government do to reduce frictional and structural unemployment?

10. Categorize each of the following according to the type of unemployment it reflects. Justify your answers.
    a. Workers are laid off when a GM factory closes due to a recession.
    b. Workers making typewriters are laid off when their firm goes bankrupt due to competition from personal computers.

c. Migrant farm workers' jobs end when the harvest is finished.

d. Lost jobs result from the movement of textile plants from Massachusetts to the South and overseas.

11. In what sense can unemployment sometimes be considered a constructive aspect of economic life?

12. What are some of the different types of costs associated with unemployment?

13. Discuss some of the problems with the way the Bureau of Labor Statistics computes the unemployment rate. In what ways might official criteria lead to an overestimate or underestimate of the actual unemployment figure?

PROBLEMS AND EXERCISES

1. Calculate the total change in a year's GDP for each of the following scenarios:

a. A family sells a home, without using a broker, for $150,000. They could have rented it on the open market for $700 per month. They buy a 10-year-old condominium for $200,000; the broker's fee on the transaction is 6 percent of the selling price. The condo's owner was formerly renting the unit at $500 per month.

b. General Electric uses $10 million worth of steel, glass, and plastic to produce its dishwashers. Wages and salaries in the dishwasher division are $40 million; the division's only other expense is $15 million in interest that it pays on its bonds. The division's revenue for the year is $75 million.

c. On March 31, you decide to stop throwing away $50 a month on convenience store nachos. You buy $200 worth of equipment, corn meal, and cheese, and make your own nachos for the rest of the year.

d. You win $25,000 in your state's lottery. Ever the entrepreneur, you decide to open a Ping Pong ball washing service, buying $15,000 worth of equipment from SpiffyBall Ltd. of Hong Kong and $10,000 from Ball-B-Kleen of Toledo, Ohio.

e. Tone-Deaf Artists, Inc. produces 100,000 new White Snake CDs that it prices at $15 apiece. Ten thousand CDs are sold abroad, but, alas, the rest remain unsold on warehouse shelves.

2. The country of Freedonia uses the same method to calculate the unemployment rate as the U.S. Bureau of Labor Statistics uses. From the data below, compute Freedonia's unemployment rate.

Population	10,000,000
Under 16	3,000,000
Over 16	
In military service	500,000
In hospitals	200,000
In prison	100,000
Worked one hour or more in previous week	4,000,000
Searched for work during previous four weeks	1,000,000

3. The Bureau of Economic Analysis (BEA), an agency of the Department of Commerce, is "the nation's economic accountant," responsible for tracking key national, international, and regional data relating to the U.S. economy. At the BEA's web site, http://www.bea.doc.gov/, follow the link "BEA News Releases" and find the most recent release about GDP. When did the release occur? Was it an "advance," "preliminary," or "final" release? For which quarter? What was the estimated rate of growth of real GDP in that quarter? What was the estimated rate of growth of nominal (current-dollar) GDP in that quarter? When will the next release occur?

CHALLENGE QUESTION

1. Suppose, in a given year, someone buys a General Motors automobile for $30,000. That same year, GM produced the car in Michigan, using $10,000 in parts imported from Japan. However, the parts imported from Japan themselves contained $3,000 in components produced in the United States.

a. How much does U.S. GDP rise?

b. Using the expenditure approach, what is the change in each component (C, I^a, G, and NX) of U.S. GDP?

c. What is the change in Japan's GDP and each of its components?

CHAPTER 13

THE MONETARY SYSTEM, PRICES, AND INFLATION

You pull into a gas station deep in the interior of the distant nation of Chaotica. The numbers on the gas pump don't make sense to you, and you can't figure out how much to pay. Luckily, the national language of Chaotica is English, so you can ask the cashier how much the gas costs. He replies, "Here in Chaotica, we don't have any standard system for measuring quantities of gas, and we don't have any standard way to quote prices. My pump here measures in my own unit, called the Slurp, and I will sell you 6 Slurps for that watch you are wearing, or a dozen Slurps for your camera." You spend the next half hour trying to determine how many Slurps there are in a gallon and what form of payment you can use besides your watch and camera.

Life in the imaginary nation of Chaotica would be difficult. People would spend a lot of time figuring out how to trade with each other, time that could otherwise be spent producing things or enjoying leisure activities. Fortunately, in the real world, virtually every nation has a *monetary system* that helps to organize and simplify our economic transactions.

THE MONETARY SYSTEM

A monetary system establishes two different types of standardization in the economy. First, it establishes a **unit of value**—a common unit for measuring how much something is worth. A standard unit of value permits us to compare the costs of different goods and services and to communicate these costs when we trade. The dollar is the unit of value in the United States. If a college textbook costs $75, while a one-way airline ticket from Phoenix to Minneapolis costs $300, we know immediately that the ticket has the same value in the marketplace as four college textbooks.

The second type of standardization concerns the **means of payment**—the things we can use as payment when we buy goods and services. In the United States, the

UNIT OF VALUE A common unit for measuring how much something is worth.

MEANS OF PAYMENT Anything acceptable as payment for goods and services.

339

means of payment include dollar bills, personal checks, money orders, credit cards like Visa and American Express, and, in some experimental locations, prepaid cash cards with magnetic strips.

These two functions of a monetary system—establishing a unit of value and a standard means of payment—are closely related, but they are not the same thing. The unit-of-value function refers to the way we *think* about and record transactions; the means-of-payment function refers to how payment is actually made.

The unit of value works in the same way as units of weight, volume, distance, and time. In fact, the same sentence in Article I of the U.S. Constitution gives Congress the power to create a unit of value along with units of weights and measures. All of these units help us determine clearly and precisely what is being traded for what. Think about buying gas in the United States—you exchange dollars for gallons. The transaction will go smoothly and quickly only if there is clarity about both the unit of fluid volume (gallons) *and* the unit of purchasing power (dollars).

The means of payment can be different from the unit of value. For example, in some countries where local currency prices change very rapidly, it is common to use the U.S. dollar as the unit of value—to specify prices in dollars—while the local currency remains the means of payment. Even in the United States, when you use a check to buy something, the unit of value is the dollar, but the means of payment is a piece of paper with your signature on it.

In the United States, the dollar is the centerpiece of our monetary system. It is the unit of value in virtually every economic transaction, and dollar bills are very often the means of payment as well. How did the dollar come to play such an important role in the economy?

HISTORY OF THE DOLLAR

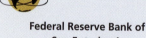

Federal Reserve Bank of San Francisco's
American Currency Exhibit
An on-line money museum where you can learn the history of money in the U.S. and view the different types of currency used since colonial times.
http://www.frbsf.org/currency/index.html

FEDERAL RESERVE SYSTEM The central bank and national monetary authority of the United States.

Prior to 1790, each colony had its own currency. It was named the "pound" in every colony, but it had a different purchasing power in each of them. In 1790, soon after the Constitution went into effect, Congress created a new unit of value called the "dollar." Historical documents show that merchants and businesses switched immediately to the new dollar, thereby ending the chaos of the colonial monetary systems. Prices began to be quoted in dollars, and accounts were kept in dollars. The dollar rapidly became the standard unit of value.

But the primary means of payment in the United States until the Civil War was paper currency issued by private banks. Just as the government defined the length of the yard, but did not sell yardsticks, the government defined the unit of value, but let private organizations provide the means of payment.

During the Civil War, however, the government issued the first federal paper currency, the greenback. It functioned as both the unit of value and the major means of payment until 1879. Then the government got out of the business of money creation for a few decades. During that time, currency was once again issued by private banks. Then, in 1913, a new institution called the **Federal Reserve System** was created to be the national monetary authority in the United States. The Federal Reserve was charged with creating and regulating the supply of money in the nation and it continues to do so today.

WHY PAPER CURRENCY IS ACCEPTED AS A MEANS OF PAYMENT

You may be wondering why people are willing to accept paper dollars as a means of payment. Why should a farmer give up a chicken, or a manufacturer give up a new car, just to receive a bunch of green rectangles with words printed on them? In fact, paper currency is a relatively recent development in the history of the means of payment.

The earliest means of payment were precious metals and other valuable commodities such as furs or jewels. These were called *commodity money* because they had important uses other than as a means of payment. The nonmoney use is what gave commodity money its ultimate value. For example, people would accept furs as payment because furs could be used to keep warm. Similarly, gold and silver had a variety of uses in industry, as religious artifacts, and for ornamentation.

Precious metals were an especially popular form of commodity money. Eventually, to make it easier to identify the value of precious metals, they were minted into coins whose weight was declared on their faces. Because gold and silver coins could be melted down into pure metal and used in other ways, they were still commodity money.

Commodity money eventually gave way to paper currency. Initially, the paper currency was just a certificate representing a certain amount of gold or silver held by a bank. At any time, the holder of a certificate could go to the bank that issued it and trade the certificate for the stated amount of gold or silver. People were willing to accept paper money as a means of payment for two reasons. First, it could be exchanged for a valuable commodity like gold or silver. Second, the issuer—either a government or a bank—could only print new money when it acquired additional gold or silver. This put strict limits on money printing, so people had faith that their paper money would retain its value in the marketplace.

Indeed, when the United States government printed greenbacks during the Civil War, they were not exchangeable into gold and quickly began to lose value in relation to gold. On the other hand, when the U.S. Federal Reserve began printing paper currency in 1913, it was fully exchangeable into gold and retained its value.

But today, paper currency is no longer backed by gold or any other physical commodity. If you have a dollar handy, put this book down and take a close look at the bill. You will not find on it any promise that you can trade your dollar for gold, silver, furs, or anything else. Yet we all accept it as a means of payment. Why? A clue is provided by the statement in the upper left-hand corner of every bill: *This note is legal tender for all debts, public and private.* The statement affirms that the piece of paper in your hands will be accepted as a means of payment (you can "tender" it to settle any "debt, public or private") by any American because the government says so. This type of currency is called **fiat money.** *Fiat,* in Latin, means "let there be" and fiat money serves as a means of payment by government declaration.

The government need not worry about enforcing this declaration. The real force behind the dollar is its long-standing acceptability by *others.* As long as you have confidence that you can exchange your dollars for goods and services, you won't mind giving up goods and services for dollars. And because everyone else feels the same way, the circle of acceptability is completed.

But while the government can declare that paper currency be accepted as a means of payment, it cannot declare the terms. Whether 10 gallons of gas will cost you 1 dollar, 10 dollars or 20 dollars is up to the marketplace. The value of the dollar—its purchasing power—does change from year to year, as reflected in the changing prices of the things we buy. In the rest of this chapter, we will discuss some of the problems created by the dollar's changing value and the difficulty economists have measuring and monitoring the changes. We postpone until later chapters the question of *why* the value of the dollar changes from year to year.

governmental action that gives our money value ↓

FIAT MONEY Anything that serves as a means of payment by government declaration.

MEASURING THE PRICE LEVEL AND INFLATION

PRICE LEVEL The average level of dollar prices in the economy.

One hundred years ago, you could buy a pound of coffee for 15 cents, see a Broadway play for 40 cents, buy a new suit for $6, and attend a private college for $200 in yearly tuition.[1] Needless to say, the price of each of these items has gone up considerably since then. Microeconomic causes—changes in individual markets—can explain only a tiny fraction of these price changes. For the most part, these price rises came about because of an ongoing rise in the **price level**—the average level of dollar prices in the economy. In this section, we begin to explore how the price level is measured, and how this measurement is used.

INDEX NUMBERS

INDEX A series of numbers used to track a variable's rise or fall over time.

Most measures of the price level are reported in the form of an **index**—a series of numbers, each one representing a different period. Index numbers are meaningful only in a *relative* sense: We compare one period's index number with that of another period and can quickly see which one is larger and by how much. The actual number for a particular period has no meaning in and of itself.

In general, an index number for any measure is calculated as

$$\frac{\text{Value of measure in current period}}{\text{Value of measure in base period}} \times 100.$$

Let's see how index numbers work with a simple example. Suppose we want to measure how violence on TV has changed over time, and we have data on the number of violent acts shown in each of several years. We could then construct a TV-violence index. Our first step would be to choose a *base period*—a period to be used as a benchmark. Let's choose 1993 as our base period, and suppose that there were 10,433 violent acts on television in that year. Then our violence index in any current year would be calculated as

$$\frac{\text{Number of violent acts in current year}}{10,433} \times 100$$

In 1993—the base year—the index will have the value $(10,433/10,433) \times 100 = 100$. Look again at the general formula for index numbers, and you will see that this is always true: *An index will always equal 100 in the base period.*

Now let's calculate the value of our index in another year. If there were 14,534 violent acts in 1998, then the index that year would have the value

$$\frac{14,534}{10,433} \times 100 = 139.3$$

Index numbers compress and simplify information, so that we can see how things are changing at a glance. Our media violence index, for example, tells us at a glance that the number of violent acts in 1998 was 139.3 percent of the number in 1993. Or, more simply, TV violence grew by 39.3 percent between 1993 and 1998.

---

1.   Scott Derks, ed., *The Value of the Dollar: Prices and Incomes in the United States: 1860–1989* (Detroit, MI: Gale Research Inc., 1994), various pages.

THE CONSUMER PRICE INDEX

The most widely used measure of the price level in the United States is the **Consumer Price Index (CPI)**. This index—which is designed to track the prices paid by the typical consumer—is compiled and reported by the Bureau of Labor Statistics (BLS).

Measuring the prices paid by the typical consumer is not easy. Two problems must be solved before we even begin. The first problem is to decide which goods and services we should include in our average. The CPI tracks only *consumer* prices; it excludes goods and services that are not directly purchased by consumers. More specifically, the CPI excludes goods purchased by businesses (such as capital equipment, raw materials, or wholesale goods), goods and services purchased by government agencies (such as fighter bombers and the services of police officers), and goods and services purchased by foreigners (U.S. exports). The CPI *does* include newly produced consumer goods and services that are part of consumption spending in our GDP—things such as new clothes, new furniture, new cars, haircuts, and restaurant meals. It also includes some things that are *not* part of our GDP because they are part of the typical family's budget. For example, the CPI includes prices for *used* goods like used cars or used books and imports from other countries—for example, French cheese, Japanese cars, and Mexican tomatoes.

The second problem is how to combine all the different prices into an average price level. In any given month, different prices will rise by different amounts. The average price of doctor's visits might rise by 1 percent, the price of blue jeans might rise by a tenth of a percent, the price of milk might fall by a half of a percent, and so on. When prices change at different rates, and when some are rising while others are falling, how can we track the change in the *average* price level?

We would not want to use a simple average of all prices—adding them up and dividing by the number of goods. A proper measure would recognize that we spend very little of our incomes on some goods—such as Tabasco sauce—and much more on others—like car repairs or rent. The CPI's approach is to track the cost of the *CPI market basket*—the collection of goods and services that the typical consumer bought in some base period. If the market basket's cost rises by 10 percent over some period, then the price level, as reported by the CPI, will rise by 10 percent. This way, goods and services that are relatively unimportant in the typical consumer's budget will have little weight in the CPI. Tabasco sauce could triple in price and have no noticeable impact on the cost of the complete market basket. Goods that are more important—such as auto repairs or rent—will have more weight. The appendix to this chapter discusses the calculation of the CPI in more detail.

CONSUMER PRICE INDEX An index of the cost, through time, of a fixed market basket of goods purchased by a typical household in some base period.

HOW THE CPI HAS BEHAVED

In recent years, the base period for the CPI has been the period 1982–1984,[2] so, following our general formula for price indexes, the CPI is calculated as

$$\frac{\text{Cost of market basket in current year}}{\text{Cost of market basket in 1982–1984}} \times 100$$

---

2. From February 1998, the market basket was updated to reflect purchasing patterns in 1993–1995. However, the *base period* used in calculation remained 1982–1984. Thus, after February 1998, the specific formula became: CPI = (Cost of 1993–1995 market basket in current year/Cost of 1993–1995 market basket in 1982–1984) × 100. The denominator requires some careful interpretation: It is what the 1993–1995 market basket *would* have cost at 1982–1984 prices. With this formula, the CPI in 1982–1984 remains equal to 100.

TABLE 1	CONSUMER PRICE INDEX, FIVE-YEAR INTERVALS, 1960–1998

Year	Consumer Price Index (December)
1960	29.6
1965	31.5
1970	38.8
1975	53.8
1980	82.4
1985	107.6
1990	130.7
1995	152.4
1998	163.0

Table 1 shows the actual value of the CPI for selected years. Because it is reported in index number form, we can easily see how much the price level has changed over different time intervals. In 1998, for example, the CPI had an average value of 163.0, telling us that the typical market basket in that year cost 63.0 percent more than it would have cost in the 1982–1984 base period. In 1960, the CPI was 29.6, so the cost of the market basket in that year was only 29.6 percent of its cost in 1982–1984.

FROM PRICE INDEX TO INFLATION RATE

INFLATION RATE The percent change in the price level from one period to the next.

DEFLATION The percent *decrease* in the price level from one period to the next when the price level is falling.

The Consumer Price Index is a measure of the price level in the economy. The **inflation rate** measures how fast the price level is changing, in percentage. When the price level is rising, as it almost always is, the inflation rate is positive. When the price level is falling, as it did during the Great Depression, we have a negative inflation rate, which is called **deflation**.

Figure 1 shows the U.S. rate of inflation—as measured by the CPI—since 1950. Notice that inflation was low in the 1950s and 1960s, was high in the 1970s and early 1980s, and has been low since then. In later chapters, you will learn what causes the inflation rate to rise and fall.

HOW THE CPI IS USED

The CPI is one of the most important measures of the performance of the economy. It is used in three major ways:

AS A POLICY TARGET. In Chapter 11, we identified price stability—or a low inflation rate—as one of the nation's important macroeconomic goals. The measure most often used to gauge our success in achieving low inflation is the CPI.

DANGEROUS CURVES

People often confuse the statement "prices are rising" with the statement "inflation is rising," but they do not mean the same thing. Remember that the inflation rate is the rate of *change* of the price level. To have rising inflation, the price level must be rising by a greater and greater percentage each period. But we can also have rising prices and *falling* inflation. For example, from 1996 to 1998, the CPI rose each year—"prices were rising." But they rose by a smaller percentage each year than the year before, so "inflation was falling"—from 3.0 percent, to 2.3 percent, and, finally, to 1.7 percent.

TO INDEX PAYMENTS. A payment is **indexed** when it rises and falls proportionately with a price index. An indexed payment makes up for the loss in purchasing power that occurs when the price level rises. It raises the nominal payment

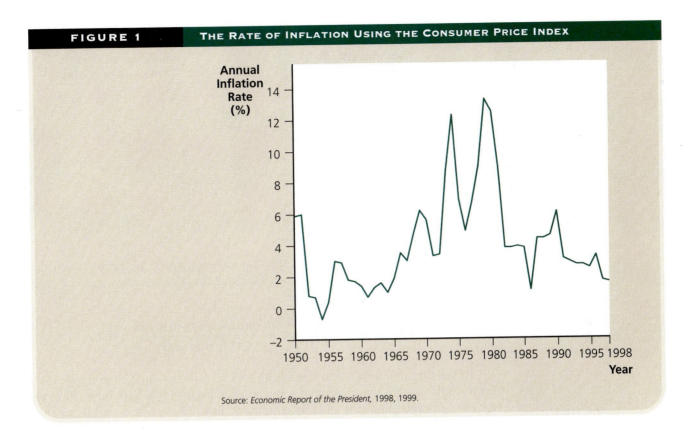

FIGURE 1   THE RATE OF INFLATION USING THE CONSUMER PRICE INDEX

Source: *Economic Report of the President,* 1998, 1999.

by just enough to keep its purchasing power unchanged. In the United States, millions of government retirees and Social Security recipients have their benefit payments indexed to the CPI. About one-quarter of all union members—more than 5 million workers—have labor contracts that index their wages to the CPI. Since the 1980s, the U.S. income tax has been indexed as well—the threshold income levels at which tax rates change automatically rise at the same rate as the CPI. And the government now sells bonds that are indexed to the CPI. The owner of an indexed bond receives a payment each year to make up for the loss of purchasing power when the CPI rises.

INDEXATION Adjusting the value of some nominal payment in proportion to a price index, in order to keep the real payment unchanged.

TO TRANSLATE FROM NOMINAL TO REAL VALUES. In order to compare economic values from different periods, we must translate *nominal variables*—measured in the number of dollars—into *real variables*, which are adjusted for the change in the dollar's purchasing power. The CPI is often used for this translation. Since calculating real variables is one of the most important uses of the CPI, we devote the next section to that topic.

REAL VARIABLES AND ADJUSTMENT FOR INFLATION

Suppose that from December 1999 to December 2000, your nominal wage—what you are paid in dollars—rises from $15 to $30 per hour. Are you better off? That depends. You are earning twice as many dollars. But you should care not about how many green pieces of paper you earn, but how many goods and services you can buy with that paper. How, then, can we tell what happened to your purchasing power? By focusing not on the **nominal wage**—the number of *dollars* you earn—but on the **real wage**—the *purchasing power* of your wage. To track your real wage, we need to look at the number of dollars you earn *relative to the price level.*

NOMINAL WAGE A wage measured in current dollars.

REAL WAGE A wage measured in terms of purchasing power.

TABLE 2	NOMINAL AND REAL WAGES		
Year	Nominal Wage (dollars per hour)	CPI	Real Wage in 1982–1984 (dollars per hour)
1960	2.09	29.6	7.06
1965	2.46	31.5	7.81
1970	3.23	38.8	8.32
1975	4.53	53.8	8.42
1980	6.66	82.4	8.08
1985	8.57	107.6	7.96
1990	10.01	130.7	7.66
1995	11.43	152.4	7.52
1998	12.77	163.0	7.83

Since the "typical worker" and the "typical consumer" are pretty much the same, the CPI is usually the price index used to calculate the real wage. The real-wage formula is as follows:

$$\text{Real wage in any year} = \frac{\text{Nominal wage in that year}}{\text{CPI in that year}} \times 100$$

To see that this formula makes sense, let's go back to our fictional example: From 1999 to 2000, your nominal wage doubles from $15 to $30. Now, suppose the price of everything that you buy doubles at the same time. It is easy to see that in this case, your purchasing power would remain unchanged. And that is just what our formula tells us: If prices double, the CPI doubles as well. With 1999 as our base year, the CPI would increase from 100 in 1999 to 200 in the year 2000. The *real* wage would be ($15/100) × 100 = $15 in 1999 and ($30/200) × 100 = $15 in 2000. The real wage would remain unchanged.

Now suppose that prices doubled between 1999 and 2000, but your nominal wage remained unchanged at $15. In this case, your purchasing power would be cut in half. You'd have the same number of dollars, but each one would buy half as much as it did before. Our formula gives us a real wage of ($15/100) × 100 = $15 in 1999 and ($15/200) × 100 = $7.50 in 2000. The real wage falls by half.

Now look at Table 2, which shows the average hourly earnings of wage earners over almost four decades. In the first two columns, you can see that the average American wage earner was paid about $4.53 per hour in 1975 and almost triple that—$12.77—in 1998. Does this mean the average hourly worker was paid more in 1998 than in 1975? In *dollars*, the answer is clearly yes. But what about in *purchasing power*? Or, using the new terminology you've learned, what happened to the *real wage* over this period?

We know that the nominal wage rose from $4.53 in 1975 to $12.77 in 1998. But—from the table—we also know that the CPI rose from 53.8 to 163.0. Using our formula, we find that

$$\text{Real wage in 1975} = \frac{\$4.53}{53.8} \times 100 = \$8.42$$

$$\text{Real wage in 1998} = \frac{\$12.77}{163.0} \times 100 = \$7.83$$

Thus, although the average worker earned more *dollars* in 1998 than in 1975, her purchasing power seems to have fallen over those years. *Why* this apparent decline in purchasing power? This is an interesting and important question, and one we'll begin to answer later in the chapter. The important point to remember here is this:

THE IMPORTANCE OF REAL VALUES

> *When we measure changes in the macroeconomy, we usually care not about the number of dollars we are counting, but the purchasing power those dollars represent. Thus, we translate nominal values into real values using the formula*
>
> $$\text{real value} = \frac{\text{nominal value}}{\text{price index}} \times 100$$

This formula, usually using the CPI as the price index, is how most real values in the economy are calculated. But there is one important exception: To calculate real GDP, the government uses a different procedure, to which we now turn.

INFLATION AND THE MEASUREMENT OF REAL GDP

In the previous chapter, we discussed the difference between nominal GDP and real GDP. After reading this chapter, you might think that real GDP is calculated just like the real wage: dividing nominal GDP by the consumer price index. But the consumer price index is *not* used to translate nominal GDP figures into real GDP figures. Instead, a special price index—which we can call the **GDP price index**—is calculated for GDP.

GDP PRICE INDEX An index of the price level for all final goods and services included in GDP.

The most important differences between the CPI and the GDP price index are in the types of goods and services covered by each index. First, the GDP price index includes some prices that the CPI ignores. In particular, while the CPI tracks only the prices of goods bought by American *consumers*, the GDP price index must also include the prices of goods and services purchased by the government, investment goods purchased by businesses, and exports, which are purchased by foreigners.

Second, the GDP price index *excludes* some prices that are part of the CPI. In particular, the GDP price index leaves out used goods and imports, both of which are included in the CPI. This makes sense, because while used goods and imports are part of the typical consumers market basket, they do not contribute to current U.S. GDP. We can summarize the chief difference between the CPI and the GDP price index this way:

> *The GDP price index measures the prices of all goods and services that are included in U.S. GDP, while the CPI measures the prices of all goods and services bought by U.S. households.[3]*

THE COSTS OF INFLATION

A high or even moderate rate of inflation—whether it is measured by the CPI or the GDP price index—is never welcome news. What's so bad about inflation? As we've seen, it certainly makes your task as an economics student more difficult: Instead of

---

3. The technical name for the GDP price index is the *chain-type annual weights GDP price index*. It differs from the CPI not only in goods covered, but also in its mathematical formula.

taking nominal variables at face value, you must do those troublesome calculations to convert them into real variables. But inflation causes much more trouble than this. It imposes important costs on society and on each of us as individuals. Yet when most people are asked what this cost is, they come up with an incorrect answer.

THE INFLATION MYTH

Most people think that inflation—merely by making goods and services more expensive—erodes the average purchasing power of income in the economy. The reason for this belief is easy to see: The higher the price level, the fewer goods and services a given income will buy. It stands to reason, then, that inflation—which raises prices—must be destroying the purchasing power of our incomes. Right?

Actually, this statement is mostly wrong. It is true that when the price level rises, the average family *would* be able to buy fewer goods . . . *if* its nominal income remained unchanged. The "if," however, is crucial. In general, nominal incomes do not remain unchanged when prices rise.

To see why, let's consider a simple example: Suppose that we can divide the economy into two distinct groups of people: wage earners and goods sellers. (In the real world, people are often both, but not in this example.) Now suppose the price level doubles, but all wages remain unchanged. The average wage earner would then see the purchasing power of his income cut in half.

But that is only part of the story. Remember that every market transaction involves *two* parties—a buyer and a seller. If wages remained constant as prices doubled, then sellers of goods and services would have a field day. They would sell their goods at higher prices, yet pay their workers the same wages as before. Sellers' profits—which are part of their incomes—would rise. In fact, the real incomes of sellers would rise by as much as the real incomes of wage earners fell. Inflation would have *redistributed* purchasing power among the population, but the average purchasing power (including both buyers and sellers in the average) would remain unchanged.

In fact, it is rare for wages to remain constant when the price level rises. And when nominal wages rise along with prices, wage earners will see a smaller decline in their real incomes. Indeed, if nominal wages rise by the same proportion as prices, wage earners will not suffer at all. But whatever happens to wages, our conclusion remains the same:

> *Inflation can redistribute purchasing power from one group to another, but it cannot—by itself—decrease the average real income in the economy.*

Why, then, do people continue to believe that inflation robs the average citizen of real income? Largely because real incomes sometimes do decline—for *other* reasons. Inflation—while not the *cause* of the decline—will often be the *mechanism* that brings it about. Just as we often blame the messenger for bringing bad news, so too, we often blame inflation for lowering our purchasing power when the real cause lies elsewhere.

Let's consider an example. In Table 2, notice the decline in real wages during the late 1970s. The real wage fell from $8.42 in 1975 to $8.08 in 1980—a decline of more than 4 percent. During this period, not only wage earners, but also salaried workers, small-business owners, and corporate shareholders all suffered a decline in their real incomes. What caused the decline?

There were several reasons, but one of the most important was the dramatic rise in the price of imported oil—from $3 per barrel in 1973 to $34 in 1981, an increase of more than 1,000 percent. The higher price for oil meant that oil-exporting countries, like Saudi Arabia, Kuwait, and Iraq, got more goods and services for each barrel of oil they supplied to the rest of the world, including the United States. But with these nations claiming more of America's output, less remained for the typical American. That is, the typical American family had to suffer a decline in real income. As always, a rise in price shifted income from buyers to sellers. But in this case, the sellers were foreigners, while the buyers were Americans. Thus, the rise in price of foreign oil caused average purchasing power in the United States to decline.

But what was the mechanism that brought about the decline? Since real income is equal to (nominal income/price index) × 100, it can decrease in one of two ways: a fall in the numerator (nominal income) or a rise in the denominator (the price index). The decline in real income in the 1970s was all from the denominator. Look back at Figure 1. You can see that this period of declining real wages in the United States was also a period of unusually high inflation; at its peak in 1979, the inflation rate exceeded 13 percent. As a result, most workers blamed *inflation* for their loss of purchasing power. But inflation was not the *cause;* it was just the *mechanism.* The cause was a change in the terms of trade between the United States and the oil exporting countries—a change that resulted in higher oil prices.

To summarize, the common idea that inflation imposes a cost on society by decreasing average real income in the economy is incorrect. But inflation *does* impose costs on society, as the next section shows.

THE REDISTRIBUTIVE COST OF INFLATION

One cost of inflation is that it often redistributes purchasing power *within* society. Because the winners and losers are chosen haphazardly—rather than by conscious social policy—the redistribution of purchasing power is not generally desirable. In some cases, the shift in purchasing power is downright perverse—harming the needy and helping those who are already well off.

How does inflation sometimes redistribute real income? An increase in the price level reduces the purchasing power of any payment that is specified in nominal terms. For example, some workers have contracts that set their dollar wage for two or three years, regardless of any future inflation. The nationally set minimum wage, too, is set for several years and specified in dollars. Under these circumstances, inflation can harm ordinary workers, since it erodes the purchasing power of their prespecified wage. Real income is redistributed from these workers to their employers, who benefit by paying a lower real wage. But the effect can also work the other way: benefiting ordinary households and harming businesses. For example, many homeowners sign fixed-dollar mortgage agreements with a bank. These are promises to pay the bank a nominal sum each month. Inflation can reduce the *real* value of these payments, thus redistributing purchasing power away from the bank and toward the average home owner.

In general,

> *inflation can shift purchasing power away from those who are awaiting future payments specified in dollars and toward those who are obligated to make such payments.*

But does inflation *always* redistribute income from one party in a contract to another? Actually, no; if the inflation is expected by both parties, it should not redistribute income. The next section explains why.

***EXPECTED* INFLATION *DOES NOT* SHIFT PURCHASING POWER.** Suppose a labor union is negotiating a 3-year contract with an employer, and both sides agree that workers should get a 3 percent increase in their real wage. If neither side anticipates any inflation, they could simply negotiate a 3 percent *nominal* wage hike. With an unchanged price level, the *real* wage would then also rise by 3 percent.

Now suppose that both sides anticipate 10 percent inflation each year for the next 3 years. Then, they must agree to *more* than a 3 percent nominal wage increase in order to raise the real wage by 3 percent. How much more?

We can answer this question with a simple mathematical rule:

> *Over any period, the percentage change in a real value (%∆Real) is approximately equal to the percentage change in the associated nominal value (%∆Nominal) minus the rate of inflation:*
>
> **%∆Real = %∆Nominal − Rate of Inflation**

If the inflation rate is 10 percent, and the real wage is to rise by 3 percent, then the change in the nominal wage must satisfy the equation

3 percent = %∆Nominal − 10 percent ⇒ %∆Nominal = 13 percent

The required nominal wage hike is 13 percent.

You can see that as long as both sides correctly anticipate the inflation and no one stops them from negotiating a 13 percent nominal wage hike, inflation will *not* affect either party in real terms:

> *If inflation is fully anticipated, and if there are no restrictions on contracts, then inflation will* not *redistribute purchasing power.*

We come to a similar conclusion about contracts between lenders and borrowers. When you lend someone money, you receive a reward—an interest payment—for letting that person use your money instead of spending it yourself. The annual *interest rate* is the interest payment divided by the amount of money you have lent. For example, if you lend someone $1,000 and receive back $1,040 one year later, then your interest payment is $40, and the interest *rate* on the loan is $40/$1,000 = 0.04, or 4 percent.

But there are actually *two* interest rates associated with every loan. One is the **nominal interest rate**—the percentage increase in the lender's *dollars* from making the loan. The other is the **real interest rate**—the percentage increase in the lender's *purchasing power* from making the loan. It is the *real* rate—the change in purchasing power—that lenders and borrowers should care about.

In the absence of inflation, real and nominal interest rates would always be equal. A 4 percent increase in the lender's dollars would always imply a 4 percent increase in her purchasing power. But if there is inflation, it will reduce the purchasing power of the money paid back. Does this mean that inflation redistributes purchasing power? Not if the inflation is correctly anticipated and if there are no restrictions on making loan contracts.

For example, suppose both parties anticipate inflation of 5 percent and want to arrange a contract whereby the lender will be paid a 4 percent *real* interest rate. What *nominal* interest rate should they choose? Since an interest rate is the *percentage change* in the lender's funds, we can use our approximation rule,

NOMINAL INTEREST RATE
The annual percent increase in a lender's *dollars* from making a loan.

REAL INTEREST RATE The annual percent increase in a lender's *purchasing power* from making a loan.

$$\%\Delta Real = \%\Delta Nominal - \text{Rate of inflation}$$

which here becomes

$$\%\Delta \text{ in Lender's purchasing power} = \%\Delta \text{ in Lender's dollars} - \text{rate of inflation}$$

or

$$\text{Real interest rate} = \text{Nominal interest rate} - \text{Rate of inflation}$$

In our example, where we want the real interest rate to equal 4 percent when the inflation rate is 5 percent, we must have

$$4 \text{ percent} = \text{Nominal interest rate} - 5 \text{ percent,}$$

or

$$\text{Nominal interest rate} = 9 \text{ percent}$$

Once again, we see that as long as both parties correctly anticipate the inflation rate and there are no restrictions on contracts (that is, they are free to set the nominal interest rate at 9 percent), then no one gains or loses.

When inflation is *not* correctly anticipated, however, our conclusion is very different.

UNEXPECTED INFLATION *DOES* SHIFT PURCHASING POWER. Suppose that, expecting no inflation, you agree to lend money at a 4 percent nominal interest rate for 1 year. You and the borrower think that this will translate into a 4 percent real rate. But it turns out you are both wrong: The price level actually rises by 3 percent, so the *real* interest rate ends up being 4 percent – 3 percent = 1 percent. As a lender, you have given up the use of your money for the year, expecting to be rewarded with a 4 percent increase in purchasing power. But you get only a 1 percent increase. Your borrower was willing to pay 4 percent in purchasing power, but ends up paying only 1 percent. *Unexpected* inflation has led to a better deal for your borrower and a worse deal for you.

That will not make you happy. But it could be even worse. Suppose the inflation rate is higher—say, 6 percent. Then your real interest rate ends up at 4 percent – 6 percent = –2 percent—a negative real interest rate. You get back less in purchasing power than you lend out—*paying* (in purchasing power) for the privilege of lending out your money. The borrower is *rewarded* (in purchasing power) for borrowing! Negative real interest rates are more than a theoretical possibility. In the late 1970s, when inflation turned out higher than expected for several years in a row, many borrowers ended up paying negative rates to lenders.

Now, let's consider one more possibility: Expected inflation is 6 percent, so you negotiate a 10 percent nominal rate. But the actual inflation rate turns out to be zero, so the real interest rate is 10 percent – 0 percent = 10 percent. In this case, inflation turns out to be *less* than expected, so the real interest rate is higher than either of you anticipated. Your borrower is harmed, and you (the lender) benefit.

These examples apply, more generally, to any agreement on future payments: to a worker waiting for a wage payment and the employer who has promised to pay it; to a doctor who has sent out a bill and the patient who has not yet paid it; or to a supplier who has delivered goods and his customer who hasn't yet paid for them.

> *When inflationary expectations are inaccurate, purchasing power is shifted between those obliged to make future payments and those waiting to be paid. An inflation rate higher than expected harms those awaiting payment and benefits the payers; an inflation rate lower than expected harms the payers and benefits those awaiting payment.*

THE RESOURCE COST OF INFLATION

In addition to its possible redistribution of income, inflation imposes another cost upon society. To cope with inflation, we are forced to use up time and other resources as we go about our daily economic activities (shopping, selling, saving) that we could otherwise have devoted to productive activities. Thus, inflation imposes an *opportunity cost* on society as a whole and on each of its members:

 **OPPORTUNITY COST**

> *When people must spend time and other resources coping with inflation, they pay an opportunity cost—they sacrifice the goods and services those resources could have produced instead.*

Let's first consider the resources used up by *consumers* to cope with inflation. Suppose you shop for clothes twice a year. You've discovered that both The Gap and Banana Republic sell clothing of similar quality and have similar service, and you naturally want to shop at the one with the lower prices. If there is no inflation, your task is easy: You shop first at The Gap and then at Banana Republic; thereafter, you rely on your memory to determine which is less expensive.

With inflation, however, things are more difficult. Suppose you find that prices at Banana Republic are higher than you remember them to be at The Gap. It may be that Banana Republic is the more expensive store, or it may be that prices have risen at *both* stores. How can you tell? Only a trip back to The Gap will answer the question—a trip that will cost you extra time and trouble. If prices are rising very rapidly, you may have to visit both stores on the same day to be sure which one is cheaper. Now, multiply this time and trouble by all the different types of shopping you must do on a regular or occasional basis—for groceries, an apartment, a car, concert tickets, compact discs, restaurant meals, and more. Inflation can make you use up valuable time—time you could have spent earning income or enjoying leisure activities.

Inflation also forces *sellers* to use up resources. First, remember that sellers of goods and services are also buyers of resources and intermediate goods. They, too, must do comparison shopping when there is inflation, and use up hired labor time in the process. Second, each time sellers raise their own prices, labor is needed to put new price tags on merchandise, to enter new prices into a computer scanning system, or to change the prices on advertising brochures, menus, and so on.

Finally, inflation makes us all use up resources managing our financial affairs. We'll try to keep our funds in accounts that pay high nominal interest rates, in order to preserve our purchasing power and minimize what we keep as cash or in low-interest checking accounts. Of course, this means more frequent trips to the bank or the automatic teller machine, to transfer money into our checking accounts or get cash each time we need it.

All of these additional activities—inspecting prices at several stores, changing price tags or price entries, going back and forth to the automatic teller machine—use up not only time, but other resources too, such as gasoline or paper. From society's point of view, these resources could have been used to produce additional goods and services that we would all enjoy. Recall our discussion at the beginning of the chapter about the large benefits of standardization in the unit of value. Some of these benefits diminish if inflation is high, because the unit of value becomes so unstable.

You may not have thought much about the resource cost of inflation, because in recent years, U.S. inflation has been so low—under 3 percent per year in the 1990s. Such low rates of inflation are often called *creeping inflation*—from week to week or month to month, the price level creeps up so slowly that we hardly notice the change. The cost of coping with creeping inflation is negligible.

But it has not always been this way. Three times during the last 50 years, we have had double-digit inflation—about 14 percent during 1947–1948, 12 percent in 1974, and 13 percent during 1979 and 1980. Going back farther, the annual inflation rate reached almost 20 percent during World War I and rose above 25 percent during the Civil War. And as serious as these episodes of American inflation have been, they pale in comparison to the experiences of other countries. In Germany in the early 1920s, the inflation rate hit thousands of percent *per month*. And more recently—in the late 1980s—several South American countries experienced inflation rates in excess of 1,000 percent annually. For a few weeks in 1990, Argentina's annual inflation rate reached 400,000 percent! Under these conditions, the monetary system breaks down almost completely. Economic life is almost as difficult as in Chaotica.

IS THE CPI ACCURATE?

The Bureau of Labor Statistics spends millions of dollars gathering data to ensure that its measure of inflation is accurate. To determine the market basket of the typical consumer every 10 years or so, the BLS randomly selects thousands of households and analyzes their spending habits. In the last household survey—completed in 1993–1995—each of about 15,000 families kept diaries of their purchases for two weeks.

But that is just the beginning. Every month, the bureau's shoppers visit 23,000 retail stores, 7,000 rental apartments, and 18,000 owner-occupied homes to record 71,000 different prices. Finally, all of the prices are combined to determine the cost of the typical consumer's market basket for the current month.

The BLS is a highly professional agency, typically headed by an economist. Billions of dollars are at stake for each 1 percent change in the CPI, and the BLS has kept its measurement honest and free of political manipulation. Nevertheless, conceptual problems and resource limitations make the CPI fall short of the ideal measure of inflation. Economists—even those who work in the BLS—widely agree that the CPI seriously overstates the U.S. inflation rate. By how much?

According to a report by an advisory committee of economists appointed by the Senate Finance Committee in 1996, the overall bias is at least 1.1 percent per year.[4] That is, in a typical year, the reported rise in the CPI is about 1 percentage point greater than the true rise in the price level.

There are several causes of this bias.

---

4.   See *Toward a More Accurate Measure of the Cost of Living,* Report to the Senate Finance Committee from the Advisory Commission to Study the Consumer Price Index, December 1996.

SOURCES OF BIAS IN THE CPI

SUBSTITUTION BIAS. The CPI has largely ignored a general principle of consumer behavior: People tend to *substitute* goods that have become relatively cheaper for those that have become relatively more expensive. For example, in the 7 years from 1973 to 1980, the price of oil-related products—like gasoline and home heating oil—increased by more than 300 percent, while the prices of most other goods and services rose by less than 100 percent. As a result, people found ways to conserve on oil products. They joined carpools, used public transportation, insulated their homes, and in many cases moved closer to their workplaces to shorten their commute. Yet throughout this period, the CPI basket—based on the 1972–1973 household survey—assumed that consumers were buying unchanged quantities of oil products.

This example illustrates the following general principle:

> *Because the CPI has been updating its market basket only every 10 years or so, it has routinely overestimated the relative importance of goods whose prices are rising most rapidly and underestimated the relative importance of goods whose prices are falling or rising more slowly. The result is an overestimate of the inflation rate.*

NEW TECHNOLOGIES. A brand-new technology often makes it cheaper to achieve a given standard of living, but the CPI is not able to take that factor into account. One problem is that goods using new technologies are introduced into the BLS market basket only after a long lag. These goods often drop rapidly in price after they are introduced, helping to balance out price rises in other goods. By excluding a category of goods whose prices are dropping, the CPI overstates the rate of inflation. For example, until 1998, the cellular phone was not included in the BLS basket of goods, so the rapid decline in its price was missed by the CPI.

But there is another issue with new technologies: They often offer consumers a lower cost alternative for obtaining the same service. For example, the introduction of cable television lowered the cost of entertainment significantly by offering a new, cheaper alternative to going out to see movies. This should have registered as a drop in the price of "seeing movies." But the CPI does not have any good way to measure this reduction in the cost of living. Instead, it treats cable television as an entirely separate service.

> *The CPI excludes many new products that lower the cost of living when they come on the market, and—when included—regards them as entirely separate from existing goods and services. The result is an overestimate of the inflation rate.*

CHANGES IN QUALITY. Many products are improving over time. Cars are much more reliable than they used to be and require much less routine maintenance. They have features like air bags and antilock brakes that were unknown in the early 1980s. The CPI struggles to deal with these changes. It knows that when cars get more expensive, some of the rise in price is not really inflation, but rather charging more because the consumer is *getting* more. But many improvements in quality are not considered in the CPI at all. When food prices rise due to better nutritional quality, or when the cost of surgery rises due to greater success rates, the BLS merely records a price increase, as if the same thing is costing more.

> *The CPI fails to recognize that, in many cases, prices rise because of improvements in quality, not because the cost of living has risen. This causes the CPI to overstate the inflation rate.*

GROWTH IN DISCOUNTING. The CPI treats toothpaste bought at a high-priced drugstore and toothpaste bought at Wal-Mart as different products. And it assumes that we continue to buy from high- and low-priced stores in unchanged proportions. But that is not what has been happening. In fact, Americans are buying more and more of their toothpaste and other products from discounters, but the CPI does not consider this in measuring inflation. The purchasing power you have lost from inflation is not as great as the CPI says if you, like most Americans, are stretching your dollar by going more often to discount outlets and warehouse stores.

> *The CPI omits reductions in the prices people pay from more frequent shopping at discount stores and so overstates the inflation rate.*

THE CONSEQUENCES OF OVERSTATING INFLATION

The impact of overstating the inflation rate by 1.1 percent per year is both serious and wide ranging. First, it means that many real variables are rising more rapidly than the official numbers suggest. For example, based on the CPI measure of inflation, the average real wage *fell* by about 7 percent between 1975 and 1998 (see Table 2). But suppose the CPI has indeed overstated the inflation rate by just 1.1 percentage points in each of those years, as the government's advisory commission has suggested. Then the real wage has not fallen at all over this period, but has actually *risen* by 18.5 percent. (See Challenge Question #3 at the end of this chapter.)

Second, remember that low inflation is an important macroeconomic goal. As you'll learn in future chapters, this goal is not always easy to achieve and may require large—if temporary—sacrifices. If the CPI overstates inflation, we may be making these sacrifices unnecessarily: We may take painful steps to bring inflation down when the real problem is that our official inflation measure is exaggerating the problem.

Finally, since many payments are indexed to the CPI, an overstatement of inflation results in *over*indexing—payments that rise *faster* than the true price level. For example, suppose a Social Security recipient's payment of $1,000 per month is indexed to the CPI in order to keep the real payment constant as prices rise. Suppose, too, that over 10 years, the CPI reports annual inflation of 3 percent. By the end of the period, the CPI will rise by 35%, and the nominal payment will rise to $1,350.[5] But what if the CPI is wrong, and the actual inflation rate was just 1.9 percent per year during the period? Then, using the initial year as the base period, an accurate price index would have risen from 100 to 120.7. This tells us that the *real* Social Security payment will rise from $1,000 to ($1,350/120.7) × 100 = $1,118—an increase of about 11 percent. This "overpayment" of $118 per month at the end of the period may suit the Social Security recipient just fine. But remember that the rest of society pays for the retired person's gain through higher real tax payments. The same general principle applies to union workers, government pensioners, or anyone else who is overindexed due to errors in the CPI:

---

5. Over 10 years, 3 percent annual inflation raises the CPI by a factor of $(1.03)^{10} = 1.35$.

When a payment is indexed, and the price index overstates inflation, inflation will increase the real payment, shifting purchasing power toward those who are indexed and away from the rest of society.

THE FUTURE OF THE CPI

The BLS has been working hard to improve the CPI and make it a more accurate measure of inflation. In recent years, BLS staff have developed sophisticated statistical techniques to account for quality improvements in computers and peripherals, clothing, and rental apartments. In January 1999, television sets were added to the list, and in coming years, the BLS hopes to extend the techniques to even more categories. Thus, slowly but surely, the BLS is planning to reduce the upward bias in inflation caused by unmeasured quality improvements.

The BLS is also planning to attack substitution bias. Beginning in January 2000, it will no longer assume that typical consumers continue to buy the same *quantity* of each good that they bought in the last household "market basket" survey. Instead, the BLS will assume that when a good's price rises by 10 percent, the typical consumer buys 10 percent less of it, so that total *expenditure* (price times quantity) of each good remains unchanged from month to month. Further, starting in 2002, the BLS will begin taking its household "market basket" survey once every two years, instead of once every ten years as it has been doing in the past. These changes will give the BLS a more accurate view of which goods and what quantities of them people are actually buying.

These changes to the CPI, and others that many economists have asked the BLS to make, require us to look at the CPI in an entirely new way. In the past, the CPI mostly tracked the cost of a fixed basket of goods, and it has done a reasonably good job of doing so. But it has *not* done a good job tracking what many people call the *cost of living,* the number of dollars a person must pay in order to enjoy a given level of economic satisfaction. When people substitute cheaper goods, take advantage of new technologies, and enjoy quality improvements, they are either getting more satisfaction for a given cost, or else attempting to prevent price hikes from decreasing their level of satisfaction. And to some extent, they are successful. In the past, the CPI has ignored our ability to increase and preserve our satisfaction from a given amount of spending, so it has not accurately told us what is happening to the cost of *living.*

On the other hand, once we try to measure the cost of living, rather than the price of a fixed basket of goods, we enter into some nebulous territory. How is the cost of living affected when our medical care is provided by an HMO that lowers the price, but gives us fewer options in choosing our own doctors? When the price of beef goes up, how much satisfaction do people lose when they substitute by buying more chicken? What about falling crime rates that enable us to protect our lives and property at lower cost? And what about other aspects of our society that affect the quality of our lives: leisure time, the state of the environment, the safety of our workplaces, the quality of our culture, and so on? Do we really want changes in these aspects of life to affect our cost-of-living measure?

For all of these reasons, fixing the CPI is controversial. Further, some groups, including Social Security recipients, union workers, and pensioners, stand to lose from any fix that will reduce the reported inflation rate. These groups have viewed suggestions to correct the CPI as a backdoor effort to reduce their benefits.

Thus, the CPI has entered the realm of politics. The voices arguing for continued changes to the CPI are getting stronger, but so are the voices of those opposed.

S U M M A R Y

Money serves two important functions. First, it is a *unit of value* that helps us measure how much something is worth and compare the costs of different goods and services. Second, it is a *means of payment* by being generally acceptable in exchange for goods and services. Without money, we would be reduced to barter, a very inefficient way of carrying out transactions.

The value of money is its purchasing power, and this changes as the prices of the things we buy change. The overall trend of prices is measured using a price index. Like any index number, a price index is calculated as: (value in current period/value in base period) × 100. The most widely used price index in the United States is the *Consumer Price Index (CPI)*, which tracks the prices paid for a typical consumer's *market basket*. The percent change in the CPI is the inflation rate.

The most common uses of the CPI are for indexing payments, as a policy target, and to translate from nominal to real variables. Many nominal variables, such as the nominal wage, can be corrected for price changes by dividing by the CPI and then multiplying by 100. The result is a real variable, such as the real wage, that is measured in units of purchasing power. Another price index in common use is the GDP price index. It includes the prices of all final goods and services included in GDP.

Inflation—a rise over time in a price index—involves costs. One of these costs is an arbitrary redistribution of income. Unanticipated inflation shifts purchasing power away from those awaiting future dollar payments and toward those obligated to make such payments. Another cost of inflation is the resource cost: People use valuable time and other resources trying to cope with inflation.

It is widely agreed that the CPI has overstated inflation—probably by more than one percentage point per year. As a result, the official statistics on real variables may contain errors, and people who are indexed to the CPI have actually been overindexed, enjoying an increase in real income that has been paid for by the rest of society. The BLS has been fixing some of those problems, and plans more repairs in the future. But the CPI's accuracy has become a political issue—and a controversial one.

K E Y   T E R M S

unit of value	price level	deflation	GDP price index
means of payment	index	indexation	nominal interest rate
Federal Reserve System	Consumer Price Index	nominal wage	real interest rate
fiat money	inflation rate	real wage	

R E V I E W   Q U E S T I O N S

1. Distinguish between the *unit of value* function of money and the *means of payment* function. Give examples of how the U.S. dollar has played each of these two roles.

2. How does the price level differ from, say, the price of a haircut or a Big Mac?

3. Explain how you might construct an index of bank deposits over time. What steps would be involved?

4. What is the CPI? What does it measure? How can it be used to calculate the inflation rate?

5. Can the inflation rate be decreasing at the same time the price level is rising? Can the inflation rate be increasing at the same time the price level is falling? Explain.

6. What are some of the main uses of the CPI? Give an example of each use.

7. Explain the logic of the formula that relates real values to nominal values.

8. What are the similarities between the CPI and the GDP price index? What are the differences?

9. What are the costs of inflation?

10. Under what circumstances would inflation redistribute purchasing power? How? When would it *not* redistribute purchasing power?

11. How is a nominal interest rate different from a real interest rate? Which do you think is the better measure of the rate of return on a loan?

P R O B L E M S   A N D   E X E R C I S E S

1. Both gold and paper currency have served as money in the United States. What are some of the advantages of paper currency over gold?

2. Which would be more costly—a steady inflation rate of 3 percent per year, or an inflation rate that was sometimes high and sometimes low, but that averaged 3 percent per year? Justify your answer.

3. Given the following *year-end* data, calculate the inflation rate for years 2, 3, and 4. Calculate the real wage in each year:

Year	CPI	Inflation Rate	Nominal Wage	Real Wage
1	100	_____	$10.00	_____
2	110	_____	12.00	_____
3	120	_____	13.00	_____
4	115	_____	12.75	_____

4. The chapter discusses the costs of inflation. Would there be any costs to a *deflation*—a period of falling prices? If so, what would they be? Give examples.

5. Given the following data, calculate the real interest rate for years 2, 3, and 4. (Assume that each CPI number tells us the price level at the *end* of each year.)

Year	CPI	Nominal Interest Rate	Real Interest Rate
1	100	_____	_____
2	110	15%	_____
3	120	13%	_____
4	115	8%	_____

If you lent $200 to a friend at the beginning of year 2 at the prevailing nominal interest rate of 15 percent, and your friend returned the money—with the interest—at the end of year 2, did you benefit from the deal?

6. Your friend asks for a loan of $100 for one year and offers to pay you 5 percent interest. Your friend expects the inflation rate over that one-year period to be 6 percent; you expect it to be 4 percent. You agree to make the loan, and the actual inflation rate turns out to be 5 percent. Who benefits and who loses?

7. If there is 5 percent inflation each year for 8 years, what is the *total* amount of inflation (i.e., the total percentage rise in the price level) over the entire 8-year period? (Hint: The answer is *not* 40 percent.)

8. Visit the Department of Labor's Minimum Wage Page at http://www.dol.gov/dol/esa/public/minwage/main.htm. When was the most recent increase in the minimum wage? What is the current nominal value of the minimum wage? What is the current real value? Be sure to specify the units correctly. What price index does the Department of Labor use to adjust for inflation? When was the real value of the minimum wage highest? What was its value then?

C H A L L E N G E   Q U E S T I O N S

1. Inflation is sometimes said to be a tax on nominal money holdings. If you hold $100 and the price level increases by 10 percent, the purchasing power of that $100 falls by about 10 percent. Who benefits from this inflation tax?

2. During the late nineteenth and early twentieth centuries, many U.S. farmers favored inflationary government policies. Why might this have been the case? (Hint: Do farmers typically pay for their land in full at the time of purchase?)

3. Look again at the first paragraph under the heading, "The Consequences of Overstating Inflation." It states that if the CPI overstated the inflation rate by 1.1 percentage points each year from 1975 to 1998, then the average real wage did not fall by 7 percent as reported, but actually grew by 18.5 percent. Prove this statement true, using numbers (as needed) from Table 2.

APPENDIX: CALCULATING THE CONSUMER PRICE INDEX

The Consumer Price Index (CPI) is the government's most popular measure of inflation. It tracks the cost of the collection of goods—called the *CPI market basket*—bought by a typical consumer in some *base year*. This appendix demonstrates how the Bureau of Labor Statistics (BLS) calculates the CPI. To help you follow the steps clearly, we'll do the calculations for a very simple economy with just two goods: medical checkups and frozen burrito dinners (not a pleasant world, but a manageable one). Table 3 shows prices for each good, and the quantities produced and consumed, in two different years: 1998 (the base year) and 1999. The market basket (measured in the base year) is given in the third column of the table: In 1998, the typical consumer buys 100 medical checkups and 1,000 frozen dinners. Our formula for the CPI in any year t is

$$\text{CPI in year } t = \frac{\text{Cost of market basket at prices in year } t}{\text{Cost of market basket at 1998 prices}} \times 100$$

Table 4 shows the calculations we must do to determine the CPI in 1998 and 1999.

In the table, you can see that the cost of the 1998 market basket at 1998 prices is \$16,000. The cost of the same market basket at 1999's higher prices is \$21,000. To determine the CPI in 1998, we use the formula with year t equal to 1998, giving us

$$\text{CPI in 1998} = \frac{\text{Cost of 1998 basket at 1998 prices}}{\text{Cost of 1998 basket at 1998 prices}} \times 100 = \frac{\$16,000}{\$16,000} \times 100 = 100$$

TABLE 3	PRICES AND QUANTITIES IN A TWO-GOOD ECONOMY				
		1998		**1999**	
		Price	Quantity	Price	Quantity
Checkups		\$110	100	\$150	96
Frozen Dinners		\$ 5	1,000	\$ 6	1,200

TABLE 4	CALCULATIONS FOR THE CPI		
		At 1998 Prices	**At 1999 Prices**
Cost of 100 medical checkups		$\$110 \times 100$ $= \$11,000$	$\$150 \times 100$ $= \$15,000$
Cost of 1,000 frozen dinners		$\$5 \times 1,000$ $= \$5,000$	$\$6 \times 1,000$ $= \$6,000$
Cost of entire market basket		$\$11,000 + \$5,000$ $= \$16,000$	$\$15,000 + \$6,000$ $= \$21,000$

That is, the CPI in 1998—the base year—is equal to 100. (The formula, as you can see, is set up so that the CPI will always equal 100 in the base year, regardless of which base year we choose.)

Now let's apply the formula again, to get the value of the CPI in 1999:

$$\text{CPI in 1999} = \frac{\text{Cost of 1998 basket at 1999 prices}}{\text{Cost of 1998 basket at 1998 prices}} \times 100 = \frac{\$21,000}{\$16,000} \times 100 = 131.3$$

From 1998 to 1999, the CPI rises from 100 to 131.3. The rate of inflation over this period is therefore 31.3 percent.

Notice that the CPI gives more weight to price changes of goods that are more important in the consumer's budget. In our example, the percentage rise in the CPI (31%) is closer to the percentage rise in the price of medical checkups (36%) than it is to the percentage price rise of frozen dinners (20%). This is because a greater percentage of our budget is spent on medical checkups than frozen dinners, so medical checkups carry more weight in the CPI.

But one of the CPI's problems, discussed in the body of the chapter, is *substitution bias*. No matter how much the relative price of checkups rises, the CPI assumes that people will continue to buy the same quantity of them. Therefore, as the price of medical checkups rises, the CPI assumes that we spend a greater and greater percentage of our budgets on them; medical checkups get *increasing weight* in the CPI. In our example, spending on checkups is assumed to rise from $11,000/$16,000 = 0.69, or 69 percent of the typical budget, to $15,000/$21,000 = 0.71, or 71 percent. In fact, however, the rapid rise in price would cause people to substitute *away* from medical checkups towards other goods. This is what occurs in our two-good example, as you can see in the last column of Table 3. In 1999, the quantity of checkups purchased drops to 96, and the quantity of frozen dinners rises to 1,200. In an ideal measure, the decrease in the quantity of checkups would reduce their weight in determining the overall rate of inflation.

But the CPI ignores this. Look back at how we've calculated the CPI in this example, and you will see that we have entirely ignored the information in the last column of Table 3, which shows the new quantities purchased in 1998. This failure to correct for substitution bias is one of the reasons the CPI overstates inflation.

CHAPTER 14

ECONOMIC GROWTH AND RISING LIVING STANDARDS

Economist Thomas Malthus, writing in 1798, came to a striking conclusion: "Population, when unchecked, goes on doubling itself every twenty-five years, or increases in a geometrical ratio. . . . The means of subsistence . . . could not possibly be made to increase faster than in an arithmetic ratio."[1] From this simple logic, Malthus forecast a horrible economic fate for the human race. There would be repeated famines and wars to keep the rapidly growing population in balance with the more slowly growing supply of food and other necessities. The prognosis was so pessimistic that it led Thomas Carlyle, one of Malthus's contemporaries, to label economics "the dismal science."

But history has proven Malthus wrong . . . at least in part. In the industrialized nations, living standards have increased beyond the wildest dreams of anyone alive in Malthus's time. Economists today are optimistic about these nations' long-run material prospects. At the same time, living standards in many of the less-developed countries have remained stubbornly close to survival level and, in some cases, have fallen below it.

What are we to make of this? Why have living standards steadily increased in some nations but not in others? And what, if anything, can governments do to speed the rise in living standards? These are questions about economic growth—the long-run increase in an economy's output of goods and services.

In this chapter, you will learn what makes economies grow. You will also see that increasing the rate of economic growth is not easy. While nations can take measures to speed growth, each measure carries an opportunity cost. As you'll see,

---

1. Thomas Robert Malthus, *Essay on the Principle of Population*, 1798.

POLICY TRADEOFFS

achieving a higher rate of growth in the long run generally requires some sacrifice in the short run.

THE IMPORTANCE OF GROWTH

Why should we be concerned about economic growth? For one simple reason:

AVERAGE STANDARD OF LIVING Total output (real GDP) per person.

*When output grows faster than the population, GDP per capita—which we call the **average standard of living**—will rise. When output grows more slowly than the population, GDP per capita, or the average living standard, will fall.*

Measuring the standard of living by GDP per capita may seem limiting. After all, as we saw two chapters ago, many important aspects of our quality of life are not captured in GDP. Leisure time, workplace safety, good health, a clean environment—we care about all of these. Yet they are not considered in GDP.

Still, many aspects of our quality of life *are* counted in GDP: food, housing, medical care, education, transportation services, and movies and video games, to name a few. It is not surprising, then, that economic growth—measured by increases in GDP—remains a vital concern in every nation.

Economic growth is especially important in countries with income levels far below those of Europe, Japan, and the United States. The average standard of living in some third-world nations is so low that many families can barely acquire the basic necessities of life, and many others perish from disease or starvation. Table 1 lists GDP per capita, infant mortality rates, life expectancies, and adult literacy rates for some of the richest and poorest countries in 1995. The statistics for the poor countries are grim enough, but even they capture only part of the story. Unsafe and unclean workplaces, inadequate housing, and other sources of misery are part of daily life for most people in these countries. Other than emigration, economic growth is their only hope.

Growth is a high priority in prosperous nations, too. As we know, resources are scarce, and we cannot produce enough of everything to satisfy all of our desires simultaneously. We want more and better medical care, education, vacations, entertainment . . . the list is endless. When output per capita is growing, everyone can enjoy an increase in material well-being without anyone having to cut back. We can also accomplish important social goals—helping the poor, improving education, cleaning up the environment—by asking those who are doing well to sacrifice part of the rise in their material well-being, rather than suffer a drop.

But when output per capita stagnates, material gains become a fight over a fixed pie: The more purchasing power my neighbor has, the less is left for me. With everyone struggling for a larger piece of this fixed pie, conflict replaces cooperation. Efforts to help the less fortunate, wipe out illiteracy, reduce air pollution—all are seen as threats, rather than opportunities.

In the 1950s and 1960s, economic growth in the wealthier nations seemed to be taking care of itself. Economists and policy makers focused their attention on short-run movements around full-employment output, rather than on the growth of full-employment output itself. The real payoff for government seemed to be in preventing recessions and depressions—in keeping the economy operating as close to its potential as possible.

| TABLE 1 | SOME INDICATORS OF ECONOMIC WELL-BEING IN RICH AND POOR COUNTRIES, 1995 |

Country	GDP per Capita	Infant Mortality Rate (per 1,000 live births)	Life Expectancy at Birth	Adult Literacy Rate
RICH COUNTRIES				
United States	$26,977	5.0	76.4	Greater than 99%
Japan	$21,930	4.0	79.9	Greater than 99%
France	$21,176	5.0	78.7	Greater than 99%
Italy	$20,174	6.0	78.0	98.1%
United Kingdom	$19,302	6.0	76.8	Greater than 99%
POOR COUNTRIES				
Pakistan	$ 2,209	95	62.8	37.8%
Ghana	$ 2,032	70	57.0	64.5%
Cambodia	$ 1,110	108	52.9	65.0%
Ethiopia	$ 455	113	48.7	35.5%
Democratic Republic of Congo	$ 355	128	52.4	77.3%

Source: United Nations Development Program, *Human Development Report, 1998* (Oxford: Oxford University Press, 1998).

All of that changed starting in the 1970s, and since then economic growth has become a national and international preoccupation. Like most changes in perception and thought, this one was driven by experience. Table 2 tells the story. It gives the average yearly growth rates of real GDP per capita for the United States and some of our key trading partners.

Over most of the postwar period, output in the more prosperous industrialized countries (such as the United States, the United Kingdom, and Canada) grew by 2 or 3 percent per year, while output in the less-wealthy ones—those with some catching up to do—grew even faster. But beginning in the mid-1970s, all of these nations saw their growth rates slip. In the late 1990s, the United States and England returned to

| TABLE 2 | AVERAGE ANNUAL GROWTH OF OUTPUT PER CAPITA (PERCENT PER YEAR) |

Country	1948–1972	1972–1988	1988–1995	1995–1998
United States	2.2	1.7	1.0	2.6
United Kingdom	2.4	2.1	0.9	2.4
Canada	2.9	2.6	0.6	1.6
France	4.3	2.1	1.2	1.8
Italy	4.9	2.8	1.6	1.2
West Germany	5.7	2.2	1.3	1.8*
Japan	8.2	3.3	2.1	0.4

*From 1995 to 1998, growth rate includes Eastern Germany.

Source: Angus Maddison, *Phases of Capitalist Development* (Oxford: Oxford University Press, 1982), and various World Bank publications.

their previous high rates of growth, while the other industrialized countries continued to grow more slowly than their historical averages.

Looking at the table, you might think that this slowing in growth was rather insignificant. Does the tiny difference between the pre-1972 and the 1972–1995 growth rates in the United States really matter? Indeed, it does. Recall our example in Chapter 11 in which a 1-percentage-point increase in the growth rate would, over 24 years, mean an additional $23,000 worth of output at today's prices for every American. Seemingly small differences in growth rates matter a great deal.

WHAT MAKES ECONOMIES GROW

Later in this book, you will learn that the economy's output cannot exceed its *potential* or *full employment* GDP for very long. Therefore, economic growth—the gradual and continual rise in our living standard over the years—requires a steady increase in our *potential* GDP.

> *To understand economic growth, we must understand how our potential output is determined, and what makes it increase.*

So how *is* the economy's potential output determined, and what makes it grow?

Economists have thought seriously about this question for more than a century. The research is ongoing, and the details continue to evolve. But in broad outlines, today's economists think about economic growth in very much the same way as did economists a hundred years ago. This thinking starts from a simple fact:

> *Goods and services are produced from resources—land, labor and capital[2]—using some known technology of production.*

Thus, our *potential* output—the maximum sustainable quantity of goods and services we can produce—depends on the quantities of resources available to firms and the available technology. This is illustrated in Figure 1. In the center of the diagram is the nation's *aggregate production function*, which shows—for a given state of technology—the maximum output we can produce from any combination of resources. When we plug the quantities of resources actually available into the aggregate production function, we obtain the nation's potential output.

As you can see in the diagram, there are only two ways for potential output to increase. One is for the quantities of resources available to firms to increase. More specifically, potential output will rise if more land becomes available (say, through a war or by clearing swampland to make it usable for farming or manufacturing), if more labor becomes available (say, through growth in the population or an increase in the fraction of the population that has jobs), or if more capital becomes available (say, because resources have been shifted from producing consumption goods toward producing capital goods).

The second way for potential output to increase is for the economy to use more and better technologies. More specifically, potential output can rise if new inputs

---

2. Entrepreneurship is often included as a fourth resource. It is not included here because it will not play a major role in the discussion that follows.

are invented and put into use (like the personal computer in the 1970s and recombinant DNA technology in the 1990s), or new ways of combining existing inputs are developed (such as the discovery of mass production techniques during the industrial revolution).

In sum,

> *Growth in potential output requires either (1) an increase in the quantities of resources available to firms; or (2) technological progress.*

At one time in human history, the acquisition of additional land through conquest was an important cause of economic growth for the acquiring nation or empire. But this is no longer true. Today, in virtually all countries enjoying rising living standards, economic growth arises from increases in employment, increases in the capital stock, and changes in technology. In the next several pages, we'll look at each of these in turn.

GROWTH IN EMPLOYMENT

As you can see in Figure 1, an increase in labor force—the quantity of labor available to firms—causes an increase in potential output. But what causes the labor force to increase?

One possibility is an increase in labor *supply:* a rise in the number of people who would like to work at any given wage. This is illustrated in Figure 2, which shows how total employment is determined in the economy. Ignore the dashed line for now and concentrate on the solid lines: the labor supply curve L_1^S, and the labor demand curve L^D.

Notice that the labor market depicted in the figure is very different from the labor markets you studied in Chapter 9. That chapter dealt with *specific* labor markets, such as the market for carpenters or the market for word processors. In Figure 2, all the different types of labor—carpenters, word processors, lawyers, factory workers, college professors, and so on—are lumped together into just "labor." We

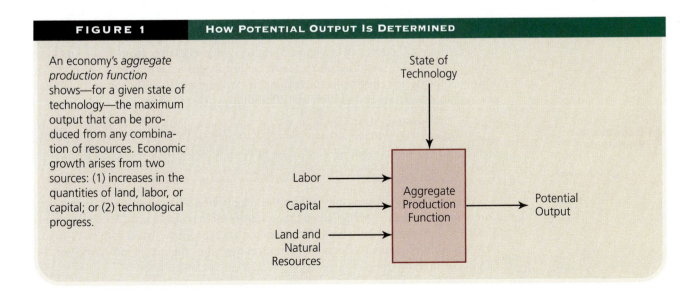

FIGURE 1   **HOW POTENTIAL OUTPUT IS DETERMINED**

An economy's *aggregate production function* shows—for a given state of technology—the maximum output that can be produced from any combination of resources. Economic growth arises from two sources: (1) increases in the quantities of land, labor, or capital; or (2) technological progress.

FIGURE 2	AN INCREASE IN LABOR SUPPLY

At point *A,* labor supply and demand determine an employment level of 100 million workers, and real GDP of $7 trillion. An increase in labor supply will raise employment to 120 million (at point *B*), although with a lower wage rate. With more people working, real GDP rises.

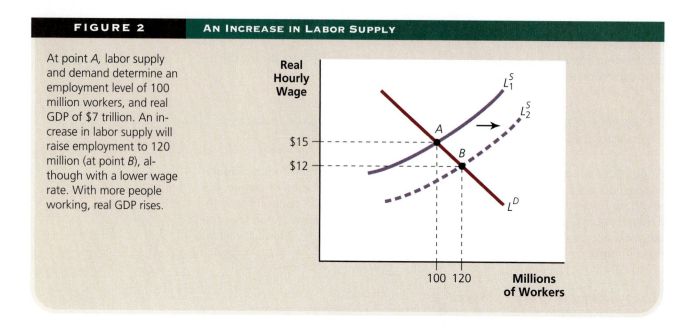

are now studying *macro*economics, and are interested in total employment rather than employment of particular types of labor.

In Figure 2, the initial equilibrium is at point *A,* where the average wage is $15, and 100 million people are working. But if labor supply increases—that is, more people decide that they want to work at any given wage—then the labor supply curve will shift rightward. For a short time, if the wage were to remain at $15, there would be an excess supply of labor—unemployed workers. But eventually, the excess supply of labor will drive down the wage. Business firms, finding that labor is now cheaper, will hire more workers, shown by a movement *along* the labor demand curve. In the figure, the new equilibrium—at point *B*—represents an increase in the labor force to 120 million people, and a decrease in the average wage to $12. But growth in employment can also arise from an increase in labor demand: a rise in the number of workers firms would like to hire at any given wage. Once again, we'll consider the *causes* of labor demand changes momentarily; here, we focus on the *consequences.*

Graphically, an increase in labor demand is represented by a rightward shift in the labor demand curve, as in Figure 3. As the wage rate rises from $15 to its new equilibrium of $17, we move along the labor supply curve from point *A* to point *B:* More people decide they want to work as the wage rises. Equilibrium employment once again rises from 100 million to 120 million workers. Thus,

**MARKETS AND
EQUILIBRIUM**

> *growth in employment can arise from an increase in labor supply (a rightward shift in the labor supply curve) or an increase in labor demand (a rightward shift of the labor demand curve).*

You may have noticed one very important difference between the labor market outcomes in Figures 2 and 3: When labor *supply* increases, the wage rate falls (from $15 to $12 in Figure 2); when labor *demand* increases, the wage rate rises (from $15 to $17 in Figure 3). Which of the figures describes the actual experience of the U.S. labor market?

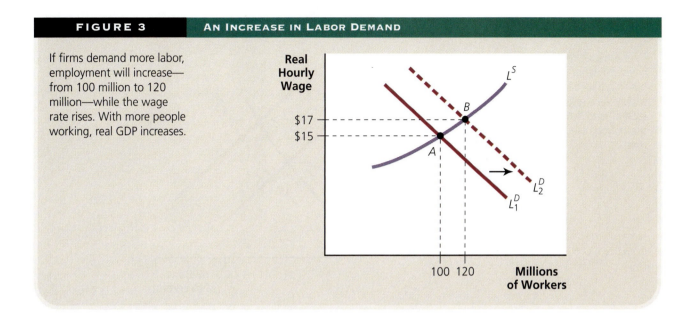

FIGURE 3 — **AN INCREASE IN LABOR DEMAND**

If firms demand more labor, employment will increase—from 100 million to 120 million—while the wage rate rises. With more people working, real GDP increases.

Actually, a combination of both: Over the past 50 years, the U.S. labor supply curve has shifted steadily rightward—sometimes slowly, sometimes more rapidly. Why the shift in labor supply? In part, the reason has been steady population growth: The more people there are, the more who will want to work at any wage. But another reason has been an important change in tastes: an increase in the desire of women (especially married women) to work.

Over the past 50 years, as the labor supply curve has shifted rightward, the labor demand curve has shifted rightward as well. Why? Throughout this period, firms have been acquiring more and better capital equipment for their employees to use. Secretaries now work with word processors instead of typewriters, accountants use lightning-fast computer software instead of account ledgers, and supermarket clerks use electronic scanners instead of hand-entry cash registers. At the same time, workers have become better educated and better trained. These changes have made workers more productive, so firms have wanted to hire more of them at any wage.

In fact, over the past century, increases in labor demand have outpaced increases in labor supply, so that, on balance, the average wage has risen and employment has increased. This is illustrated in Figure 4, which shows a shift in the labor supply curve from L_1^S to L_2^S, and an even greater shift in the labor demand curve from L_1^D to L_2^D.

The impact of these changes on total employment has been dramatic. Between 1947 and 1998, the *labor force participation rate*—the fraction of the adult population that is either working or looking for work—rose from 58.3 percent to 67.0 percent. The increased participation rate was due partly to women's increased tastes for working, as mentioned and partly to the increase in the average wage rate that made work more rewarding. Together, growth in the population and in the participation rate have increased the U.S. labor force from 59.5 million workers in 1947 to 138 million workers at the end of 1998.

Currently, the U.S. Bureau of Labor Statistics predicts employment growth of 1 percent per year until the year 2010. Is there anything we can do to make employment grow even *faster* and thus increase our rate of economic growth? Can we speed up the rightward shifts in labor supply and labor demand? Yes, we can. But

| **FIGURE 4** | **THE U.S. LABOR MARKET OVER A CENTURY** |

Over the past century, increases in labor demand have outpaced increases in supply. As a result, both the level of employment and the average wage have risen.

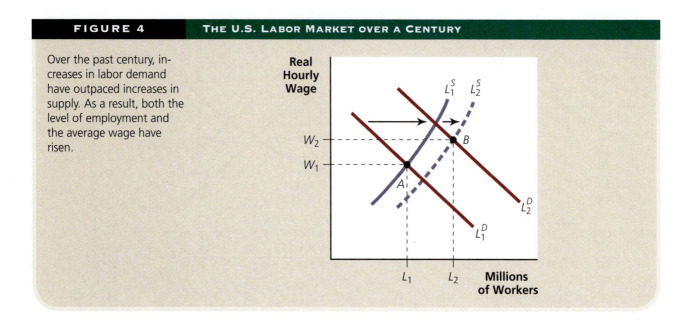

HOW TO INCREASE EMPLOYMENT

One set of policies to increase employment focuses on changing labor supply. One often-proposed example of this type of policy is a decrease in income tax rates. Imagine that you have a professional degree in accounting, physical therapy, or some other field, and you are considering whether to take a job. Suppose the going rate for your professional services is $30 per hour. If your average tax rate is 33 percent, then one-third of your income will be taxed away, so your take-home pay would be only $20 per hour. But if your tax rate were cut to 20 percent, you would take home $24 per hour. Since your take-home pay is what you care about, you will respond to a tax cut in the same way you would respond to a wage increase—even if the wage your potential employer pays does not change at all. If you would be willing to take a job that offers a take home pay of $24, but not one that offers $20, then the tax cut would be just what was needed to get you to seek work.

When we extend your reaction to the population as a whole, we can see that a cut in the income tax rate can convince more people to seek jobs at any given wage, shifting the labor supply curve rightward. This is why economists and politicians who focus on the economy's long-run growth often recommend lower taxes on labor income to encourage more rapid growth in employment. They point out that many American workers must pay combined federal, state, and local taxes of more than 40 cents out of each additional dollar they earn, and that this may be discouraging work effort in the United States.

In addition to tax rate changes, some economists advocate changes in government transfer programs to increase labor supply. They argue that the current structure of many government programs creates disincentives to work. For example, families receiving welfare payments, food stamps, unemployment benefits, and Social Security retirement payments all face steep losses in their benefits if they go to

as you read on, keep in mind that these measures to increase employment are not necessarily socially desirable. They, would, most likely, accomplish the goal, but they would also have costs—costs that Americans may or may not be willing to pay. Later, we'll discuss these costs.

work or increase their work effort. Redesigning these programs might therefore stimulate growth in labor supply.

This reasoning was an important motive behind the sweeping and highly controversial reforms in the U.S. welfare system passed by Congress and signed by President Clinton in August 1996. Among other things, the reforms reduced the number of people who were eligible for benefits, cut the benefit amount for many of those still eligible, and set a maximum coverage period of five years for most welfare recipients. Later in this chapter, we'll discuss some of the costs of potentially growth-enhancing measures like this. Here, we only point out that changes in benefit programs, whether "right" or "wrong," have the potential to change labor supply.

> *A cut in tax rates increases the reward for working, while a cut in benefits to the needy increases the hardship of* not *working. Either policy can cause a greater rightward shift in the economy's labor supply curve than would otherwise occur and speed the growth in employment and output.*

Government policies can also affect the labor demand curve. In recent decades, subsidies for education and training, such as government-guaranteed loans for college students or special training programs for the unemployed, have helped to increase the skills of the labor force and have made workers more valuable to potential employers. In some cases, government subsidizes employment more directly. The government contributes part of the wage when certain categories of workers are hired—the disabled, college work-study participants, and, in some experimental programs, inner-city youth. By enlarging these programs, government could increase the number of workers hired at any given wage and thus shift the labor demand curve to the right:

> *Government policies that help increase the skills of the workforce or that subsidize employment more directly shift the economy's labor demand curve to the right, increasing employment and output.*

Efforts to speed employment growth are controversial. In recent decades, those who prefer an activist government have favored policies to increase labor *demand* through government-sponsored training programs, more aid to college students, employment subsidies to firms, and similar programs. Those who prefer a more laissez-faire approach have generally favored policies to increase labor *supply* by *decreasing* government involvement—lower taxes or a less generous social safety net.

EMPLOYMENT GROWTH AND PRODUCTIVITY

Increases in employment have been an important source of economic growth in the United States and many other countries. But growth from this source has a serious drawback: It does not necessarily raise a nation's standard of living. Indeed, it can even cause living standards to fall. Why? Because living standards are closely tied to **labor productivity** (sometimes just called **productivity**)—the nation's total output divided by the total number of workers that produce it. Productivity is the output produced by the average worker in a year.[3]

LABOR PRODUCTIVITY Total output, real GDP, per worker.

---

3. Productivity is more often defined as total output divided by total *labor hours*—the output produced by the average worker in an hour. But our calculations will be easier if we use the definition given in the text. As long as the typical worker's hours remain unchanged, the two definitions of productivity—output per hour or output per worker per year—will rise or fall by the same percentage.

If employment rises, and there is no other change in the economy, then productivity is bound to fall. Why? Because with more workers, but the same total amount of capital, each worker has less and less capital equipment with which to work, and the average worker's output falls. If 100 ditchdiggers have 100 shovels, then each has his own shovel. If we double the number of ditchdiggers, but hold constant the number of shovels, then each worker must share his shovel with another and digs fewer ditches in any period. Labor productivity decreases:

> *When employment increases, while the capital stock remains constant, the amount of capital available to the average worker will decrease, and labor productivity will fall.*

Falling labor productivity is bad news for a society. If output per worker falls, then the average standard of living will ordinarily fall as well. What can be done to prevent the fall in labor productivity as employment grows? Or—even better—can anything be done to *increase* labor productivity even as more people are working? The answer is yes.

GROWTH OF THE CAPITAL STOCK

The key to increasing labor productivity is to increase the nation's stock of capital. Has your college or university acquired more computers, desks, or campus-patrol vehicles in the past year? Did it install a new phone system? Build a new classroom or dormitory? If the answer to any of these questions is yes, then your institution has participated in the growth of the U.S. capital stock. With more capital—more assembly lines, bulldozers, computers, factory buildings, and the like—a given number of workers can produce more output. Notice that while increases in employment and increases in capital both cause output to grow, they do so in very different ways. An increase in employment, on its own, tends to *lower* productivity. An increase in the capital stock, by contrast, *raises* productivity.

> *An increase in the capital stock causes labor productivity and living standards to increase.*

So far, we've considered growth in the capital stock and growth in the labor force separately. But in the real world, both the capital stock and the labor force grow each year. What happens to labor productivity when both changes occur simultaneously? That depends on what happens to **capital per worker**—the total quantity of capital divided by total employment. Greater capital per worker means greater productivity: You can dig more ditches with a shovel than with your bare hands and even more with a backhoe.

CAPITAL PER WORKER The total capital stock divided by total employment.

> *If the capital stock grows faster than employment, then capital per worker will rise, and labor productivity will increase along with it. But if the capital stock grows more slowly than employment, then capital per worker will fall, and labor productivity will fall as well.*

In the United States and most other developed countries, the capital stock has grown more rapidly than the labor force. As a result, labor productivity has risen over time. But in some developing countries, the capital stock has grown at about the same rate, or even more slowly than, the population, and labor productivity has remained stagnant or fallen. We will return to this problem in the "Using the Theory" section of the chapter.

INVESTMENT AND THE CAPITAL STOCK

Now you can see why an increase in the capital stock plays such a central role in economists' thinking about growth: It works by raising labor productivity and thus unambiguously helps to raise living standards. But how does a nation's capital stock grow?

Remember that capital is a stock variable—it represents the total amount of plant and equipment that exists at any moment in time. Investment, on the other hand, is a flow variable, telling us how rapidly we are producing new plant and equipment over some period. The relationship between the two is similar to that between the flow of water into a bathtub and the total amount of water in the tub itself. As long as investment is greater than depreciation (more water flows into the tub than drains out), the total stock of capital (the quantity of water in the tub) will rise. Moreover, the greater the flow of investment, the faster will be the rise in the capital stock. Can the government do anything to raise investment by business firms? Actually, it can, and it has many methods from which to choose. In order to understand how investment spending is determined and how economic policy can increase it, we must take a temporary detour and explore an important market in the macro-economy: the market for loanable funds.

THE LOANABLE FUNDS MARKET

The **loanable funds market** is where business firms obtain funds for investment. When Avis wants to add cars to its automobile rental fleet, when McDonald's wants to build a new beef-processing plant, or when the local dry cleaner wants to buy new dry-cleaning machines, it will likely raise the funds in the loanable funds market. Firms may take out bank loans, sell bonds, or sell new shares of stock. In all of these cases, they are going to the loanable funds market as *demanders* of funds. Thus, the total amount of funds demanded by firms is equal to their investment purchases.[4]

> **LOANABLE FUNDS MAR-KET** The market in which business firms obtain funds for investment.

Where do the funds that business firms demand come from? Largely from household saving. When you save—that is, when you have income left over after paying taxes and buying consumption goods—you will do *something* with your surplus funds. You might put your funds in a bank, or buy bonds or shares of stock. In any of these cases, you would be a *supplier* of funds.

Our picture of the loanable funds market would be very simple if this were all there was to it. We would have firms demanding funds for investment, and households supplying them. But there is one more sector involved in this market: the government.

The government acts as a *demander* of funds when it runs a **budget deficit**—that is, when its tax revenue is not sufficient to pay for its total outlays (on final goods and services as well as transfer payments). After all, if the government cannot meet its bills with the tax revenue it has collected, it must get the funds from somewhere. By law, it has no choice: It must *borrow* the money (demand loanable funds) by issuing U.S. government bonds.

> **BUDGET DEFICIT** The amount by which the government's total outlays (on goods, services, and transfer payments) exceeds its total tax revenue.

---

4.   By making this assumption, we are ignoring investment purchases that firms make with their own funds. But with a slight reinterpretation, even this source of investment spending can be included in the demand for loanable funds. The firm that finances its investment spending with its own funds can be regarded as both supplying funds to the market and then demanding them for itself.

BUDGET SURPLUS The amount by which the government's total tax revenue exceeds its total outlays (on goods, services, and transfer payments).

But the government can also be on the other side of the loanable funds market. It acts as a *supplier* of funds when it runs a **budget surplus**—when its tax revenues *exceed* its total outlays. In this case, the surplus funds are either put in a bank account (the government has its own bank accounts, just like households and businesses do), or else used to purchase government bonds. In either case, the funds are being made available to those who want to borrow—loanable funds are being supplied.

It's easy to see that the government's surplus is also its supply of loanable funds when the surplus funds end up in a bank, since the bank simply lends the funds (supplies them) to someone else. But even when the government uses its surplus to purchase government bonds, it once again supplies loanable funds. Those who were holding the bonds—and previously lending to the U.S. government—will now get their funds back, and they will no doubt lend them (supply them) to someone else.

For now, we'll assume that the government is a *demander* of funds. That is, we'll assume that the government is running a budget deficit, and not a surplus, just as it has for most of the last quarter century. In 1998, however, the government budget turned from deficit to surplus, and—for the first time in 30 years—the government became a *supplier* of funds to the loanable funds market. We'll explore the case of a budget surplus at the end of this chapter. As you will see, it does not change any of our conclusions in this chapter.

We can summarize our view of the loanable funds market so far with the following two points:

- *The supply of funds is equal to household saving.*
- *The demand for funds is equal to the business sector's investment spending and the government sector's budget deficit (if any).*

There is just one more piece of the puzzle to discuss before we analyze the loanable funds market more formally. Those who supply funds—households, in our model—receive a reward for doing so. Those who demand funds—business firms and the government—must pay this reward. When funds are transferred from suppliers to demanders via banks or the bond market, the funds are *loaned* and the payment is called *interest*. When the funds are transferred via the stock market, the suppliers become part owners of the firm and their payment is called *dividends*. To keep our discussion simple, we'll assume that all funds transferred are loaned and that the payment is simply interest.

- *Demanders of funds pay interest to suppliers of funds.*

SUPPLY OF FUNDS CURVE Indicates the level of household saving at each interest rate.

THE SUPPLY OF FUNDS CURVE. Since interest is the reward for saving and supplying funds to the loanable funds market, a rise in the interest rate *increases* the quantity of funds supplied (household saving). Similarly, a drop in the interest rate should decrease it. This relationship is illustrated by the upward-sloping **supply of funds curve** in Figure 5. When the interest rate is 3 percent, households save $1.5 trillion, and if the interest rate rises to 5 percent, saving (and the supply of funds) rises to $1.75 trillion.

The quantity of funds supplied to the loanable funds market depends positively on the interest rate. This is why the saving, or supply of funds, curve slopes upward.

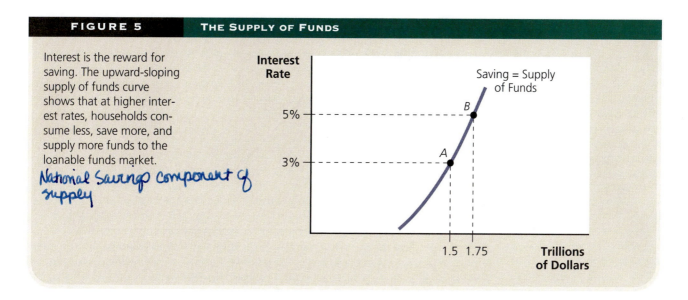

FIGURE 5   **THE SUPPLY OF FUNDS**

Interest is the reward for saving. The upward-sloping supply of funds curve shows that at higher interest rates, households consume less, save more, and supply more funds to the loanable funds market.

National Savings component of supply

Of course, other things can affect saving besides the interest rate—tax rates, expectations about the future, and the general willingness of households to postpone consumption, to name a few. In drawing the supply of funds curve, we hold each of these variables constant. In the next section, we'll explore what happens when some of these variables change.

THE DEMAND FOR FUNDS CURVE. Like saving, investment also depends on the interest rate. This is because businesses buy plant and equipment when the expected benefits of doing so exceed the costs. Since businesses obtain the funds for their investment spending from the loanable funds market, a key cost of any investment project is the interest rate that must be paid on borrowed funds. As the interest rate rises and investment costs increase, fewer projects will look attractive, and investment spending will decline. This is the logic of the downward-sloping **investment demand curve** in Figure 6. At a 5-percent interest rate, firms would borrow $1 trillion and spend it on capital equipment; at an interest rate of 3 percent, business borrowing and investment spending would rise to $1.5 trillion.

> *When the interest rate falls, investment spending and the business borrowing needed to finance it rise. The investment demand curve slopes downward.*

What about the government's demand for funds? Will it, too, be influenced by the interest rate? Probably not very much. Government seems to be cushioned from the cost–benefit considerations that haunt business decisions. Any company president who ignored interest rates in deciding how much to borrow would be quickly out of a job. U.S. presidents and legislators did so for years with little political cost.

For this reason, we can treat government borrowing as independent of the interest rate: No matter what the interest rate, the government sector's deficit—and its borrowing—remain constant. This is why we have graphed the **government's demand for funds curve** as a vertical line in panel (a) of Figure 7.

INVESTMENT DEMAND CURVE Indicates the level of investment spending firms plan at each interest rate.

GOVERNMENT'S DEMAND FOR FUNDS CURVE Indicates the amount of governmental borrowing at each interest rate.

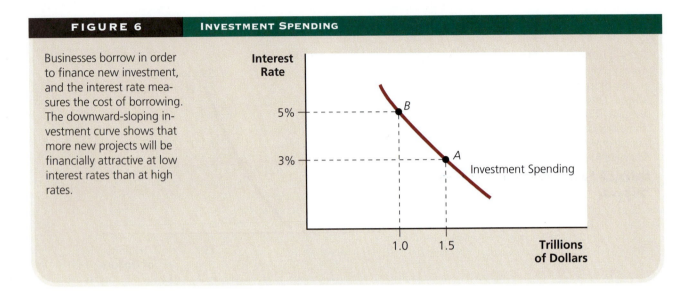

Businesses borrow in order to finance new investment, and the interest rate measures the cost of borrowing. The downward-sloping investment curve shows that more new projects will be financially attractive at low interest rates than at high rates.

FIGURE 6   **INVESTMENT SPENDING**

> *The government sector's deficit and, therefore, its demand for funds are independent of the interest rate.*

TOTAL DEMAND FOR FUNDS CURVE Indicates the total amount of borrowing at each interest rate.

In the figure, the government deficit—and hence the government's demand for funds—is equal to $0.75 trillion at any interest rate.

In panel (c) of Figure 7, the **total demand for funds curve** is found by horizontally summing the government demand curve (panel [a]) and the business demand curve (panel [b]). For example, if the interest rate is 5 percent, firms demand $1 trillion in funds, and the government demands $0.75 trillion, so that the total quantity

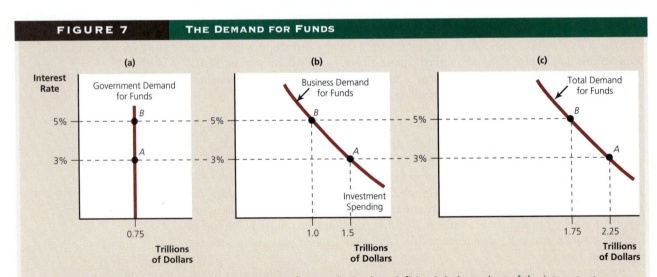

FIGURE 7   **THE DEMAND FOR FUNDS**

In panel (a), the government's demand for funds—to finance the budget deficit—is independent of the interest rate. Businesses' demand for funds—for investment—is inversely related to the interest rate in panel (b). The total demand for funds in panel (c) is the horizontal sum of government and business demand. At lower interest rates, more funds are demanded than at higher rates.

of loanable funds demanded is $1.75 trillion. A drop in the interest rate—to 3 percent—increases business borrowing to $1.5 trillion, while the government's borrowing remains at $0.75 trillion, so the total demand for funds rises to $2.25 trillion.

As the interest rate decreases, the quantity of funds demanded by business firms increases, while the quantity demanded by the government remains unchanged. Therefore, the total quantity of funds demanded rises.

Equilibrium in the Loanable Funds Market. In the loanable funds market—like other markets—we can expect the price to adjust until quantity demanded and quantity supplied are equal. In this case, the price of funds—the interest rate—will rise or fall until the quantities of loanable funds supplied by households and the quantity demanded by firms and the government are equal. In Figure 8, which combines the supply and demand curves together, equilibrium occurs at point *E,* with an interest rate of 5 percent and total saving equal to $1.75 trillion. But notice that we can also read investment off of the graph: The investment curve (the thinner red line) tells us that when the interest rate is 5%, investment spending is equal to $1.0 trillion. That is, of the total $1.75 billion saved, $1 trillion goes to business firms for capital purchases and $0.75 trillion goes to the government to cover its deficit.

Don't be confused by point *A* in the figure. It shows us where the equilibrium in the loanable funds market *would* be if there were no budget deficit. In that case, the thin red line representing business borrowing would be the *total* demand for loanable funds, the interest rate would equal 3%, and investment spending would be $1.5 trillion. But as long as the government is borrowing funds as well as firms, point *A* is not the equilibrium. We'll come back to this idea again a bit later when we explore the effects of the budget deficit on investment spending.

Figure 8 is important because it shows us just how the level of investment spending is determined in the loanable funds market. But it also gives us a framework for analyzing policies designed to *increase* investment, speed the growth of the capital stock, and make our living standards grow faster.

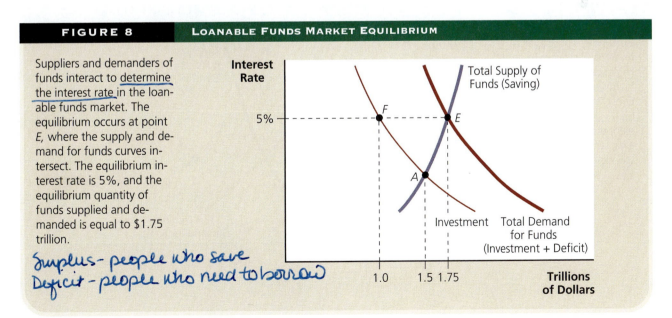

FIGURE 8 **Loanable Funds Market Equilibrium**

Suppliers and demanders of funds interact to determine the interest rate in the loanable funds market. The equilibrium occurs at point *E*, where the supply and demand for funds curves intersect. The equilibrium interest rate is 5%, and the equilibrium quantity of funds supplied and demanded is equal to $1.75 trillion.

Surplus - people who save
Deficit - people who need to borrow

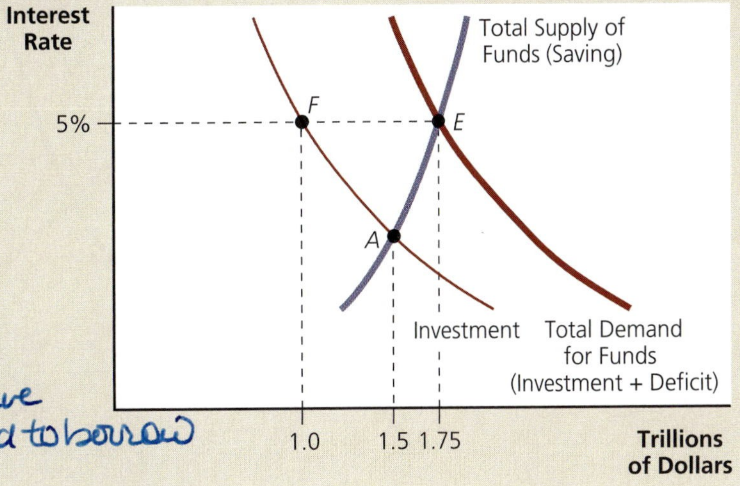

HOW TO INCREASE INVESTMENT

A government seeking to spur investment spending can direct its efforts toward three different targets: toward business firms, toward households, or toward its own budget. Let's explore each of these types of policies in turn.

TARGETING BUSINESSES: INCREASING THE INCENTIVE TO INVEST.

One way to increase investment is to target the business sector itself. Figure 9 shows how this works. The figure shows a simplified view of the loanable funds market where—to focus on investment—we assume that there is no budget deficit, so there is no government demand for funds. The initial equilibrium in the market is at point A, where household saving (the supply of funds) and investment (the demand for funds) are both equal to $1.5 trillion and the interest rate is 3 percent. Now suppose that a government policy move (to be discussed soon) makes investment more profitable, so that—at any interest rate—firms will want to purchase $0.75 trillion more in capital equipment than before. Then the investment curve would shift rightward by $0.75 trillion—from I_1 to I_2. If the interest rate were to remain unchanged, investment spending would rise from $1.5 trillion (point A) to $2.25 trillion (point C). But because of the shift in the investment curve, the equilibrium interest rate *will* rise, from 3 percent to 5 percent. As the interest rate rises, some—but not all—of the original increase in investment is choked off. In the end, investment rises from $1.5 trillion to $1.75 trillion, and so each year $0.25 trillion more is added to the capital stock than would otherwise be added.

These are the mechanics of a rightward shift in the investment curve. But what government measures would *cause* such a shift in the first place? That is, how could the government help to make investment spending more profitable for firms?

One such measure would be a reduction in the **corporate profits tax,** which would allow firms to keep more of the profits they earn from investment projects. Another, even more direct, policy is an **investment tax credit,** which subsidizes corporate investment in new capital equipment.

CORPORATE PROFITS TAX
A tax on the profits earned by corporations.

INVESTMENT TAX CREDIT
A reduction in taxes for firms that invest in certain favored types of capital.

FIGURE 9	**INVESTMENT-ORIENTED PUBLIC POLICY**

Government policies that make investment more profitable will increase investment spending at each interest rate. The resulting rightward shift of the investment demand curve leads to a higher level of investment spending, at point *B*.

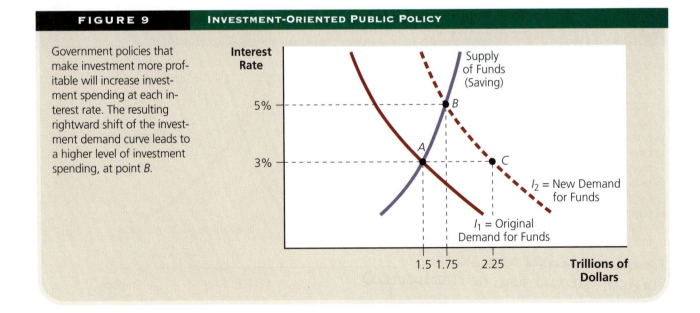

> *Reducing business taxes or providing specific investment incentives can shift the investment curve rightward, speed growth in physical capital, and increase the growth rate of living standards.*

Over the past half century, the U.S. government has experimented with both of these types of policy changes to spur investment spending.

Of course, the same reasoning applies in reverse: An *increase* in the corporate profits tax or the *elimination* of an investment tax credit would shift the investment curve to the left, slowing the rate of investment, the growth of the capital stock, and the rise in living standards.

TARGETING HOUSEHOLDS: INCREASING THE INCENTIVE TO SAVE. While firms make decisions to purchase new capital, it is largely households that supply the firms with funds via personal saving. Thus, an increase in investment spending can originate in the household sector through an increase in the desire to save. This is illustrated in Figure 10. If households decide to save more of their incomes at any given interest rate, the supply of funds curve will shift rightward, from S_1 to S_2. The increase in saving drives down the interest rate, from 5 percent to 3 percent, which, in turn, causes investment to increase. With a lower interest rate, NBC might decide to borrow funds to build another production studio, or the corner grocery store may finally decide to borrow the funds for a new electronic scanner at the checkout stand. In this way, an increase in the desire to save is translated—via the loanable funds market—into an increase in investment and faster growth in the capital stock.

What might cause households to increase their saving? The answer is found in the reasons people save in the first place. And to understand these reasons, you needn't look further than yourself or your own family. You might currently be saving for a large purchase (a car, a house, the next year of college tuition) or to build a financial cushion in case of hard times ahead. You might even be saving to support yourself during retirement, though this may be a distant thought for most

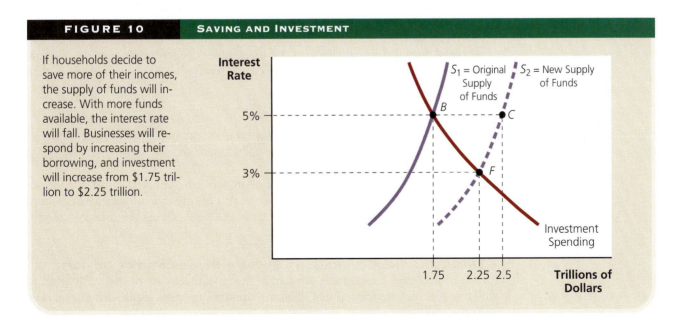

FIGURE 10   **SAVING AND INVESTMENT**

If households decide to save more of their incomes, the supply of funds will increase. With more funds available, the interest rate will fall. Businesses will respond by increasing their borrowing, and investment will increase from $1.75 trillion to $2.25 trillion.

CAPITAL GAINS TAX A tax on profits earned when a financial asset is sold at more than its acquisition price.

college students. Given these motives, what would make you increase your saving? Several things: greater uncertainty about your economic future, an increase in your life expectancy, anticipation of an earlier retirement, a change in tastes toward big-ticket items, or even just a change in your attitude about saving. Any of these changes—if they occurred in many households simultaneously—would shift the saving curve (the supply of funds curve) to the right, as in Figure 10.

But government policy can increase household saving as well. One often-proposed idea is to decrease the **capital gains tax**. A capital gain is the profit you earn when you sell an asset, such as a share of stock or a bond, at a higher price than you paid for it. If the capital gains tax rate is decreased, you would be able to keep more of the capital gains when you sell your stocks and bonds. As a result, these assets would become more rewarding to own, and you might decide to buy more of them. But in order to buy more stocks and bonds, you would have to reduce your current spending and *save* more. If other households react in the same way, total saving would rise, and the supply of funds to the loanable funds market would increase.

CONSUMPTION TAX A tax on the part of income that households spend.

Another frequently proposed measure is to switch from the current U.S. income tax—which taxes all income whether it is spent or saved—to a **consumption tax,** which would tax only the income that households spend. A consumption tax could work just like the current income tax, except that you would deduct your saving from your income and pay taxes on the remainder. This would increase the reward for saving, since, by saving, you would earn additional interest on the part of your income that would have been taxed away under an income tax.

In the 1980s, government policy inched in the direction of a consumption tax by establishing Individual Retirement Accounts, or IRAs. These allow households to deduct *limited* amounts of saving from their incomes before paying taxes. A general consumption tax, however, would go much further and allow *all* saving to be deducted. The United States is far from this now.

Another proposal to increase household saving is to restructure the U.S. Social Security system, which provides support for retired workers who have contributed funds to the system during their working years. Because Social Security encourages people to rely on the government for income during retirement, they have less incentive to save for retirement themselves. The proposed restructuring would link workers' Social Security benefits to their actual contributions to the system, whereas under the current system some people receive benefits worth far more than the amount they have contributed.

> *Government can alter the tax and transfer system to increase incentives for saving. If successful, these policies would make more funds available for investment, speed growth in the capital stock, and speed the rise in living standards.*

(Do any of these methods of increasing saving disturb you? Remember, we are not advocating any of them here. Rather, we're just noting that such measures would increase saving and promote economic growth. We'll discuss the *costs* of growth-promoting measures later.)

TARGETING THE GOVERNMENT BUDGET: SHRINKING THE DEFICIT. A final pro-investment measure is directed at the government sector itself. Flip back to Figure 8, which we used to first illustrate equilibrium in the loanable funds market. At the equilibrium (point *E*), the interest rate is 5 percent, and total saving is $1.75

trillion. The thin red investment line tells us that, at an interest rate of 5 percent, investment spending is $1.0 trillion.

Now suppose the government eliminates its budget deficit. Then the thin red investment curve also becomes the *total* demand for funds curve. (The government is no longer a borrower). The equilibrium moves from point *E* to point *A,* and the interest rate drops (to some unidentified level), and investment spending increases from $1.0 trillion to $1.5 trillion.

What has happened here? By balancing its budget, the government no longer needs to borrow in the loanable funds market, which frees up funds to flow to the business sector instead. Initially, this creates a surplus of funds. But—as the loanable funds market clears—the interest rate drops, and the surplus of funds disappears. (Why does a drop in the interest rate make the surplus disappear? Hint: What happens to saving and to investment as the interest rate declines?)

The link between the budget deficit, the interest rate, and investment spending is the major reason why the U.S. government, and governments around the world, keep a watchful eye on their budget deficits. They have learned that

> *a shrinking deficit tends to reduce interest rates and increase investment, thus speeding the growth in the capital stock.*

This is an important lesson. As these words are being written (early 1999), the U.S. government budget was in surplus for the first time in 28 years, and the surpluses were expected to continue for several more years. But the forecasted surpluses could disappear if taxes are cut, or new spending programs are introduced. By the time you read this, the budget may even have gone back into deficit. If so, there will be voices calling to reduce the deficit once again, and now you understand why. Just as a shrinking budget deficit speeds economic growth, a rising budget deficit will slow growth.

AN IMPORTANT PROVISO ABOUT DEFICIT REDUCTION. Deficit reduction, even if it stimulates private investment, is not *necessarily* a pro-growth measure. It depends on *how* the deficit is reduced. By an increase in taxes? A cut in government spending? And if the latter, which government programs will be cut? Welfare? National defense? Highway repair? The answers can make a big difference to the impact on growth.

For example, in our discussions of the capital stock in this chapter, we've ignored government capital—roads, communication lines, bridges, and dams. To understand the importance of government capital, just imagine what life would be like without it. How would factories obtain their raw materials or distribute their goods without public roads? How would contracts between buyers and sellers be enforced if there were no public buildings to house courts and police departments? Government capital supports private economic activity in more ways than we can list here.

> *Government investment in new capital and in the maintenance of existing capital makes an important contribution to economic growth.*

This important observation complicates our view of deficit reduction. It is still true that a decrease in government spending will lower the interest rate and increase private investment. But if the budget cutting falls largely on government *investment,* the negative effect of smaller public investment will offset some of the positive impact of greater private investment. Shrinking the deficit will then alter the *mix* of capital—more private and less public—and the effect on growth could go either way. A society rife with lawlessness, deteriorating roads and bridges, or an unreliable communications network might benefit from a shift toward public capital. For example, a study of public budgets in African nations—which are notorious for having poor road conditions—found that each one-dollar-per-year cut in the road-maintenance budget increased vehicle operating costs by between $2 and $3 per year, and in one case, by as much as $22 per year.[5] This is an example where a cut in government spending—even if it reduces the deficit—probably hinders growth. By contrast, a stable society (Sweden comes to mind) with a fully developed and well-maintained public infrastructure might benefit from shifting the mix toward private capital.

> *The impact of deficit reduction on economic growth depends on which government programs are cut. Shrinking the deficit by cutting government investment will not stimulate growth as much as would cutting other types of government spending.*

HUMAN CAPITAL AND ECONOMIC GROWTH

So far, our discussion of capital has been limited to physical capital—the plant and equipment workers use to produce output. But when we think of the capital stock most broadly, we include *human capital* as well. **Human capital**—the skills and knowledge possessed by workers—is as central to economic growth as is physical capital. After all, most types of physical capital—computers, CAT scanners, and even shovels—will contribute little to output unless workers know how to use them. And when the stock of human capital grows (i.e., when more workers gain skills or improve their existing skills), output rises just as it does from growth in the stock of physical capital:

HUMAN CAPITAL Skills and knowledge possessed by workers.

> *An increase in human capital causes economic growth much like an increase in physical capital: it raises labor productivity and increases potential output.*

There is another similarity between human and physical capital: Both are *stocks* that are increased by *flows* of investment. The stock of human capital increases whenever investment in new skills during some period, through education and training, exceeds the depreciation of existing skills over the same period, through retirement, death, or deterioration. Therefore, greater investment in human capital will speed the growth of the human capital stock, the growth in productivity, and the growth in living standards.

Human capital investments are made by business firms (when they help to train their employees), by government (through public education and subsidized training), and by households (when they pay for general education or professional training). Human capital investments have played an important role in recent U.S. economic growth. Can we do anything to increase our rate of investment in human capital?

---

5. This World Bank study was cited in the *Economist*, June 10, 1995, p. 72.

In part, we've already answered this question: Some of the same policies that increase investment in *physical* capital also work to raise investment in human capital. For example, a decrease in the budget deficit would lower the interest rate and make it cheaper for households to borrow for college loans and training programs. A change in the tax system that increases the incentive to save would have the same impact, since this, too, would lower interest rates. And an easing of the tax burden on business firms could increase the profitability of *their* human capital investments, leading to more and better worker training programs.

But there is more: Human capital, unlike physical capital, cannot be separated from the person who possesses it. If you own a building, you can rent it out to one firm and sell your labor to another. But if you have training as a doctor, your labor and your human capital must be sold together, as a package. Moreover, your wage or salary will be payment for both your labor and your human capital. This means that income tax reductions—which we discussed earlier as a means of increasing labor supply—can also increase the profitability of human capital to households, and increase their rate of investment in their own skills and training.

For example, suppose an accountant is considering whether to attend a course in corporate financial reporting, which would increase her professional skills. The course costs $4,000 and will increase the accountant's income by $1,000 per year for the rest of her career. With a tax rate of 40 percent, her take-home pay would increase by $600 per year, so her annual rate of return on her investment would be $600/$4,000 = 15 percent. But with a lower tax rate—say, 20 percent—her take-home pay would rise by $800 per year, so her rate of return would be $800/$4,000 = 20 percent. The lower the tax rate, the greater is the rate of return on human capital investments, and the more likely people will decide to acquire new skills. Thus,

> *many of the pro-growth policies discussed earlier—policies that increase employment or increase investment in physical capital—are also effective in promoting investment in human capital.*

TECHNOLOGICAL CHANGE

So far, we've discussed how economic growth arises from greater quantities of resources—more labor, more physical capital, or more human capital. But another important source of growth is **technological change**—the invention or discovery of new inputs, new outputs, or new methods of production. Indeed, it is largely because of technological change that Malthus's horrible prediction (cited at the beginning of this chapter) has not come true. In the last 60 years, for example, the inventions of synthetic fertilizers, hybrid corn, and chemical pesticides have enabled world food production to increase faster than population.

New technology affects the economy in much the same way as do increases in the capital stock: by increasing productivity. In some cases, the new technology requires the acquisition of physical and human capital before it can be used. For example, a new technique for destroying kidney stones with ultrasound, rather than through time-consuming surgery, can make doctors more productive—but not until they spend several thousand dollars to buy the ultrasound machine and take a course on how to use it. In other cases, a new technology can be used without any

It's All in Your Head
A discussion of the importance of ideas and the profit motive in the process of technological change by Professor Paul Romer of Stanford University.
http://www.ac.com/overview/
Outlook/6.98/over_currentf2.html

TECHNOLOGICAL CHANGE
The invention or discovery of new inputs, new outputs, or new production methods.

additional equipment or training, as when a factory manager discovers a more efficient way to organize workers on the factory floor. In either case, technological change will increase labor productivity. It follows that

> *the faster the rate of technological change, the greater the growth rate of productivity, and the faster the rise in living standards.*

It might seem that technological change is one of those things that just happens. Thomas Edison invents the electric light bulb, or Steve Jobs and Steve Wozniak develop the first practical personal computer in their garage. But the pace of technological change is not as haphazard as it seems. For example, the transistor was invented as part of a massive research and development effort by AT&T to improve the performance of communications devices. Similarly, the next developments in computer technology, transportation, and more will depend on how much money is spent on research and development (R&D) by the leading technology firms:

> *The rate of technological change in the economy depends largely on firms' total spending on R&D. Policies that increase R&D spending will increase the pace of technological change.*

What can the government do to increase spending on R&D? First, it can increase its own direct support for R&D by carrying out more research in its own laboratories or increasing funding for universities and tax incentives to private research labs.

PATENT PROTECTION A government grant of exclusive rights to use or sell a new technology.

Second, the government can enhance **patent protection,** which increases rewards for those who create new technology by giving them exclusive rights to use it or sell it. For example, when the DuPont Corporation discovered a unique way to manufacture Spandex, it obtained a patent to prevent other firms from copying its technique. This patent has enabled DuPont to earn millions of dollars from its invention. Without the patent, other firms would have copied the technique, competed with DuPont, and taken much of its profit away. Hundreds of thousands of new patents are issued every year in the United States: to pharmaceutical companies for new prescription drugs, to telephone companies for new cellular technologies, and to the producers of a variety of household goods ranging from can openers to microwave ovens.

Since patent protection increases the rewards that developers can expect from new inventions, it encourages them to spend on R&D. By *broadening* patent protection (issuing patents on a wider variety of discoveries) or by *lengthening* patent protection (increasing the number of years during which the developer has exclusive rights to market the invention), the government could increase the expected profits from new technologies. That would increase total spending on R&D and increase the pace of technological change. Currently in the United States, patents give inventors and developers exclusive marketing rights over their products for a period of about 20 years. Increasing patent protection to 30 years would certainly increase R&D spending at many firms.

Finally, R&D spending is in many ways just like other types of investment spending: The funds are drawn from the loanable funds market, and R&D programs require firms to buy something now (laboratories, the services of research scientists, materials to build prototypes) for the uncertain prospect of profits in the future. Therefore, almost any policy that stimulates investment spending in general will also increase spending on R&D. Cutting the tax rate on capital gains or on corporate profits, or lowering interest rates by encouraging greater saving or by reducing the budget deficit, can both help to increase spending on R&D and increase the rate of technological change.

ECONOMIC GROWTH IN THE UNITED STATES

In the preceding sections, we've discussed several potential contributors to a nation's economic growth. In practice, which of these causes has been most important to growth in the United States? In a well-known study, the late Edward F. Denison addressed this question, using data from 1929 to 1982. During these years, total output grew, on average, by 2.92 percent per year. Denison attributed this growth to the various factors shown in Table 3.

What is important in this table? First, it shows that most of the average yearly growth rate over the period studied (2.46 percent out of 2.92 percent) can be explained by the leading causes discussed in this chapter: increases in employment, increases in the capital stock (physical and human), and technological change. But notice also that these three cannot explain *all* growth. Almost a half-percentage point of growth per year is explained by "other" factors. What are they? The two most important factors are improvements in the allocation of resources (such as the movement of workers to industries and geographic areas where their productivity is higher) and growth economies of scale (greater productivity made possible by growth in the *size* of firms). In both cases, productivity rises because of an increase in the economy's operating efficiency.

Notice, too, that most of our economic growth comes from sources that increase productivity. Indeed, the only source of growth that tends to decrease productivity is greater employment, leaving the productivity-increasing sources responsible for 1.68 percentage points out of the total 2.92 percentage points of yearly output growth.

This highlights the role of productivity in economic growth. Earlier, you learned that increases in productivity help to raise living standards. Now you can see that most of the rise in our living standard has been caused by increases in productivity. It is not surprising, then, that higher productivity is usually viewed as the most direct route to higher living standards, both in the wealthy industrialized countries and in the poorer, less-developed countries. In the "Using the Theory" section we will focus our attention on the special problems of increasing productivity and living standards in the less-developed countries.

TABLE 3	PERCENTAGE POINTS OF TOTAL GROWTH IN OUTPUT EXPLAINED BY VARIOUS FACTORS, 1929–1982
Factor	**Percentage Points per Year**
Increases in employment	1.24
Increases in physical capital	0.56
Increases in human capital and technological change	0.66
Other	0.46

Source: *Trends in American Economic Growth, 1929–1982* (Washington, D.C.: Brookings Institution, 1985).

THE COST OF ECONOMIC GROWTH

This chapter has presented a variety of policies that could increase the rate of economic growth and speed the rise in living standards. Why don't all nations pursue these policies and push their rates of economic growth to the maximum? Why did the United States grow by 2.92 percent per year between 1929 and 1982? Why not 5 percent per year? Or 10 percent? Or even more?

The answer hinges on one of the basic principles of economics, policy trade-offs, which was first introduced in Chapter 3. In this section, you'll see how this principle of policy tradeoffs can be applied to economic growth. You'll learn that while a variety of policies can increase a nation's rate of economic growth, each of these policies imposes a cost on some group within society or on society as a whole.

POLICY TRADEOFFS

> *Promoting economic growth involves unavoidable tradeoffs: It requires some groups, or the nation as a whole, to give up something else that is valued. In order to decide how fast we want our economy to grow, we must consider growth's costs as well as its benefits.*

What are the costs of growth?

BUDGETARY COSTS

If you look back over this chapter, you'll see that many of the pro-growth policies we've analyzed involve some kind of tax cut. Cutting the income tax rate will likely increase labor supply; cutting taxes on capital gains or corporate profits will increase investment directly; and cutting taxes on saving will increase household saving, lower interest rates, and thus increase investment spending indirectly. Unfortunately, implementing any of these tax cuts would force the government to choose among three unpleasant alternatives: increase some other tax to regain the lost revenue, cut government spending, or permit the budget deficit to rise.

Who will bear the burden of this budgetary cost? That depends on which alternative is chosen. Under the first option—increasing some other tax—the burden falls on those who pay the other tax. For example, if income taxes are cut, real estate taxes might be increased. A family might pay lower income taxes, but higher property taxes. Whether it comes out ahead or behind will depend on how much income the family earns relative to how much property it owns.

The second option, cutting government outlays on goods, services, or transfer payments will impose the burden on those who currently benefit from government programs. These include not only those who receive money from the government directly—like welfare recipients, social security recipients, and many farmers—but also those who benefit from government spending more indirectly. Even though you may earn your income in the private sector, if government spending is cut, you may suffer from a deterioration of public roads, decreased police protection, or poorer schools for your children.

The third option—a larger budget deficit—is more complicated. Under this option, government borrowing will increase, and the total amount of government debt outstanding—called the **national debt**—will rise more rapidly. As a result, future generations will have to make larger interest payments, which will require them to pay higher taxes. But that is not all. Earlier in this chapter, you learned

NATIONAL DEBT The total amount of government debt outstanding as a result of financing earlier budget deficits.

that a rise in the deficit increases the demand for funds and drives up the interest rate. The higher interest rate will reduce investment in physical capital by businesses, as well as investment in human capital by households. Both effects will work to decrease economic growth. It is even possible that private investment will decrease so much that the tax cut, originally designed to boost economic growth, ends up slowing growth instead. At best, the growth-enhancing effects of the tax cut will be weakened. This is why advocates of pro-growth tax cuts usually propose one of the other options—a rise in some other tax or a cut in government spending—as part of the policy.

In sum,

> *properly targeted tax cuts can increase the rate of economic growth, but will force us to either redistribute the tax burden or cut government programs.*

POLICY TRADEOFFS

CONSUMPTION COSTS

Any pro-growth policy that works by increasing investment requires a sacrifice of current consumption spending. The land, labor, and capital we use to produce new cloth-cutting machines, oil rigs, assembly lines, training facilities, college classrooms, or research laboratories could have been used instead to produce clothing, automobiles, video games, and other consumer goods. In other words, we face a tradeoff: The more capital goods we produce in any given year, the fewer consumption goods we can enjoy in that year.

The role of this tradeoff in economic growth can be clearly seen with a familiar tool from Chapter 2: the production possibilities frontier (PPF). Figure 11 shows the PPF for a nation with some given amounts of land, labor, and capital that must be allocated to the production of two types of output: capital goods and consumption goods. At point *K*, the nation is using all of its resources to produce capital goods and none to produce consumption goods. Point *C* represents the opposite extreme—all resources are used to produce consumption goods and none to produce capital goods. Ordinarily, a nation will operate at an intermediate point such as *A*, where it is producing both capital and consumption goods.

Now, as long as capital production at point *A* exceeds the depreciation of existing capital, the capital stock will grow. In future periods, the economy—with more capital—can produce more output, as shown by the outward shift of the PPF to the dashed line in the figure. If a nation can produce more output, then it can produce more consumption goods for the same quantity of capital goods (moving from point *A* to point *B*) or more capital goods for the same quantity of consumption goods (from point *A* to point *D*) or more of both (from point *A* to point *E*).

Let's take a closer look at how this sacrifice of current consumption goods might come about. Suppose that some change in government policy—an investment tax credit or a lengthening of the patent period for new inventions—successfully increases investment spending and shifts the demand for loanable funds curve to the right (go back to Figure 9). What will happen? Businesses—desiring more funds for investment—will drive up the interest rate. With a higher interest rate, households all over the country will find that saving has become more attractive. As families increase their saving, we move rightward along the economy's supply of funds curve. In this way, firms get the funds they need to purchase new capital.

FIGURE 11	CONSUMPTION, INVESTMENT, AND ECONOMIC GROWTH

In the current period, a nation can choose to produce only consumer goods (point C), or it can produce some capital goods by sacrificing some current consumption. If investment at point A exceeds capital depreciation, the capital stock will grow, and the production possibilities frontier will shift outward. After it does, the nation can produce more consumption goods (point B), more capital goods (point D), or more of both (point E).

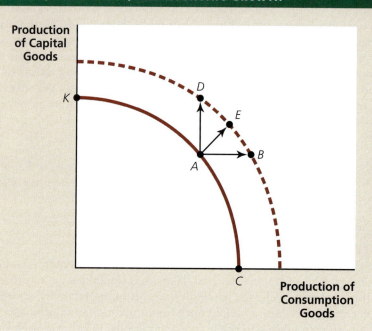

But when households *save more*, they also *spend less*. Thus, by driving up the interest rate, *the increase in investment spending causes a voluntary decrease in consumption spending by households.* Resources are freed from producing consumption goods and diverted to producing capital goods instead.

Although this decrease in consumption spending is voluntary, it is still a cost that we pay. And in some cases, a painful cost: Some of the increase in the household sector's net saving is actually a decrease in household borrowing. At higher interest rates, many people can no longer afford to finance purchases of homes, cars, or furniture. In sum,

POLICY TRADEOFFS

> *greater investment in physical capital, human capital, or R&D will lead to faster economic growth and higher living standards in the future, but we will have fewer consumer goods to enjoy in the present.*

OPPORTUNITY COSTS OF WORKERS' TIME

Suppose that economic growth arises not because of a shift from consumption to investment goods, but rather because of an increase in employment among the current population. In particular, imagine that a greater fraction of the population begins working or those who already have jobs begin working longer hours. In either case, there will be more output to divide among the same population, and the standard of living will rise without any need to sacrifice current consumption. Have we escaped the basic principle of policy tradeoffs—achieved growth without cost? Not at all. In this case, we sacrifice the time we spend in *non*market activities. If a greater fraction of the population works, then students might be working at summer jobs instead of studying, elderly workers might be postponing their retirement, or more previously nonworking spouses might be entering the labor force. Alternatively, if average working hours rise, then the average worker will have less time for other activities—less time to watch television, read novels, garden, fix up the house, raise his or her children, or do volunteer work.

Thus, when economic growth comes about from increases in work effort by the current population, we face a tradeoff: On the one hand, we can enjoy higher incomes and more goods and services. On the other hand, we will have less time to do things other than work at our jobs. In a market economy, the choice is voluntary. If people work longer hours or more people decide to work, then the value of the income gained must be greater than the value of the time given up. Any worker who takes either of these actions must be better off for doing so. Still, we must recognize that *something* of value is always given up when employment increases:

> *An increase in the fraction of the population with jobs or a rise in working hours will increase output and raise living standards, but also will require us to sacrifice time previously spent in nonmarket activities.*

POLICY TRADEOFFS

SACRIFICE OF OTHER SOCIAL GOALS

Rapid economic growth is an important social goal, but it's not the only one. Some of the policies that quicken the pace of growth require us to sacrifice other goals that we care about. For example, you've seen that restructuring Social Security benefits would increase saving, leading to lower interest rates, greater investment, and faster growth. But such a move would cut the incomes of those who benefit from the current system and increase the burden on other social programs, such as welfare and food stamps. Extending patent protection would increase incentives for research and development. But it would also extend the monopoly power exercised by patent holders and force consumers to pay higher prices for drugs, electronic equipment, and even packaged foods.

Of course, the argument cuts both ways: Just as government policies to stimulate investment require us to sacrifice other goals, so, too, can the pursuit of other goals impede investment spending and economic growth. Most of us would like to see a cleaner environment and safer workplaces. But government safety and environmental regulations have increased in severity, complexity, and cost over time, reducing the rate of profit on new capital and shrinking investment spending.

Does this mean that business taxes and government regulations should be reduced to the absolute minimum? Not at all. As in most matters of economic policy, we face a tradeoff:

> *We can achieve greater worker safety, a cleaner environment, and other social goals, but we may have to sacrifice some economic growth along the way. Alternatively, we can achieve greater economic growth, but we will have to compromise on other things we care about.*

POLICY TRADEOFFS

Does this sound a bit familiar? It is very much like the tradeoff discussed in the "Using the Theory" section in Chapter 12. Whether we want a greater GDP (as in Chapter 12), or a greater *growth rate* of GDP (as in this chapter), we must pay an opportunity cost. We will have to sacrifice other things we value. And when values differ, people will disagree on just how much we should sacrifice for economic growth or how much growth we should sacrifice for other goals.

ECONOMIC GROWTH IN THE LESS DEVELOPED COUNTRIES

In most countries, Malthus's dire predictions have not come true. An important part of the reason is that increases in the capital stock have raised productivity and increased the average standard of living. Increases in the capital stock are even more important in the less developed countries (LDCs), which have relatively little capital to begin with and where even small increases in capital formation can have dramatic effects on living standards.

But how does a nation go about increasing its capital stock? As you've learned, there are a variety of measures, all designed to accomplish the same goal: shifting resources away from consumer-goods production toward capital-goods production. A very simple formula.

Some countries that were once LDCs—like the four Asian tigers (Hong Kong, Singapore, South Korea, and Taiwan)—have applied the formula very effectively. Output per capita in these countries has grown by more than 5 percent per year over the past 25 years. While a financial crisis threw these countries into recession in the late 1990s, it was a minor setback in an otherwise stellar record of growth. How was the growth achieved? Largely through the the growth-enhancing measures discussed in this chapter. In particular, these nations provided large subsidies for human and physical capital investments, gave pro-growth tax cuts to encourage saving and investment, and sacrificed other social goals—especially a clean environment—for growth.[6]

But other LDCs have had great difficulty raising living standards. Table 4 shows growth rates for several of them. In some cases—such as Pakistan—growth is slow, but picking up steam. In others—like Ghana—the standard of living has remained stagnant at very low levels for years. In still other cases—for example, Zaire and, more recently, Ethiopia—output per capita has been falling steadily. Why do some LDCs have such difficulty achieving economic growth?

Much of the explanation for the low growth rates of many LDCs lies with three characteristics that they share:

1. *Very low current output per capita.* Living standards are already so low in some LDCs that they cannot take advantage of the tradeoff between producing consumption goods and producing capital goods. In these countries, pulling resources out of consumption would threaten the survival of many households. At the level of the individual household, the problem is seen as an inability to save: Incomes are so low that households must spend all they earn on consumption.

2. *High population growth rates.* Low living standards and high population growth rates are linked together in a cruel circle of logic. On the one hand, population growth by itself tends to reduce living standards, since it decreases the capital-labor ratio and decreases productivity. On the other hand, low living standards tend to increase population growth. Why? First, the poor are often uneducated in matters of family planning. Second, high mortality rates among infants and children encourage families to have many offspring to ensure the survival of at least a few to care for parents in their old age. As a result, while the average woman in the United States will have fewer than two children in her

---

6. The Asian tigers also had some special advantages—such as a high level of human capital to start with.

TABLE 4	ECONOMIC GROWTH IN SELECTED POOR COUNTRIES	
	Average Annual Growth in Output per Capita	
Country	**1965–1980**	**1980–1993**
Pakistan	1.8%	3.1%
Ghana	-0.8%	0.1%
Bangladesh	-0.3%	2.1%
Ethiopia	0.4%	-1.9%
Democratic Republic of Congo	-1.3%	-1.8%
All of Sub-Saharan Africa	1.5%	-0.6%

Source: United Nations Development Program, *Human Development Reports, 1995–1997* (Oxford: Oxford University Press, 1995–1997), Table 25.

lifetime, the average woman in Haiti will have about five children, and the average woman in Rwanda will have more than six.

3. *Poor social infrastructure.* A variety of social factors make LDCs unprofitable places in which to invest. These include political instability, corruption, adverse government regulations, and poor law enforcement. The last problem—poor law enforcement—is an especially serious economic problem in many LDCs. Citizens must spend valuable time guarding against thievery and trying to induce the government to let them operate businesses—time they could otherwise spend producing output.

These three characteristics—low current production, high population growth, and poor social infrastructure—interact to create a vicious circle of continuing poverty, which we can understand with the help of the familiar PPF between capital goods and consumption goods. Look back at Figure 11, and now imagine that it applies to a poor, developing country. In this case, an outward shift of the PPF does not, in itself, guarantee an increase in the standard of living. In the LDCs, the population growth rate is often very high, and—with a constant fraction of the population in the labor force—employment grows at the same rapid rate as the population.

Now, suppose employment growth is so rapid that the number of workers rises faster than the capital stock. Then even though the PPF is shifting outward, capital per worker will decline. The result is falling labor productivity and a general decline in living standards. Even though the PPF shifts outward, it does not shift outward fast enough to keep up with population growth.

In order to have rising living standards, a nation's stock of capital must not only grow, but grow faster than its population.

To explore this idea more fully, look at Figure 12. Point N shows the minimum amount of investment needed to maintain capital per worker, labor productivity, and living standards for a given rate of population growth. For example, if the population is growing at 4 percent per year, then point N indicates the investment needed to increase the total capital stock by 4 percent per year. If investment is just equal to N, then capital per worker—and living standards—remains

---

FIGURE 12   **LDC GROWTH AND LIVING STANDARDS**

In order to increase capital per worker when population is growing, yearly investment spending must exceed some minimum level N. In any year, there is a minimum level of consumption, S, needed to support the population. If output is currently at point H, capital per worker and living standards are stagnant. But movement to a point like J—which would enable the standard of living to grow—would require an unacceptably low level of consumption.

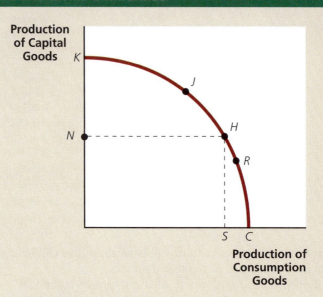

constant. If investment exceeds N, then capital per worker—and living standards—will rise. Of course, the greater the growth in population, the higher point N will be on the vertical axis, since greater investment will be needed just to keep up with population growth.

The PPF in Figure 12 has an added feature: Point S shows the minimum acceptable level of consumption—the amount of consumer goods the economy *must* produce in a year. For example, S might represent the consumption goods needed to prevent starvation among the least well off or to prevent unacceptable social consequences, such as violent revolution.

Now we can see the problem faced by the most desperate of the less-developed economies. Output is currently at a point like H in the figure, with consumption at its minimum acceptable level and investment just equal to N. The capital stock is growing just fast enough to maintain the level of capital per worker, and so labor productivity and living standards are stagnant. In this situation, the PPF shifts outward each year, but not quickly enough to improve people's lives. People are no worse off each year, but no better off either.

Another (even worse) possibility is that the economy is operating at point R. In this case, the average standard of living declines even though the capital stock is growing—that is, even though the PPF will shift outward in future periods. Why? Because at R, capital is growing *more slowly* than the population, so labor productivity is falling.

The solution to this problem appears to be an increase in capital production beyond point N—a movement *along* the PPF from point H to a point such as J. As investment rises above N, capital per worker rises, and the PPF shifts outward rapidly enough over time to raise living standards. In a wealthy country, like the United States, such a move could be engineered by changes in taxes or other government policies. But in the LDCs depicted here, such a move would be intolerable: At point H, consumption is already equal to S, the lowest acceptable level. Moving to point J would require reducing consumption *below S*.

The poorest LDCs are too poor to take advantage of the tradeoff between consumption and capital production in order to increase their living standards. Since they cannot reduce consumption below current levels, they cannot produce enough capital to keep up with their rising populations.

In recent history, countries have attempted several methods to break out of this vicious circle of poverty. During the 1930s, the dictator Joseph Stalin simply *forced* the Soviet economy from a point like *H* to one like *J*. His goal was to shift the Soviet Union's PPF outward as rapidly as possible. But, as you can see, this reduced consumption below the minimum level *S*, and Stalin resorted to brutal measures to enforce his will. Many farmers were ordered into the city to produce capital equipment. With fewer people working on farms, agricultural production declined, and there was not enough food to go around. Stalin's solution was to confiscate food from the remaining farmers and give it to the urban workforce. Of course, this meant starvation for millions of farmers. Millions more who complained too loudly, or who otherwise represented a political threat, were rounded up and executed.

A less-brutal solution to the problem of the LDCs is to make the wealthy bear more of the burden of increasing growth. If the decrease in consumption can be limited to the rich, then total consumption can be significantly reduced—freeing up resources for investment—without threatening the survival of the poor. This, however, is not often practical, since the wealthy have the most influence with government in LDCs. Being more mobile, they can easily relocate to other countries, taking their savings with them. This is why efforts to shift the sacrifice to the wealthy are often combined with restrictions on personal liberties, such as the freedom to travel or to invest abroad. These moves often backfire in the long run, since restrictions on personal and economic freedom are remembered long after they are removed and make the public—especially foreigners—hesitant to invest in that country.

A third alternative—and the one used increasingly since the 1940s—is *foreign investment* or *foreign assistance*. Suppose that wealthier nations, individually or through international organizations such as the World Bank or the International Monetary Fund, provide an LDC with capital. Then the capital available to the LDC increases, with *no* cutbacks in consumption. This is illustrated in panel (a) of Figure 13. The LDC *makes use* of capital and consumption goods at a point like *F* in Figure 13(a), even though its *production* remains—for the moment—at point *H*.

A variation of this strategy is for foreign nations to provide consumer goods so that the poorer nation can shift its *own* resources away from producing them (and into capital production) without causing consumption levels to fall. Once again, if capital production exceeds point *N* during the year, capital per worker will grow, setting the stage for continual growth to higher standards of living.

Finally, there is a fourth alternative. Consider a nation producing at point *H* in Figure 13(b). Once again, capital production is just sufficient to keep up with a rising population, so the PPF shifts outward each year, but not rapidly enough to raise living standards. If this nation can reduce its population growth rate, however, then less capital production will be needed just to keep up with population growth. In the figure, point *N* will move downward to *N'*. If production remains at point *H*, the PPF will continue to shift outward as before, but now—with slower population

FIGURE 13	GROWTH OPTIONS FOR LDCS

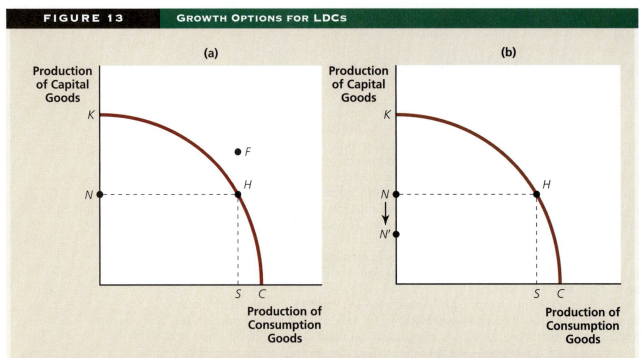

Panel (a) shows an LDC producing at point *H*, where the available consumption goods are just sufficient to meet minimum standards (point *S*), but capital production just keeps up with population growth. The economy is stagnant. If the nation can obtain goods externally—through foreign investment or foreign assistance—it can *make use* of capital and consumption goods at a point like *F*—outside of its PPF.

Panel (b) shows another case where capital production at point *H* is just sufficient to keep up with a rising population, but not great enough to raise capital per worker and living standards. If this nation can reduce its population growth rate, then the same rate of capital production will increase capital per worker and shift the PPF outward.

growth—productivity and living standards will rise. Slowing the growth in population has been an important (and successful) part of China's growth strategy, although it has required severe restrictions on the rights of individual families to have children—policy tradeoffs, once again.

SUMMARY

The growth rate of real GDP is a key determinant of economic well-being. If output grows faster than the population, then the average standard of living will rise. Output can grow because of increases in employment, increases in physical and human capital, and improvements in technology.

Employment will rise if either labor supply or labor demand increases. Labor supply is determined by the size of the working-age population and by individuals' willingness to forgo leisure in return for a wage. Population growth is something that occurs naturally, but the amount of work effort supplied by a given population is sensitive to after-tax labor earnings. A decrease in the income tax rate would stimulate labor supply.

Labor demand is influenced by productivity. Any factor that makes labor more productive will increase the demand for labor, raise employment, and contribute to economic growth. If employees become better trained, or if they are given more capital to work with, their productivity will increase.

An increase in the capital stock contributes to economic growth by making workers more productive. Whenever investment exceeds depreciation, the capital stock will grow. And if the capital stock grows faster than the labor force, then labor productivity will rise.

Investment spending—which is financed by funds obtained in the loanable funds market—can be encouraged by government policies. Investment can be stimulated directly through reductions in the corporate profits tax or through subsidies to new capital. Investment can also be stimulated indirectly. If the government reduces its budget deficit, the demand for loanable funds will fall, the interest rate will decline, and investment will increase. Finally, policies that encourage household saving will lower the interest rate, increase investment, and contribute to capital formation.

The third factor that contributes to economic growth is technological change—the application of new inputs or new methods of production. Technological change increases productivity and raises living standards by permitting us to produce more output from a given set of inputs. Technological improvements can be traced back to spending on research and development, either by the government or by private firms.

Economic growth is not costless. Government policies that stimulate employment, capital formation, or technological progress require either tax increases, cuts in other spending programs, or an increase in the national debt. More broadly, any increase in investment requires the sacrifice of consumption today. Any increase in employment from a given population requires a sacrifice of leisure time and other nonmarket activities.

KEY TERMS

average standard of living
labor productivity
capital per worker
loanable funds market
budget deficit

budget surplus
supply of funds curve
investment demand curve
government's demand for
    funds curve

total demand for funds curve
corporate profits tax
investment tax credit
capital gains tax
consumption tax

human capital
technological change
patent protection
national debt

REVIEW QUESTIONS

1. Discuss the three ways a country can increase its level of potential output.

2. Why can population growth be a mixed blessing in terms of economic growth?

3. Explain how a tax cut could lead to *slower* economic growth.

4. Given that a country's PPF is shifting outward, is it necessarily the case that the country's standard of living is rising? Why or why not?

5. Who are the two major players on the demand side of the loanable funds market? Why does each seek funds there? What is the "price" of these funds?

6. What is the source of funds supplied to the loanable funds market? Explain why the supply of funds curve slopes up, and why the curve depicting business demand for funds slopes down.

7. Will the *slope* of the demand for funds curve be affected if the government runs a deficit? Why or why not?

8. Why did Malthus's dire prediction fail to materialize? Do you think it could still come true? Explain your reasoning.

9. "Faster economic growth can benefit everyone and need not harm anyone. This is a rare violation of the basic principle of policy tradeoffs." True or false? Explain.

10. Discuss some of the factors that contribute to rapid population growth in LDCs.

11. Explain the following statement: "In some LDCs, it can be said that a significant cause of continued poverty is poverty itself."

12. Describe four ways in which LDCs have tried to improve their growth performance. Discuss the opportunity cost that must be borne in each case and identify the group that is most likely to bear it.

PROBLEMS AND EXERCISES

1. Discuss the effect (holding everything else constant) each of the following would have on potential output, productivity, and the average standard of living. Use the appropriate graphs (e.g., labor market, loanable funds market) and state your assumptions when necessary.
   a. Increased immigration
   b. An aging population with an increasing proportion of retirees
   c. A baby boom
   d. A decline in the tax rate on corporate profits
   e. Reduction of unemployment compensation benefits
   f. A balanced budget amendment to the U.S. Constitution
   g. Expanding the scope of the federal student loan program
   h. Easier access to technical information on the Internet

2. Below are GDP and growth data for the United States and four other countries:

	1950 per Capita GDP (in constant dollars)	1990 per Capita GDP (in constant dollars)	Average Yearly Growth Rate
United States	$9,573	$21,558	2.0%
France	$5,221	$17,959	3.0%
Japan	$1,873	$19,425	5.7%
Kenya	$ 609	$ 1,055	1.3%
India	$ 597	$ 1,348	2.0%

Source: Angus Maddison, *Monitoring the World Economy, 1820–1992.* Paris, OECD, 1995.

   a. For both years, calculate each country's per capita GDP as a percentage of U.S. per capita GDP. Which countries appear to be catching up to the United States, and which are lagging behind?
   b. If these countries continue to grow at the average growth rates given, how long will it take France to catch up to the United States? How long will it take India? Kenya?

3. The following data are for the country of Barrovia, which has long been concerned with economic growth.

	Population (millions)	Employment (millions)	Labor Productivity	Total Output
1996	100	50	$ 9,500	_____
1997	104	51	$ 9,500	_____
1998	107	53	$ 9,750	_____
1999	108	57	$ 9,750	_____
2000	110	57	$10,000	_____

   a. Fill in the entries for total output in each of the five years.
   b. Calculate the following for each year (except 1996):
      (1) Population growth rate (from previous year)
      (2) Growth rate of output (from previous year)
      (3) Growth rate of per capita output (from previous year)

Suppose the government is running a budget surplus instead of a deficit. Draw graphs of the loanable funds market to illustrate each of the following:

   c. Government policies that successfully increase firms' incentives to invest.
   d. Government policies that successfully increase households' incentives to save.
   e. A decrease in government spending with no change in taxes.

4. In 1992 Professor Gary Becker of the University of Chicago won the Nobel Prize in Economics for extending economic analysis to a wide range of human behavior and interaction.
   a. Read the press release, including a brief synopsis of Professor Becker's research, at http://www.nobel.se/laureates/economy-1992-press.html. Pay special attention to the sections "Human Capital" and "Household and Family."
   b. How does Professor Becker explain declining fertility as countries become increasingly industrialized? If decreased fertility leads to slower population growth, how will labor productivity be affected? At the same time, if parents increase investment in their children's human capital, how will labor productivity be affected?

CHALLENGE QUESTIONS

1. Harvard economist Amartya Sen has argued that famines in underdeveloped countries are not simply the result of crop failures or natural disasters. Instead, he suggests that wars, especially civil wars, are linked to most famine episodes in recent history. Using a framework similar to Figure 12, discuss the probable effect of war on a country's PPF. Explain what would happen if the country were initially operating at or near a point like S, the minimum acceptable level of consumption.

2. All else equal, why might a country with a small capital stock actually attract more investment than a country with more capital?

CHAPTER 15

BOOMS AND RECESSIONS

If you are like most college students, you will be looking for a full-time job when you graduate. As you are no doubt aware, your prospects will depend partly on the type of job you seek and your qualifications relative to others in that line of work. But it will *also* depend—importantly—on the overall level of economic activity in the country.

If the economy always operated at its potential output, with the labor force fully employed, you'd have nothing to worry about. You could be confident of getting a job within a reasonable time at the going wage for someone with your skills and characteristics. Unfortunately, this is not how the world works. *Potential* output increases every year, but *actual* output does not always grow, or grow at the same rate as potential output. Instead, as far back as we have data, the United States and similar countries have experienced *economic fluctuations*.

In Figure 1, look first at the red line. It shows full-employment or potential output since 1960. As a result of technological change and growth in the capital stock and population, full-employment output rises steadily. But now look at the blue line, which shows *actual* output. You can see that actual GDP fluctuates above and below its potential. During *contractions*, which are shaded in the figure, output declines, occasionally sharply. During *expansions*, the unshaded periods, output rises quickly—usually faster than potential output is rising.

Figure 2 shows another characteristic of expansions and contractions: fluctuations in unemployment. Notice the bulge of unemployment that occurs during each contraction. When GDP falls, the unemployment rate increases. The worst bulge in unemployment was in 1982, when more than 10 percent of the labor force was looking for work. In expansions, on the other hand, the unemployment rate falls. During the long expansion of the mid- and late-1990s, for example, unemployment dropped as low as 4.1 percent. In some expansions, the unemployment rate can drop even lower than the full-employment level. In the sustained expansion of the

FIGURE 1   POTENTIAL AND ACTUAL REAL GDP, 1960–1998

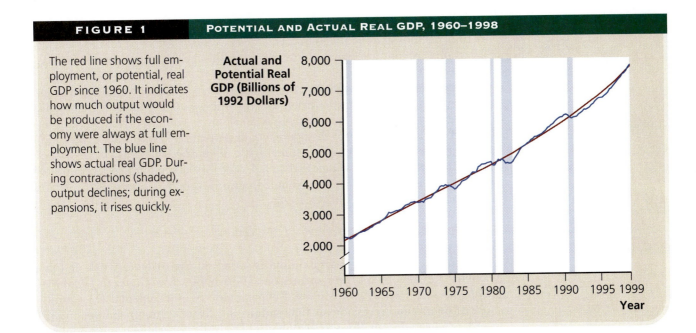

The red line shows full employment, or potential, real GDP since 1960. It indicates how much output would be produced if the economy were always at full employment. The blue line shows actual real GDP. During contractions (shaded), output declines; during expansions, it rises quickly.

late 1960s, for example, it reached a low of just over 3 percent. At the same time, output exceeded its potential, as you can verify in Figure 1.

The terms "expansion" and "contraction" refer to *changes* in GDP: GDP *rises* in an expansion and *falls* in a contraction. But it is also useful to label periods when output is above and below its potential. In this book, we'll use the term **boom** to indicate a period during which GDP *exceeds* its full employment, potential level. During a boom, the *un*employment rate is unusually low. A *recession*, by contrast, is a period during which GDP is *below* potential.[1] During recessions, the unemployment

BOOM A period of time during which real GDP exceeds full employment, potential GDP.

---

1. Formally, the term "recession" is a synonym for "contraction"—a period during which *output is falling*. But economists and the media often use it to mean a period during which output *is below its potential*. We follow that convention in this book.

FIGURE 2   U.S. UNEMPLOYMENT RATE, 1960–1998

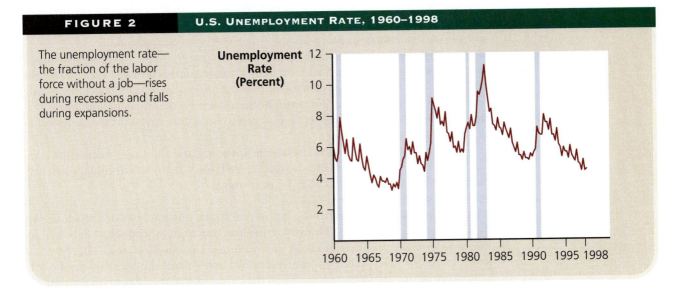

The unemployment rate—the fraction of the labor force without a job—rises during recessions and falls during expansions.

John Maynard Keynes on the Internet

Links to material by and about Keynes can be found on Professor Brad de Long's Keynes Web page.
http://econ161.berkeley.edu/Economists/keynes.html

rate is unusually high. As you can see in Figure 1, expansions often cause the economy to overshoot its potential—that is, *expansions often lead to booms*. During contractions, by contrast, the economy often operates below its potential—*contractions often lead to recessions*.

Figure 1 also shows something else: Booms and recessions don't last forever. Indeed, sometimes they are rather brief. The recession of 1990–1991, for example, ended within a year.

But if you look carefully at the figure, you'll see that the back-to-back recessions of the early 1980s extended over 3 full years. And during the Great Depression of the 1930s (not shown), it took more than a decade for the economy to return to full employment. Booms can last for extended periods, too. The boom of the 1980s lasted about 7 years, from 1983 to 1990.

SPENDING AND ECONOMIC FLUCTUATIONS

Why are there booms and recessions?

Much of our current understanding is based on the original work of John Maynard Keynes. In his very influential 1936 book, *The General Theory of Employment, Interest, and Money,* Keynes made two arguments: (1) a major cause of booms and recessions is fluctuations in private sector *spending*; and (2) in order to keep output close to its potential level, the government must counteract changes in private sector spending by adjusting either its own spending or taxes.

The second of these two arguments has always been controversial, but the first is accepted by most economists today. Keynes showed how shocks that initially affect spending in one sector of the economy quickly influence spending in other sectors, causing changes in total output and employment.

The basic logic of Keynes's argument is straightforward. Business firms will not continue producing output that they cannot sell. When total spending in the economy suddenly *decreases*, some firms find themselves producing more output than they are selling. They respond by reducing output and laying off workers.

But the story does not end there. The laid-off workers—even those who collect some unemployment benefits—will see their incomes decline. As a consequence, they will spend less on a variety of consumer goods. This will cause *other* firms—the ones that produce those consumer goods—to cut back on *their* production, lay off some of their workers, and so on. On a national level, the economy contracts and—if the contraction is sharp enough—we may enter a recession.

Similarly, when total spending suddenly *increases*, some firms will produce *more* output and hire additional workers (or rehire some who were previously laid off.) When these workers spend some of their additional income on consumer goods produced by other firms, the latter will begin to increase *their* production, hire more workers, and so on. The result is an economic expansion, and—if the expansion is sharp enough—a boom.

The focus of this chapter is changes in spending and their role in creating economic fluctuations. In Chapters 16 and 17, we'll look at some additional causes of economic fluctuations besides changes in spending.

THINKING ABOUT SPENDING. Before we begin our analysis of spending, we have two choices to make. The first concerns our basic approach. There are so many different types of spenders in the economy: city dwellers and suburbanites; government agencies like the Department of Defense and the local school board; and businesses of all types, ranging from the corner convenience store to a huge corporation such as AT&T. How should we organize our thinking about spending? Macro-economists have found that the most useful approach is to divide spending into four broad *aggregates*:

- Consumption spending (*C*)
- Investment spending (*I*)
- Government purchases (*G*)
- Net exports (*NX*)

These categories should seem familiar to you. They were the same ones we used to break down GDP in the expenditure approach. In the first part of this chapter, we'll take another look at each of these aggregates with our eye on *spending* rather than production. Then, we'll combine them to explore the behavior of total spending in the economy and, finally, look at the relationship between total spending and output.

Our second choice in analyzing spending is whether to look at *nominal* or *real* spending. (Recall that a nominal variable is measured in current dollars, while a real variable is measured in the constant dollars of some base year.) Ultimately, we care more about real variables, such as real output and real income, because they are more closely related to our economic well-being. For example, a rise in *nominal* output might mean that we are producing more goods and services, or it might just mean that prices have risen and production has remained the same or fallen. But a rise in *real* output always means that production has increased. For this reason, we will think about real variables right from the beginning. When we discuss "consumption spending," we mean "real consumption spending"; "investment spending" means "real investment spending"; and so on.

CONSUMPTION SPENDING

A natural place for us to begin our look at spending is with its largest component: *consumption spending.* In all, household spending on consumer goods—groceries, restaurant meals, rent, car repairs, furniture, telephone calls, and so forth—is about two-thirds of total spending in the economy. Because we are interested in the macro-economy, we don't concern ourselves with the differences between one consumer good and another. Instead, we want to know: What determines the *total* amount of consumption spending?

Of all the factors that might influence consumption spending, the most important is **disposable income,** the income of the household sector after taxes. More formally, disposable income is defined as follows:

DISPOSABLE INCOME The part of household income that remains after paying taxes.

$$\text{Disposable Income} = \text{Total Income} - \text{Net Taxes}$$

Notice the word "net" that modifies taxes. **Net taxes** are the taxes the government collects *minus* the transfer payments the government pays out, such as social security payments or unemployment insurance:

NET TAXES The taxes the government collects *minus* the transfer payments the government pays out.

$$\text{Net Taxes} = \text{Tax Revenue} - \text{Transfer Payments}$$

In macroeconomics, we are interested in the tax dollars that flow from the household sector to the government. Transfer payments, however, are collected from one set of households and given to another, so we treat them as if they were never taken from the household sector at all. Thus, when we calculate disposable income, we subtract transfer payments from taxes before we subtract the result from total income.

THE CONSUMPTION FUNCTION

The relationship between consumption and disposable income is a positive one. All else equal, you'd certainly spend more on consumer goods if your *own* disposable income were $50,000 per year than if it were $20,000 per year. The same is true for the nation as a whole. A rise in aggregate disposable income causes a rise in aggregate consumption spending. (Here, as elsewhere, we are speaking about aggregate *real* variables: *real* consumption and *real* disposable income.)

Figure 3 shows the relationship between real consumption spending and real disposable income in the United States from 1960 to 1998. (The figures are in 1992 dollars.) Each point in the diagram represents a different year. For example, the point labeled "1982" represents a disposable income in that year of $3,496 billion and consumption spending of $3,082 billion. Notice that each time disposable income rises, consumption spending rises as well. Indeed, almost all of the variation in consumption spending from year to year can be explained by variations in disposable income.

There is something even more interesting about Figure 3: The relationship between consumption and disposable income is almost perfectly *linear*—the points lie remarkably close to a straight line. This almost-linear relationship between consumption and disposable income has been observed in a wide variety of historical periods and a wide variety of nations. This is why, when we represent the relation-

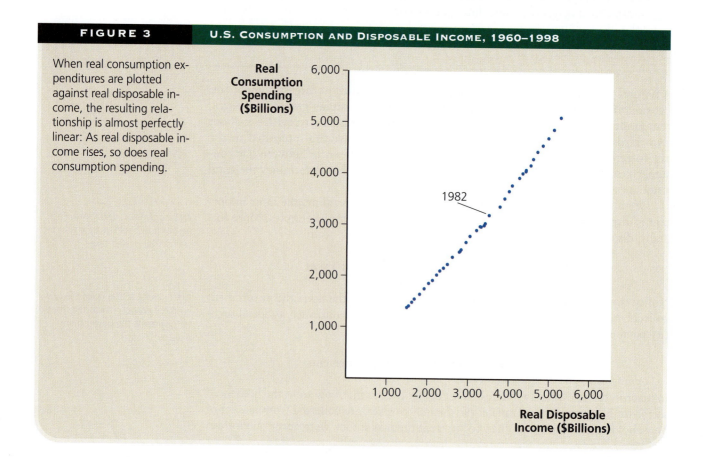

FIGURE 3   **U.S. CONSUMPTION AND DISPOSABLE INCOME, 1960–1998**

When real consumption expenditures are plotted against real disposable income, the resulting relationship is almost perfectly linear: As real disposable income rises, so does real consumption spending.

TABLE 1	HYPOTHETICAL DATA ON DISPOSABLE INCOME AND CONSUMPTION	
	Disposable Income (billions of dollars per year)	**Consumption Spending (billions of dollars per year)**
	0	2,000
	1,000	2,600
	2,000	3,200
	3,000	3,800
	4,000	4,400
	5,000	5,000
	6,000	5,600
	7,000	6,200
	8,000	6,800

ship between disposable income and consumption with a diagram or an equation, we use a straight line.

Our discussion will be clearer if we move from the actual data in Figure 3 to the hypothetical example in Table 1. Each row in the table represents a combination of real disposable income and consumption we might observe in an economy. For example, the table shows us that if disposable income were equal to $7,000 billion in some year, consumption spending would equal $6,200 billion in that year. In Figure 4, where the data are plotted on a graph, this combination of disposable income and consumption is represented by point *A*. When all of the other points in the table are plotted in the figure, the result is a straight line. This line is called the **consumption function**, because it illustrates the functional relationship between consumption and disposable income.

Like every straight line, the consumption function in Figure 4 has two main features: a vertical intercept and a slope. Mathematically, the intercept—in this case, $2,000 billion—tells us how much consumption spending there would be in the economy if disposable income were zero. However, the real purpose of the vertical intercept is not to identify what would actually happen at zero disposable income, but rather to help us determine which particular line represents consumption spending in the diagram. After all, there are many lines we could draw that have the same slope as the one in the figure. But only one of them has a vertical intercept of $2,000.

The vertical intercept in the figure also has a name: **autonomous consumption.** It represents the combined impact on consumption spending of everything *other than* disposable income. We'll discuss some of these other factors a bit later. The second important feature of Figure 4 is the slope, which shows the change along the vertical axis divided by the change along the horizontal axis as we go from one point to another on the line. If we use ΔC to represent the change in real consumption spending and ΔDI to represent the change in real disposable income, then the slope of the consumption function is given by

$$\text{slope} = \Delta C / \Delta DI$$

CONSUMPTION FUNCTION A positively sloped relationship between real consumption spending and real disposable income.

AUTONOMOUS CONSUMPTION The part of consumption spending that is independent of income; also, the vertical intercept of the consumption function.

As you can see in the table, each time disposable income rises by $1,000 billion, consumption spending rises by $600 billion, so that the slope is $\Delta C / \Delta DI$ = $600 billion/ $1,000 billion = 0.6.

The slope in Figure 4 is an important feature not just of the consumption function itself, but of the macroeconomic analysis we will build from it. This is why

| FIGURE 4 | THE CONSUMPTION FUNCTION |

Real consumption spending is linearly related to real disposable income. The vertical axis intercept of the line, a = $2,000 billion, shows autonomous consumption spending. The slope of the line, b = 0.6, is the marginal propensity to consume.

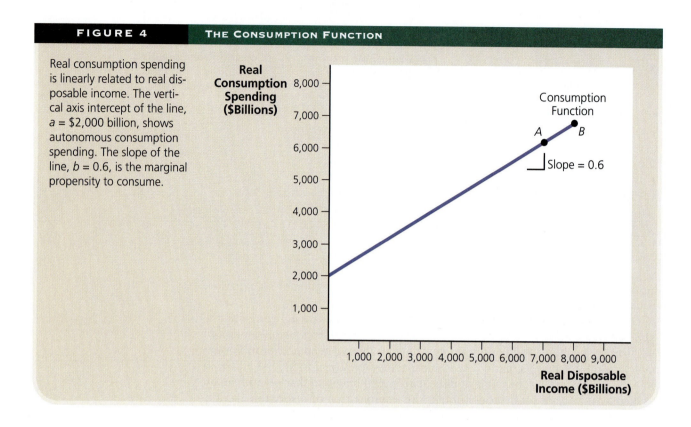

economists have given this slope a special name, the *marginal propensity to consume,* abbreviated *MPC.* In our example, the *MPC* is 0.6.

We can think of the *MPC* in three different ways, but each of them has the same meaning:

> The **marginal propensity to consume (MPC)** is (1) the slope of the consumption function; (2) the change in consumption divided by the change in disposable income ($\Delta C/\Delta DI$); and (3) the amount by which consumption spending rises when disposable income rises by one dollar.

MARGINAL PROPENSITY TO CONSUME The amount by which consumption spending rises when disposable income rises by one dollar.

Logic suggests that the *MPC* should be larger than zero (when income rises, consumption spending will rise), but less than 1 (the rise in consumption will be *smaller* than the rise in disposable income). This is certainly true in our example: With an *MPC* of 0.6, a one-dollar rise in disposable income causes spending to rise by 60 cents. It is also observed to be true in economies throughout the world. Accordingly,

> We will always assume that 0 < MPC < 1.

REPRESENTING CONSUMPTION WITH AN EQUATION. Sometimes, we'll want to use an equation to represent the straight-line consumption function. The most general form of the equation is

$$C = a + bDI$$

The term *a* is the vertical intercept of the consumption function, which you've learned is called *autonomous consumption spending*. The equation clearly shows that autonomous consumption (*a*) is the part of consumption that does *not* depend on disposable income.

The other term, *b*, is the slope of the consumption function. This is our familiar marginal propensity to consume (*MPC*), telling us how much consumption *increases* each time disposable income rises by a dollar. In our example in Figure 4, *b* is equal to 0.6.

SHIFTS IN THE CONSUMPTION FUNCTION

As you've learned, consumption spending depends positively on disposable income: If disposable income rises, consumption spending will rise with it.

In Figure 4, this change in consumption spending would be represented by a *movement along* the consumption function. For example, a rise in disposable income from $7,000 billion to $8,000 billion would cause consumption spending to increase from $6,200 billion to $6,800 billion, moving us from point *A* to point *B* along the consumption–income line.

But other factors besides disposable income influence consumption spending. For example, suppose your disposable income is $50,000 per year. How much of that sum will you spend, and how much will you save? Since the *interest rate* determines your reward for saving, you would probably save less at a lower interest rate like 2 percent than at a higher interest rate like 10 percent. But since you'd be saving less at a lower interest rate, you'd be spending more. The same is true for the nation as a whole: For any given level of disposable income, *we can expect a drop in the interest rate to cause an increase in consumption spending*. Graphically, this is represented as an *upward shift* in the consumption function. Figure 5 shows an example in which, at each level of disposable income, consumption spending rises by $800 billion.

Another determinant of consumption is *wealth*—the total value of household assets (home, stocks, bonds, bank accounts, and the like) minus total outstanding liabilities (mortgage loans, credit card debt, student loans, and so on). Even if your disposable income stayed the same, a rise in your wealth—say, because your stocks or bonds became more valuable—would probably cause you to spend more. The same is true for the nation as a whole: For any level of disposable income, a rise in household wealth will cause an upward shift in the consumption function.

Expectations about the future will also affect consumption spending. If households become more optimistic about their job security or expect higher future incomes, they are likely to spend more of their income now, shifting the consumption function upward. Similarly, increased pessimism, such as greater worries about job loss, would lead to a downward shift of the consumption function.

Notice, in Figure 5, that the new, dashed consumption function is parallel to the original. That is, after the shift, the *slope* of the consumption function—which is equal to the *MPC*—remains unchanged. Another way of saying this is that, when any of the factors we've discussed causes the consumption function to shift, it changes *autonomous consumption*—the vertical intercept of the line—represented by *a* in the consumption equation $C = a + bDI$. This corresponds to what economists have observed about the real world. While autonomous consumption spending changes quite frequently, the *MPC* tends to remain the same over time.

| FIGURE 5 | AN UPWARD SHIFT IN THE CONSUMPTION FUNCTION |

A variety of factors can shift the consumption function upward: a drop in the interest rate, an increase in real wealth, or optimism about the future of the economy. If the changes occur in the opposite direction (e.g., a *rise* in the interest rate), the consumption function will shift downward.

In this figure, the consumption function shifts upward by $800 billion. For example, at a disposable income of $7,000 billion, consumption spending increases from $6,200 billion (point *A*) to $7,000 billion (point *D*).

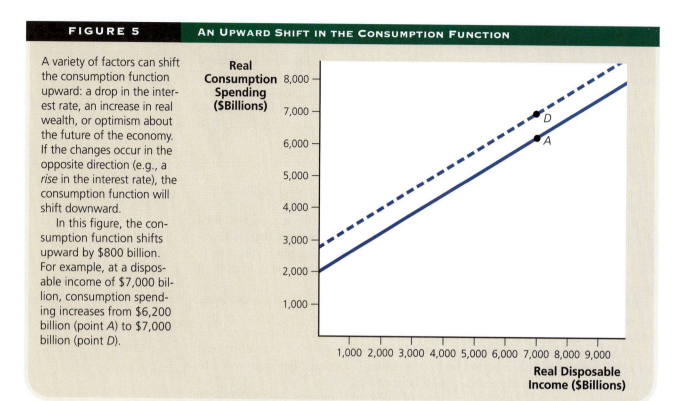

We can summarize our discussion of changes in consumption spending as follows:

When a change in disposable income causes consumption spending to change, we move along the consumption function. When a change in anything else besides disposable income causes consumption spending to change, the consumption function will shift.

Table 2 provides a more specific summary of how different types of changes affect consumption spending in a graph such as Figure 5. Remember that all of the changes that *shift* the line work by increasing or decreasing autonomous consumption (*a*).

| TABLE 2 | CHANGES IN CONSUMPTION SPENDING AND THE CONSUMPTION–FUNCTION |

Rightward Movement along the Line	Leftward Movement along the Line	Entire Line Shifts Upward	Entire Line Shifts Downward
Disposable Income ↑	Disposable Income ↓	Taxes ↓	Taxes ↑
		Household wealth ↑	Household wealth ↓
		Interest rate ↓	Interest rate ↑
		Greater optimism	Greater pessimism

GETTING TO TOTAL SPENDING

In addition to household consumption spending, there are three other types of spending on goods and services produced by American firms: investment, government purchases, and purchases by foreigners. Let's consider each of these types of spending in turn.

INVESTMENT SPENDING

In the definition of GDP, we used the term *actual investment* (I^a), which consists of three components: (1) business spending on plant and equipment; (2) purchases of new homes; and (3) accumulation of unsold inventories. In this chapter, we focus not on actual investment, but on planned investment spending (I)—business purchases of plant and equipment and construction of new homes. Why do we leave out inventory accumulation?

When we look at how spending influences the economy, we are interested in the purchases households, firms, and the government *want* to make. Inventory changes, however, are most often an *un*planned and undesired occurrence that firms try to avoid. While firms want to have some inventories on hand, sudden *changes* in inventories are not desirable. Accordingly, we exclude inventory investment when we measure spending in the economy.

> When analyzing total spending in the economy, we define investment spending as planned plant and equipment purchases by business firms and new home construction. Inventory investment is treated as unintentional and undesired and is therefore excluded from our definition of investment spending.

What determines the level of investment spending in a given year? In this chapter, we will regard investment spending as a *fixed value,* determined by forces outside of our analysis. This may seem a bit surprising. After all, aren't there variables that affect investment spending in predictable ways? Indeed, there are.

For example, in our discussion of long-run growth in the previous chapter, you learned that investment is likely to be affected by the interest rate. Indeed, in the real world, the investment–interest rate relationship is quite strong. Investment is also influenced by the general level of optimism or pessimism about the economy and by new technological developments. But if we introduce all of these other variables into our analysis, we would find ourselves working with a very complex framework, and much too soon. In future chapters, we'll explore some of the determinants of investment spending; but in this chapter, to keep things simple, we assume that investment spending is some given amount. We'll explore what happens when that amount changes, but we will not, in this chapter, try to explain what causes investment spending.

GOVERNMENT PURCHASES

Government purchases include all of the goods and services that government agencies—federal, state, and local—buy during the year. We treat government purchases in the same way as investment spending: as a given value, determined by forces outside of our analysis. Why?

The relationship between government purchases and other macroeconomic variables—particularly income—is rather weak. In recent decades, the biggest changes in government purchases have involved military spending. These changes have been based on world politics, rather than macroeconomic conditions. So when we assume that government spending is a given value, independent of the other variables in our model, our assumption is actually realistic.

> *When analyzing total spending in the economy, government purchases are treated as a given value, determined by forces that are outside of our analysis.*

As with investment spending, we'll be exploring what happens when the "given value" of government purchases changes. But we will not try to explain what causes it to change.

NET EXPORTS

If we want to measure total spending on U.S. output, we must also consider the international sector. First, about 12 percent of American goods are sold to *foreign* consumers, businesses, and government. These are *exports* from the U.S. point of view, and they must be included in our measure of total spending.

But international trade in goods and services also requires us to make an adjustment to the other components of spending. A portion (about 13 percent) of the output bought by *American* consumers, firms, and government agencies was produced abroad. From the U.S. point of view, these are *imports*—spending on foreign, rather than U.S., output. These imports are included in our measures of consumption, investment, and government spending, giving us an exaggerated measure of spending on *American* output. But we can easily correct for this overcount by simply deducting imported consumption goods from our measure of consumption, deducting imported investment goods from our measure of investment and imported government purchases from our measure of government purchases. Of course, this means we will be deducting total imports from our measure of total spending.

In sum, to incorporate the international sector into our measure of total spending, we must add U.S. exports and subtract U.S. imports. These two adjustments can be made together by simply including *net exports* (NX) as the foreign sector's contribution to total spending.

Net Exports = total exports − total imports

By including net exports, we simultaneously ensure that we have included U.S. output that is sold to foreigners, and excluded consumption, investment and government spending on output produced abroad.

Net exports can change for a variety of reasons: changes in tastes toward or away from a particular country's goods, changes in the price of foreign currency on world foreign exchange markets, and more. Later in the book—in Chapter 17—we'll discuss what caused net exports to change in 1997 and 1998. But in this chapter, to keep things simple, we assume that net exports—like investment spending and government purchases—are some given amount. We'll explore what happens when that amount changes, but we will not, in this chapter, try to explain what causes net exports to change. For now, we regard net exports as a given value, determined by forces outside of our analysis.

SUMMING UP: TOTAL SPENDING

We've used the phrase *total spending* several times in this chapter, and now we're ready to define it more formally.

Total spending is the sum of spending by households, businesses, the government, and the foreign sector on final goods and services produced in the United States.

TOTAL SPENDING The sum of spending by households, businesses, the government, and the foreign sector on American final goods and services, or $C + I + G + NX$.

Remembering that C stands for household consumption spending, I for investment spending, G for government purchases, and NX for net exports, we have

$$Total\ Spending = C + I + G + NX$$

Total spending plays a key role in explaining economic fluctuations. Why? Because over several quarters or even a few years, business firms tend to respond to changes in total spending by changing their level of output. That is, a rise in total spending leads firms throughout the economy to raise their output level, while a drop in total spending causes a decrease in output throughout the economy. While these changes are temporary, they persist long enough to create the kinds of booms and recessions that you saw in Figures 1 and 2. In the next section, we'll explore just how changes in spending create these economic fluctuations.

The definition of total spending looks *very* similar to the definition of GDP presented in Chapter 12. Does this mean that total spending and total output are, in fact, the same thing? Not at all. There is a slight—but important—difference in the definitions. GDP is defined as $C + I^a + G + NX$. Total spending, by contrast, is defined as $C + I + G + NX$. The difference is that GDP adds *actual* investment spending (I^a), which includes business firms' inventory investment. Total spending adds just "investment spending" (I), which excludes inventory investment. As you are about to learn, the two numbers will be equal only when we are producing our *equilibrium* GDP. In that case, business firms' inventories will not be changing over the year, so inventory investment is zero and I^a and I are equal.

DANGEROUS CURVES

TOTAL SPENDING AND EQUILIBRIUM GDP

Imagine that—after graduating from college—you go into business manufacturing cellular phones. You set up a factory, hire a dozen workers, decide on a price to charge for your phones, prepare your advertising, and begin producing.

Now suppose that, after producing phones for a few weeks or months, you notice that you aren't selling as many as you're producing. What will you do? If you are like many firms, you will decrease your output of phones and lay off some of your workers. If the problem persists, you may take other steps as well—including lowering your price. But you may hesitate to change your price, because it can be costly for you. (For example, changing prices will require you to change all of your advertising brochures, inform all of your wholesalers, etc.) Moreover, price changes can be even more costly to reverse if sales pick up again in a few months. Not only will you have to change your advertising brochures once again, but by raising prices you risk alienating customers who got used to lower prices. For these reasons, you may be hesitant to drop your price in the first place, and respond first by cutting back on production.

Now imagine the opposite scenario: After producing phones for a few weeks or months, and building up a reasonable inventory for filling orders, you begin selling *more* than you're producing. For a few days, you fill the orders by running down your inventories. But then what? Most likely, you'll *increase* your output of phones and hire some additional workers. If the situation continues for many months, you may take other steps as well—including raising your price. But, once again, price hikes can be costly and alienating to customers. You may want to wait until you are reasonably sure that your high sales will continue indefinitely before raising prices. For these reasons, your first response may be to increase production.

Under what conditions would you continue to produce an unchanged level of output? Only when your sales are equal to your production. And what is true for you is true for firms throughout the country.

Now let's consider the same line of reasoning on a macroeconomic level. Total spending in the economy is the same as total sales by all business firms. GDP is the same as total production by all business firms. We come to the following macroeconomic conclusion:

> *When total spending is less than GDP, firms in general will decrease production and GDP will drop. When total spending is greater than GDP, firms will increase production, and GDP will rise. When total spending is equal to GDP, firms will continue producing at the same rate, and GDP will remain unchanged.*

We can carry this one step further by remembering that an *equilibrium* is a situation that tends to remain unchanged, unless the underlying conditions change. In microeconomics, we are interested in the equilibrium price and quantity in individual markets—such as the market for maple syrup that we studied in Chapter 3. In macroeconomics, we use the same concept in defining equilibrium GDP.

EQUILIBRIUM GDP A level of output that is equal to total spending in the economy.

> *Equilibrium GDP is a level of GDP that tends to remain unchanged—that is, a level of GDP at which total spending and total output in the economy are equal.*

We can summarize our discussion about the relationship between GDP and total spending in this way:

$$C + I + G + NX > GDP \Rightarrow GDP \uparrow$$

$$C + I + G + NX < GDP \Rightarrow GDP \downarrow$$

$$C + I + G + NX = GDP \Rightarrow No\ \Delta GDP$$

Note that the economy's *equilibrium* output need not be its *potential* output. In fact, equilibrium GDP will equal potential GDP only if there is sufficient spending for firms to *sell* all the output they would produce when they are fully employing the economy's resources. But whether they will be able to sell this output or not depends on the behavior of spenders in the economy. Indeed, even when the economy is happily producing at potential GDP, a change in spending can throw it off course, into a boom or recession. We explore this possibility in the next section.

WHAT HAPPENS WHEN THINGS CHANGE?

SPENDING SHOCK A change in spending that ultimately affects the entire economy.

Imagine that the economy is humming along at its potential output level, with the labor force fully employed. Then, there is a **spending shock**—a sudden change in one or more of the components of total spending. What will happen? To make our analysis more concrete, we'll explore a specific type of spending shock: a change in investment spending. Then, we'll generalize our results to other types of spending shocks.

A CHANGE IN INVESTMENT SPENDING

Suppose that business firms decide to increase yearly investment purchases by $100 billion above the original level. What will happen? First, output at firms that manufacture investment goods—firms like IBM, Bethlehem Steel, Caterpillar, and Westinghouse—will increase by $100 billion. However, as you learned in Chapter 12, the economy's total output and total income are equal. Each time a dollar in output is produced, a dollar of income (factor payments) is created. Thus, the $100 billion in additional output will become $100 billion in additional income. This income will be paid out as wages, rent, interest, and profit to the households who own the resources these firms have purchased.[2]

What will households—as consumers—do with their $100 billion in additional income? How much will they spend, and how much will they save? That depends on two things: First, what happens to the taxes they must pay? To keep our discussion simple, we'll assume that household tax payments do not change at all with their additional income. We imagine that the government wants to collect a certain amount of taxes, and—if income rises—it will lower the income tax *rate* in order to keep the total income tax payment constant.

Second, what is the *marginal propensity to consume (MPC) in the economy?* Let's suppose that the *MPC* is 0.6. Then consumption spending will rise by 60 percent of the $100 billion in additional household income, or $0.6 \times \$100$ billion = $60 billion. Households will save the remaining $40 billion.

But that is not the end of the story. When households spend an additional $60 billion, firms that produce consumption goods and services—firms such as McDonald's, Coca Cola, American Airlines, and Disney—will produce and sell an additional $60 billion in output, which, in turn, will become an equal amount of income for the households that supply resources to these firms. And when *these* households see *their* incomes rise by $60 billion, they will spend part of it as well. With an *MPC* of 0.6, consumption spending in this phase will rise by $0.6 \times \$60$ billion = $36 billion, resulting in still more production at other firms, and so on and so on. . . .

As you can see, an increase in investment spending will set off a chain reaction, leading to successive rounds of increased spending and income. The process is illustrated in Figure 6: After the $100 billion increase in investment spending, there is a $60 billion increase in consumption, then a $36 billion increase in consumption, and on and on. Each successive round of additional spending is 60 percent of the round before. Each time spending increases, output rises to match it. These successive increases in spending and output occur quickly—the process is largely completed within a year. At the end of the process, when the economy has reached its new equilibrium, spending and output will have increased considerably. But by how much?

Table 3 gives us the answer. The second column shows us the additional spending in each round, while the third column shows the cumulative rise in spending. As

---

2. Some of the sales revenue of these firms will be spent on intermediate goods, such as raw materials, electricity, and supplies. But the producers of these intermediate goods will themselves pay wages, rent, interest, and profit for *their* resources, so that household income will still rise by the full $100 billion.

| FIGURE 6 | THE EFFECT OF A CHANGE IN INVESTMENT SPENDING |

An increase in investment spending sets off a chain reaction, leading to successive rounds of increased spending and income. As shown here, a $100 billion increase in investment first causes real GDP to increase by $100 billion. Then, with higher incomes, households increase consumption spending by the *MPC* times the change in disposable income. In round 2, spending and GDP increase by $60 billion. In succeeding rounds, increases in income lead to further changes in spending, but in each round the increase in income is smaller than in the preceding round.

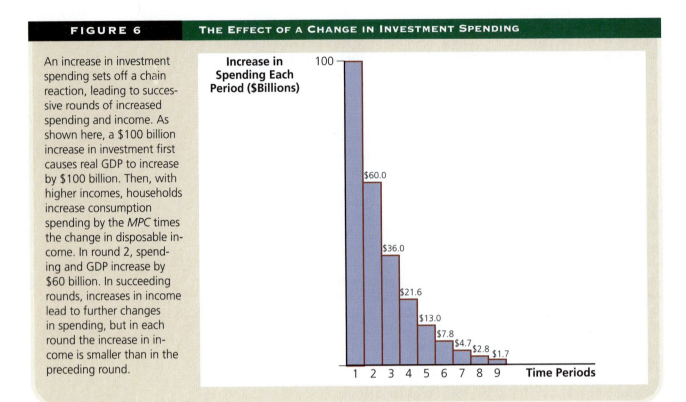

you can see, the cumulative increase becomes larger and larger with each successive round, but it grows by less and less each time. Eventually, the additional spending in a given round is so small that we can safely ignore it. At this point, the cumulative increase in spending and output will be very close to $250 billion—so close that we can ignore any difference.

| TABLE 3 | CUMULATIVE INCREASES IN SPENDING WHEN INVESTMENT INCREASES BY $100 BILLION |

Round	Additional Spending in This Round (billions of dollars)	Additional Spending in All Rounds (billions of dollars)
Initial increase in investment	100	100
Round 2	60	160
Round 3	36	196
Round 4	21.6	217.6
Round 5	13	230.6
Round 6	7.8	238.4
Round 7	4.7	243.1
Round 8	2.8	245.9
Round 9	1.7	247.6
Round 10	1.0	248.6
.	.	.
.	.	.
.	.	.
All other rounds	Very close to 1.4	Very close to 250

THE SPENDING MULTIPLIER

Let's go back and summarize what happened in our example: Business firms increased their investment spending by $100 billion, and as a result, spending and output rose by $250 billion. GDP increased by *more* than the initial increase in investment spending. In our example, the increase in GDP ($250 billion) was 2.5 times the initial increase in investment spending ($100 billion). As you can verify, if investment spending had increased by half as much ($50 billion), GDP would have increased by 2.5 times *that* amount ($125 billion). In fact, *whatever* the rise in investment spending, GDP would increase by a factor of 2.5, so we can write

$$\Delta GDP = 2.5 \times \Delta I$$

The change in investment spending must be *multiplied by* the number 2.5 in order to get the change in GDP that it causes. For this reason, 2.5 is called the *spending multiplier* in this example.

> The **spending multiplier** is the number by which a change in spending (e.g., investment spending) must be multiplied to get the change in equilibrium GDP.

SPENDING MULTIPLIER The amount by which equilibrium real GDP changes as a result of a one-dollar change in autonomous consumption, investment, or government purchases.

The value of the spending multiplier depends on the value of the *MPC* in the economy. If you look back at Table 3, you will see that each round of additional spending would have been larger if the *MPC* had been larger. For example, with an *MPC* of 0.9 instead of 0.6, spending in round 2 would have risen by $90 billion, in round 3 by $81 billion, and so on. The result would have been a larger cumulative change in GDP and a larger multiplier.

There is a very simple formula we can use to determine the multiplier for *any* value of the *MPC*. To obtain it, let's start with our numerical example in which the *MPC* is 0.6. When investment spending rises by $100, the change in equilibrium GDP can be written as follows:

$$\Delta GDP = \$100 \text{ billion} + \$60 \text{ billion} + \$36 \text{ billion} + \$21.6 \text{ billion} + \ldots$$

Factoring out the $100 billion change in investment, this becomes

$$\Delta GDP = \$100 \text{ billion } [1 + 0.6 + 0.36 + 0.216 + \ldots]$$
$$= \$1,000 \text{ billion } [1 + 0.6 + 0.6^2 + 0.6^3 + \ldots]$$

In this equation, $100 billion is the change in investment (ΔI), and 0.6 is the *MPC*. To find the change in GDP that applies to *any* ΔI and *any MPC*, we can write

$$\Delta GDP = \Delta I \times [1 + (MPC) + (MPC)^2 + (MPC)^3 + \ldots]$$

Now we can see that the term in brackets—the infinite sum $1 + MPC + (MPC)^2 + (MPC)^3 + \ldots$—is our multiplier. But what is its value?

The Mathematical Appendix at the back of this book shows that an infinite sum

$$1 + H + H^2 + H^3 + \ldots$$

always has the value $1/(1 - H)$ as long as H is a fraction between zero and 1. When we replace H with the *MPC*—which is always between zero and 1—we obtain a value for the multiplier of $1/(1 - MPC)$.

> *For any value of the MPC, the formula for the spending multiplier is*
> *1/(1 − MPC).*

In our example, the *MPC* was equal to 0.6, so the spending multiplier had the value 1/(1 − 0.6) = 1/0.4 = 2.5. If the *MPC* had been 0.9 instead, the spending multiplier would have been equal to 1/(1 − 0.9) = 1/0.1 = 10. The formula 1/(1 − *MPC*) can be used to find the multiplier for any value of the *MPC* between zero and 1.

Using the general formula for the spending multiplier, we can restate what happens when investment spending increases:

$$\Delta GDP = [1/(1 - MPC)] \times \Delta I$$

The multiplier effect is a rather surprising phenomenon. It tells us that an increase in investment spending ultimately affects GDP by *more* than the initial increase in investment. Moreover, the multiplier can work in the other direction, as you are about to see.

THE MULTIPLIER IN REVERSE

Suppose, in Table 3, that investment spending had *decreased* instead of increased. Then the initial change in spending would be −$100 billion ($\Delta I$ = −$100 billion). This would cause a $100 billion decrease in output at firms that produce investment goods, and they, in turn, would pay out $100 billion less in factor payments. In the next round, households—with $100 billion less in income—would spend $60 billion less on consumption goods, and so on. The final result would be a $250 billion *decrease* in equilibrium GDP.

> *Just as increases in investment spending cause GDP to rise by a multiple of the change in spending, decreases in investment spending cause GDP to fall by a multiple of the change in spending.*

The multiplier formula we've already established will work whether the initial change in spending is positive or negative.

OTHER SPENDING SHOCKS

Shocks to the economy can come from other sources besides investment spending. In fact, when *any* sector's spending behavior changes, it will set off a chain of events similar to that in our investment example. Let's see how an increase in government spending could set off the same chain of events as an increase in investment spending.

Suppose that government agencies increased their purchases above previous levels. For example, the Department of Defense might raise its spending on new fighter jets, or state highway departments might hire more road repair crews, or cities and towns might hire more teachers. If total government purchases rise by $100 billion, then, once again, household income will rise by $100 billion. As before, households will spend 60 percent of this increase, causing consumption—in the next round—to rise by $60 billion, and so on. The chain of events is exactly like that of Table 3, with one exception: The first line in column 1 would read, "Initial Increase in Government Spending" instead of "Initial Increase in Investment." Once again, output would increase by $250 billion.

Changes in autonomous consumption (*a*), which shift the consumption function upward, or changes in net exports (*NX*), will set off the same process. In both cases, after the initial spending increase of $100 billion, we would see further increases in consumption spending of $60 billion, then $36 billion, and so forth. The first line in column 1 of Table 3 would read, "Initial Increase in Autonomous Consumption," or "Initial Increase in Net Exports," but every entry in the table would be the same.

> *Changes in investment, government purchases, autonomous consumption, or net exports lead to a multiplier effect on GDP. The spending multiplier—1/(1 − MPC)—is what we multiply the initial change in spending by in order to get the change in equilibrium GDP.*

The following four equations summarize how we use the spending multiplier to determine the effects of the four different types of spending shocks. Keep in mind that these formulas work whether the initial change in spending is positive or negative.

$$\Delta GDP = [1/(1 - MPC)] \times \Delta I$$
$$\Delta GDP = [1/(1 - MPC)] \times \Delta G$$
$$\Delta GDP = [1/(1 - MPC)] \times \Delta a$$
$$\Delta GDP = [1/(1 - MPC)] \times \Delta NX$$

CHANGES IN NET TAXES

In addition to the spending changes we've considered so far, there is one additional factor that can change total spending and lead to a multiplier effect on output: net taxes. Suppose that the government either decreases its tax revenue or increases its transfer payments. Either of these changes will *decrease* net taxes. Since disposable income (DI) is equal to total income minus net taxes, the cut in net taxes will *raise* disposable income for any given total income.

What will happen?

With more income, households will spend more, leading business firms to produce more, creating more income, and so on. Thus, a decrease in net taxes raises output in the economy by a multiple of the original tax cut. Sounds very much like all the other spending changes we've considered. There is one difference, however: The multiplier for a tax cut turns out to be *smaller* than the multiplier for other spending changes.

To understand why, let's compare two specific changes: a $100 billion increase in government purchases versus a $100 billion tax cut. Will they have the same impact on

It's easy to become confused about the relationship between spending and output (or income). Do changes in spending cause changes in output? Or do changes in output cause changes in spending? Actually, the causation runs in both directions. The key is to recognize that there are *two* types of spending changes.

Some spending changes happen for reasons *other* than a change in income. These are the *spending shocks* that can set off the multiplier process. Changes in investment, government purchases, and net exports all fall into this category. So do changes in consumption spending *when* they are caused either by changes in autonomous consumption or changes in net taxes. In the cases of spending shocks, a change in spending *causes* a change in output.

But another kind of spending change is *caused by* a change in output. In this chapter, we've considered one example: the changes in consumption spending that occur automatically during the multiplier process. This is a change in spending, but not a spending shock.

Whenever you discuss a change in spending, make sure you know which type of spending change you are discussing: one caused by something *other* than a change in income (a spending shock) or one caused by a change in income.

DANGEROUS CURVES

GDP? No. When *G* increases, the initial change in spending—which sets off the multiplier process—is $100 billion. But when *T* drops, the initial change in spending will be *less* than $100 billion. That is because households—when they get the tax cut—will spend only *part* of it and save the rest. The fraction that they spend will depend on the *MPC*. If the *MPC* is 0.9, for example, then households will spend $900 billion of the tax cut, so the initial change in spending in Table 3 will be $90 billion, not $100 billion. The final result is a smaller change in GDP—and a smaller multiplier. The special multiplier for changes in tax is derived in the appendix to this chapter. Here, we can note the following important conclusion:

> *Changes in net taxes lead to a multiplier effect on GDP, although the multiplier for tax changes is smaller than for other spending changes. A cut in net taxes causes GDP to rise, while a rise in net taxes causes GDP to fall.*

SPENDING SHOCKS IN RECENT HISTORY

In the real world, the economy is constantly buffeted by spending shocks. As you've learned, these shocks have a multiplied effect on output and income and they often cause full-fledged recessions and booms. Table 4 lists some of the recessions and booms of the last 50 years, along with the spending shocks that are thought to have caused them or at least contributed heavily. You can see that each of these shocks began in one or more specific sectors of the economy. For example, several recessions have been set off by increases in oil prices, which caused a decrease in spending on products that depend on oil and energy, such as automobiles, trucks, and new factory buildings. Other recessions have been precipitated

TABLE 4		BOOMS, RECESSIONS, AND THE SHOCKS THAT CAUSED THEM	
Period		**Event**	**Spending Shock**
Early 1950s	Boom	Korean War	Defense Spending ↑
1953	Recession	End of Korean War	Defense Spending ↓
Late 1960s	Boom	Vietnam War	Defense Spending ↑
1970	Recession	Financial Crisis	Spending on New Homes ↓
1974	Recession	Dramatic Increase in Oil Prices	Spending on Energy-using Products ↓
1980	Recession	Dramatic Increase in Oil Prices	Spending on Cars and Other Energy-using Products ↓
1981–82	Recession	Financial Crisis	Spending on New Homes, Cars, and Business Investment ↓
Early 1980s	Boom	Military Buildup	Defense Spending ↑
Late 1980s	Boom	Huge Decline in Oil Prices	Spending on Energy-using Products ↑
1990	Recession	Large Increase in Oil Prices; Collapse of Soviet Union	Spending on Cars and Other Energy-using Products ↓; Defense Spending ↓

by military cutbacks and by financial crises—sudden increases in interest rates—that led to decreased spending on new homes. Booms, on the other hand, have been caused by military buildups and by falling oil prices that stimulated spending on energy-related products. But in each case, the spending shock quickly spread to the economy as a whole through the multiplier process that you've learned about in this chapter.

As you can see in Table 4, the economy barely has time to adjust to one shock before it is hit by another. But we can usually see the beginnings of the adjustment process, and sometimes we can follow it through to its end. In the case of an adverse shock, large numbers of workers lose their jobs. Then, there is a long and gradual period of **recovery,** during which output and employment rise back to their full-employment levels. Unemployed workers are gradually reabsorbed into the economy until full employment is restored.

RECOVERY The period after a recession during which output and employment return to their full-employment levels.

But notice the word "gradually." The process of adjustment back to full employment can take surprisingly long. It can take—and has taken—years for the economy to return to full employment after a recession, as we saw in Figures 1 and 2. For example, the unemployment rate exceeded 10 percent in 1982 and did not fall below 6 percent until 1986.

A positive shock triggers a boom—a rise in output beyond its potential and a drop in unemployment below its full-employment rate. Output will gradually return to its full-employment level, but once again, the process of adjustment can take years.

What brings the economy back to its potential output after a boom or a recession? And why does the process take so long? These questions will be answered in Chapter 17, "Aggregate Demand and Aggregate Supply."

AUTOMATIC STABILIZERS

In this chapter, we've analyzed an important piece of the macroeconomic puzzle: how spending shocks are transmitted throughout the economy and ultimately have a multiplier effect on total output. However, to keep our discussion as simple as possible, we've ignored many real-world factors that interfere with, and reduce the size of, the multiplier. These forces are called **automatic stabilizers** because, with a smaller multiplier, spending shocks will cause a much smaller change in GDP. As a result, booms and recessions will be milder. Or, to put it another way: if not for automatic stabilizers, the deviations away from potential output would have been greater than the ones we've actually experienced, as seen in Figure 1.

AUTOMATIC STABILIZERS Forces that reduce the size of the spending multiplier and diminish the impact of spending shocks.

> *Automatic stabilizers reduce the size of the multiplier and therefore reduce the impact of spending shocks on the economy. With milder booms and recessions, the economy is more stable.*

How do automatic stabilizers work? They shrink the additional spending that occurs in each round of the multiplier, and thereby reduce the final multiplier effect on equilibrium GDP. In Table 3, automatic stabilizers would reduce each of the numerical entries after the first $100 billion and lead to a final change in GDP smaller than $250 billion.

Here are some of the real-world automatic stabilizers we've ignored in our discussion.

Taxes. We've been assuming that—as the multiplier process works its way through the economy, and income rises—taxes remain constant. But some taxes (like the personal income tax) rise with income. As a result, in each round of the multiplier, the increase in disposable income will be smaller than the increase in total income. With a smaller rise in disposable income, there will be a smaller rise in consumption spending as well.

Transfer Payments. Some government transfer payments fall as income rises. For example, many laid-off workers receive unemployment benefits, which help support them for several months while they are unemployed. But when income and output rise, employment rises too, and newly hired workers must give up their unemployment benefits. As a result, a rise in income will cause a smaller rise in *disposable* income. Consumption will then rise by less in each round of the multiplier.

Interest Rates. Increase in output often leads to rising interest rates. As a result, investment spending may drop even as output expands. When the drop in investment spending is accounted for, the rise in total spending in each round of the multiplier process will be smaller.

Prices. In a later chapter, you'll learn that the price level tends to rise as spending and production increase. This, in turn, works to decrease spending. The net effect is a smaller increase in spending in each round of the multiplier process.

Imports. Some of the additional spending in the multiplier process is on goods and services imported from abroad. This will increase the revenue of foreign firms and the incomes of foreign workers, but will not contribute to higher incomes for U.S. workers. As a result, the increase in output and spending in each round of the multiplier process will be smaller.

Forward-looking Behavior. Consumers may be *forward looking*. If they realize that recessions and booms are temporary, their consumption spending may be less sensitive to changes in their current income. Therefore, any change in income will cause a smaller change in consumption spending and lead to a smaller multiplier effect.

Remember that each of these automatic stabilizers reduces the size of the multiplier, making it smaller than the simple formulas given in this chapter. For example, the simple formula for the spending multiplier is $1/(1 - MPC)$. With an MPC of about 0.9—which is in the ballpark for the United States and many other countries—we would expect the multiplier to be about 10 . . . *if the simple formula were accurate.* In that case, every time a spending shock hit the economy, output would change by 10 times the initial shock. But after we take account of all of the automatic stabilizers, the multiplier is considerably smaller. How much smaller? Most of the forecasting models used by economists in business and government predict that the multiplier effect takes about 3 quarters of a year to work its way through the economy. At the end of the process, the multiplier has a value of about 1.5. This means that a $100 billion increase in, say, government spending should cause GDP to increase by only about $150 billion in a year. This is much less than the $1,000 billion increase predicted by the simple formula $1/(1 - MPC)$ when the MPC is equal to 0.9.

> *In the real world, due to automatic stabilizers, spending shocks have much weaker impacts on the economy than our simple multiplier formulas would suggest.*

Finally, there is one more automatic stabilizer you should know about, perhaps the most important of all: the *passage of time*. Why is this an automatic stabilizer? Because, as you'll see in later chapters, the impact of spending shocks on the economy is *temporary*. A few months after a shock, corrective mechanisms begin to operate, and the economy begins to return to full employment. As time passes, the impact of a spending shock gradually disappears. And if we wait long enough—a few years or so—the effects of the shock will be gone entirely. That is, after a shock pulls us away from full-employment GDP, the economy will eventually return to full-employment GDP—right where it started. We thus conclude that

> *in the long run, our multipliers have a value of zero: No matter what the change in spending or taxes, output will return to full employment, so the change in equilibrium GDP will be zero.*

SHORT-RUN VERSUS LONG-RUN OUTCOMES

COUNTERCYCLICAL FISCAL POLICY

What you've learned about the multiplier not only helps to explain what *causes* economic fluctuations: It also suggests a method of *preventing them*. After all, if a spending shock sends output spiraling downward, the government should be able to create its *own* spending shock in the opposite direction, by changing government purchases or net taxes. Changes in the government's budget designed to affect the macro-economy are called *fiscal policy*. When the changes are specifically designed to counteract economic fluctuations, they are called *countercyclical fiscal policy*.

> *Countercyclical fiscal policy is any change in government purchases or net taxes designed to counteract spending shocks and keep the economy close to potential output.*

COUNTERCYCLICAL FISCAL POLICY Any change in government purchases or net taxes designed to counteract spending shocks.

Here is an example of how countercyclical fiscal policy might work. Suppose that the economy is hit by an adverse spending shock—say, a decrease in investment spending of $100 billion. Suppose, too, that the multiplier in the economy is 1.5. If the government did nothing, output would ultimately decrease by $100 billion × 1.5 = $150 billion.

If the government wanted to counteract this spending shock, it could raise its *own* spending on goods and services by $100 billion. This would tend to *increase* GDP by $100 billion × 1.5 = $150 billion—the same amount by which the adverse shock is pulling GDP down. With the countercyclical fiscal policy, the net effect of the adverse shock and the change in government purchases would be . . . no change in GDP!

In addition to changing its purchases, the government has another option: It could decrease net taxes. This could be accomplished either by cutting taxes or by increasing transfer payments. However, since the multiplier for changes in net taxes is smaller than the spending multiplier, the tax cut or the rise in transfers would have to be greater than $100 billion.

In the 1960s and early 1970s, many economists and government officials believed that countercyclical fiscal policy could be an effective tool to counteract the business cycle. Today, however, very few economists hold this position. Instead, they would leave the job of fighting the business cycle to the U.S. Federal Reserve—an institution discussed first in Chapter 13 and to which we will return in great detail in the next chapter. Indeed, the last clear use of countercyclical fiscal policy occurred in 1975, when the government gave tax rebates in the depths of a serious recession in order to stimulate consumption. Why do economists recommend against using countercyclical fiscal policy, and why does Washington follow their advice? There are several reasons.

TIMING PROBLEMS. It takes many months or even longer for a fiscal change to be enacted. Consider, for example, a decision to change taxes in the United States.

A tax bill originates in the House of Representatives and then goes to the Senate, where it is usually modified. Then a conference committee irons out the differences between the House and Senate versions, and the tax bill goes back to each chamber for a vote. Even if all goes smoothly—and the president does not veto the bill—this process can take many months.

But in most cases, it will *not* go smoothly: The inevitable political conflicts will cause further delays. First, there is the thorny question of distributing the cost of a tax hike, or the benefits of a tax cut, among different income groups within the country. Each party may argue for changes in the tax bill in order to please its constituents. And some senators and representatives will see the bill as an opportunity to improve the tax system in more fundamental ways, causing further political debate.

All of these problems create the danger that the tax change will take effect long after it is needed. And changes in transfer payments or government purchases would suffer from similar delays. As a result, a fiscal stimulus might take effect after the economy has recovered from a recession and is headed for a boom; or a fiscal contraction might take effect just as the economy is entering a recession. Fiscal changes would then be a *de*stabilizing force in the economy—stepping on the gas when we should be hitting the brakes, and vice versa.

As you will see in the next chapter, the Federal Reserve can make decisions that begin to influence the economy *on the very day it decides that the change is necessary*. While there are time lags in the *effectiveness* of the Federal Reserve's policy moves, its ability to execute its policy in short order gives it an important advantage over fiscal policy for stabilizing the economy.

IRREVERSIBILITY. To be truly *countercyclical*, fiscal policy moves would have to be temporary. This is because the forces they are designed to counteract—spending shocks—are themselves temporary. If the government increases its purchases to fight an adverse shock, it must reverse course and cut its purchases as the adverse shock subsides. But reversing changes in government purchases, transfer payments or taxes can be extraordinarily difficult, for political reasons.

Spending programs that create new government departments or expand existing ones tend to become permanent, or at least difficult to terminate because those who benefit from the programs will lobby to preserve them. Many temporary tax changes become permanent as well—the public is never happy to see a tax cut reversed, and the government is often reluctant to reverse a tax hike that has provided additional revenue for government programs.

THE REACTION OF THE FEDERAL RESERVE. Even if the government attempted to stabilize the economy with fiscal policy, it could not do so very effectively, because—to put it simply—the Fed will not allow it. As you will learn in the next chapter, the Federal Reserve sees its own goal as keeping the economy as close to potential output as possible. Its officials view any change in fiscal policy as just another spending shock threatening to create a boom or recession, to be neutralized as quickly as possible. For example, if the government cuts taxes, which tends to increase output, the Fed will counteract it with its own policies, designed to *decrease* output. As long as the Fed is free to set its own course, and as long as it continues to take responsibility for stabilizing the economy, there is simply no opportunity—and no need—for countercyclical fiscal policy.

Our discussion about countercyclical policy has probably raised several questions in your mind. What gives the Federal Reserve the audacity to claim countercylical policy for itself and to shamelessly counteract the government's fiscal policy? What policies does it use to accomplish its goals? And how do its policies affect the economy? These are important questions, and we'll address them in the next chapter.

THE RECESSION OF 1990–1991

Our most recent recession began in the second half of 1990 and continued into 1991. Table 5 tells the story. The second column shows real GDP in 1992 dollars in each of several quarters. For example, "1990:2" denotes the second quarter of 1990, and during that three-month period, GDP was $6,174 billion at an annual rate. (That is, if we had continued producing that quarter's GDP for an entire year, we *would* have produced a total of $6,174 billion worth of goods and services in that year.)

As you can see, real GDP began to fall in the third quarter of 1990, and it continued to drop until the second quarter of 1991. In all, GDP fell for three consecutive quarters. During this time, real output fell by $100 billion, a drop of about 1.6 percent. At the same time, the unemployment rate rose, from 5.1 percent in June of 1990 to 7.7 percent in June of 1992. The economy had not completely recovered by the presidential election of November 1992, and many observers believe that the recession and slow recovery were the deciding factors in George Bush's loss to Bill Clinton.

Can our insights about spending help us understand what caused this recession? Very much so. In retrospect, we can see that there were two separate spending shocks to the economy in early 1990.

First, for a variety of reasons, a financial crisis had developed, in which some banks and savings and loan associations were near bankruptcy. Many banks, playing it safe, responded by cutting back on loans for new home purchases, as well as for business expansion. The media began to speak of a "credit crunch," in which homebuyers and businesses were forced to pay very high interest rates on loans or were unable to borrow at all. The consequence was a sizable decrease in the demand for new housing and for plant and equipment—an investment spending shock. (Remember that investment spending includes new-housing construction as well as plant and equipment.)

The second shock resulted from global politics. In the summer of 1990, Iraqi troops invaded and occupied much of Kuwait. The United States responded by sending troops to Kuwait and, in early 1991, launched an attack on Iraqi troops. Americans began to fear a prolonged and costly war in the Middle East, one that

TABLE 5	THE RECESSION OF 1990–1991			
Quarter	Real GDP (billions of 1992 dollars)	Change in Real GDP from Previous Quarter (billions of 1992 dollars)	Real Investment Spending (billions of 1992 dollars)	Consumer Confidence Index
1990:2	6,174		811	105
1990:3	6,145	−29	803	90
1990:4	6,081	−64	774	61
1991:1	6,048	−33	742	65
1991:2	6,074	+26	739	77

would, among other things, cause a large increase in the price of oil. They remembered that in the early 1970s, the last time that oil prices had risen substantially, the U.S. economy plunged into recession. As a result, American households became less confident about the economy.

The fifth column of Table 5 shows the rapid decline in the *consumer confidence index* that was occurring at the time. The index is based on a survey of about 5,000 households. Each month, these households respond to questions about their job and career prospects in the months ahead, their expected income, their spending plans, and so forth. A drop in consumer confidence decreases household consumption spending at *any* level of disposable income. Or, put another way, households wanted to *save more* at any level of disposable income. Viewed either way, the drop in consumer confidence caused a decrease in autonomous consumption, *a*. This was the second spending shock to the economy.

In sum, in early 1990, there were two spending shocks to the economy: a decline in investment and a decline in autonomous consumption. Each of these shocks had a multiplier effect on the economy, causing income and spending to decline in successive rounds for almost a year. Beginning in 1992, the credit crunch began to subside, increasing investment spending, and the Gulf War ended, increasing consumer confidence. These factors helped the economy to recover in 1992 and on into 1993.

SUMMARY

Over periods of a few years, national economies experience booms and recessions—economic fluctuations in which output rises above or falls below its long-term growth path. And when real GDP fluctuates, the unemployment rate fluctuates as well.

The key to explaining booms and recessions is changes in total spending. The largest component of total spending is consumption spending (C), which depends on disposable income—total income minus net taxes. When disposable income rises by a dollar, consumption spending rises by a fraction of a dollar. The fraction is called the *marginal propensity to consume,* or *MPC.* The consumption function is a graph that shows how consumption spending depends on disposable income. The consumption function is a straight line, and its vertical intercept is called *autonomous consumption.* The slope of the line is the *MPC.*

Besides consumption, the other three components of total spending are investment spending (I), government purchases (G), and net exports (NX). In this chapter, none of these three variables depends on income.

Deviations from the full-employment level of output are often caused by *spending shocks*—changes in autonomous consumption, investment, government purchases, or net exports. These initially affect one sector and then work their way through the entire economy. Negative or adverse shocks can cause recessions, while positive shocks can cause booms. Eventually, output will return to its potential, full-employment level, but it does not do so immediately.

After a spending shock, output changes by a multiple of the initial change in spending. The multiple is called the *spending multiplier.* The simple formula for the multiplier is 1/(1 – MPC). But this formula ignores a variety of automatic stabilizers, and in reality, the multiplier is considerably smaller than the simple formula suggests. There is also a multiplier for changes in taxes, but it is smaller than the spending multiplier.

Countercyclical fiscal policy is any change in government purchases, taxes, or transfer payments designed to stabilize the economy. Until about 25 years ago, economists believed that countercyclical fiscal policy had great promise as a stabilizing force. Today, most economists and government policy makers believe that stabilizing the economy should be the job of the Federal Reserve.

KEY TERMS

boom
disposable income
net taxes
consumption function

autonomous consumption
marginal propensity to consume (MPC)
total spending

equilibrium GDP
spending shock
spending multiplier

recovery
automatic stabilizer
countercyclical fiscal policy

R E V I E W   Q U E S T I O N S

1. How does a *recession* differ from a *boom*? Describe the typical behavior of GDP and the unemployment rate during these periods?

2. Briefly describe the four main categories of spending.

3. List, and briefly explain, the main determinants of consumption spending. Indicate whether a change in each determinant causes a movement along, or a shift of, the consumption function.

4. What are the main components of investment spending? How does actual investment differ from planned investment?

5. Why are exports added, and imports subtracted, in measuring total spending?

6. Why are transfer payments subtracted in measuring net taxes?

7. What is the *spending multiplier*? Why does the multiplier for a change in taxes have a different value than the multiplier for a change in government purchases?

8. "Today, the business cycle is dead. The government can neutralize any spending shock with a well-timed, counter-cyclical change in government spending or net taxes." Comment.

9. "During the last half century economic fluctuations in the United States have been caused entirely by changes in military spending." True or false? Explain.

P R O B L E M S   A N D   E X E R C I S E S

1.

DI	C
7,000	6,600
8,000	7,400
9,000	8,200
10,000	9,000
11,000	9,800
12,000	10,600
13,000	11,400

a. What is the marginal propensity to consume implicit in this data?

b. What is the value of autonomous consumption spending? (Hint: if the data in the table were extrapolated, what would be the value of C when DI is zero?)

c. What is the numerical value of the multiplier in this economy? (Assume there are no automatic stabilizers in this economy, i.e., use the simple formula from the chapter.)

d. In this economy, if government purchases decreased by 600, what would happen to total output?

2. Using the data given in problem 1, construct a table similar to Table 3 in the chapter.

a. Show what would happen in the first five rounds following an increase in investment spending from 400 to 800.

b. What would be the ultimate effect of that increase in investment spending on total output?

c. If consumption spending was 10,600 before the increase in investment, what would be the new value of consumption spending after the multiplier process has finished?

3. Suppose that households become more thrifty—that is, they now wish to save 500 more at any level of disposable income.

a. In the table in problem 1, which column of data would be affected? How?

b. What would be the new value of the MPC?

c. What would be the new value of autonomous consumption?

4. Economists both in industry and government have great interest in predicting the cyclical ups and downs of the economy. One approach to doing this is to use the *Index of Leading Indicators* published by the Conference Board.

a. Visit their Web site at http://www.tcb-indicators.org/index.htm. Click on "Full List of Articles" and select "Using Cyclical Indicators." What is a leading indicator? Why is an index of indicators used rather than the indicators themselves? How is the index used to forecast recessions?

b. Now return to http://www.tcb-indicators.org/index.htm and follow the "Latest Leading Economic Indicators" link. What are the components of the leading index? What is your forecast for the economy based on the most recent behavior of the index?

CHALLENGE QUESTION

Suppose that net taxes depend on income. Specifically, each time household income increases by $100, the government's net taxes increase by $25. What is the new value for the multiplier? (Hint: Construct a table similar to Table 3, but incorporating the change in taxes. Also Note: In each round of the multiplier, the rise in disposable income will equal the rise in income *minus* any rise in taxes.)

APPENDIX: THE SPECIAL CASE OF THE TAX MULTIPLIER

You learned in this chapter how changes in autonomous consumption, investment, and government purchases affect the economy's GDP. But there is another type of change that can influence GDP: a change in taxes. For this type of change, the formula for the multiplier is a bit different from the one presented in the chapter.

Let's suppose that household taxes (T) *decrease* by $100 billion. The immediate impact is to increase households' *disposable income* (DI) by $100 billion. As a result, consumption spending will increase. But by how much?

The answer is, by *less* than $100 billion. When households get a tax cut, they increase their spending *not* by the full amount of the cut, but only by a *part* of it. The amount by which spending initially increases depends on the *MPC*. If the *MPC* is 0.6, and disposable income rises by $100 billion, the initial change in consumption spending is just $60 billion. *This is the first change in spending that occurs after the tax cut.* Of course, once consumption spending rises, every subsequent round of the multiplier will work just as in Table 3: In the next round, consumption spending will rise by $36 billion, and then $21.6 billion, and so on.

Now let's compare what happens when taxes are cut by $100 billion with what happens when spending rises by $100 billion. As you can see from Table 3, when investment rises by $100 billion, the initial change in spending is, by definition, $100 billion. But when taxes are cut by $100 billion, the initial change in spending is *not* $100 billion, but *$60 billion*. Thus, the first line of the table is missing in the case of a $100 billion tax cut. All subsequent rounds of the multiplier are the same, however. Therefore, we would expect the $100 billion tax cut to cause a $150 billion increase in equilibrium GDP—not the $250 billion increase listed in the table.

Another way to say this is: For each dollar that taxes are cut, equilibrium GDP will increase by $1.50 rather than $2.50—the increase is one dollar less in the case of the tax cut. This observation tells us that the tax multiplier must have a numerical value *1 less than* the spending multiplier of the chapter.

Finally, there is one more difference between the spending multiplier of the chapter and the tax multiplier: While the spending multiplier is a positive number (because an increase in spending causes an increase in equilibrium GDP), the tax multiplier is a negative number, since a tax cut (a negative change in taxes) must be multiplied by a *negative* number to give us a *positive* change in GDP. Putting all this together, we conclude that

> *the tax multiplier is 1.0 less than the spending multiplier and negative in sign.*

Thus, if the *MPC* is 0.6 (as in the chapter), so that the spending multiplier is 2.5, then the tax multiplier will have a value of $-(2.5 - 1) = -1.5$.

More generally, since the tax multiplier is 1 less than the spending multiplier and is also negative, we can write

Tax multiplier = –(spending multiplier – 1)

Because the spending multiplier is $1/(1 - MPC)$, we can substitute to get

$$\text{Tax multiplier} = -\left[\frac{1}{1 - MPC} - 1\right] = -\frac{1 - (1 - MPC)}{1 - MPC} = \frac{-MPC}{1 - MPC}$$

Hence,

the general formula for the tax multiplier is

$$\frac{-MPC}{1 - MPC}$$

For any change in taxes, we can use the formula to find the change in GDP as follows:

$$\Delta GDP = \left[\frac{-MPC}{1 - MPC}\right] \times \Delta T$$

In our example, in which taxes were cut by $100 billion, we have $\Delta T = -\$100$ billion and $MPC = 0.6$. Plugging these values into the formula, we obtain

$$\Delta GDP = \left[\frac{-0.6}{1 - 0.6}\right] \times -\$100 \text{ billion} = \$150 \text{ billion}$$

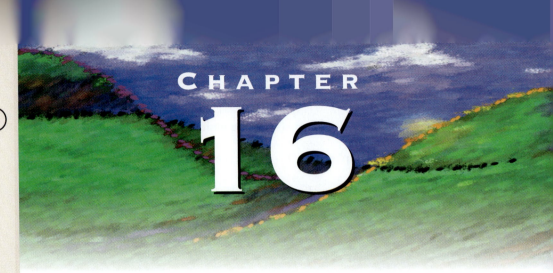

CHAPTER 16

THE BANKING SYSTEM, THE FEDERAL RESERVE, AND MONETARY POLICY

Everyone knows that money doesn't grow on trees. But where does it actually come from? You might think that the answer is simple: The government just prints it. Right?

Sort of. It is true that much of our money supply is, indeed, paper currency printed by our national monetary authority. But most of our money supply is not paper currency at all and is not printed by anyone. Moreover, the monetary authority in the United States—the Federal Reserve System—is not technically a part of the government, but a quasi-independent agency that operates *along side* of the government.

This chapter is about money, the institutions that help create it, and how changes in the nation's money supply affect the economy. What you learn here will deepen your understanding of economic fluctuations and help you understand our policy choices in dealing with them. We will begin by taking a look at what money is and how it is measured. Then, we turn our attention to the private banking system and the U.S. Federal Reserve. Next, we'll consider how the Federal Reserve works through the private banking system to change the money supply. Finally, we'll explore how the Federal Reserve uses its control over the money supply to help stabilize the economy.

WHAT IS COUNTED AS MONEY?

Money, loosely defined, is the means of payment in the economy. As you will learn in this chapter, the amount of money in circulation can affect the macro-economy. This is why governments around the world like to know how much money is available to their citizens.

In practice, the standard definition of money is *cash, checking account balances, and travelers' checks.*[1] What do these have in common and why are they included in the definition of money when other means of payment—such as credit cards—are not included?

First, only *assets*—things of value that people own—are regarded as money. Paper currency, travelers' checks, and funds held in checking accounts are all examples of assets. But *the right to borrow* is not considered an asset, so it is not part of the money supply. This is why the credit limit on your credit card and your ability to go into a bank and borrow money are not considered part of the money supply.

Second, only things that are widely *acceptable* as a means of payment are regarded as money. Currency, travelers' checks, and personal checks can all be used to buy things or pay bills. Other assets—such as the funds in your savings account—cannot generally be used to pay for goods and services, and so they fail the acceptability test.

The money supply is constantly changing. The Federal Reserve—the institution responsible for controlling the money supply—keeps track of the total and reports it each week. For example, on January 18, 1999, the total U.S. money supply (as reported by the Fed) was $1,083 billion—slightly more than one trillion dollars.

Let's take a closer look at the different components of the money supply.

THE COMPONENTS OF THE MONEY SUPPLY

When we think about money, the first image that pops into our minds is *cash*. More specifically, we count as money **cash in the hands of the public**. Excluded are cash held by banks and cash held by the Federal Reserve itself.

CASH IN THE HANDS OF THE PUBLIC Currency and coins held outside of banks.

The Fed has a fairly easy time keeping track of the total amount of currency in circulation, because the Fed itself has issued it. (It is also the institution that collects and destroys worn-out or damaged bills.) In January, 1999, the Fed reported that cash in the hands of the public totaled $462 billion in cash.

However, there is one very important detail about this number. Almost half of this cash—more than $200 billion—was circulating in foreign countries.[2] Foreigners in many countries prefer to hold their wealth in U.S. dollars because the dollar's purchasing power is more stable than their own currency. Even though this cash is circulating outside our own country, it is still counted as part of the U.S. money supply.

Travelers' checks are specially printed checks that you can buy from banks or other private companies, like American Express. Travelers' checks can be easily spent at almost any hotel or store and you can often cash them at a bank. You need only show an I.D. and countersign the check. In January 1999, the public held about $8 billion in travelers' checks.

The remaining component of the money supply is checking account balances. Most are **demand deposits**, which are checking accounts that don't pay interest held by households and business firms at commercial banks. These accounts are called "demand" deposits because when you write a check to someone, that person can

DEMAND DEPOSITS Checking accounts that do not pay interest.

---

1.   This corresponds to the official money supply measure known as *M1*. There are other, broader measures of the money supply as well. For example, *M2* includes not only cash, checking accounts, and travelers' checks, but also savings accounts, money market funds, and small (under $100,000) certificates of deposit.
2.   Money supply data are from the Federal Reserve Board of Governors' Web site: http://www.bog.frb.fed.us. The Fed's estimate of currency held abroad is based on Richard D. Porter, and Gretchen C. Weinbach, "Currency Ratios and U.S. Underground Economic Activity," *Federal Reserve Board Finance and Economics Discussion Series*, July 1998. They estimate cash in the hands of foreigners was $210 billion in May 1998.

go into a bank and, on demand, be paid in cash. The U.S. public held $368 billion in demand deposits in January 1999.

Other checkable deposits is the catchall category for several types of checking accounts that work very much like demand deposits. These include *negotiable order of withdrawal (NOW) accounts,* which are like demand deposits but pay some interest, and *automatic transfer from savings accounts (ATS accounts),* which are interest-paying savings accounts that automatically transfer funds into checking accounts when needed. In January 1999, the U.S. public held $245 billion of these types of checkable deposits.

Adding up all of the components we've discussed gives us the total U.S. money supply:

Money Supply = cash in the hands of the public + travelers' checks + demand deposits + other checkable deposits

In January 1999, this amounted to:

Money Supply = $462 billion + $8 billion + $368 billion + $245 billion = $1,083 billion

It is important to understand that our measure of the money supply excludes many things that people use regularly as a means of payment. Credit cards, for example, are not included in any of the official measures. But for many of us, unused credit is a means of payment, to be lumped together with our cash and our checking accounts. As credit cards were issued to more and more Americans over the last several decades, the available means of payment increased considerably, much more than the increase in the money supply suggests.

Technological advances—now and in the future—will continue the trend toward new and more varied ways to make payments. For example, at the 1996 Olympics, people used electronic cash to make small transactions, smaller than would make sense with credit cards. You could buy a card worth $5, $10, or $20 and use it in place of cash or checks. You could even put the card in a machine and add purchasing power to it by tapping into your Visa or Mastercard credit line. Electronic cash is clearly a means of payment, even though it is yet not included in any measure of the money supply. If and when electronic cash becomes important in the economy, it will probably be counted as money.

THE BANKING SYSTEM

Think about the last time you went into a bank. Perhaps you deposited a paycheck or withdrew cash to take care of your shopping needs for the week. We make these kinds of transactions dozens of times every year without ever thinking about what a bank really is, or how our own actions at the bank—and the actions of millions of other bank customers—might contribute to a change in the money supply.

FINANCIAL INTERMEDIARIES

FINANCIAL INTERMEDIARY
A business firm that specializes in brokering between savers and borrowers.

Let's begin at the beginning: What are banks? They are important examples of **financial intermediaries**—business firms that specialize in accepting loanable funds from households and firms whose revenues exceed their expenditures, and channeling the funds to households, firms, and government agencies whose expenditures exceed their revenues. Financial intermediaries make the economy work much more efficiently than would be possible without them.

To understand this more clearly, imagine that Boeing, the U.S. aircraft maker, wants to borrow a billion dollars for 5 years. If there were no financial intermediaries, Boeing would have to make individual arrangements to borrow small amounts of money from thousands—perhaps millions—of households, each of which wants to lend money for, say, 3 months at a time. Every 3 months, Boeing would have to renegotiate the loans with new lenders. Borrowing money in this way would be quite cumbersome. Lenders, too, would find this arrangement troublesome. All of their funds would be lent to one firm. If that firm encountered difficulties, the funds might not be returned at the end of 3 months.

An intermediary helps to solve these problems by combining a large number of small savers' funds into custom-designed packages and then lending them to larger borrowers. The intermediary can reduce the risk to savers by spreading its loans among a number of different borrowers. If one borrower fails to repay its loan, that will have only a small effect on the intermediary and its depositors. Intermediaries also offer depositors the convenience of being able to withdraw funds whenever they want. This is possible because the intermediary can predict—from experience—the pattern of inflows and outflows of funds. On any given day, some funds may be withdrawn, and some deposited, but the overall total available for lending tends to be quite stable. In addition, intermediaries keep a certain level of funds available—called *reserves*—in case of a period of unusually high withdrawals. The reserves are held as cash, or in accounts that can be quickly and easily converted into cash. For some financial institutions, the level of reserves is even mandated by law. We'll come back to reserves—and the legal requirements to hold them—later in this chapter. Of course, intermediaries must earn a profit for providing brokering services. They do so by charging a higher interest rate on the funds they lend than the rate they pay to depositors. But they are so efficient at brokering that both lenders and borrowers benefit. Lenders earn higher interest rates, with lower risk and greater liquidity, than if they had to deal directly with the ultimate users of funds. And borrowers end up paying lower interest rates on loans that are specially designed for their specific purposes.

The United States boasts a wide variety of financial intermediaries. Some of these intermediaries—called *depository institutions*—accept deposits from the general public and lend the deposits to borrowers. There are four types of depository institutions:

1. *Savings and loan associations (S&Ls)* obtain funds through their customers' time, savings, and checkable deposits and use them primarily to make mortgage loans.
2. *Mutual savings banks* accept deposits (called *shares*) and use them primarily to make mortgage loans. They differ from S&Ls because they are owned by their depositors, rather than outside investors.
3. *Credit unions* specialize in working with particular groups of people, such as members of a labor union or employees in a specific field of business. They acquire funds through their members' deposits and make consumer and mortgage loans to other members.
4. *Commercial banks* are the largest group of depository institutions. They obtain funds mainly by issuing checkable deposits, savings deposits, and time deposits and use the funds to make business, mortgage, and consumer loans.

Since commercial banks will play a central role in the rest of this chapter, let's take a closer look at how they operate.

COMMERCIAL BANKS

A commercial bank (or just "bank" for short) is a private corporation, owned by its stockholders, that provides services to the public. For our purposes, the most important service is to provide checking accounts, which enable the bank's customers to pay bills and make purchases without holding large amounts of cash that could be lost or stolen. Checks are one of the most important means of payment in the economy. Every year, U.S. households and businesses write trillions of dollars worth of checks to pay their bills, and many wage and salary earners have their pay deposited directly into their checking accounts. If you look back at the components of the U.S. money supply, you'll see that the public holds more money in the form of demand deposits and other checking-type accounts than it holds in cash.

Banks provide checking account services in order to earn a profit. And bank profits come from *lending.* The more of its deposits a bank lends out, the higher its profits will be. But banks do not lend out *every* dollar of deposits they receive; they hold some back as reserves.

BANK RESERVES AND THE REQUIRED RESERVE RATIO

RESERVES Vault cash plus balances held at the Fed.

A commercial bank's **reserves** are funds that it has *not* lent out, but instead keeps in a form that is readily available to its depositors. In practice, a bank holds its reserves in two places: in its vault (as cash), or in a special *reserve account* managed by the Federal Reserve. In either case, the reserves pay no interest. Why, then, does the bank hold reserves?

There are two explanations. First, on any given day, some of the bank's customers might want to withdraw more cash than other customers are depositing. The bank must always be prepared to honor its obligations for withdrawals, so it must have some cash on hand to meet these requirements. This explains why it holds vault cash.

REQUIRED RESERVES The minimum amount of reserves a bank must hold, depending upon the amount of its deposit liabilities.

Second, banks are required by law to hold reserves. The amount of reserves a bank must hold are called **required reserves.** The more funds its customers hold in their checking accounts, the greater the amount of required reserves. The **required reserve ratio,** set by the Federal Reserve, tells banks the fraction of their checking accounts that they must hold as required reserves.

REQUIRED RESERVE RATIO The minimum fraction of checking account balances that banks must hold as reserves.

For example, suppose a bank has $100 million in demand deposits. If the required reserve ratio is 0.1, this bank's required reserves are $0.1 \times \$100$ million = $10 million in reserves. The bank must hold *at least* this amount in reserves—as the sum of its vault cash and its accounts with the Federal Reserve.

More generally, the relationship between a bank's required reserves (RR), demand deposits (DD), and the required reserve ratio (RRR) is:

$$RR = RRR \times DD$$

As you are about to see, the required reserve ratio plays a key role in the Fed's control over the money supply. But first, it's time to stop hinting around about the Federal Reserve—about what it is and what it does—and take a systematic look at this important institution.

THE FEDERAL RESERVE SYSTEM

CENTRAL BANK A nation's principal monetary authority.

Every large nation controls its banking system with a **central bank.** Most of the developed countries established their central banks long ago. For example, England's central bank—the Bank of England—was created in 1694. France was one of the latest, waiting until 1800 to establish the Banque de France. But the United States was even later. Although we experimented with central banks at various times in our history, we did not get serious about a central bank until 1913, when Congress established the *Federal Reserve System*.

Why did it take the United States so long to take control of its monetary system? Part of the reason is the suspicion of central authority that has always been part of U.S. politics and culture. Another reason is the large size and extreme diversity of our country and the fear that a powerful central bank might be dominated by the interests of one region to the detriment of others. These special American characteristics help explain why our own central bank is different in form from its European counterparts.

One major difference is indicated in the very name of the institution—the Federal Reserve System. It does not have the word "central" or "bank" anywhere in its title, making it less suggestive of centralized power.

Another difference is the way the system is organized. Instead of a single central bank, the United States is divided into 12 different Federal Reserve districts, each one served by its own Federal Reserve Bank. The 12 districts and the Federal Reserve Banks that serve them are shown in Figure 1. For example, the Federal Reserve Bank of Dallas serves a district consisting of Texas and parts of New Mexico and Louisiana, while the Federal Reserve Bank of Chicago serves a district including Iowa and parts of Illinois, Indiana, Wisconsin, and Michigan.

Another interesting feature of the Federal Reserve System is its peculiar status within the government. Strictly speaking, it is not even a *part* of the government, but rather a corporation whose stockholders are the private banks that it regulates.

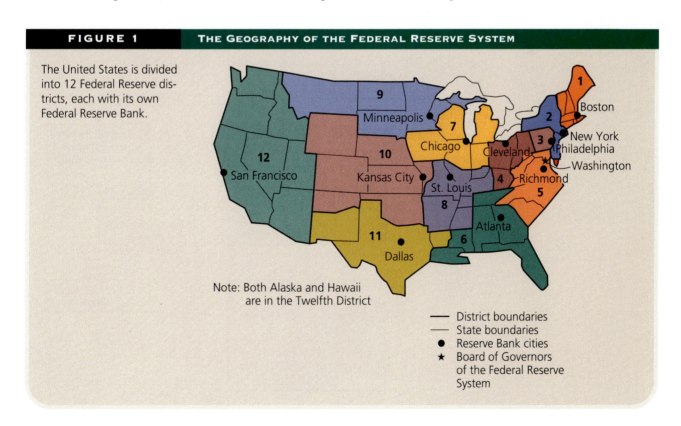

FIGURE 1   **THE GEOGRAPHY OF THE FEDERAL RESERVE SYSTEM**

The United States is divided into 12 Federal Reserve districts, each with its own Federal Reserve Bank.

Note: Both Alaska and Hawaii are in the Twelfth District

—— District boundaries
—— State boundaries
● Reserve Bank cities
★ Board of Governors of the Federal Reserve System

But it is unlike other corporations in several ways. First, the *Fed* (as the system is commonly called) was created by Congress and could be eliminated by Congress if it so desired. Second, both the president and Congress exert some influence on the Fed through their appointments of key officials in the system. Finally, the Fed's mission is not to make a profit for its stockholders like an ordinary corporation, but rather to serve the general public.

THE STRUCTURE OF THE FED

Figure 2 shows the organizational structure of the Federal Reserve System. Near the top is the Board of Governors, consisting of seven members who are appointed by the president and confirmed by the Senate for a 14-year term. The most powerful person at the Fed is the chairman of the Board of Governors—one of the seven governors who is appointed by the president, with Senate approval, to a 4-year term as chair. In order to keep any president or Congress from having too much influence over the Fed, the 4-year term of the chair is *not* coterminous with the 4-year term of the president. As a result, every newly elected president inherits the Fed chair appointed by his predecessor, and waits several years before making an appointment of his own.

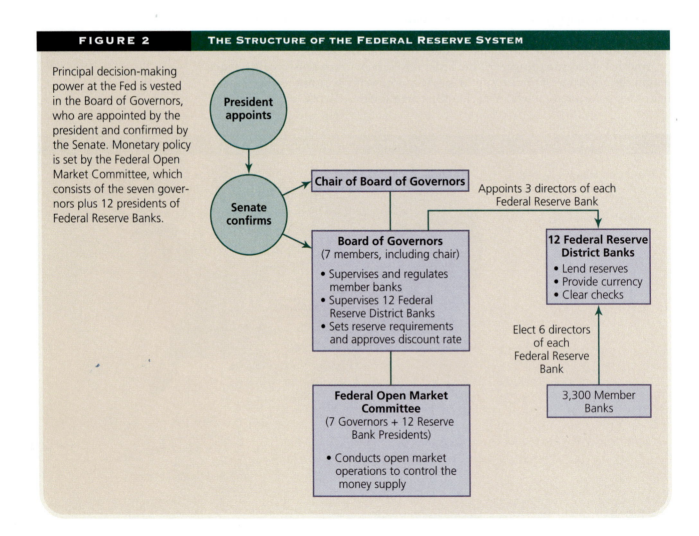

| FIGURE 2 | THE STRUCTURE OF THE FEDERAL RESERVE SYSTEM |

Principal decision-making power at the Fed is vested in the Board of Governors, who are appointed by the president and confirmed by the Senate. Monetary policy is set by the Federal Open Market Committee, which consists of the seven governors plus 12 presidents of Federal Reserve Banks.

President appoints

Senate confirms

Chair of Board of Governors

Appoints 3 directors of each Federal Reserve Bank

Board of Governors
(7 members, including chair)

- Supervises and regulates member banks
- Supervises 12 Federal Reserve District Banks
- Sets reserve requirements and approves discount rate

12 Federal Reserve District Banks

- Lend reserves
- Provide currency
- Clear checks

Elect 6 directors of each Federal Reserve Bank

Federal Open Market Committee
(7 Governors + 12 Reserve Bank Presidents)

- Conducts open market operations to control the money supply

3,300 Member Banks

For example, the current chairman of the Board of Governors is Alan Greenspan. He was originally appointed by President Reagan in 1987 for a term lasting until 1991, well into George Bush's term as president. In 1991, President Bush re-appointed Greenspan to another 4-year term, which included the first 3 years of Bill Clinton's administration. In 1995, President Clinton reappointed Greenspan yet again, for a term lasting until 1999.

Each of the 12 Federal Reserve Banks is supervised by nine directors, three of whom are appointed by the Board of Governors. The other six are elected by private commercial banks—the official stockholders of the system. The directors of each Federal Reserve Bank choose a *president* of that bank, who manages its day-to-day operations.

Notice that Figure 2 refers to "member banks." Only about 3,300 of the 11,000 or so commercial banks in the United States are members of the Federal Reserve System. But they include all *national banks* (those chartered by the federal government) and some *state banks* (chartered by their state governments). All of the largest banks in the United States (e.g., Citibank, Bank of America, and Bank-Boston) are nationally chartered banks and therefore member banks as well.

THE FEDERAL OPEN MARKET COMMITTEE

Finally, we come to what most economists regard as the most important part of the Fed—the **Federal Open Market Committee (FOMC)**. As you can see in Figure 2, the FOMC consists of all seven governors of the Fed, along with the 12 district bank presidents.[3] The committee meets about eight times a year to discuss current trends in inflation, unemployment, output, interest rates, and international exchange rates. After determining the current state of the economy, the FOMC sets the general course for the nation's money supply.

The word "open" in the FOMC's name is ironic, since the committee's deliberations are private. Summaries of its meetings are published only after a delay of a month or more. In some cases, the committee will release a brief public statement about its decisions on the day they are made. But not even the president of the United States knows the details behind the decisions, or what the FOMC actually discussed at its meeting, until the summary of the meeting is finally released. The reason for the word "open" is that the committee controls the nation's money supply by buying and selling bonds in the public ("open") bond market. Later, we will discuss how and why the FOMC does this.

FEDERAL OPEN MARKET COMMITTEE A committee of Federal Reserve officials that establishes U.S. monetary policy.

THE FUNCTIONS OF THE FEDERAL RESERVE

The Federal Reserve, as the overseer of the nation's monetary system, has a variety of important responsibilities. Some of the most important follow.

SUPERVISING AND REGULATING BANKS. We've already seen that the Fed sets and enforces reserve requirements, which all banks—not just Fed members—must obey. The Fed also sets standards for establishing new banks, determines what sorts of loans and investments banks are allowed to make, and closely monitors banks' financial activities.

Managed Fiat Currency

ACTING AS A "BANK FOR BANKS." Commercial banks use the Fed in much the same way that ordinary citizens use commercial banks. For example, we've

Provide liquidity in a financial panic

3.   Only five of the 12 presidents can vote on FOMC decisions. The president of the Federal Reserve Bank of New York has a permanent vote, because New York is such an important financial center. But the remaining four votes rotate among the other district presidents.

DISCOUNT RATE The interest rate the Fed charges on loans to banks.

already seen that banks hold some of their reserves in reserve accounts with the Fed. In addition, banks can borrow from the Fed, just as we can borrow from our local bank. The Fed charges a special interest rate, called the **discount rate,** on loans that it makes to member banks. In times of financial crisis, the Fed is prepared to act as *lender of last resort,* to make sure that banks have enough reserves to meet their obligations to depositors.

ISSUING PAPER CURRENCY. The Fed doesn't actually *print* currency; that is done by the government's Bureau of Engraving and Printing. But once printed, it is shipped to the Fed (under *very* heavy guard). The Fed, in turn, puts this currency into circulation. This is why every U.S. bill carries the label *Federal Reserve Note* on the top.

CHECK CLEARING. Suppose you write a check for $500 to pay your rent. Your building's owner will deposit the check into *his* checking account, which is probably at a different bank than yours. Somehow, the funds for your rent payment must be transferred from your bank account to your landlord's account at the other bank—a process called *check clearing.* In some cases, the services are provided by private clearinghouses. But in many other cases—especially for clearing out-of-town checks—it's done by the Federal Reserve. To clear checks, the Fed simply transfers funds from one bank's reserve account to another's.

CONTROLLING THE MONEY SUPPLY. The Fed, as the nation's monetary authority, is responsible for controlling the money supply. Since this function is so important in macroeconomics, we explore it in detail in the next section.

THE FED AND THE MONEY SUPPLY

Suppose the Fed wants to change the nation's money supply. (*Why* might the Fed want to do this? We'll get to that in the next section.) There are many ways this could be done. To increase the money supply, the Fed could print up currency and give it to Fed officials, letting them spend it as they wish. Or it could hold a lottery and give all of the newly printed money to the winner. To decrease the money supply, the Fed could require that all citizens turn over a portion of their cash to Fed officials who would then feed it into paper shredders.

These and other methods would certainly work, but they hardly seem fair or orderly. In practice, the Fed uses a more organized, less haphazard method to change the money supply: *open market operations.*

OPEN MARKET OPERATIONS Purchases or sales of bonds by the Federal Reserve System.

When the Fed wishes to increase or decrease the money supply, it buys or sells *government bonds in the open market.* These actions are called **open market operations.**

HOW THE FED INCREASES THE MONEY SUPPLY

To increase the money supply, the Fed will *buy* government bonds. This is called an *open market purchase.* To understand how an open market purchase works, let's start with a specific example. We'll assume that:

1. The Fed buys a government bond worth $1,000 from Acme Bond Dealers.
2. Acme has a checking account at First National Bank.
3. First National Bank is the only bank in its town.
4. The required reserve ratio (*RRR*) is 0.10.

Now, when the Fed buys the government bond, it will pay Acme Bond Dealers with a $1,000 check, which Acme will deposit into its account at First National. First National, in turn, will send the check to the Fed, which will credit First National's reserve account by $1,000.

At this point, First National's reserves have *increased* by $1,000. With more reserves, the bank can legally increase its total demand deposits. But how does a bank increase its demand deposits? By creating new loans. When a bank makes a loan, it credits the checking account of the borrower. For example, suppose the borrower is a businesswoman who wants to open a new business—Ilene's Ice Cream. When Ilene is granted a loan, First National will simply credit her checking account by the amount of the loan. Ilene is then free to spend the funds on rent, set-up costs, advertising, ingredients, and so forth.

How much can First National lend out? Remember that the required reserve ratio in our example is 0.10. That is, for each dollar of demand deposits, the bank must hold 10 cents in reserves. Or, to put it another way, for each dollar of reserves, the bank can have $10 in demand deposits. Thus, when the bank's reserves rise by $1,000, its demand deposits can rise by $10,000. Now, its demand deposits have *already* risen by $1,000 (the deposit from Acme Bond Dealers). Therefore, the bank will lend Ilene $9,000 by adding that sum to her checking account, bringing the total increase in demand deposits to $10,000.

But wait. . . . Won't Ilene spend what she borrows? And won't First National therefore *lose* its new reserves when the money is spent? For example, when Ilene writes a $500 check for advertising to the local newspaper, and the newspaper presents its check to First National, won't the bank lose $500 in reserves? The answer is no, as long as First National is the only bank in town. When Ilene pays the newspaper, the paper will just deposit her check into its *own* account at First National. Unless the newspaper wants to keep its earnings in cash, which is doubtful, all the bank must do is move funds from Ilene's account to the newspaper's account. The entire $1,000 in reserves stays at the bank, and the total increase in demand deposits remains at $10,000.

We conclude that—*if First National is the only bank in town*—*then the Fed's $1,000 open market purchase increases the money supply by $10,000.* In this case, the entire increase in demand deposits occurs at First National.

Now let's be a bit more realistic. What if there are *many* banks in town? First National will know that, when Ilene spends her loan, many of those who get her checks will deposit them in other banks. For example, Ilene might use some of her loan to buy milk and sugar, and pay by writing a check to the supermarket. The supermarket, in turn, would deposit the check into its own account at another bank—let's call it SecondBank. When SecondBank submits the check to the Fed for clearing, the Fed will transfer some reserves from First National's reserve account to SecondBank's reserve account. Will this change the results of our story? Will demand deposits rise by a different amount when there are more than one bank involved?

Not at all. The total increase in demand deposits will remain the same: $10,000. How do we know? Because the Fed—with its open market purchase—has put $1,000 in new reserves into the banking system. While the Fed may transfer these reserves from one bank to another as it clears checks, this has no effect on the total amount of reserves. Each dollar of the $1,000 in new reserves ends up at *some* bank, where it enables that bank to create $10 in new demand deposits. First National itself will lend less and create less in new demand deposits when there are other banks in town. But these other banks will just do the lending *instead* of First National. The total amount of new reserves—and the total

Demand deposits are a means of payment, and banks create them. This is why we say that banks "create deposits" and "create money." But don't fall into the trap of thinking that banks create *wealth*. No one gains any additional wealth as a result of money creation.

To see why, think about what happened in our story when Acme Bond Dealers deposited the $1,000 check from the Fed into its account at First National. *Acme* was no wealthier: It gave up a $1,000 check from the Fed and ended up with $1,000 more in its checking account, for a net gain of zero. Similarly, the *bank* gained no additional wealth: It had $1,000 more in cash, but it also *owed* Acme $1,000—once again, a net gain of zero.

The same conclusion holds for any other step in the money-creation process. In our simple, one-bank story, when Ilene borrows $9,000, she is no wealthier: She has $9,000 more in her checking account, but owes $9,000 to First National. And once again, the bank is no wealthier: It has $9,000 more in demand deposits—which are owed to Ilene—matched by $9,000 in loans—which Ilene owes to the bank. Always remember that while banks can "create money," in doing so they do not create wealth.

increase in demand deposits—remains the same, whether there is only one bank or many. Once again, we conclude that *when the Fed injects $1,000 in reserves into the banking system with an open market purchase, total checking accounts—and the money supply—will rise by $10,000.*

Let's go back and summarize what happened in our example. The Fed, through its open market purchase, injected $1,000 in reserves into the banking system. As a result, demand deposits rose by $10,000—10 times the injection in reserves. As you can verify, if the Fed had injected twice the amount of reserves ($2,000), demand deposits would have increased by 10 times *that* amount ($20,000). In fact, *whatever* the injection of reserves, demand deposits will increase by a factor of 10, so we can write:

$$\Delta DD = 10 \times \text{reserve injection}$$

where "*DD*" stands for demand deposits. The injection of reserves must be *multiplied by* the number 10 in order to get the change in demand deposits that it causes. For this reason, 10 is called the *demand deposit multiplier* in this example.

> The *demand deposit multiplier* is the number by which we must multiply the injection of reserves to get the total change in demand deposits.

The size of the demand deposit multiplier depends on the value of the required reserve ratio set by the Fed. If the *RRR* had been 0.20 instead of 0.10, then each dollar of demand deposits would require 20 cents in reserves, or each dollar of additional reserves would support an additional (1 / 0.20) = $5 in demand deposits. In that case, our formula would be

$$\Delta DD = 5 \times \text{reserve injection}$$

Generalizing, we can say that:

> For any value of the required reserve ratio (RRR), the formula for the demand deposit multiplier is 1/RRR.

In our example, the *RRR* was equal to 0.1, so the deposit multiplier had the value 1/0.1 = 10. If the *RRR* had been 0.2 instead, the deposit multiplier would have been equal to 1/0.2 = 5.

Using our general formula for the demand deposit multiplier, we can restate what happens when the Fed injects reserves into the banking system as follows:

$$\Delta DD = (1/RRR) \times \Delta \text{Reserves}$$

As long as all of the changes involve checking accounts (one component of the money supply), and the public does not change its holdings of cash (the other component of the money supply), then $\Delta DD = \Delta$ Money Supply. In that case, we can also write:

$$\Delta \textbf{Money Supply} = (1/RRR) \times \Delta \textbf{Reserves}$$

HOW THE FED DECREASES THE MONEY SUPPLY

Just as the Fed can increase the money supply by purchasing government bonds, it can also *decrease* the money supply by *selling* government bonds—an *open market sale*.

Where does the Fed get the government bonds to sell? It has trillions of dollars worth of government bonds from open market purchases it has conducted in the past. Since, on average, the Fed tends to increase the money supply each year, it conducts more open market purchases than open market sales, and its stock of bonds keeps growing. So we needn't worry that the Fed will run out of bonds to sell.

Suppose the Fed sells a $1,000 government bond to the familiar Acme Bond Dealers, which still has its checking account at First National Bank—the only bank in town. Acme pays for the bond with a $1,000 check drawn on its account at First National. When the Fed gets Acme's check, it will present the check to First National and deduct $1,000 from First National's reserve account. In turn, First National will deduct $1,000 from Acme's checking account.

Now First National has a problem. It's reserves have decreased by $1,000. Therefore, with $RRR = 0.10$, its demand deposits must decrease by $10,000. But—after it deducts the funds from Acme's checking account—its demand deposits *actually* decrease by only $1,000. Thus, First National must somehow reduce its demand deposits by another $9,000. How can it do this?

First National will have to *call in a loan*—that is, ask for repayment—in the amount of $9,000. In theory, the bank would tell Ilene, "You know that $9,000 in new loans we gave you? Actually, we need it back. So we're going to cancel the $9,000 credit to your checking account, and you no longer owe us the money." In this case, the bank's demand deposits would fall by a total of $10,000 after the Fed's open market sale.

In reality, bank loans are for specified time periods, and a bank cannot actually demand that a loan be repaid early. Our conclusion still holds, however. Most banks have a large volume of loans outstanding, with some being repaid each day. Typically, the funds will be lent out again the very same day they are repaid. A bank that needs to reduce its total demand deposits will simply reduce its rate of new lending on that day, thereby reducing its total amount of loans outstanding. This has the same effect as "calling in a loan."

What if First National is one of *many* banks in town? Then First National will know that, as it reduces its volume of lending, some of the loans paid back will result in a transfer of reserves from other banks to First National. Thus, First National's reserves will not fall by the full $1,000, as in our simple story. Will this

In this section, you learned how the Fed sells government bonds to decrease the money supply. It's easy to confuse this with another type of government bond sale, which is done by the U.S. Treasury.

When the government runs a budget deficit, the U.S. Treasury raises the funds to cover it by issuing and selling government bonds. These are *new* government bonds, and their sale represents *new lending* to the government. By contrast, when the Fed conducts an open market sale, it does not sell *newly* issued bonds, but rather "second-hand bonds"—those already issued by the Treasury to finance past deficits. Thus, open market sales are *not* government borrowing; they are strictly an operation designed to change the money supply, and they have no direct effect on the government budget.

change the results? No. The total decrease in demand deposits will remain the same: $10,000. How do we know? Because the Fed—with its open market sale—has taken $1,000 in reserves out of the banking system. Each dollar of these reserves comes from *some* bank, where it was supporting $10 in demand deposits. Regardless of how many banks are in the system, when the Fed removes $1,000 in reserves from the banking system with an open market sale, total checking accounts—and the money supply—will fall by $10,000.

Keeping in mind that a withdrawal of reserves is a *negative change in reserves,* we can still use our demand deposit multiplier—$1/(RRR)$—and our general formula:

$$\Delta DD = (1/RRR) \times \Delta\text{Reserves}$$

Applying it to our example, we have:

$$\Delta DD = [1/0.1] \times (-\$1,000) = -\$10,000$$

In other words, the Fed's $1,000 open market sale causes a $10,000 decrease in demand deposits. As long as the public's cash holdings do not change, the money supply decreases by $10,000 as well.

SOME IMPORTANT PROVISOS ABOUT THE DEMAND DEPOSIT MULTIPLIER

Although the process of money creation and destruction as we've described it illustrates the basic ideas, our formula for the demand deposit multiplier—$1/RRR$—is oversimplified. In reality, the multiplier is likely to be smaller than our formula suggests, for two reasons.

First, we've assumed that as the money supply changes, the public does *not* change its holdings of cash. But as the money supply increases, the public typically will want to hold part of the increase as demand deposits, and part of the increase as cash, where it cannot be used by banks as reserves against new demand deposits. As a result, an open market purchase of, say, $1,000, will inject *less* than $1,000 of new reserves into the banking system, and create *less* than $10,000 of new demand deposits. The demand deposit multiplier will be smaller than $1/RRR$.

Second, we've assumed that banks are always "fully loaned up"—that is, they hold only the minimum reserves required by law and create the maximum amount of new demand deposits (the maximum amount of new loans). In reality, banks may want to hold **excess reserves**—reserves beyond those legally required. For example, they may want some flexibility to increase their loans in case interest rates—their reward for lending—rise in the near future. Or they may prefer not to lend the maximum legal amount during a recession, because borrowers are more likely to declare bankruptcy and not repay their loans. Banks end up with excess reserves when they

EXCESS RESERVES Reserves in excess of required reserves.

lend out *less* than the maximum amount allowed by law, thereby creating *less* than the maximum amount of new demand deposits. In this case, the money supply will expand by less than in our simple story, and the demand deposit multiplier turns out to be smaller than 1/*RRR*.

OTHER TOOLS FOR CONTROLLING THE MONEY SUPPLY

Open market operations are the Fed's primary means of controlling the money supply. But there are two other tools that the Fed can use to increase or decrease the money supply.

- *Changes in the Required Reserve Ratio.* In theory, the Fed can set off the process of deposit creation, similar to that described earlier, by lowering the required reserve ratio. For example, suppose the Fed lowered the required reserve ratio from 0.10 to 0.05. Suddenly, every bank in the system would find that its reserves—which used to support 10 times their value in demand deposits—can now support 20 times their value. To earn the highest profit possible, banks would increase their lending, creating new demand deposits. The money supply would increase.

  On the other side, if the Fed raised the required reserve ratio, the process would work in reverse: All banks would suddenly find that—given their reserves—their demand deposits exceed the legal maximum. They would be forced to call in loans, and the money supply would decrease.

- *Changes in the Discount Rate.* The discount rate, mentioned earlier, is the rate the Fed charges banks when it lends them reserves. In principle, a lower discount rate—enabling banks to borrow reserves from the Fed more cheaply—might encourage banks to borrow more. An increase in borrowed reserves works just like any other injection of reserves into the banking system: It increases the money supply. On the other side, a rise in the discount rate would make it more expensive for banks to borrow from the Fed and decrease the amount of borrowed reserves in the system. This withdrawal of reserves from the banking system would lead to a decrease in the money supply.

Changes in either the required reserve ratio or the discount rate *could* change the money supply by causing banks to expand or contract their lending, in much the same way outlined in this chapter. In reality, neither of these policy tools is used very often. The most recent change in the required reserve ratio was in April 1992, when the Fed lowered the ratio for most demand deposits from 12 percent to 10 percent. Changes in the discount rate are more frequent. For example, in late 1998, the Fed lowered the discount rate two months in a row—first from 5 percent to 4.75 percent, and then from 4.75 percent to 4.5 percent. But it is not unusual for the Fed to leave the discount rate unchanged for a year or more. Indeed, before the changes in late 1998, the discount rate had remained unchanged at 5 percent for almost 3 years. Why are these other tools used so seldom? Part of the reason is that they can have such unpredictable effects. When the required reserve ratio changes, all banks in the system are affected simultaneously. Even a tiny error in predicting how a typical bank will respond can translate into a huge difference for the money supply.

A change in the discount rate has uncertain effects as well. Many bank managers do not like to borrow reserves from the Fed, since it puts them under closer Fed scrutiny. And the Fed discourages borrowing of reserves unless the bank is in difficulty. Thus, a small change in the discount rate is unlikely to have much of an impact on bank borrowing of reserves, and therefore on the money supply.

Open market operations, by contrast, have more predictable impacts on the money supply. They can be fine-tuned to any level desired. Another advantage is that they are covert. No one knows exactly what the FOMC decided to do to the money supply at its last meeting. And no one knows whether it is conducting more open market purchases or more open market sales on any given day (it always does a certain amount of both to keep bond traders guessing). By maintaining secrecy, the Fed can often change its policies without destabilizing financial markets and also avoid the pressure that Congress or the president might bring to bear if its policies are not popular.

> *While other tools can affect the money supply, open market operations have two advantages over them: precision and secrecy. This is why open market operations remain the Fed's primary means of changing the money supply.*

The Fed's ability to conduct its policies in secret—and its independent status in general—is controversial. Some argue that secrecy and independence are needed so that the Fed can do what is best for the country—keeping the price level stable—without undue pressure from Congress or the president. Others argue that there is something fundamentally undemocratic about an independent Federal Reserve, whose governors are not elected and who can, to some extent, ignore the popular will. In recent years, because the Fed has been so successful in guiding the economy, the controversy has largely subsided.

THE MONEY MARKET

At this point, you may be wondering: How *does* the Fed guide the economy? Granted, the Fed can raise or lower the money supply. But so what? How does control over the money supply translate into control over the economy? These are important questions. In order to answer them, we must consider *both* sides of the market for money: not just the supply of money, which is controlled by the Fed, but also the demand for money, which depends on the behavior of the public.

THE DEMAND FOR MONEY

Reread the title of this subsection. Does it appear strange to you? Don't people always want as much money as possible? Isn't their demand for money infinite?

Actually, no. The "demand for money" does not mean how much money people would *like* to have in the best of all possible worlds. Rather, it means *how much money people would like to hold, given the constraints that they face.* Let's first consider the demand for money by an individual, and then turn our attention to the demand for money in the entire economy.

AN INDIVIDUAL'S DEMAND FOR MONEY. Money is one of the ways that each of us, as individuals, can hold our *wealth.* Unfortunately, at any given moment, the total amount of wealth we have is a given; we can't just snap our fingers and have more of it. Therefore, if we want to hold more wealth in the form of money, we must hold less wealth in other forms—in savings accounts, money market funds, stocks, bonds, and so on. Indeed, individuals exchange one kind of wealth for another millions of times a day, in banks, stock markets, and bond markets. If you sell shares in the stock market, for example, you give up wealth in the form of corporate stock and acquire money. The buyer of your stock gives up money and acquires the stock.

These two facts—that wealth is given, and that you must give up one kind of wealth in order to acquire more of another—determine an individual's **wealth constraint.** Whenever we speak about the demand for money, the wealth constraint is always in the background. This is why we say:

> You've been reminded before, but since it's a very common mistake, another reminder won't hurt. Money and wealth are *stock variables,* not flow variables. They refer to amounts held *at a particular moment in time.* Do not confuse them with flow variables such as *income* or *saving.* Your income is what you earn *over a period of time.* Your saving is the part of your income that you don't spend *over a period of time.*

DANGEROUS CURVES

WEALTH CONSTRAINT At any point in time, wealth is fixed.

> *An individual's demand for money is the amount of wealth that the individual chooses to hold as money, rather than as other assets.*

Why do people want to hold some of their wealth in the form of money? The most important reason is that money is a *means of payment;* you can buy things with it. Other forms of wealth, by contrast, cannot be used for purchases. (Imagine trying to pay for your groceries with stocks or bonds.) However, the other forms of wealth provide a financial return to their owners. For example, bonds and savings deposits pay interest, while stocks pay dividends. Money, by contrast, pays either very little interest (on some types of checking accounts) or none at all (cash and most checking accounts). Thus,

OPPORTUNITY COST

> *when you hold money, you bear an opportunity cost—the interest or other financial return you could have earned if you held your wealth in some other form.*

Each of us must continually decide how to divide our total wealth between money and other assets. The upside to money is that it can be used as a means of payment. The more of our wealth we hold as money, the easier it is to buy things at a moment's notice, and the less often we will have to pay the costs (in time, trouble, and commissions to brokers) to change our other assets into money. The downside to money is that it pays little or no interest.

To keep our analysis as simple as possible, we'll use *bonds* as our representative nonmoney asset. Bonds have been mentioned several times in this book, but now it's time for a formal definition. A **bond** is an IOU issued by a corporation or a government agency when it borrows money. The bond promises to pay back the loan either gradually (e.g., each month) or all at once at some future date. In either case, the sum the borrower pays back exceeds what was borrowed, and the difference is the *interest* on the bond.

BOND An IOU issued by a corporation or government agency when it borrows funds.

While bonds pay interest, we'll assume money pays *no interest at all.* In our discussion, therefore, people will choose between two assets that are mirror images of each other. Specifically,

> *individuals choose how to divide wealth between two assets: (1) money, which can be used as a means of payment but earns no interest; and (2) bonds, which earn interest, but cannot be used as a means of payment.*

This choice involves a clear tradeoff: The more money we hold, the less often we'll have to go through the inconvenience of changing our bonds into money . . . but the less interest we will earn.

Since interest is the opportunity cost of holding money, it follows that *the greater the interest rate, the less money an individual will want to hold.*

THE DEMAND FOR MONEY BY BUSINESSES. Our discussion of money demand has focused on the typical individual. But some money (not a lot in comparison to what individuals hold) is held by businesses. Stores keep some currency in their cash registers, and firms generally keep funds in business checking accounts. Businesses face the same types of constraints as individuals: They have only so much wealth, and they must decide how much of it to hold in money rather than in other assets. The quantity of money demanded by businesses follows the same principles we have developed for individuals: They want to hold more money when the opportunity cost (the interest rate) is lower and less money when the interest rate is higher.

THE ECONOMY-WIDE DEMAND FOR MONEY. When we use the term "demand for money" without the word "individual," we mean the total demand for money by all wealth holders in the economy—businesses and individuals. And just as each person and each firm in the economy has only so much wealth, so, too, there is a given amount of wealth in the economy as a whole at any given time. In our analysis, this total wealth must be held in one of two forms: money or bonds.

> The (economy-wide) demand for money is the amount of total wealth in the economy that all households and businesses, together, choose to hold as money rather than as bonds.

The demand for money in the economy depends on the interest rate in the same way as it does for individuals and businesses. That is,

> a rise in the interest rate will decrease the (economy-wide) quantity of money demanded, and a drop in the interest rate will increase the quantity of money demanded.

MONEY DEMAND CURVE A curve indicating how much money will be willingly held at each interest rate.

THE MONEY DEMAND CURVE. Figure 3 shows a **money demand curve**, which tells us *the total quantity of money demanded in the economy at each interest rate.* Notice that the curve is downward sloping. As long as the other influences on money demand don't change, a drop in the interest rate—which lowers the opportunity cost of holding money—will increase the quantity of money demanded. (We'll discuss some of the other influences on money demand later in this chapter and in the next chapter.)

Point *E*, for example, shows that when the interest rate is 10 percent, the quantity of money demanded is $500 billion. If the interest rate falls to 5 percent, we move to point *F*, where the quantity demanded is $800 billion. As we move along the money demand curve, the interest rate changes, but other determinants of money demand (such as the price level and real income) are assumed to remain unchanged.

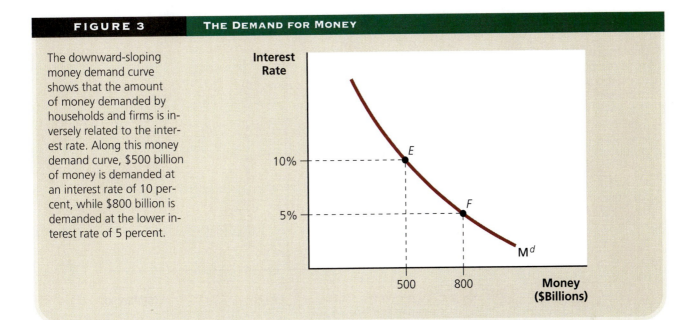

FIGURE 3   **THE DEMAND FOR MONEY**

The downward-sloping money demand curve shows that the amount of money demanded by households and firms is inversely related to the interest rate. Along this money demand curve, $500 billion of money is demanded at an interest rate of 10 percent, while $800 billion is demanded at the lower interest rate of 5 percent.

THE SUPPLY OF MONEY

Just as we did for money demand, we would like to draw a curve showing the quantity of money *supplied* at each interest rate. Earlier in this chapter, you learned how the Fed controls the money supply: It uses open market operations to inject or withdraw reserves from the banking system and then relies on the demand deposit multiplier to do the rest. Since the Fed decides what the money supply will be, we treat it as a fixed amount. That is, the interest rate can rise or fall, but the money supply will remain constant unless and until the Fed decides to change it.

Look at the solid vertical line in Figure 4. This is the economy's **money supply curve**, which shows the total money supply at each interest rate. The line is vertical because once the Fed sets the money supply, it remains constant until the Fed changes it. In the figure, the Fed has chosen to set the money supply at $500 billion. A rise in the interest rate from, say, 5 percent to 10 percent would move us from point *J* to point *E* along the solid money supply curve, leaving the money supply unchanged.

Now suppose the Fed, for whatever reason, were to *change* the money supply. Then there would be a *new* vertical line, showing a different quantity of money supplied at each interest rate. Recall from the previous chapter that the Fed raises the money supply by purchasing bonds in an open market operation. For example, if the demand deposit multiplier is 10, and the Fed purchases government bonds worth $20 billion, the money supply increases by 10 × $20 billion = $200 billion. In this case, the money supply curve shifts rightward, to the dashed line in the figure.

MONEY SUPPLY CURVE A line showing the total quantity of money in the economy at each interest rate.

Open market purchases of bonds inject reserves into the banking system and shift the money supply curve rightward by a multiple of the reserve injection. Open market sales have the opposite effect: They withdraw reserves from the system and shift the money supply curve leftward by a multiple of the reserve withdrawal.

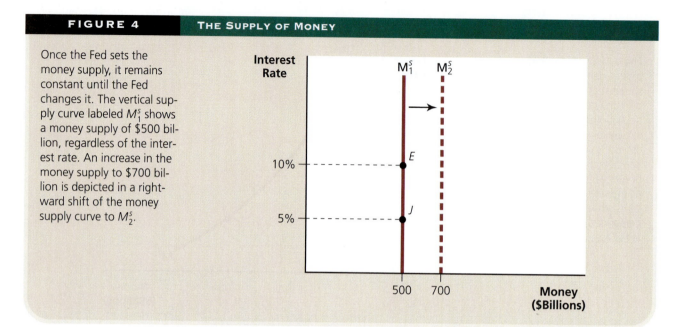

FIGURE 4   **THE SUPPLY OF MONEY**

Once the Fed sets the money supply, it remains constant until the Fed changes it. The vertical supply curve labeled M_1^s shows a money supply of $500 billion, regardless of the interest rate. An increase in the money supply to $700 billion is depicted in a rightward shift of the money supply curve to M_2^s.

EQUILIBRIUM IN THE MONEY MARKET

Now we are ready to combine what you've learned about money demand and money supply to find the interest rate in the economy. More specifically, we want to find the *equilibrium* interest rate—the rate at which the quantity of money demanded and the quantity of money supplied are equal.

Figure 5 combines the money supply and demand curves. By now, you've seen enough economics diagrams to know that the equilibrium occurs at point *E*, where the two curves intersect. At this point, with an interest rate of 10 percent, the quantity of money demanded and the quantity supplied are both equal to $500 billion.

But before rushing through this figure, it's important to understand what equilibrium in the money market actually means. First, remember that the money supply curve tells us the quantity of money, determined by the Fed, that *actually exists* in the economy. Every dollar of this money—either in cash or in checking account balances—is held by *someone*. Thus, the money supply curve, in addition to telling us the quantity of money supplied by the Fed, also tells us the quantity of money that people *are actually holding* at any given moment. The money demand curve, on the other hand, tells us how much money people *want* to hold at each interest rate. Thus, when the quantity of money supplied and the quantity demanded are equal, all of the money in the economy is being *willingly held*. That is, people are *satisfied* holding the money that they are *actually* holding.

🔑 **MARKETS AND EQUILIBRIUM**

> *Equilibrium in the money market occurs when the quantity of money people are actually holding (quantity supplied) is equal to the quantity of money they want to hold (quantity demanded).*

Can we have faith that the interest rate will reach its equilibrium value in the money market, such as 10 percent in our figure? Indeed we can. In the next section, we explore the forces that drive the money market toward its equilibrium.

HOW THE MONEY MARKET ACHIEVES EQUILIBRIUM. To understand how the money market reaches equilibrium, suppose that the interest rate, for some rea-

FIGURE 5	MONEY MARKET EQUILIBRIUM

Money market equilibrium occurs when households and firms are content to hold the amount of money they are actually holding. At point *E*—at an interest rate of 10 percent—the quantity of money demanded equals the quantity supplied, and the market is in equilibrium. At a higher interest rate, such as 15 percent, there would be an excess supply of money, and the interest rate would fall. At a lower interest rate, such as 5 percent, there would be an excess demand for money, and the interest rate would rise.

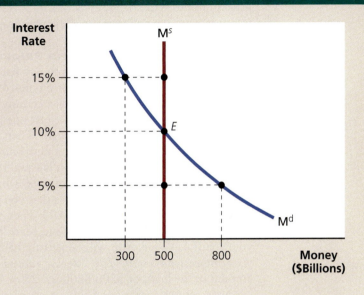

son, were *not* at its equilibrium value. For example, suppose the interest rate in Figure 5 were 15 percent—higher than the equilibrium value of 10 percent. As you can see, at 15 percent, the quantity of money demanded would be $300 billion, while the quantity supplied would be $500 billion. Or, put another way, people would *actually* be holding $500 billion of their wealth as money, but they would *want* to hold only $300 billion as money. There would be an **excess supply of money** (the quantity of money supplied would exceed the quantity demanded) equal to $500 billion – $300 billion = $200 billion.

Now comes an important point. Remember that in our analysis, money and bonds are the only two assets available. If people want to hold *less* money than they are currently holding, then, by definition, they must want to hold *more* in bonds than they are currently holding—an **excess demand for bonds.**

> When there is an excess supply of money in the economy, there is also an excess demand for bonds.

So far, we've established that if the interest rate were 15 percent, which is higher than its equilibrium value, there would be an excess supply of money and an excess demand for bonds. What would happen? The public would try to convert the undesired money into the desired bonds. That is, people would try to buy bonds. Just as there is a market for money, there is also a market for bonds. And as the public begins to demand more bonds, making them scarcer, *the price of bonds will rise.* We can illustrate the steps in our analysis so far as follows:

EXCESS SUPPLY OF MONEY The amount of money supplied exceeds the amount demanded at a particular interest rate.

EXCESS DEMAND FOR BONDS The amount of bonds demanded exceeds the amount supplied at a particular interest rate.

Interest rate higher than equilibrium	→	Excess supply of money	→	Excess demand for bonds	→	Public tries to buy bonds	→	Price of bonds ↑

We conclude that, when the interest rate is higher than its equilibrium value, the price of bonds will rise. Why is this important? In order to take our story further, we must first take a detour for a few paragraphs.

AN IMPORTANT DETOUR: BOND PRICES AND INTEREST RATES. A bond, in the simplest terms, is a promise to pay back borrowed funds at a certain date or dates in the future. There are many types of bonds. Some promise to make payments each month or each year for a certain period and then pay back a large sum at the end. Others promise to make just one payment—one, five, ten, or even more years from the date the bond is issued. When a large corporation or the government wants to borrow money, it issues a new bond and sells it in the marketplace for a price. Thus, the amount of the loan is equal to the price paid for the bond.

Let's consider a very simple example: a bond that promises to pay to its holder $1,000 in exactly one year. Suppose that you purchase this bond from the issuer—a firm or government agency—for $800. Then you are lending $800 to the issuer, and you will be paid back $1,000 in one year. What interest rate are you earning on your loan? Let's see: You will be getting back $200 more than you lent, so that is your *interest payment*. The interest *rate* is the interest payment divided by the amount of the loan, or $200/$800 = 0.25 or 25 percent.

Now, what if instead of $800, you paid a price of $900 for this very same bond. The bond still promises to pay $1,000 in one year, so your interest payment would now be $100, and your interest rate would be $100/$900 = 0.11 or 11 percent—a considerably lower interest rate. As you can see, the interest rate that you will earn on your bond depends entirely on the *price* of the bond. *The higher the price, the lower the interest rate.*

This general principle applies to virtually all types of bonds, not just the simple one-time-payment bond we've considered here. Bonds promise to pay various sums to their holders at different dates in the future. Therefore, the more you pay for any bond, the lower your overall rate of return, or interest rate, will be. Thus:

> When the price of bonds rises, the interest rate falls; when the price of bonds falls, the interest rate rises.[4]

The relationship between bond prices and interest rates helps explain why the government, the press, and the public are so concerned about the *bond market*, where bonds issued in previous periods are bought and sold. This market is sometimes called the *secondary* market for bonds, to distinguish it from the *primary* market where newly issued bonds are bought and sold. When you hear that "the bond market rallied" on a particular day of trading, it means that prices rose in the secondary bond market. This is good news for bond holders. But it is also good news for any person or business that wants to borrow money. When prices rise in the secondary market, they immediately rise in the primary market as well, since newly issued bonds and previously issued bonds are perfect substitutes for each other. Therefore, a bond market rally not only means lower interest rates in the secondary market, it also means lower interest rates in the primary market, where firms borrow money by issuing new bonds. Sooner or later, it will also lead to a drop in the

---

4.   In our macroeconomic model of the economy, we refer to *the* interest rate. In the real world, there are many types of interest rates—a different one for each type of bond, and still other rates on savings accounts, time deposits, car loans, mortgages, and more. However, all of these interest rates move up and down together, even though some may lag behind a few days, weeks, or months. Thus, when bond prices rise, interest rates *generally* will fall, and vice versa.

interest rate on mortgages, car loans, credit card balances, and even many student loans. This is good news for borrowers. But it is bad news for anyone wishing to lend money by buying bonds, for now they will earn less interest.

Now that you understand the relationship between bond prices and interest rates, let's return to our analysis of the money market.

BACK TO THE MONEY MARKET. Look back at Figure 5, and let's recap what you've learned so far. If the interest rate were 15 percent, there would be an excess sup-

A question may have occurred to you. Haven't we already discussed how the interest rate is determined? Indeed, we have. In Chapter 14, we used the loanable funds market—where a flow of loanable funds is offered by lenders to borrowers—to explain how the interest rate is determined. But in that chapter, we were discussing how the economy operates in the long run. Here, we are interested in how the interest rate is determined in the short run, so we must change our perspective.

DANGEROUS CURVES

Chapter 14 ignored an important idea discussed in this chapter: that the public continuously chooses how to divide its wealth between money and bonds. In the short run, the public's preferences over money and bonds can change, and this, in turn, can change the interest rate. But since these changes tend to be short-lived, when we focus on the long run, we can ignore them. Our view of the interest rate depends on the time period we are considering. Over the long run, the interest rate is determined in the market for loanable funds, where household saving is lent to businesses and the government. In the short run, the interest rate is determined in the money market, where wealth holders adjust their wealth between money and bonds.

ply of money and an excess demand for bonds. The public would try to buy bonds, and the price of bonds would rise. Now we can complete the story. As you've just learned, a rise in the price of bonds means a *decrease* in the interest rate. The complete sequence of events is:

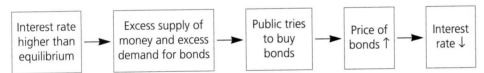

Thus, if the interest is 15 percent in our figure, it will begin to fall. Therefore, 15 percent is *not* the equilibrium interest rate.

How far will the interest rate fall? As long as there continues to be an excess supply of money and an excess demand for bonds, the public will still be trying to acquire bonds and the interest rate will continue to fall. But notice what happens in the figure as the interest rate falls: The quantity of money demanded *rises*. Finally, when the interest rate reaches 10 percent, the quantity of money demanded is finally equal to the quantity supplied. The excess supply of money, and therefore the excess demand for bonds, is eliminated. At this point, there is no reason for the interest rate to fall further. Ten percent is, indeed, our equilibrium interest rate.

We can also do the same analysis from the other direction. Suppose the interest rate were *lower* than 10 percent in the figure. Then, as you can see in Figure 5, there would be an *excess demand for money* and an *excess supply of bonds*. In this case, the following would happen:

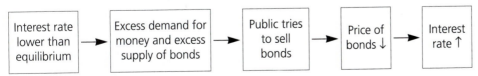

The interest rate would continue to rise until it reached its equilibrium value: 10 percent.

WHAT HAPPENS WHEN THINGS CHANGE?

In this section, we'll focus on two questions: (1) How does the Fed change the interest rate? and (2) What are the macroeconomic *consequences* of a change in the interest rate?

HOW THE FED CHANGES THE INTEREST RATE

Suppose the Fed wants to lower the interest rate. Fed officials cannot just *declare* that the interest rate should be lower. To change the interest rate, the Fed must change the *equilibrium* interest rate in the money market, and it does this by changing the money supply.

Look at Figure 6. Initially, with a money supply of $500 billion, the money market is in equilibrium at point *E,* with an interest rate of 10 percent. To lower the interest rate, the Fed *increases* the money supply through open market purchases of bonds. In the figure, the Fed raises the money supply to $800 billion, shifting the money supply curve rightward to the dashed line. (This is a much greater shift than the Fed would engineer in practice, but it makes the graph easier to read.) At the old interest rate of 10 percent, there would be an excess supply of money and an excess demand for bonds. This will drive the interest rate down until it reaches its new equilibrium value of 5 percent, at point *F.* The process works like this:

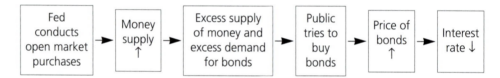

| FIGURE 6 | AN INCREASE IN THE MONEY SUPPLY |

If the Fed wishes to lower the interest rate, it can do so by increasing the money supply. At point *E,* the money market is in equilibrium at an interest rate of 10 percent. To lower the rate, the Fed could increase the money supply to $800 billion. At the original interest rate, there would be an excess supply of money (and an excess demand for bonds). Bond prices would rise, and the interest rate would fall until a new equilibrium is established at point *F* with an interest rate of 5 percent.

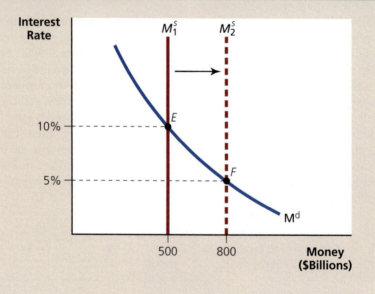

The Fed can raise the interest rate as well, through open market *sales* of bonds. In this case, the money supply curve in Figure 6 would shift leftward (not shown), setting off the following sequence of events:

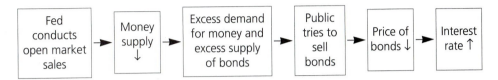

If the Fed increases the money supply by buying government bonds, the interest rate falls. If the Fed decreases the money supply by selling government bonds, the interest rate rises. By controlling the money supply through purchases and sales of bonds, the Fed can also control the interest rate.

THE FED IN ACTION

When the Fed tries to achieve a macroeconomic goal by controlling or manipulating the money supply, it is conducting **monetary policy**. During periods of economic calm, such as 1993 through 1997, the Fed's monetary policy tends to be stable, and the interest rate remains at about the same level from year to year. Occasionally, however, the Fed sees the need to act dramatically—to adjust the money stock aggressively and engineer large changes in interest rates. Such an episode occurred in the period from 1988 to 1990. In 1988, the Fed believed that the economy was becoming overheated and that it needed to be slowed down by a rise in the interest rate (you'll learn why a higher interest rate slows the economy in the next section).

Figure 7 shows what happened. Starting in July 1988, the Fed began to conduct open market sales of bonds, withdrawing reserves from the banking system. As you can see in panel (a) of the figure, from mid-1988 to mid-1989, banking system reserves fell by about $2 billion. This, in turn, shrank demand deposits and similar checking account balances by about $20 billion—10 times the withdrawal of reserves. (An earlier section of this chapter explained why the decrease in checking-type accounts is greater than the decrease in reserves.)

Because checking account balances are part of the money supply, the Fed's action shifted the money supply curve leftward. This, in turn, caused the interest rate to rise. Panel (c) of the figure shows changes in the *federal funds rate*—a key interest rate in the economy. The **federal funds rate** is the interest rate that banks with excess reserves charge for lending reserves to other banks. The federal funds rate varies closely with other interest rates in the economy, so it gives us a good idea of how interest rates in general were changing during this period. As you can see, the federal funds rate rose sharply, from less than 8 percent to almost 10 percent over the period.

Starting in July 1989, the Fed reversed course. It began to *purchase* government bonds, thereby injecting reserves into the banking system. This caused checking account balances to rise and shifted the money supply curve rightward. As a result, the federal funds rate fell back to a little over 8 percent.

Another dramatic change in monetary policy (not shown in the figure) occurred toward the end of 1998. The Fed began to fear that the U.S. economy might be sliding into recession and wanted to *lower* interest rates. Beginning in September 1998, the Fed increased the money supply—and lowered interest rates—three times over less than 3 months. By November, the federal funds had fallen from 5.5% to

MONETARY POLICY Action or inaction by the Federal Reserve designed to control the money supply and thereby influence the economy.

FEDERAL FUNDS RATE The interest rate charged for loans of reserves among banks.

FIGURE 7   **THE FED IN ACTION**

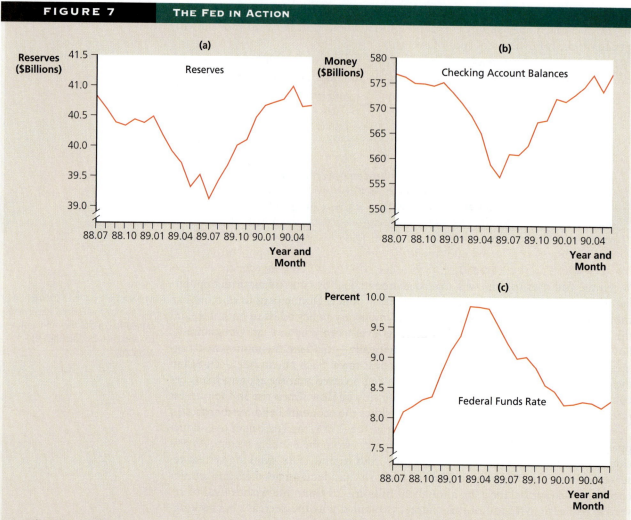

In July 1988, the Fed began to sell bonds and withdraw reserves from the banking system. As a result, checking account balances fell and the federal funds rate increased. In July 1989, the Fed reversed course and injected reserves. Checking balances rose and the federal funds rate fell.

4.75%. The Fed seemed happy with this move and left interest rates unchanged for the rest of the year.

These contractions and expansions of the money supply—and the resulting changes in interest rates—raise an important question. Why would the Fed feel the need to raise or lower interest rates in the first place? But we can begin to understand the Fed's motives by learning how interest rate changes affect the economy, which is the subject of the next section.

HOW INTEREST RATE CHANGES AFFECT THE ECONOMY

Suppose the Fed increases the money supply through open market purchases of bonds. The interest rate falls, for the reasons discussed earlier in this chapter and strongly confirmed by the data shown in Figure 7. But what then? How is the macro-economy affected? The answer is: *A drop in the interest rate will boost several different types of spending in the economy.*

HOW THE INTEREST RATE AFFECTS SPENDING. First, a lower interest rate stimulates business spending on plant and equipment. This idea came up a few chapters ago when we studied long-run economic growth, but we will go back over it here.

Remember that the interest rate is one of the key costs of any investment project. If a firm must borrow funds, it will have to pay for them at the going rate of interest—for example, by selling a bond at the going price. If the firm uses its *own* funds, so it doesn't have to borrow, the interest rate *still* represents a cost: Each dollar spent on plant and equipment could have been lent to someone else at the going interest rate. Thus, whether a firm has its own funds or must borrow them, the interest rate is the *opportunity cost* of funds spent on plant and equipment.

A firm deciding whether to spend on plant and equipment compares the benefits of the project—the increase in future income—with the costs (opportunity costs) of the project. With a lower interest rate, the costs of funding investment projects are lower, so more projects will get the go-ahead. Other variables can and do affect investment spending as well. But for given values of these other variables, a drop in the interest rate will cause an increase in spending on plant and equipment.

Interest rate changes also affect another kind of investment: spending on new houses and apartments that are built by developers or individuals. Most people borrow to buy houses or condominiums, and most developers borrow to build apartment buildings. The loan agreement for housing is called a *mortgage,* and mortgage interest rates move closely with other interest rates. Thus, when the Fed lowers the interest rate, families find it more affordable to buy homes, and landlords find it more profitable to build new apartments. Total investment in new housing increases.

Finally, in addition to investment spending, the interest rate affects consumption spending on "big ticket" items such as new cars, furniture, and dishwashers. Economists call these *consumer durables* because these goods usually last several years. People often borrow to buy consumer durables, and the interest rate they are charged tends to rise and fall with other interest rates in the economy. Spending on new cars, the most expensive durable that most of us buy, is especially sensitive to interest rate changes.

When the interest rate falls, consumption spending rises at *any* level of disposable income. It causes a *shift* in the consumption function, not a movement along it. Therefore, we consider this impact on consumption to be a rise in autonomous consumption spending, called *a* in our discussion of the consumption function.

We can summarize the impact of monetary policy as follows:

> *When the Fed increases the money supply, the interest rate falls and spending on three categories of goods increases: plant and equipment, new housing, and consumer durables (especially automobiles). When the Fed decreases the money supply, the interest rate rises and these categories of spending fall.*

MONETARY POLICY AND THE ECONOMY. Now we can finally see how monetary policy affects the economy overall. The only remaining step is one you learned in the last chapter: how a change in spending affects output and employment.

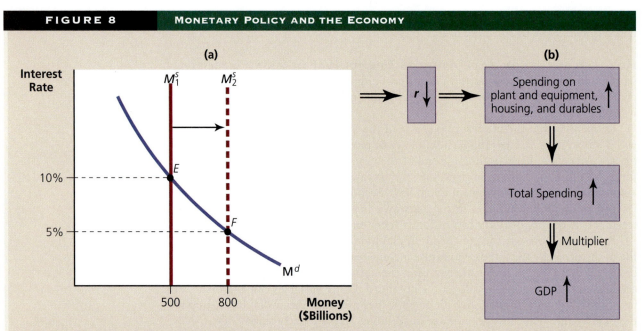

| FIGURE 8 | MONETARY POLICY AND THE ECONOMY |

Monetary policy involves an interaction between the interest rate and equilibrium real GDP. Initially, the Fed has set the money supply at $500 billion, so the interest rate is 10 percent (point *E*). If the Fed increases the money supply to $800 billion, money market equilibrium moves to point *F*, and the interest rate falls, stimulating interest-sensitive spending and driving total expenditures up. Through the multiplier process, real GDP increases.

Figure 8 puts the entire picture together. The left-hand side of the figure shows the money market, where the Fed has initially set the money supply at $500 billion. Equilibrium is at point *E*, with an interest rate (*r*) of 10 percent.

Now we suppose that the Fed increases the money supply to $800 billion. (This is an unrealistically large change in the money supply, but it makes it easier to see the change in the figure.) Equilibrium in the money market moves from point *E* to point *F*, and the interest rate drops to 5 percent. The drop in the interest rate causes spending on plant and equipment, new housing, and consumer durables (especially automobiles) to rise. That is, both investment spending (*I*) and autonomous consumption spending (*a*) will rise, setting off the multiplier effect and increasing equilibrium GDP by a multiple of the initial, interest-rate-driven rise in spending.

The new equilibrium in the money market will be at point *F*, with the interest rate driven down to 5 percent and total spending and GDP higher than they were initially. In the end, we see that the Fed, by increasing the money supply and lowering the interest rate, has increased output and employment.[5]

We've covered a lot of ground to reach our conclusion, so let's review the highlights of how monetary policy works. This is what happens when the Fed conducts open market purchases of bonds:

---

5. There is one additional step which we are not showing here. The rise in GDP—which is also a rise in total income—will cause the money demand curve to shift rightward. This is because, as income rises, and spending rises, individuals tend to want more of their wealth in the form of money at *any* interest rate. If we include this rightward shift in money demand, the interest rate will still fall, but not by as much as it does in Figure 8.

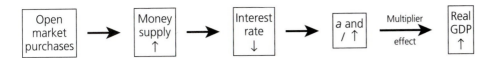

Open market *sales* by the Fed have exactly the opposite effects. In this case, the money supply curve in Figure 8 would shift leftward (not shown), driving the interest rate up. The rise in the interest rate would cause a decrease in interest-sensitive spending (*a* and *I*), ultimately causing total spending to drop by a multiple of the decrease in *a* and *I*, and causing equilibrium GDP to drop as well.

SHIFTS IN THE MONEY DEMAND CURVE

So far, we've considered changes in the interest rate engineered by the Fed. Here, we discuss an additional source of interest rate changes: a *shift in the money demand curve.*

We can imagine several causes of a spontaneous shift in money demand. For example, suppose the public began to fear that criminals would steal their credit card numbers and began to prefer making payments by cash or check. This would cause an increase in tastes for holding money, and the demand for money curve would shift rightward. On the other hand, new technology (such as electronic money cards) can lead to new substitutes for money, *decreasing* tastes for holding money and shifting the money demand curve leftward. Finally, *expectations about the future interest rate* can dramatically affect the demand for money in the present. This is the case we'll explore in detail.

EXPECTATIONS AND MONEY DEMAND. Why should expectations about the future interest rate affect money demand *today*? Because bond prices and interest rates are negatively related. If you expect the interest rate to rise in the future, then you also expect the price of bonds to fall in the future.

To see this more clearly, imagine (pleasantly) that you hold a bond promising to pay you $100,000 in exactly one year and that the interest rate is currently 10 percent. Now you decide you wish to sell the bond. The going price for your bond will be $90,900. Why? At that price, a buyer would earn $100,000 − $90,900 = $9,100 in interest. Since the bond cost $90,900, the buyer's rate of return would be $9,100/$90,900 = 0.10 or 10 percent—the going rate of interest. If you tried to charge more than $90,900 for the bond, its rate of return would be less than 10 percent, so no one would buy it—they could always earn 10 percent by buying another bond that pays the going rate of interest.

Now suppose that you *expect* the interest rate to rise to 15 percent in the near future, say, next week. (This is an unrealistically large change in the interest rate in so short a time, but it makes the point dramatically.) If you are right, then next week the going price for your bond will be only about $87,000. At that price, a buyer would earn $100,000 − $87,000 = $13,000 in interest, so the buyer's rate of return would be $13,000/$87,000 = 0.15 or 15 percent. Thus, if you believe that the interest rate is about to rise from 10 to 15 percent, you also believe the price of your bond is about to fall from $90,900 to $87,000—a drop of almost $4,000.

What would you do?

Logically, you would want to sell your bond *now,* before the price drops. If you still want to hold this type of bond later, you can always buy it back next week at the lower price, and gain from the transaction. Thus, if you expect the interest rate to rise in the future, you will want to exchange your bonds for money *today.* Your demand for money will *increase.*

Of course, if *you* expect the interest rate to drop, and your expectation is reasonable, others will probably feel the same way. They, too, will want to trade in their bonds for money. Thus, if the expectation is widespread, there will be an increase in the demand for money economy-wide.

> *A general expectation that interest rates will rise (bond prices will fall) in the future will cause the money demand curve to shift rightward in the present.*

Notice that when people expect the interest rate to rise, we *shift* the money demand curve, rather than move along it. People will want to hold more money at any *current* interest rate.

Figure 9 shows what will happen in the money market when people expect the interest rate to rise. Initially, with the money supply equal to $500 billion, the equilibrium is at point *E* and the interest rate is 10 percent. But the expected rise in the interest rate shifts the money demand curve rightward. After the shift, there is an excess demand for money and an excess supply of bonds at the original interest rate of 10 percent. As the public attempts to sell bonds, the price of bonds will fall, which means the interest rate will rise.

How far will the interest rate rise? That depends. Imagine a simple case where *everyone* in the economy expected the interest rate to rise to 15 percent next week. Then *no one* would want to hold bonds at any *current* interest rate less than 15 percent. For example, if the interest rate rose to 14 percent, people would still expect it to rise further, so they would still want to sell their bonds. Therefore, to return the money market to equilibrium, the interest rate would rise to exactly the level that people expected. This is the case we've illustrated in Figure 9, where the money demand curve shifts rightward by just enough to raise the interest rate to 15 percent. More generally:

> *When the public as a whole expects the interest rate to rise in the future, they will drive up the interest rate in the present.*

When information comes along that makes people believe that interest rates will rise and bond prices fall in the near future, the result is an immediate rise in the interest rate and a fall in bond prices. This principle operates even if the information is false and there is ultimately no reason for the interest rate to rise. Thus, a general expectation that interest rates will rise can be a *self-fulfilling prophecy:* Because people believe it, it actually happens. Their expectation alone is enough to drive up the interest rate.

This immediate response to information about the future—and the possibility of a self-fulfilling prophecy—works in the opposite direction as well:

> *When the public expects the interest rate to drop in the future, they will drive down the interest rate in the present.*

FIGURE 9	INTEREST RATE EXPECTATIONS

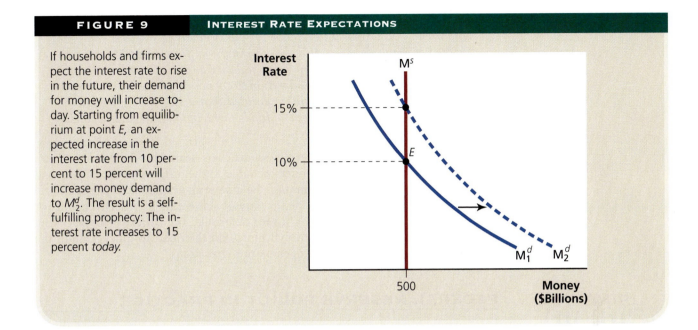

If households and firms expect the interest rate to rise in the future, their demand for money will increase today. Starting from equilibrium at point *E,* an expected increase in the interest rate from 10 percent to 15 percent will increase money demand to M_2^d. The result is a self-fulfilling prophecy: The interest rate increases to 15 percent *today.*

In this case, the public expects bond prices to rise, so they try to shift their wealth from money to bonds. In Figure 9, the money demand curve would shift leftward (not shown). The price of bonds would rise, and the interest rate would fall, just as was originally expected.

EXPECTATIONS AND THE FED. Changes in interest rates due to changes in expectations can have important consequences. Fortunes can be won and lost depending on how people bet on the future. For example, suppose you believe the interest rate is about to drop, so you buy bonds, thinking that bond prices are about to rise. But suppose you are wrong, the interest rate actually *rises* instead, and bond prices *drop*. Then your bonds will be worth less than what you paid for them. In fact, it is not unusual for major bondholders—such as pension funds or money market mutual funds—to gain or lose millions of dollars in a single day based on a good or a bad bet.

Another consequence of changes in expectations is the effect on the overall economy. When a change in expectations becomes a self-fulfilling prophecy, it causes *current* interest rates to change. As you've learned, this will affect total spending and output. Fortunately, the Fed can counteract these changes with open market purchases or sales of bonds, as needed, and we'll discuss this a bit later.

Still, the public's ever-changing expectations about future interest rates make the Fed's job more difficult. Expectations can change interest rates, and changes in interest rates can affect individual fortunes as well as the economy as a whole. This observation helps explain some seemingly mysterious Fed behavior. Public policy statements made by the Fed's chair (currently Alan Greenspan) or by other Fed officials are remarkably tentative and sometimes downright confusing. You can read them again and again and still have no idea what the Fed intends to do about interest rates in the future. For example, in December 1998, the Federal Reserve's Open Market Committee (FOMC) released a summary of the minutes of its November 1998 meeting. Here is the part of the statement explaining the Fed's future intentions regarding the money supply and interest rates. See if you can tell what the Fed planned to do.

At the conclusion of the Committee's discussion, all except one member supported . . . a proposal to remove the bias toward easing that had been adopted at the previous meeting. Accordingly, in the context of the Committee's long-run objectives for price stability and sustainable economic growth, and giving careful consideration to economic, financial, and monetary developments, the Committee decided that a slightly higher federal funds rate or a slightly lower federal funds rate would be acceptable during the intermeeting period.[6]

This is the kind of writing that gives English teachers heartache. But from the Fed's point of view, the obfuscation is understandable. If the officials of the FOMC had given stronger hints about their thinking, the money and bond markets might have gone into overdrive, as people rushed to buy or sell bonds in order to profit (or avoid loss) from the Fed's action. On rare occasions, Fed officials—by speaking more clearly—have given unintentional hints and then had to quickly undo the damage with further statements or open market operations.

USING THE THEORY

FEDERAL RESERVE POLICY IN PRACTICE

The Fed's overall guidelines have changed over the years. In the past, it has followed a policy of stabilizing the interest rate at a low level in order to enable the business and government sectors to borrow cheaply. At other times, it has set targets for the growth rate of the money supply and tried to stick to them. But in the 1990s, under Chairman Alan Greenspan, the Fed has switched its focus toward real GDP.

The Fed's goal over the past decade has been to keep GDP as close to potential GDP as possible and to prevent short-run fluctuations around potential GDP. When the economy seems in danger of expanding beyond potential (a boom), the Fed uses monetary policy to decrease total spending and reign the economy in. When the economy is in danger of slipping into recession, the Fed uses monetary policy to increase total spending and expand the economy.

Why is the Fed so intent on keeping the economy at its potential output—no more and no less? Because it is very costly for the economy to deviate in either direction. The economic and human costs of recessions were outlined earlier, in Chapter 12. But a boom, too, imposes significant costs on society. In the next chapter, you will see how booms—if allowed to continue—inevitably lead to inflation. And inflation, as you learned in Chapter 13, creates economic inefficiencies and redistributes purchasing power rather haphazardly among the population.

Here, we'll consider how the Fed tries to keep the economy on track in the face of two different types of challenges: shifts in the money demand curve and spending shocks.

THE FED'S RESPONSE TO CHANGES IN MONEY DEMAND

Earlier in the chapter, you saw that changes in the expected future interest rate can shift the money demand curve. Changes in tastes for holding money and other assets, or changes in technology, can also shift the money demand curve. For exam-

6.   These comments can be found at the Board of Governors' Web site: http://www.bog.frb.fed.us.

ple, the increasing use of substitutes for money—such as credit cards or, in the future, electronic money cards—can decrease the demand for money.

Money demand shifts—if ignored—would create problems for the economy. A look back at Figure 9 shows why. In that figure, the money supply is $500 billion and the money market is initially in equilibrium at point E, with an interest rate of 10 percent. Then, the money demand curve shifts rightward. If the Fed does nothing, the interest rate will rise—to 15 percent in the figure.

But if the Fed's goal is to stabilize real GDP, it cannot sit by while these events occur. For if the Fed does nothing, the rise in the interest rate will *decrease* investment and interest-sensitive consumption spending, thereby decreasing total spending. Real GDP will decrease. What can the Fed do to keep real GDP constant? It must *neutralize* the change in the interest rate.

Figure 10 illustrates how the Fed—by increasing the money supply—can neutralize a rightward shift of the money demand curve. In this case, a money supply of $700 billion will do the trick. (As in all of our examples, this is an unrealistically huge change in the money supply, but it makes the graph easier to read.) With the equilibrium interest rate back at 10 percent, there is no reason for total spending to drop, and the recession is avoided.

> *To stabilize real GDP when money demand changes on its own (not in response to a spending shock), the Fed must change the money supply. Specifically, it must increase the money supply in response to an increase in money demand, and decrease the money supply in response to a decrease in money demand.*

Notice an interesting (and pleasant) by-product of this policy. In order to stabilize real GDP, the Fed must also stabilize the interest rate. This gives it an easy guideline to follow when disturbances to the economy arise from changes in money demand:

Federal Reserve Bank of Minneapolis's *United States Monetary Policy Page*

Links covering everything you could ever want to know about US monetary policy—and more.

http://woodrow.mpls.frb.fed.us/info/policy/

| **FIGURE 10** | **THE FED'S RESPONSE TO CHANGES IN MONEY DEMAND** |

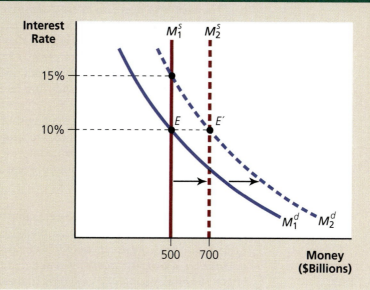

A spontaneous increase in money demand would disturb the equilibrium at point E. In the absence of a Fed response, the interest rate would increase to 15 percent. The Fed can offset this increase in the interest rate by raising the money supply (from $500 billion to $700 billion). At E', the interest rate is the same as it was originally.

> *To prevent changes in money demand from affecting real GDP, the Fed should set a target for the interest rate, and adjust the money supply as necessary to maintain that target.*

In normal times, when there are no significant spending shocks to the economy, the Fed can concentrate its efforts on maintaining its interest rate target. This was the Fed's main activity during the period from 1994 through 1997. In practice, keeping the interest rate constant during such periods is straightforward. When the interest rate rises, the Fed knows the money demand curve has shifted to the right. When the interest rate falls, it knows the money demand curve has shifted leftward.

The Fed does not even need to know the precise amount of the shift in the money demand curve in order to stabilize the interest rate. It can operate successfully with educated guesses. A mistake that it makes one day can be fixed the next day, because the mistake will show up in the interest rate. (For example, suppose the Fed had increased the money supply to $800 billion in Figure 10. What would have happened to the interest rate? How would the Fed have responded?) Since the Fed conducts open market operations each day, it is able to use continuous feedback to keep the interest rate relatively constant. While small changes occur between one day and the next, the changes largely disappear when the interest rate is averaged over several weeks.

THE FED'S RESPONSE TO SPENDING SHOCKS

As you've learned, shifts in total spending—due to changes in autonomous consumption, investment, taxes, or government purchases—cause changes in real GDP. How can the Fed keep real GDP close to potential output when there are spending shocks to the economy?

Figure 11 provides the answer. Initially, the money market is in equilibrium at point *E*, with a money supply of $500 billion and an interest rate of 10 percent. Now suppose a positive spending shock hits the economy, say, an increase in government purchases. If the Fed does nothing, the economy will head into a boom, so real GDP would still rise. To prevent this, the Fed will have to *raise* its interest rate target. The idea is to decrease interest-sensitive spending by the same amount that spending increased due to the shock—in the case, a government spending shock.

The Fed can hit its new, higher interest rate target by *decreasing* the money supply. In Figure 11, an interest rate target of 15 percent will do the trick, so that the Fed must decrease the money supply from $500 billion to $300 billion. With the new, lower money supply, the equilibrium interest rate is the required 15 percent (point *H*).

What if there were a *negative* spending shock to the economy, say, a decrease in government purchases? Then the Fed—to keep real GDP constant—would follow the opposite policy. It would *lower* its interest rate target and *increase* the money supply to hit it. In this way, it could prevent any decrease in total spending and thereby prevent a recession.

> *To stabilize real GDP, the Fed must change its interest rate target in response to a spending shock, and change the money supply to hit its new target. Specifically, it must raise its interest rate target (decrease the money supply) in response to a positive spending shock and lower the interest rate target (increase the money supply) in response to a negative spending shock.*

FIGURE 11   THE FED'S RESPONSE TO SPENDING SHOCKS

Initially, the Fed is maintaining an interest rate target of 10 percent. When a spending shock threatens to cause a boom, the Fed can neutralize it by raising its interest rate target and decreasing the money supply to hit the new, higher target. Interest-sensitive spending will decrease, preventing GDP from rising above potential output.

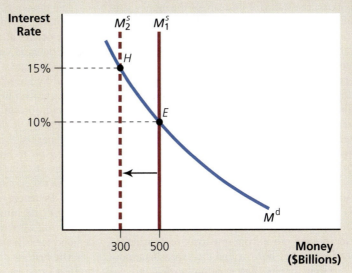

The Federal Reserve faced a serious negative spending shock in late 1998. Actually, the problem had begun more than a year earlier, with a financial crisis that had spread from Asia to Russia to South America. Nations in these areas were sliding into recession, and by late 1998, the U.S. economy was affected in two ways: (1) U.S. exports were decreasing, as foreign firms and households cut their spending, including spending on goods from the United States; (2) U.S. imports were increasing, as foreign firms—finding it increasingly difficult to sell their goods locally—began aggressively marketing their products in the United States. Both of these changes—the decrease in U.S. exports and the increase in U.S. imports—caused a fall in *net exports*.

There were other causes for concern as well. The financial crisis was making consumers pessimistic. They worried that the decrease in total spending on U.S. output might cause a recession, threatening their own jobs. If consumers responded by cutting their *own* spending, there would be another negative spending shock.

In the face of these events, the Fed responded: In late 1998, it decreased its target for the federal funds rate from 5.5 percent to 4.75 percent over 3 months. By early 1999, it appeared as if the Fed's policy had succeeded, and that the economy had managed to avoid the threatened recession.

Notice that the Fed's policy of stabilizing real GDP comes at a price: fluctuations in the interest rate. In Figure 11, in response to a positive spending shock, the Fed raises the interest rate all the way to 15 percent. When the shock is a decrease in spending—as occurred in late 1998—the Fed must decrease its interest rate target.

Fluctuations in the interest rate are costly in some ways. They make it more difficult for households and businesses to plan, and they increase the risks to bondholders (remember that changes in interest rates translate into changes in bond prices). They can also cause problems for the interest-sensitive sectors of the economy, especially housing construction and automobiles. Nevertheless, fluctuations in real GDP are costly too, and the Fed—especially in recent decades—has concluded that it is a good idea to adjust its interest rate targets aggressively when necessary to stabilize real GDP.

SUMMARY

In the United States, the standard measure of the money supply consists of cash in the hands of the public, checking account balances, and travelers' checks. Each of these assets is widely acceptable as a means of payment.

The amount of money in the economy is controlled by the Federal Reserve, operating through the banking system. Banks and other financial intermediaries are profit-seeking firms that collect loanable funds from households and businesses, then repackage them to make loans to other households, businesses, and governmental agencies.

The Federal Reserve injects money into the economy mostly through open market operations. When the Fed wants to increase the money supply, it buys bonds in the open market and pays for them with a check. This is called an *open market purchase*. When the Fed's check is deposited in a bank, the bank obtains reserves and can create new loans. The reserves may move from one bank to another, as borrowers spend what they borrow and the proceeds are deposited into different banks. But eventually, demand deposits, and the money supply, increase by some multiple of the original injection of reserves by the Fed. The *demand deposit multiplier*—the inverse of the required reserve ratio—gives us that multiple.

The Fed can decrease the money supply by selling government bonds—an open market sale—causing demand deposits to shrink by a multiple of the initial reduction in reserves. The Fed can also change the money supply by changing either the required reserve ratio or the discount rate it charges when it lends reserves to banks.

In the short run, the supply and demand for money interact to determine the interest rate. On one side of the market is the demand for money. An individual's demand for money indicates the fraction of wealth that person wishes to hold in the form of money, for different interest rates. Money is useful as a means of payment, but holding money means sacrificing the interest that could be earned by holding bonds instead. The higher the interest rate, the larger the fraction of their wealth people will hold in the form of bonds, and the smaller the fraction they will hold as money.

The money supply is under the control of the Fed and is independent of the interest rate. Equilibrium in the money market occurs at the intersection of the downward-sloping money demand curve and the vertical money supply curve. The interest rate will adjust so that the quantity of money demanded by households and firms just equals the quantity of money supplied by the Fed and the banking system.

Conditions in the money market mirror conditions in the bond market. If the interest rate is above equilibrium in the money market, there will be an excess supply of money there. People *want to* hold less money than they actually *do* hold, which means that they wish to hold more bonds than they do hold. An excess supply of money means an excess demand for bonds. As people try to obtain more bonds, the price of bonds rises and the interest rate falls. Thus an excess supply of money will cause the interest rate to fall. Similarly, an excess demand for money will cause the interest rate to rise.

The Fed, by changing the money supply, can change the interest rate. An increase in the money stock creates an excess supply of money. Very quickly, the interest rate will fall so that the public is willing to hold the now-higher money supply. A decrease in the money stock will drive up the interest rate.

Changes in the interest rate affect interest-sensitive forms of spending—firms' spending on plant and equipment, new housing constructions, and households' purchases of "big ticket" consumer durables. By lowering the interest rate, the Fed can stimulate aggregate expenditures and increase GDP through the multiplier process.

For the past decade, the Fed has used monetary policy to counteract booms and recessions. In normal times—when the only disturbances to the economy are shifts in money demand—the Fed will adjust the money supply to maintain an unchanged interest rate target. By preventing changes in the interest rate, the Fed prevents shifts in money demand from affecting the economy. But to deal with spending shocks, the Fed *changes* its interest rate target, and changes the money supply to meet its new target.

KEY TERMS

cash in the hands of the
    public
demand deposits
financial intermediary
reserves
required reserves

required reserve ratio
central bank
Federal Open Market
    Committee
discount rate
open market operations

demand deposit multiplier
excess reserves
wealth constraint
bond
money demand curve

money supply curve
excess supply of money
excess demand for bonds
monetary policy
federal funds rate

R E V I E W Q U E S T I O N S

1. Describe the main characteristics of money. What purpose does money serve in present-day economies?

2. Which of the following is considered part of the U.S. money supply?
   a. A $10 bill you carry in your wallet
   b. A $100 travelers' check you bought but did not use
   c. The $325.43 balance in your checking account
   d. A share of General Motors stock worth $40

3. What is a financial intermediary?

4. What are the main functions of the Federal Reserve System?

5. Explain how the Federal Reserve can use open market operations to change the level of bank reserves. How does a change in reserves affect the money supply? (Give answers for both an increase and a decrease in the money supply.)

6. Suppose that the money supply is $1 trillion. Decision makers at the Federal Reserve decide that they wish to reduce the money supply by $100 billion, or by 10 percent. If the required reserve ratio is 0.05, what does the Fed need to do to carry out the planned reduction?

7. Why do individuals choose to hold some of their wealth in the form of money? Besides individual tastes, what factors help determine how much money an individual holds?

8. Why is the money demand curve downward sloping? Why does a change in the expected interest rate cause the money demand curve to shift?

9. Why is the economy's money supply curve vertical? What causes the money supply curve to shift?

10. What sequence of events brings the money market to equilibrium if there is an excess supply of money? An excess demand for money?

11. The text mentions that starting in July 1989 the Fed began purchasing government bonds, and as a result, the interest rate fell to a little over 8 percent. Explain how the Fed's purchase of bonds led to a lower interest rate.

12. Describe how an increase in the interest rate affects spending on the following:
    a. plant and equipment
    b. new housing
    c. consumer durables

13. In the face of increased government spending, what could the Fed do to maintain a stable level of real GDP? In the case of a decrease in government spending, how can the Fed maintain a stable level of real GDP?

P R O B L E M S A N D E X E R C I S E S

1. Suppose the required reserve ratio is 0.2. If an extra $20 billion in reserves is injected into the banking system through an open market purchase of bonds, by how much can demand deposits increase? Would your answer be different if the required reserve ratio were 0.1?

2. Suppose total bank reserves are $100 billion, the required reserve ratio is 0.2, and banks are "fully loaned up." What is the total amount of demand deposits in the economy? Now suppose that the required reserve ratio is lowered to 0.1 and that banks once again become fully "loaned up" with no excess reserves. What is the new level of demand deposits?

3. For each of the following situations, determine whether the money supply will increase, decrease, or stay the same.
   a. Depositors become concerned about the safety of depository institutions and begin withdrawing cash.

   b. The Fed lowers the required reserve ratio.
   c. The economy enters a recession and banks have a hard time finding credit-worthy borrowers.
   d. The Fed sells $100 million of bonds to First National Bank of Ames, Iowa.

4. A bond promises to pay $500 one year from now. For the following prices, find the corresponding interest payments and interest rates that the bond offers.

Price	Amt. Paid in One Year	Interest Payment	Interest Rate
$375	$500	_____	_____
$425	$500	_____	_____
$450	$500	_____	_____
$500	$500	_____	_____

As the price of the bond rises, what happens to the bond's interest rate?

5. "A general expectation that the interest rate will fall can be a self-fulfilling prophecy." Explain what this means.

6. Suppose that the money demand curve shifts leftward, instead of rightward as in Figure 10.
   a. If the Fed did nothing, would the economy be in danger of a boom or a recession?
   b. Illustrate graphically, using a diagram similar to Figure 10, how the Fed can prevent the money demand shift from affecting the economy.
   c. Which would cause the money demand curve to shift leftward: an *increase* or a *decrease* in the expected interest rate? Why?

7. The government, thinking the economy is below potential GDP, decides to raise GDP, so it cuts taxes. The Fed, believing the economy was *already* at potential GDP, wants to neutralize the impact of the tax cut on the economy. What should the Fed do? Illustrate on a graph.

8. Assume that the Fed's goal is to stabilize GDP. How would it respond to the following changes in money demand? How will the interest rate and GDP be affected in each case? Illustrate each case with a diagram.
   a. People believe the interest rate will fall in the near future, so money demand falls.
   b. Many credible financial advisors recommend buying bonds, and consequently the demand for bonds increases.
   c. Tired of credit card debt, the general public begins to use credit cards less frequently and money more frequently.

9. Follow the link to "FOMC Minutes" on the Federal Reserve Bank of Minneapolis's *United States Monetary Policy Page* at http://woodrow.mpls.frb.fed.us/info/policy/. On what date did the most recent meeting for which minutes are available occur? What was the Fed's view of the state of the economy at that time? Did the Fed decide to take any policy actions at the meeting? Do you expect the Fed to tighten or loosen monetary policy in the next few months? Why?

CHALLENGE QUESTION

Sometimes banks wish to hold reserves in excess of the legal minimum. Suppose that banks are initially fully loaned up and the required reserve ratio is 0.1. Then the Fed makes an open market purchase of $100,000 in government bonds, and each bank decides to hold excess reserves equal to 5 percent of its deposits.

a. Derive the demand deposit multiplier in this case. Is it larger or smaller than when banks hold no excess reserves?
b. What is the ultimate change in demand deposits in the entire banking system?

CHAPTER

17

AGGREGATE DEMAND AND AGGREGATE SUPPLY

Booms and recessions are a fact of life. If you need a reminder, look back at Figure 1 in Chapter 15. There you can see that while potential GDP rises steadily year after year—due to economic growth—*actual* GDP tends to fluctuate around its potential.

But Figure 1 also reveals another important fact about the economy: Booms and recessions don't last forever. When output dips below or rises above potential, the economy always returns to potential output after a few quarters or years. True, in some of these episodes, government policy—either fiscal or monetary—helped the economy return to full employment more quickly. But even without corrective policies—such as during long parts of the Great Depression of the 1930s—the economy shows a remarkable tendency to begin moving back toward potential output. Why? And what is the mechanism that brings us back to our potential when we have strayed from it? These are the questions we will address in this chapter. We'll do this by studying the behavior of a variable that we've put aside for several chapters: the price level.

The chapter begins by exploring the relationship between the price level and output. This is a two-way relationship, as you can see in Figure 1. On the one hand, changes in the price level cause changes in real GDP. This causal relationship is captured in the *aggregate demand curve*, which we will discuss shortly. On the other hand, changes in real GDP cause changes in the price level. This relationship is summarized by the *aggregate supply curve*, to which we will turn later.

Once we've developed the aggregate demand and supply curves, we'll be able to use them to understand how changes in the price level—sometimes gently, other times more harshly—steer the economy back toward potential output.

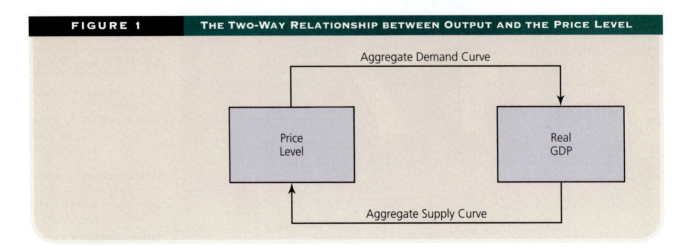

FIGURE 1   **THE TWO-WAY RELATIONSHIP BETWEEN OUTPUT AND THE PRICE LEVEL**

THE AGGREGATE DEMAND CURVE

In this section, we'll focus on how changes in the price level affect real GDP. We'll postpone till later the question of *why* the price level might change.

THE PRICE LEVEL AND THE MONEY MARKET

The first effect of a change in the price level occurs in the money market. When the price level rises, the money demand curve shifts rightward. Why? Remember the money demand curve tells us how much of their wealth people want to hold as money (as opposed to bonds) at each interest rate. People hold bonds because of the interest they pay; people hold money because of its convenience. Each day, as we make purchases, we need cash or funds in our checking account to cover them. If the price level rises, and the average purchase becomes more expensive, we'll need to hold more of our wealth as money just to achieve the same level of convenience. Thus, at any given interest rate, the demand for money increases, and the money demand curve shifts rightward.

> *A rise in the price level—because it makes purchases more expensive—increases the demand for money and shifts the money demand curve rightward. Conversely, a drop in the price level makes purchases cheaper, decreases the demand for money, and shifts the money demand curve leftward.*

Now, its time for a bit of review. Look back at Figure 9 in the previous chapter. There you saw that, when the money demand curve shifts rightward, the interest rate rises. You also learned that a rise in the interest rate reduces interest-sensitive spending—on plant and equipment, new housing, and consumer durables. Finally, you learned that a decrease in spending causes a (multiplied) decrease in equilibrium GDP. Putting all of this together:

> *A rise in the price level causes the interest rate to rise and interest-sensitive spending to fall. Equilibrium GDP decreases by a multiple of the decrease in interest-sensitive spending.*

THE PRICE LEVEL AND NET EXPORTS

The second effect of a higher price level brings in the foreign sector. When the U.S. price level rises, American goods become more expensive to foreigners, so U.S. exports decrease. At the same time, foreign goods become *relatively* cheaper to Americans, so U.S. imports increase. The decrease in U.S. exports, and the increase in U.S. imports, each contributes to a decrease in *net exports*—one of the components of total spending. When total spending drops, so does equilibrium GDP.

> A rise in the price level causes net exports to drop and equilibrium GDP to decrease by a multiple of the drop in net exports.

DERIVING THE AGGREGATE DEMAND (*AD*) CURVE

Now let's combine these insights about the price level and output in a graph. Figure 2 plots the price level on the vertical axis and the economy's real GDP on the horizontal axis. We'll assume that initally, the price level is 100, and equilibrium GDP is $6 trillion, represented by point *J*. Then—for some reason that we will not yet identify—the price level rises to 140. As you've just learned, the rise in the price level will raise the interest rate and raise the price of U.S. goods relative to foreign goods. Both of these will contribute to a drop in total spending and a (multiplied) drop in equilibrium GDP. In Figure 2, we assume that equilibrium GDP decreases to $5 trillion, so the economy moves to point *K*.

If we continued to change the price level to other values—raising it further to 150, lowering it to 85, and so on—we would find that each different price level results in a different equilibrium GDP. This is illustrated by the downward-sloping curve in the figure, which we call the *aggregate demand curve*.

> The **aggregate demand (AD) curve** tells us the equilibrium real GDP at any price level.

AGGREGATE DEMAND (AD) CURVE A curve indicating equilibrium GDP at each price level.

FIGURE 2	DERIVING THE AGGREGATE DEMAND CURVE

With a price level of 100, equilibrium GDP is $6 trillion, so the economy is at point *J*. As the price level rises to 140, output decreases to $5 trillion, at point *K*. Output falls because the rise in the price level: (1) increases money demand, raises the interest rate, and reduces interest sensitive spending; and (2) makes U.S. goods more expensive relative to foreign goods and decreases U.S. net exports. Connecting points like *J* and *K* yields the downward-sloping aggregate demand (*AD*) curve.

MOVEMENTS ALONG THE *AD* CURVE

As you will see later in this chapter, a variety of events can cause the price level to change, and move us along the *AD* curve. It's important to understand what happens in the economy as we make such a move.

Look again at the *AD* curve in Figure 2. Suppose the price level rises, and we move from point *J* to point *K* along this curve. Then the following sequence of events occurs: The rise in the price level increases the demand for money, raises the interest rate, decreases autonomous consumption (*a*) and investment spending (*I*), and works through the multiplier to decrease equilibrium GDP. At the same time, the rise in the price level raises the price of U.S. goods, decreases U.S. exports, and raises U.S. imports, which also works through the multiplier to decrease equilibrium GDP. The process can be summarized as follows:

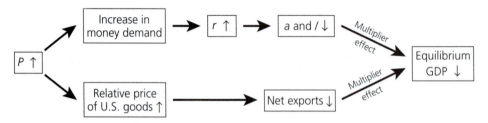

The opposite sequence of events will occur if the price level falls, moving us rightward along the *AD* curve:

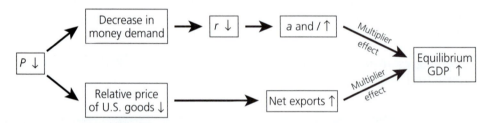

SHIFTS OF THE *AD* CURVE

When we move along the *AD* curve in Figure 2, we assume that the price level changes, but that other influences on equilibrium GDP remain constant. When any of these other influences on GDP changes, the *AD* curve will shift. The distinction between movements along the *AD* curve and shifts of the curve itself is very important. Always keep the following rule in mind:

> *When a change in the price level causes equilibrium GDP to change, we move along the* AD *curve. Whenever anything* other *than the price level causes equilibrium GDP to change, the* AD *curve itself shifts.*

What are these other influences on GDP? They are the very same changes you learned about in previous chapters. Specifically, equilibrium GDP will change whenever there is a change in any of the following:

- government spending
- taxes
- autonomous consumption spending
- investment spending

- the money supply curve
- the money demand curve

Let's consider some examples and see how each causes the *AD* curve to shift.

SPENDING SHOCKS. Spending shocks initially affect the economy by changing total spending and then changing output by a multiple of that original change in spending. For example, a positive spending shock—say, an increase in government spending—causes an increase in total spending and an increase in equilibrium GDP. But now that we've introduced the price level into our analysis, we can be more precise: A positive spending shock raises equilibrium GDP *at any given price level.* Thus, a positive spending shock *shifts* the *AD* curve rightward.

Figure 3 illustrates a rightward shift in the *AD* curve. We assume that the economy begins at a price level of 100, with equilibrium GDP at $6 trillion—point *J* on AD_1.

Now let's increase government purchases by $1 trillion and ask what happens if the price level remains at 100. Let's suppose that the multiplier is 2.5. Then equilibrium GDP rises by $2.5 trillion to $8.5 trillion—point *N*. This point lies to the right of our original curve AD_1. Point *N*, therefore, must lie on a *new AD* curve—a curve that tells us equilibrium GDP at any price level *after the increase in government spending*. The new *AD* curve is the dashed line, AD_2, which goes through point *N*. What about the other points on AD_2? They tell us that, if we had started at any *other* price level, an increase in government spending would have increased equilibrium GDP at that price level, too. We conclude that *an increase in government purchases shifts the entire AD curve rightward.*

Other spending shocks can shift the *AD* curve rightward just as in Figure 3. More specifically,

> *the AD curve shifts rightward when government purchases, investment spending, autonomous consumption spending, or net exports increase, or when taxes decrease.*

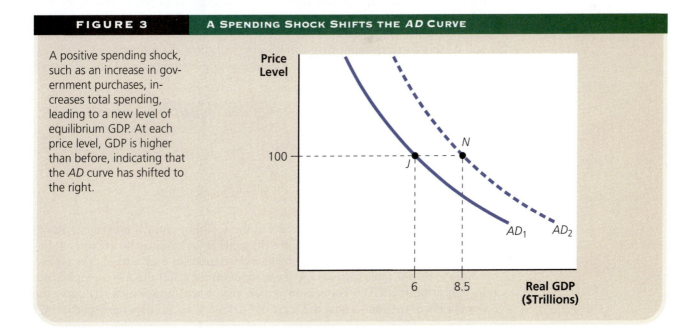

| **FIGURE 3** | **A SPENDING SHOCK SHIFTS THE *AD* CURVE** |

A positive spending shock, such as an increase in government purchases, increases total spending, leading to a new level of equilibrium GDP. At each price level, GDP is higher than before, indicating that the *AD* curve has shifted to the right.

Our analysis also applies in the other direction. For example, at any given price level, a *decrease* in government spending decreases total spending and, decreases equilibrium GDP. This in turn shifts the *AD* curve leftward.

More generally,

> *the AD curve shifts leftward when government purchases, investment spending, autonomous consumption spending, or net exports decrease, or when taxes increase.*

CHANGES IN THE MONEY MARKET. Changes that originate in the money market will also shift the aggregate demand curve. To see why, imagine once again that the economy begins at point *J* in Figure 3.

Now suppose the Fed conducts an open market purchase of bonds, thereby increasing the money supply. As you learned in the last chapter, this will shift the money supply curve rightward. (If you need to refresh your memory, flip back to Figure 8 in the previous chapter.) As the interest rate drops, total spending rises, increasing equilibrium GDP *at any given price level*. In Figure 3, at the initial price level P = 100, equilibrium GDP rises from $6 trillion to $8.5 trillion, so the economy moves—once again—from point *J* to point *N*. As you can see, the *AD* curve has *shifted* from AD_1 to AD_2.

A decrease in the money supply would have the opposite effect in Figure 3: The money supply curve would shift leftward. As a result, the interest rate would rise, total spending would fall, and *equilibrium GDP at any price level would fall*. We conclude that

> *an increase in the money supply shifts the* AD *curve rightward. A decrease in the money supply shifts the* AD *curve leftward.*

Changes in the money demand curve can also shift the *AD* curve. For example, if the public *expects* the interest rate to rise (the price of bonds to fall), they will want to sell bonds and acquire money. To test your understanding, put down the book and see if you can trace out the effects of an expected rise in the interest rate. If you do this correctly, your new equilibrium will show the following: The money demand curve has shifted rightward, the interest rate is higher, and the *AD* curve has shifted leftward.

> *Changes in money demand cause the* AD *curve to shift. If money demand increases, the* AD *curve shifts leftward. If money demand decreases, the* AD *curve shifts rightward.*

SHIFTS VERSUS MOVEMENTS ALONG THE *AD* CURVE: A SUMMARY

Table 1 summarizes how different events in the economy cause a movement along, or a shift in, the *AD* curve. You can use the table as an exercise by drawing a diagram similar to Figure 3, and providing an explanation for each entry in the table.

Notice that the table tells us how a variety of events affect the *AD* curve, but *not* how they affect *real* GDP. The reason is that, even if we know which *AD* curve the economy is on, we don't know the level of GDP until we know *where* on that *AD*

TABLE 1	EFFECTS OF KEY CHANGES ON THE AGGREGATE DEMAND CURVE									
	Price Level		Government Purchases, Autonomous Consumption, Investment Spending, or Net Exports		Taxes		Money Supply		Money Demand	
	Increases	Decreases	Increases	Decreases	Increase	Decrease	Increases	Decreases	Increases	Decreases
Effect on AD Curve	Movement upward along curve	Movement downward along curve	Shifts rightward	Shifts leftward	Shifts leftward	Shifts rightward	Shifts rightward	Shifts leftward	Shifts leftward	Shifts rightward

curve we are operating. And that, in turn, depends on the value of the price level. But how is the price level determined? Our first step in answering that question is to understand the other side of the relationship between GDP and the price level.

THE AGGREGATE SUPPLY CURVE

Look back at Figure 1, which illustrates the *two-way* relationship between the price level and output. On the one hand, changes in the price level affect output. This is the relationship—summarized by the *AD* curve—that we explored in the previous section. On the other hand, changes in output affect the price level. This relationship—summarized by the *aggregate supply curve*—is the focus of this section.

The effect of changes in output on the price level is complex, involving a variety of forces. Current research is helping economists get a clearer picture of this relationship. Here, we will present a simple model of the aggregate supply curve that focuses on the link between prices and costs. Toward the end of the chapter, we'll discuss some additional ideas about the aggregate supply curve.

PRICES AND COSTS IN THE SHORT RUN

The price *level* in the economy results from the pricing behavior of millions of individual business firms. In any given year, some of these firms will raise their prices, and some will lower them. For example, during the 1990s, personal computers and long-distance telephone calls came down in price, while college tuition and the prices of movies rose. These types of price changes are subjects for *micro*economic analysis, because they involve individual markets.

But often, all firms in the economy are affected by the same *macro*economic event, causing prices to rise or fall throughout the economy. This change in the price *level* is what interests us in macroeconomics.

To understand how macroeconomic events affect the price level, we begin with a very simple assumption:

A firm sets the price of its products as a markup over average total cost (ATC).

For example, if it costs Burger King $2.00, on average, to produce a Whopper (*ATC* is $2.00), and Burger King's percentage markup is 10 percent, then it will charge $2.00 + (0.10 × $2.00) = $2.20 per Whopper.[1]

The percentage markup in any particular industry will depend on the degree of competition there. If there are many firms competing for customers in a market, all producing very similar products, then we can expect the markup to be relatively small. Thus, we expect a relatively low markup on fast-food burgers or personal computers. In industries where there is less competition—such as daily newspapers or jet aircraft—we would expect higher percentage markups.

In macroeconomics, we are not concerned with how the markup differs in different industries, but rather with the *average percentage markup* in the economy:

> *The average percentage markup in the economy is determined by competitive conditions in the economy. The competitive structure of the economy changes very slowly, so the average percentage markup should be stable from year to year.*

But a stable markup does not necessarily mean a stable price level, because firms' average costs can change. For example, if Burger King's markup remains at 10 percent, but the average cost of a Whopper rises from $2.00 to $3.00, then the price of a Whopper will rise to $3.00 + (0.1 × $3.00) = $3.30. Extending this example to all firms in the economy, we can say:

> *In the short run, the price level rises when there is an economy-wide increase in average costs, and the price level falls when there is an economy-wide decrease in average costs.*

Our primary concern in this chapter is how changes in *output* affect average costs and, therefore, the price level. Why should a change in output affect average costs and the price level? We'll focus on three key reasons. As total output in the economy increases:

Greater Amounts of Inputs May Be Needed to Produce a Unit of Output. As output increases, firms hire new, untrained workers who may be less productive than existing workers. Firms also begin using capital and land that are less well-suited to their industry. As a result, greater amounts of labor, capital, land, and raw materials are needed to produce each unit of output. Even if the prices of these inputs remain the same, average total cost will rise. For example, imagine that Intel increases its output of computer chips. Then it will have to be less picky about the workers it employs, hiring some who are less well-suited to chip production than those already working there. Thus, more labor hours will be needed to produce each chip. Intel may also have to begin using older, less efficient production facilities, which require more silicon and other raw materials per chip. Even if the prices of all of these inputs remain unchanged, average cost will rise.

---

1.   In the microeconomic chapters of this book, you learned a more sophisticated theory of how prices are determined. In competitive markets, prices are determined by the intersection of supply and demand curves. In imperfectly competitive or monopoly markets, each firm sets its price using marginal analysis. But the simple markup model in this chapter captures a central conclusion of those theories: that an increase in costs will result in higher prices.

The Prices of Nonlabor Inputs Rise. This is especially true of inputs like land and natural resources, which may be available only in limited quantities in the short run. An increase in the production of final goods raises the demand for these inputs, causing their prices to rise. Firms that produce final goods experience an increase in average costs and raise their own prices accordingly.

The Nominal Wage Rate Rises. Greater output means higher employment, leaving fewer unemployed workers looking for jobs. As firms compete to hire increasingly scarce workers, they must offer higher nominal wage rates to attract them. Higher nominal wages increase average costs, and therefore result in a higher price level. Notice that we use the nominal wage, rather than the real wage we've emphasized elsewhere in this book. That's because we are interested in explaining how firms' prices are determined. Since price is a nominal variable, it will be marked up over *nominal* costs.

A decrease in output affects average costs through the same three forces, but with the opposite result. As output falls, firms can be more selective in hiring the best, most efficient workers and in choosing other inputs, thereby decreasing input requirements per unit of output. Decreases in demand for land and natural resources will cause their prices to drop. And as unemployment rises, wages will fall as workers compete for jobs. All of these contribute to a drop in average costs and a decrease in the price level.

All three of our reasons are important in explaining why a change in output affects the price level. However, they operate within different time frames. When total output increases, new, less-productive workers will be hired rather quickly. Similarly, the prices of certain key inputs—such as lumber, land, oil, and wheat—may rise within a few weeks or months.

But our third explanation—changes in the nominal wage rate—is a different story. While wages in some lines of work might respond very rapidly, we can expect wages in many industries to change very little or not at all for a year or more after a change in output.

> *For a year or so after a change in output, changes in the average nominal wage are less important than other forces that change average costs.*

Here are some of the more important reasons why wages in many industries respond so slowly to changes in output:

- Many firms have union contracts that specify wages for up to 3 years. While wage increases are often built into these contracts, a rise in output will not affect the wage increase. When output rises or falls, these firms continue to abide by the contract.
- Wages in many large corporations are set by slow-moving bureaucracies.
- Wage changes in either direction can be costly to firms. Higher wages must be widely publicized in order to attract more job applicants to the firm. Lower wages can reduce the morale of workers—and their productivity. Thus, many firms are reluctant to change wages until they are reasonably sure that any change in demand for their output will be long-lasting.
- Firms may benefit from developing reputations for paying stable wages. A firm that raises wages when output is high and labor is scarce may have to lower wages when output is low and labor is plentiful. Such a firm would develop a reputation for paying unstable wages and have difficulty attracting new workers.

In this section, we focus exclusively on the short run—a time horizon of a year or so after a change in output. Since the average wage rate changes very little over the short run, we'll make the following simplifying assumption: *The nominal wage rate is fixed in the short run.* More specifically,

> *we assume that changes in output have no effect on the nominal wage rate in the short run.*[2]

Keep in mind, though, that our assumption of a constant wage holds only in the short run. As you will see later, wage changes play a very important role in the economy's adjustment over the long run.

Since we assume a constant nominal wage in the short run, a change in output will affect average costs through the other two factors we mentioned earlier. Specifically, in the short run, a rise in real GDP raises firms' average costs because (1) the prices of nonlabor inputs rise, and (2) input requirements per unit of output rise. With a constant percentage markup, the rise in average costs translates into a rise in the price level. Thus,

> *in the short run, a rise in real GDP, by causing average costs to increase, will also cause a rise in the price level.*

In the other direction, a drop in real GDP lowers average costs because (1) the prices of nonlabor inputs fall, and (2) input requirements per unit of output fall. With a constant percentage markup, the drop in average costs translates into a fall in the price level.

> *In the short run, a fall in real GDP, by causing average costs to decrease, will also cause a decrease in the price level.*

DERIVING THE AGGREGATE SUPPLY CURVE

Figure 4 summarizes our discussion about the effect of output on the price level in the short run. Suppose the economy begins at point *A*, with output at $6 trillion and the price level at 100. Now suppose that output rises to $8 trillion. What will happen in the short run? Even though wages are assumed to remain constant, the price level will rise because of the other forces we've discussed. In the figure, the price level rises to 140, indicated by point *B*. If, instead, output *fell* to $4 trillion, the price level would fall—to 80 in the figure, indicated by point *C*.

As you can see, each time we change the level of output, there will be a new price level in the short run, giving us another point on the figure. If we connect all of these points with a line, we obtain the economy's *aggregate supply curve:*

AGGREGATE SUPPLY (AS) CURVE A curve indicating the price level consistent with firms' average costs and markups for any level of output over the short run.

> *The **aggregate supply curve** (or **AS curve**) tells us the price level consistent with firms' average costs and their percentage markup at any level of output over the short run.*

---

2.   This simplifying assumption is not entirely realistic. In some industries, wages will respond to changes in output, at least somewhat, even in the short run. However, assuming that the nominal wage remains constant in the short run makes our model much simpler, without affecting any of our essential conclusions.

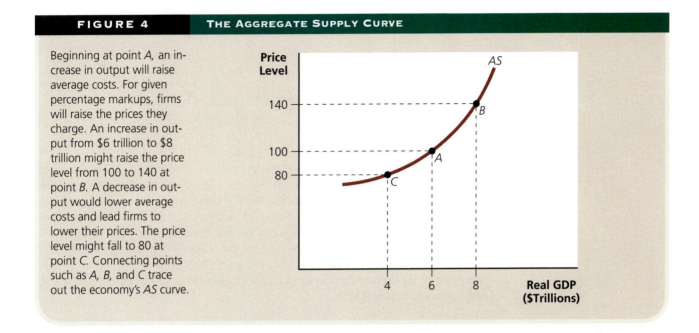

| FIGURE 4 | THE AGGREGATE SUPPLY CURVE |

Beginning at point *A*, an increase in output will raise average costs. For given percentage markups, firms will raise the prices they charge. An increase in output from $6 trillion to $8 trillion might raise the price level from 100 to 140 at point *B*. A decrease in output would lower average costs and lead firms to lower their prices. The price level might fall to 80 at point *C*. Connecting points such as *A*, *B*, and *C* trace out the economy's *AS* curve.

A more accurate name for the *AS* curve would be the "short-run-price-level-at-each-output-level" curve, but that is not a very catchy name. The *AS* curve gets its name because it *resembles* a microeconomic market supply curve. Like the supply curve for maple syrup we discussed in Chapter 3, the *AS* curve is upward sloping, and it has a price variable (the price level) on the vertical axis, and a quantity variable (total output) on the horizontal axis. But there, the similarity ends.

MOVEMENTS ALONG THE *AS* CURVE

When a change in output causes the price level to change, we *move along* the economy's *AS* curve. But what happens in the economy as we make such a move?

Look again at the *AS* curve in Figure 4. Suppose we move from point *A* to point *B* along this curve in the short run. The increase in output raises the prices of raw materials and other (nonlabor) inputs and also raises input requirements per unit of output at many firms. Both of these changes increase average costs. As long as the markup remains somewhat stable, the rise in unit costs will lead firms to raise their prices, and the price level will increase. Thus, as we move upward along the *AS* curve, we can represent what happens as follows:

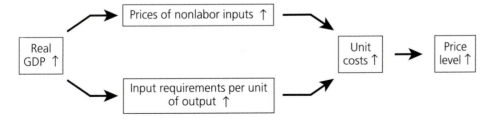

The opposite sequence of events occurs when real GDP falls, moving us downward along the *AS* curve:

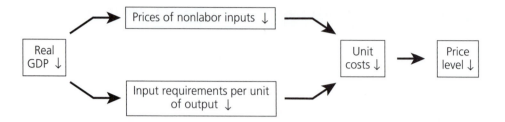

SHIFTS OF THE *AS* CURVE

When we drew the *AS* curve in Figure 4, we assumed that a number of important variables remained unchanged. In particular, we assumed that the only changes in unit costs were those caused by a change in output. But in the real world, unit costs—and the price level—sometimes change for reasons *other* than a change in output. When this occurs, unit costs—and the price level—will change at *any* level of output, so the *AS* curve will shift.

In general, we distinguish between a movement along the *AS* curve, and a shift of the curve itself, as follows:

> *When a change in real GDP* causes *the price level to change, we* move along the AS *curve. When anything other than a change in real GDP causes the price level to change, the* AS *curve itself* shifts.

Figure 5 illustrates the logic of a shift in the *AS* curve. Suppose the economy's initial *AS* curve is AS_1. Now suppose that some economic event *other* than a change in output—for the moment, we'll leave the event unnamed—causes firms to raise their prices. Then the price level will be higher at *any* level of output we might imagine, so the *AS* curve must shift *upward*—for example, to AS_2 in the figure. At an

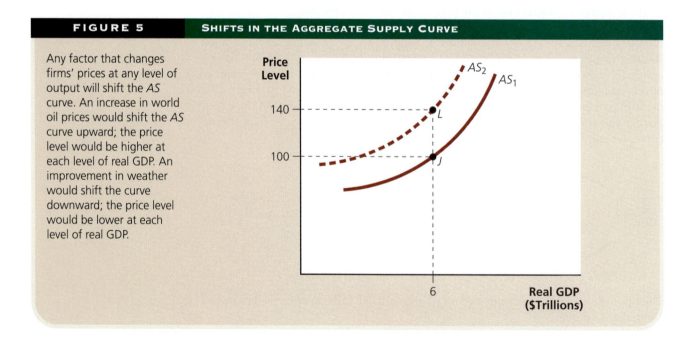

| FIGURE 5 | SHIFTS IN THE AGGREGATE SUPPLY CURVE |

Any factor that changes firms' prices at any level of output will shift the *AS* curve. An increase in world oil prices would shift the *AS* curve upward; the price level would be higher at each level of real GDP. An improvement in weather would shift the curve downward; the price level would be lower at each level of real GDP.

output level of $6 trillion, the price level would rise from 100 to 140. At any other output level, the price level would also rise.

In practice, we can distinguish two different types of events that cause the *AS* curve to shift.

SHORT-RUN CHANGES IN UNIT COSTS. You've seen that as we move along the *AS* curve, unit costs are changing *because* output is changing. But unit costs can change for other reasons, too.

Changes in World Oil Prices. Oil is traded on a world market, where prices can fluctuate even when output in the United States does not. Indeed, over the last few decades, changes in world oil prices have caused major shifts in the *AS* curve. An oil embargo by Arab oil-producing nations in 1973–1974, the Iranian revolution in 1978–1979, and Iraq's invasion of Kuwait in 1990 all caused large jumps in the price of oil. Each time, unit costs rose and, at any output level, firms charged higher prices than before. As in Figure 5, the *AS* curve shifted upward. Conversely, in 1991, the price of oil decreased dramatically. This caused unit costs to decrease at many firms, shifting the *AS* curve downward.

Changes in the Weather. Good crop-growing weather increases farmers' yields for any given amounts of land, labor, capital, and other inputs used. This decreases farms' unit costs, and the price of agricultural goods falls. Since many of these goods are final goods (such as fresh fruit and vegetables), a drop in their prices will contribute directly to a drop in the overall price level, and a downward shift of the *AS* curve. Additionally, agricultural products are important inputs in the production of many other goods. (For example, corn is an input in beef production.) Good weather thus leads to a drop in input prices for many other firms in the economy, causing their unit costs—and their prices—to decrease. For these reasons, we can expect good weather to shift the *AS* curve downward. Bad weather, which decreases crop yields, increases unit costs at any level of output, and shifts the *AS* curve upward.

CHANGES IN UNIT COSTS DURING ADJUSTMENT TO THE LONG RUN. We've assumed that, in the short run, the nominal wage remains unchanged as output changes. But as we extend our time horizon beyond the first year after a change in output, our assumption of a constant wage becomes increasingly unrealistic. As you will see a bit later, when output rises beyond its full-employment level, we can expect nominal wage rates to rise as part of the long-run adjustment process in the economy. Similarly, if output falls below potential, wage rates will eventually fall, shifting the *AS* curve, since we assume that the wage is constant when we draw the curve.

SHIFTS VERSUS MOVEMENTS ALONG THE *AS* CURVE: A SUMMARY

Table 2 summarizes how different events in the economy cause a movement along, or a shift in, the *AS* curve.

The *AS* curve tells only half of the economy's story: It shows us the price level *if* we know the level of output. The *AD* curve tells the other half of the story: It shows us the level of output *if* we know the economy's price level. In the next section, we finally put the two halves of the story together, allowing us to determine both the price level and output.

TABLE 2	EFFECTS OF KEY CHANGES ON THE AGGREGATE SUPPLY CURVE				
	Short-Run Changes in Average Costs Caused by Changes in Output		Short-Run Changes in Average Costs *Not* Caused by Changes in Output		Adjustment over the Long Run	
	Average Costs Increase	Average Costs Decrease	Average Costs Increase	Average Costs Decrease	Wage Rate Increases	Wage Rate Decreases
Effect on *AS* Curve	Movement upward along curve	Movement downward along curve	Shifts upward	Shifts downward	Shifts upward	Shifts downward

AD AND *AS* TOGETHER: SHORT-RUN EQUILIBRIUM

Where will the economy settle in the short run? That is, where is our **short-run macroeconomic equilibrium**? Figure 6 shows how to answer that question, using both the *AS* curve and the *AD* curve. If you suspect that the equilibrium is at point *E*, the intersection of these two curves, you are correct. At that point, the price level is 100, and output is $6 trillion. But it's worth thinking about *why* point *E*—and only point *E*—is our short-run equilibrium.

First, we know that the economy must be at some point on the *AD* curve. Otherwise, real GDP would not be at its equilibrium value. For example, consider point *A*, which lies to the right of the *AD* curve. At this point, the price level is 130, and output is $8 trillion. But the *AD* curve tells us that with a price level of 130, *equilibrium* output is $5.3 trillion. Thus, at point *A*, real GDP would be greater than its equilibrium value. Or—to put it another way—at point *A*, given the price level, there is not enough spending for firms to sell all of their output. As you learned two

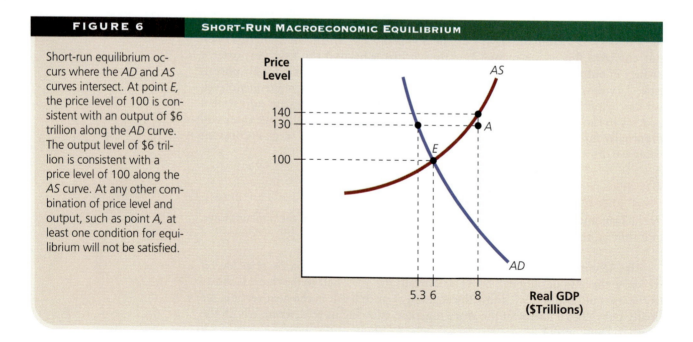

FIGURE 6   SHORT-RUN MACROECONOMIC EQUILIBRIUM

Short-run equilibrium occurs where the *AD* and *AS* curves intersect. At point *E*, the price level of 100 is consistent with an output of $6 trillion along the *AD* curve. The output level of $6 trillion is consistent with a price level of 100 along the *AS* curve. At any other combination of price level and output, such as point *A*, at least one condition for equilibrium will not be satisfied.

chapters ago, this situation cannot persist for long, since inventories would pile up and firms would be forced to cut back on their production. Thus, point *A* cannot be our short-run equilibrium.

Second, short-run equilibrium requires that the economy be operating on its *AS* curve. Otherwise, firms would not be charging the prices dictated by their average costs and the average percentage markup in the industry. For example, point *A* lies *below* the AS curve. But the *AS* curve tells us that when output is $8 trillion, based on the average percentage markup and average costs, the price level should be 140, not 130, as at point *A*. That is, prices are *too low* for equilibrium. This situation will not last long either.

We could make a similar argument for other points that are off the *AS* and *AD* curves, always coming to the same conclusion: Unless the economy is on *both* the *AS* and the *AD* curve, the price level and the level of output will change. Only when the economy is at point *E*—on *both* curves—will we have reached a sustainable level of real GDP and the price level.

WHAT HAPPENS WHEN THINGS CHANGE?

Now that we know how the short-run equilibrium is determined, and armed with our knowledge of the *AD* and *AS* curves, we are ready to put the model through its paces. In this section, we'll explore how different types of events cause the short-run equilibrium to change.

Our short-run equilibrium will change when either the *AD* curve, the *AS* curve, or both *shift*. Since the consequences for the economy are very different for shifts in the *AD* curve as opposed to shifts in the *AS* curve, economists have developed a shorthand language to distinguish between them:

> *An event that causes the* AD *curve to shift is called a **demand shock**. An event that causes the* AS *curve to shift is called a **supply shock**.*

DEMAND SHOCK Any event that causes the *AD* curve to shift.

SUPPLY SHOCK Any event that causes the *AS* curve to shift.

In much of this section, we'll explore the effects of demand shocks, both in the short run and during the adjustment process to the long run. Then, we'll take up the issue of supply shocks.

DEMAND SHOCKS IN THE SHORT RUN

Table 1, which lists the reasons for a shift in the *AD* curve, also serves as a list of demand shocks to the economy. Let's consider some examples.

AN INCREASE IN GOVERNMENT PURCHASES. You've learned that an increase in government purchases shifts the *AD* curve rightward. Now we can see how it affects the economy in the short run. Figure 7 shows the initial equilibrium at point *E*, with the price level equal to 100 and output at $6 trillion. Now, suppose that government purchases rise by $1 trillion. Table 1 tells us that the *AD* curve will shift rightward. What will happen to equilibrium GDP?

Let's suppose that the *MPC* is 0.6, so that the multiplier is $1/(1 - 0.6) = 2.5$. Also, let's suppose that the price level remains unchanged. Then a $1 trillion rise in government purchases would increase output by $2.5 trillion to $8.5 trillion. The *AD* curve would shift, and the economy would move from point *E* to point *F* in Figure 7. Would we stay there? Absolutely not. Point *F* lies below the *AS* curve, telling

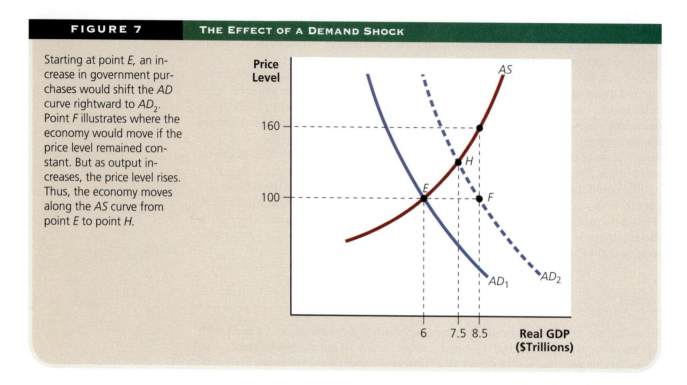

FIGURE 7   **THE EFFECT OF A DEMAND SHOCK**

Starting at point *E,* an increase in government purchases would shift the *AD* curve rightward to *AD₂.* Point *F* illustrates where the economy would move if the price level remained constant. But as output increases, the price level rises. Thus, the economy moves along the *AS* curve from point *E* to point *H.*

us that when GDP is $8.5 trillion, the price level consistent with firms' average costs and average markup is 160, not 100. Firms would soon raise prices, and this would cause a movement upward along AD_2. The price level would keep rising, and output would keep falling, until we reached point *H.* At that point—with output at $7.5 trillion—we would be on both the *AS* and *AD* curves. There would be no reason for a further rise in the price level, and no reason for a further fall in output.

However, the process we've just described is not entirely realistic. It assumes that when government purchases rise, output *first* increases (the move to point *F*), and *then* the price level rises (the move to point *H*). In reality, output and the price level tend to rise *together.* Thus, the economy would likely *slide along* the *AS* curve from point *E* to point *H.* As we move along the *AS* curve, output rises, increasing average costs and the price level. At the same time, the rise in the price level *reduces equilibrium GDP—the level of output toward which the economy is heading on the* AD *curve—from point *F* to point *H.*

We can summarize the impact of a rise in government purchases this way:

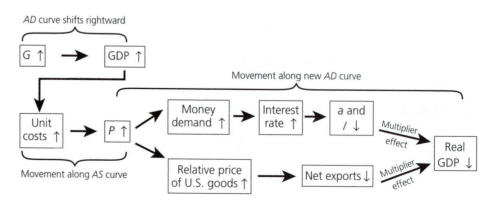

Let's step back a minute and get some perspective on this example of fiscal policy. This is the second time in this text that we've considered fiscal policy in the short run. Here, our discussion is more realistic, because we're incorporating changes in the price level—and we've seen that the effect of fiscal policy becomes weaker. More specifically, a rise in government purchases *increases* the price level. The rise in the price level causes the other components of total spending—consumption, investment, and net exports—to drop. The result is: Real GDP rises by less than the simple multiplier suggests. (In our example, a $1 trillion increase in government purchases increases equilibrium GDP by $1.5 trillion, so the multiplier would be 1.5.) Or, to put it another way, the multiplier is not really as large as our simple formula—$1/(1 - MPC)$—would suggest. However, as you can see in Figure 7, a rise in government purchases—even when we include the rise in the price level—still raises GDP in the short run.

We can summarize the impact of price-level changes this way:

> When government purchases increase, the horizontal shift of the AD curve measures how much real GDP would *increase* if the price level remained constant. But because the price level rises, real GDP rises by less than the shift in the AD curve.

Now let's switch gears into reverse: How would we illustrate the effects of a *decrease* in government purchases? In this case, the AD curve would shift *leftward,* causing the following to happen:

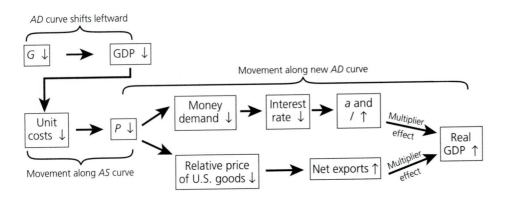

As you can see, the same sequence of events occurs in the same order, but each variable moves in the opposite direction. A decrease in government purchases decreases equilibrium GDP, but the multiplier effect is smaller because the price level falls.

AN INCREASE IN THE MONEY SUPPLY. Monetary policy stimulates the economy through a different channel than fiscal policy. But once we arrive at the AD and AS diagram, the two kinds of policy look very much alike. For example, an increase in the money supply, which reduces the interest rate, will stimulate interest-sensitive consumption and investment spending. Real GDP then increases, and the

AD curve shifts rightward, just as in Figure 7. Once output begins to rise, we have the same sequence of events as in fiscal policy: The price level rises, so the increase in GDP will be smaller. We can represent the situation as follows:

*Positive Demand Shock .
Increase in money supply*

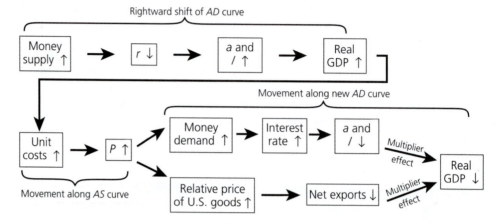

OTHER DEMAND SHOCKS. You may want to go through the other demand shocks in Table 1 on your own and explain the sequence of events in each case that causes output and the price level to change. This will help you verify the following general conclusion about demand shocks:

> *A positive demand shock—one that shifts the* AD *curve rightward—increases both real GDP and the price level in the short run. A negative demand shock—one that shifts the* AD *curve leftward—decreases both real GDP and the price level in the short run.*

AN EXAMPLE: THE GREAT DEPRESSION. The U.S. economy collapsed far more seriously during 1929 through 1933—the onset of the Great Depression—than it did at any other time in the country's history. Because the price level fell during the contraction, we know that the contraction was caused by an adverse demand shock. An adverse supply shock would have caused the price level to *rise* as GDP fell.

What specific demand shock caused the depression? This question has been debated by economists almost continuously in the 70 years since the contraction began. The candidates are numerous, and it appears that a combination of bad developments was responsible. The 1920s were a period of optimism—with high levels of investment by businesses and spending by families on houses and cars. The stock market soared. But in the fall of 1929, the bubble of optimism burst. The stock market crashed, and investment and consumption spending plummeted. Similar events occurred in other countries, and the demand for products exported by the United States fell. The Fed—then only 16 years old—reacted by cutting the money supply sharply, which added an adverse monetary shock to all of the cutbacks in spending. Each of these events contributed to a leftward shift of the *AD* curve, causing both output and the price level to fall.

DEMAND SHOCKS: ADJUSTING TO THE LONG RUN

In Figure 7, point *H* shows the new equilibrium after a positive demand shock *in the short run*—a year or so after the shock. But point *H* is not necessarily where the economy will end up in the long run. For example, suppose full-employment output is $6 trillion, and point *H*—representing an output of $7.5 trillion—is above full-employment output. Then—with employment unusually high and unemployment unusually low—business firms will have to compete to hire scarce workers, driving up the wage rate. It might take a year or more for the wage rate to rise significantly—recall our earlier list of reasons that wages adjust only slowly. But when we extend our horizon to several years or more, we must recognize that if output is beyond its potential, the wage rate will rise. Since the *AS* curve is drawn for a *given wage*, a rise in the wage rate will *shift* the curve upward, changing our equilibrium.

Alternatively, we could imagine a situation in which short-run equilibrium GDP was *below* its potential. In this case, with abnormally high unemployment, workers would compete to get scarce jobs, and eventually the wage rate would fall. Then the *AS* curve would shift downward, once again changing our equilibrium GDP.

> *In the short run, we treat the wage rate as given. But in the long run, the wage rate can change. When output is above full employment, the wage rate will rise, shifting the AS curve upward. When output is below full employment, the wage rate will fall, shifting the AS curve downward.*

SHORT-RUN VERSUS LONG-RUN OUTCOMES

Now we are ready to explore what happens over the long run in the aftermath of a demand shock. Figure 8 shows an economy in equilibrium at point *E*. We assume that the initial equilibrium is at full-employment output (Y_{FE}), since—as you are about to see—this is where the economy always ends up after the long-run adjustment process is complete. To make our results as general as possible, we'll use symbols, rather than numbers, to represent output and price levels.

FIGURE 8	THE LONG-RUN ADJUSTMENT PROCESS

Beginning at point *E*, a positive demand shock would shift the aggregate demand curve to AD_2, raising both output and the price level. At point *H*, output is above the full-employment level, Y_{FE}. Firms will compete to hire scarce workers, thereby driving up the wage rate. The higher wage rate will shift the *AS* curve to AS_2 and then to AS_3. Only when the economy returns to full-employment output at point *K* will there be no further shifts in *AS*.

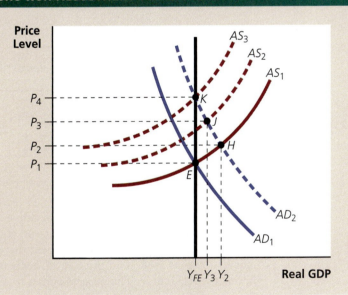

Now suppose the *AD* curve shifts rightward, say, due to an increase in government purchases. In the short run, the equilibrium moves to point *H,* with a higher price level (P_2) and a higher level of output (Y_2). Point *H* tells us where the economy will be about a year after the increase in government purchases, before the wage rate has a chance to adjust. (Remember, along any given *AS* curve, the wage rate is assumed to be constant.)

But now let's extend our analysis beyond a year. Notice that Y_2 is greater than Y_{FE}. The wage will begin to rise, raising average costs at any given output level and causing firms to raise prices. In the figure, the *AS* curve would begin shifting upward. The new aggregate supply curve, AS_2, shows where the economy might be 2 years after the shock, after the long-run adjustment process has begun. With this *AS* curve, the economy would be at point *J,* with output at Y_3. The rise in the price level has moved us along the new aggregate demand curve, AD_2.

Is point *J* our final, long-run equilibrium? No, it cannot be. At Y_3, output is *still* greater than Y_{FE}, so the wage rate will continue to rise, and the *AS* curve will continue to shift upward. At point *J,* the long-run adjustment process is not yet complete. When will the process end? Only when the wage rate stops rising—that is, only when output has returned to Y_{FE}. This occurs when the *AS* curve has shifted all the way to AS_3, moving the economy to point *K*—our new, long-run equilibrium.

As you can see, the increase in government purchases has no effect on equilibrium GDP in the long run: The economy returns to full employment, which is just where it started. This is why the long-run adjustment process is often called the economy's **self-correcting mechanism.** And this mechanism applies to any demand shock, not just an increase in government purchases:

> *If a demand shock pulls the economy away from full employment, changes in the wage rate and the price level will eventually cause the economy to correct itself and return to full-employment output.*

For a positive demand shock that shifts the *AD* curve rightward, the self-correcting mechanism works like this:

Change in short-run equilibrium

Positive demand shock → $P \uparrow$ and $Y \uparrow$

$Y > Y_{FE}$ → Wage $\uparrow$ → Unit costs $\uparrow$ → $P \uparrow$ → $Y \downarrow$ until $Y = Y_{FE}$

Long-run adjustment process

Figure 9 illustrates the case of a negative demand shock, in which the *AD* curve shifts leftward. In this case, the short-run equilibrium GDP is *below* Y_{FE}. Over the long run, unusually high unemployment drives the wage rate down, shifting the *AS* curve down as well. The price level decreases, causing equilibrium GDP to rise along the AD_2 curve. The process comes to a halt only when output returns to Y_{FE}.

(margin note)

Classical Economists

SELF-CORRECTING MECHANISM The adjustment process through which price and wage changes return the economy to full-employment output in the long run.

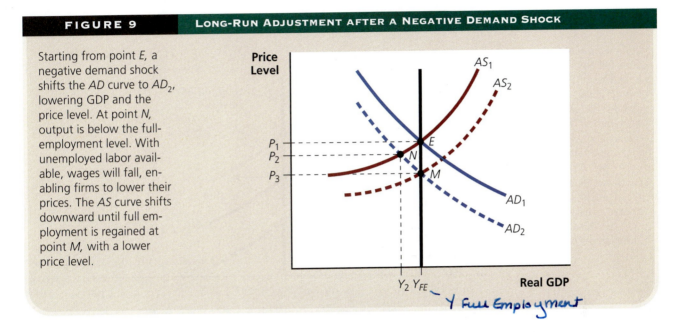

| FIGURE 9 | LONG-RUN ADJUSTMENT AFTER A NEGATIVE DEMAND SHOCK |

Starting from point *E*, a negative demand shock shifts the *AD* curve to *AD₂*, lowering GDP and the price level. At point *N*, output is below the full-employment level. With unemployed labor available, wages will fall, enabling firms to lower their prices. The *AS* curve shifts downward until full employment is regained at point *M*, with a lower price level.

Thus, in the long run, the economy moves from point *E* to point *M*, and the negative demand shock causes no change in equilibrium GDP. The complete sequence of events after a negative demand shock looks like this:

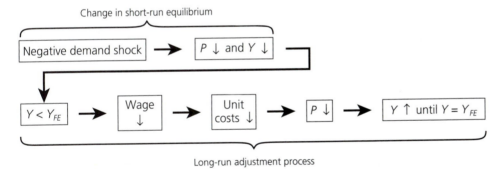

Pulling all of our observations together, we can summarize the economy's self-correcting mechanism as follows:

> *Whenever a demand shock pulls the economy away from full employment, the self-correcting mechanism will eventually bring it back. When output exceeds its full-employment level, wages will eventually rise, causing a rise in the price level and a drop in GDP until full employment is restored. When output is less than its full-employment level, wages will eventually fall, causing a drop in the price level and a rise in GDP until full employment is restored.*

THE LONG-RUN AGGREGATE SUPPLY CURVE

The self-correcting mechanism provides an important link between the economy's long-run and short-run behavior. It helps us understand why booms and recessions

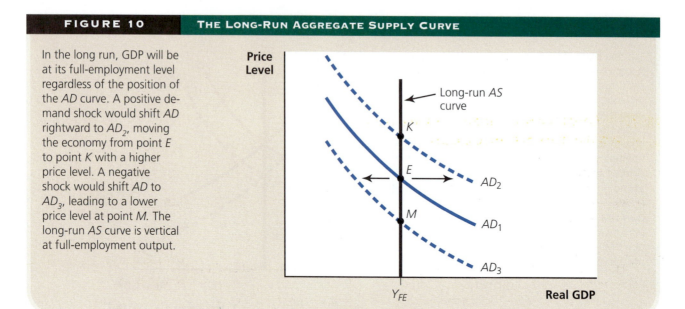

| FIGURE 10 | THE LONG-RUN AGGREGATE SUPPLY CURVE |

In the long run, GDP will be at its full-employment level regardless of the position of the *AD* curve. A positive demand shock would shift *AD* rightward to *AD₂*, moving the economy from point *E* to point *K* with a higher price level. A negative shock would shift *AD* to *AD₃*, leading to a lower price level at point *M*. The long-run *AS* curve is vertical at full-employment output.

LONG-RUN AGGREGATE SUPPLY CURVE A vertical line indicating all possible output and price-level combinations at which the economy could end up in the long run.

don't last forever. Often, however, we are primarily interested in the long-run effects of a demand shock. In these cases, we may want to skip over the self-correcting mechanism and go straight to its end result. A new version of the *AS* curve helps us do this.

Look again at Figure 8, which illustrates the impact of a positive demand shock. The economy begins at full employment at point *E,* then moves to point *H* in the short run (before the wage rate rises), and then goes to point *K* in the long run (after the rise in wages). If we skip over the short-run equilibrium, we find that the positive demand shock has moved the economy from *E* to *K,* which is vertically above *E.* That is, in the long run, the price level rises, but output remains unchanged.

Now look at Figure 10, which shows another way of illustrating this long-run result. In the figure, the vertical line is the economy's **long-run aggregate supply curve.** It summarizes all possible output and price-level combinations at which the economy could end up in the long run. It is vertical because, in the long run, GDP will be the same—full-employment output—*regardless* of the position of the *AD* curve. The price level, however, will depend on the position of the *AD* curve. In the figure, a positive demand shock would shift the *AD* curve rightward, moving the economy from *E* to *K*: a higher price level, but the same level of output. A negative demand shock would shift the *AD* curve leftward, moving the economy from *E* to *M*: a lower price level with the same level of output.[3]

Figure 10 tells us something very important about the economy: In the long run, after the self-correcting mechanism has done its job, *neither fiscal nor monetary policy has any influence on the level of output or employment.* In the long run, these policies shift the *AD* curve along a vertical *AS* curve, changing the price level, but without affecting real GDP.

3.   Of course, full-employment output can increase from year to year, as you learned in the chapter on economic growth. When the economy is growing, the long-run *AS* curve will shift rightward. In that case, the level of output at which the economy will eventually settle increases from year to year.

But notice the words "long run" in the previous statement. It can take several years before the economy returns to full employment after a demand shock. This is why governments around the world are reluctant to rely on the self-correcting mechanism alone to keep the economy on track. Instead, they often use fiscal and monetary policy in an attempt to return the economy to full employment more quickly.

SOME IMPORTANT PROVISOS ABOUT THE ADJUSTMENT PROCESS

The upward-sloping aggregate supply curve we've presented in this chapter gives a realistic picture of how the economy actually behaves after a demand shock. In the short run, positive demand shocks that increase output also raise the price level. Negative demand shocks that decrease output generally put downward pressure on prices.

However, the story we have told about what happens as we move along the *AS* curve is somewhat incomplete.

First, we made the assumption that prices are completely flexible—that they can change freely over short periods of time. In fact, however, some prices take time to adjust, just as wages take time to adjust. Firms print catalogs containing prices that are good for, say, 6 months. The regulatory commission in your state generally sets the prices of electricity, gas, water, and basic telephone service in advance for a year or more.

Second, we assumed that wages are completely *inflexible* in the short run. But in *some* industries, wages respond quickly. For example, in the construction industry, contractors hire workers for projects lasting a few months. When they can't find the workers they want, they immediately offer higher wages—they don't wait for a year.

Third, there is more to the process of recovering from a shock than the adjustment of prices and wages. During a recession, many workers lose their jobs at the same time. It takes time for those workers to become re-established in new jobs. As time passes, and job losers become job finders, the economy tends to recover. This process, in addition to the changes in wages and prices we've discussed, is part of the long-run adjustment process and helps to bring the economy back to full employment after a demand shock.

SUPPLY SHOCKS

In recent decades, supply shocks have been important sources of economic fluctuations. The most dramatic supply shocks have resulted from sudden changes in world oil prices. As you are about to see, supply shocks affect the economy differently than demand shocks.

SHORT-RUN EFFECTS OF SUPPLY SHOCKS. Figure 11 shows an example of a supply shock: an increase in world oil prices that shifts the aggregate supply curve upward, from AS_1 to AS_2. As rising oil prices increase average costs, firms will begin raising prices, and the price level will increase. The rise in the price level decreases equilibrium GDP along the *AD* curve. In the short run, the price level will continue to rise, and the economy will continue to slide leftward along its *AD* curve, until we reach the AS_2 curve at point *R*. At this point, the price level is consistent with firms' average costs and average markup (we are on the *AS* curve), and total output is equal to total spending (we are on the *AD* curve). As you can see, the short-run impact of higher oil prices is a rise in the price level and a fall in output. We call this a *negative* supply shock, because of the negative effect on output.

Economic Report of the President
Submitted to Congress early each year, the *Economic Report of the President* offers the Administration's view on the current state and future outlook for the economy. An excellent source for macroeconomic data and analysis.
http://www.access.gpo.gov/eop/index.html

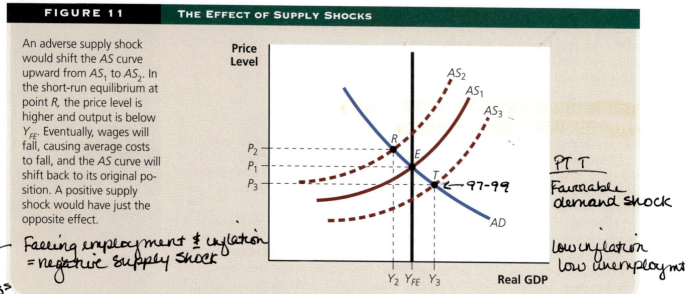

FIGURE 11   **THE EFFECT OF SUPPLY SHOCKS**

An adverse supply shock would shift the *AS* curve upward from AS_1 to AS_2. In the short-run equilibrium at point *R*, the price level is higher and output is below Y_{FE}. Eventually, wages will fall, causing average costs to fall, and the *AS* curve will shift back to its original position. A positive supply shock would have just the opposite effect.

[Handwritten notes on figure:]
PT R — Falling employment & inflation = negative supply shock
PT T — Favorable demand shock — low inflation low unemploymt
97-99

[Handwritten note left margin:]
In 70s
Substantial increase in oil prices that initially raised costs across the economy resulting in unexpected higher prices & lower employment

---

In the short run, a negative supply shock shifts the AS curve upward, decreasing output and increasing the price level.

Notice the sharp contrast between the effects of negative supply shocks and negative demand shocks in the short run. After a negative demand shock (see, for example, Figure 9), both output and the price level fall. After a negative supply shock, however, output falls, but the price level rises. Economists and journalists have coined the term **stagflation** to describe a *stag*nating economy experiencing in*flation*.

A negative supply shock causes stagflation in the short run.

STAGFLATION The combination of falling output and rising prices.

Stagflation caused by increases in oil prices is not just a theoretical possibility. Three of our recessions in the last quarter century—in 1973–1974, 1978–1979, and 1990–1991—followed increases in world oil prices. And each of these three recession also saw jumps in the price level.

Positive supply shocks increase output by shifting the *AS* curve downward, as in the shift from AS_1 to AS_3 in Figure 11. As you can see in the figure,

a positive supply shock shifts the AS curve downward, increasing output and decreasing the price level.

Unusually good weather or a drop in oil prices are examples of positive supply shocks. In addition, a positive supply shock can sometimes be caused by government policy. A few chapters ago, we discussed how the government could use tax incentives and other policies to increase the rate of economic growth. These policies work by shifting the *AS* curve downward, thus increasing output while tending to decrease the price level.

Another type of policy tries to deal directly with negative supply shocks. For example, after the oil price shocks of the 1970s, the federal government decided to accumulate a strategic reserve of oil in huge underground storage areas. The idea was to release oil from the reserve if another oil price shock hit, in order to stabilize the price. The reserve was used in this way in 1990, but it was not enough to make much difference in the world oil price.

LONG-RUN EFFECTS OF SUPPLY SHOCKS. What about the effects of supply shocks in the long run? In some cases, we need not concern ourselves with this question, because some supply shocks are temporary. For example, except in unusual cases, periods of rising oil prices are followed by periods of falling oil prices. Similarly, supply shocks caused by unusually good or bad weather, or by natural disasters, are always short lived. A temporary supply shock causes only a temporary shift in the AS curve; over the long run, the curve simply returns to its initial position, and the economy returns to full employment. In Figure 11, the AS curve would shift back from AS_2 to AS_1, and the economy would move from point R back to point E.

In other cases, however, a supply shock can last for an extended period. One example was the rise in oil prices during the 1970s, which persisted for several years. In cases like this, is there a self-correcting mechanism that brings the economy back to full employment after a long-lasting supply shock? Indeed, there is, and it is the same mechanism that brings the economy back to full employment after a demand shock.

Look again at Figure 11. At point R, output is below full-employment output. In the long run, as workers compete for scarce jobs, the wage rate will decline. This will cause the AS curve to shift *downward*. The wage will continue to fall until the economy returns to full employment; that is, until we are back at point E.

> *In the long run, the economy self-corrects after a supply shock, just as it does after a demand shock. When output differs from its full-employment level, the wage rate changes, and the* AS *curve shifts until full employment is restored.*

SHORT-RUN VERSUS LONG-RUN OUTCOMES

THE RECESSION AND RECOVERY OF 1990–1992

The aggregate demand and aggregate supply curves are not just graphs and concepts; they are tools that help us understand important economic events. In this section, we'll look at how we can use these tools to understand our most recent recession.

Our story begins in mid-1990, when Iraq invaded Kuwait, a major oil producer. During this conflict, Kuwait's oil was taken off the world market, and so was Iraq's. The reduction in oil supplies resulted in an immediate and substantial increase in the price of oil, a key input to many industries. Panel (a) of Figure 12 shows that the price of oil rose from $14 to $27 per barrel in 1990.

Figure 13 shows our AS–AD analysis of the shock. Initially, the economy was on both AD_1 and AS_1, with equilibrium at point E and output at its full-employment level. Then, the oil price shock shifted the AS curve upward, to AS_2. As the short-run equilibrium moved to point R, real GDP fell and the price level rose. Going back to Figure 12, we see that this is indeed what happened. Panel (b) shows that real GDP did fall in the period after the shock, from $6.175 trillion in mid-1990 to about $6.05 trillion in early 1991. In panel (c), you can see that the Consumer Price Index rose especially rapidly during this period. Late 1990 through early 1991 was clearly a period of stagflation.

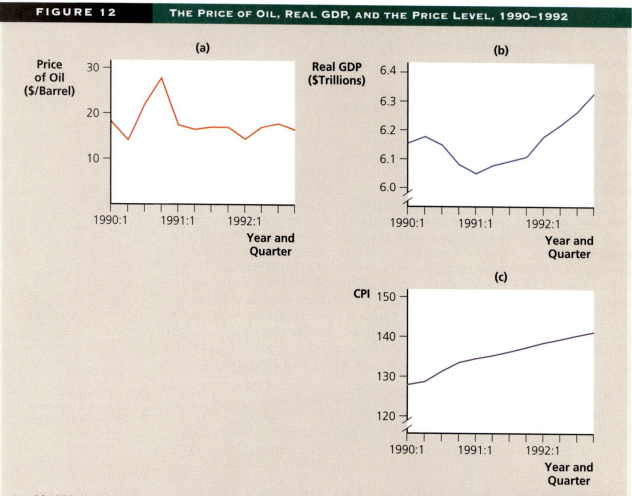

| FIGURE 12 | THE PRICE OF OIL, REAL GDP, AND THE PRICE LEVEL, 1990–1992 |

In mid-1990, Kuwaiti and Iraqi oil was taken off the world market, resulting in a substantial increase in the world price of oil, as shown in panel (a). U.S. GDP fell, and the Consumer Price Index rose. When oil prices fell in 1991, GDP recovered.

Now let's return to our *AS–AD* analysis in Figure 13. At point *R*, output was below its full-employment level. If the price of oil had remained high, our theory tells us, the self-correcting mechanism would have begun to work: Falling wages would have decreased average costs, shifting the *AS* curve back down to *AS₁*. However, the self-correcting mechanism wasn't needed in this case: As you can see in Figure 12, the oil price shock was temporary. Oil prices fell back down in early 1991, shifting the *AS* curve back to *AS₁*. In panel (b) of Figure 12, you can see that real GDP began to recover in early 1991, and continued moving back to its full-employment level in the succeeding years.

But something looks fishy here. In our *AS–AD* analysis, the price level should have risen when the negative supply shock hit and then gradually *fallen* back to its original level when the shock proved temporary. But panel (c) of Figure 12 shows that this prediction was not borne out by the experience of 1990–1992. Instead, while the price level rose more rapidly in the year after the shock, it *continued to rise* in the next 2 years as the economy self-corrected. Have we missed something?

| **FIGURE 13** | **AN *AD–AS* ANALYSIS OF THE OIL PRICE SHOCK** |

Beginning at point *E*, the increase in the world price of oil shifted the *AS* curve from *AS₁* to *AS₂*. Output fell and the price level rose. When oil prices fell in 1991, the *AS* curve shifted back to *AS₁*. Because the Fed simultaneously increased the money supply, the *AD* curve shifted rightward. By 1992, output was back to Y_{FE}, but with a higher price level at point *T*.

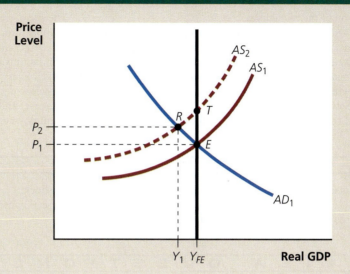

Yes, we have. In our analysis of demand and supply shocks in this chapter, we've been focusing on only one change at a time. And here, too, we've been looking at the events of 1990–1992 by considering *only* the shift in the *AS* curve. In particular, as the *AS* curve shifted upward and then downward, we've assumed that the *AD* curve stayed put.

But that is not what happened in the early 1990s. Instead, in the period after the shock, the Fed decided to intervene. Rather than wait for the self-correcting mechanism and endure a painful recession, the Fed increased the money supply, shifting the *AD* curve rightward. Thus, instead of moving from point *R* back to *E*, the economy moved from *R* to *T*. (You can draw in the new *AD* curve to help you see the move.) Output rose, but the price level rose as well.

S U M M A R Y

The model of aggregate supply and demand explains how the price level and output are determined in the short run—a period of a year or so following a change in the economy—and how the economy adjusts over longer time periods as well.

The aggregate demand (*AD*) curve shows how changes in the price level affect equilibrium real GDP. A change in the price level has two effects on output. First, it shifts the money demand curve and alters the interest rate in the money market. The change in the interest rate, in turn, affects interest-sensitive forms of spending, triggers the multiplier process, and leads to a new level of equilibrium real GDP. The second effect works through the foreign sector: A change in the price level changes the price of U.S. goods relative to foreign goods, which causes a change in net exports. The change in net exports, in turn, triggers the multiplier process and leads to a new level of equilibrium GDP.

A lower price level means a higher equilibrium real GDP, and a higher price level means lower GDP. The downward-sloping *AD* curve is drawn for given values of government spending, taxes, autonomous consumption spending, investment spending, the money supply, and the public's preferences for holding money and bonds. Changes in any of those factors will cause the *AD* curve to shift.

The aggregate supply (*AS*) curve summarizes the way changes in output affect the price level. To draw the *AS* curve, we assume that firms set the price of individual products as a markup over their average cost, and that the economy's average markup is determined by competitive conditions. We also assume that the nominal wage rate is fixed in the short run. As we move upward along the *AS* curve, a rise in real GDP—by raising average costs—causes the price level to increase. When anything other than a change in real GDP causes the price level to change, the entire *AS* curve shifts.

AD and *AS* together determine real GDP and the price level. The economy must be on the *AD* curve or real GDP would not be at its equilibrium level. It must be on the *AS* curve or firms would not be charging prices dictated by their average costs and markups. Both conditions are satisfied at the intersection of the two curves.

The AD–AS equilibrium can be disturbed by a demand shock. An increase in government purchases, for example, shifts the AD curve rightward. As a result, the price level rises, and so does real GDP. In the long run, if GDP is above potential, wages will rise. This causes average costs to rise and shifts the AS curve upward. Eventually, GDP will return to potential and the only long-run result of the demand shock is

a higher price level. This implies that the economy's long-run aggregate supply curve is vertical at potential output.

The short-run AD–AS equilibrium can also be disturbed by a supply shock, such as an increase in world oil prices. With average costs higher at each level of output, the AS curve shifts upward, decreasing real GDP and increasing the price level. Eventually, the shock will be self-correcting: With output below potential, the wage rate will fall, average costs will decrease, and the AS curve will shift back downward until full employment is restored.

K E Y   T E R M S

aggregate demand (AD) curve

aggregate supply (AS) curve

short-run macroeconomic equilibrium

demand shock

supply shock

self-correcting mechanism

long-run aggregate supply curve

stagflation

R E V I E W   Q U E S T I O N S

1. What causal relationship does the aggregate demand curve describe? Why is the AD curve downward sloping?

2. "Only changes in spending shift the aggregate demand curve." True or false? Explain.

3. List three reasons why a change in output affects average costs and subsequently the price level.

4. What causal relationship does the aggregate supply curve describe? Why is the AS curve upward sloping?

5. Why does equilibrium occur only where the AD and AS curves intersect?

6. What is meant by the economy's *self-correcting mechanism* after a demand shock?

7. What is the long-run aggregate supply curve? Why is it vertical?

8. How does an economy recover from a negative supply shock?

P R O B L E M S   A N D   E X E R C I S E S

1. Illustrate graphically how an increase in the use of credit cards affects the interest rate and the aggregate demand curve. (Assume that the price level does not change.)

2. Describe how an increase in taxes affects real GDP and the aggregate demand curve. (Assume that the price level does not change.) What other spending changes would result in these same effects?

3. Suppose firms become pessimistic about the future and consequently investment spending falls. Describe the short-run effects on GDP and the price level. If the price level were constant, how would your answer change?

4. Explain, using graphs, the short-run effect of a decrease in the money supply on GDP and the price level. What is the effect in the long run? Assume the economy begins at full employment.

5. A new government policy successfully lowers average costs to firms. What are the short-run and the long-run effects of such a policy? (Assume full-employment output does not change.)

6. Go to the Bureau of Economic Analysis (BEA) Web site at http://www.bea.doc.gov/ and follow "GDP and related data" for links to National Accounts Data. Then go to "Selected NIPA Tables" (HTML) for links to data on real GDP and price indexes for GDP.

   a. Find real GDP and the price index in the two most recent years for which the data are available.

   b. On a diagram with real GDP along the horizontal axis and the price level on the vertical axis, plot the data points for each year.

   c. Draw AD and AS curves for each year that are consistent with the points you plotted.

   d. Describe shifts in AD and/or AS that could explain the changes in real GDP and the price level that have occurred. Has the long-run AS curve shifted?

CHALLENGE QUESTIONS

1. Suppose that wages were slow to adjust downward but rapidly adjust upward. What would the *AS* curve look like? How would this affect the economy's adjustment to spending shocks (compared to the analysis given in the chapter)?

2. Because of increases in the capital stock, technological change, and population growth, full-employment output grows every year. Using this fact, illustrate the long-run effects of a positive spending shock. (Hint: What happens to the long-run *AS* curve over time?)

CHAPTER 18

COMPARATIVE ADVANTAGE AND THE GAINS FROM TRADE

Consumers love bargains. And the rest of the world offers U.S. consumers bargains galore—cars from Japan, computer memory chips from Korea, shoes from China, tomatoes from Mexico, lumber from Canada, and sugar from the Caribbean. But Americans' purchases of foreign-made goods have always been a controversial subject. Should we let these bargain goods into the country? Consumers certainly benefit when we do let them in. But don't cheap foreign goods threaten the jobs of American workers and the profits of American producers? How do we balance the interests of specific workers and producers on the one hand with the interests of consumers in general? These questions are important not just in the United States, but in every country of the world.

Over the post–World War II period, there has been a worldwide movement toward a policy of *free trade*—the unhindered movement of goods and services across national boundaries. A new international body, the World Trade Organization (WTO), has been created as a forum for negotiations to remove restrictions on trade all over the world.

Thanks to the WTO and earlier efforts, import taxes, import limitations, and all kinds of crafty regulations designed to keep out imports are gradually falling away. In addition, a new mechanism for settling trade disputes has been put in place. At the end of 1998, 133 countries belonged to the WTO. And some 30 other countries, including China and Russia, seemed eager to join the free-trade group.

But while many barriers have come down, others are being put up. Asian governments have been dragging their feet on allowing U.S. firms to sell financial services there. The United States has renewed its long-standing quota on sugar imports and—in early 1999—was considering moves to reduce imports of steel from Russia, Brazil, and Japan. Europeans have restricted the sale of American satellite communications services. Poor countries have imposed tariffs on computers, semiconductors, and software exported by rich countries. Rich countries have announced their intention to maintain, at least through the year 2005, existing quotas on textiles and clothing sold by poor countries.

Looking at the contradictory mix of trade policies that exist in the world, we are left to wonder: Is free international trade a good thing that makes us better off, or is it bad for us and something that should be kept in check? In this chapter, you'll learn some of the tools economists use to analyze the issues surrounding international trade.

THE LOGIC OF FREE TRADE

Many of us like the idea of being self-reliant. A very few even prefer to live by themselves in a remote region of Alaska or the backcountry of Montana. But consider the defects of self-sufficiency: If you lived all by yourself, you would be poor. You could not *export* or sell to others any part of your own production, nor could you *import* or buy from others anything they have produced. You would be limited to consuming the goods and services that you produced. Undoubtedly, the food, clothing, and housing you would manage to produce by yourself would be small in quantity and poor in quality—nothing like the items you currently enjoy. And there would be many things you could not get at all—electricity, television, cars, airplane trips, or the penicillin that could save your life.

The defects of the self-sufficient state explain why most people choose *not* to be self-sufficient, but rather to specialize and trade with each other. In Chapter 2, you learned the *basic principle of specialization and exchange:*

> *Specialization and exchange enable us to enjoy greater production and higher living standards than would otherwise be possible. As a result, all economies exhibit high degrees of specialization and exchange.*

This principle applies not just to individuals, but also to *groups* of individuals, such as those living within the boundaries that define cities, counties, states, or nations. That is, just as we all benefit when *individuals* specialize and exchange with each other, so too can we benefit when *groups of* individuals specialize in producing different goods and services and exchange them with other *groups.*

Imagine what would happen if the residents of your state switched from a policy of open trading with other states to one of self-sufficiency, refusing to import anything from "foreign states" or to export anything to them. Such an arrangement would be preferable to individual self-sufficiency—at least there would be specialization and trade *within* the state. But the elimination of trading between states would surely result in many sacrifices. Lacking the necessary inputs for their production, for instance, your state might have to do without bananas, cotton, or tires. And the goods that *were* made in your state would likely be produced inefficiently. For example, while residents of Vermont *could* drill for oil, and Texans *could* produce maple syrup, they could do so only at great cost of resources.

Thus, it would make no sense to insist on the economic self-sufficiency of each of the 50 states. And the founders of the United States knew this. They placed prohibitions against tariffs, quotas, and other barriers to interstate commerce right in the U.S. Constitution. The people of Vermont and Texas are vastly better off under free trade among the states than they would be if each state were self-sufficient.

What is true for states is also true for entire nations. The members of the WTO have carried the argument to its ultimate conclusion: National specialization and exchange can expand world output through free *international* trade. Such trade involves the movement of goods and services across national boundaries. Goods and services produced domestically, but sold abroad, are called **exports;** those produced abroad, but consumed domestically, are called **imports.** The long-term goal of the WTO is to remove all barriers to exports and imports in order to encourage among nations the specialization and trade that has been so successful within nations.

EXPORTS Goods and services produced domestically, but sold abroad.

IMPORTS Goods and services produced abroad but consumed domestically.

THE THEORY OF COMPARATIVE ADVANTAGE

Economists who first considered the benefits of international trade focused on a country's *absolute advantage*.

ABSOLUTE ADVANTAGE The ability to produce a good using fewer resources than another country.

> *A country has an **absolute advantage** in a good when it can produce it using fewer resources than another country.*

As the early economists saw it, the citizens of every nation could improve their economic welfare by specializing in the production of goods in which they had an absolute advantage and exporting them to other countries. In turn, they would import goods from countries that had an absolute advantage in those goods.

Way back in 1817, however, the British economist David Ricardo disagreed. Absolute advantage, he argued, was not a necessary ingredient for mutually beneficial international trade. The key was *comparative advantage:*

COMPARATIVE ADVANTAGE The ability to produce a good at a lower opportunity cost than elsewhere.

> *A nation has a **comparative advantage** in producing a good if it can produce it with a lower opportunity cost than some other country.*

Notice the difference between the definitions of absolute advantage and comparative advantage. While absolute advantage in a good is based on the resources used to produce it, comparative advantage is based on the *opportunity cost* of producing it. And we measure the opportunity cost of producing a good not by the resources used to produce it, but rather by the *other goods* whose production must be sacrificed.

Ricardo argued that a potential trading partner could be absolutely inferior in the production of every single good—requiring more resources per unit of each good than any other country—and still have a comparative advantage in some good. The comparative advantage would arise because the country was *less* inferior at producing some goods than others. Likewise, a country that had an absolute advantage in producing everything could—contrary to common opinion—still benefit from trade. It would have a comparative advantage only in some—but not all—goods.

 **OPPORTUNITY COST**

> *Mutually beneficial trade between any two countries is possible whenever one country is relatively better at producing a good than the other country is. Being relatively better means having the ability to produce a good at a lower opportunity cost—that is, at a lower sacrifice of other goods forgone.*

TABLE 1	COSTS OF PRODUCTION	
	Per Camera	**Per Computer**
Germany	DM125	DM2,500
United States	$100	$1,000

OPPORTUNITY COST AND COMPARATIVE ADVANTAGE

To illustrate Ricardo's insight, let's consider a hypothetical world of two countries, Germany and the United States. Both are producing only two goods, cameras and computers. Could they better themselves by trading with one another? Ricardo would have us look at opportunity costs. To find them, let's consider what it costs to produce these goods in each country. To keep our example simple, we assume that the costs per unit—for both cameras and computers—remain the same no matter how many units are produced.

The relevant cost information is provided in Table 1. Since German firms keep books in deutsche marks (DM) and American firms in dollars, our cost data are expressed accordingly. We can use the data in the table to calculate the opportunity cost of producing more of each good in each country.

First, suppose Germany were to produce one additional computer. Then it would have to divert DM2,500 of resources from the camera industry. This, in turn, would require Germany to produce fewer cameras. How many fewer? Since each camera uses up DM125 in resources, using DM2500 for one computer would require producing DM2,500/DM125 = 20 fewer cameras.

In the United States, producing an additional computer requires diverting $1,000 of resources from camera making, losing $1,000/$100, or 10 cameras. Thus, the U.S. opportunity cost is smaller (10 < 20), and *the United States has a comparative advantage in making computers.*

We can do the same calculation for cameras, determining the opportunity cost in terms of *computers forgone.* Our computations are summarized in Table 2. The numbers allow us to see which country has the lower opportunity cost in which good. Thus, Germany has the comparative advantage in cameras, and the United States has it in computers.

Now we can use our conclusions about comparative advantage to show how both countries can gain from trade. The explanation comes in two steps. First, we show that if Germany could be persuaded to produce more cameras and the United States more computers, the world's total production of goods will increase. Second, we show how each country can come out ahead by trading with the other.

SPECIALIZATION AND WORLD PRODUCTION

According to Table 2, if Germany produced say, 20 more cameras, it would have to sacrifice the production of one computer as resources were shifted between the two

TABLE 2	OPPORTUNITY COSTS	
	Per Camera	**Per Computer**
Germany	1/20 computer	20 cameras
United States	1/10 computer	10 cameras

TABLE 3	A SMALL CHANGE IN PRODUCTION	
	Camera Production	**Computer Production**
Germany	+20	−1
United States	−10	+1
World	+10	0

industries. If the United States, simultaneously, produced one extra computer, it would have to sacrifice 10 cameras—again because fully employed resources would have to be moved. But note: As a result of even this small change, the world output of cameras would increase by 10, while computer production would be unchanged—despite the fact that no more resources were used than before. Table 3 summarizes the changes.

The extra cameras in this example represent the gain from specializing according to comparative advantage—a gain, as the next section will show, that the two trading partners will share. It is also the kind of gain that, multiplied a million times, lies behind the substantial benefits countries enjoy from free trade.

The particular example given here is not the only one that can be derived from our table of opportunity costs. For example, if Germany produced 10 more cameras and, therefore, cut back by half a computer, the world output of cameras would be unchanged, while computer production would rise. Other examples illustrate simultaneous increases in the world output of both goods. As an exercise, try to create such an example on your own.

In all cases, however, the key insight remains the same:

SPECIALIZATION AND EXCHANGE

> *If countries specialize according to comparative advantage, a more efficient use of given resources occurs. As a result, the world output of at least one good rises, without decreasing that of any other good.*

GAINS FROM INTERNATIONAL TRADE

Now we proceed to the second step in Ricardo's case, showing that both sides can gain from trade. In our example so far, each country would have more of one good but *less* of another. However, because of the increase in *world* output, international trade flows could be arranged so that each country would share in the gain in total output. Many different arrangements are possible; here is one that would apportion the world output gain equally:

> **Germany exports (and the U.S. imports) 15 cameras.**
>
> **Germany imports (and the U.S. exports) 1 computer.**

Table 4 summarizes the end result. The second column in the table shows the changes in *production* in each country. The third column shows how much of each good is exported or imported. Finally, the last column shows how much more of each good the citizens of each country end up with. In our example, Germany and the United States each end up with 5 additional cameras, with no sacrifice in computers. Notice that if we add up these gains from trade (10 cameras total), the sum is precisely equal to the gain in world output noted earlier. This is no coincidence: With only two countries in our example, when world output rises by 10 cameras, one country or the other must end up with the additional cameras.

TABLE 4	THE GAINS FROM SPECIALIZATION AND TRADE		
	Production	**Loss from Exports (–) or Gain from Imports (+)**	**Net Gain**
Germany			
Cameras	+20	–15	+5
Computers	–1	+1	none
United States			
Cameras	–10	+15	+5
Computers	+1	–1	none

It is worth reiterating that the mutually beneficial changes summarized in Table 4 are based on *comparative* advantage, not *absolute* advantage. To make this point even clearer, let's look at the information in Table 1 from another perspective. Instead of thinking about the *cost* of producing a good, we'll look directly at the resources used up in making it. To keep things simple, we'll suppose that the only resource countries use in production is labor. Further, we'll suppose arbitrarily that an hour of labor costs DM10 in Germany and $10 in the U.S. Then the DM125 it costs to make a camera in Germany would mean that 12.5 hours of labor are needed to make a camera there, since 12.5 hours × DM10 per hour = DM125. Thus, in Table 5, we enter 12.5 hours for the labor needed per camera in Germany.

Making similar calculations, we find that it takes 250 hours to make a computer in Germany; and in the United States, it takes 10 hours to make a camera and 100 hours to make a computer.

Now it's easy to see that the United States has an absolute advantage—using less input per unit of output than Germany—in the production of *both* goods. Would specialization and mutually beneficial trade still be possible? Very much so. The opportunity cost data in Table 2 would be unchanged (verify this on your own), and so would be all the conclusions we derived from that table. Thus,

> *as long as opportunity costs differ, specialization and trade can be beneficial to all involved. This remains true regardless of whether the parties involved are nations, states, counties, or individuals. It remains true even if one party holds an all-round absolute advantage or disadvantage.*

 **SPECIALIZATION AND EXCHANGE**

THE TERMS OF TRADE

In our ongoing example, Germany exports 15 cameras in exchange for 1 computer. This exchange ratio (15 cameras for 1 computer) is known as the **terms of trade**. Our particular choice of 15 to 1 for the terms of trade happened to apportion the gain in world output equally between the two countries. (See Table 4.) With different terms of trade, however, the benefit would have been distributed unequally. We

TERMS OF TRADE The ratio at which a country can trade domestically produced products for foreign-produced products.

TABLE 5	LABOR INPUTS NEEDED	
	Per Camera	**Per Computer**
Germany	12.5 hours	250 hours
United States	10 hours	100 hours

won't consider here precisely *how* the terms of trade are determined (it is a matter of supply and demand), but we can establish the limits within which they must fall.

Look again at Table 2. Germany would never give up *more than* 20 cameras to import 1 computer. Why not? Because it could always get 1 computer for 20 cameras *domestically*, by shifting resources into computer production.

Similarly, the United States would never export a computer for *fewer than* 10 cameras, since it can substitute 1 computer for 10 cameras domestically (again, by switching resources between the industries). Therefore, the equilibrium terms of trade must lie *between* 20 cameras for 1 computer and 10 cameras for 1 computer. Outside of that range, one of the two countries would refuse to trade. Note that in our example, we assume terms of trade of 15 cameras for 1 computer—well within the acceptable range.

TURNING POTENTIAL GAINS INTO ACTUAL GAINS

So far in this chapter, we have discussed the *potential* advantages of specialization and trade among nations, but one major question remains: How is that potential realized? Who or what causes a country to shift resources from some industries into others and then to trade in the world market?

Do foreign trade ministers at WTO meetings decide who should produce and trade each product? Does some group of omniscient and benevolent people in Washington and other world capitals make all the necessary arrangements? Not at all. Within the framework of the WTO, government officials are supposed to create the environment for free trade, but they do not decide who has a comparative advantage in what, or what should be produced in this or that country. In today's market economies around the world, it is individual consumers and firms who decide to buy things—at home or abroad. By their joint actions, they determine where things are produced and who trades with whom. That is, the promise of Ricardo's theory is achieved through markets. People only have to do what comes naturally: buy products at the lowest price. Without their knowing it, they are promoting Ricardo's dream!

Let's see how this works. In the absence of trade, the prices of goods within a country will generally reflect their opportunity costs. That is, if producing one more computer in the United States requires the sacrifice of 10 cameras, then the price of a computer should be about 10 times the price of a camera.

Let's imagine the situation before trade between two countries begins. We'll suppose that prices in each country are precisely equal to the costs of production in each country, as given earlier in Table 1. These prices are shown again in Table 6, in bold type. For the moment, ignore the prices in parentheses.

TABLE 6	PRICES IN GERMANY AND THE UNITED STATES WITH AN EXCHANGE RATE OF DM2 FOR $1	
	Per Camera	**Per Computer**
Germany	**DM125** ($62.50)	**DM2,500** ($1,250)
United States	**$100** (DM200)	**$1,000** (DM2,000)

Now suppose we allow trade to open up between the two countries. Consider the decision of a U.S. consumer, who can choose to purchase cameras and computers in either country. To buy goods from German producers, Americans must pay in deutsche marks. In order to obtain that currency, Americans must go to the *foreign exchange market* and trade their dollars for deutsche marks at the going **exchange rate**—the rate at which one currency can be exchanged for another. Let's assume that the exchange rate is 2 deutsche marks for 1 dollar.

Now, at this exchange rate, an American can purchase a German camera priced at DM125 by exchanging $62.50 for DM125 and then buying the camera. Thus, to the American, the *dollar price of a German camera* is $62.50, which appears in parentheses below the price in deutsche marks. Similarly, the dollar price of a DM2,500 German computer is $1,250—also in parentheses. Looking at the table, you can see that, to an American, German cameras at $62.50 are cheaper than U.S. cameras at $100, so *Americans will prefer to buy cameras from Germany.* But when it comes to computers, we reach the opposite conclusion: A U.S. computer at $1,000 is cheaper than a German computer at $1,250, so *Americans will prefer to buy computers in the United States.*

Now take the viewpoint of a German consumer who can buy U.S. or German goods. To buy U.S. goods, German consumers will need dollars, which they can obtain at the going exchange rate: DM2 for $1. The bottom row of the table shows the prices in deutsche marks of the U.S. goods, in parentheses. German cameras at DM125 are cheaper than U.S. cameras at DM200, while U.S. computers at DM2,000 are cheaper than German computers at DM2,500. Thus, *a German, just like an American, will prefer to buy computers from the United States and cameras from Germany.*

Now suppose that trade in cameras and computers had previously been prohibited, but is now opened up. Everyone would buy cameras in Germany and computers in the United States, and the process of specialization according to comparative advantage would begin. German camera makers would expand their production, while German computer makers would suffer losses, lay off workers, and even exit the industry. Unemployed computer workers in Germany would find jobs in the camera industry. Analogous changes would occur in the United States, as production of computers expanded there. These changes in production patterns would continue until Germany specialized in camera production and the United States specialized in computer production—that is, until each country produced according to its comparative advantage.

Our example illustrates a general conclusion:

When consumers are free to buy at the lowest prices, they will naturally buy a good from the country that has a comparative advantage in producing it. The country's industries respond by producing more of that good and less of other goods. In this way, countries naturally tend to specialize in those goods in which they have a comparative advantage.[1]

EXCHANGE RATE The amount of one currency that is traded for one unit of another currency.

---

1.   Something may be bothering you about the way we reached this conclusion: We merely *asserted* that the exchange rate was DM2 for $1. What if we had chosen another exchange rate? With a little work, you can verify that at any exchange rate between DM1.25 for $1 and DM2.5 for $1, our conclusion will still hold: Countries will automatically produce according to their comparative advantage. Further, you can verify that if the exchange rate went *beyond* those bounds, the residents of both countries would want to buy both goods from just one country. This would increase the demand for deutsche marks and force the exchange rate back between DM1.25 for $1 and DM2.5 for $1.

SOME IMPORTANT PROVISOS

Look back at Tables 3 and 4. There you saw how a small change in production—one less computer in Germany, and one more in the United States—caused world production of cameras to rise, with no sacrifice of computers. But if this can happen once, why not again? . . . and again? . . . and again? In fact, our simple example seems to suggest that countries should specialize *completely*, producing *only* the goods in which they have a comparative advantage. In our example, it seems that Germany should get out of computer production *entirely*, and the United States should get out of camera production *entirely*.

But the real world is much more complicated than our simplified examples might suggest. Despite divergent opportunity costs, sometimes it does *not* make sense for two countries to trade with each other, or it might make sense to trade, but *not* completely specialize. Following are some real-world considerations that can lead to reduced trade or incomplete specialization.

COSTS OF TRADING. If there are high transportation costs or high costs of making deals across national boundaries, trade may be reduced and even become prohibitively expensive. High transportation costs are especially important for perishable goods, such as ice cream, which must be shipped frozen, and most personal services, such as haircuts, eye exams, and restaurant meals. None of these are typically traded internationally. (Imagine the travel cost for an American barber who would like to sell a haircut to a resident of Germany.)

The costs of making deals are generally higher for international trade than for trade within domestic borders. For one thing, different laws must be dealt with. In addition, there are different business and marketing customs to be mastered. High transportation costs and high costs of making deals help explain why nations continue to produce some goods in which they do not have a comparative advantage and why there is less than complete specialization in the world.

One final cost of international trade arises from the need to exchange domestic for foreign currency. In international trade, either importers or exporters typically take some risk that the exchange rate might change. For example, suppose a U.S. importer of German cameras agrees in advance to pay DM10,000 for a shipment of cameras. At the time the agreement is made, the exchange rate is half a dollar per deutsche mark, so the importer figures the shipment will cost him $5,000. But suppose that, before he pays, the exchange rate changes to $0.75 per deutsche mark. Then the camera shipment—for which the importer must still pay DM10,000—will cost him $7,500. The rise in costs could wipe out the importer's profit or even cause him to lose money on the shipment.

The risk and other costs of dealing with foreign currency transactions were a primary reason behind the creation of a new, single currency—the *Euro*—to be shared by 11 European countries, including France, Germany, Holland, and Italy. The Euro was introduced into commerce in early 1999. By July 2002, the separate national currencies of the "Euroland" countries will be phased out of existence, and the French Franc, the Italian Lira, the German mark and several other national currencies will become relics of the past. The move to a single currency will eliminate all the costs and risks of foreign exchange transactions from intra-European trade. This should enable countries to specialize more completely according to their comparative advantage, and increase the gains from trade even further.

SIZES OF COUNTRIES. Our earlier example featured two large economies capable of fully satisfying each other's demands. But sometimes a very large country, such as the United States, trades with a very small one, such as the Pacific island nation of Tonga. If the smaller country specialized completely, its output would be insufficient to fully meet the demand of the larger one. The larger country would continue to produce both goods and would specialize only in the sense of producing *more* of its comparative-advantage good rather than *nothing but* that good. The smaller country would specialize completely. This helps to explain why the United States continues to produce bananas, even though we do so at much higher opportunity cost than many small Latin American nations.

INCREASING OPPORTUNITY COST. In all of our tables, we have assumed that opportunity cost remains constant as production changes. For example, in Table 2, the opportunity cost of a camera in Germany is 1/20th of a computer—regardless of how many cameras or computers Germany makes. But more typically, the opportunity cost of a good rises as more of it is produced. (Why? You may want to review the law of increasing opportunity cost in Chapter 2.) In that case, each step on the road to specialization would change the opportunity cost. A point might be reached—before complete specialization—in which opportunity costs become *equal* in the two countries, and trading for mutual gain would no longer be possible. (Remember: Opportunity costs must *differ* in the two countries in order for trade to be mutually beneficial.) In the end, while trading will occur, there will not be complete specialization. Instead, each country will produce both goods, just as Germany and the United States each produce cameras *and* computers in the real world.

GOVERNMENT BARRIERS TO TRADE. Governments can enact barriers to trading. In some cases, these barriers increase trading costs; in other cases, they make trade impossible. We'll consider government-imposed barriers a bit later in the chapter.

THE SOURCES OF COMPARATIVE ADVANTAGE

We've just seen how nations can benefit from specialization and trade when they have comparative advantages. But what determines comparative advantage in the first place? In many cases, the answer is differences in natural resources. The top part of Table 7 contains some examples. Saudi Arabia has a comparative advantage in the production of oil because it has oil fields with billions of barrels of oil that can be extracted at low cost. Canada is a major exporter of timber because its climate and geography make its land more suitable for growing trees than other crops. Canada is a good example of comparative advantage without absolute advantage—it grows a lot of timber not because it can do so using fewer resources than other countries, but because its land is even more poorly suited to growing other crops.

The bottom part of Table 7 shows examples of international specialization in which comparative advantage arises from some cause *other* than natural resources. Japan has a huge comparative advantage in making automobiles—over 40 percent of the world's automobiles are made there. And that number would be even larger, except for laws that limit the import of Japanese cars into Europe. Yet none of the natural resources needed to make cars are available in Japan; the iron ore, coal, and oil that provide the basic ingredients for cars are all imported.

TABLE 7	EXAMPLES OF NATIONAL SPECIALTIES IN INTERNATIONAL TRADE

Country	Specialty Resulting from Natural Resources or Climate
Saudi Arabia	Oil
Canada	Timber
United States	Grain
Spain	Olive oil
Mexico	Tomatoes
Jamaica	Aluminum ore
Italy	Wine
Israel	Citrus fruit

	Specialties Not Based on Natural Resources
Japan	Cars, consumer electronics
United States	Software, movies, music
Switzerland	Watches
Korea	Steel, ships
Hong Kong	Textiles
Great Britain	Financial services

Countries often specialize in products based on their own particular endowments of natural resources. But natural resources are not the only basis for comparative advantage.

Explaining the origins of the specialties in the bottom part of Table 7 is not easy. For example, if you think you know why Japan completely dominates the world market for VCRs and other consumer electronics—say, some unique capacity to develop technical expertise—be sure you have an explanation for why Japan is a distant second in computer printers. The company that dominates the market for printers—Hewlett-Packard—is a U.S. firm. Moreover, the ability to mass-produce high-quality products is not unique to Japan, as Switzerland showed long ago in developing its international specialty in watches.

In even the most remote corner of the world, the cars, cameras, and VCRs will be Japanese, the movies and music American, the clothing from Hong Kong, and the bankers from Britain. Although we can't explain the reasons behind these countries' comparative advantages, we *can* explain why a country retains its comparative advantage once it gets started. Japan today enjoys a huge comparative advantage in cars and consumer electronics in large part because it has accumulated a capital stock—both physical capital and human capital—well suited to producing those goods. The physical capital stock includes the many manufacturing plants and design facilities that the Japanese have built over the years. But Japan's human capital is no less important. Japanese managers know how to anticipate the features that tomorrow's buyers of cars and electronic products will want around the world. And Japanese workers have developed skills adapted for producing these products. The stocks of physical and human capital in Japan sustain their comparative advantage in much the way that stocks of natural resources lead to comparative advantages in other countries. More likely than not, Japan will continue to have a comparative advantage in cars and electronics, just as Saudi Arabia will continue to have a comparative advantage in producing oil.

> *Countries often develop strong comparative advantages in the goods they have produced in the past, regardless of why they began producing those goods in the first place.*

WHY SOME PEOPLE OBJECT TO FREE TRADE

Given the clear benefits that nations can derive by specializing and trading, why would anyone *ever* object to free international trade? Why do the same governments that join the WTO turn around and create roadblocks to unhindered trade? The answer is not too difficult to find: Despite the benefit to the nation as a whole, some groups within the country, in the short run, are likely to lose from free trade, even while others gain a great deal more. In the language of Chapter 10, we can say that opening up trade is a *potential Pareto improvement*—a change in which the gains to the gainers are greater than the losses to the losers. We know this because trade increases *total* production and *total* consumption within the country, so it must create net gains for the country's residents as a whole.

But opening up trade is rarely a *simple* Pareto improvement, in which no one loses. And unfortunately, instead of finding a way to compensate the losers—to make them better off as well—we often allow them to block free-trade policies. The simple model of supply and demand helps illustrate this story.

In our earlier example, after trade opens up, the U.S. exports computers and Germany imports them. Figure 1 illustrates the impact on the computer market in the two countries. To keep things simple, we'll let the vertical axis represent the *dollar* price of computers in both countries, even though computers in Germany are actually sold for deutsche marks. (To obtain the dollar prices of computers in Germany, we would translate from deutsche marks, using the exchange rate between the two currencies.)

Before trade opens up, the U.S. computer market is in equilibrium at point E, with price equal to P_N (for "no trade") and quantity equal to Q_N. The German computer market is in equilibrium at point F, with price P_N' and quantity Q_N'. Notice that before trade opens up, the price is lower in the United States—the country with a comparative advantage in computers.

Now, when trade opens up, Germans will begin to buy U.S. computers, driving the price of U.S. computers upward. As the price in the United States rises from P_N to P_T (T for "trade"), U.S. producers increase their output of computers, moving from E to B along the supply curve, and U.S. consumers decrease their purchases of computers, moving from E to A along the demand curve. This seems to create an "excess supply" of computers in the United States, equal to AB, but it is not *really* an excess supply, because AB is precisely the number of computers that are exported to Germany. That is, the entire output of computers—Q_3—is purchased by either Americans or Germans.

Now let's consider the effects in Germany. There, consumers are switching from German computers to U.S. ones. With less demand for German computers, their price will fall. With free trade, Germans must be able to buy U.S. computers at the same price as Americans (ignoring transportation costs), so the price of German computers must fall to P_T. As the price falls, German producers will decrease their

---

FIGURE 1   **THE IMPACT OF TRADE**

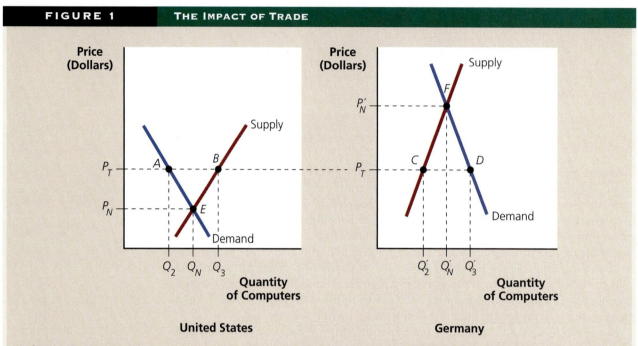

Before trade, the U.S. computer market is in equilibrium at point *E,* and the German market is in equilibrium at *F.* When trade begins, Germans buy the cheaper U.S. computers, driving up their price. In response, U.S. computer manufacturers increase output and U.S. consumers decrease their purchases. At world equilibrium price P_T, Americans buy Q_2 computers, Germans buy $Q_3 - Q_2$ American computers, and the total quantity of American computers produced and sold is Q_3. Distance *CD*, which shows German imports of computers, equals distance *AB*, which shows U.S. exports.

As a result of trade, U.S. computer producers sell more units at a higher price, but U.S. consumers pay more for computers. In Germany, computer producers are worse off, but computer buyers benefit from the lower price there.

---

output, from *F* to *C* along the supply curve, and German consumers will increase their purchases, from *F* to *D* along the demand curve. This seems to create a shortage of computers in Germany, equal to *CD*, but it is not a shortage: *CD* is precisely the number of computers imported from the United States.

Now let's see how different groups are affected by the opening up of trade.

THE IMPACT OF TRADE IN THE EXPORTING COUNTRY

When trade opens up in computers, the United States is the exporting country. How are different groups affected there?

U.S. Computer Producers and Workers Are Better Off. Before international trade, producers sold Q_N computers at price P_N, but with trade, they sell the higher quantity Q_3 at the higher price P_T. The industry's workers are equally delighted because they undoubtedly share in the bonanza as the number of workers demanded rises along with the level of production. Both management and labor in the U.S. computer industry are likely to favor free trade.

U.S. Computer Buyers Are Worse Off. Why? Before trade, they bought Q_N computers at price P_N, and now they must pay the higher price P_T and consume the smaller quantity Q_2. If the harm is great enough, consumers may band together and lobby the government to restrict free trade:

> *When the opening of trade results in increased exports of a good, the producers of the good are made better off and will support increased trade. Consumers of the good will be made worse off and will oppose increased trade.*

The story told here is anything but hypothetical. A dramatic example is provided by American agriculture, which for decades exported a large percentage of various crops to the former Soviet Union. Growers of wheat, rye, and corn did everything they could to promote this trade. All kinds of people in grain-growing areas, ranging from car dealers to sellers of fertilizer, were equally behind the Russian trade deal; they benefited indirectly. American consumers, however, complained bitterly. Bread, cereals, and flour were more expensive. So were eggs and chicken, because chickens were fed with more expensive grain.

THE IMPACT OF TRADE IN THE IMPORTING COUNTRY

Now let's consider the impact of free trade in computers on Germany, the importing country. Once again, it is easy to figure out who is happy and who is unhappy with the new arrangement.

German Computer Producers and Workers Are Worse Off. They used to sell quantity Q_N' at price P_N', but now they are furious because they sell the lower quantity Q_2' at the lower price P_T. The industry's workers suffer, too, because the number of workers demanded falls with the level of production. Both management and labor are likely to oppose free trade.

German Computer Buyers Are Better Off. They used to buy quantity Q_N' at price P_N', but now they pay the lower price, P_T and consume the larger quantity, Q_3'. German consumers will favor free trade:

> *When the opening of trade results in increased imports of a product, the domestic producers of the product are made worse off and will oppose the increased trade. Consumers are better off and will favor the increased trade.*

This story, too, is anything but hypothetical. A vivid example was provided recently by the American clothing industry. A Ukrainian clothing maker produced stylish, high-quality women's coats and sold them in the United States. With the coats priced between $89 and $139, over a million of them were sold. When American coat makers complained bitterly about the new competitor, the U.S. government stepped in. A tight import limitation killed off half of the Ukrainian imports in 1995. On top of that, the United States imposed a 21.5 percent tax on the offending coats. The interests of U.S. coat makers prevailed over the interests of U.S. coat consumers.

ATTITUDES TOWARD FREE TRADE: A SUMMARY

In our examples, we've been discussing the impact of free trade in computers. We could tell the same story about free trade in cameras. In this case, Germany has the role of exporter, and the United States is the importer. But our conclusions about the impacts on different groups in exporting and importing countries would remain the same. And so would our conclusions about who favors, and who opposes, free trade. Table 8 summarizes the stance toward trade we can expect from these different groups.

World Trade Organization (WTO)
Established in 1995 and located in Geneva, the WTO is the only international organization devoted to the rules of trade between nations. The WTO is an important forum for trade negotiations, and for settling trade disputes, among its 132 members. Visit the WTO Web site to learn more about current issues in international trade. For an excellent introduction to the organization, go to the "downloads" section and get their interactive electronic guide, "Trading into the Future," available at http://www.wto.org/wto/download/download.htm

TABLE 8	ATTITUDES TOWARD FREE TRADE	
	In Export Sectors That Enjoy Comparative Advantage	**In Import Sectors That Suffer from Comparative Disadvantage**
Pro Trade	Owners of firms, workers	Consumers
Antitrade	Consumers	Owners of firms, workers

HOW FREE TRADE IS RESTRICTED

So far in this chapter, you've learned that specialization and trade according to comparative advantage can dramatically improve the well-being of entire nations. This is why governments generally favor free trade. Yet international trade can, in the short run, hurt particular groups of people. These groups often induce governments to restrict free trade.

When governments decide to accommodate the opponents of free trade, they are apt to use one of two devices to restrict trade: tariffs or quotas.

TARIFFS

TARIFF A tax on imports.

A **tariff** is a tax on imported goods. It can be a fixed dollar amount per physical unit, or it can be a percentage of the good's value. In either case, the effect in the tariff-imposing country is similar.

Figure 2 illustrates the effects of a German tariff on U.S. computers. Initially, before the tariff is imposed, the price of computers in both countries is P_T, and the United States exports AB computers while Germany imports the same number (represented by the distance CD in the German market). Now, suppose Germany imposes a tariff on U.S. computers that raises the price there to P_3. In Germany, the rise in price will increase the quantity of computers supplied and decrease the quantity demanded. German imports are accordingly cut back to KL. In the United States, exports must shrink to the new level of German imports, so the new U.S. export level is HJ. With fewer computers exported, the price in the U.S. market will fall to P_2.

As you can see, German consumers are worse off—they pay a higher price for fewer computers. German producers, on the other hand, are much better off: They sell more computers at a higher price. In the United States, the impact is the opposite: The price of computers falls, so U.S. producers lose and U.S. consumers gain.

But we also know this: Since the volume of trade has decreased, the gains from trade according to comparative advantage have been reduced as well. Both countries, as a whole, are worse off as a result of the tariff:

POLICY TRADEOFFS

> *Tariffs reduce the volume of trade and raise the domestic prices of imported goods. In the country that imposes the tariff, producers gain and consumers lose. But the world as a whole loses, because tariffs decrease the volume of trade and therefore decrease the gains from trade.*

QUOTAS

A **quota** is a government decree that limits the imports of a good to a specified maximum physical quantity, such as 500,000 Ukrainian coats per year. Because

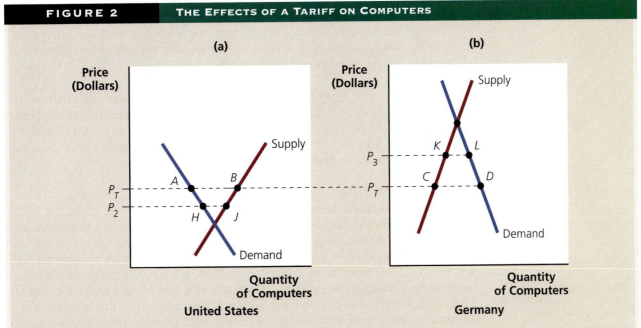

FIGURE 2	THE EFFECTS OF A TARIFF ON COMPUTERS

A German tariff on imports of U.S. computers raises the price in Germany from P_T to P_3. As a result of the price increase, German imports fall to *KL*, which equals U.S. exports of *HJ*. With fewer computers produced, the U.S. price falls to P_2.

the goal is to restrict imports, a quota is usually set below the level of imports that would occur under free trade. Its general effects are precisely the same as those of a tariff.

QUOTA A limit on the physical volume of imports.

Figure 2, which we used to illustrate tariffs, can also be used to analyze the impact of a quota. In this case, we suppose that the German government simply decrees that it will only allow *KL* computers into the country and that it is able to enforce this quota. Once again, the market price in Germany will rise to P_3. (Why? Because at any price lower than P_3, total imports of *KL* plus the domestic quantity supplied, given by the supply curve, would be smaller than quantity demanded. This would cause the price to rise.) And once again, the decrease in German imports translates into a shrinkage in U.S. exports—down to *HJ*. Both countries' computer markets end up in exactly the same place as if Germany had imposed a tariff that raised the German price to P_3.

The previous discussion seems to suggest that tariffs and quotas are pretty much the same. But even though prices in the two countries may end up at the same level with a tariff or a quota, there is one important difference between these two trade-restricting policies. When a government imposes a tariff, it collects some revenue every time a good is imported. (See if you can determine the amount of tariff revenue in Figure 2.) This revenue can be used to fund government programs or reduce other taxes, to the benefit of the country as a whole. When a government imposes a quota, however, it gains no revenue at all.[2]

---

2. In theory, a government could *auction off* the right to import, granting permission to the highest bidders to buy goods abroad and resell them in the domestic country. In this way, the government could collect just as much revenue under a quota as it could under a tariff. However, this does not happen in the United States.

> *Quotas have effects similar to tariffs—they reduce the quantity of imports and raise domestic prices. While both measures help domestic producers, they reduce the benefits of trade to the nation as a whole. However, a tariff has one saving grace: increased government revenue.*

Economists, who generally oppose measures such as quotas and tariffs to restrict trade, argue that, if one of these devices must be used, tariffs are the better choice. While both policies reduce the gains that countries can enjoy from specializing and trading with each other, the tariff provides some compensation in the form of additional government revenue.

PROTECTIONISM

This chapter has outlined the *gains* that arise from international trade, but it has also outlined some of the *pain* trade can cause to different groups within a country. While the country as a whole benefits, some citizens in both the exporting and importing countries are harmed. The groups who suffer from trade with other nations have developed a number of arguments against free trade. Together, these arguments form a position known as **protectionism**—the belief that a nation's industries should be *protected* from free trade with other nations. Some protectionist arguments are rather sophisticated and require careful consideration. We'll consider some of these a bit later. But antitrade groups have also promulgated a number of myths to support their protectionist beliefs. Let's consider some of these myths.

PROTECTIONISM The belief that a nation's industries should be protected from foreign competition.

MYTHS ABOUT FREE TRADE

> *A high-wage country cannot afford free trade with a low-wage country. The high-wage country will either be undersold in everything and lose all of its industries, or else its workers will have to accept equally low wages and equally low living standards.*

It's true that some countries have much higher wages than others. Here are 1997 figures for average hourly wages, including benefits such as holiday pay and health insurance: Germany $28.28; Japan $19.37; United States $18.24; Korea $7.22, Mexico $1.75; and less than a dollar in Russia, China, and India. As you can see, the wealthier, more-developed countries have wages far higher than poorer, less-developed countries. This leads to the fear that the poorer countries will be able to charge lower prices for their goods, putting American workers out of jobs unless they, too, agree to work for low wages.

But this argument is incorrect, for two reasons. First, workers in different countries are not equally productive. American workers, for example, are more highly skilled than their counterparts in China and work with more sophisticated machinery. If an American could produce 80 times as much output as a Chinese worker in an hour, then even though wages in the United States are about 70 times greater, cost *per unit* produced would still be lower in the United States.

But even if cost per unit *were* lower in China, there is another, more basic argument against the fear of a general job loss or falling wages in the United States: comparative advantage. Let's take an extreme case. Suppose that labor productivity were the same in the United States and China, so that China—with lower wages—could produce *everything* more cheaply than the United States could. Both would still gain if China specialized in products in which its cost advantage was relatively large and the United States specialized in goods in which China's cost advantage was relatively small. That is, even though China would have an absolute advantage in everything, the United States would still have a comparative advantage in some things. The mutual gains from trade arise not from absolute advantage, but from comparative advantage.

A low-productivity country cannot afford free trade with a high-productivity country. The former will be clobbered by the latter and lose all of its industries.

This argument is the flip side of the first myth. Here, it is the poorer, less-developed country that is supposedly harmed by trade with a richer country. But this myth, like the first one, confuses absolute advantage with comparative advantage. Suppose the high-productivity country (say, the United States) could produce *every* good at lower cost per unit than the low-productivity country (say, China). Once again, the low-productivity country would *still* have a comparative advantage in *some* goods. It would then gain, just as China does, by producing those goods and trading with the high-productivity country.

To make the point even clearer, let's bring it closer to home. Suppose there is a small, poor town in the United States where workers are relatively uneducated and work with little capital equipment, so their productivity is very low. Would the residents of this town be better off sealing their borders and not trading with the rest of the United States, which has higher productivity? Before you answer, think what this would mean: The residents of the poor town would have to produce everything on their own: grow their own food, make their own cars and television sets, and even provide their own entertainment. Clearly, they would be worse off in isolation. And what is true *within* a country is also true *between* different countries: Closing off trade will make a nation, as a whole, worse off, regardless of its level of wages or productivity. Even a low-productivity country is made better off by trading with other nations.

In recent times, America's unskilled workers have suffered because of ever-expanding trade between the United States and other countries.

True enough, unskilled workers have been losing ground since around 1980, for *some* reason. College graduates have enjoyed growing purchasing power from their earnings, while those with only a grade school education have lost about 25 percent of their 1980 purchasing power. Rising trade with low-wage countries has been blamed for this adverse trend.

But before we jump to conclusions, let's take a closer look. Our discussion earlier in this chapter tells us where to look for effects that come through trade. If the opening of trade has harmed low-skilled workers in the United States, it would have done so by lowering the prices of products that employ large numbers of those workers. For example, we should see a decline in U.S. clothing prices and reductions in earnings among clothing workers, who tend to be less skilled. But a recent study taking this approach found almost no change in the relative prices of products in this country that employ large numbers of unskilled workers. Studies that take other approaches have found only modest effects. In general, economists who have looked at the relation between changes in trade patterns and the depressed earnings of unskilled American workers have concluded that foreign trade is a small contributor.[3]

---

3.   The studies include Robert Z. Lawrence and Matthew J. Slaughter, "Trade and U.S. Wages: Giant Sucking Sound or Small Hiccup?" *Brookings Papers on Economic Activity: Microeconomics 2: 1993,* pp. 161–210, and Jeffrey D. Sachs and Howard J. Shatz, "Trade and Jobs in U.S. Manufacturing," *Brookings Papers on Economic Activity 1: 1994,* pp. 1–84.

SOPHISTICATED ARGUMENTS FOR PROTECTION

While most of the protectionist arguments we read in the media are based on a misunderstanding of comparative advantage, some more recent arguments for protecting domestic industries are based on a more sophisticated understanding of how markets work. These arguments have become collectively known as *strategic trade policy.* According to its proponents, a nation can gain in some circumstances by assisting certain "strategic" industries that benefit society as a whole but that may not thrive in an environment of free trade.

Strategic trade policy is most effective in situations where a market is dominated by a few large firms.[4] With few firms, the forces of competition—which ordinarily reduce profits in an industry to very low levels—will not operate. Therefore, each firm in the industry may earn high profits. These profits benefit not only the owners of the firm, but also the nation more generally, since the government will be able to capture some of the profit with the corporate profits tax. When a government helps an industry compete internationally, it increases the likelihood that high profits—and the resulting general benefits—will be shifted from a foreign country to its own country. Thus, interfering with free trade—through quotas, tariffs, or even a direct subsidy to domestic firms—might actually benefit the country as a whole.

An argument related to strategic trade policy is the *infant industry argument.* This argument begins with a simple observation: In order to enjoy the full benefits of trade, markets must allocate resources toward those goods in which a nation has a comparative advantage. This includes not only markets for resources such as labor and land, but also *financial markets,* where firms obtain funds for new products. But in some countries—especially developing countries—financial markets do not work very well. Poor legal systems or incomplete information about firms and products may prevent a new industry from obtaining financing, even though the country would have a comparative advantage in that industry once it was formed. In this case, government assistance to the "infant industry" may be warranted until the industry can "stand on its own feet."

Strategic trade policy and support for infant industries are controversial. Opponents of these ideas stress three problems:

1. Once the principle of government assistance to an industry is accepted, special-interest groups will lobby to get the assistance, whether it benefits the general public or not.
2. When one country provides assistance to an industry by keeping out foreign goods, other nations may respond in kind. If they respond with tariffs and quotas of their own, the result is a shrinking volume of world trade and falling living standards. If subsidies are used to support a strategic industry, and another country responds with its own subsidies, then both governments lose revenue, and neither gains the sought-after profits.
3. Strategic trade policy assumes that the government has the information to determine which industries, infant or otherwise, are truly strategic and which are not.

This last point—insufficient information—is the one that opponents of free trade policy cite most often. They point to the European firm Airbus as an example

---

4. Why might there be only a few firms in a market? In Chapter 8, you learned some of the reasons. These include economies of scale, legal barriers like patent protection, and strategic behavior on the part of existing firms to keep out competitors.

of a costly government mistake. During the 1970s, Airbus received $1.5 billion from European governments to help it produce the A300 aircraft, in competition with Boeing's 767 aircraft. In the end, in spite of the subsidy, Airbus suffered a loss, Boeing continued to produce the 767, and European governments had spent a lot of money with very little return.

Still, the arguments related to strategic trade policy suggest that government protection or assistance *may* be warranted in some circumstances, even if putting this support into practice proves difficult. Moreover, the arguments help to remind us of the conditions under which free trade is most beneficial to a nation:

> *Production is most likely to reflect the principle of comparative advantage when firms can obtain funds for investment projects and when they can freely enter industries that are profitable. Thus, free trade, without government intervention, works best when markets are working well.*

This may explain, in part, why the United States, where markets function relatively well, has for decades been among the strongest supporters of the free-trade ideal.

TRADE RESTRICTIONS IN THE UNITED STATES

No country has completely free trade with the rest of the world; every government limits trade in one way or another. And in spite of its strong protrade stance, the United States has restricted imports in many cases. Among the trade restrictions currently imposed by the U.S. government are the following:

- Foreign airlines may not carry domestic passengers from one point to another inside the United States.
- Canadian lumber can enter the United States only in limited quantities.
- Imports of fibers and textiles are tightly limited.
- Importers of many products have to pay tariffs.
- The amount of sugar that can be imported is tightly limited and is far less than would occur with free trade.

In addition, the government often takes temporary steps to limit certain kinds of imports or to raise their prices. For example, the United States has required Japan to limit exports of automobiles during certain periods, and the government required Asian manufacturers of computer memory chips to double the U.S. prices of their products for a time. Again, these practices, though restrictive, are not nearly as severe as those of many other governments: Japanese carmakers sell millions of cars in the United States, but almost none in Europe, where there is a flat ban on imports of their cars.

As we learned earlier in the chapter (see Table 8), protection benefits those who make the protected product, but it is bad for consumers. As a result, there is a tug-of-war between consumer interests and producer interests. Generally, in the United States, consumers have won the tug-of-war. Because so many imports are allowed into the country free of tariffs, the average U.S. tariff rate for all imports (which once approached 50 percent) was down to 3 percent by the mid-1990s. Thus, U.S. consumers enjoy the benefits of importing many of the products listed in Table 7—olive oil from Spain, tomatoes from Mexico, and cars and VCRs from Japan. Consumers also benefit indirectly when domestic producers buy inputs abroad, such as oil, aluminum, timber, and steel.

On the other side of the ledger, U.S. consumers suffer, and U.S. producers gain, from some persistent quotas, such as the sugar import quota. As you saw in Figure 2, a quota on imports raises the price to domestic residents. It is no surprise that the price of sugar in the United States is about ten times higher than the world market price.

But quotas—like the U.S. sugar quota—create further problems of their own. First, because a quota raises the domestic price above prices elsewhere in the world, importers have an incentive to buy the good on the international market, violating the quota. The U.S. sugar quota, for example, has to be enforced by "sugar police"—customs inspectors. Their job is to prevent the importation of extra sugar that would eliminate the price differential and reduce the price of sugar in the United States to the free-trade price, like P_T in Figure 2. In this way, valuable resources—such as the labor of customs inspectors—are used up to enforce the quota.

Another problem with a quota is how to decide who gets to import the restricted good. Importers have a lot to gain, since they can buy at the lower world price and sell at the artificially high domestic price. One logical approach would be to auction tickets that entitle the holder to import a given amount of the restricted good. Then the government would collect the difference between the U.S. and world price as revenue, making the quota similar to a tariff in its total impact. But this approach is never used in practice. Instead, the right to import is typically *given* away by the government, as in the case of sugar.

The impact of quotas in general can be understood by looking closely at the harm caused by the U.S. sugar quota:

1. It denies U.S. consumers the benefits of free trade—the ability to buy sugar cheaply from countries that have comparative advantages in sugar production.
2. It lowers the incomes of sugar producers in the generally poor, tropical countries that have comparative advantages in sugar production.
3. The gap between the U.S. and world market price creates an incentive for illegal and wasteful activities, such as smuggling sugar, bribing the "sugar police," or importing candy and refining it back into sugar. (Some people are actually in jail for defying the sugar import quota.)
4. The government's power to grant sugar-importing rights causes people to waste resources lobbying for those rights, and it may cause corruption of the government officials in charge.
5. The government does not collect revenue that it could.

Who benefits from the sugar quota? A look back at Table 8 provides the answer: U.S. sugar producers and foreign sugar consumers. But as the principle of comparative advantage shows, the world as a whole is the loser.

S U M M A R Y

International specialization and trade enable people throughout the world to enjoy greater production and higher living standards than would otherwise be possible. The benefits of unrestrained international trade can be traced back to the idea of comparative advantage. Mutually beneficial trade is possible whenever one country can produce a good at a lower opportunity cost than its trading partner can. Whenever opportunity costs differ, countries can specialize according to their comparative advantage, trade with each other, and end up consuming more.

Despite the net benefits to each nation as a whole, some groups within each country lose while others gain. When trade leads to increased exports, domestic producers gain and domestic consumers are harmed. When imports increase as a result of trade, domestic producers suffer and domestic consumers gain. The losers often encourage government to block or reduce trade through the use of tariffs—taxes on imported goods—and quotas—limits on the volume of imports.

A variety of arguments have been proposed in support of protectionism. Some are clearly invalid and fail to recognize the principle that both sides gain when countries trade according to their comparative advantage. More sophisticated arguments for restricting trade may have merit in certain circumstances. These include strategic trade policy—the notion that governments should assist certain strategic industries—and the idea of protecting "infant" industries when financial markets are imperfect.

K E Y   T E R M S

exports
imports
absolute advantage

comparative advantage
terms of trade

exchange rate
tariff

quota
protectionism

R E V I E W   Q U E S T I O N S

1. Describe the theory of comparative advantage.

2. What is the difference between absolute advantage and comparative advantage?

3. What are the terms of trade and why are they important?

4. What are the sources of comparative advantage?

5. What is a tariff? What are its main economic effects? How does a quota differ from a tariff?

6. What arguments have been made in support of protectionism? Which of them may be valid and under what circumstances?

7. List the ways in which a quota on imported coffee would harm the nation that imposes it.

P R O B L E M S   A N D   E X E R C I S E S

1. Suppose that the costs of production of winter hats and wheat in two countries are as follows:

	Per Winter Hat	Per Bushel of Wheat
United States	$10	$1
Russia	5,000 rubles	2,500 rubles

a. What is the opportunity cost of producing one more winter hat in the United States? In Russia?
b. What is the opportunity cost of producing one more bushel of wheat in the United States? In Russia?
c. Which country has a comparative advantage in winter hats? . . . in wheat?
d. Construct a table similar to Table 3 that illustrates how a change in production in each country would increase world production.
e. If the exchange rate were 1,000 rubles per dollar, would mutually beneficial trade occur? If yes, explain what mechanism would induce producers to export according to their country's comparative advantage. If no, explain why not, and explain in which direction the exchange rate would change. (Hint: Construct a table similar to Table 6.)
f. Answer the same questions for an exchange rate of 100 rubles per dollar.

2. The following table gives information about the supply and demand for beef in Paraguay and Uruguay. (You may wish to draw the supply and demand curves for each country to help you visualize what is happening.)

Paraguay			Uruguay		
Price	Quantity Supplied	Quantity Demanded	Price	Quantity Supplied	Quantity Demanded
0	0	1200	0	0	1800
5	200	1000	5	0	1600
10	400	800	10	0	1400
15	600	600	15	0	1200
20	800	400	20	200	1000
25	1000	200	25	400	800
30	1200	0	30	600	600
35	1400	0	35	800	400
40	1600	0	40	1000	200
45	1800	0	45	1200	0

a. In the absence of trade, what is the equilibrium price and quantity in Paraguay? In Uruguay?
b. If the two countries begin to trade, what will happen to the price of beef? How many sides of beef will be purchased in Paraguay and how many in Uruguay at that price?

c. How many sides of beef will be produced in Paraguay and how many in Uruguay? Why is there a difference between quantity purchased and quantity produced in each country?

d. Who benefits and who loses from the opening of trade between these two countries?

3. Use the data on supply and demand given in question 2 to answer the following questions:

a. Suppose that Uruguay imposed a tariff that raised the price of beef imported from Paraguay to $25 per side. What would happen to beef consumption in Uruguay? To beef production there? How much beef would be imported from Paraguay?

b. How would the tariff affect Paraguay? What would happen to the price of beef there after Uruguay imposed its tariff? How would domestic production and consumption be affected?

c. Suppose, instead, that Uruguay imposed a quota on the import of beef from Paraguay—only 200 sides of beef can be imported each year. What would happen to the price of beef in Uruguay? What would happen to beef consumption in Uruguay? To beef production there?

d. How would the quota affect Paraguay? What would happen to the price of beef there after Uruguay imposed its quota? How would domestic production and consumption be affected?

4. Under the Omnibus Trade and Competitiveness Act of 1988, every year the State Department must send Congress a detailed report on economic policies and trade practices of every country trading with the United States. The State Department makes these reports available on the Web at http://www.state.gov/www/issues/economic/trade_reports/index.html.

a. Go to this State Department site and click on the most recent year available. Read about the common contents and format for all country reports.

b. Select a country that interests you and pull up its report. Read the introductory material, then turn to Section 5, "Significant Barriers to U.S. Exports."

c. What instruments does this country use to limit imports? Does it rely primarily on tariffs or quotas? Does it have significant "non-tariff barriers," such as licensing or health code restrictions? Are this country's tariffs and/or quotas imposed in an even-handed, non-discriminatory manner, to products arriving from all countries, or does the country target the products of specific countries?

d. Would you describe this country as "protectionist" or "pro-free trade"? Why do you think the government of this country maintains this set of policies?

C H A L L E N G E   Q U E S T I O N

Suppose that the Marshall Islands does not trade with the outside world. It has a competitive domestic market for VCRs. The market supply and demand curves are reflected in this table:

Price ($/VCR)	Quantity Demanded	Quantity Supplied
500	0	500
400	100	400
300	200	300
200	300	200
100	400	100
0	500	0

a. Plot the supply and demand curves and determine the domestic equilibrium price and quantity.

b. Suddenly, the islanders discover the virtues of free exchange and begin trading with the outside world. The Marshall Islands is a very small country, and so its trading has no effect on the price established in the world market. It can import as many VCRs as it wishes at the world price of $100 per VCR. In this situation, how many VCRs will be purchased in the Marshall Islands? How many will be produced there? How many will be imported?

c. After protests from domestic producers, the government decides to impose a tariff of $100 per imported VCR. Now how many VCRs will be purchased in the Marshall Islands? How many will be produced there? How many will be imported?

d. What is the government's revenue from the tariff described in part (c)?

MATHEMATICAL APPENDIX

TABLES AND GRAPHS

A brief glance at this text will tell you that graphs are important in economics. Graphs provide a convenient way to display data. Take the example of Len & Harry's, an up-and-coming manufacturer of high-end ice cream products, located in Texas. Suppose that you've just been hired to head Len & Harry's advertising department, and you want to learn as much as you can about how advertising can help the company's sales. One of the simplest things you can do as you begin to analyze the data that have been collected is to organize the information in the form of a table.

Table A1 records the company's total advertising outlay per month in the left-hand column, and the company's ice cream sales during that same month are shown in the right-hand column. Notice that the data are organized so that advertising outlay increases as we move down the first column. Often, just looking at such a table can reveal useful patterns. In this case, it seems that higher advertising outlays are associated with higher monthly sales. This suggests that there may be some *causal relationship* between advertising and sales.

To explore this relationship further, we might decide to plot the data and draw a graph. First, we need to choose units for our two variables. We'll measure both advertising and sales in thousands of dollars. Different values of one variable are then measured along the horizontal axis, increasing as we move rightward from the origin. The corresponding values of the other variable are measured along the vertical axis, increasing as we move upward, away from the origin.

Using the data in the table, let X stand for advertising outlay per month, and let Y stand for sales per month. Notice that each row of the table gives us a pair of numbers: The first is always the value of the variable we are calling X, and the second is the value of the variable we are calling Y. We often write such pairs in the form (X,Y). For example, we would write the first three rows of the table as (2,46), (3,49) and (6,58), respectively.

To plot the pair (X,Y) on a graph, begin at the origin, where the axes cross. Count rightward X units along the horizontal axis, then count upward Y units parallel to the vertical axis, and then mark the spot. For example, to plot the pair (2,46), we go rightward 2 units along the horizontal axis and then upward 46 units along the vertical axis, arriving at the point marked A in Figure A1. To plot the next pair, (3,49), we go rightward from the origin 3 units and then upward 49 units, arriving at the point marked B. Carrying on in just this way, we can plot all remaining pairs in Table A1 as the points C, D, E, and F.

If we connect points A through F, we see that they all lie along the same straight line. Now we are getting somewhere. The relationship we've discovered appears from the graph to be very regular, indeed.

Study the graph closely. You will notice that each time advertising increases (moves rightward) by $1,000, Y moves upward by $3,000. For example, when advertising rises from $2,000 to $3,000, sales rise from $46,000 to $49,000. By checking between any other two points on the graph, you will see that every time X increases horizontally by one unit (here, a unit is $1,000), Y increases vertically by three units (here, by $3,000). Thus, we conclude that that the *rate of change* in Y is three units of Y for every one-unit increase in X.

TABLE A1

ADVERTISING AND SALES AT LEN & HARRY'S

Advertising ($1,000s per month)	Sales ($1,000s per month)
2	46
3	49
6	58
7	61
11	73
12	76

FIGURE A1

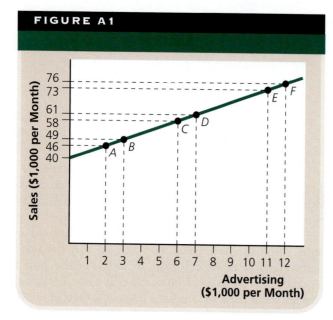

NONLINEAR GRAPHS

Although many of the relationships we encounter in economics have straight-line graphs, many do not. Still, graphs can help us understand the underlying relationships, and the concept of slope remains very useful.

As an example, look at the data in Table A2, which records the price of a share of Len and Harry's stock at different points in time since the stock first appeared on the market. To understand how the price of this stock has behaved over time, we might again start by plotting a graph of the data in the table. It seems natural to measure time—in "weeks since launch"—on the X-axis and stock price—in "dollars per share"—on the Y-axis. As you can see in Figure A2, Len and Harry's has had a rocky ride since it came on the market. In its first 10 weeks, the stock's price rose, so the slope of the underlying relationship was positive during that time. Over the next 10 weeks, the story changed. The stock's price decreased, so the slope of the relationship was negative then. Between weeks 20 and 30, things leveled off. There was no change in the stock's price, so the slope of the graph was zero during that time. However, between weeks 30 and 40 things picked up, and once again the slope turned positive, since the price of the stock increased.

From this example, we can see the following:

• *The slope is positive whenever an increase in* X *is associated with an increase in* Y.

• *The slope is negative whenever an increase in* X *is associated with a decrease in* Y.

• *The slope is equal to zero whenever an increase in* X *is associated with no change in* Y.

The *slope* of a graph tells us the rate at which the Y-variable changes for every one-unit change in the X-variable. The slope of a straight line between any two points (X_1, Y_1) and (X_2, Y_2) is defined as the change in Y—the vertical "rise"—divided by the change in X—the horizontal "run." This is why the slope is often described as "rise over run." Supposing we start at (X_1, Y_1) and end at (X_2, Y_2); then the change in the X-variable is $(X_2 - X_1)$. The corresponding change in the Y-variable is $(Y_2 - Y_1)$. We therefore compute the slope as follows:

$$\text{Slope of the line from } (X_1, Y_1) \text{ to } (X_2, Y_2) = \frac{\text{Rise along vertical axis}}{\text{Run along horizontal axis}}$$

$$= \frac{Y_2 - Y_1}{X_2 - X_1}$$

We sometimes use the capital Greek letter, Δ ("delta"), to denote a change in a variable. Here we would write $\Delta X = X_2 - X_1$ to denote the change in X, and $\Delta Y = Y_2 - Y_1$ to denote the corresponding change in Y. We then could write that same formula for the slope more compactly as

$$\text{Slope of the line from } (X_1, Y_1) \text{ to } (X_2, Y_2) = \frac{\Delta Y}{\Delta X}.$$

TABLE A2

PRICE OF LEN & HARRY'S STOCK SINCE LAUNCH

Weeks Since Launch	Stock Price
3	$20
10	50
18	35
20	20
25	20
30	20
40	75

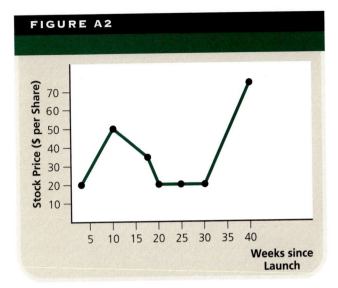

FIGURE A2

LINEAR EQUATIONS

Let's go back to the relationship between advertising and sales, as shown in Table A1. What if you need to know how much sales the firm could expect if it spent $5,000 on advertising next month? What if it spent $8,000? How about $9,000? Wouldn't it be nice to be able to answer questions like this without having to pull out tables and graphs to do it? As it turns out, any time the relationship you are studying has a straight-line graph, it is easy to figure out the equation for the entire relationship. You then can use the equation to answer any such question that might be put to you.

All straight lines have the same general form. If Y stands for the variable on the vertical axis and X for the variable on the horizontal axis, every straight line has an equation of the form

$$Y = a + bX,$$

where a stands for some number and b for another number. The number a is called the vertical *intercept*, because it marks the point where the graph of this equation hits (intercepts) the vertical axis; this occurs when X takes the value zero. (If you plug $X = 0$ into the equation, you will see that, indeed, $Y = a$.) The number b is the slope of the line, telling us how much Y will change every time X changes by one unit. To confirm this, note that as X increases from 0 to 1, Y goes from a to $a + b$. The number b is therefore the change in Y corresponding to a one-unit change in X—exactly what the slope of the graph should tell us.

More generally, if X changes from some value X_1 to some other value X_2, Y will change from

$$Y_1 = a + bX_1$$

to

$$Y_2 = a + bX_2.$$

If we subtract Y_1 from Y_2 to compute how much Y has changed (ΔY), we find that

$$\begin{aligned}\Delta Y = Y_2 - Y_1 &= (a + bX_2) - (a + bX_1)\\ &= a + bX_2 - a - bX_1\\ &= b(X_2 - X_1)\\ &= b\Delta X.\end{aligned}$$

Dividing both sides of the equation $\Delta Y = b\Delta X$ by ΔX, we get

$$\frac{\Delta Y}{\Delta X} = b,$$

confirming that b really does measure the slope.

If b is a positive number, a one-unit increase in X causes Y to increase by b units, so the graph of our line would slope upward, as illustrated by the red line in panel (a) of Figure A3. If b is a negative number, then a one-unit increase in X will cause Y to *decrease* by b units, so the graph would slope downward, as the blue line does in panel (a). Of course, b could equal zero. If it does, a one-unit increase in X causes no change in Y, so the graph of the line is flat, like the black line in panel (a).

The value of a has no effect on the slope of the graph. Instead, different values of a determine the graph's position. When a is a positive number, the graph will intercept the vertical Y-axis above the origin, as the red line does in panel (b) of Figure A3. When a is negative, however, the graph will intercept the Y-axis *below* the origin, like the blue line in panel (b). When a is zero, the graph intercepts the Y-axis right at the origin, as the black line does in panel (b).

Let's see if we can figure out the equation for the relationship depicted in Figure A1. There, X denotes advertising and Y denotes sales. On the graph, it is easy to see that when advertising expenditure is zero, sales are $40,000. Therefore, our equation will have a *vertical intercept* of $a = 40$. Earlier, we calculated the slope of this graph to be 3. Therefore, the equation will have $b = 3$. Putting these two observations together, we find that the equation for the line in Figure A1 is

$$Y = 40 + 3X.$$

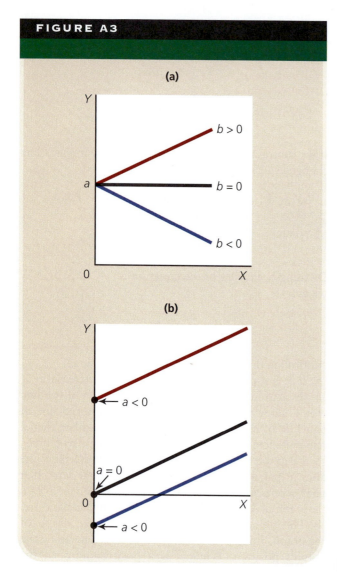

FIGURE A3

(a)

(b)

of interest to us is actually affected by more than just one other variable. When Y is affected by both X and some third variable, changes in that third variable will usually cause a *shift* in the graph of the relationship between X and Y. This is because whenever we draw the graph between X and Y, we are holding fixed every other variable that might possibly affect Y.

> *A graph between two variables* X *and* Y *is only a picture of their relationship when all other variables affecting* Y *are constant. Changes in any one or more of those other variables will shift the graph of* X *and* Y.

Think back to the relationship between advertising and sales. Earlier, we supposed sales depend only on advertising. But suppose we make an important discovery: Ice cream sales are *also* affected by how hot the weather is. What's more, all of the data in Table A1 on which we previously based our analysis turns out to have been from the month of June, when the average temperature in Texas is always 80 degrees. What's going to happen in July, when the average temperature rises to 100 degrees?

In Figure A4 we've redrawn the graph from Figure A1, this time labeling the line "June." Often, a good way to determine how a graph will shift is to perform a simple experiment like this: Put your pencil tip anywhere on the graph labeled June, let's say at point C. Now ask the following question: If I hold advertising constant at $6,000, do I expect to sell more or less ice cream as temperature rises in July? If you expect to sell

Now if you need to know how much in sales to expect from a particular expenditure on advertising, you'd be able to come up with an answer: You'd simply multiply the amount spent on advertising by 3, add $40,000, and that would be your sales. To confirm this, plug in for X in this equation any amount of advertising from the left-hand column of Table A1. You'll see that you get the corresponding amount of sales in the right-hand column.

HOW LINES AND CURVES SHIFT

So far, we've focused on relationships where some variable Y depends on a single other variable, X. But in many of our theories, we recognize that some variable

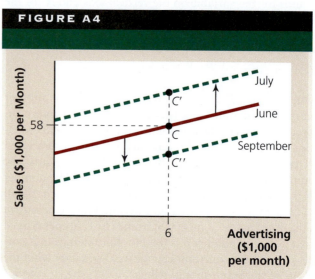

FIGURE A4

Sales ($1,000 per Month)

58

July

June

September

C'

C

C''

6

Advertising ($1,000 per month)

FIGURE A5

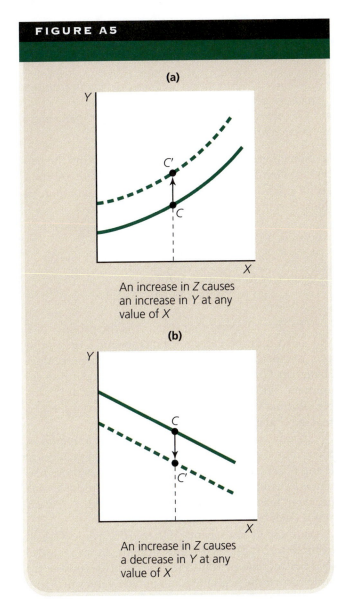

(a)

An increase in Z causes
an increase in Y at any
value of X

(b)

An increase in Z causes
a decrease in Y at any
value of X

the graph of the relationship between X and Y shifts upward as Z increases. We often phrase it this way: "An increase in Z causes an increase in Y, *with X held constant*." In panel (b), an increase in Z *decreases* the value of Y, at any value of X, so the graph of the relationship between X and Y shifts *downward* as Z increases.

SOLVING EQUATIONS

When we first derived the equation for the relationship between advertising and sales, we wanted to know what level of sales to expect from different amounts of advertising. But what if we're asked a slightly different question? Suppose, this time, you are told that the sales committee has set an ambitious goal of $64,000 for next month's sales. The treasurer needs to know how much to budget for advertising, and you have to come up with the answer.

Since we know how advertising and sales are related, we ought to be able to answer this question. One way is just to look at the graph in Figure A1. There, we could first locate sales of $64,000 on the vertical axis. Then, if we read over to the line and then down, we find the amount of advertising that would be necessary to generate that level of sales. Yet even with that carefully drawn diagram, it is not always easy to see just exactly how much advertising would be required. If we need to be precise, we'd better use the equation for the graph, instead.

According to the equation, sales (Y) and advertising (X) are related as follows:

$$Y = 40 + 3X.$$

In the problem before us, we know the value for sales, and we need to solve for the corresponding amount of advertising. Substituting the sales target of $64,000 for Y, we need to find that value of X for which

$$64 = 40 + 3X.$$

Here, X is the unknown value for which we want to solve.

Whenever we solve one equation for one unknown, say, X, we need to *isolate* X on one side of the equals sign and everything else on the other side of the equals sign. We do this by performing identical operations on both sides of the equals sign. Here, we can first subtract 40 from both sides, getting

$$24 = 3X.$$

more, then the amount of sales corresponding to $6,000 of advertising will be *above* point C, at a point such as C'. From this, we can tell that the graph will shift upward as temperature rises. In September, however, when temperature falls, the amount of sales corresponding to $6,000 in advertising would be less than it is at point C. It would be shown by a point such as C". In that case, the graph would shift downward.

The same procedure works well whether the original graph slopes upward or downward, and whether it is a straight line or a curved one. Figure A5 sketches two examples. In panel (a), an increase in some third variable, Z, increases the value of Y for each value of X, so

We can then divide both sides by 3 and get

$$8 = X.$$

This is our answer; if we want to achieve sales of $64,000, we'll need to spend $8,000 on advertising.

By looking back over what we just did, we can come up with a useful formula that will help to solve similar equations. Starting with an equation of the form

$$Y = a + bX,$$

we first subtracted a from both sides to get

$$Y - a = bX.$$

We then divided both sides by b to get our answer:

$$\frac{Y - a}{b} = X.$$

This is a formula you can use to solve for X whenever X and Y are linearly related and whenever b is not equal to zero. Of course, not all relationships are linear, so this formula will not work in every situation. But no matter what the underlying relationship, the idea remains the same:

> To solve for X in any equation, rearrange the equation, following the rules of algebra, so that X appears on one side of the equals sign and everything else in the equation appears on the other side.

PERCENTAGE CHANGES

It is often convenient to express changes in percentage terms, rather than absolute terms. While we are all quite used to thinking in percentages, a quick review of how to calculate them may be helpful. If some variable X starts at one value and ends at another, the percentage change in X, denoted, $\%\Delta X$, is computed as follows:

$$\%\Delta X$$
$$= \frac{\text{ending value of } X - \text{starting value of } X}{\text{starting value of } X} \times 100$$

Look at this formula for a moment. It says that, to calculate the *percentage* change in X, first compute the *change* in X by subtracting the ending value from the starting value, and then divide by the "base," or starting value, of X. The resulting fraction is then multiplied by 100. The formula shows us that:

- *Whenever a variable decreases, the percentage change in its value will be negative.*
- *Whenever a variable increases, the percentage change in its value will be positive.*

Sometimes, we are interested in computing the percentage change in a product or a ratio. There are some useful rules of thumb that can simplify those computations. Specifically, we have:

Product Rule: If $A = B \times C$,
then $\%\Delta A = \%\Delta B + \%\Delta C$.

Quotient Rule: If $A = B/C$,
then $\%\Delta A = \%\Delta B - \%\Delta C$.

The first rule says that when A is the product of B and C, to find the percentage change in A, we simply *add* the percentage change in B to the percentage change in C. The second rule says that when A is the quotient, B/C, to find the percentage change in A, simply *subtract* the percentage change in C from the percentage change in B.

Strictly speaking, these rules are *approximations*. They are most accurate when the percentage changes in B and C are extremely small. Yet, as long as those percentage changes remain "relatively small," the rules will provide "reasonably good" approximations. A few examples will help to convince you.

Suppose B rises from 100 to 103, while C rises from 20 to 21. To keep things straight, we've recorded the relevant data in Table A3. The first two rows of the table record the beginning and ending values of B and C, and the percentage change in each variable. The last

TABLE A3

RULES OF THUMB FOR PERCENTAGE CHANGES

Variable	Beginning value	Ending value	Calculated percentage change
B	100	103	+3
C	20	21	+5
$B \times C$	2,000	2,163	+8.15
B/C	5	4.905	−1.90

two rows show the beginning and ending values for the product $B \times C$ and the quotient B/C, respectively, and the percentage change in each of these, calculated exactly.

Now look at what we have. Moving across the third row, we see that $B \times C$ rises from 2,000 to 2,163, a percentage increase of 8.15% when computed exactly. Notice that this is very close to what we would get if, instead, we just applied our product rule, adding the 3% change in B to the 5% change in C to get an estimate of 8% for the change in the product $B \times C$. Thus, our approximation is very close. Similarly, moving across the fourth row, we find that the quotient B/C declines from 5 to 4.905, a percentage decrease of exactly 1.9%. Had we applied our quotient rule instead, we would have taken the 3% increase in B and subtracted the 5% increase in C to get $3\% - 5\% = -2\%$—again, very close to the exact result of -1.9%.

A SPECIAL SUM

In economics, we sometimes need to evaluate the sum of an infinite number of terms. A common example is the sum of a *geometric series,* in which some number or expression is raised to higher and higher powers. If H is the number we are raising to higher powers, then we can write the sum (S) of the geometric series as

$$S = 1 + H + H^2 + H^3 + H^4 + \ldots.$$

In all of the geometric series you will encounter in this book, H will be a fraction between 0 and 1. For example, when H is the fraction ½, the sum of the geometric series is

$$S = 1 + ½ + (½)^2 + (½)^3 + (½)^4 + \ldots$$
$$= 1 + 1/2 + 1/4 + 1/8 + 1/16 + \ldots.$$

Notice that each time we add a term, it is smaller than the term before. Eventually, as we continue to add terms, they will become so small that we can safely ignore them. That is, the sum *converges* (becomes closer and closer to) some finite number, which we are calling S.

It turns out that, as long as H is a fraction between 0 and 1, we can use a very simple formula to calculate S. To get this formula, we'll start with the equation for S itself:

$$S = 1 + H + H^2 + H^3 + H^4 + \ldots.$$

Next, we multiply both sides of the previous equation by H, to get

$$H \times S = H(1 + H + H^2 + H^3 + H^4 + \ldots)$$
$$= H + H^2 + H^3 + H^4 + H^5 + \ldots.$$

Now we subtract this expression from the original expression, yielding

$$S = 1 + H + H^2 + H^3 + H^4 + \ldots$$
$$- (H \times S) = \quad - H - H^2 - H^3 - H^4 - \ldots$$

You can see that all the terms cancel out except for "1" from the first equation. Therefore, we end up with

$$S - HS = S(1 - H) = 1.$$
$$\text{or} \quad S(1 - H) = 1$$

Finally, we divide both sides by $(1 - H)$ to get the formula for S, the sum of the geometric series that we've been seeking:

$$S = 1/(1 - H)$$

When H is a fraction between 0 and 1, our formula gives us a very simple way to compute a rather complicated-looking sum:

> When H *is a positive fraction less than 1, the sum of the infinite geometric series*
>
> $$S = 1 + H + H^2 + H^3 + H^4 + \ldots.$$
>
> *resolves to the simple expression*
>
> $$S = 1/(1 - H)$$

When we use this formula in the text, H will sometimes be an expression involving other variables. For example, suppose $H = (1 - a)$, so that our geometric series is

$$S = 1 + (1 - a) + (1 - a)^2 + (1 - a)^3 + (1 - a)^4 + \ldots.$$

Then, as long as $(1 - a)$ is a fraction between 0 and 1, we can still use our formula. The sum of the infinite geometric series will be $1/(1 - H) = 1/[1 - (1 - a)] = 1/a$.

GLOSSARY

A

Absolute Advantage The ability to produce a good or service using fewer resources than other producers use.

Accounting Profit Total revenue minus accounting costs.

Agent A person hired to do a job.

Aggregate Demand (*AD*) Curve A curve indicating equilibrium GDP at each price level.

Aggregate Supply (*AS*) Curve A curve indicating the price level consistent with firms' average costs and markups for any level of output over the short run.

Aggregation The process of combining different things into a single category.

Alternate Goods Other goods that a firm could produce, using some of the same types of inputs as the good in question.

Automatic Stabilizers Forces that reduce the size of the spending multiplier and diminish the impact of spending shocks.

Autonomous Consumption The part of consumption spending that is independent of income; also, the vertical intercept of the consumption function.

Average Fixed Cost (AFC) Total fixed cost divided by the quantity of output produced.

Average Standard of Living Total output (real GDP) per person.

Average Total Cost (ATC) Total cost divided by the quantity of output produced.

Average Variable Cost (AVC) Total variable cost divided by the quantity of output produced.

B

Basic Principles of Economics A small set of basic ideas that are used repeatedly in analyzing economic problems. They form the foundation of economic theory.

Black Market An illegal market in which goods are sold at prices above the legal ceiling.

Bond An IOU issued by a corporation or government agency when it borrows funds.

Boom A period of time during which real GDP exceeds full employment, potential GDP.

Budget Constraint The different combinations of goods a consumer can afford with a limited budget, at given prices.

Budget Deficit The amount by which the government's total outlays (on goods, services, and transfer payments) exceeds its total tax revenue.

Budget Line The graphical representation of a budget constraint.

Budget Surplus The amount by which the government's total tax revenue exceeds its total outlays (on goods, services, and transfer payments).

Business Cycles Fluctuations in real GDP around its long-term growth trend.

Business Firm A firm, owned and operated by private individuals, that specializes in production.

C

Capital Long-lasting tools used in producing goods and services.

Capital Gains Tax A tax on profits earned when a financial asset is sold at more than its acquisition price.

Capital per Worker The total capital stock divided by total employment.

Capital Stock The total value of all goods that will provide useful services in future years.

Capitalism A type of economy in which most resources are owned privately.

Cartel A group of firms that selects a common price that maximizes total industry profits.

Cash in the Hands of the Public Currency and coins held outside of banks.

Central Bank A nation's principal monetary authority.

Change in Demand A shift of a demand curve in response to a change in some variable other than price.

Change in Quantity Demanded A movement along a demand curve in response to a change in price.

Change in Quantity Supplied A movement along a supply curve in response to a change in price.

Change in Supply A shift of a supply curve in response to some variable other than price.

Command Economy An economy in which resources are allocated according to explicit instructions from a central authority.

Communism A type of economy in which most resources are owned in common.

Comparative Advantage The ability to produce a good at a lower opportunity cost than elsewhere.

Compensating Wage Differential A difference in wages that makes two jobs equally attractive to workers.

Complement A good that is used together with some other good.

Constant Returns to Scale Long-run average total cost is unchanged as output increases.

Consumer Price Index An index of the cost, through time, of a fixed market basket of goods purchased by a typical household in some base period.

Consumption The part of GDP purchased by households as final users.

Consumption Function A positively sloped relationship between real consumption spending and real disposable income.

Consumption Tax A tax on the part of their income that households spend.

Copyright A grant of exclusive rights to sell a literary, musical, or artistic work.

Corporate Profits Tax A tax on the profits earned by corporations.

Corporation A firm owned by those who buy shares of stock and whose liability is limited to the amount of their investment in the firm.

Countercyclical Fiscal Policy Any change in government purchases or net taxes designed to counteract spending shocks.

Critical Assumption Any assumption that affects the conclusions of a model in an important way.

Cyclical Unemployment Joblessness arising from changes in production over the business cycle.

D

Deflation The percent decrease in the price level from one period to the next when the price level is falling.

Demand Curve The graphical depiction of a demand schedule; a curve showing the quantity of a good or service demanded at various prices, with all other variables held constant.

Demand Curve Facing a Firm A curve that indicates, for different prices, the quantity of output that customers will purchase from a particular firm.

Demand Deposit Multiplier The number by which a change in reserves is multiplied to determine the resulting change in demand deposits.

Demand Deposits Checking accounts that do not pay interest.

Demand Schedule A list showing the quantities of a good that consumers would choose to purchase at different prices, with all other variables held constant.

Demand Shock Any event that causes the *AD* curve to shift.

Depression An unusually severe recession.

Diminishing Marginal Returns to Labor The marginal product of labor decreases as more labor is hired.

Discount Rate The interest rate the Fed charges on loans to banks.

Discouraged Workers Individuals who would like a job, but have given up searching for one.

Discrimination When a group of people have different opportunities because of personal characteristics that have nothing to do with their abilities.

Diseconomies of Scale Long-run average total cost increases as output increases.

Disposable Income The part of household income that remains after paying taxes.

Diversification The process of reducing risk by spreading sources of income among different alternatives.

Dominant Strategy A strategy that is best for a firm no matter what strategy its competitor chooses.

Duopoly An oligopoly market with only two sellers.

E

Economic Efficiency A situation in which every Pareto improvement has occurred.

Economic Profit Total revenue minus all costs of production, explicit and implicit.

Economic System A system of resource allocation and resource ownership.

Economics The study of choice under conditions of scarcity.

Economies of Scale Long-run average total cost decreases as output increases.

Equilibrium A state of rest; a situation that, once achieved, will not change unless some external factor, previously held constant, changes.

Equilibrium GDP A level of output that is equal to total spending in the economy.

Excess Demand At a given price, the excess of quantity demanded over quantity supplied.

Excess Demand for Bonds The amount of bonds demanded exceeds the amount supplied at a particular interest rate.

Excess Reserves Reserves in excess of required reserves.

Excess Supply At a given price, the excess of quantity supplied over quantity demanded.

Excess Supply of Money The amount of money supplied exceeds the amount demanded at a particular interest rate.

Exchange The act of trading with others to obtain what we desire.

Exchange Rate The amount of one currency that is traded for one unit of another currency.

Excludability The ability to exclude those who do not pay for a good from consuming it.

Expansion A period of increasing real GDP.

Expenditure Approach Measuring GDP by adding the value of goods and services purchased by each type of final user.

Explicit Collusion Cooperation involving direct communication between competing firms about setting prices.

Explicit Costs Money actually paid out for the use of inputs.

Exports Goods and services produced domestically but sold abroad.

Externality A by-product of a good or activity that affects someone not immediately involved in the transaction.

F

Factor Payments Payments to the owners of resources that are used in production.

Factor Payments Approach Measuring GDP by summing the factor payments made by all firms in the economy.

Federal Funds Rate The interest rate charged for loans of reserves among banks.

Federal Open Market Committee A committee of Federal Reserve officials that establishes U.S. monetary policy.

Federal Reserve System The central bank and national monetary authority of the United States.

Fiat Money Anything that serves as a means of payment by government declaration.

Final Good A good sold to its final user.

Financial Intermediary A business firm that specializes in brokering between savers and borrowers.

Firm's Supply Curve A curve that shows the quantity of output a competitive firm will produce at different prices.

Fixed Costs Costs of fixed inputs.

Fixed Input An input whose quantity remains constant, regardless of how much output is produced.

Flow Variable A measure of a process that takes place over a period of time.

Frictional Unemployment Joblessness experienced by people who are between jobs or who are just entering or reentering the labor market.

Friendly Takeover When a firm's management arranges a takeover by another firm deemed unlikely to fire them.

Full Employment A situation in which there is no cyclical unemployment.

G

Game Theory An approach to modeling the strategic interaction of oligopolists in terms of moves and countermoves.

GDP Price Index An index of the price level for all final goods and services included in GDP.

Government Franchise A government-granted right to be the sole seller of a product or service.

Government Purchases Spending by federal, state, and local governments on goods and services.

Government's Demand for Funds Curve A curve indicating the amount of governmental borrowing at each interest rate.

Gross Domestic Product (GDP) The total value of all final goods and services produced for the marketplace during a given year, within the nation's borders.

H

Hostile Takeover When outsiders buy up a firm's shares with the goal of replacing the management team and increasing profits.

Human Capital The skills and training of the labor force.

I

Imperfect Competition A market structure with more than one firm, but in which one or more of the requirements of perfect competition are violated.

Imperfectly Competitive Market A market in which a single buyer or seller has the power to influence the price of the product.

Implicit Costs The cost of inputs for which there is no direct money payment.

Imports Goods and services produced abroad but consumed domestically.

Income The amount that a person or firm earns over a particular period.

Income Effect As the price of a good decreases, the consumer's purchasing power increases, causing a change in quantity demanded for the good.

Increasing Marginal Returns to Labor The marginal product of labor increases as more labor is hired.

Index A series of numbers used to track a variable's rise or fall over time.

Indexation Adjusting the value of some nominal payment in proportion to a price index in order to keep the real payment unchanged.

Individual Demand Curve A curve showing the quantity of a good or service demanded by a particular individual at each different price.

Inelastic Demands A price elasticity of demand between 0 and −1.

Inferior Good A good that people demand less of as their income rises.

Inflation Rate The percent change in the price level from one period to the next.

Intermediate Goods Goods used up in producing final goods.

Investment Demand Curve A curve that indicates the level of investment spending firms plan at each interest rate.

Investment Tax Credit A reduction in taxes for firms that invest in certain favored types of capital.

Involuntary Part-Time Workers Individuals who would like a full-time job, but who are working only part time.

L

Labor The time human beings spend producing goods and services.

Labor Force Those people who have a job or who are looking for one.

Labor Productivity Total output, real GDP, per worker.

Land The physical space on which production occurs and the natural resources that come with it.

Law of Demand As the price of a good increases, the quantity demanded decreases.

Law of Diminishing Marginal Returns As more and more of any input is added to a fixed amount of other inputs, its marginal product will eventually decline.

Law of Diminishing Marginal Utility As consumption of a good or service increases, marginal utility decreases.

Law of Increasing Opportunity Cost The more of something that is produced, the greater is the opportunity cost of producing one more unit.

Law of Supply As the price of a good increases, the quantity supplied increases.

Loanable Funds Market The market in which business firms obtain funds for investment.

Long Run A time horizon long enough for a firm to vary all of its inputs.

Long-Run Aggregate Supply Curve A vertical line indicating all possible output and price-level combinations at which the economy could end up in the long run.

Long-Run Average Total Cost (LRATC) The cost per unit of output in the long run, when all inputs are variable.

Long-Run Supply Curve A curve indicating the quantity of output that all sellers in a market will produce at different prices, after all long-run adjustments have taken place.

Long-Run Total Cost (LRTC) The cost of producing each quantity of output when the least-cost input mix is chosen in the long run.

Loss A negative profit—when total cost exceeds total revenue.

M

Macroeconomics The study of the economy as a whole.

Marginal Approach to Profit A firm maximizes its profit by taking any action that adds more to its revenue than to its cost.

Marginal Cost (MC) The increase in total cost from producing one more unit of output.

Marginal Product of Labor (MPL) The additional output produced when one more worker is hired.

Marginal Propensity to Consume The amount by which consumption spending changes when disposable income changes by one dollar.

Marginal Revenue (MR) The change in total revenue from producing one more unit of output.

Marginal Utility The change in total utility an individual obtains from consuming an additional unit of a good or service.

Market A group of buyers and sellers with the potential to trade.

Market Economy An economy in which resources are allocated through individual decision making.

Market Failure A market equilibrium that fails to take advantage of every Pareto improvement.

Market Signals Price changes that cause firms to change their production to more closely match consumer demand.

Market Structure The characteristics of a market that influence how trading takes place.

Market Supply Curve A curve indicating the quantity of output that all sellers in a market will produce at different prices.

Market System An economic system involving resource allocation by the market and private resource ownership.

Means of Payment Anything acceptable as payment for goods and services.

Microeconomics The study of the behavior of individual households, firms, and governments, the choices they make, and their interaction in specific markets.

Minimum Efficient Scale (MES) The level of output at which economies of scale are exhausted and minimum LRATC is achieved.

Model An abstract representation of reality.

Monetary Policy Action or inaction by the Federal Reserve designed to control the money supply and thereby influence the economy.

Money Demand Curve A curve indicating how much money will be willingly held at each interest rate.

Money Supply Curve A line showing the total quantity of money in the economy at each interest rate.

Monopolistic Competition A market structure in which there are many firms selling products that are differentiated, yet are still close substitutes, and in which there is free entry and exit.

Monopoly Firm The only seller of a good or service that has no close substitutes.

Monopoly Market The market in which a monopoly firm operates.

N

National Debt The total amount of government debt outstanding as a result of financing earlier budget deficits.

Natural Monopoly A market in which, due to economies of scale, one firm can operate at lower average cost than can two or more firms.

Net Exports Total exports minus total imports.

Net Investment Spending Total investment spending minus depreciation.

Net Taxes The taxes the government collects minus the transfer payments the government pays out.

Nominal Interest Rate The annual percent increase in a lender's dollars from making a loan.

Nominal Variable A variable measured without adjustment for the dollar's changing value.

Nominal Wage A wage measured in current dollars.

Nonmarket Production Goods and services that are produced, but not sold in a market.

Nonmonetary Job Characteristic Any aspect of a job—other than the wage—that matters to a potential or current employee.

Nonprice Competition Any action a firm takes to increase the demand for its product, other than cutting its price.

Normal Good A good that people demand more of as their income rises.

Normal Profit Another name for zero economic profit

Normative Economics The study of what should be; it is used to make value judgments, identify problems, and prescribe solutions.

O

Oligopoly A market structure in which a small number of firms are strategically interdependent.

Open Market Operations Purchases or sales of bonds by the Federal Reserve System.

Opportunity Cost The value of the best alternative sacrificed when taking an action.

P

Pareto Improvement An action that makes at least one person better off and harms no one.

Partnership A firm owned and usually operated by several individuals who share in the profits and bear personal responsibility for any losses.

Patent A temporary grant of monopoly rights over a new product or scientific discovery.

Patent Protection A government grant of exclusive rights to use or sell a new technology.

Payoff Matrix A table showing the payoffs to each of two firms for each pair of strategies they choose.

Peak The point at which real GDP reaches its highest level during an expansion.

Perfect Competition A market structure in which there are many buyers and sellers, the product is standardized, and sellers can easily enter or exit the market.

Perfectly Competitive Labor Market A labor market with a great many buyers and sellers and no barriers to entry or exit and in which all workers appear the same to firms.

Perfectly Competitive Market A market in which no buyer or seller has the power to influence the price.

Plant The collection of fixed inputs at a firm's disposal.

Positive Economics The study of what *is*, of how the economy works.

Potential Output The level of output the economy could produce if operating at full employment.

Potential Pareto Improvement An action in which the gains to the gainers would exceed the losses to the losers.

Price The amount of money that must be paid to a seller to obtain a good or service.

Price Ceiling A government-imposed price that may not legally be exceeded.

Price Discrimination Charging different prices to different customers for reasons other than production costs.

Price Floor A government-imposed minimum price below which a good or service may not be sold.

Price Leadership A form of tacit collusion in which one firm sets a price that other firms copy.

Price Level The average level of dollar prices in the economy.

Price Setter Any firm that faces a downward-sloping demand curve and so can choose the price it charges.

Price Taker Any firm that treats the price of its product as given and beyond its control.

Principal A person or group that hires someone to do a job.

Principle of Opportunity Cost The correct way to measure the cost of a choice is its opportunity cost—that which is given up to make the choice.

Principal-Agent Problem The situation that arises when an agent has interests that conflict with the principal's and has the ability to pursue those interests.

Private Good A good that can be, and should be, provided by private firms.

Private Investment Spending The sum of business plant and equipment purchases, new home construction, and inventory changes.

Production Function A function that indicates the maximum amount of output a firm can produce over some period of time from each combination of inputs.

Production Possibilities Frontier (PPF) A curve showing all combinations of two goods that can be produced with the resources and technology currently available.

Profit Total revenue minus total cost.

Protectionism The belief that a nation's industries should be protected from foreign competition.

Public Good A good that private firms cannot, and should not, provide.

Q

Quantity Demanded The total amount of a good that all buyers in a market would choose to purchase at a given price.

Quantity Supplied The total amount of a good or service that all producers in a market would choose to produce and sell at a given price.

Quota A limit on the physical volume of imports.

R

Rational Preferences Preferences that satisfy two conditions: (1) Any two alternatives can be compared and either one is preferred or the two are valued equally, and (2) the comparisons are logically consistent.

Real Interest Rate The annual percent increase in a lender's purchasing power from making a loan.

Real Variable A variable adjusted for changes in the dollar's value.

Real Wage A wage measured in terms of purchasing power.

Recession A period of declining or abnormally low real GDP.

Recovery The period after a recession during which output and employment return to their full-employment levels.

Relative Price The price of one good relative to the price of another.

Rent Controls A government-imposed maximum on rents that may be charged for apartments or homes.

Repeated Play A situation in which strategically interdependent sellers compete over many time periods.

Required Reserve Ratio The minimum fraction of checking account balances that banks must hold as reserves.

Required Reserves The minimum amount of reserves a bank must hold, depending upon the amount of its deposit liabilities.

Reserves Vault cash plus balances held at the Fed.

Resource Allocation A method of determining which goods and services will be produced, how they will be produced, and who will get them.

Resource Markets Markets in which households sell resources—land, labor, and natural resources—to firms.

Resources The land, labor, and capital that are used to produce goods and services.

Rivalry A situation in which one person's consumption of a good or service means that no one else can consume it.

S

Scarcity A situation in which the amount of something available is insufficient to satisfy the desire for it.

Seasonal Unemployment Joblessness related to changes in weather, tourist patterns, or other seasonal factors.

Self-Correcting Mechanism The adjustment process through which price and wage changes return the economy to full-employment output in the long run.

Short Run A time horizon during which at least one of the firm's inputs cannot be varied.

Short-Run Macroeconomic Equilibrium A combination of price level and GDP consistent with both the *AD* and *AS* curves.

Short Side of the Market At a given price, the smaller of quantity demanded and quantity supplied.

Shutdown Price The price at which a firm is indifferent between producing and shutting down.

Shutdown Rule In the short run, the firm should continue to produce if total revenue exceeds total variable costs; otherwise, it should shut down.

Simplifying Assumption Any assumption that makes a model simpler without affecting any of its important conclusions.

Socialism A type of economy in which most resources are owned by the state.

Sole Proprietorship A firm owned by a single individual.

Specialization A method of production in which each person concentrates on a limited number of activities.

Spending Multiplier The amount by which equilibrium real GDP changes as a result of a one-dollar change in autonomous consumption, investment, or government purchases.

Spending Shock A change in spending that ultimately affects the entire economy.

Stagflation The combination of falling output and rising prices.

Statistical Discrimination When individuals are excluded from an activity based on the statistical probability of behavior in their group, rather than their personal characteristics.

Stock Options Rights to purchase shares of stock at a prespecified price.

Stock Variable A measure of an amount that exists at a moment in time.

Stockholder Revolt When owners, dissatisfied with the profits they are earning, replace the firm's management team.

Structural Unemployment Joblessness arising from mismatches between workers' skills and employers' requirements or between workers' locations and employers' locations.

Substitute A good that can be used in place of some other good and that fulfills more or less the same purpose.

Substitution Effect As the price of a good decreases, the consumer substitutes that good in place of other goods whose prices have not changed.

Sunk Cost A cost that was incurred in the past and does not change in response to a present decision.

Supply Curve A graphical depiction of a supply schedule; a curve showing the quantity of a good or service supplied at various prices, with all other variables held constant.

Supply of Funds Curve A curve that indicates the level of household saving at each interest rate.

Supply Schedule A list showing the quantities of a good or service that firms would choose to produce and sell at different prices, with all other variables held constant.

Supply Shock Any event that causes the *AS* curve to shift.

T

Tacit Collusion Any form of oligopolistic cooperation that does not involve an explicit agreement.

Tariff A tax on imports.

Technical Efficiency A situation in which the maximum possible output is being produced from a given collection of inputs.

Technological Change The invention or discovery of new inputs, new outputs, or new production methods.

Technology A method by which inputs are combined to produce a good or service.

Terms of Trade The ratio at which a country can trade domestically produced products for foreign-produced products.

Tit for Tat A game-theoretic strategy of doing to another player this period what he has done to you in the previous period.

Total Cost (TC) The costs of all inputs—fixed and variable.

Total Demand for Funds Curve A curve that indicates the total amount of borrowing at each interest rate.

Total Fixed Cost (TFC) The cost of all inputs that are fixed in the short run.

Total Product The maximum quantity of output that can be produced from a given combination of inputs.

Total Revenue The total inflow of receipts from selling a given amount of output.

Total Spending The sum of spending by households, businesses, the government and the foreign sector on American final goods and services, or C + I + G + NX.

Total Variable Cost (TVC) The cost of all variable inputs used in producing a particular level of output.

Traditional Economy An economy in which resources are allocated according to long-lived practices from the past.

Transaction Costs The time costs and other costs required to carry out market exchanges.

Transfer Payments Funds the government gives to people or organizations but not as payment for goods or services.

Trough The point at which real GPD reaches its lowest level during a recession.

U

Unemployment Rate The fraction of the labor force that is without a job.

Unit of Value A common unit for measuring how much something is worth.

Utility Pleasure or satisfaction obtained from consuming goods and services.

V

Value Added The revenue a firm receives minus the cost of the intermediate goods it buys.

Value-Added Approach Measuring GDP by summing the value added by all firms in the economy.

Variable Costs Costs of variable inputs.

Variable Input An input whose usage changes as the level of output changes.

W

Wealth The total value of everything a person or firm owns at a point in time, minus the total value of everything owed.

Wealth Constraint At any point in time, wealth is fixed.

White Knight A firm that undertakes a friendly takeover.

INDEX

Note: Italicized letters *f* and *t* following page references indicate figures and tables, respectively.